THE UNIVERSITIES
OF EUROPE
IN THE MIDDLE AGES

THE

UNIVERSITIES OF EUROPE

IN THE

MIDDLE AGES

BY THE LATE

HASTINGS RASHDALL

DEAN OF CARLISLE

A NEW EDITION IN THREE VOLUMES

EDITED BY

F. M. POWICKE

Regius Professor of Modern History
in the University of Oxford

AND

A. B. EMDEN

Principal of St. Edmund Hall, Oxford

VOLUME I

SALERNO–BOLOGNA–PARIS

OXFORD
AT THE CLARENDON PRESS

Oxford University Press, Walton Street, Oxford OX2 6DP

Oxford New York Toronto
Delhi Bombay Calcutta Madras Karachi
Petaling Jaya Singapore Hong Kong Tokyo
Nairobi Dar es Salaam Cape Town
Melbourne Auckland

and associated companies in
Beirut Berlin Ibadan Nicosia

Oxford is a trade mark of Oxford University Press

Published in the United States
by Oxford University Press, New York

First published 1936
Re-issued 1987

British Library Cataloguing in Publication Data

Rashdall, Hastings
Universities of Europe in the Middle
Ages.—New ed.
1. Universities and colleges—Europe—
History   2. Education, Medieval
I. Title   II. Powicke, Sir Maurice
III. Emden, A. B.
378.4   LA627
ISBN 0-19-822981-X v. 1

Library of Congress Cataloging in Publication Data
Rashdall, Hastings, 1858–1924
Universities of Europe in the Middle Ages.
Includes bibliographies.
Contents: v. 1. Salerno–Bologna–Paris—v. 2.
Italy–Spain–France–Germany–Scotland, etc.—v. 3.
English universities–student life.
1. Universities and colleges—Europe— History.
2. Learning and scholarship—Europe—History—
Medieval, 500–1500.   3. Education, Medieval—Europe.
I. Powicke, F. M. (Frederick Maurice), 1879–1963.
II. Emden, Alfred Brotherston, 1888–   .   III. Title
LA177.R25 1987   378.4   87–1603
ISBN 0-19-822981-X (v. 1)

Printed and bound in
Great Britain by Biddles Ltd,
Guildford and King's Lynn

PREFACE TO THE FIRST EDITION

THE writing of this book is a task in which I became involved through winning the Chancellor's Prize at Oxford for an English Essay in 1883. I entered upon it with no intention of undertaking anything more than such a revision and expansion of my Essay as would justify its publication in book form. The Essay was, of course, written in less than a year: the revision has occupied more than eleven. Twelve years will seem none too much to any one acquainted with the extent and the difficulties of the subject; but it is fair to myself to state that I have been throughout pretty fully occupied in teaching subjects quite unconnected with medieval history.

Part of the difficulty has been occasioned by the rapidity with which materials and literature have of late poured from the press. When I began to work at the medieval universities, no really critical book had appeared on the subject as a whole or on any large section of it. Much labour was therefore expended in discovering for myself the non-existence of the University of Paris during the greater part of that period of its history which it has taken Du Boulay two bulky folios to chronicle. The publication of Father Denifle's great work, *Die Entstehung der Universitäten des Mittelalters*, in 1885, disclosed to me masses of fresh authorities for which I should probably have hunted in vain for myself. Later on, the publication of new documents in the successive volumes of Denifle and Chatelain's magnificent *Chartularium Universitatis Parisiensis* (1889, 1891), when I thought that my work was nearly at an end, involved much revision of the Paris chapter, and the addition of references to my citations from already published documents. The third volume came into my hands when most of the sheets had been already printed off. The Bologna octocentenary of 1888 produced a crop of new literature relating to that university, and in particular Malagola's edition of the statutes, only partially published before. Fournier's great collection of documents for the

French universities (the three volumes of which were published in 1890, 1891, and 1892 respectively) involved the re-
writing of the chapter on the French universities other than
Paris. Statute books, matriculation books, chartularia, and
histories of particular universities have also appeared in rapid
succession. Since I began to write, the amount of printed
matter demanding notice must have about doubled itself.
There are now few universities of which we have not at least
the statutes in print, while in very many cases all the extant
documents have been edited with a completeness which leaves
nothing to be desired. Unfortunately this cannot be said with
regard to our own universities.

With this growing mass of printed material before me, I
felt that it would be unnecessary to occupy myself to any great
extent with manuscript sources. To have done so with any
thoroughness, I should have had to bury myself for years in
foreign libraries and muniment rooms; and even so most of
the material would have been printed before my book could
have appeared. I have made exceptions to this rule in respect
of Oxford, Cambridge, S. Andrews, and (to a very limited
extent) Paris. At Paris I have not attempted to deal with
original documents beyond a slight study of some manuscript
registers: the *Chartularium* has now made this unnecessary for
the greater portion of the period embraced within this volume:
I have, however, read through the important manuscript histories of that university preserved in the Bibliothèque Nationale
(see below, vol. i, p. 269). With regard to the British universities, I have, I believe, made myself acquainted with all the unpublished manuscript material which was likely to throw any
light upon their history, or upon that of the colleges so far as
the history of the latter is dealt with in these volumes. With
regard to Oxford the mass of manuscript material is very large
indeed. My task has been much facilitated by the transcripts
of those indefatigable antiquaries Robert Hare and Bryan
Twyne (see below, vol. iii, p. 1); but after all I feel the
truth of Mark Pattison's remark, 'History cannot be written
from manuscripts.' This is particularly the case with masses of
official documents which require to be seen together and to

be arranged in chronological order for their full significance to be easily appreciated. It is to be hoped that Oxford will soon cease to be almost the only important university in the world (exclusive, perhaps, of the Spanish Peninsula) whose earlier history cannot be studied in a tolerably complete series of published documents. The work can only be done by the university itself. It is too extensive for private Societies, and in England there is no political capital to be made out of Government aid to scientific undertakings. At Cambridge the amount of unpublished material is smaller, though still considerable.

The plan of this book is to describe with tolerable fullness the three great archetypal universities—Bologna, Paris, Oxford—and to give short notices of the foundation, constitution, and history of the others, arranged in national groups. Even of the three great universities, however, I do not profess to have written a history. Exception may possibly be taken to the place assigned to particular universities. Many of them were, of course, situated in territories which did not then strictly belong to any of the larger divisions of the existing map of Europe, or belonged at one time to one of them, at another time to another. In these cases I have simply endeavoured to assign each university to the group to which it seemed on the whole most naturally to belong.

In endeavouring to cover so large an extent of ground in a work of moderate compass, it was inevitable that many aspects of university history should be dealt with slightly or not at all. The point of view from which I have approached the subject has been primarily that of constitutional history; but I could hardly have hoped to interest any but a few specialists in my subject had I not endeavoured to give some account of the intellectual history of the period. I have, however, touched upon the growth of the scholastic philosophy and theology and the development of legal and medical science just sufficiently to make intelligible my account of the educational organization of the Middle Ages, and to suggest its historical significance. The condensed treatment of seventy-three universities in 316 pages has, of course, rendered that part of my work of little interest except for purposes of reference; but to have ignored all but the most famous *studia* would have left the reader with a very inadequate impression of the extent and variety of the medieval university system, and of the importance of the part which it played in the making of civilized Europe. Moreover, it would have been impossible to write satisfactorily the history of even one university without an acquaintance with the documents of all the rest. The great defect of university histories has been the non-application of the comparative method. As matters stand, even students will probably skip the greater part of vol. ii. The 'general reader' will perhaps find most that will interest him in the last chapter of vol. iii.

Nobody can be better aware than myself of the great deficiencies of my work. Many years more might well have been spent in removing them. I could, of course, indicate point after point which demands further investigation. But I felt that the time had come when the book must be published, if I were not prepared to make it the work of a lifetime. Ten or twenty years hence it will perhaps be possible to base a history of the medieval universities upon an almost complete collection of printed materials. Meanwhile, I hope my Essay will be of some use to the now considerable number of students who are at work on portions of the subject.

It is needless to say that such a work as the present owes a great deal to the researches of others. My obligations to the historians of particular universities are expressed in the bibliographical notices. But I am particularly anxious to state accurately the extent of my debt to Father Denifle, the only modern writer on the subject as a whole to whom I am under important obligations. If I had not had Father Denifle as a predecessor, my work might have possessed more novelty and originality than it can now claim, since there were large masses of traditional error and misconception which must have been dispelled by the first serious modern student who should take up the subject; but it would assuredly have been very much more incomplete and inadequate than it actually is. At the same time, in justice to myself, I may perhaps point out the following facts:

1. I had already reached for myself the most important of the corrections which Father Denifle has made in the hitherto received version of the early history of Paris. Some of them were just indicated or implied in a very slight article on universities which I contributed to the *Dictionary of English History* in 1884.

2. The amount of my indebtedness naturally varies with the extent to which Father Denifle has been an original worker. In some cases the history of a minor university has been re-written or discovered for the first time by Father Denifle's researches in the Vatican or other archives. In such cases I could do no more than epitomize his results. But where his work is based on the researches of others or on published documents, I have endeavoured to make an independent use of them. I believe I have read every published document relating to any medieval university which I could succeed in getting hold of; and I have, of course, verified (wherever possible) all citations which I owe to other writers. I am, however, everywhere indebted to Father Denifle for bibliographical information, by no means the least difficult or important part of his work.

3. Father Denifle's *Entstehung* is only the first of a series which is to extend to five volumes. It deals only with the 'origines' of the universities founded up to 1400. It does not describe in detail their mature constitution, organization, or history. Here, therefore, I have been without the advantage of Father Denifle's guidance, as also in all that relates to the universities founded after 1400.

4. To Oxford Father Denifle devotes only twenty pages, and he does not profess to add anything to our knowledge of that university. The view I have taken of its origin and early history is entirely independent of his work.

5. The whole plan and arrangement of my book is different from Father Denifle's.

The English universities form the only part of the subject in which Father Denifle has left scope for much originality to his successors, so far at least as the all-important question of 'origines' is concerned. On details I have sometimes ventured to differ from him. But, as he has been severely criticized and unjustly disparaged by several writers on the same subject, I feel it a duty to give expression to the admiration with which a careful comparison of his book with the authorities upon which it is based has filled me, not merely for the immensity of his learning and for the thoroughness of his work, but for the general soundness of his conclusions. In particular, I think it right to add that, though Father Denifle is a Dominican and Under-Archivist of the Holy See, I have hardly ever discovered any ground for the insinuation of an ultramontane bias.

Throughout the work I have received an amount of help from my friends which I have been almost ashamed to accept, and which it is difficult for me adequately to acknowledge. My greatest debt is perhaps to the constant advice and assistance of Mr. Reginald Lane Poole, Ph.D., Lecturer in Jesus College, Oxford, whose great learning in everything that relates to the Middle Ages has always been accessible to me, and who has kindly read through nearly the whole of my proofs. My proofs have also been read by Mr. T. Tout, Professor of History in Owens College, Manchester, whose wide knowledge of general history has constantly supplied the deficiencies in mine, and by Mr. C. H. Turner, Fellow of Magdalen College, Oxford, who has generously devoted an immense amount of labour to the final correction for the press of a book on a subject quite remote from his own studies. These volumes owe more than I can easily explain to the accuracy and diligence of his revision. My thanks are also due for kind assistance with portions of the revision to my colleague, Mr. S. G. Hamilton, Fellow of Hertford, to Mr. C. W. C. Oman, Fellow of All Souls, and to the Rev. Andrew Clark, late Fellow of Lincoln, who has often helped me with his unrivalled knowledge of the materials for Oxford history.

The nature of my task has necessarily compelled me to touch upon many subjects with which I could not aspire to more than a very second-hand acquaintance. If I have escaped serious error in dealing with the history of medieval Law and Medicine, I owe it largely to the kindness of Professor Maitland, of Cambridge, and of Dr. J. F. Payne, late Fellow of Magdalen College, Oxford, Physician of S. Thomas's Hospital, who were good enough to read through the portions of my proofs relating to their respective subjects. I have also to thank Lord Acton for several valuable suggestions in regard to chap. v, § 6. I have to acknowledge the great assistance which I have at all times received from all the authorities of the Bodleian Library, especially from Mr. F. Madan, Sub-Librarian, and Fellow of Brasenose, to whose help in matters bibliographical and palaeographical I am under great obligations. I am indebted to the Society of Antiquaries for access to the Smith MSS. in their Library. I must acknowledge the never-failing courtesy with which the Rev. T. Vere Bayne, Student of Christ Church and Keeper of the Archives at Oxford, has met my, I fear, somewhat troublesome applications for the use of documents under his charge. I must also express my gratitude for similar assistance to the late Rev. Dr. Luard, formerly Registrary of the University of Cambridge, and to his successor, Mr. J. W. Clark; to Mr. F. J. H. Jenkinson, Librarian of the University of Cambridge; to his Grace the Archbishop of Canterbury and his Librarian, Mr. Kershaw; to the Lord Bishop of Lincoln and his Secretary, Mr. S. S. Smith; to the Lord Bishop of Ely and his Registrar, Mr. W. J. Evans; to the Venerable Archdeacon Chapman, of Ely; to the Rev. C. Leeke, Chancellor of Lincoln Cathedral; and to Mr. J. M. Anderson, Registrar and Librarian of the University of S. Andrews, who was kind enough to facilitate my researches by allowing me to make free use of the transcripts which he had made for his work on that university. For the invariable courtesy which I have met with from the Librarians and other authorities of colleges at Oxford and Cambridge to whom I have applied for access to manuscripts or for information on various points, I must ask them to be kind enough to accept this general acknowledgement. Some of these obligations are mentioned in the notes or bibliographical notices. I must not, however, omit to thank Father Denifle and Monsieur Chatelain, Librarian of the Sorbonne, for their kindness in answering inquiries which I have occasionally ventured to address to them.

To my friend and former pupil the Rev. S. Holmes I owe a large part of the Index.

The lists of authorities which are prefixed to each university do not pretend to anything like bibliographical completeness.

H. RASHDALL.

OXFORD:
June 24, 1895.

CONTENTS OF VOLUME I

CHAPTER III
SALERNO

CHAPTER IV
BOLOGNA

§ 1. IRNERIUS AND THE CIVIL LAW REVIVAL

§ 2. GRATIAN AND THE CANON LAW

§ 3. THE ORIGINES OF THE JURIST UNIVERSITIES

CHAPTER V
PARIS

§ 1. THE ORIGINS OF THE UNIVERSITY

I. The Rise of the University

II. Development of the University from 1210 to 1249: Origin of the Four Nations

The Faculty of Theology:

§ 5. THE COLLEGES OF PARIS

§ 6. THE PLACE OF THE UNIVERSITY IN EUROPEAN HISTORY

APPENDICES

ILLUSTRATION

TABLE OF UNIVERSITIES (with references)

	ITALY. SALERNO. BOLOGNA. Reggio, 1188*. (ii. 5).	FRANCE, ETC. PARIS. Montpellier (?) (ii. 116).	GREAT BRITAIN. OXFORD.	SPAIN AND PORTUGAL.	GERMANY, BOHEMIA, AND THE LOW COUNTRIES.	OTHER COUNTRIES.
12th Cent. *Studia Generalia before or without Bulls.*	Vicenza, 1204*. (ii. 6). Arezzo, 1215*. (ii. 8). Padua, 1222*. (ii. 9). Vercelli, 1228*. (ii. 26). Siena (1246: I. in 1357)*. (ii. 31).	Orleans, ante 1231. (ii. 139). Angers*. (ii. 151).	Cambridge, 1209*. (P. in 1318.)	(?) Valladolid, c. 1250. (P. in 1346). (ii. 69).		
13th Century.	Naples, 1224, I. (ii. 21). Curia Romana, 1244–5, P. (ii. 27). Piacenza, 1248, P. (ii. 35).	Toulouse, 1229, 1233, P. (ii. 160).		Palencia, 1212–1214, R. (ii. 65). Salamanca, ante 1230, R. (ii. 74). Seville, 1254, R.: P. in 1260 (Latin and Arabic). (ii. 90). Lisbon-Coimbra, 1290, P. (ii. 108).		
14th Century. *Studia Generalia founded by Papal or Imperial Bull (or in Spain by Royal Charter).*	Rome (Studium Urbis), 1303, P. (ii. 38). Perugia, 1308, P. (ii. 40). Treviso, 1318, P. (ii. 43). Pisa, 1343, P. (ii. 45). Florence, 1349, P. (ii. 47). Pavia, 1361, I. (ii. 51). Ferrara, 1391, P. (ii. 53).	Avignon, 1303, P. (ii. 173). Cahors, 1332, P. (ii. 182). Grenoble, 1339, P. (ii. 183). Orange, 1365, I. (ii. 184).		Lerida, 1300, R. (ii. 91). Perpignan, 1349, P. (ii. 96). Huesca, 1359, R. (ii. 98).	Prague, 1347–8, P. I. (ii. 211). Vienna, 1365, P. (ii. 234). Erfurt, 1379, 1392, P. (ii. 245). Heidelberg, 1385, P. (ii. 250). Cologne, 1388, P. (ii. 254).	Cracow (Poland), 1364, 1397, P. (ii. 289). Pécs or Fünfkirchen (Hungary), 1367, P. (ii. 294). Buda (Hungary), 1389, P. (ii. 295).
15th Century.	Turin, 1405, P. (ii. 55). Catania, 1444, P. (ii. 57).	Aix, 1409, P. (ii. 186). Dôle, 1422, P. (ii. 190). Poitiers, 1431, P*. (ii. 193). Caen, 1432, P. (ii. 195). Bordeaux, 1441, P. (ii. 199). Valence, 1452, 1459, P. (ii. 203). Nantes, 1460, P. (ii. 205). Bourges, 1464, P. (ii. 205). [Besançon, 1485, P. (ii. 207).]	S. Andrews, 1413, P. (ii. 301). Glasgow, 1451, P. (ii. 311). Aberdeen, 1494, P*. (ii. 318).	Barcelona, 1450, P. (ii. 100). Saragossa, 1474 (Arts). (ii. 101). Palma (Majorca), 1483, R. (ii. 102). Sigüenza, 1489, P. (ii. 104). Alcalá, 1499, P. (ii. 105). Valencia, 1500, P. (ii. 106).	Würzburg. (ii. 257). Leipzig, 1409. P*. (ii. 258). Rostock, 1419, P. (ii. 260). Louvain, 1425, P. (ii. 265). Trier, 1454, 1473, P. (ii. 268). Greifswald, 1428*, 1456, P*. (ii. 269). Freiburg-im-Breisgau, 1455–6, P. (ii. 272). Basel, 1459, P. (ii. 275). Ingolstadt, 1459, 1472, P. (ii. 275). Mainz, 1476, P. (ii. 278). Tübingen, 1476–7, P. (ii. 278).	Poszony or Pressburg (Hungary), 1465–7, P. (ii. 297). Upsala (Sweden), 1477, P. (ii. 298). Copenhagen (Denmark), 1478, P. (ii. 299).

* Known to have been founded by or in connexion with a migration from some other university.

P. = founded by Papal Bull.   I. = founded by Imperial Bull.   R. = founded by Royal Charter.

For Bulls granted but not executed see vol. ii, Appendix I, p. 325, and for some universities wrongly so called vol. ii, Appendix II, p. 331.

INTRODUCTION

DR. RASHDALL, in the preface to the first edition of his book, described the circumstances in which he wrote and elaborated it.[1] He claimed that twelve years of a life largely concerned with other duties were not too many for its composition, and, after ten years' work, in the midst of similar distractions, upon the task of revision, his editors may well trace a touch of irony in the under-statement. Few books, indeed, which have secured an enduring place in our historical literature, can have been written so quickly, for the twelve years given by Rashdall to his subject included the period of preparation as well as the time required for the final composition of his treatise.

The task of preparing a second edition has not been an easy one. In addition to the work of coping with the literary output of forty years, we had to face the perplexities involved in the treatment of Rashdall's text. His book is not a 'classic', like Gibbon's *Decline and Fall of the Roman Empire* or Macaulay's *History of England*, whose every word and comma must be preserved. Rashdall was a vigorous and often a delightful writer, but he did not possess the infallible composure which is characteristic of a fine or distinctive literary style. Sometimes he wrote hurriedly and carelessly; occasionally he made grammatical slips; and, although he arranged the contents of his book with obvious care, he had little sense of form. He frequently repeated himself or tucked away a significant observation, as it occurred to him, in a place which was not the most relevant to its significance. On the other hand, Rashdall was incapable of writing anything dry or impersonal. He put himself into his books, and he liked to expatiate and to indulge in a genial jibe. He lived in a time, and was trained in a university, in which the study of history was an expression of interest in the 'humanities', and, while

---

[1] Above, pp. v–viii. See also P. E. Matheson, *The Life of Hastings Rashdall* (Oxford, 1928), pp. 70–5.

it had begun to take account of scientific method, had not yet become professional. His success, it is true, was due to robust good sense rather than to the critical perception which a great historical scholar, as, for example, his older contemporary, Stubbs, instinctively applies to fresh problems; but his good sense combined with his wide interests and capacity for hard work to produce a living and powerful book. Hence it is impossible to deal with his study as though it were a standard treatise of an almost impersonal kind, such as Ueberweg's history of philosophy, which can be edited and re-edited until the original work is barely traceable. Treatment of this kind would have done injustice alike to the author and to his future readers.

Accordingly, in this second edition, Rashdall's text has in general been preserved, but has not been regarded as sacrosanct. We have not hesitated to correct it and to delete erroneous or misleading passages. Here and there, particularly in the first volume, we have substituted new sentences for the old, and, more rarely, we have interpolated new matter.[1] To have called attention to these numerous changes, however trivial or brief, would have been pedantic and might well have irritated the reader, but the more significant alterations and additions have been enclosed within square brackets. Similarly, in the footnotes editorial additions and comments have been enclosed in square brackets, but deletions and minor corrections have been made silently. We have naturally allowed ourselves much more freedom in the footnotes, especially in the third volume, where Rashdall's treatment in the text of the Universities of Oxford and Cambridge has deliberately been retained more faithfully than his earlier treatment of the continental universities. He attached much importance to his views on the origins and history of the University of Oxford, and, just as he lingered with pleasure over this part of his work, so it has become the most familiar to English readers. At the same time, no section of his book requires more criticism and correction. The result

[1] The longest of these insertions refers to the Dominican schools (below, vol. i, pp. 371, 372).

is a lavish annotation which sometimes assumes the form of a running debate with the author.[1]

Many of Rashdall's casual comments are too characteristic to be omitted, yet are not apposite forty years later. We have in such cases inserted the date [1895] of the first edition between square brackets.

The bibliographies have been brought up to date (generally to 1934) and new material has been discussed in the foot-notes, and in the 'additional notes' which are occasionally inserted at the end of a section.[2] Rashdall's own additional notes to his first volume have been incorporated, in substance or *verbatim*, in the body of the volume. Some of the appendixes, which in the first edition were grouped together at the end of the book, have been omitted as now unnecessary or out of date; those which we have retained have been distributed between the three volumes. The clumsy division of the second volume into two separate parts with a continuous pagination has been abandoned; this edition appears in three volumes, each of which is paged separately. The original arrangement of the text has been retained, except that, in the second volume, the section on Valladolid now precedes that on Salamanca, and Rashdall's general observations upon the Italian and Spanish universities have been grouped somewhat differently. The figures within square brackets, which will be found on the inner margin of every fifth page, are references to the pages of the first edition, and will, we hope, assist readers who already possess that edition or may wish to consult it.

Rashdall, in an interleaved copy, made contributions, from time to time, towards a second edition, but he was not able to do very much. The most serious work was done on Valladolid and on Salamanca, where he was allowed to study the

---

[1] A list of references to discussion and notes on particular points will be found in the Index, *s.v.* Rashdall.

[2] Many important books and articles have appeared while this edition was passing through the press. Among those to which we have not been able to refer, J. Destrez, *La Pecia dans les manuscrits universitaires du XIIIe et du XIVe siècle* (Paris, 1935) should especially be noted. Cf. below, pp. 189, 421-2.

printed, but unpublished, text of the revised statutes of Pope Martin V (1422). His additions on these universities[1] and a few other notes which he made on various sections of his book (e.g. in the section on Abelard) have been incorporated in this edition.

The plans of the Latin Quarter at Paris and of medieval Oxford have been omitted as out of date. A rather more satisfactory plan of the former will be found in S. d'Irsay's *Histoire des universités* (vol. i), and of the latter in Sir C. E. Mallet's *A History of the University of Oxford* (vol. i). A fine and detailed map of medieval Oxford has recently been published by Dr. H. E. Salter. The Index has been carefully revised and extended. With a few outstanding exceptions, to which cross-references are given, the names of persons have been indexed under the surname, not the Christian name.

A few observations on the progress which has been made in the study of medieval academic thought and history since 1895 may not be out of place. In this introduction the history of Oxford and Cambridge is not discussed. Our readers will find an estimate of the bearing of recent work upon the history of the ancient English universities in Mr. Emden's introduction to the third volume.

Rashdall, as he says in his preface, wrote his book while new and important work was appearing. It would have been better, indeed, if he could have foreseen the output of the next few years and had delayed the arrangement of his material until Malagola's edition of the statutes of the University of Bologna and the four volumes of the *Chartularium Universitatis Parisiensis* had appeared; for, although he was able to make use of the former and of two volumes of the latter, it is obvious that he grafted the results of new studies upon a work which was already growing under his hands. When he began his investigations he realized that, in the absence of reliable guides, he must work afresh from the texts. In his study of Bologna, he relied to a considerable extent upon the jurist statutes of Padua for 1463, published

---

[1] Vol. ii, pp. 69–74, *passim*, 86–8.

in 1551, and, in his treatment of Paris, upon the great collection of texts published by Du Boulay in 1665–73. The success with which he used Du Boulay's great work is very remarkable, and is creditable to Du Boulay, whom he rather ungratefully described as 'perhaps the stupidest man that ever wrote a valuable book',[1] no less than to himself. In the meantime (1885) Denifle's epoch-making and solitary volume of his projected work, *Die Entstehung der Universitäten des Mittelalters*, appeared. Henceforward Rashdall felt on safer ground, and, although he rightly adhered to his own method of treating the subject, he could handle with more confidence the texts which appeared while his work was in course of preparation. But this process of gradual absorption left its marks upon his book. It accounts for the impression of unevenness, for the qualifications and repetitions, and for the fact that though nearly everything which the reader may want is to be found somewhere, he cannot be sure of finding it where he would reasonably expect to find it. Moreover, if Rashdall had been able to study the texts in good editions both with fresh eyes and with the aid of later critical scholarship, he would have been better able to draw out at leisure the implications of his material as a contribution to the history of corporate life in the Middle Ages.[2] Many fine passages show that Rashdall was exceptionally well fitted for this congenial task; but his approach to his subject involved him in the critical discussion of institutions rather than in a study of the society which created and expressed itself in them. One of our helpers once exclaimed, in a moment of not unnatural impatience with the institutional details which fill the second volume, that Rashdall devoted most of his time to the things that do not matter. This criticism, if it had been seriously intended, would have been unjust, but it contains an element of truth of which Rashdall was probably well aware. His realistic mind frequently sought relief in picturesque detail which would have had more significance in

[1] Below, vol. i, p. 269.
[2] Cf. F. M. Powicke, 'Some problems in the history of the medieval university', in *Transactions of the Royal Historical Society* (1934), p. 4.

a wider setting. His human interests had to find expression in the decoration rather than in the substance of his book. He must often have sympathized with the fourteenth-century scribe who wrote at the end of one of the registers of the English nation in the University of Paris: *nota quod supra multa continentur quae modicum valebunt post mille annos persicos*.

The embarrassment which Rashdall felt in trying to compose a comprehensive work upon a continuously and rapidly growing subject still perplexes his successors. Here, however, it is necessary to make a distinction. The new learning has affected the intellectual far more than the constitutional history of the medieval universities. Comparatively little has been published about the institutions to which Rashdall devoted so much attention. The numerous volumes of the magnificent *Chartularium Studii Bononiensis*, which began to appear in 1909, and the valuable series of *Studi e memorie per la storia della università di Bologna*, would doubtless have led Rashdall, if he had had them before him, to alter his treatment, both in structure and detail, of the history of the University of Bologna, but the documents in the former, though they are all medieval, and the articles in the latter, do not seriously disturb the conclusions which he drew from his study of Sarti, Denifle, and Malagola's edition of the statutes. The detailed history of the medieval University of Bologna will largely be based upon them and other material unknown to Rashdall, but this history has yet to be written. It could not be attempted by Rashdall's editors.[1] It is more unfortunate that Rashdall was unable to make full use of the third and fourth volumes of the *Chartularium Universitatis Parisiensis*, and especially of the *Auctarium*, which contains the earlier records of the English nation at Paris, but, here also, he succeeded, on the whole, and within the limits which he had imposed upon his work, in giving a fairly accurate account of later constitutional developments.[2] The most im-

[1] We have made considerable use of the *Studi e memorie*, and especially of the notarial acts in the fourth volume of the *Chartularium*.

[2] In the interpretation of some of the texts used by Rashdall we have ventured to differ from him, e.g. in his depreciation of the im-

portant criticism which can be made of his description of the University of Paris in the later Middle Ages is that, too frequently, he read back into medieval history the evidence collected by Du Boulay from the records of the sixteenth century. The University of Paris, like the University of Bologna, still awaits its historian. There are no histories of the universities of Italy and Spain, which displace the works of Denifle and La Fuente, upon whom Rashdall mainly relied; and, among the numerous studies and articles, the editions of the documents of Pavia and Valladolid stand out like isolated peaks.[1] When we turn to France the prospect is even more bleak. Here, again, we find a fair number of local studies, but, since 1895, no university, except the University of Orleans,[2] seems to have shown the energy which Rashdall applauded at Montpellier. This is the more to be regretted, because the indispensable collection of documents published by Marcel Fournier in 1890–2, *Les Statuts et privilèges des universités françaises depuis leur fondation jusqu'en 1789*, cries out for a new editor. The texts, as printed, are unreliable and their critical presentation is inadequate. On the other hand, few literary enterprises have been so laudable in their intention as Fournier's, and, in the interests of the

---

portance of the chancellor (Gerson would surely have been surprised to be told that the chancellor was not an official of the university), and in his description of the early history of the proctors. Other criticisms of his chapter on Paris are generally the outcome of study of the *Auctarium*, and of the unassuming but excellent little study by Boyce of the English-German nation. For example, Rashdall erroneously believed that 'sub-determination', which he did not understand, was peculiar to Oxford and was not allowed in Paris. Finally, the discussion on the period of 'determination', on sophistical disputations, text-books, and similar matters, has been corrected in the light of recent

work upon the contents of scholastic texts.

[1] Below, vol. ii, pp. 51, 69. Rashdall based his revision of the section on Valladolid upon the documents published by Alcácer Martínez.

[2] At Orleans activity has been shown in the arrangement and cataloguing of documents, and in the transactions of a vigorous local society. Professor D. M. Quynn (Miss Dorothy Mackay), a pupil of the late Professor Paetow, has in hand a work on the history of the university. Professor Prentout's short history of the University of Caen, written on the occasion of its fifth centenary, is a good example of recent work on French universities.

comparative study of medieval university life, similar collections might well be made in other countries. At present university statutes can only be studied in separate and scattered publications, ranging from sumptuous centenary volumes to modest contributions to local periodicals.

Rashdall's plan—'to describe with tolerable fullness the three great archetypal universities', and 'to give short notices of the foundation, constitution and history of the others, arranged in national groups'[1]—makes it difficult, if not impossible, to correlate the notices in his second volume with later work. We have revised the text as well as it was in our power to do so, and we have made the bibliographical notes as complete as we could; but we have not attempted, save in the sections on the Universities of S. Andrews and Glasgow, to recast what Rashdall wrote. Indeed, an exhaustive revision of the notices of the Italian, Spanish, and French universities would have required us to depart unduly from Rashdall's plan, and drastic revision was quite out of the question in the notices on the German universities and the Universities of Louvain, Prague, and Cracow. Later scholarship has made accessible far more documentary evidence on the history of these than on that of the southern and French universities, and has exhausted itself in treatises and monographs. If we had tried to cope with all the literature described in the bibliographical notes, the universities which were established within the borders of the Empire would have demanded a large volume to themselves. Fortunately, Rashdall, within the limits of his somewhat meagre plan, was as successful in his characterization of the German as of other universities. Most of the material especially relevant to his particular purpose had been published when he wrote. He used independently the same texts as Georg Kaufmann used in the second volume of his *Geschichte der deutschen Universitäten* (1896), and it is not without significance that, in spite of its age, Kaufmann's book, which is constructed on a plan quite different from Rashdall's, is still the only comparative survey of the history of German academic institutions. Later German

---

[1] Above, p. vii.

literature, although it has revealed much new detail, is important as a contribution to wider aspects of university life; it has not seriously modified the work either of Rashdall or of his German contemporary.[1]

Rashdall, as a theologian and a philosopher, was greatly interested in the history of medieval thought. Beyond the slow and intricate development of university institutions he was acutely aware of the great scholars and thinkers, of Irnerius, Gratian, Abelard, Aquinas, Occam, and many more; and he has explained in his preface why he felt constrained to interleave his history of the universities with sections on the intellectual movements associated with these great names. It is no secret that the friend upon whose help Rashdall especially relied urged him to confine himself to a study of the medieval university as a social organism, and it is easy to appreciate the practical wisdom of this advice. In rejecting it Rashdall incurred the risk that his book would lack unity and balance. He had to combine a theme which could be elaborated, if not exhaustively, at least with adequate comprehension, with another theme whose study was still in its infancy, and whose implications, when compared with the clear-cut issues supplied by his institutional material, were elusive and largely unexplored. Yet it is impossible to regret that he held to his purpose. The pages which he wrote on medieval thought and learning are perhaps the most vigorous, incisive, and interesting in the book. To the specialist, with his painful experience of the pitfalls and uncertainties of the way, they may often seem to be one-sided, over-confident, even perverse, but they never fail to reveal the working of a sagacious and masterful mind. Their argument is clear and forcible; and has first opened the eyes of many of its readers to wider and richer prospects in medieval history. On the other hand, these sections are dated. They belong incorrigibly to the year 1895. They reflect the outlook of their author in a particular period and environment, a fact which,

[1] Rashdall does not allow sufficient importance to Italian influence upon the origin and statutes of some German universities, just as Kaufmann draws too hard and fast his distinction between ecclesiastical and secular authority.

while it does not, of course, affect their significance as speculative criticism, seriously impairs their value as contributions to a history of universities. It is worth while to give a few examples of the change in method and exposition which Rashdall would probably have made if he had been writing to-day.

Rashdall rightly emphasized the part played by great men in the history of the medieval schools, but it is not unfair to say that he approached the problem of their relation to the rise and growth of organized universities in an *a priori* manner. He consulted their writings, and he tried to master the literature which purported to analyse their place in the development of thought. He had one great guide in Savigny's classical work on the history of Roman law in the Middle Ages. But he lived in the early days of the learned movement which was to absorb and transcend the traditions of Savigny and other pioneers, such as Prantl, Hauréau, and Renan. He was the philosopher interested in the development of ideas rather than the historian patiently tracing out the intricate pattern of thought. Although his successors have to depend as he had upon the results reached by the specialists, they can appreciate, as Rashdall could not, the bearing of the new learning. They can breathe its atmosphere and form some idea of the difficulties which beset its investigations. The historian who would trace the influence of a great man and the influences which the great man felt himself must do more than read his books and compare them with the books of other great men. He must go behind later printed texts to the manuscripts, follow their migrations, and find out who used them; he must acquaint himself with the lives and thoughts of the obscure teachers and scholars who worked in isolation or wandered from place to place, or formed transient or permanent societies of learned men. If a new influence appears, whether it is the Digest or a group of medieval texts, a translation of a book of Aristotle or a new version of the pseudo-Dionysius, a commentary of Averroës or a mathematical tract from Spain, he must try to understand how, when, and why it made itself felt, if he is to make his humble contribution to the history of scholasticism or heresy or scientific speculation. And, if he would see how this leaven worked in the eager life of the schools, he must sit in the schools, listen to lectures and disputations, and master their rules and practices. In short, he must live in the valley and mix with the crowd before he follows the great teacher to the heights, not take his stand on the high ground and peer with casual curiosity at the insignificant life below. Only so can the work of a great man, as a formative element in the history of the society in which he lived or which he influenced, be understood. Our bibliographies and notes will, we hope, give some guidance to those who may wish to examine the results of these painful investigations. A few examples may be noted here. (1) The medical school of Salerno has been given a more precise place in history, as the source of an influence more than medical; it both passed on the work of a great man, Constantinus Africanus, and was one of the doors by which the new Aristotle entered the West; its authoritative texts, comprised in the *ars medicinae* of Constantinus, directed the studies of Paris and the course of later teaching in the universities of Europe. But it was Montpellier that transmitted the more theoretical conception of medicine, as a science among sciences, a conception which, if it delayed the empirical study of medicine, helped to spread the knowledge of Arab and Jewish science and philosophy as a whole. (2) Again, the impressive figure of Irnerius dominates the early history of the schools at Bologna. Many of the details are still in dispute, and some scholars view with strong disfavour the clear-cut fabric which H. Kantorowicz and others have raised among the ruins of old theories, but the remarkable work of Irnerius and of the long line of glossators, with their far-reaching influence on medieval statecraft and political discussion and official correspondence, has undoubtedly become more vivid and portentous in recent years.[1] It has

[1] Seckel is outstanding among the numerous scholars who have carried on the work whose foundations were laid by Savigny. See especially the masterly survey of his pupil, Professor Erich Gensmer of Königsberg, 'Die Justinianische Kodifikation und die Glossatoren', in the *Atti del Congresso internazionale di diritto romano* (held at

become something to be reckoned with not only in Italy, but also in France, where its influence, with comparable effects upon the French monarchy, took root and developed, as E. M. Meijer has shown, in the law schools of Orleans.[1] Rashdall worked hard and faithfully on the problem of the origins of the university at Bologna and, with less pertinacity, dealt with the glossators, but he conveys a very imperfect idea of the significance of Bologna and Orleans in the life of Europe during the thirteenth and fourteenth centuries. (3) The early scholasticism of the twelfth century touched only the 'periphery' of this development of civil law, and later scholasticism affected its method in France more than in Italy,[2] but, especially in the earlier period, the systematization of theology and canon law proceeded in constant interaction. Hence the theologian Peter the Lombard at Paris, a secular priest and bishop, and the canonist Gratian at Bologna, a monk, were embedded more deeply in long tradition, as was also that bold and independent thinker, Abelard, than Irnerius was. The Lombard at Paris, in his Sentences and exegesis, notably of the epistles of S. Paul, precipitated, so to speak, the Biblical and theological studies of his time and brought them into the lecture-room. Gratian, a disciple of papalism, carried on the work of great predecessors, Burchard of Worms and Ivo of Chartres, and compiled the standard exposition of the canon law. The story of their work and antecedents may be read in the treatises of Grabmann, Ghellinck, Robert, and in the important history of early canon law by the late Paul Fournier and Gabriel le Bras. (4) Numerous students have been and are at work upon the

Bologna in April, 1933), Pavia, 1934, i. 347–430. The influence of the early scholastics, so far as it went, upon the glossators is discussed on pp. 347–68, 381–4.

[1] Below, vol. ii, p. 139.

[2] Meijer, in the articles mentioned above (*Tijdschrift voor rechtsgechiedenis*, ii. 491–2 n.), cites the criticism by the Paduan civilian, Ricardus Malumbra, of the growth of syllogistic, sophistic, and dialectical methods in legal study. The new style 'originem habuit a doctoribus ultra-montanis', i.e. in the French schools of law. It was, in Richard's view, very inferior to the method of John Bassianus, subtle though he was (*qui satis fuit subtilis*) and of masters like Azo, Bulgarus, Martinus, and Odofredus who 'arguerunt ex textibus legum vicinis ad materiam de qua agebatur'—an admirable definition.

later course of scholastic thought and method, both for its own sake and in its relations to the schools, and at the same time others, equally numerous, have explored the obscure developments of medieval interests in cosmology, astronomy, physics, and mathematics, always pursued under the guidance of dialectic. The result of their labours is that the intense intellectual life of the Middle Ages is no longer presented as a long and weary orgy of barren chatter, interrupted by the orderly argument of a few men of genius who are as isolated in history as they are great, but as a process of incessant wisdom and folly with distinguishable lines of development in it, a process which did not come to a sudden close on the appearance of Erasmus and Luther, nor linger fruitlessly in obsolete schools, but threw up ideas and ways of thought and speech which have profoundly influenced the science and philosophy of the modern world.[1]

Most of this activity took place in the medieval university. It is true enough that much of it was sterile, as much academic discussion always is, had no roots in fact or experience, or was merely perverse. Rashdall emphasizes the reaction of men like Petrarch against it and would have sympathized with the criticisms of Aeneas Sylvius and the humanists.[2] Even if the whole course of medieval thought could be described as thoroughly and minutely as the ordnance survey of London, men would still continue to differ about its value. The only moral to be drawn here is that this intellectual activity is inseparable from the history of the medieval universities, or rather that any historian of the medieval university is compelled to reckon with it at every step. If Rashdall

---

[1] We are especially indebted to the work of Mandonnet, Haskins, and Duhem, and to many more scholars whose books and articles are mentioned in the bibliographies and notes. The best guide to literature before 1928 is Geyer's edition of Ueberweg. Lynn Thorndike's *History of Magic and Experimental Science* is very helpful. The third and fourth volumes unfortu-nately appeared too late to be used.

[2] Apropos of Aeneas Sylvius's oration, delivered in the *aula* of the University of Vienna in 1445, O. Redlich refers to Thomas Ebendorfer of Vienna, who lectured for twenty-two years on the book of Isaiah with no visible result (*Das akademische Deutschland*, i. 403). Later parallels could doubtless be found.

were writing his book to-day, and if he were not prepared to limit his subject even more rigidly than he did,[1] he would write a book differing in treatment, emphasis, and arrangement from the book which he completed in 1895. As it is impossible to separate thought and action, closer attention to the processes of thought would be found to lead to a more careful treatment of the bearing of their expression in action upon the origin and growth of universities. For example, we can see in the early history of Bologna and Paris the continuous influence of ecclesiastical ideas, not merely as external influences upon alien material, but as an expression, both in deliberate policy and in more or less conscious application, of that movement which we generally describe as the development of the papal system. As a matter of course, the organized Church, as it grew in strength and complexity, took cognizance of every form of educational life. From one point of view the concentration of students and teachers in cathedral schools, of which Paris was one, was made possible by the papal concern for the clergy which was to grow into the system of provisions. From another, the formation of 'universities' of masters who lived on their fees raised the issue of the legal standing of corporate bodies within the Church.[2] From another, the early history of Bologna is an illustration of the *modus vivendi* which had to be reached between ecclesiastical authority, imperial legislation, civic control, and a new kind of organization, the 'university' of foreign students.[3] Denifle had seen the importance of these problems, and Rashdall, with his own independent outlook, followed Denifle;

---

[1] As it is perhaps needless to add, a 'constitutional history' of the medieval university could not be written without constant regard to contemporary movements of thought, both in the study of university origins, as is shown above, and in the description of university institutions. For example, the statutes which prescribe the exercises necessary before inception follow and take account of the methods of disputation evolved to display scholastic forms of argument. Other examples will occur to the reader.

[2] See Gaines Post in *Speculum*, ix (1934), 421–45; cf. below, vol. i, p. 298, n. 2, and *passim*.

[3] We have suggested that the formation of a 'university' of students at Paris was at one time more likely than Rashdall supposed; see below, vol. i, pp. 298 n., 316 n.

but, as Manacorda and other scholars have suggested, the issues had a wider setting, and were at the same time more significant and more consciously debated than has been realized. They illustrate the attitude of ecclesiastical power and its adjustment to new forms of life. They reveal thought in action at a critical period in the history of western Europe.

On the whole, however, recent investigation has not followed the earlier historians in their juristic discussions on the *criteria* of a university. These discussions were and are important enough, but they tend to a false separation between the studies which were pursued within the societies legally definable as universities and the intellectual life outside these societies. Separation suggests independence if not opposition, and the suggestion, with all respect to Petrarch and Erasmus, can be very misleading. The Spanish scholar who has argued that the European universities were the outcome of Islamic influence seems to us to be in error, but his argument may at least remind us that one of the greatest forces in the medieval university, Mohammedan learning, found a footing in the West in centres, especially Toledo, which were under royal and episcopal influence, in Jewish and other circles in the south of France and, to some extent, in the royal court in Sicily. Again, the study of theology owed almost as much to the Dominican and Franciscan *scolae* outside the universities as to their houses in university centres; yet it would be absurd to separate the former from the latter. The hard and fast distinction drawn by Rashdall between the Italian universities and educational developments in Italy as a whole vitiates his criticism of the learned interests of the medieval Italian, whether he was a university man or not. Rashdall, indeed, spent so much time and energy on legal and constitutional problems that he had little to give to the other academic developments of the later Middle Ages. And, in any case, as we must always remember, he was treading here on almost unknown ground. Since he wrote, every aspect of his subject or of what he might have comprised within his subject has been illuminated, fitfully, but powerfully, by later scholars. The conflicts of medieval scholasticism in the

fourteenth and fifteenth centuries, the interactions of humanism and older studies in Germany, Italy, France, and Spain, the
influence of the Renaissance upon university life everywhere,
the appropriation and transcendence of medieval thought by
the philosophers and scientists of the sixteenth and seventeenth centuries—all these problems are being explored. One
result of this learned activity has been to change our views
about the universities of Europe in the fourteenth and fifteenth centuries. Some of them, perhaps especially in France,
lived vacantly on their past, but as a whole they played their
part, and an important part, in the transition from the
medieval to the modern world. Indeed, Rashdall's rather
pedantic adherence to the year 1500 as a closing date, and
his somewhat weary treatment, which gives the impression of
a long and melancholy cadence, of the history of the universities in the later Middle Ages, were not justified, as he occasionally seems to have realized himself. Recent scholarship
has broken down the artificial barrier which was set for so
long by men's minds between the centuries.[1]

Even so, the medieval university was but one expression
of medieval life, both active and contemplative. If we rightly
refuse to allow that the medieval scholar, who had spent his
life in the university schools, was cut off from the society
around him, we must not place him in the centre of things
and regard the microcosm of which he was part as an exhaustive reflection of the wider world. He might be influential in the counsels of kings, or even be able to appreciate the
beauties of good Latin prose, and yet be remote from all
those spiritual things in which men of loftier minds would
have had him take delight. S. Anselm, Abelard, S. Bernard,
Hugh of S. Victor, S. Francis, Dante, Master Eckhart, and

---

[1] It is fitting to mention in this
connexion the *Histoire des universités françaises et étrangères des
origines à nos jours*, by the late
Stephen d'Irsay (vol. i, Paris, 1933).
Though slightly constructed, if
compared with the work of Denifle
and Rashdall, it approaches the
subject, often very suggestively,
and with considerable charm, from
this newer point of view. The
second volume, dealing with modern times prior to 1860 has recently appeared (1935). Manacorda's
Storia della scuola in Italia, frequently noted in the pages of this
edition of Rashdall, is important,
if often disputable.

Nicholas of Cues, some of them men of the schools, others not, each in his time, knew what the ordinary scholar never knew. And there is still much work to be done which may not touch the life of the schools, yet none the less will take us into the heart of the Middle Ages. We have mentioned Nicholas of Cues, the great scholar-preacher and cardinal-statesman of the fifteenth century. Nicholas found his own way, which was neither the *via antiqua* nor the *via moderna* of his contemporaries in the schools. The vision of the incomprehensible 'to be embraced incomprehensibly in learned ignorance' came to him at sea on his way home from Greece —'a heavenly gift from the father of lights'. His 'negative theology' was the culmination of a long process, which, while it had passed through and taken the colour of the schools, had its own independent impetus. Nicholas read John the Scot and Eckhart, while other men read Duns Scotus and Occam. His religious and intellectual experience contained within it a Platonic tradition which, if its exponents speak truly, has entered deeply into modern thought. But, if Nicholas made himself independent of the schools, he did not, like Luther, repudiate them. His theory of knowledge was inseparable in his mind from the love of one's neighbour which is to be sought and found in membership of the Church which is the body of Christ; his attitude to the learning of the schools was not that it was false but that it must be transcended by a higher learning. The subtleties of human reasoning were natural to man in his pagan state,[1] and the knowledge of this world was none the less a knowledge of incorruptible truths.

Professor Powicke is responsible for the revision of the first and second volumes of Rashdall's book, Mr. Emden for

[1] 'Si vis in Christo Dei filius renasci, accedere te et venire oportet ad hunc solem, tu qui es gentilis in subtilitate racionum humanarum.' From the sermon *Dies Sanctificatus* of 1439, edited with a commentary, by E. Hoffmann and R. Klibansky in the *Sitzungsberichte der Heidelberger Akademie der Wissenschaften*, philos.-hist. Klasse, 1928–9, Abhandl. 3, p. 39. For Luther's views on the university teaching of his day and of the true university, see Hanns Rückert's short essay, *Die Stellung der Reformation zur mittelalterlichen Universität*, Stuttgart, 1933.

the revision of the chapters on Oxford and Cambridge in the third volume. We revised the two concluding chapters of the work jointly. At every stage in the progress of our task we have discussed its problems together, and both of us have read the proofs of the whole work. In the revision of the proofs we have owed much to the careful and intelligent scrutiny of the readers of the Clarendon Press. We have received assistance from many other quarters, and desire, in this introduction, to make our grateful acknowledgement to our helpers.

Professor G. R. Potter, of the University of Sheffield, has given ungrudgingly and invaluable help throughout. He prepared detailed lists of corrections and submitted notes which embodied, so far as he considered that they would help us, the results of his own investigations into the history of the German universities. Also, he has revised the proofs of the first and second volumes. Other scholars have helped us in the revision of particular chapters. Professor C. C. J. Webb revised the proofs of the chapter on Abelard, Professor C. Foligno those on Bologna and the Italian universities, and Professor H. Kantorowicz those on Irnerius (with particularly helpful results). In the preparation of the long chapter on Paris, we have been especially assisted by Father Franz Pelster, S.J., Mr. Gaines Post, formerly of Harvard University, and Professor Ch. Samaran of the École des Chartes in Paris. The late Professor L. J. Paetow had also undertaken to send us notes on the University of Paris, to whose history he had given much attention, and before his death he was able to send us helpful contributions to the section on the colleges. One of his notes has been incorporated as it stood, and we have profited by everything that he sent and by his published work. Professor W. J. Entwistle took charge of the chapter on the universities of Spain and Portugal. For the presentation of his material we are responsible, but the chapter, as revised, is, with the exception of a few notes, his work or the work of Rashdall himself.[1] We are deeply

---

[1] Professor Entwistle desires to acknowledge help received from several correspondents in Spain, America, and the British Isles.

indebted to him. Similar acknowledgement is due to the Historiographer Royal, Professor R. K. Hannay, of the University of Edinburgh, who not only took charge of the sections on the Universities of S. Andrews and Glasgow, but, in accordance with his own wish, completely re-wrote them.[1] Professor A. Odložilík of the Charles University, Prague, revised the proofs of the section on Prague, and Professor Stanislaw Kot, member of the Polish Academy, the proofs of the section on Cracow. The revision of the chapter on Oxford shows on every page our indebtedness to the writings of the Rev. Dr. H. E. Salter and of the Keeper of the Archives, Mr. Strickland Gibson, who have also given valuable advice. In the preparation of the chapter on Cambridge we received help from many quarters, especially from the late Mr. A. Attwater, of Pembroke College, Cambridge.

Miss Helen Briggs gave us help on the history of *dictamen* in Italy, Miss Mary Rixon allowed us to use her unpublished dissertation on the Dominican schools, Professor Dorothy Mackay Quynn, of Duke University, sent criticisms of Rashdall's section on the University of Orleans, and Miss Hilda Moyns collected material for the revision of the last two chapters on numbers and university life. The late Monsignor G. Lacombe summarized for us the results of his laborious investigation into the medieval translations of Aristotle.

We have received corrections and information upon particular points from Mrs. H. M. Allen, Mr. G. Barraclough, Professor J. H. Baxter, Dr. G. G. Coulton, Mr. Richard Hunt, Professor E. F. Jacob, Dr. A. G. Little, the late Professor Max Manitius, Mr. W. A. Pantin, Mr. R. F. Young, Count Roberto Weiss, and Professor F. de Zulueta.

Mrs. Rashdall, with a view to a new edition, entrusted her husband's annotated copy of his book to the Delegates of

[1] Professor Hannay has incorporated a few characteristic passages from the original chapter on the universities of Scotland. He prepared the section on S. Andrews with the aid of Professor J. H. Baxter, and that on Glasgow after consultation with Sir Robert Rait. The section on Aberdeen and the concluding observations in this chapter have been revised, not re-written.

the Clarendon Press more than ten years ago. We fear that she must often have wondered whether the new edition would ever appear. Apologies for delay are always tedious and are rarely convincing. We shall offer none, but venture to hope that she will welcome our work, in spite of all its imperfections, as a tribute to the learning, and also to the memory, of a great Oxford scholar.

CHAPTER I

WHAT IS A UNIVERSITY?

Of the older works on universities in general the most important are— CONRINGIUS, *De Antiquitatibus Academicis Dissertationes Septem* (ed. Heumannus, with HEUMANNI, *Bibliotheca Historica Academica*, Göttingen, 1739; and *Opera*, Brunswick, 1730, vol. v); MIDDENDORPIUS, *Academiarum Orbis Christiani Libri duo*, Cologne, 1567 (*Libri iv*, 1594; *Libri viii*, 1602); LAUNOIUS, *De Scholis Celebrioribus*, Paris, 1672.

The following may also be mentioned: HAGELGANS, *Orbis Literatus Academicus Germano-Europaeus*, Frankfurt, 1737; ITTERUS, *De Honoribus Academicis Liber*, Frankfurt, 1685.

MEINERS, *Geschichte der Entstehung und Entwickelung der hohen Schulen* (Göttingen, 1802–5), long remained the only modern work on this subject as a whole, and that a completely uncritical one. SAVIGNY began the scientific investigation of the subject, in his *Geschichte des römischen Rechts im Mittelalter* (Heidelberg, 2. Aufl. 1834, &c.); but he is only valuable for the Italian universities and the legal faculties. MALDEN, *On the Origin of Universities* (London, 1835), is full of blunders; more valuable contributions to university history were made by Sir William HAMILTON in his polemical articles in the *Edinburgh Review* (1831–4), reprinted in *Discussions on Philosophy and Literature, Education, and University Reform* (London, 1852). VALLET DE VIRIVILLE, *Histoire de l'instruction publique en Europe* (Paris, 1849), hardly pretends to be a serious history of the universities. The subject has naturally been the theme of many academical addresses, pamphlets, &c., but it will be enough to mention DÖLLINGER, *Die Universitäten sonst und jetzt* (Munich, 1867; *Universities Past and Present*, translated by APPLETON, Oxford, 1867).

The subject remained practically *terra incognita* till the appearance of DENIFLE'S great work, *Die Entstehung der Universitäten des Mittelalters bis 1400* (Berlin, 1885), the first and only volume of a colossal undertaking which was never continued. I have expressed my sense of the value of this great work in the Preface.

Of the critics of Denifle the most important is GEORG KAUFMANN. His *Geschichte der Deutschen Universitäten* (Stuttgart, 1888–96) forms an interesting, well-written, and not unimportant contribution to the history of medieval universities in general. The controversy between him and DENIFLE (which was unfortunately violent) was conducted by KAUFMANN in *Göttingische Gelehrte Anzeigen* (1886, p. 97 *sq*.), *Zeitschrift d. Savigny-Stiftung* (VII. Germ. Abth. Heft i, p. 124 *sq*.), *Historisches Jahrbuch* (x, 1888, 349–60), *Deutsche Zeitschrift für Geschichtswissenschaft* (1889, I. i, 118 *sq*.); and by DENIFLE in *Hist. Jahrbuch* (x. 72–98, 361–75), *Archiv für Litteratur- und Kirchengeschichte des Mittelalters* (ii. 337 *sq*.).

LAURIE, *Lectures on the Rise and Early Constitution of Universities* (London, 1886), is a brilliantly written little book, but is unfortunately full of inaccuracies and misconceptions, old and new. MULLINGER's article on *Universities* in the *Encyclopaedia Britannica* (ninth edition) deserves mention as the first tolerably correct (though very brief) account of the subject which has appeared in English.

[The most suggestive contribution to the subject since 1895 is to be found

CHAP. I. in Giuseppe MANACORDA's *Storia della scuola in Italia*, vol. i; *Il medio evo*, in two parts, published in the series 'Pedagogisti ed Educatori' (Remo Sandron, editore, Milan, n.d. The preface is dated October 1913). This book, however, should be used with care, for MANACORDA's main contentions have been strongly criticized; see especially V. ROSSI's review in the *Giornale storico della letteratura italiana*, lxvi (1915), 182–99; reprinted in his *Scritti di critica letteraria*, iii. 71 *sqq*. Stephen D'IRSAY, *Histoire des universités françaises et étrangères des origines à nos jours*, volume i (Paris, 1933), is good within its limits, and especially useful for the development of studies.

Among other recent works may be noted Ch.-V. LANGLOIS's essay in the first series of his *Questions d'histoire et d'enseignement* (Paris, 1902); C. H. HASKINS, *The Rise of Universities* (New York, 1923), a good popular sketch. Paul SIMON's rectorial address, *Die Idee der mittelalterlichen Universität und ihre Geschichte* (Stuttgart, 1932), is thoughtful and interesting.

The subject is treated at more or less length in the general histories of education: K. A. SCHMID, *Geschichte der Erziehung vom Anfang an bis auf unsere Zeit* (Berlin, 1884–1902); Th. ZIEGLER, *Geschichte der Pädagogik mit besonderer Rücksicht auf das höhere Unterrichtswesen* (3rd ed., Munich, 1909); cf. articles in WATSON's *The Encyclopaedia and Dictionary of Education* (4 volumes, London, 1920).]

Importance of subject. *S*ACERDOTIUM, *Imperium*, *Studium* are brought together by a medieval writer[1] as the three mysterious powers or 'virtues', by whose harmonious co-operation the life and health of Christendom are sustained. This 'Studium' did not to him, any more than the 'Sacerdotium' or the 'Imperium' with which it is associated, represent a mere abstraction. As all priestly power had its visible head and source in the city of the Seven Hills, as all secular authority was ultimately held of the Holy Roman Empire, so could all the streams of knowledge by which the Universal Church was watered and fertilized, be ultimately traced as to their fountain-head to the great universities, especially to the University of Paris. The history of an institution which held such a place in the imagination of a medieval scholar is no mere subject of antiquarian curiosity; its origin, its development, its decay, or rather the transition to its modern form, are worthy of the same serious investigation which

---

[1] 'Hiis si quidem tribus, scilicet sacerdotio imperio et studio, tanquam tribus uirtutibus, uidelicet uitali naturali et animali, sancta ecclesia katholica spiritualiter uiuificatur augmentatur et regitur. Hiis etiam tribus, tanquam fundamento pariete et tecto, eadem ecclesia quasi materialiter perficitur.' Jordan of Osnaburg, *De prerogatiua Romani Imperii*, ed. Waitz (1869), p. 70. [For the authorship of this tract see below, p. 23, where the passage is again cited.]

has been abundantly bestowed upon the Papacy and the Empire.

Like the Papacy and the Empire, the university is an institution which owes not merely its primitive form and traditions, but, in a sense, its very existence to a combina- tion of accidental circumstances; and its origin can only be understood by reference to those circumstances.[1] But the subsequent development of each of these institutions was determined by, and reveals to us, the whole bent and spiritual character of the age to whose life it became organic. The university, no less than the Roman Church and the feudal hierarchy headed by the Roman Emperor, represents an attempt to realize in concrete form an ideal of life in one of its aspects. Ideals pass into great historic forces by embodying themselves in institutions. The power of embodying its ideals in institutions was the peculiar genius of the medieval mind, as its most conspicuous defect lay in the corresponding tendency to materialize them. The institutions which the Middle Age has bequeathed to us are of greater and more imperishable value even than its cathedrals. And the university is distinctly a medieval institution—as much so as constitutional kingship, or parliaments, or trial by jury. The universities and the immediate products of their activity may be said to constitute the great achievement of the Middle Ages in the intellectual sphere. Their organization and their traditions, their studies and their exercises affected the progress and intellectual development of Europe more powerfully, or (perhaps it should be said) more exclusively, than any schools in all likelihood will ever do again. A complete history of the universities of the Middle Ages would be in fact a history of medieval thought—of the fortunes, during four centuries, of literary culture, of the whole of the

---

[1] [The possibility that the medieval university owed much to conscious imitation from the Arabian system of education has been urged by the Spanish scholar, J. Ribera y Tarragó. See his collected *Disertaciones y opúsculos*, i. 243 (Madrid, (1928). He lays stress upon the rapidity of the development from the twelfth century, the mingling of papal direction with free institutions, suggesting a mingling of two types of civilization, and the grant of titles or degrees (cf. the *ichaza* or licence, *ibid.*, pp. 334-40). His argument is not convincing.]

scholastic philosophy and scholastic theology, of the revived study of the civil law, of the formation and development of the canon law, of the faint, murky, cloud-wrapped dawn of modern mathematics, modern science, and modern medicine. Hardly more than a glance can be given at many of these subjects in the present work. Its paramount object will be to study the growth of the university as an institution, to trace the origin of the various universities, and to sketch the most important changes which passed over their form and their spirit during the period before us. Our attention will be for the most part confined to the parent or typical universities; no more than a slight sketch will be attempted of their derivatives or descendants. Even so, our subject is in some respects an inconveniently extended one. But if this diffusion of interest involves some sacrifice of that thoroughness in research, of that concentration of view, and that vividness of local colouring which might have been possible in a monograph on a single university, something will be gained if it becomes clear, as we compare Bologna with Paris, and Paris with Oxford or Prague, that the universities of all countries and all ages are in reality adaptations under various conditions of one and the same institution; that if we would completely understand the meaning of offices, titles, ceremonies, organizations preserved in the most modern, most practical, most unpicturesque of the institutions which now bear the name of 'university', we must go back to the earliest days of the earliest universities that ever existed, and trace the history of their chief successors through the seven centuries that intervene between the rise of Bologna or Paris, and the foundation of the new University of Strasbourg or of the new universities in England.

Meaning of *univer-sitas.* The word *universitas* is one to which a false explanation is often assigned for polemical purposes by controversial writers, while the true explanation of it at once supplies us with a clue to the nature and historical origin of the institution itself. The notion that a university means a *universitas facultatum*—a school in which all the faculties or branches of knowledge are represented—has, indeed, long

since disappeared from the pages of professed historians; but
it is still persistently foisted upon the public by writers with
whom history is subordinate to what may be called intellectual edification. However imposing and stimulating may be
the conception of an institution for the teaching or for the cultivation of universal knowledge, however imperative the necessity of such an institution in modern times, it is one which can
gain little support from the facts of history. A glance into
any collection of medieval documents reveals the fact that
the word 'university' means merely a number, a plurality, an
aggregate of persons. *Universitas vestra*, in a letter addressed
to a body of persons, means merely 'the whole of you'; in a
more technical sense it denotes a legal corporation[1] or juristic
person; in Roman law (though in strictness a wider term)
it is for most purposes practically the equivalent of *collegium*. At the end of the twelfth and beginning of the thirteenth centuries, we find the word applied to corporations
either of masters or of students; but it long continues to be
applied to other corporations as well, particularly to the then
newly formed guilds and to the municipalities of towns;
while as applied to scholastic guilds it is at first used inter-
changeably with such words as 'community' or 'college'.
In the earliest period it is never used absolutely. The phrase
is always 'University of Scholars', 'University of Masters and
Scholars', 'University of Study', or the like. It is a mere accident that the term has gradually come to be restricted to a
particular kind of guild or corporation, just as the terms
'convent', 'corps', 'congregation', 'college', have been
similarly restricted to certain specific kinds of association.
It is particularly important to notice that the term was generally in the Middle Ages used distinctly of the scholastic
body whether of teachers or scholars, not of the place in
which such a body was established, or even of its collective
schools. The word used to denote the academic institution

[1] Long after the rise of the
scholastic universities, *universitas*
is used (absolutely) of the town corporations or guilds. Thus Boniface
VIII writes 'Universitatibus et
populo dicti Regni' (Franciae). Even
so vague a body as 'all faithful
Christian people' is often addressed
as 'Universitas vestra'.

CHAP. I. in the abstract—the schools or the town which held them—was *studium* rather than *universitas*. To be a resident in a university would be *in studio degere* or *in scolis militare*. The term which most nearly corresponds to the vague and indefinite English notion of a university as distinguished from a mere school, seminary, or private educational establishment, *Studium generale.* is not *universitas*, but *studium generale*; and *studium generale* means, not a place where all subjects are studied, but a place where students from all parts are received. As a matter of fact, very few medieval *studia* possessed all the faculties. Even Paris in the days of her highest renown possessed no faculty of civil law; while throughout the thirteenth century graduation in theology was in practice the almost exclusive privilege of Paris and the English universities.[1]

Changes of meaning. The term *studium generale* does not become common till the beginning of the thirteenth century.[2] At that time the

[1] Though nominally shared by Naples, Toulouse, and the university of the Roman Court. Bulls for the erection of *studia generalia* usually specified the faculties in which the *Facultas ubique docendi* was granted; or it was 'in quavis licita facultate'.

[2] 'Universale', and more rarely 'commune', are common synonyms for 'generale'. The allusion in Guibert de Nogent (†1124), *De vita sua*, l. i, c. 4 (ed. G. Bourgin, 1907, p. 13), 'Cum nocte dormiret in cubiculo, cuius et ego memini, in quo totius nostri oppidi generale studium regebatur, . . .', is clearly a non-technical use of the word. The earliest instance of the technical expression that I have noticed is in the Chronicle of Emo in relation to Oxford, *c.* 1190 (*Monumenta Germaniae Historica, Scriptores*, xxiii. 467; below, vol. ii, ch. xii, § 1), where the word is 'commune'. *Studium solempne* is sometimes used as a synonym for *generale*, but occasionally it seems to be distinguished from it, meaning an important or frequented school which

was not technically 'general'. See Denifle and Chatelain, *Chartul. Univ. Paris.*, 1889, &c., ii, No. 1015, 'in nullo conventu, ubi non est studium generale aut aliud studium solempne'. See the definition in the Siete Partidas of Alfonso X of Castile, below, vol. ii, ch. vii, § 2. The Canonist 'Hostiensis' (Henricus de Segusia), writing at about the same time (†1271), discusses the limits of the privilege of dispensation from residence for the purpose of study, and lays it down: 'Hoc autem arg. potest hinc elici, quod istud intelligatur de generali, non de particulari. Et dicitur generale, quando triuium et quadriuium, Theologia et sacri canones ibidem leguntur. Sed certe et hoc putamus ad arbitrium boni judicis redigendum,' &c. Hostiensis, *in Decretalium Libros*, ii, Venice, 1581, f. 13. The requirement that theology should be taught is curious, since Bologna could only satisfy the test by its Friar doctors, who did not graduate at Bologna. He goes on to ask: 'Nunquid enim si propter guerram non audent ad presens ad scholas

term was a perfectly vague one, as vague and indefinable CHAP. I.
as the English term Public School or the German *Hoch-
schule*. In the main, however, the term seems to have
implied three characteristics: (1) That the school attracted
or at least invited students from all parts, not merely
those of a particular country or district; (2) that it was a
place of higher education; that is to say, that one at least
of the higher faculties—theology, law, medicine—was
taught there;[1] (3) that such subjects were taught by a
considerable number—at least by a plurality—of masters.
Of these ideas the first was the primary and fundamental
one: a *studium generale* meant a school of general resort,
but in its origin the expression was a wholly popular and
extra-legal one. The question whether a particular school
was or was not a *studium generale* was one settled by
custom or usage, not by authority. There were, however,
at the beginning of the thirteenth century three *studia* to
which the term was pre-eminently applied and which enjoyed
a unique and transcendent prestige: they were Paris for
theology and arts, Bologna for law, and Salerno for
medicine. A master who had taught and been admitted
to the magisterial guild in one of those places was certain
of obtaining immediate recognition and permission to teach

Bononie accedere, licebit eis citra
montes etiam in castris si compe-
tentem magistrum habeant studere?' A gloss declares that the
laws may be read anywhere:
'talis tamen locus non habebit
priuilegium studii generalis, nisi
ei concedatur a principe, vel consuetudine immemoriali, ut not. Bat.'
&c. It was no doubt largely the
necessity of defining a *studium
generale* for the purpose of dispensation from residence on account
of study which led to a definite and
precise meaning being given to the
term.

[1] [Cf. the words of Pope Innocent
VI, in his *privilegium* establishing
a theological faculty at Bologna
(1360): 'auctoritate apostolica statuimus et ordinamus quod in dicta
civitate deinceps existat *studium
generale in eadem theologica facultate*'; Ehrle, *I più antichi statuti della
facoltà teologica dell'università di
Bologna* (1932), p. 3.] There are
at least two instances of a *studium
generale* in arts only: (1) Sara-
gossa, which Denifle somewhat
arbitrarily excludes from the category of Universities—see below,
vol. ii, p. 101; (2) Erfurt, which we
learn from a document of 1362 was
'populari sermone' spoken of as a
studium generale. Since the recognition is in this case equivocal, I
have considered Erfurt as founded
by the Bull of 1379. See below, vol.
ii, p. 248.

CHAP. I. in all other inferior studia, while these *studia* themselves would not receive masters from other schools without fresh examination. Thus to the original conception of a *studium generale* there was gradually added a vague notion of a certain ecumenical validity for the mastership which it conferred. But at the same time there was nothing to prevent any school which thought itself entitled to the designation from assuming it. In the thirteenth century many schools besides Bologna and Paris claimed the rank of *studium generale*: it was in fact—at least in Italy, where the term was most in use—assumed by any school which wanted to intimate that it gave an education equal to that of Bologna or Paris.[1] And the extension of this usage was facilitated by the fact that most of these early schools were founded by masters who had actually taught at one of these places.

The *ius ubique docendi.* In the latter half of the thirteenth century this unrestricted liberty of founding *studia generalia* gradually ceased; and the cessation brought with it an important change in the meaning of the term. It so happened that at about the same time the two great 'world-powers' of Europe conceived the idea of creating a school which was to be placed by an exercise of authority on a level with the great European centres of education. In 1224 the Emperor Frederick II founded a *studium generale* at Naples; in 1229 Gregory IX did the same at Toulouse; while in 1244 or 1245 Innocent IV established a *studium generale* in the Pontifical Court itself. These foundations would appear to have suggested the idea that the erection of new *studia generalia* was one of the papal and imperial prerogatives, like the power of creating

---

[1] There were many such schools in Italy during the thirteenth century, but most of them early died out. ˏWhere they maintained their ground, the later and more technical ideas about *studia generalia* were naturally applied to them, since the change in the meaning was gradual and unconscious. Out of Italy there were no doubt many schools which *de facto* were as much *studia generalia* as Arezzo or Vercelli, but the name does not happen to have been applied to them: hence when the technical interpretation of *studium generale* gained ground, they lost their claims to the privileges which it conferred. Such schools were Lyons and Reims, for whose inclusion Kaufmann is urgent.

notaries public. Moreover, in order to give the graduates of Toulouse (in so far as parchment and wax could secure it) the same prestige and recognition which were enjoyed by the graduates of Paris and Bologna, a Bull was issued (in 1233) which declared that any one admitted to the mastership in that university should be freely allowed to teach in all other *studia* without any further examination. In the course of the century other cities anxious to place their schools on a level with these privileged universities applied for and obtained from Pope or Emperor Bulls constituting them *studia generalia*. The earlier of these Bulls simply confer the position of *studium generale* without further definition or confer the privileges of some specified university such as Paris or Bologna. The most prominent practical purpose of such Bulls seems at first to have been to give beneficed ecclesiastics the right of studying in them while continuing to receive the fruits of their benefices[1]— a privilege limited by canonical law or custom to *studia* reputed 'general'.[2] But gradually the special privilege of the *ius ubique docendi* came to be regarded as the principal object of papal or imperial creation. It was usually,

---

[1] The first Bull for a *studium* not actually created to forward some special purpose of Pope or Emperor was that for Piacenza in 1248, which conferred the privileges of Paris and other *studia generalia*. The Bull for Rome (*studium urbis*) in 1303 confers the right to receive fruits and other privileges, but no express *ius ubique*; those for Pamiers (1295) and Perugia (1308) simply create a *studium generale*. On the other hand, Montpellier (1289) and Avignon (1303) received the *ius ubique docendi*, which gradually became the usual form.

[2] Honorius III in 1219 (Decretal. Greg. IX. lib. v, tit. 5, c. 5; cf. lib. iii, tit. 5, c. 32) provided that teachers *of theology* as long as they were teaching, or students for five years, might receive their fruits, and prelates and chapters were required

to send 'docibiles' (i.e. canons) to study theology. There was no express limitation to *studia generalia*; but Honorius III clearly had recogized *scolae* in mind; and in 1207 Innocent III had ruled (Decretal. Greg. IX, lib. iii, tit. 4, c. 12) that the privilege of receiving the fruits of their prebends did not apply to those who 'se transferunt ad villas vel castella, in quibus nullum est vel minus competens studium literarum'. This was only intended to prevent fraud, but as time went on it could be interpreted to mean *studia* which were not general. (See the comment of Hostiensis, above, p. 6 note.)

Later, particular universities often obtained special Bulls confirming the dispensation from residence, and the right to receive all fruits except the 'daily distribution'.

CHAP. I. but not quite invariably, conferred in express terms by the original foundation-bulls; and was apparently understood to be involved in the mere act of erection even in the rare cases where it is not expressly conceded. In 1291–2 even the old archetypal universities themselves—Bologna and Paris—were formally invested with the same privilege by Bulls of Nicholas IV. From this time the notion gradually gained ground that the *ius ubique docendi* was of the essence of a *studium generale*, and that no school which did not possess this privilege could obtain it without a Bull from Emperor or Pope.[1] At the same time there were some of the older *studia*[2]—such as Oxford and Padua—which, without having been founded by Pope or Emperor and without having procured a subsequent recognition of their *ius ubique docendi*, had obtained a position as *studia generalia* too secure to be successfully attacked. Hence, with their habitual respect for established facts, the fourteenth-century jurists, to whom is chiefly due the formulation of the medieval ideas about universities, declared that such schools were *studia generalia* 'by custom' (*ex consuetudine*).[3]

Studia generalia respectu regni. The view of the fourteenth-century Italian jurists no doubt, on the whole, represents the dominant medieval theory on the subject. At the same time it is only natural

---

[1] The Bull for Paris is given in *Chartul. Univ. Paris.* ii, No. 578 (in Bulaeus, iii. 449, wrongly ascribed to Nicholas III); the Bologna Bull by Sarti, *De claris Archigymnasii Bononiensis Professoribus*, t. i, p. ii, Bologna, 1772, p. 59, renewed by Clement V in 1310, *Reg. Clem. V*, Rome, 1885, &c., No. 5275. In the latter case the privilege extended only to the two legal faculties. Bologna never obtained this privilege for her faculty of medicine or arts, yet this made no difference in practice to the estimation of the degrees—an illustration of the anomalies with which the matter abounds.

[2] Denifle holds (i. 777) that no *studium generale* arose without a Bull after the middle of the thirteenth century. There are one or two cases where this is doubtful: they are discussed in vol. ii.

[3] In some cases these prescriptive *studia generalia* assumed the right of conferring the *licentia docendi hic et ubique*. This appears to have been done by Reggio as early as 1276 (see the diploma in Tacoli, *Memorie storiche d. Reggio*, iii. 215), a circumstance which would suggest that the formula was used at Bologna before the grant of the papal Bull. In other cases, however, no such change appears to have taken place, e.g. at Oxford, if we may trust the evidence of the extant *formulae*. Padua eventually (in 1346) obtained a Bull. (See below, vol. ii, p. 15.)

to find that these ideas were less rapidly and less firmly established in countries which recognized the supremacy of the Holy Roman Empire at most in some shadowy and honorary way, and where the national Churches possessed most independence. Thus we find the Spanish kings erecting *studia generalia* without consulting Pope or Emperor. They do not, indeed, claim to confer a *ius ubique docendi*, which would be an absurd pretension on the part of a merely local sovereign. The jurists conceded to such universities all that they could possibly claim when they held them to be *studia generalia respectu regni*. If (as is insisted by Kaufmann)[1] there are instances of attempts on the part of a city

[1] Kaufmann (*Die Gesch. d. deutschen Universitäten*, i. 371–409) labours to show that the papal or imperial brief was not necessary to the legitimacy of a *studium generale* according to medieval notions— that the essential thing was recognition by the sovereign of the place. This theory is put forward in opposition to Denifle's view, which I have, in the main, adopted. Upon Kaufmann's arguments I remark: (1) That the discussions by Baldus and Bartolus in the extracts which he gives (i. 383, 384) turn not upon the question what constitutes a *studium generale,* but upon the question whether the teaching of the civil law was still restricted, as the constitution *omnem* (Digesta, ed. Mommsen, Berlin, 1872, i. xvi) provided, to *civitates regiae*, and what constituted a *civitas regia*. No doubt this constitution, and the claims which Bologna based upon it, powerfully contributed to the growth of the custom of applying for papal and imperial Bulls of erection and to the eventual belief in their necessity. But to say that the laws might be taught 'ex permissione eius tacita vel expressa qui est princeps' is not the same thing as to say that any 'princeps' could create a *studium generale* (in the full sense, not merely

'respectu regni'). There were scores of Italian cities (as Denifle has shown over and over again) in which law was taught by a number of state-authorized teachers which never pretended to be *studia generalia*. (2) That all passages and instances taken from the thirteenth-century writers or documents are not *ad rem*. It is admitted that at this time no Bull or Brief was thought to be necessary. But then so far *studium generale* meant merely 'a place of higher education of European or more than local repute'. And equally little is there any general notion (though such a view is undoubtedly expressed by the *Siete Partidas*) that a *studium generale* required a charter from King or sovereign-city. Undoubtedly it might have been held that it required the sovereign's 'permissio tacita', though this might have been denied by a Hildebrandine Churchman. There was no more general agreement as to the limits of the authority of Church and State than there is at the present moment between Father Denifle and Prof. Kaufmann. The fact is that this whole discussion as to the educational right of 'the State' in the Middle Ages involves something of an anachronism. I am bound to say

CHAP. I. republic to erect a *studium generale* without papal or imperial permission, if in one or two cases we even have diplomas granted by such bodies purporting to confer the *licentia ubique docendi*,[1] these are merely the exceptions which prove

that Kaufmann's treatment of the subject is far more vitiated by an infusion of ideas suggested by the *Kulturkampf*, than Denifle's is distorted by any desire to find support for those of the Syllabus [1895].

(3) It is useless to quote documents in which a king or town purports to erect a *studium generale* without express allusion to Emperor or Pope, unless it is shown (*a*) that no Bull was actually applied for, and (*b*) that a school actually came into existence without such Bull which was looked upon as a *studium generale*. Royal charters for the erection of a university are usually expressed in this form even where a Bull was applied for or already granted. It would be as reasonable to quote a written agreement between two persons to enter into marriage as evidence that they thought marriage would be legal without the intervention of priest or registrar. Even Denifle does not contend that it was considered lawful, or at all events possible, for the Pope to erect a university without consulting the local sovereign.

(4) The case of the Spanish universities is no exception to Denifle's view, since it is admitted that they were *studia generalia respectu regni*.

(5) Even if it could be shown that in isolated instances a city did purport to erect a *studium generale* without a Bull (after 1300), this would only show that they used the word in its older and less technical sense. In this older sense it is impossible to decide dogmatically what was a *studium generale* and what was not. It is therefore better to confine the word (in dealing with the period 1300–1500) to its technical sense of a *studium* which

possessed the *ius ubique docendi* at least *respectu regni*—even if this sense of the word was not universally accepted. As to the impossibility of a mere city (even if really sovereign) granting such a right, I have said enough. The case of the Parmese diploma merely proves the arrogance or ignorance of the scribe who copied it from some diploma or form-book of a real university, even if it was not intended to apply for a Bull.

(6) The only evidence that may possibly require some modification of Denifle's view is the language used by the *imperial* Bull (the Papacy at this time always assumes the necessity of a Bull) in the foundation of Siena (1357), where the Emperor treats the *studium generale* of that place as already existing. But if its position as *studium generale* was established before 1250, Denifle would admit it to be *studium generale ex consuetudine*. Although Denifle does not admit this to have been the case, the correction involves no change of principle. See below, ch. vi, § 9.

(7) It must be conceded to Kaufmann that when Denifle, while fully admitting the imperial prerogative of founding universities, insinuates (i. 384) that 'Allein gerade dieses letztere Recht war theilweise durch das Gutdünken des Papstes bedingt', the Vatican Archivist does for once get the better of the historian. For Denifle's view of the whole question, see especially *Die Entstehung*, &c., pp. 763–91, and for his controversy with Kaufmann, the articles mentioned above, p. 1.

[We leave this characteristic note; but see the Additional Note at the end of the chapter.]

[1] As to Reggio see above, p. 10, note 3; cf. below, vol. ii, p. 6.

the rule. A claim on the part of officials or corporations chartered by a mere local authority to confer rights of teaching in universities which lay beyond their jurisdiction is too extravagant to have been seriously made, much less to have obtained general recognition.

The fluctuations of meaning which the term *studium* Subject *generale* underwent in the course of the Middle Age make it no easy task in all cases to adjudicate upon the claims of particular schools to that title. In the thirteenth century we are obliged to include in the category of 'universities' all bodies which we find expressly styled *studia generalia* in medieval writers, though there were no doubt many schools (especially in parts of Europe where the term was less current) which had in point of fact quite as good claims to 'generality', in the sense in which it was then understood, as some of those to which the term is actually applied; and some of them may have been actually so called, though evidence of the fact does not happen to have come down to us.[1] But from the beginning of the fourteenth century I accept the juristic definition, and exclude from the category of universities all bodies which were not founded by Pope or Emperor. *Studia generalia respectu regni* are, however, included, but these in nearly every case sooner or later strengthened their position by a papal Bull.

A wrong impression would, however, be given of the whole matter if it were supposed that, even when the *ius ubique docendi* was most indisputably assured by papal or imperial authority, it really received the respect which juristic theories claimed for it. The great primeval universities

---

[1] Such as Lyons, Reims, Erfurt, &c. It is highly probable—and this must be conceded to Kaufmann—that in the thirteenth century these schools were sometimes or always called *studia generalia*. A Paris Statute of 1279 (Bulaeus, iii. 447; Denifle and Chatelain, *Chartul.* i, No. 485) requires candidates for the licence in arts to have determined either at Paris or in some other *studium generale* where there were not less than twelve regents: this points to the existence of many small *studia generalia*. But if we begin to include in our enumeration schools which are not expressly described as *studia generalia* or created such by Bull, it would be impossible to know where to draw the line.

CHAP. I. perhaps never recognized the doctorates conferred by the younger bodies.[1] At Paris, even Oxford degrees failed to command incorporation without fresh examination and licence, and Oxford repaid the compliment by refusing admission to Parisian doctors, the papal Bull notwithstanding.[2] Even in less illustrious universities the statutes provide for some preliminary test before the reception of a graduate from another university which can hardly be distinguished from the 'examination' which the papal Bulls forbade,[3] since it is always implied that the university reserved the right of refusing permission to lecture and exercise other magisterial rights to any foreign graduate of whose competence it was not satisfied.[4] It should be added

The ius ubique docendi not always respected.

[1] When Paris complained of the rights given to the graduates of Toulouse, Gregory IX himself explained that the privileges of the new university were not intended to interfere with those of Paris. *Chartul. Univ. Paris.* i, No. 101. In granting the *ius ubique docendi* to Salamanca, Alexander IV expressly excepted Paris and Bologna. See below, vol. ii, p. 78.

[2] 'Qui Parisius uel alibi ubi Oxonienses a resumpcione maliciose excluduntur, nec ipsi Oxonie admittantur' (*Statuta Antiqua*, ed. S. Gibson, pp. 53, 54; see the comment in the introduction, p. cxviii and note), and Paris complains to the Pope that her *ius ubique docendi* is not respected everywhere 'ut in Anglia et apud Montem Pessulanum'. *Chartul. Univ. Paris.* ii, No. 728. Attempts were made in 1296 and 1317 to procure the *ius ubique docendi* by papal Bull. Documents in Lincoln Register (Bishop Sutton's *Memoranda*, f. 141 *b*); Wood, *Hist. and Antiq. of Oxford*, ed. Gutch, i. 155; *Chartul. Univ. Paris.* ii, No. 756. As the attempt was not made at a later date, we may perhaps assume that Oxford was satisfied with its position as a *studium generale ex consuetudine*; yet Oxford never

actually conferred the *licentia ubique docendi*, nor (of course) did she confer degrees 'Apostolica auctoritate'. At Bologna we find the personal intervention of Charles II of Naples necessary to obtain recognition for Jacobus de Belvisio, who had graduated at Naples in 1298 or 1299; and even then he appears to have gone through the ceremony of promotion *de novo*. Savigny, c. xlix.

[3] See e.g. Kink, *Gesch. der Univ. Wien*, ii. 167. At Angers it is expressly provided that no graduates from another university shall lecture before 'per scholasticum et doctores examinentur diligenter', but 'si repetant alia examinatione non indigent'. Rangeard, *Hist. de l'Un. d'Angers*, ii. 221.

[4] In 1321 Orleans enacted 'quod nullus doctor extrinsecus veniens, ad actum regendi ordinarie . . . in nostra Universitate admittatur, vel ad alios actus doctorales, nisi per collationem doctorum, ut moris est, fuerit approbatus, et hic insignia receperit doctoratus'—Fournier, *Stat. et privilèges des univ. françaises* (Paris, 1890) i, No. 78. It is true that there is a 'salvo honore . . . sancte sedis apostolice'. In 1463 (*ibid.*, No. 320) we find the Pope interfering to prevent a

CHAP. I.

that in proportion as the real privileges of the mastership were restricted (as was eventually more or less the case in the majority of universities) to a limited body of salaried doctors, the ecumenical rights conferred by graduation in a *studium generale* came to possess a purely honorary value. The mastership was reduced to a universally recognized honour, but nothing more.[1]

It remains to point out the relation of the term 'studium generale' to the term 'universitas'. There was originally no necessary connexion between the institution denoted by the term *universitas* and that denoted by the term *studium generale*. Societies of masters or clubs of students were formed before the term *studium generale* came into habitual use; and in a few instances such societies are known to have existed in schools which never became *studia generalia*.[2] The university was originally a scholastic guild whether of masters or students. Such guilds sprang into existence, like other guilds, without any express authorization of king, pope, prince, or prelate. They were spontaneous products of that instinct of association which swept like a great wave over the towns of Europe in the course of the eleventh and twelfth centuries.[3] But in two places

Universitas and *studium generale*; originally distinct, afterwards synonymous.

'doctor bullatus', i.e. made by the Pope, from assuming the rights of a regent at Orleans. Cf. *Chartul. Univ. Paris.* ii, No. 1174.

[1] Kaufmann (i. 366 *sq.*) has the merit of first pointing out the very limited respect which was actually paid to these papal Bulls.

[2] Thus at Cremona it is provided by the town-statutes of 1387 'quod duo rectores possint eligi per scholares legum vel unus, secundum quod placuerit dictis scholaribus' (*Statuta Civ. Crem.*, Cremona, 1678, p. 135 [for the schools at Cremona see the bibliography in Manacorda, *op. cit.* ii. 295–6]); and the privileges accorded by the town are as ample as those enjoyed by masters and scholars in *studia generalia*. So at Perugia and at Pisa (see below, ch. vi, §§ 11, 12)

before they became *studia generalia*. It should be added that a *studium privilegiatum*—even with papal privileges—was not necessarily a *studium generale*, unless the Bull expressly created it such. Thus in 1247 the Pope gave 'doctoribus et scholaribus universis Narbonne in studio commorantibus', the privilege of absence from benefices, as though they were scholars in a *studium generale*. *Reg. Innocent IV*, ed. Berger, Paris, 1884, &c., No. 2717. Fournier prints a Bull of 1329 exempting the *studium* of Arts at Gaillac from the control of the Bishop of Albi and 'rectoris et magistrorum studii Albiensis' (*loc. cit.*, No. 1573). As to Valencia, see below, vol. ii, p. 107.

[3] Among general historians, no

CHAP. I. especially—Bologna and Paris—the scholastic guilds obtained a development and importance which they possessed nowhere else. And, as we shall see, nearly all the secondary *studia generalia* which arose spontaneously without papal or imperial charter, were established by secessions of masters or students from Paris or Bologna. The seceders carried with them the customs and institutions of their *alma mater*. Even in the few cases where the germs of a university or college of doctors may have originated independently of the influence of Paris and Bologna, their subsequent development was due to more or less direct and conscious imitation of the scholastic guilds of these two great schools. Thus it came about that a *universitas*, whether of masters or of students, became in practice the inseparable accompaniment of the *studium generale*—and a *universitas* of a particular and definite type formed more or less on the model of one of these great archetypal universities.[1] Thus in the later Middle Ages the term *studium generale* came practically to denote not merely a school with the *ius ubique docendi* (though this remained its legal and technical differentia), but a scholastic organization of a particular type and

one has so fully appreciated this essential fact as the learned, if unsympathetic, Church-historian Mosheim: 'They who had satisfied all the demands of this academical law, and gone through the formidable trial with applause, were solemnly invested with the dignity of professors, and were saluted masters with a certain round of ceremonies, that were used in the societies of illiterate tradesmen, when their company was augmented by a new candidate. This vulgar custom had been introduced, in the preceding century, by the professors of law in the academy of Bologna; and in this century it was transmitted to that of Paris, where it was first practised by the divinity colleges, and afterwards by the professors of physic and the

liberal arts.' *Ecclesiastical History*, trans. by Maclaine, 1826, iii. 137. This last distinction is, however, unfounded.

[1] It is clear that graduation in its stricter sense could only exist where there was a *universitas*. A *licentia docendi* of purely local validity might of course have continued to be given by *studia* which were not general, but gradually the *licentia docendi* seems usually to have disappeared with the growing employment of university graduates to teach in the smaller *studia*. This seems to me a truer mode of statement than to say (with Denifle, i. 21) that *studia particularia* could only enjoy the 'Promotionsrecht' by special papal privilege or special custom.

endowed with more or less uniform privileges. By the CHAP. I.
fifteenth century the original distinction between the two
terms was pretty generally lost; and *universitas* gradually
became a mere synonym for *studium generale*.[1] In the
following pages the term university will be used in this
comprehensive sense except where it is necessary expressly
to distinguish the *studium* from the *universitas* proper.

Paris and Bologna are the two archetypal—it might Paris and
almost be said the only *original* universities: Paris sup- Bologna the two
plied the model for the universities of masters, Bologna arche-
for the universities of students. Every later university types.
from that day to this is in its developed form a more or
less close imitation of one or the other of these two types,
though in some few cases[2] the basis of the organization
may be independent. In the case of the earlier universities the imitation was, with whatever adaptation to local circumstances, conscious and deliberate; while the most purely
utilitarian of new universities retains constitutional features
or usages which are only explained by the customs and institutions either of the Bologna students or of the Parisian
masters at the end of the twelfth or the beginning of the
thirteenth centuries. It is clear therefore that a somewhat
minute study of these two typical bodies is essential to a
proper understanding of the university as an institution.

The two great parent universities arose at about the same Order of
time—during the last thirty years of the twelfth century. treatment.
They arose out of different sides of that wonderful deepening
and broadening of the stream of human culture which may
be called the Renaissance of the twelfth century. In Italy
this Renaissance found its expression most conspicuously
in a revival of the study of the Roman law, which started
from Bologna; in France it took the form of a great outburst of dialectical and theological speculation which

[1] The way for the identification was prepared by the intermediate term *universitas studii*, which was used at first distinctly of the society, as at Perugia in 1316, afterwards more loosely.

[2] Chiefly some of the older French universities, such as Angers and Orleans. See below, vol. ii, ch. viii. Denifle will ·not admit this except in the case of Oxford, where the contention is doubtful.

found its ultimate, though not its earliest, home in Paris. The Bologna university of students, though perhaps later than the first rudimentary germ of the Parisian society of masters, completed its organization earlier. And though each type of constitution was affected in its development by the influence of the other, Bologna in all probability exerted more influence over Paris than Paris over Bologna. Bologna therefore shall be dealt with first. With regard to the derivative universities, it might seem natural to divide them into two great classes, and to deal first with the universities of students, and then with the universities of masters. When, however, we come to examine the various constitutions in detail, it will be found that it is not always possible, without a very arbitrary treatment, to assign a given university definitively either to the Bolognese or the Parisian group. Many universities were influenced both by Paris and by Bologna. For it must be remembered that, though at Bologna the student-guild eventually established complete supremacy over the magisterial body, the masters always had a college of their own, to which alone belonged the right of admitting new masters or (in the modern phrase) 'granting degrees'. There might therefore be, and in fact there were, great variations in the distribution of academic power between the magisterial college and the student-guild. Moreover, this distribution might vary at different times; so that some *studia* approximate at one period of their history to the Bolognese, at another to the Parisian type. Hence, though a classification into student-universities and master-universities would bring into prominence the curious fact that the French universities are mostly children of Bologna rather than of Paris, and that the Scottish universities are in certain points more closely affiliated to Bologna than to Paris or Oxford, I have deemed it best on the whole (after dealing with the great model-universities) to group together the universities of each country in Europe, which naturally have certain features in common, though the differences between these national varieties are often far smaller than the fundamental distinction between the student and the magisterial type. Our own universities shall be reserved to the last, because, though belonging wholly to the magisterial type, and originally modelled on Paris, they exhibit from the first such marked constitutional peculiarities as almost to constitute a separate natural order of universities, distinct alike from the Bologna and the Parisian groups.

There is, however, one great *studium generale*, older in Salerno. a sense than either Paris or Bologna, which stands absolutely by itself. Its original constitution, of which, indeed, not much is known, appears to have had little resemblance to that of any other; and it never enjoyed that reproductive power which is so remarkable a characteristic of Bologna and Paris. The Medical School of Salerno did not (so far as it is known) influence the constitution even of the medical universities or the medical faculties. Such treatment as can be given to it must precede our account of Bologna. But, before entering upon the universities in detail, it will be convenient to give some general sketch of the great intellectual movement out of which in a sense all the universities, though pre-eminently that of Paris, arose, and, as an introduction to it, of the state of European education, especially in France, before the rise of the universities proper.

Before closing this preliminary survey of our subject, it The may be well to point out that the three titles, master, doctor, synonyms *master,* professor, were in the Middle Ages absolutely synonymous. *doctor,* *professor.* At Paris and its derivative universities we find *magister* the prevailing title in the faculties of theology, medicine, and arts; the title *professor* is, however, pretty frequently, that of *doctor* more rarely, employed.[1] The teachers of law at Bologna, however, specially affected the title *doctor*; they were also called *professores* and *domini*, but not as a rule *magistri*. The same usage was transferred to Paris. In the Acts of the faculty of canon law, we find the term *doctor* habitually used. Thus, when letters are addressed 'Rectori, Magistris, *Doctoribus* et Scolaribus Universitatis Parisiensis',

---

[1] That is, after the rise of the university. At an earlier period it had been common; *Hist. lit. de la* *France*, ix. 81. [It again became more frequent in the fifteenth century.]

CHAP. I. the order makes it plain that the theological teachers are included in the *magistri*, while the teachers of canon law are specially designated by the *doctores*. The same distinction was observed at Oxford; but in the fifteenth century—at least in the English universities—the practice gradually arose of appropriating the title *doctor* to all the superior faculties and reserving that of *magister* for the inferior faculties of arts and grammar. In Italy the term *doctor* soon spread from the faculty of law to all the other faculties. The same was eventually the case in Germany, where the master of arts is still styled doctor of philosophy. The purely accidental character of the distinction is strikingly illustrated by the fact that in the English universities the doctor of music, who in spite of his gorgeous plumage is not a member of Convocation and only ranks above the modest bachelor of arts, enjoys that imposing prefix of *doctor*, while his superior, the teacher of arts, is confined to the (in popular estimation) humbler style of *master*. German diplomas often confer the style 'Doctor of Philosophy and Master of Arts'.[1]

Additional Note to Chapter I

[Rashdall in the main accepted Denifle's conclusions on the origin of universities. Later investigation has done little to shake these conclusions. It tends to emphasize the importance of the *licentia docendi* and to strengthen the connexion between the early universities and ecclesiastical authority. It suggests that the sharp distinction between the *studium* and the *studium generale* can easily be exaggerated and that it obscures the growing control of the Pope and the bishops over the whole field of educational activity in the twelfth and thirteenth centuries. Manacorda (*Storia della scuola in Italia*, I. i, c. vii) discusses the various views of previous writers and argues that, even in Bologna, where Denifle traced the origin of the university to the communal schools, the evidence for con-

[1] In the above chapter, I am under exceptional obligations to Denifle, and have with some reserves adopted his position; but I have put the matter in my own way, and do not hold myself responsible for his views except so far as I have actually reproduced them. Denifle hardly recognizes sufficiently the prominence of the dispensation from residence in the earlier conception of a *studium generale*. See the Bull for Rome, cited below, vol. ii, p. 28 n., and above, p. 6, n. 2.

tinuous intervention by the ecclesiastical authority, and particularly by the Pope, is considerable. His conclusion, anticipated on
p. 165, that the medieval universities were in origin 'trasforma-
zioni delle scuole vescovili', cannot be literally accepted as a universal
truth. It is true of Paris, but it cannot be established, on existing
evidence, in the cases of Oxford and Montpellier, nor is it clear that,
in the early twelfth century, the masters who taught at Bologna had
any connexion with an episcopal school (cf. Haskins, on the *dictamen* of Albert of Samaria, *c.* 1111–18, in *Studies in Mediaeval
Culture*, Oxford, 1929, p. 175). On the other hand, Manacorda's
main contention, that the continuity of the schools, in Bologna and
elsewhere, was mainly due to the oversight of the diocesan authorities
who gave the licence to teach, and whose powers at this time were
steadily enforced, may be accepted, although, according to one view,
Montpellier provides an exception (see below, vol. ii, p. 122). It
should be remembered, in this regard, that the importance of the
episcopal schools, especially north of the Alps, in the twelfth century has been better realized than it was when Rashdall wrote. Until
late in the century Paris was by no means the outstanding centre of
higher learning in France, nor was Oxford in England. Why the
schools of Paris or Oxford grew into a university, while those of
Chartres and Laon, of Exeter and Lincoln did not, is a separate
problem, but the groups within which the university organization
developed were in the twelfth century given permanence by the
licentia docendi, and the licence was granted by the *magiscola*,
chancellor or archdeacon, as the case might be.

In the formative period the schools were fostered by the ecclesiastical authority and, like the universities into which some of them
developed, depended upon this authority for the right to exercise
their activity. There were exceptional cases, and these should be
regarded as exceptional. In Italy the city schools began too late
to be responsible for early developments; outside Italy such schools
hardly existed. In the later decades of the twelfth century ecclesiastical control of education was complete.

A long series of papal decrees provided for the creation of schools
under episcopal control. It begins with a letter of Eugenius II
(*c.* 826), embodied by Gratian in his *Decretum* (pars i, dist. xxxvii,
c. 2). The control of education by the secular power in Carolingian
times was first shared by, and then gave way to ecclesiastical control.
By the end of the twelfth century the ecclesiastical sanction behind
the licence to teach was undisputed. (The evidence for the undoubted existence of lay schools, and for the probable existence of
lay masters, in the twelfth century is discussed by Manacorda in
his fifth chapter; see below, p. 92, n. 1.) Pope Alexander III, in the
third Lateran Council in 1179 (see *Decretals*, lib. v, tit. v, c. 1) and
in various letters, emphasized the importance of the cathedral schools
and laid down rules for the grant of the licence. (See Gaines Post,
'Alexander III, the *licentia docendi* and the rise of the Universities'

CHAP. I. in *Haskins Anniversary Essays*, Boston, 1929, pp. 254–77.) As Post points out, too much stress has been laid on the point that the licence was to be gratuitous; whether this injunction was observed or not is not really of great importance in the history of university development. The important matter is the continuous guidance and encouragement given by the Papacy. When, on 28 June 1219, Honorius III in a letter to Grazia, the archdeacon of Bologna, decreed 'ut nullus ulterius in civitate predicta ad docendi regimen assumatur, nisi a te obtenta licentia, examinatione praehabita diligenti', he was not initiating a new policy. Manacorda (p. 208) is probably right in urging that the novelty here is the insistence upon a careful examination, not in the application to Bologna of a general practice which had not hitherto prevailed in the schools of that city. (See his quotations from the published and unpublished *summae* of S. Raymond of Pennaforte and the other evidence cited; Post, p. 266, accepts the earlier view that Honorius III was using precedents to bring the Law School of Bologna 'within the papal system'; and see Rossi's criticism of Manacorda, noted in the bibliographical note above, p. 2.)

The papal position in the thirteenth century was defined by Clement IV, in his letter 'contra venerabilem fratrem' of 31 May 1268, addressed to James I, king of Aragon (Potthast, No. 20366; edited by Martène, *Thesaurus anecdotorum*, ii. 603; see Manacorda, *op. cit.*, p. 217 *passim*). The bishop of Maguellone had excommunicated a civilian who had, in accordance with earlier usage (cf. Post, p. 267), received the licence to teach from the king, after he had taken counsel with *iuris prudentes* in the faculty at Montpellier. The Pope rebuked the king for his rancour against the bishop and upheld the claim of the latter to grant the licence in the faculty of law as in the other faculties, in which the episcopal licence had been given *a largissimis retro temporibus*. He did not deny that it had been customary at Montpellier for the king to grant the licence to civilians: 'de licentiandis quibus doctoribus in scientiarum facultatibus aliud canonica iura diffiniunt, aliud principum sanctiones', for local custom had differed and the secular authority at one time had dealt even with matrimonial questions, when the 'censura ecclesiae non vigebat'. On the other hand, the policy of the Church has been laid down by Eugenius II and the general rule applies to new specific conditions, although the species did not exist at the time when the rule was made, just as, if new kinds of corn are grown, the old law of tithe applies to them. 'Cancellarius caput studentium, post episcopum, in quacunque legat vel doceat facultate, ab episcopo ordinatur.'

The issue in debate between Denifle and Kaufmann (above, p. 11, note) may best be considered from the historical standpoint taken by Pope Clement IV. In the thirteenth and fourteenth centuries the *studia* were regarded as ecclesiastical foundations. In S. Thomas's words the *collegium scholasticum* was a *collegium ecclesiasticum*. But this is to be interpreted in the light of the medieval conception that CHAP. I. the Christian *ecclesia* was synonymous with Christian society. While the *studium* belonged to the *sacerdotium* rather than to the *imperium*, it was, like both, a part of the Christian society, which acquired a dignity of its own and deserved the fostering attention of *sacerdotium* and *imperium* alike. Thus, kings founded universities in co-operation with and after gaining the approval of the Popes (cf. Lérida, below, ii. 92). Where the spirit of co-operation existed, no burning question need arise if the chancellor was appointed by the king or bishop or masters. After expounding the curious historical view that Charles the Great had transferred the 'studium philosophiae et liberalium artium' from Rome to Paris, in part recompense to the king of the western Franks for the loss of his Empire (*regnum*), a German patriot (probably Alexander of Roes, in the year 1281) concludes: 'Hiis siquidem tribus, scilicet sacerdotio imperio et studio, tamquam tribus virtutibus, videlicet vitali naturali et animali, sancta ecclesia catholica spiritualiter vivificatur augmentatur et regitur' (*De translatione imperii*, ed. H. Grundmann, Leipzig, 1930, p. 27; cf. Cecil Woolf, *Bartolus of Sassoferrato*, Cambridge, 1913, p. 239). This wider conception made any dispute about the particular rights of lay or ecclesiastical authority a matter of local or temporary interest only, so long as the Pope and lay rulers cooperated in the foundation and development of universities. (F. von Bezold, following Gebhardt, has some pertinent remarks to this effect in his review of Kaufmann's work, *Aus Mittelalter und Renaissance*, Munich, 1918, p. 226.) An early instance of co-operation is the confirmation by Alexander III of the immunity granted by the Emperor Frederick I in 1158 to the students of Bologna (below, p. 145, n.). Just as the two powers co-operated in the repression of heresy, so they co-operated in the encouragement of learning. Papal privileges for the German universities, frequently founded by lay rulers, are found throughout the Middle Ages. That the grant of the licence was regarded as an ecclesiastical act is clear from the protest against the practice entered by Marsiglio of Padua: 'conferendi licentias in disciplinis iam dicto episcopo et alteri cuicumque presbytero ac ipsorum soli collegio debeat et licite potest revocari potestas. Est enim hoc humani legislatoris aut eius auctoritate principantis officium', and again, 'nolentes enim aut dubitantes viri literati suorum magisteriorum titulos perdere, appetitu commodi et gloriae consequentis, hosque sibi episcoporum Romanorum aut aliorum auctoritate advenisse, non aliunde, credentes, votis horum assequuntur' (*Defensor Pacis*, II. xxi, ed. Previté-Orton, Cambridge, 1928, pp. 340, 341).

That, as time went on, secular princes exercised authority over universities in virtue of their position as founders, or in the public interest, is undoubted; but it is important to distinguish action which can be construed as a deliberate interference with ecclesiastical or quasi-ecclesiastical privilege from co-operation which can be

CHAP. I. traced throughout the Middle Ages in all kinds of social activity, and which raised no controversial issues. It would not be difficult, if no regard were paid to this distinction, to show that the university of Oxford was under the control as well as the patronage of the king of England, and the more so, because the Chancellor was invested with a measure of temporal jurisdiction. Blackstone, indeed, traced the grant by the Crown of privileges to universities back to the Authenticum '*Habita*' or imperial constitution of 1158 (see Strickland Gibson, 'The Great Charter of Charles I', *Bodleian Quarterly Record*, vii. 1933).]

CHAPTER II

ABELARD AND THE RENAISSANCE OF THE TWELFTH CENTURY

For the general literary and educational history of the period with which this chapter deals, the most important authorities are the immense mass of material collected by BULAEUS in vols. i and ii of his *Historia Universitatis Parisiensis*, Paris, 1665; the *Histoire littéraire de la France*, par les Bénédictins de Saint-Maur, 1733, &c.;[1] JOLY, *Traité historique des écoles épiscopales et ecclésiastiques*, Paris, 1678; OZANAM, *La Civilisation chrétienne chez les Francs*, Paris, 1849; AMPÈRE, *Histoire littéraire de la France avant le douzième siècle*, Paris, 1839; MAITLAND, *The Dark Ages*, London, 1844; MAÎTRE (Léon), *Les Écoles épiscopales et monastiques de l'Occident*, Paris, 1866; MULLINGER, *The Schools of Charles the Great*, London, 1877 (also the Introduction to his *University of Cambridge to 1535*, Cambridge, 1873); POOLE (R. L.), *Illustrations of the History of Medieval Thought*, London, 1884 (ed. 2, 1920); COUSIN, *Ouvrages inédits d'Abélard*, Paris, 1836, and *Petri Abaelardi Opera*, Paris, 1849; SCHAARSCHMIDT, *Johannes Saresberiensis*, Leipzig, 1862; DE RÉMUSAT, *Abélard*, Paris, ed. 2, 1855; COMPARETTI, *Virgilio nel Medio Evo*, Leghorn, 1872 (English trans., London, 1895), ed. 2, Florence, 1896. Among the more recent writers my greatest acknowledgements are perhaps due to Mr. Poole. I am also considerably indebted to Mr. Mullinger.

For the history of the scholastic philosophy and theology in the Middle Ages, I have used chiefly BAUR, *Die christliche Lehre von der Dreieinigkeit und Menschwerdung Gottes*, Theil 2, Tübingen, 1842; DEUTSCH (S. M.), *Peter Abälard*, Leipzig, 1883; ERDMANN, *Grundriss der Geschichte der Philosophie*, Berlin, 1866 (Eng. trans. by Hough, London, 1890, &c.); HAGENBACH, *Lehrbuch der Dogmengeschichte*, Leipzig, 1840 (E.T., ed. Buch, Edinburgh, 1846–7); HAMPDEN, *The Scholastic Philosophy considered in its relation to Christian Theology*, Oxford, 1833; HAURÉAU, *Histoire de la philosophie scolastique*, Paris, P. I, 1872, P. II, 1880; JOURDAIN (Amable), *Recherches critiques sur l'âge et l'origine des traductions latines d'Aristote*, Paris, 1843; JOURDAIN (Charles Bréchillet), *La Philosophie de Saint Thomas d'Aquin*, Paris, 1858; MAURICE, *Moral and Metaphysical Philosophy*, vol. iii, ed. 2, 1857; MORIN, *Dictionnaire de philosophie et de théologie scolastique*, Paris, 1856; MUNK, *Mélanges de philosophie juive et arabe*, Paris, 1859; PRANTL, *Geschichte der Logik im Abendlande*, Leipzig, 1870 (ed. 2, 1885); ROUSSELOT, *Études sur la philosophie dans le moyen-âge*, Paris, 1840–2; RENAN, *Averroès et l'Averroïsme*, Paris, 1866; WERNER, *Die Scholastik des späteren Mittelalters*, Vienna, 1881–3. Among these works I am most indebted to Hauréau, Erdmann, and Renan. Among general ecclesiastical historians, I need only mention my obligations to GIESELER, *Lehrbuch der Kirchengeschichte*, Bonn, 1827–57 (E.T., from ed. 4, Edinburgh, 1853–4).

[Since the first edition of this work was published so much has been written upon the history of medieval thought that it would be quite impossible to include, in a book devoted to the history of medieval universities or

---

[1] This work, with its continuation 'by members of the Institute', may here be mentioned, once for all, as an authority for many parts of my subject.

CHAP. II. institutions, a systematic bibliography. Reference may be made once for all
to the latest or eleventh edition of F. UEBERWEG, *Grundriss der Geschichte
der Philosophie*, vol. ii (ed. 11, edited by Bernhard Geyer, Berlin, 1928), and
to Maurice DE WULF, *History of Mediaeval Philosophy*, translated E. C.
MESSENGER (2 vols., London, 1926). Both contain full bibliographies. Other
references will be given when required in later sections and in the footnotes.
  The study of the twelfth century has been revolutionized since Rashdall
wrote. The most important works are the following: J. DE GHELLINCK, *Le
Mouvement théologique du xii*e *siècle* (Paris, 1914); M. GRABMANN, *Die
Geschichte der scholastischen Methode* (Freiburg i. B., vol. i, 1909, and
especially vol. ii, 1911). C. H. HASKINS, *The Renaissance of the Twelfth
Century* (Cambridge, Mass., 1927), a popular sketch, and some of the chapters in the same scholar's *Studies in the History of Mediaeval Science* (ed. 2,
Cambridge, Mass., 1927). For work on more particular subjects see the
bibliographies in UEBERWEG-GEYER and DE WULF. Other references will be
given in the notes, but A. CLERVAL, *Les Écoles de Chartres au moyen âge*
(Chartres, 1895), and G. ROBERT, *Les Écoles et l'enseignement de la théologie
pendant la première moitié du xii*e *siècle* (Paris, 1909), should be mentioned
here; also, as most important of all, *La Renaissance du xii*e *siècle: les écoles
et l'enseignement*, by G. PARÉ, A. BRUNET, and P. TREMBLAY (Paris and
Ottawa, 1933), a drastic revision of Robert's book, with a suggestive preface
by M.-D. CHENU. A new edition of Maître's book appeared in 1924.
  It appears from a few notes made with a view to the revision of this chapter
that Rashdall gave considerable attention to F. PICAVET, particularly to the
*Essais sur l'histoire générale et comparée des théologies et des philosophies
médiévales* (Paris, 1913).]

The Bene-
dictine
Age.

THE period which intervenes between the time of Charles
the Great and the eleventh century has been called the
Benedictine Age. The phrase exactly expresses its position in the history of education: it was the age, and the only
age, during which European education was mainly in the
hands of monks. With the progress of the barbarian invasions, the old imperial and municipal schools had everywhere disappeared: their place had been taken by the episcopal and monastic schools which the imperative needs of
the Church had called into existence. In transalpine Europe,
at all events, the old educational system was completely
swept away, though some of its traditions for a time survived
in the Christian schools by which it was supplanted.

Attitude of
the Church
towards
education.

It is generally acknowledged that the age which immediately followed the completion of the barbarian conquests
is the darkest age in the intellectual history of Europe.
Whatever view may be taken of the part played by Christian theology in bringing about that rapid evanescence of
intellectual light which culminated in the almost total night

of the seventh century, it is at least certain that so much of the culture of the old Roman world as survived into medieval Europe survived by virtue of its association with Christianity. The truth is that the hostility of Christian theologians to secular culture was to a very great extent merely the reflection within the sphere of theology of the political and social conditions of the time. If Gregory the Great interpreted the advance of the barbarian hosts, the slaughter and pillage which they brought in their train, as sure signs of the coming end, the events themselves were sufficiently calculated to discourage study and education apart altogether from any theological interpretation which might be put upon them. All culture that was not obviously and immediately useful was doomed to extinction. Christianity at least considerably widened the limits assigned to utility. The christianized barbarian recognized the spiritual, if he did not recognize the intellectual, needs of humanity; and some measure of intellectual cultivation was made necessary to the satisfaction of those spiritual needs by the narrowest interpretation of a religion whose principles had to be gathered from books, and whose services formed a small literature by themselves. Narrow as may have been the Churchman's educational ideal, it was only among Churchmen that an educational ideal maintained itself at all. The tendency of the Church's teaching was undoubtedly to depreciate secular, and especially literary, education—at least for the only class which still possessed education of any sort; but the grossest ignorance of the Dark Ages was not due to the strength of the ecclesiastical system but to its weakness. The improvement of education formed a prominent object with every zealous Churchman and every ecclesiastical reformer from the days of Gregory the Great to the days when the darkness passed away under the influence of the ecclesiastical revival of the eleventh and twelfth centuries. If the monastic system of Cassian retained something of the ascetic and obscurantist traditions of the Egyptian desert, the Benedictine monasticism which superseded it created almost the only homes of learning and education, and constituted by far the most

CHAP. II. powerful civilizing agency in Europe until it was superseded as an educational instrument by the growth of the universities.

Educational reform of Charles the Great. The ecclesiastical character of medieval education was in the first instance due solely to the fact that, in the general extinction of Roman civilization, the clergy were almost the only class which possessed or desired to possess even the rudiments of knowledge.[1] The intimate connexion between the Church and the school was stereotyped by the legislation of Charles the Great. A revival of education formed a prominent part of the wise and far-reaching scheme of ecclesiastical reform which originated with that monarch.[2] The centre of the Carolingian educational system was the Palace School, whose head, the famous Alcuin, was a sort of Minister of Education as well as the actual teacher of the young courtier-nobles and even of the great monarch himself. But this school hardly constitutes an exception to the ecclesiastical character of the system: it was primarily intended as a nursery for the future bishops and abbots of the Frankish Empire: it was perhaps in its origin an outgrowth of the royal chapel.[3] But though under Alcuin in the days of

The Palace School.

---

[1] These generalizations apply in their full extent to northern Europe only. As to Italy see below, ch. iv.

[2] [The standard work on this subject is M. Roger, *L'Enseignement des lettres classiques d'Ausone à Alcuin* (Paris, 1905). For the *scola* in the Merovingian Palace see E. Vacandard's papers in the *Revue des questions historiques*, lxi, lxii, lxxvi. The most convenient short account of early medieval schools is Margaret Deanesly's chapter in the *Cambridge Medieval History*, v. 765–79; bibliography on pp. 934–6. See also S. D'Irsay, *op. cit.*, ch. 2.]

[3] [For the training given to laity in the royal household and the episcopal *familia* in this period see Deanesly, *op. cit.*, p. 773. The cathedral and monastic schools were not intended for the laity, and

grammar schools outside these did not become common until the thirteenth century, although they are found before that time. 'As a rule the teaching of laymen and laywomen before 1300 was individual' (*ibid.*, p. 779). In a formulary of the early twelfth century we find a reference to a schoolmaster in the castle of Hugh of Gournai, recommended by the Count of Clermont, but he seems primarily to have been intended to teach the household clerks (Haskins, 'An Early Bolognese Formulary', in *Mélanges offerts à Henri Pirenne*, Brussels, 1926, p. 207). An important exception to the general conclusion that there were very few systematic educational arrangements for the benefit of the laity is the evidence for the education of merchants in the Flemish towns

Charles the Great and again under Erigena in the days of
Charles the Bald, the Palace School took the lead and served
as a sort of normal school to the whole Empire, a more permanently influential part of the Carolingian reform lay in
the enactment that every monastery and every cathedral
should have a school for the education of young clerks.[1] Of
these two classes of schools by far the most important were
the schools of the monasteries which now, for the first time,
opened their doors to non-monastic students. Nearly all
the schools which possessed more than a local importance
were monastic. From the beginning of the ninth century
all the more famous monasteries had two distinct schools
—one of its own *oblati*, the other for outsiders.[2] All the
enlightened ecclesiastics of the time were educated in
monasteries, and most of them were monks: it was from
the monasteries that the episcopal schools derived their
teachers. On the other hand, it was, as we shall see, from
the cathedral schools that the universities were at length
developed when the intellectual enthusiasm of the Middle
Age began to flow in a distinct channel from its religious
enthusiasm. The cathedral schools were, of course, as
ecclesiastical in their character and aims as the monastic; and
this ecclesiastical character of the pre-university education
should be remembered as the first of the conditions which
determined, at least in northern Europe, the form of the

in the twelfth and thirteenth centuries; see the interesting paper by
Pirenne in *Annales d'histoire écono-
mique et sociale*, i. 13–26 (Jan.
1929).]

[1] [L. Maître, *Les Écoles épiscopales et monastiques en Occident
avant les universités*, ed. 2
(Ligugé and Paris, 1924); Deanesly,
op. cit., pp. 774–9.]

[2] For the evidence see Joly,
p. 144 *sq.*; Mullinger, *Schools of
Charles the Great*, p. 130. [Also,
in addition to the authors cited in
the preceding note, U. Berlière, in
the *Revue Bénédictine*, vi. 499 (1889),
and his later paper in the *Bulletin*

*de la classe des lettres de l'acadé-
mię royale de Belgique*, 1921, pp.
550–72.] Sometimes this distinction between the external and internal school extended to the cathedrals. Thus at Reims: 'Praefatus
denique praesul honorabilis Fulco
... duas scholas Remis, canonicorum scilicet loci, atque ruralium
clericorum, jam pene delapsas restituit, et evocato Remigio Autissio-
dorensi magistro, liberalium artium
studiis adolescentes clericos exer-
ceri fecit, ipseque cum eis lectioni
ac meditationi sapientiae operam
dedit.'—Flodoardus, *Chron.*, lib.
iv, c. 9 (*Patrol. Lat.* cxxxv. 289).

CHAP. II. intellectual movement out of which the universities grew and the shape of the university-system itself. In Italy and southern Europe generally, neither the education of the pre-university era nor the movement which gave rise to the universities was so predominantly ecclesiastical as was the case beyond the Alps. For the present, however, we shall confine ourselves to the countries whose educational system was most powerfully and permanently affected by the traditions of the school of Alcuin and his successors, and especially to the original home of European scholasticism, northern France.

Retrogression after Charles. Thanks to Charles the Great and the little group of learned ecclesiastics promoted by him, Europe was never again plunged into intellectual darkness quite as profound as that of the Merovingian epoch. But, as in the political, so in the intellectual world, the bright auguries which might have been drawn from the enlightened administration of the great barbarian were not destined to immediate fulfilment. The revival of intellectual life which might have been expected as the outcome of the Carolingian schools was thrown back for nearly two centuries by the political confusion consequent upon the break-up of the Frankish Empire, by the renewal of Scandinavian devastations in the north, and by the Saracen invasions in the south. But though the general level of education among the clergy throughout large parts of Europe may have sunk in the tenth century to very nearly the eighth-century level, there were always at least a few monasteries or cathedrals which kept alive a succession of comparatively well-educated ecclesiastics. It may be broadly stated that whatever knowledge was possessed by Alcuin was never allowed entirely to die out. The torch was handed on from one generation to another: the seeds of a new order of things had been sown, though it was not till the beginning of the eleventh century that even the first-fruits of harvest were reaped.[1]

[1] [Rashdall was later inclined to modify the sharp distinction which he drew between the eleventh and the preceding centuries here and in the following paragraphs. Since he wrote, the intellectual history

The change which began to pass over the schools of France in the eleventh century and culminated in the great intellectual Renaissance of the following age was but one effect of that general revivification of the human spirit which should be recognized as constituting an epoch in the history of European civilization not less momentous than the Reformation or the French Revolution. It is, indeed, only the absence of any clearly marked breach of political or ecclesiastical continuity that can excuse the designation by a common name of two periods so utterly dissimilar in their social, intellectual, and religious conditions, as the period before the eleventh century and the period after it. It is only the first of these periods that can with any propriety be called the Dark Age of European history: it would conduce to stamp the distinction between the two periods in the popular mind if the term 'Middle Age' were reserved for the latter.

The eleventh century forms the transition between one of the darkest and what was in many respects the brightest of all the centuries generally included in 'the Middle Age'; but in the main it belongs to the second—to the period of progress, not to the period of stagnation or retrogression. It cannot be too emphatically stated that there is no historical evidence for the theory which connects the new birth of Europe with the passing away of the fateful millennial year and with it of the awful dread of a coming end of all things.[1] Yet, although there was no breach of historical

The new birth of Europe in the eleventh century.

The millenial year.

of the ninth and tenth centuries has been investigated, notably by Traube and his pupils, and the significance of the monastic movements stimulated by the work of Benedict of Aniane and the Irish monks has been appreciated. See for the bibliographical material M. Manitius, *Geschichte der lateinischen Literatur des Mittelalters,* vol. ii (Munich, 1923); and F. J. E. Raby, *Christian-Latin Poetry* (Oxford, 1927); and the same writer's *A History of Secular Latin Poetry in the Middle Ages,* 2 vols. (Oxford, 1934). On the subject in general see E. K. Rand, *Founders of the Middle Ages* (Cambridge, Mass., 1928), C. Foligno, *Latin Thought during the Middle Ages* (Oxford, 1929), M. L. W. Laistner, *Thought and Letters in Western Europe A.D. 500 to 900* (London, 1931), and D'Irsay, *op. cit.,* ch. 2. Cf. U. Berlière, *L'Ordre monastique des origines au xiie siècle* (ed. 3, Maredsous, Lille and Paris, 1924). Rashdall noted the observations of Picavet, *Essais,* p. 14.]

[1] [For the curiously abundant literature on this subject see the long note in Hefele-Leclercq,

CHAP. II. continuity at the year 1000, the date will serve as well as any other that could be assigned to represent the turning-point of European history, separating an age of religious terror and theological pessimism from an age of hope and vigour and active religious enthusiasm. Monasticism renewed its life in the Cluniac and a century later in the Cistercian reforms. A revival of architecture heralded, as it usually does, a wider revival of art. The schools of Christendom became thronged as they were never thronged before. A passion for inquiry took the place of the old routine. The Crusades brought different parts of Europe into contact with one another and into contact with the new world of the East—with a new religion and a new philosophy, with the Arabic Aristotle, with the Arabic commentators on Aristotle, and eventually even with Aristotle in the original Greek.

Pre-existing causes of the Renaissance.   Of the complex causes of this astonishing new birth of Europe, some were no doubt in operation before the mysterious thousandth year of grace. The conversion of the Scandinavian pirates into Christian and civilized Normans was one of them. In Germany, under the enlightened rule of the Ottos, the symptoms of a better order of things may already be traced before the middle of the tenth century. To the Ottos, too, was due the regeneration of the Papacy. In Italy the very necessity of fortifying the towns against the Saracenic and Hungarian raids had begun to develop that civic life which there played so large a part in the intellectual revival. All these causes contributed to that restoration of political order, of ecclesiastical discipline, and of social tranquillity which began with the close of the tenth century. Order and peace, leisure and security are the most indispensable conditions of intellectual activity,[1] and after

Histoire des conciles, vol. iv, pt. 2 (Paris, 1911), pp. 901–3.]
[1] I do not ignore the stimulating intellectual effects of political revolutions and social upheavals; but this will not apply to such devastation as was wrought by Danes or Saracens. When an abbey was in constant danger of pillage by Danes or robber-nobles, the monks were not likely to think much about logic or verse-making, though a modern war may interfere but little with professorial studies. [1895.]

all it is for the most part the conditions only, and not the
originating causes of great spiritual movements, which admit
of analysis at the hands of the historian.

Whatever the causes of the change, the beginning of the
eleventh century represents, as nearly as it is possible to fix
it, the turning-point in the intellectual history of Europe.
But it must not be supposed that the change at once manifested itself in any great 'movement' or discovery. The fact
that the tide has turned reveals itself solely in the increased
efficiency and wider diffusion of an education such as the
Church schools had never wholly ceased to impart, at least
since the time of Alcuin; in the increasing vigour of the
theological controversies in which the Dark Ages had expended whatever intellectual activity they possessed; in
the increased volume and more vigorous movement of that
stream of theological literature which had never entirely
ceased to flow. It was not, however, till the very end of the
eleventh or the beginning of the following century that the
improvement becomes rapid[1] and surprising; it is not till
then that we trace the first beginnings of that great scholastic movement out of which grew the northern university-
system. To enable the reader to appreciate the causes and
the character of that movement, it is essential to give some
account of the educational system which it eventually transformed. The revival of educational activity in the course
of the eleventh century was, as has been said, but one side of
a far wider movement—of the reawakening of the European
mind from the torpor of centuries, of the triumph of order
and civilization over disorder and barbarism. But the particular direction which was taken by the reawakened intellectual energies of Europe was completely determined by the

---

[1] How rapid may be judged from the change which Guibert of Nogent (1053–1124) notices as having taken place within his own lifetime. 'Erat paulo ante id temporis, et adhuc partim sub meo tempore tanta grammaticorum charitas, ut in op- pidis prope nullus, in urbibus vix aliquis reperiri potuisset, et quos inveniri contigerat, eorum scientia tenuis erat, nec etiam moderni temporis clericulis vagantibus com- parari poterat.' *De Vita Sua*, l. i, c. iv [ed. Bourgin, Paris, 1907, pp. 12, 13. Bourgin dates the autobiography 1114–17, p. xlix].

CHAP. II. character of the traditional education which it had inherited from the past.

Theological education. Of the ecclesiastical character and objects of this education enough has already been said. The end and object which the teacher set before himself was to enable the future ecclesiastic to understand and expound the canonical Scriptures, the Fathers, and other ecclesiastical writings. But beyond the elementary instruction in the Psalter and church music, we hear little of any systematic training in theology. In truth theology at this time had not yet become a system. The object of an ecclesiastical education was to enable the priest or monk to read and meditate upon the Bible and Fathers for himself: the theological writings of the times are for the most part either refutations of prevalent errors or abridgements of the patristic commentaries or treatises. What regular theological teaching there was, assumed of course a similarly positive and traditional character. But for the proper understanding of these sacred writings a certain amount of secular culture was considered to be necessary.[1] The maximum secular knowledge which the ordinary schools imparted is represented by that celebrated division of the 'Seven Arts'[2]

The Trivium and Quadrivium.

[1] The theory finds expression in the Capitulary of Charles the Great: 'Cum autem in sacris paginis schemata, tropi, et caetera his similia inserta inveniantur, nulli dubium est quod ea unusquisque legens tanto citius spiritualiter intelligit, quanto prius in litterarum magisterio plenius instructus fuerit.' Pertz, Leges, i. 52, 53.

[2] The idea of the Seven Liberal Arts dates, according to Ozanam (La Civilisation chrétienne, p. 389) from Philo, De Congressu (ed. Mangey, IV. Erlangen, 1788, p. 148 sq.). But in any case it owed its popularity mainly to the De Nuptiis Philologiae et Mercurii of Martianus Capella (ed. Eyssenhardt, Leipzig, 1866), in which the Seven Arts appear as the attendant Virgins of philology upon her marriage with Mercury. [The main source of this work, written between 410 and 439, is Varro, architecture and medicine being excluded from the latter's novem disciplinae. P. Rajna has shown that the effective division of the Seven Arts into the Trivium and the Quadrivium dates from the time of Alcuin (Studi medievali, i (1928), 4–36. See, for the literature on the subject, Schanz, Geschichte d. röm. Lit., iv. 166–70 (Munich, 1920), and for the history of the Seven Arts, D'Irsay, i. 32–8, especially the bibliographical note on p. 38, and J. Mariétan, Problème de la classification des sciences d'Aristote à Saint Thomas (Paris, 1901). H. Parker's article in the English Historical Review for 1890 requires considerable correction. The bibliographies in Manitius (vols. ii, iii) and in Ueberweg-Geyer should be consulted for particular writers.]

into the elementary *Trivium* and the more advanced *Quad-* CHAP. II. *rivium*. The *Trivium* consisted of grammar, rhetoric, and dialectic; the *Quadrivium* of music, arithmetic, geometry, and astronomy. What was known of these arts may be estimated from the contents of the ordinary text-books of the age—the work of three writers who, living in the dim twilight which intervened between the daylight of ancient culture and the total night of barbarism, had occupied themselves with reducing to compendiums so much as they could save or so much as they could appreciate of the intellectual treasures destined otherwise to be buried for centuries or lost for ever. These three writers were Boethius, the popularity of whose The text-works was largely increased by his fame as a theologian and books. Christian martyr,[1] the Christian Cassiodorus, and the half-pagan Martianus Capella. Of the *Quadrivium* even Boethius gives but a meagre outline, the other two but the scantiest smattering.[2] In the Dark Ages arithmetic and astronomy found their way into the educational curriculum chiefly because they taught the means of finding Easter. Music included but a half-mystical doctrine of numbers and the rules of plain-song: under geometry Boethius gives little but a

---

The scope of some of the arts was wider than is indicated by modern usage. Rhetoric included the elements of law as well as prose and verse composition (see below, ch. iv, § 1); so 'Geometria est ars disciplinata quae omnium herbarum graminumque experimentum enuntiat: unde et medicos hac fretos geometres vocamus, id est, expertos herbarum'. Virgilius Maro (the Toulouse grammarian of the seventh century), *Epistolae*, iv, ed. Huemer, Leipzig, 1886, p. 22.

[1] [Rashdall, following Charles Jourdain in rejecting the claim of Boethius to the theological works ascribed to him, wrote 'supposititious fame'. But the evidence of a fragment of Cassiodorus, available since 1877 in H. Usener's *Anecdoton Holderi* (Bonn, 1877), is now generally accepted and the importance of Usener's work realized. See the edition of the theological tractates by H. F. Stewart and E. K. Rand (London, 1918). Rand now accepts the authenticity of the tract *De Fide Catholica*, which in 1901 he rejected (*Jahrbücher für klass. Phil.*, xxvi. 437 *sqq.*; Supplementband). It is not easy to exaggerate the influence of Boethius in late medieval thought. His definition of theological terms, his classification of the sciences, as well as his logical translations and commentaries are of great importance.]

[2] [D'Irsay (p. 36 n.) suggests a deliberate intention, citing Cassiodorus, 'ut simplicibus viribus famuletur etiam mundanarum peritia litterarum'.]

CHAP. II. selection of propositions from Euclid without the demonstrations. Historically speaking, the *Quadrivium* is chiefly important as supplying the skeleton outline of a wider course of study which was afterwards filled up by the discoveries or rediscoveries of the twelfth-century Renaissance. The real secular education of the Dark Ages was the *Trivium*—grammar, rhetoric, and dialectic. Under grammar had long been included, not merely the technical rules of grammar as formulated by Priscian and Donatus, but all that we should include in the studies known as classical or philological—the systematic study and interpretation of the classical writers of ancient Rome. Before the age of Charles the Great, whatever secular culture survived the wreck of ancient civilization had, in spite of the frowns of the severer Christian teachers, been based upon the Latin classics. Alcuin, though certainly himself well acquainted with the principal Roman poets, in later life condemned the teaching of pagan poetry to the Christian youth; and the tendency of the age which he inaugurates was on the whole in the same direction, though the more enlightened teachers of the Dark Ages took a more liberal view, and it is probable that in practice boys continued to be taught grammatical Latin by reading a classical author, such as Virgil or Ovid;[1] and in the best schools, notably at Ferrières, under Alcuin's pupil, the Abbot Servatus Lupus, a wider study of classical literature was pursued with some enthusiasm.[2] Under the head of rhetoric the treatises of Cicero, such as the Topics (with the commentary of Boethius),

The pagan literature.

[1] See *Vita Alcuini* (*M.G.H. Scriptores*, xv. 193), where a story is told of Alcuin (when Abbot of Tours) detecting his *scholasticus* Sigulfus secretly teaching Virgil to his pupils (cf. letter to Richbod, Archbishop of Trier, in Epistles, ed. Dümmler, *M.G.H. Epistolae*, iv. 38, No. 13), while in Lupus, Abbot of Ferrières, we find as keen a devotee of classical literature and collector of manuscripts as any Italian scholar of the Renaissance. See his letters, *passim*, ed. Dümmler in *M.G.H. Epistolae*, vi. 7–126. For the toleration of classics cf. Rabanus Maurus, *De Clericorum Institutione*, *Patrol. Lat.* cvii. 396.

[2] Lupus Ferrarensis, *Epp.* lxii, ciii (Dümmler, pp. 62, 91). The passages are interesting as showing that Quintilian, though little known, was not so entirely lost as is sometimes supposed. [Cf. Manitius, i. 486; ii. 713; and Webb's preface to his edition of John of Salisbury's *Metalogicon*, p. xv.]

the *De Oratore* and the pseudo-Ciceronian *ad Herennium*, CHAP. II. were largely read. The elements of Roman law were often added, and all schoolboys were exercised in writing prose and what passed for verse. But the heart and centre of the secular education of the time in northern Europe was the study of dialectic or logic. Here the teacher was untram- Promi-melled by the lurking uneasiness of conscience which haunted logic. the medieval monk who loved his Virgil: there was nothing pagan about syllogisms: the rules of right reasoning were the same for Christian and for pagan alike, and were (as was thought) essential for the right comprehension and inculca-tion of Christian truth. Under cover of this idea teacher and pupil alike were enabled in the study of dialectic, and per-haps in dialectic only, to enjoy something of the pleasure of knowledge for its own sake. The mysteries of logic were indeed intrinsically better calculated to fascinate the intellect of the half-civilized barbarian than the elegancies of classical poetry and oratory. At all events, in this department a richer material, meagre as even that undoubtedly seems to us, was placed at his disposal than in most other branches of secular knowledge. Boethius (481–524) had translated the *De Interpre-* Know-*tatione* and the *Categoriae* as well as the *Isagoge* of Porphyry, but Aristotle. in the time of Alcuin only the translations of Porphyry and the *De Interpretatione* (with the commentary of Boethius) were generally known, together with an abridgement of the Cate-gories falsely ascribed to S. Augustine,[1] and some logical writings of Boethius. Such were the chief sources of the scholar's secular inspiration down to the eleventh century. Even Abelard knew only the *Categoriae* and the *De Inter-pretatione* in actual translations: the rest of the *Organon* he knew only from the Boethian *De Syllogismis Categoricis*, *De Syllogismis Hypotheticis*, *De Differentiis Topicis*, and *De Divi-sionibus*.[2]

---

[1] Hauréau, pt. i, p. 95 *sq.* Jour-dain (*Recherches*, p. 379) treats this work as an actual translation. Some knowledge of the *Physics* and *Metaphysics* was also obtainable through a collection of axioms

ascribed to Bede (Jourdain, p. 21).
[2] [See Abelard's own words in Cousin, *Ouvrages inédits d'Abélard*, 1836, p. 228. Geyer (*Philosophischer Jahrbuch*, xxx. 32) shows that he knew the *Sophistici Elenchi* also

CHAP. II.   Though in a sense the authority of Aristotle was supreme
Influence throughout this as well as the later medieval period, in the
of Plato. formation of the scholastic philosophy the influence of Plato
and still more of Plotinus and the Neoplatonists upon
medieval thought counted for at least as much as that of the
Stagirite. The authority of Aristotle was in the first instance
due to his position as a logician, and Plato was the author of
no logical system that could rival that of Aristotle; while the
later Middle Ages had before them in the writings of Aristotle
a whole encyclopedia of subjects upon which Plato had
written nothing. Of Plato's own writings none were known
at any period of the Middle Ages, except the *Timaeus* in the
translation by Chalcidius, the *Phaedo* and the *Meno*,[1] and
even of these the circulation was not very wide—certainly not
in the seed-time of the scholastic philosophy. [The immense
influence which Platonism exercised upon medieval thought
was mainly derived from accounts or reproductions of
Platonic or Neoplatonic teaching in such Latin writers as
Cicero, Apuleius, Augustine,[2] Macrobius, and Boethius, from
the references made by Aristotle himself to his master's
teaching, from Erigena's, and later translations of the
pseudo-Dionysius, from the translations of Arabic writings

and quotes a non-Boethian translation of the *Prior Analytics*. For
the writings of Boethius and their
importance in transmitting much of
the Aristotelian logic cf. Manitius,
i. 26 *sqq.* and the references in his
index. Boethius translated the
Analytics; his translation was very
little known, but the *Prior Analytics*
are included in the *Heptateuchon*
or manual of the Seven Arts written
by the well-known *scholasticus*,
Theodoric or Thierry of Chartres
in the first half of the twelfth century (Clerval, *Les Écoles de Chartres*,
p. 222). For the dialectical works
studied at Chartres in the eleventh
century see the list given by Clerval
from a Chartres manuscript (*ibid.*,
p. 117). On the whole question of
the transmission of the *Organon*

see Haskins, *Studies in Mediaeval
Science*, pp. 223–34, and the
authorities there given; and below,
pp. 353–62, and notes.]
  [1] [Haskins, *op. cit.*, pp. 88, 165–
71. The prologues to the translations of the *Phaedo* and the *Meno*,
made by Henricus Aristippus (1156–
60), who was in the service of
William I of Sicily, were discovered
by Valentin Rose in 1866.] Plato
was *never* the subject of medieval
lectures.
  [2] [The influence of Plotinus
over S. Augustine was much
greater than that of Plato, and
Plato was known to him chiefly
through Plotinus. Cf. M. Grand-
george, *Saint Augustin et Le Néo-
Platonisme*, Paris, 1896.]

which were inspired by Neoplatonic influence (e.g. the *Fons* CHAP. II.
vitae of the Jew, Gebirol, or Avicebron), and from the translations of Neoplatonic works made from the Greek by
William of Moerbeke in the thirteenth century.] Of Plato
himself little was known besides his doctrine of ideas; but
the controversy between Aristotle and Plato upon this matter
supplied the Middle Ages with the great central subject—in
the earlier period of its development the main subject—of
its metaphysical controversies. The concentration of intellectual interest upon a single topic of ancient philosophy
originated the never-ending controversy over the reality of
universals.[1]

Thus the whole scholastic training of the pre-university Origin of
era paved the way for the absorption of the intellectual the scho-
lastic phi-
energies of entire generations by this highly speculative losophy.
question, and the other speculative questions which grew out
of it or were connected with it. The most stimulating and
interesting morsel which the monastic teacher could place
before the hungry intellect of the inquiring student was a
morsel of logic. Logic was the one treasure snatched from
the intellectual wreckage of a bygone civilization which he
was encouraged to appropriate. The one fragment of 'the
Philosopher' (as Aristotle was called in the Middle Ages) was
a fragment of his logic. And at the very threshold of logic
the student was encountered by this question of the reality of
universals—on the face of it (as it is apt to appear to the
modern mind) a dry, abstract, uninviting topic—a topic
which at first sight might seem to belong rather to the theory
of grammar than to logic or metaphysic. Yet no sooner
does he approach it than the student finds himself led by

---

[1] M. Picavet declares as the
result of recent studies that 'la
question des universaux ne fut
guère traitée que de 1080 à 1160
et elle n'eut même pas alors l'importance que lui attribuent encore
la plupart des historiens' (*Essais*,
p. 10). I have modified a few
phrases which might suggest such
an exaggeration in my first edition,
but M. Picavet recognizes that the
question was revived in the later
Middle Ages and its intrinsic importance for medieval and for all
philosophy it would not be easy to
exaggerate. [Note by Rashdall,
1921. On Platonic and Neoplatonic
influences generally see Baeumker,
Der Platonismus im Mittelalter
(Munich, 1916).]

CHAP. II. imperceptible steps from logic into physics, and from physics into metaphysics, and from metaphysics into theology. Indeed, the solution of the most momentous questions to which the human intellect can address itself is inextricably bound up with the solution of a question which 'common sense' will undertake to clear up in five minutes, or which it will indignantly pronounce too trifling to be asked or answered. Yet he who has given his answer to it has implicitly constructed his theory of the universe.

The scholastic problem. In the introduction to the logic of Aristotle which was in the hands of every student even in the Dark Ages, the *Isagoge* of Porphyry, the question was explicitly raised in a very distinct and emphatic manner. The words in which this writer states, without resolving, the central problem of the scholastic philosophy, have played perhaps a more momentous part in the history of thought than any other passage of equal length in all literature outside the canonical Scriptures. They are worth quoting at length: 'Next, concerning genera and species, the question indeed whether they have a substantial existence, or whether they consist in bare intellectual concepts only, or whether if they have a substantial existence they are corporeal or incorporeal, and whether they are separable from the sensible properties of the things (or particulars of sense), or are only in those properties and subsisting about them, I shall forbear to determine. For a question of this kind is a very deep one and one that requires a longer investigation.'[1]

The scholastic philosophy before Roscellinus. Such was the central question of the scholastic philosophy. At what period are we to say that the great debate was opened? In a sense the history of the scholastic philosophy begins with the revival of Aristotelian dialectic in the Carolingian schools, but its characteristic question about the reality of universals did not come into great prominence till

---

[1] 'Mox de generibus ac speciebus illud quidem, sive subsistunt sive in solis nudisque intellectibus posita sunt, sive subsistentia corporalia sunt an incorporalia, et utrum separata a sensibilibus an in- sensibilibus posita et circa ea constantia, dicere recusabo: altissimum enim est huiusmodi negotium et majoris egens inquisitionis.' (In trans. Boethii.)

the far-reaching issues of the conflict were brought out by the teaching of the realist Johannes Scotus Erigena in the second half of the ninth century. From this time onwards there is a succession of dialecticians by whom the question is more or less distinctly raised. But the hottest battles of the long campaign do not open until we come to that great intellectual revival of the eleventh and twelfth centuries with which we are chiefly concerned. The second and by far the most brilliant period in the history of scholasticism is opened up by the teaching of the nominalist Roscellinus at the end of the eleventh and beginning of the twelfth centuries. With Roscellinus we enter upon the most important period of the scholastic *philosophy*, while the scholastic *theology* can hardly be said to begin before this epoch. There had been indeed a growing tendency to apply the weapons of dialectic to the discussion of theological questions before this period. Johannes Scotus had pushed the realist argument very near to the borders of Pantheism, but he had not directly either assailed or questioned the truths of revealed religion. He was rather a somewhat unorthodox Christian Platonist or Plotinian or a belated gnostic than a dialectical theologian. A nearer anticipation of the scholastic conflicts is the controversy which broke out in the middle of the eleventh century—just before the period from which we have seen reason to date the intellectual new birth of Europe—in consequence of Berengar's attack upon the doctrine of the real presence of Christ in the Eucharist; but this controversy was in the main conducted upon the basis of authority—at least in the hands of the chief defender or (since the dogma had not yet been authoritatively defined) the chief formulator of the orthodox doctrine, Lanfranc, the famous teacher of the great monastic school of Bec. It was not till the time of Lanfranc's great successor, Anselm of Aosta, that a marked change took place in the character of the theological teaching and the theological controversies of the Church's schools.[1]

[1] [The John who is said to have preceded Roscellinus in his nominalism (see the anonymous *His-* *toria francica* in *Recueil des historiens de France*, xi. 160, xii. 3) was probably, as Prantl thought, John

CHAP. II.

The scholastic theology.

The scholastic theology grew out of the concentration upon theological study of minds whose only or chief secular culture was supplied by logic. In the intellectual torpor of the Dark Ages young ecclesiastics might be taught to think or to argue by the teacher of dialectic, and to repeat doctrinal formulae or mystical interpretations of Scripture by the teacher of theology without feeling the temptation to apply to the subject-matter of the one school the weapons which they had learned to use in the other. But when once real intellectual activity was roused, this state of things could not last much longer. And as soon as the combustible materials which had long lain side by side without mixing were brought into contact, an explosion was inevitable. Intellectual activity stimulated by dialectic, intellectual curiosity aroused by the glimpses of old-world philosophy which were afforded by the traditional education of the age, had no material on which to expend themselves, except what was supplied by the Scriptures, the Fathers, and the doctrinal system of the Church. To investigate and to interpret, to attack or defend what was found there, was the natural impulse of the cloister-bred ecclesiastic of northern Europe. At about the same period this tendency found marked expression in the writings of two great teachers—the orthodox Anselm and the heretical Roscellinus. In Anselm we are perhaps met for the first time with the spectacle of an orthodox teacher expending his utmost intellectual ingenuity in first raising and then meeting objections to the doctrine which he himself unhesitatingly accepted. With Anselm, author of the famous *Credo ut intelligam*, this effort was made entirely for the instruction of the believer: his object was to add knowledge to a pre-existing faith: reason was entirely subordinated to authority. In Roscellinus reason undertook the task of criticizing and (where it seemed needful) modifying the doctrines of the received theology.[1]

the Scot; cf. Poole, *Illustrations*, pp. 99, 321, 336. Otto of Freising, on the other hand, states that Roscellinus 'sententiam vocum instituit' (*De gestis Friderici*, i. 47; cf. John of Salisbury, *Policraticus*, vii. 2, ed. Webb, ii. 142, and *Metalogicon*, ii. 17, ed. Webb, p. 92). For other views on John see Ueberweg-Geyer, pp. 206, 207; Clerval, pp. 121–3; De Wulf, i. 110.]

[1] A complete account of the

From Roscellinus the speculative impulse was communi- cated to Abelard, in whose hands the scholastic treatment of theology attained its full development. Anselm and Roscellinus were the precursors, Abelard was the true founder of the scholastic theology. With Abelard the great scholastic movement reaches a point at which it begins to identify itself with what we may call the university movement. Most emphatically it must be asserted that universities, even in their most rudimentary form, did not exist till at least a generation after Abelard. But Abelard inaugurated the intellectual movement out of which they eventually sprang. The method of inquiry and of teaching of which he was the originator was the method which essentially characterized the teaching of the medieval universities—a method transferred by Abelard from philosophy to theology, and afterwards (in a greater or less degree) to the whole cycle of medieval studies. Even from the point of view of external organization Abelard may in a sense be said to inaugurate the university movement. Anselm was the last of the great monastic teachers. A generation later the monasteries began to shut their doors upon secular students; and their educa- tional activity was taken up by the cathedrals and their more

growth of scholasticism would have to take into consideration the influence of John of Damascus, in the eighth century, who already exhibits the two changes introduced (at different periods) into Western theology by scholasticism, viz. (1) the introduction of dialectical processes, and (2) the prominence of the Aristotelian philosophy. He originates scholasticism in the Eastern Church, and was by no means without influence in the West. [See J. de Ghellinck, *Le Mouvement théologique*, pp. 245–67. It is not possible to revise this chapter, with its almost exclusive emphasis on dialectic, in the light of later work. The interplay of theological developments and canon law has been treated by Ghellinck, and, more recently, by le Bras in the *Histoire des collections canoniques en Occident*, by P. Fournier and G. le Bras (Paris, 1932), ii. 314 *sqq.* The best introduction to the new methods of teaching, the development of the *sententiae* and *summae*, and the use of sources, &c., is in *Les Écoles et l'enseignement*, edited by G. Paré and others. The following passage, concluding a discussion of the place of the Seven Arts in medieval teaching, sums up the position: 'Mais la vie est ailleurs, et, dès le XIIᵉ siècle, mine peu à peu les vieilles catégories. C'est dans ce contexte qu'il faut lire Abélard, et non pas enclore en la turbulence du chevalier de l'"art" dialectique l'esprit de la philosophie du XIIᵉ siècle' (*op. cit.*, p. 101).]

CHAP. II. independent secular teachers. It was the cathedral school in which Abelard had taught—the Cathedral School of Paris —which eventually developed into the earliest and greatest university of northern Europe. Abelard, though not in any strict sense the founder, was at least the intellectual progenitor of the University of Paris.

Relations of philosophy to theology. A slight sketch of the life and teaching of this extraordinary man will be the best introduction to the investigation of our main subject. But to appreciate Abelard's position in the history of medieval thought, it will be well to start with some clear ideas as to the relations between the old speculative problems which in the age of Abelard were being debated with a fury hitherto unknown in the history of philosophy and the new problems of the scholastic theology. We have defined the scholastic theology as the result of an attempt to apply dialectical methods to the discussion of theological problems. But it was not only philosophical methods, but philosophical conclusions, that were now imported into the schools of theology. At this period it was in the main the question of the reality of universals that troubled the traditional repose of the theological schools: at a later date, as we shall see, the whole of the Aristotelian philosophy was re-imported into the schools of Europe, and demanded that its relations with theology should be adjusted. At present we need only deal with the theological bearings of the great problem raised by the earlier scholasticism. The modification of theological doctrine by ancient philosophy was, indeed, no new thing in the history of Christian thought. Philosophy had just begun to colour the expression of Christian doctrine before the close of the New Testament canon: in the hands of the Fathers it entered into its substance. It was, indeed, largely the discrepancies between the traditional Augustinian theology based upon a Platonic philosophy and the conclusions to which more independent thinkers were led by the study of Aristotle that created many of the problems with which the scholastic theologian was confronted. But none of the recognized answers to the great scholastic problem was without its theological difficulties. Without an apprecia-

tion of the theological bearing of the questions at issue be- CHAP. II.
tween medieval realism and medieval nominalism, the inner
history of the movement of which the universities were
originally the outgrowth and afterwards became the organs,
nay, it is no exaggeration to say the whole ecclesiastical history of the Middle Ages, will be unintelligible. Unless we Theo-
see clearly the theological rocks on which the combatants on difficulties
either side were alternately in danger of being wrecked, we of different
shall be unable to understand either the alarm with which the phical
rise of scholastic theology in the twelfth century was re- positions.
garded by old-fashioned and conservative Churchmen, or the
way in which now one, now another, metaphysical position
was proscribed in the interests of orthodoxy.

In the first place, the dialectician who maintained (with Realism.
Scotus) that reality belonged only to the idea or universal
while the particulars are mere phantasms, was liable to be
confronted with this line of argument. If the reality which
the class-name 'Table' stands for is the immaterial self-sub-
sistent idea of a table, the name principle must clearly be
applied to the class-name 'Man'. The real thing in man must
then be the humanity which is shared alike by Socrates, by
Plato, and by every other individual man: individuality thus
belongs merely to the phenomenal world, to the seeming and
the transitory. What then, the realist was liable to be asked,
becomes of the immortality of the soul? One step more and the
personality of God disappears with the personality of man.
If the reality of the individual is constituted merely by its
participation in the essence of the species, must not the reality
of the species in like manner be absorbed into that of the
genus, and the reality of the genus into that of the more
comprehensive genus in which it is embraced, and so on?
The *summum genus* would thus appear to be ultimately the
only reality: all substances become mere forms or modes of
the being of the one substance: all material things and all
individual minds must be regarded as essentially and fundamentally one: mind and matter alike are reduced to modes of
the One, the Absolute Being. There are, of course, innumerable ways of evading the consequences of the realistic

CHAP. II. premisses: one dialectician or another might stop here or there in the chain of argument. But in proportion as his mind was logical, in proportion to the clearness and fearlessness of his intellect, pantheistic—or at least what we now call absolutist—tendencies were sure to become apparent. All realism *which starts with denying the reality of the particular* is essentially (as M. Hauréau has said of more than one scholastic system) an 'undeveloped Spinozism'.[1]

Nominal-
ism. On the other hand, the opposite extreme of nominalism, the theory which declared that universals are mere sounds (*merae voces*) and that predication has to do with nothing but names, is a doctrine whose sceptical tendency lies upon the surface. In Roscellinus the heretical tendency of the doctrine became immediately evident [however little that thinker intended to push his speculative conclusions to the denial of the traditional theology]. Starting with the assumption that only the individual was real and that intellectual relations had no existence, he required the theologian to choose between [the doctrine that the three Persons were but names for one and the same being, so that it would be as true to say of the Father as of the Son that he was incarnate], and the admission that the Persons of the Holy Trinity are 'tres res', himself [accepting the latter alternative which his opponents not unnaturally described as tritheistic]. The same rigorous logic was applied to the doctrine of the real presence in the Eucharist. But, even apart from its application to particular dogmas, the destructive tendency of a doctrine which declared the particular, the isolated, unrelated atom to be the only reality was sufficient to alarm the medieval theologian at first sight: his instinct was right in rejecting a doctrine of which the sensationalistic scepticism of Hume or the crudest modern materialism is but an illogical attenuation. Strange as it may appear, nominalism was to have its fleeting triumph even within the pale of the Church; but when it was first broached, it was heresy.

[1] In attributing this tendency to realism in general, M. Hauréau (who writes from a strongly nominalist point of view) omits what seems to me to be the necessary qualification. There is a realism which does not deny that the particular is real, though it may be there is no such thing as a particular apart from universal relations.

It might seem that the cautious dialectician who wished CHAP. II.
to keep on good terms with the Bishops and the theologians Yet realism more
must fall back upon the peripatetic view which acknowledged or less necessary to
the reality of the universals while it denied that the universal orthodoxy.
had any reality apart from the particulars. And the logical
position of the most orthodox dialecticians who immediately
followed Scotus was in the main of a peripatetic cast, while
they fenced themselves off against the attacks of the ever-
watchful theologian by drawing a sharp line between the
province of theology and that of philosophy. But tendencies
were at work which by the time of Abelard had resulted in
making realism the orthodox philosophy of the Church's
schools. The pantheistic tone of Erigena's own writings was,
indeed, too obvious to escape notice. Nevertheless, this same
Erigena contributed largely by his translation of the pseudo-
Dionysian treatises *De hierarchiâ coelesti* and *De nominibus
divinis* to a modification in the philosophical attitude of the
orthodox theology. The mingled mysticism and sacerdotal-
ism of these works, further recommended in France by the
identification of their author with S. Denis of Paris, was so
attractive to the medieval mind that the current theology
became largely coloured by the Neoplatonic ideas which had
given so much offence in the original writings of their translator. Moreover, since the time of Erigena a change had passed
over the sacramental teaching of the Church, which was
destined eventually to make some form of realism almost
essential to the dialectician who aimed at giving a philosophical explanation of the doctrines which he accepted as a
theologian.

First revealed perhaps by a chance word or two of the Realism and sacra-
Platonist Justin, the belief in a physical though mysterious mentalism.
and vaguely conceived change in the consecrated elements in
the Eucharist had found some support among later Fathers,
though a more spiritual view was upheld by theologians of
as great or greater authority, such as S. Augustine and Pope
Gelasius. Both in the popular and in the clerical mind the
growth of the belief kept pace with the decay of education,
the advance of sacerdotal pretension, the deepening paganism

of popular religion. The belief in an actual transformation of the consecrated elements into the very body and blood of Christ was perhaps for the first time fully and formally promulgated in the writings of Paschasius Radbertus (†853) about the middle of the ninth century. Though strongly opposed by Rabanus, Ratramnus, and others, the dogma now took firm hold of the popular imagination. In the darkness of the succeeding age of ignorance it became the very central truth of popular orthodoxy. The first indication of the reawakening of the European mind after its long slumber is the denial of the popular superstition by Berengar of Tours. When conservative theologians like Lanfranc attempted a scientific defence of the popular creed, the necessity of more accurate definition was felt. Berengar's attack rested upon a nominalistic basis: with Lanfranc began the attempt to defend and at the same time to sublimate the coarse materialism of the current doctrine[1] by introducing the realistic distinction between the substance—the impalpable universal which was held to inhere in every particular included under it—and the accidents or sensible properties which came into existence when the pure form clothed itself in matter. Thus was gradually built up the fully developed doctrine of *transubstantiation*.[2] The substances of the bread and wine were changed, it was held, by the act of the priest into the substance of the body and blood of Christ, while the sensible appearances, which had been the accidents of the bread and wine, remained the same.

[1] Thus Berengar was compelled at a synod of Rome in A.D. 1059 to declare that the body and blood of Christ 'sensualiter, non solum sacramento, sed in veritate manibus sacerdotum tractari et frangi et fidelium dentibus atteri'. (Mansi, *SS. Conciliorum Ampliss. Collectio*, xix, Venice, 1774, c. 900.)

It will be seen that the doctrine of transubstantiation was originally a refinement upon a stronger and coarser identification of the Eucharistic elements with the body and blood of Christ.

[2] According to Gieseler, the word transubstantiation first occurs in Damiani (†1072), *Expositio canonis Missae* (*Patrol. Lat.* cxlv. 883). [But this work is now not regarded as Damiani's. On the history of the use of the word see Herzog-Hauck, *Realencyklopädie für protestantische Theologie und Kirche*, xx (1908), 57 (including a criticism of Denifle), and Ghellinck, 'Eucharistie au xiie siècle en occident' in Vacant and Mangenot, *Dictionnaire de théologie catholique*, vol. v.]

Thus realism bespoke the favour of the theologian by supply- ing a much-needed philosophical dress for his cherished doctrine. However jealously he might defend the claims of authority against reason, in his exposition of theological doctrine Anselm leant to the same side. In fact, from this time forward, though reactionary theologians declaimed against all philosophy, the tendency to introduce dialectical distinctions and methods of argument into theology became more and more irresistible; and in whatever proportion this was done, the philosophy which was made use of among the orthodox was sure to be of a more or less realistic cast.

The outburst of pure, unadulterated, extravagant nominal- Roscellinus. ism in Roscellinus—nominalism as crude as the realism of William of Champeaux—was the first wholly new idea which had moved upon the surface of philosophic thought since the time of Johannes Scotus, afterwards known as Erigena.[1] But Scotus is a solitary genius emerging from the dead level of traditional education and passing away without founding a school or inspiring a successor. Roscellinus, by his doctrine that universals are mere sounds (*flatus vocis*), supplied that powerful shock to established beliefs and modes of thought in which great speculative movements usually have their origin. His teaching awoke the schools of Europe to a consciousness of the speculative issues of the logical question which they had been languidly discussing since the time of Alcuin, as well as to the speculative possibilities of the dialectical weapons whose use they had long made it their chief business to teach. In Abelard—at once the pupil, the successor, and the antagonist of Roscellinus—this consciousness of the power of thought, which now began to take the place of the timid dialectic and conventional theology of the Dark Ages, found its fullest and most brilliant exponent.

Peter Abelard was a Breton, born at the village of Palais Life of near Nantes in 1079. It is a sign of the change which was Abelard. coming over the face of Europe that the eldest son of a

---

[1] [For Roscellinus (born at Compiègne, *c.* 1050) see Picavet, *Roscelin, philosophe et théologien* (Paris, ed. 2, 1911) and the works cited in De Wulf, i. 114; also Ueberweg-Geyer, pp. 206–9.]

CHAP. II. seigneur, himself destined to the profession of arms, should be given the education of a clerk. The boy soon discovered so ardent a zeal for knowledge that he was content to be disinherited rather than abandon his studious life. After the fashion of the age, he wandered from one school to another,[1] and it was in the course of these early wanderings that he was for a time the pupil of the great nominalist Roscellinus.[2] At last, at about the age of twenty, he was attracted by the fame of William of Champeaux to the Cathedral School of Paris.

Collision with William of Champeaux. His new master had done more than any one else to formulate that realistic doctrine which was more and more assuming the position of an orthodox or official philosophy. His teaching, if we may accept Abelard's interpretation of it, was the very quintessence of crude, uncompromising realism. He maintained that the whole thing, i.e. the idea represented by each specific or generic name, was 'essentially' present in each individual of the genus or species. His brilliant pupil, imbued with at least the critical side of Roscellinus's doctrine, ventured, with a presumption which shocked an age disposed to apply the principles of feudal loyalty to the warfare of the schools, openly to combat the principles of his teacher.[3] At

[1] 'Proinde diversas disputando perambulans provincias, ubicunque huius artis (sc. Dialecticae) vigere studium audieram, Peripateticorum aemulator factus sum.' Ep. i, c. 1. For the facts of Abelard's life I may refer to this autobiography or *Historia Calamitatum* which stands as the first of his letters, and to Rémusat's most interesting Life. [For recent work on Abelard see Manitius, *Gesch. d. latein. Literatur*, iii (1931), 105–12, Ueberweg-Geyer, pp. 214–26, 702–3, De Wulf, i. 161–6, and J. G. Sikes, *Peter Abailard* (Cambridge, 1932); cf. C. Ottaviano, *Pietro Abelardo* (Rome, 1932). Interesting studies will be found in the works of Grabmann and Ghellinck, in E. Gilson, *Études de philosophie médiévale* (Strasbourg, 1921), pp. 20–9, and, with excellent biblio-

graphical notes, in G. Paré, &c., *Les Écoles et l'enseignement*, pp. 275–312. The most important advance in the study of Abelard has been due to Geyer's new edition of his philosophical works, including the rediscovered glosses on Porphyry, in the *Beiträge zur Geschichte der Philosophie des Mittelalters*, xxi, parts 1–4 (Münster, 1919–33: in progress). For recent discussion on Abelard's so-called rationalism see below, pp. 59–60, note.]

[2] The fact, though stated by Otto of Freising (*De Gestis Frid.* i, c. 47), was formerly doubted, but is put beyond dispute by the letter from Roscellinus to his pupil published by Cousin, *Opp.* ii. 792–803.

[3] 'Primo ei acceptus, postmodum gravissimus extiti, cum nonnullas ... eius sententias refellere conarer,

what was then accounted an unusually early age, long before the completion of the ordinary period of study, the ambitious and self-confident youth became anxious to set up as an independent teacher. But in France education was the monopoly of the Church. No one could teach, at least in the neighbourhood of any recognized school, without the permission of its duly appointed head; and William was naturally not disposed to admit so presumptuous a pupil to a participation in his privileges. At Paris Abelard could not venture to defy the established custom: he succeeded, however, in establishing himself as a master at Melun without opposition, if not with the assent of the ecclesiastical authorities of the place. As his fame spread, he ventured to move nearer Paris, to Corbeil. An illness compelled him to retire for some years to his native Brittany, whither he was followed by many of his enthusiastic disciples. Disgusted at the success of his conceited pupil, the old master became more than ever convinced of the vanity of secular knowledge[1]—a suspicion which often haunted the teacher of the old school even while he was spending his life in imparting it. When Abelard returned to Paris, he found that the famous Archdeacon of Paris, the 'Column of the Doctors' as he was called, had retired from his preferment to the little chapel of S. Victor which grew into the famous abbey of that name.[2] But the passion for dialectic had invaded even this new retreat of mystical and sanctified learning, and William was persuaded to resume his lectures for the benefit of the canons of his house as well as of outsiders. Professing a desire to learn rhetoric, but more probably thirsting for fresh laurels, Abelard placed himself again under the instruction of his former master. The old conflicts were resumed. Abelard contended that if the whole 'thing', i.e. the whole of the universal, were

et ratiocinari contra eum saepius aggrederer et nonnunquam superior in disputando viderer.' *Hist. calamitatum*, c. 2.

[1] Abelard as usual assigns a more sinister motive: 'ut quo religiosior crederetur, ad maiorem praelationis gradum promoveretur, sicut in proximo contigit.' *Ibid*.

[2] As to the early history of this House [see Fourier-Bonnard, *Histoire de l'abbaye royale et de l'ordre des chanoines réguliers de Saint-Victor de Paris* (Paris, 1904)].

'essentially' present in each individual of the genus or species, none of it was left to be present in any other individual at the same time. [Crude indeed must have been a realism which could be refuted by such an argument; yet so formidable did it seem], if we may trust to its author's account of the matter, that the master was obliged to retract and amend his formula by substituting the vaguer 'indifferently'[1] for the more definite 'essentially'. This retraction gave the death-blow to what was left of the older schoolman's reputation. The distinction which Abelard gained by the encounter was such that William's successor in the schools of Notre Dame offered to resign in his favour and to sit at the feet of the young master. Abelard was therefore duly installed in the Cathedral School. But the cowl had not made a genuine 'religious' of the ex-Archdeacon, and he succeeded in procuring the removal of the master who had lent Abelard his chair, and the substitution of a jealous rival in his place. Abelard was thus obliged to retire once more to Melun. But now William also retired for a time with his disciples into the country—as Abelard suggests, to convince sceptical critics of the reality of his 'conversion'. Abelard thereupon ventured to set up his chair, not indeed within the walls of the city, but in the precincts of Ste Geneviève on the southern bank of the Seine. The immunities of this church, at that time in the hands of a chapter of secular canons, enabled it to offer an asylum to masters who were excluded from teaching by the cathedral authorities; and henceforth the 'Mountain' of Ste Geneviève became and long remained the head-quarters of philosophical teaching in Paris. [William returned once more to Paris, but according to his rivals lost nearly all his pupils and gave up

Abelard at Ste Geneviève.

---

[1] *Hist. cal.*, c. 2. Such is no doubt the right reading. (See Cousin, *Œuvres inéd.*, p. cxvii.) [It is confirmed by William's *Sententiae*, edited by G. Lefèvre, *Les Variations de Guillaume de Champeaux* (Lille, 1898). For William and the literature on him see Ueberweg-Geyer, pp. 206, 210–11, 701–2; De Wulf, i. 149, 156. The term *indifferenter* was taken not directly from the translation of the *Topics*, but from Boethius on the *De Interpretatione*. The gloss on Porphyry shows that in his later teaching Abelard, while attacking their realistic use, availed himself of the conceptions of indifference and of its development 'status'.]

teaching altogether. Abelard's private affairs compelled him
to return to Brittany for a time: when he returned the old
scholastic had become a bishop.]

Abelard had hitherto been a teacher of dialectic and
grammar, or, as we should express it, of logic and latin.
But no sooner had the promotion of William of Champeaux
to the see of Châlons (in 1113) left him without a rival in
this field than he became ambitious of attaining distinction
as a theologian. With this view he put himself under the
instruction of the most famous theological master of his day
—Anselm of Laon.[1] The great philosopher was not, however,
long content to be a student in his new faculty under an aged
master of whose powers he appears to have formed the lowest
possible estimate.[2] He soon ceased to attend lectures
regularly, and at length, in the course of conversation with
some of his fellow students, freely expressed his surprise
that educated men should not be able to study the Scriptures
for themselves without any other aid than the text and the
gloss. The unheard-of doctrine was received with derision,
and Abelard was jestingly challenged to make the attempt.
He took the students at their word, and offered, if they would

---

[1] [On Anselm of Laon and the literature see De Wulf, i. 199 sq.; Ueberweg-Geyer, p. 700. His Sentences have been edited by F. Bliemetzrieder in the Beiträge, xviii. 2–3 (Münster, 1919). Their systematic arrangement is now regarded as a stage of some significance in the development of scholastic method; see especially Grabmann, ii. 136 sqq. On the fame of the School of Laon under Anselm and his brother Ralph, and on Anselm's glosses on scripture, see the authorities cited by Poole, Illustrations of Medieval Thought, pp. 112, 135 n. Anselm's authorship of the glossa interlinearia found in medieval Bibles cannot be literally accepted, although his glosses, e.g. of the Pauline Epistles, largely influenced the interlinear. His glosses, in their turn influenced

especially by Remi of Auxerre, were the basis of his systematic Sententiae or systematic tabulation of scriptural doctrine from the patristic sources compiled by commentators in previous centuries. Hence Anselm helped to prepare the way for the Lombard. See Hans Glunz, History of the Vulgate in England (Cambridge, 1933), pp. 201–11, 317, &c.; cf. G. Paré, &c., Les Écoles et l'enseignement, pp. 231, 248–9.]

[2] 'Accessi igitur ad hunc senem, cui magis longaevus usus quam ingenium vel memoria nomen comparaverat. Ad quem si quis de aliqua quaestione pulsandum accederet incertus, redibat incertior.' Hist. cal., c. 3. He afterwards compares him to the barren fig-tree of the Gospel.

CHAP. II. provide him with one of the usual commentaries, to begin lecturing on the most difficult book of the Bible that they might choose, the very next day. They pitched upon the book of Ezekiel. Abelard fulfilled his promise. The attempt was at first regarded as a mere piece of braggadocio, but after a few lectures, the reports of those who came attracted a large audience, and Abelard became almost as formidable a rival to Anselm as he had been to William of Champeaux. Abelard had, however, 'incepted' or begun to teach in defiance of all established custom without any authorization; and he was compelled to give up lecturing in Laon.

Abelard at Paris.   He returned to Paris, and was now allowed to lecture without interruption as a duly authorized master in the schools of Notre Dame; and his fame as a theologian soon equalled that which he had won in earlier days as a philosopher. Abelard had reached the zenith of his glory; and now began his rapid and terrible downfall—a moral downfall which prepared the way for his undeserved persecutions, and gave some colour to the arguments of men to whom that spirit of rationalism which Abelard represented seemed a direct inspiration of the Evil One. It is, however, surprising how little his treacherous crime seems to have shocked the men who professed such a holy horror of his theological enormities.[1] The tragic story of Abelard—of his connexion with his pupil Heloise and the terrible revenge by which it was terminated —is too well known to need repetition, and does not directly concern us here. Nor need we follow the pathetic story of the quarrels with his abbot as a monk of S. Denis—where the whole convent was roused to fury against him by his denial of their founder's identity with Dionysius the companion of S. Paul—of his hermit life near Nogent at the oratory of the Paraclete built for him with their own hands by his faithful disciples, of his troubled career as abbot of the poor, remote and unruly Breton monastery of S. Gildas de Rhuys, of his half-imprisonment, half-retirement at Cluny. This part of his life belongs rather to the general ecclesiastical history of the

---

[1] [He is, however, reproached with the incident by Roscellinus (Cousin, *Petri Abailardi Opera*, ii. 801).]

time than to the history of universities. All through his later
years S. Bernard was preaching a crusade against him: he
was almost as much done to death by S. Bernard as if he had
died at the stake.[1]

It is unnecessary for us to estimate the exact extent of Abelard's
Abelard's heresy. As has been already pointed out, nominal- heresies.
ism had become associated in Berengar with the denial of
transubstantiation, and in Roscellinus with heretical views
of the Holy Trinity. As to the Eucharist, Abelard's position
amounted to a somewhat mystical form of transubstantiation;[2] but comparatively little was made of this point against
him. From the tritheism of Roscellinus he most emphatically
dissociated himself: Roscellinus, indeed, was one of his
accusers at the Council of Soissons. His teaching on the
Trinity is not essentially different from the doctrine of the
'Master of the Sentences' solemnly affirmed by a general
council: in its general tone and spirit it is substantially
(certain metaphysical technicalities apart) the teaching of
S. Thomas Aquinas.[3] One of the passages to which most

---

[1] But see Denifle in *Archiv*, i.
595, note 1. It is probable that
in Ep. 189 the Saint does not
hesitate to incur the 'venial sin'
of lying to accomplish the object of his pious zeal, by represent-
ing that the appeal to the Holy See
was made after the condemnation;
whereas from his own statement it
appears that it was before. Cf.
Rémusat, i. 223. [The order of the
proceedings at Sens is too obscure
to warrant this judgement. See
Poole, *Illustrations*, ed. 2, p. 143
note, and the bibliographical notes
in Hefele-Leclercq, *Histoire des
conciles*, v. i. 754 and *passim*.]

[2] If we may trust the so-called
Epitome Theologiae Christianae as
containing Abelard's teaching,
though probably not his work
(*Opera*, ed. Cousin, ii. 578). See also
the 'Capitula errorum' in Bernard
(*Patrol. Lat.* clxxxii. 1052). Large
extracts from Walter of S. Victor's

polemic against Abelard are printed
by Bulaeus (ii. 404).

[3] The explanation of the 'tres
personae' as 'tres proprietates', i.e.
Potentia, Sapientia, and Bonitas or
(as Aquinas said) Amor, which together form the one 'substantia'
or 'essentia' of God. The main
distinction of Aquinas's position is
that he recognizes 'tres substantiae'
or even 'tres res' (for which poor
Roscellinus suffered so much),
though adhering to the one 'essentia', and admitting that 'substantia'
may be used in the sense of 'essentia'. Yet Innocent III in the Lateran
Council of 1215 issued a decree,
permanently embodied in the
canon law (Decret. Greg. IX, lib.
i, tit. i, c. 2), in favour of Peter the
Lombard's doctrine (attacked by
the Abbot Joachim) that the three
Persons form 'una substantia,
essentia, seu natura divina', and
even 'una res'.

CHAP. II. exception was taken at Soissons turned out, on further inspection, to be a citation from S. Augustine himself. The charge of Sabellianism at one council is sufficiently refuted by the charge of Arianism founded upon precisely the same expressions at another. What may perhaps be thought his most indefensible heresy, the doctrine known as nihilianism, which may be construed into an obscuration of the real humanity of Christ, was shared by his disciple Peter the Lombard, the 'Master of the Sentences', the author of the accredited medieval text-book of theology.[1] His view of redemption, one of his most damnable heresies in the eyes of S. Bernard, was partly shared by no less a person than S. Anselm.[2] Twice Abelard was condemned; the first time in 1121 at the Synod of Soissons,[3] afterwards by the Prelates

[1] Alexander III directed the Archbishop of Sens to condemn certain propositions of the Lombard, among others the doctrine of *nihilianismus*, i.e. the 'quod Christus secundum quod est homo non est aliquid' (Bulaeus, ii. 403; *Chartul. Univ. Paris.*, Introd., No. 3. Cf. *Sententiarum*, lib. iii, dist. 10). Again, in 1177 the Archbishop of Reims is directed to condemn the doctrine, 'convocatis magistris scolarum Parisiensium et Remensium et aliarum circumpositarum civitatum' (*Chartul.*, Introd., No. 9). The Pope had once taught the doctrine himself (Denifle, *Archiv*, i. 617). The historical explanation of nihilianism is that it was a reaction from the 'adoptionism' of a preceding age. Though the medieval Church formally repudiated the Lombard's teaching, the Christology of both medieval and modern Churches received from this time an Apollinarian taint from which they have never completely emancipated themselves. This was, however, due far more to the turn given to the doctrine by the Lombard than to the much more rational form which it assumes in Abelard. See the valuable chapter in Dorner,

Hist. of the Development of the Doct. of the Person of Christ, Eng. trans. by Simon, div. 2, vol. i, p. 309 *sq.*

[2] His denial that the death of Christ was a price paid to the Devil for the redemption of man from his just dominion (though Anselm held a theory of satisfaction which Abelard rejects). Cf. Anselm, *Cur Deus Homo*, i, c. vii. (*Patrol. Lat.* clviii. 367 *sq.*), with Bernard, *ibid.* clxxxii. 1063 *sq.* For the theological teaching of Abelard see Deutsch, p. 192 *sq.* [Also C. C. J. Webb, *Studies in the History of Natural Theology* (Oxford, 1915); H. Rashdall, *The Idea of Atonement in Christian Theology* (London, 1919); and the elaborate essay of J. Cottaux in the *Revue d'hist. ecclésiastique*, xxviii (1932), 247–95, 788–828.]

[3] The actual work condemned on this occasion, the *Tractatus de unitate et trinitate divina*, was discovered and edited by Dr. Remigius Stölzle of Würzburg (Freiburg i. B. 1891); the *Theologia Christiana* is now seen to be a revised form of this treatise with a few highly significant omissions and much amplification, especially in the way of apology.

of France—aroused against him by his indefatigable enemy CHAP. II.
S. Bernard—at Sens in 1141.[1] On the first occasion Abelard
had to submit to the humiliation of burning his book with
his own hands, and was imprisoned in a monastery; on the
second, after the condemnation had been confirmed by the
Pope, he was again sentenced to imprisonment in a monastery,
though upon the intercession of Peter the Venerable, the
good Abbot of Cluny, he was allowed a more honourable
retirement in that illustrious house.

In the estimation of men like Bernard and Norbert, the *His
rational-
ism the
real cause
of offence.* real grievance against Abelard was not this or that particular
error, but the whole tone, spirit, and method of his theological
teaching.[2] He had presumed to endeavour to understand, to
explain the mystery of the Trinity: he had dared to bring all
things in heaven and earth to the test of reason.[3]   For his
conservative opponents that was heresy enough: to accept the
doctrines of the Church because they were rational was
hardly less offensive than to reject them as irrational.   The
well-known story of the proceedings at Sens, when drowsy
bishops woke up from their slumbers at each pause of the
reader's voice to mutter ' 'namus', ' 'namus'[4] against theological positions which they were incapable of understanding,
has become the typical illustration of the methods by which

---

[1] Not 1140, as has been shown
by Deutsch in his pamphlet *Die
Synode von Sens 1141*, Berlin,
1880, p. 50 *sq.*; though Vacandard
defends 1140 (*Rev. des ques. hist.*,
vol. l, 1891, p. 235).

[2] Cf. the words of S. Bernard:
'Irridetur simplicium fides, evisce-
rantur arcana Dei, quaestiones de
altissimis rebus temerarie ventilan-
tur, insultatur Patribus, quod eas
magis sopiendas quam solvendas
censuerint.' (Ep. 188, *Patrol. Lat.*
clxxxii. 353.) And again: 'Nihil
videt per speculum et in aenigmate,
sed facie ad faciem omnia intuetur.'
(Ep. 192, *ibid.*, c. 358.)

[3] Bernard, *Opera, ibid.* clxxxii.
359 *sq.*, 539 *sq.*

[4] 'Inter haec sonat lector, stertit

auditor. Alius cubito innititur, ut
det oculis suis somnum, alius super
molle cervical dormitionem palpe-
bris suis molitur, alius super genua
caput reclinans dormitat. Cum itaque lector in Petri satis [? scriptis]
aliquod reperiret spinetum, surdis
exclamabat auribus Pontificum:
Damnatis? Tunc quidam vix ad
extremam syllabam expergefacti,
somnolenta voce, capite pendulo,
Damnamus, aiebant. Alii vero
damnantium tumultu excitati,
decapitata prima syllaba, *namus*
inquiunt.' Berengarius Scholasticus, *Apologeticus pro magistro*, ap.
Bulaeum, ii. 183; Abael. *Opp.* ii.
773, 774. The writer is of course
a partisan.

CHAP. II. an intolerant ecclesiastical imbecility has sometimes endeavoured to stifle theological inquiry. But the Council of Sens was no fair representative even of the Church of the twelfth century. It is evident that the intellect of the age was with Abelard; and the heresy of one generation became the orthodoxy of the next.

Abelard and the Lombard. It is from one point of view little more than an accident that the odour of heresy still cleaves to the name of Abelard, while Peter the Lombard lived to be Bishop of Paris, to be consulted by a Pope on a question of theology, and to see his 'Sentences' already becoming the very canon of orthodoxy for all succeeding ages. Not only had the Lombard shared Abelard's most serious deviation from Catholic teaching: he had adopted from his persecuted master that dialectical treatment of theology—that system of fully and freely stating difficulties before attempting their solution—which had given so much umbrage to Bernard and the obscurantists. By opponents of the next generation, such as Walter of S. Victor, Peter the Lombard is classed with Abelard and two other victims of Bernard's theological malice among the 'sophists' and enemies of the faith—the four 'Labyrinths' of France.[1] So far, it was the principle soon to be embodied in the University of Paris which was condemned at Soissons and which triumphed when the new university became recognized as the first school of the Church, and its most illustrious teachers as Saints and accredited 'Doctors of the Church'. From another point of view we must pronounce that the estimate which orthodox opinion has formed of the relative position of Abelard and the Lombard is amply justified. From this point of view Abelard was a confessor in a losing cause. In Abelard we must recognize incomparably the greatest intellect of the Middle Ages, one of the great minds which mark a period in the world's intellectual history:

[1] Walter of S. Victor wrote a treatise 'Contra manifestas et damnatas etiam in conciliis haereses, quas Sophistae Abelardus, Lombardus, Petrus Pictavinus et Gilbertus Porretanus libris Sententiarum suarum acuunt, limant, roborant'; in which he declares them, 'dum ineffabilia Trinitatis et Incarnationis scholastica levitate tractarent, multas haereses olim vomuisse.' Bulaeus, ii. 402. Cf. p. 200.

in the Lombard we descend from the mountain to the plain. CHAP. II.
Not only did the nominalism of which Abelard was the
champion long remain under the ban of the Church, but the
spirit of free inquiry, for the moment associated with nominalism, was crushed with it. Abelard, a Christian thinker to the
very heart's core (however irredeemable the selfishness and
overweening vanity of his youth), was at the same time the
representative of the principle of free, though reverent,
inquiry in matters of religion and individual loyalty to truth.
To say that Abelard anticipated the spirit of Protestant theology would be scant praise. He was not of course altogether
exempt from the traditionalism of his age: still at times a
note of criticism may be discerned in his methods of exegetical
and historical discussion.[1] And on such subjects as the Holy
Trinity, the Atonement,[2] and the doctrine of Grace, we should
have to come down to very recent times indeed for more
enlightened attempts at the philosophical presentation of
Christian doctrine.

Peter the Lombard inherited the form but not the spirit Peter the
of Abelard's theological methods.[3] The attempt to appeal Lombard.

[1] The whole principle of six-
teenth-century Protestantism is
contained in the declaration that
the 'ecclesiastici doctores' are to be
read 'non cum credendi necessitate,
sed cum iudicandi libertate'—a
principle which he does not extend to the canonical scriptures,
though even there he recognizes
(with Jerome) the possibility that
'aut codex mendosus est, aut inter-
pres erravit'. Sic et Non (Œuv.
inéd., p. 14). [On the other hand,
Abelard was not alone in the view
that some authorities had more
weight than others, and that the
authority of Scripture was supreme. Cf. for the previous period
G. Robert, Les Écoles et l'enseignement de la théologie (1909), pp. 155,
161–6. On the authority of the
fathers see Glunz, op. cit., passim.]
[2] I cannot forbear to quote one
of the 'blasphemies' against which

Bernard exhausts the resources of
his pious scurrility: 'Puto ergo quod
consilium et causa incarnationis
fuit, ut mundum luce suae sapientiae illuminaret, et ad amorem
suum accenderet.' Bernard, Opera,
Patrol. Lat. clxxxii. 1050, 1051).
For the Saint's reply see ibid., c.
1062 sq.
[3] [In several respects Rashdall
unduly emphasized the unique
quality of Abelard. In the first
place his rationalism was by no
means so far-reaching as is here
represented. Like S. Anselm he
regarded reason as the servant of
faith. See especially Poole's correction from Balliol College MS.
296 of Cousin's text of the Intro-
ductio ad theologiam (Illustrations of
Med. Thought, 2nd ed., 1920, p.
180 note, and on the main issue,
pp. 138–41). Cf. Gilson, Études,
pp. 20–7, and especially Cottaux in

CHAP. II. from recent tradition to the ancient Fathers, and from the ancient Fathers to Scripture and to reason, is abandoned. With the Master of the Sentences scholasticism ceases to wear the aspect of a revolt against authority. There remains, indeed, a deep conviction of the necessity for a rationalization of Christian doctrine, and the method of boldly stating and attempting to answer the most formidable objections to received opinions; but, with the Lombard, theology returns to her earlier habit of unquestioning submission to patristic and ecclesiastical authority when once the balance of authority has been determined. It is the object of the 'Sententiae' to collect and harmonize the opinions of the Fathers upon every point of Christian theology, and to extract from their scattered and sometimes conflicting *dicta* a precise and explicit answer to every question which the dialectical activity of the age had suggested. Of the scholastic theology which henceforth expressed itself chiefly in the form of lectures and comments upon the 'Sentences', Abelard is unquestionably the father; but the child only partially reproduced the intellectual characteristics of its parent. It was from Abelard's 'Theologia' that the Lombard derived the idea of reducing theology from a chaotic literature to a philosophical system: it was in Abelard's audacious 'Sic et Non' that he found a precedent for the marshalling of argument against argument and authority against authority; but in the 'Sentences' the critical attitude of Abelard is exchanged for the more modest attempt to harmonize the apparently conflicting authorities by the aid

the essay mentioned above (p. 56 n.), e.g. p. 824, 'la théologie n'atteint que du vraisemblable, c'est-à-dire une représentation contingente de la réalité'. In the second place, the method of *Sic et Non* was not original in Abelard, whose work, here as elsewhere, was a masterly comprehension and appropriation of existing tendencies. (See below, p. 128 n.) Lastly, the intellectual life of the twelfth century, both before and after Abelard, was much more active and vigorous than Rash-dall represents. Perhaps the most striking text is the analysis given by John of Salisbury in the *Historia Pontificalis* (ed. Poole, pp. 16–41) of the position of Gilbert of La Porrée during his conflict with S. Bernard; but the whole history of the twelfth-century renaissance, in theology as in literature and science, as elaborated in recent works, brings the great figure of Abelard into clearer relations with his time.]

of subtle distinction and ingenious inference. If (as was CHAP. II. undoubtedly the case[1]) the Lombard's object was to appease the raging sea of theological speculation and disputation on which his lot was cast, he succeeded singularly ill; but the publication of the 'Sentences' did largely tend to that gradual limitation of the controversial area which accompanied the eventual triumph of the scholastic method throughout the Western Church. In the generation after Abelard, and still more emphatically in the thirteenth century, the philosophy and philosophical theology against which Bernard had arrayed all the ecclesiastical chivalry of Europe finally triumphed over the mystical or positive teaching of the monasteries. Were S. Bernard at this moment to revisit the banks of the Seine, he would be nearly as much shocked at the 'solvuntur objecta' of S. Sulpice as he would be at the philosophical speculations of the now secularized Sorbonne.[2] But the triumph of scholasticism was a 'Cadmeian victory':

[1] See the Prologue to the *Sententiae*. [The Lombard's relation to and dependence upon his environment have been much discussed since Rashdall wrote. See especially the works of Ghellinck and Grabmann, and, for the development of the *Sententiae* on a scriptural basis, Glunz, *The Vulgate in England*. From a *formal* point of view the Lombard probably owed as much to Abelard's despised master, Anselm of Laon, as to Abelard himself.]

[2] How offensive the new theology still seemed to old-fashioned Churchmen up to the very end of the twelfth century may be judged from the letters of Stephen, Bishop of Tournai, who complains that nowadays 'discipuli solis novitatibus applaudunt, et magistri glorie potius invigilant quam doctrine. Novas recentesque summulas et commentaria firmantia super theologia passim conscribunt, quibus auditores suos demulceant, detineant, decipiant, quasi nondum suffecerint sanctorum opuscula Patrum, quos eodem spiritu sacram Scripturam legimus exposuisse, quo eam composuisse credimus apostolos et prophetas ... Disputatur publice contra sacras constitutiones,de incomprehensibili deitate; de incarnatione Verbi verbosa caro et sanguis irreverenter litigat; individua Trinitas in triviis secatur et discepitur; ut tot iam sint errores quot doctores, tot scandala quot auditoria, tot blasphemie quot platee.' Edit. J. Desilve (1893), pp. 344, 345; *Chartul. Univ. Paris.*, Introd., No. 48. Such is the way in which orthodox and conservative Churchmen greeted the introduction of the theology now taught in every Roman Catholic seminary. Even Gregory IX in 1228 writes in much the same strain to warn the theologians of Paris 'quatinus ... sine fermento mundane scientie doceatis theologicam puritatem, non adulterantes verbum Dei philosophorum figmentis'; *Chartul. Univ. Paris.* i, No. 59.

CHAP. II. it cost the vanquished hardly more than the victors. If the University of Paris was born of the spirit of which Abelard is the foremost representative, every increase of her material splendour and ecclesiastical importance was bought by some fresh departure from that principle of free inquiry which it is the highest function of a university to enshrine.[1]

Growth of the Parisian schools. The career of Abelard at Paris just coincided with the first steps in the rapid rise to commercial and political importance of the ancient stronghold of the Counts of Paris. The military strength of the Island-city was the principal instrument in the rapid aggrandizement of the descendants of Hugh Capet. The increasing importance of the place had already (as we have seen) lent fame to its schools before the wandering Breton scholar of twenty appeared for the first time in the cloisters of Notre Dame. The renown of Abelard drew crowds of students from the remotest parts of Europe;[2] it is said that twenty of his pupils became cardinals and more than fifty of them bishops.[3] He attracted to himself all the new-born enthusiasm for learning which was everywhere springing up, and which itself resulted from the operation of vaster forces than the genius of the greatest of its representatives. Though crowds of enthusiastic disciples followed their per-

[1] S. Bernard puts his case against Abelard in a nutshell when he says, 'Ita omnia usurpat sibi humanum ingenium, fidei nil reservans . . . et quidquid sibi non invenit pervium, id putat nihilum, credere dedignatur.' Ep. 188 *Patrol. Lat.* clxxxii. 353). In judging of Bernard's attitude towards Abelard, we must remember that, as Otto of Freising has it, the good man was 'tam ex Christianae religionis fervore zelotypus, quam ex habitudinali mansuetudine quodammodo credulus'. (*Gest. Frid.* i. 47, ap. *M.G.H.*, *Scriptores*, xx. 376.)

[2] 'Roma suos tibi docendos transmittebat alumnos: . . . Anglorum turbam juvenum mare . . . non terrebat . . . Remota Brittania (probably Brittany) sua ani-

malia erudienda destinabat. Andegavenses eorum edomita feritate tibi famulabantur in suis. Pictavi, Vuascones et Hiberi; Normania, Flandria, Theutonicus et Suevius tuum calere ingenium, laudare et praedicare assidue studebat.' Letter of Fulk, Prior of Deuil, to Abelard, in Cousin, *Abailardi Opp.* i. 703, 704 (for 'calere' read 'colere').

[3] *Hist. Lit.* ix. 85. [The ascendancy of Paris, as 'the centre of European thought and culture', is exaggerated in this eloquent paragraph. To say nothing of literary and scientific activity elsewhere, e.g. in Sicily, the school of Chartres was probably as influential as that of Paris for some years after the death of Abelard.]

secuted master from one retreat to another—even when he sought to bury himself like an anchorite in the desert—it was at Paris that his teaching began and at Paris that his largest audiences were gathered. The stream of pilgrim scholars which set in towards Paris in the days of Abelard flowed continuously for at least a century and a half, when its volume began to be somewhat abated by the growth of daughter-universities in other parts of Europe. Had Paris been no more than a mere ecclesiastical city clustering round some ancient sanctuary, the fame which Abelard had won for its schools might have passed away like the scholastic fame of Tours or of Chartres. But the process was already beginning by which the successors of the Counts of Paris were to become the real Kings of France; and one of the effects of this movement was to make Paris incomparably the greatest and most important city of Transalpine Europe. This increase of political and commercial importance had a decisive influence in constituting the city the permanent head-quarters of the movement which Abelard had inaugurated. The university, the corporation of masters (as we have so often to remark), existed as yet hardly even in germ; but from the days of Abelard Paris was as decidedly the centre of European thought and culture as Athens in the days of Pericles, or Florence in the days of Lorenzo de' Medici.

In order to understand the character of that mighty stirring Character of the twelfth-century Renaissance. of the human spirit which Abelard represents, it is essential to form as accurate a conception as possible of the nature and subject-matter of the teaching which awakened so much enthusiasm. There is the broadest distinction between the culture of the twelfth century and the culture of the thirteenth century. Though the former period was the epoch of the highest or at all events of the most varied intellectual activity which the schools of the Middle Ages ever knew, the greater part of the books which were to absorb all the energies of the universities for the three following centuries were not yet known in Western Christendom. The Renaissance of the twelfth century began, like the more brilliant but not more real Renaissance of the fifteenth, with a revived interest in a

CHAP. II. literature which had never passed into total oblivion: like that later Renaissance, it culminated in the rediscovery of a literature which had been practically lost, or at least buried, for centuries. Abelard belongs to the first half of this movement. Of the works of Aristotle he knew little more than had been known to Alcuin or Erigena.[1] It was not till the generation after Abelard that the whole of the *Organon*, in old or new translations, was generally known in northern Europe.[2] By the time of John of Salisbury, the new logic (as it was called) took the foremost place among the acknowledged text-books of the schools. Abelard concentrated his attention upon the old question of the schools—the question of the reality of universals. And on this subject he did little

Abelard's logical position. more than continue with more moderation and more common sense the polemic inaugurated by Roscellinus against the crudities of a realism which understood the Aristotelian doctrine of the priority of the universal as a priority in order of time.[3] He may be said to have formulated the position which in modern times would be described as conceptualism, though in the Middle Ages this position was always looked upon as a form of nominalism. This teaching had the stimulating effect of all teaching which clears away time-honoured cobwebs, however little the reformer may discern the truth which lies buried beneath the rubbish. And with

---

[1] See above, p. 37, n. 2.

[2] [The new logic was known to Thierry of Chartres and Otto of Freising. Gilbert of La Porrée, a rather close contemporary of Abelard, refers to the *Prior Analytics*, as Abelard does. It is probable that the version of Boethius was rediscovered and in general use, in spite of the translations of James of Venice (*c.* 1128). On the whole subject see the important paper of Haskins, 'Versions of Aristotle's Posterior Analytics' in *Studies in the History of Mediaeval Science*, pp. 223–41.]

[3] His logical position is fairly expressed by the following sentences: 'Clarum itaque ex supradictis arbi-

tror esse, res aliquas non esse ea, quae a propositionibus dicuntur ... Non itaque propositiones res aliquas designant simpliciter quemadmodum nomina. Imo qualiter sese ad invicem habeant, utrum scilicet sibi conveniant annon, proponunt ...; et est profecto ita in re, sicut dicit vera propositio, sed non est res aliqua, quod dicit; unde quasi quidam rerum modus habendi se per propositiones exprimitur, non res aliquae designantur' (*Dialect.* ap. *Œuv. inéd.*, p. 245). 'Aliud enim in nomine Socratis quam in nomine hominis vel caeteris intelligitur; sed non est alia res unius nominis quod Socrati inhaeret quam alterius' (*ibid.*, p. 248).

the cobwebs in which the older dialecticians had been im-meshed there disappeared also the caution and timidity which, since the time of Erigena, had characterized their attitude towards theology. The weapon of dialectic was now freely applied to the problem of revealed as well as of natural religion: the boundaries which had hitherto divided philosophy and theology were broken down: the sovereignty of reason was proclaimed.

But it was not only as the clear-headed logician, the bold and independent moral philosopher,[1] and the daring theologian that Abelard cast such a spell over the student of his generation. Anticipating the sixteenth century in his advocacy of the rights of private judgement, Abelard (though less than some of his contemporaries) anticipated it also in his enthusiasm for the study of classical literature. He was at least one, if not the most prominent, of the little band of scholars who imparted fresh vigour to the teaching of grammar as well as to philosophy and theology. Though he was not (as has sometimes been supposed) a Greek scholar, Virgil and Ovid, Seneca and parts of Cicero were as familiar to him as Boethius and Augustine; and even the great classical law-texts were included among the subjects which divided the attention of this many-sided teacher.[2] Abelard was an orator and a stylist as well as a logician and dialectical theologian; and, even on the subjects of the old

His many-sidedness.

---

[1] The *Scito te ipsum* is an original treatise on moral philosophy, more valuable and interesting perhaps than anything which the Middle Ages produced after the recovery of the Nicomachean Ethics.

[2] When and where Abelard appeared in the character of a teacher of law we do not know, but the traditional story about him in this capacity by Odofredus is, except in the different sequel of the boast, so exactly parallel to the story of his relations to Anselm of Laon that it may conveniently be given here. Odofredus remarks, *Com. in Cod.* iii, tit. 39, l. 5 (Lugd. 1550, iii, f.

184 b): 'In lege ista . . . fuit deceptus quidam qui magnus philosophus putabatur: et dicitur quod fuit quidam qui vocabatur magister Petrus Baiardi . . . et valde deridebat legistas, et iactabat se quod nulla lex esset in corpore iure (*sic*) quantumcunque esset difficilis in litera quin in ea poneret casum et de ea traheret sanum intellectum. Unde una die fuit sibi ostensa a quodam ista lex, et tunc ipse dixit: Nescio quid velit dicere ista lex, unde derisus fuit.' I owe the reference to Chiappelli, *Lo Studio Bolognese*, p. 82.

CHAP. II. traditional curriculum, his lectures no doubt owed their popularity as much to the attractiveness of the manner[1] as to the novelty of the matter.

Breadth of twelfth-century studies. There was no one among Abelard's immediate successors who united the same variety of gifts to the same extraordinary charm of voice and manner; but there is hardly any period in the history of the schools of France when so many famous masters were teaching at the same time, and certainly no period in which their teaching extended over so varied a field as in the middle of the twelfth century. The subsequent predominance of an all-absorbing scholasticism has almost thrown into oblivion the fact that for about half a century classical Latin was taught—not merely to young boys, but to advanced students—with almost as much thoroughness in at least one school of medieval France, as it was afterwards taught in the universities of the Reformation, or in the Jesuit colleges of the Counter-reformation.

Studies of John of Salisbury. The Englishman, John of Salisbury, has left us a full and complete account of his education in France between 1137 and 1149.[2] He is indeed the typical scholar of the period. In those days there was no regular curriculum of studies. Scholars wandered from school to school, and from subject to subject, at their pleasure. They were no more bound to spend a fixed number of years upon any one branch of knowledge than the students at Rhodes or at Athens in the days of Cicero. John of Salisbury's studies extended over a period of twelve years, though during part of the time he was engaged in teaching privately as well as in attending the public lectures of eminent masters. First he went

---

[1] Cf. the words of Heloise: 'Duo autem . . . tibi specialiter inerant, quibus feminarum quarumlibet animos statim allicere poteras; dictandi videlicet et cantandi gratia; quae caeteros minime philosophos assecutos esse novimus.' Abael. Ep. 2, *Opera*, i. 76. Abelard's Latin hymns are printed in *loc. cit.*, p. 295, and he appears also to have composed vernacular songs. Another side of Abelard as a lecturer is brought out by Otto of Freising: 'Inde magistrum induens Parisius venit, plurimum in inventionum subtilitate non solum ad philosophiam necessariarum, sed et pro commovendis ad iocos hominum animis utilium valens.' *De Gestis Frid.* i. 48 (*M.G.H., Scriptores*, xx. 377).

[2] *Metalogicon*, ii. 10 (ed. Webb, pp. 77–83).

to Paris, and applied himself to the study of logic. Abelard CHAP. II. had just managed to escape from his uncongenial retreat at S. Gildas, and had resumed his lectures at Ste Geneviève, where for a short time John was able to sit at his feet. The departure of Abelard (S. Bernard was no doubt upon his track) compelled him to fall back upon the teaching of the orthodox realistic dialecticians, Alberic of Reims and Robert of Melun, the last an Englishman and afterwards Bishop of Hereford. After two years he left Paris, and spent three years under the famous 'grammarian' William of Conches, at Chartres. At Chartres too he went on to the *Quadrivium* under the learned Richard l'Evêque, and (at a later date) studied both dialectic and theology under Gilbert of La Porrée, the first logician of the day, afterwards Bishop of Poitiers, 'the one man whom saint Bernard of Clairvaux unsuccessfully charged with heresy'.[1] Afterwards he returned to Paris, and heard theology under Robert Pullus and Simon of Poissy. The order and varieties of these studies present the strongest contrast to the fashions of the next century, with its strict distinction of 'faculties' and invariable succession of studies, which reduced 'grammar' to a mere schoolboy preparation for dialectic, and practically compelled the student to abandon for ever each subject in the course when he had heard the regulation lectures upon it.

Among these varied studies what really interested our Twelfth-author most were the classical, or, as they were then called, century human-grammatical lectures. He has left us a very full and highly ism: Method of interesting account of the teaching of William of Conches.[2] Bernard of Chartres.

---

[1] Poole, p. 133. [For William of Conches and his predecessor, Bernard of Chartres (who is to be distinguished from Bernard Silvester), see Poole, 'The Masters of the Schools at Paris and Chartres in John of Salisbury's Time' (*English Hist. Rev.* xxxv. 1920, 321–42); lso his *Illustrations*, ed. 2, ch. iv; and the works of Clerval, G. Robert, Haskins, &c. William's encyclopaedic interests are brought out by Duhem, and by Thorndike,

History of Magic and Experimental Science, ii. 50 sqq. On the range of classical authors known in the twelfth century and the attitude to humanism, see, besides Haskins, the prolegomena to C. C. J. Webb's edition of the *Policraticus*, § 5, and Robert's interesting book, especially in the new edition, as re-written by G. Paré, &c.]

[2] *Metalogicon*, i. 24 (ed. Webb, pp. 53–8). [Clerval (p. 225) has given a good summary of the

CHAP. II. This teacher followed a method invented by his master, Bernard of Chartres, and based on the recommendations of Quintilian, a method which bears a striking resemblance to that most thoroughgoing application of the principle of classical education which gained such a marvellous popularity in later days for the schools of the Jesuits. The lectures (or at least the course of reading recommended) covered pretty well the whole field of classical Latin.[1] After questions on parsing, scansion, construction, and the grammatical figures or 'oratorical tropes' illustrated in the passage read, the lecturer noticed the 'varieties of phraseology' occurring therein, and pointed out the 'different ways in which this or that may be expressed'—in short subjected the whole diction of the author to an elaborate and exhaustive analysis with the view of stamping it upon the memory of his audience. He then proceeded to comment on or explain the subject-matter,

chapter, and brings out the distinction between the evening lesson, in which the real teaching was done, and the morning résumé and repetition. The *declinatio* or exposition was followed, in this evening exercise, by the *collatio* or conference, which was to have a great future. For both see especially Robert, pp. 50–61. Robert argues from John of Salisbury's studies that the masters in the schools had, both in grammar and in logic, an elementary and also an advanced class.] The whole chapter in the *Metalogicon* throws a most interesting light on the schools of the period— would that we had an equally full and graphic account of the schools of any later period in the Middle Ages!

[1] Peter of Blois, Archdeacon of Bath, John of Salisbury's pupil, tells us that he read 'praeter caeteros libros qui celebres sunt in scholis', Trogus Pompeius, Josephus (translated), Suetonius, Hegesippus, Q. Curtius, Cornelius Tacitus, and T. Livius, besides the Latin poets. (Ep. 101, *Patrol. Lat.* ccvii. 314;

Chartul. Univ. Paris. Introd., No. 25. This list, however, seems to be taken from John of Salisbury, *Policraticus*, viii. 18, ed. Webb, ii. 364, who does not explicitly say that he had read them, and must be looked upon with some suspicion, since John makes Suetonius and Tranquillus into two distinct authors.) The only modern author whom John's pupils were encouraged to read was Hildebert of Lavardin, Bishop of Le Mans (1096–1125), Archbishop of Tours (1125–33). 'Profuit mihi quod Epistolas Hildeberti Cenomanensis Episcopi styli elegantia et suavi urbanitate praecipuas firmare corde tenus reddere adolescentulus compellebar.' Peter of Blois, *loc. cit.* The compliment seems to be well merited and supplies another illustration of the classical taste of Abelard's generation. (See his *Epp.* ap. *Patrol. Lat.* clxxi. 141 sq.) [On Hildebert in general see A. Dieudonné, *Hildebert de Lavardin*, Paris, 1898, and Manitius, iii. 853 *sq.* and *passim.*]

enlarging upon any incidental allusions to physical science CHAP. II. or any ethical questions touched on by the author. The next morning the pupils were required, under the severest penalties, to repeat what they had been taught on the preceding day; and there was daily practice in Latin prose and verse composition in imitation of specified classical models, and frequent conversation or discussion among the pupils on a given subject, with a view to the acquisition of fluency and elegance of diction.

The Latinity of the great writers of this intermediate period—of Abelard's letters, and still more of Hildebert of Tours, and John of Salisbury—though Latin was to them too much of a living language to permit of a dilettante Ciceronianism, was often more classical than the Latinity of the African Fathers. A revival of serious study had raised their style out of the barbarism of ignorance; and even in their logical and philosophical writings it was as yet but little disfigured by the barbarism of the new scholastic terminology. A combination of circumstances narrowed the culture and the education of the succeeding age. Even in the hey-day of the twelfth-century Renaissance, the humanists (if one may so call them) were in a minority, just as they were in the days of Erasmus and Reuchlin. John of Salisbury's *Metalogicon* was largely written to vindicate the claims of 'grammar' or humane letters. His writings are full of lamentation over the prevailing passion for frivolous, subtle, and sophistical disputation. Fully as he appreciated the value of logic as an instrument of education, he recognized, as his contemporaries for the most part did not recognize, the intellectual barrenness of logical training for minds ignorant of everything besides logic.[1] All his reflections on education —which may be almost said to amount to a treatise on the subject—imply that he is the advocate of a losing cause. The humanists of the sixteenth century had a battle to fight,

Latinity of the twelfth century.

[1] 'Expertus itaque sum, quod liquido colligi potest, quia, sicut dialectica alias expedit disciplinas, sic, si sola fuerit, jacet exsanguis et sterilis, nec ad fructum philosophie fecundat animam, si aliunde non concipit.' *Metalogicon*, ii. 10 (ed. Webb, pp. 82, 83).

CHAP. II. but the opposing cause was then no longer intellectually formidable; the world was sick of syllogisms. In the twelfth century the scholastic philosophy was in its vigorous youth; a majority of the best intellects of the age were devoted to its pursuit; the humanists themselves were philosophers too. The revived classicism of that day was not crushed by an opposing obscurantism such as vainly attempted to resist the humanism of the Reformation period; it was simply crowded out in the 'conflict of studies'.

The new Aristotle. By the beginning of the thirteenth century, in consequence of the opening up of communications with the East —through intercourse with the Moors in Spain, through the conquest of Constantinople, through the Crusades, through the travels of enterprising scholars—the whole of the works of Aristotle were gradually making their way into the Western world. Some became known in translations direct from the Greek: more in Latin versions of older Syriac or Arabic translations. And now the authority which Aristotle had long enjoyed as a logician—nay, it may almost be said the authority of logic itself—communicated itself in a manner to all that he wrote. Aristotle was accepted as a wellnigh final authority upon metaphysics, upon moral philosophy, and with far more disastrous results upon natural science. The awakened intellect of Europe busied itself with expounding, analysing, and debating the new treasures unfolded before its eyes, and the classics dropped again, for the mass of students whose readings was bounded by the prescribed curriculum of the universities, into the obscurity from which they had for a brief period emerged. Not only did bad translations of a writer whom the best translator would perhaps have found it impossible to clothe in a dress Decadence of elegant Latinity take the foremost place in education, of classical studies. but the eagerness to drink of what seemed the fountain of all wisdom, and to reach the more and more coveted honours of the mastership in arts or philosophy, reduced to a minimum the time that could be bestowed upon the mere acquisition of the language. As soon as the student had learnt the rules of grammar and the vocabulary of the conversa-

tional Latin in ordinary use, he hastened to acquire the subtle CHAP. II.
but unliterary jargon which would enable him to hold his
own in the arena of the schools.[1] The humanists who wrote
towards the close of the twelfth century are full of complaints
at the increasing neglect of grammatical and historical training and the undisciplined rawness of the young philosophers.
At times, indeed, their chief grievance is that the study of
law is destroying all liberal education. This last tendency
the discovery of the new Aristotle at the beginning of the
thirteenth century did something to arrest, but the fresh
vigour thus imparted to speculation only added to the growing contempt for classical study and for all literature as such.
For the attainment of the mastership in the liberal arts,
logic and philosophy were the essential requisites; and at
that early period in the history of the examination-system it
was soon found that the establishment of a prescribed curriculum of studies and the offer of a premium to those who
pursue it is fatal to all subjects excluded therefrom.

The new Aristotle in fact proved simply so much addi- The new
tional fuel thrown upon the all-consuming dialectical fire of Aristotle:
gain and
loss.

[1] 'Sufficiebat ad uictoriam ver-
bosus clamor; et qui undecumque
aliquid inferebat, ad propositi per-
ueniebat metam. Poete historio-
graphi habebantur infames, et si
quis incumbebat laboribus antiquo-
rum, notabatur, et non modo asello
Archadie tardior, sed obtusior
plumbo uel lapide, omnibus erat
in risum. Suis enim aut magistri
sui quisque incumbebat inuentis.
Nec hoc tamen diu licitum, cum
ipsi auditores in breui coerrantium
impetu urgerentur, ut et ipsi, spretis
his que a doctoribus suis audierant,
cuderent et conderent nouas sectas.
Fiebant ergo summi repente philo-
sophi; nam qui illiteratus accesserat,
fere non morabatur in scolis ulterius quam eo curriculo temporis,
quo auium pulli plumescunt. Itaque
recentes magistri e scolis . . . sicut
pari tempore morabantur, sic
pariter auolabant. . . . Solam "con-
uenientiam" siue "rationem" loque-
bantur. . . . Impossibile credebatur
"conuenienter" et ad "rationis"
normam dicere quicquam, aut
facere, nisi "conuenientis" et "rationis" mentio expressim esset inserta. Sed nec argumentum fieri
licitum, nisi praemisso nomine
argumenti. Ex arte et de arte agere
idem erat.' John of Salisbury,
Metalogicon, i. 3 (ed. Webb, pp. 11,
12). Cf. the extremely interesting
preface to the Speculum Ecclesiae
of Giraldus Cambrensis (written
c. 1220, in old age), ed. Brewer,
Opera, iv, 1873, p. 3 sq.); for
Wood's account of the unmutilated
passage (Hist. and Antiq. Univ.
Oxon., i. 56) see below, p. 293 n.
[On the Sophists and Utilitarians
or Cornificians, attacked by John
of Salisbury, see Robert, op. cit.,
pp. 69–76.]

CHAP. II. the philosophical schools. While it enormously widened the range of study, it did nothing to improve its method. The psychology, the metaphysics, and the theology which the enlarged Aristotle of the thirteenth century made possible was certainly a more nutritious intellectual diet than the mere endless, purposeless logic-chopping which John of Salisbury had denounced. It must not be too hastily assumed that Europe would have gained more from an earlier Renaissance than it gained from the scholasticism of the thirteenth and fourteenth centuries. But advance in one direction had to be bought by retrogression in another. Freshness, originality, style, culture, solidity—such as we find in the great writers of the twelfth century—all these were crushed beneath the dead weight of a semi-authoritative literature of barbaric translations. A comparison of John of Salisbury's account of his education in the first half of the twelfth century with the earliest university statute at the beginning of the next century enables us to trace the startling rapidity of this decline in literary culture.[1] Grammar is prescribed as one of the subjects of examination, but grammar is represented solely by the works of Priscian and Donatus. Rhetoric receives hardly more than a complimentary recognition: the classics are not taken up at all. The student's whole attention is concentrated upon logic and Aristotle. Boys in grammar schools might still learn their grammar by construing Ovid or 'Cato',[2] but henceforth the poets, the historians, the orators of ancient Rome were considered unworthy of the attention of ripe students of fourteen or sixteen in the university schools.[3]

[1] Bulaeus, iii. 82; *Chartul*. i, No. 20.

[2] The work commonly styled 'Dionysii Catonis Disticha de moribûs ad filium', a work of unknown origin which served as the universal Delectus of the Middle Ages. [See Manitius, iii. 713 and Index; Haskins, *Studies in Mediaeval Science*, p. 317 and note.]

[3] [The most significant contributions to this difficult subject are L. J. Paetow's *The Arts Course at Medieval Universities with special reference to Grammar and Rhetoric* (Champaign, Illinois, 1910); and his edition of 'Two Medieval Satires on the University of Paris', *La Bataille des vii ars of Henri d'Andeli, and the Morale Scolarium of John of Garland* (Berkeley, California, 1927). Paetow, while

he shows that academic protests were raised, agrees on the whole with Rashdall's view. John Garland's protest (1241) against the *Doctrinale* and the *Grecismus* (see below, p. 443) is especially important. It should be mentioned, on the other hand, that the exclusion of the classics from the arts course and the inclusion of the new works on grammar, &c., do not prove that the love and study of the classics which undoubtedly continued in the thirteenth century were not fostered by members of the university. Apart from the evidence which comes from Orleans and Toulouse, it is impossible to suppose that the classical learning of the time was maintained without some guidance from the masters in the schools. This subject, which Rashdall had to neglect, still awaits adequate treatment. The reader will find general guidance in E. Faral, *Les Arts poétiques du xiie et du xiiie siècle* (Paris, 1923), E. K. Rand, 'The Classics in the Thirteenth Century' (*Speculum*, iv (1929), 249–69), and B. L. Ullman, 'A project for a new edition of Vincent of Beauvais' (*ibid*. viii (1933), 312–26); cf. also Ullman's papers 'Classical Authors in Mediaeval Florilegia', reprinted from *Classical Philology*, xxiii–vii (1928–32).]

CHAPTER III

SALERNO

The first considerable account of the School is that given by NAPOLI-SIGNORELLI, *Vicende della coltura nelle due Sicilie*, Naples, 1784, ii. 147 *sq.*, 257 *sq.* Cf. also MURATORI, *Antiq. Italicae*, Milan, 1740, iii, c. 935 *sq.* The School receives more systematic treatment in ACKERMANN, *Regimen Sanitatis Salerni*, Stendal, 1790,[1] and *Institutiones Historiae Medicinae*, Nuremberg, 1792; and from TIRABOSCHI, *Storia della letteratura italiana*, Milan, 1822, &c., iii. 576–90. But the most important authority is the *Collectio Salernitana* (including the medical treatises discovered by HENSCHEL, the *Regimen Sanitatis Salerni*, &c.) of Salvatore DE RENZI, Naples, 1852–8, in five volumes, who has also published a *Storia documentata della Scuola Medica di Salerno*, ed. 2, Naples, 1857. [Other treatises are in P. GIACOSA, *Magistri Salernitani nondum editi*, Turin, 1901, and P. CAPPARONI, *Magistri Salernitani nondum cogniti*, London, 1923; cf. F. HARTMANN, *Die Literatur von Früh- und Hoch-Salerno*, Leipzig, 1919.] I have also consulted MEAUX, *L'École de Salerne* (an edition and translation of the *Regimen Sanitatis* with Introduction by DAREMBERG), Paris, 1880; HAESER, *Lehrbuch der Geschichte der Medicin*, Jena, ed. 3, 1875, i. 645 *sq.*), and *Grundriss der Gesch. d. M.*, Jena, 1884, p. 114 *sq.*; LECLERC, *Histoire de la médecine arabe*, Paris, 1876; POUCHET, *Histoire des sciences naturelles au moyen âge*, Paris, 1853; the article *Médecine (Histoire de la)* in the *Dict. encycl. des sciences méd.* (Sér. ii, vol. xvi, Paris, 1877) by BEAUGRAND (which see for a very full bibliography), and the very interesting and learned article on the same subject by Dr. J. F. PAYNE in the *Encyclopaedia Britannica*. [For recent work on Salerno see Charles and Dorothea SINGER, 'The Origin of the Medical School of Salerno', in *Essays in the History of Medicine presented to K. Sudhoff*, edited by C. SINGER and H. E. SIGERIST, Zürich, 1924, pp. 121–38; also their article on 'The School of Salerno' in *History*, Oct. 1925, x. 242–6 (reprinted, without the bibliography, in C. SINGER, *From Magic to Science*, London, 1928, pp. 240–8). The most important work has been done by SUDHOFF in articles contributed to the *Archiv für Geschichte der Medizin*, Leipzig (see additional note). See also Lynn THORNDIKE, *A History of Magic and Experimental Science*, New York, 1923, especially chapters 31 and 32, in vol. i, pp. 731 *sqq.*; and the excellent sketch in S. D'IRSAY, *Histoire des universités*, i. 99–110.]

CONSIDERATIONS of chronological sequence make it desirable to introduce in this place a short notice of the School of Salerno. For more than two centuries Salerno as a school of medicine stood fully on a level in point of academic fame with Bologna as a school of law, and Paris as the head-quarters of scholasticism. The eleventh century was marked

The revival of medicine.

---

[1] I am indebted for the use of a copy of this rare work to the Library of the Royal College of Surgeons.

CHAP. III. by a revival of medicine as well as by a revival of legal, theological, and dialectical study. And in point of time the
medical revival seems to have been the earliest phase of the
movement. At all events, the unique fame of Salerno as a
school of medicine was fully established long before the
dialectical movement centred in Paris or the legal in Bologna.
The subject of medieval medicine is so obscure and technical
that the reader will not expect any detailed history of its rise
and progress; while so little is known of the origin and development of the School as an educational institution that
we are absolved from taking more than a passing notice of its
place in the academic system of medieval Europe.

Date of   The origin of the School of Salerno is veiled in impene-
medical
school at   trable obscurity. There are some traces of the study or at
Salerno. least the practice of medicine here as early as the ninth century,[1] but of course the fact that the town possessed a
physician does not show the existence of a medical school.
In the tenth century the place was certainly famous for the
skill of its physicians;[2] while in the first half of the twelfth
century the School is described by Ordericus Vitalis as 'existing from ancient times'.[3] Its European celebrity dates at

[1] The name of a Salerno physician occurs in a charter of 848
(De Renzi, *Storia documentata*, No.
22), but the names in De Renzi's list
do not become frequent till after
1050 (*Coll. Salern.* ii. 797). Perhaps the earliest indication of a
repute for medical skill occurs towards the middle of the tenth century (before 946), when a French
Bishop 'in arte medicinae peritissi-
mus', and 'quidam Salernitanus
medicus', met at the court of Louis
IV. It is noticeable that while the
Bishop was 'litterarum artibus eruditus', the Salerno practitioner
'licet nulla litterarum scientia pre-
ditus, tamen ex ingenio naturae
multam in rebus experientiam
habebat'. (Richerus, *Hist.* ap.
M.G.H., Scriptores, iii. 600.) It
would thus seem that the earliest
Salerno physicians were empiric

rather than scientific. For other
early notices of the School see
De Renzi, *Coll. Salern.* i. 121 *sq.*,
and the signatures collected from
the *Codex Diplomaticus Cavensis*
(Naples, 1873) by Gloria, *Monumenti della Università di Padova*
(1222–1318), p. 91.

[2] Adalbero, Bishop of Verdun
(985–8) went to Salerno *curationis
gratia* (Chronicle of Hugh of Fla-
vigny in *M.G.H., Scriptores*, viii.
367).

[3] 'Physicae quoque scientiam
tam copiose habuit ut in urbe
Psalernitana, ubi maximae medicorum scolae ab antiquo tempore
habentur, neminem in medicinali
arte, praeter quamdam sapientem
matronam, sibi parem inveniret.'
Hist. Eccles. P. ii, l. iii. 11 (*Patrol.
Lat.* clxxxviii. 260). The statement relates to one Rodulfus Mala-

least from the middle of the eleventh century—about half a CHAP. III.
century before the teaching of Irnerius and the earliest dawn
of the scholastic fame of Paris.

Salerno was purely a medical school; and in the other Its origin.
faculties southern Italy never possessed a university of more
than the third rank. It is no doubt at first sight tempting to
trace the medical knowledge and skill of Salerno to contact
with the Saracens of Southern Italy or Sicily; but it appears
to be well established by the researches of Henschel, Daremberg, de Renzi, and their successors, that no external cause
can be assigned to the beginnings of the movement, any more
than to the somewhat later revival of dialectical and literary
culture north of the Alps, or to the revival of the civil law
in the Lombard cities. The medical traditions of the old
Roman world lingered on amidst the material civilization of
Magna Graecia, just as the traditions of legal culture lingered
in the freer and more political atmosphere of northern Italy.
The theory which attributes the rise of the School of Salerno
to the introduction of Arabic writings by Constantinus
Africanus, towards the end of the eleventh century, is a
legend of the same order as the legend (to which we shall have
to return hereafter) about the discovery of the Roman law
at the capture of Amalfi, and is as completely inconsistent
with facts and dates as the theory which assumes the northern

---

Corona, *sub anno* 1059. In about
1173 Benjamin of Tudela speaks
of Salerno as 'the College of the
Physicians of the Sons of Edom'
(*Itinerary*, trans. by Asher, 1840,
i. 43, 'the principal university of
Christendom', but there is, I believe, nothing corresponding to
'principal' in the original). He
speaks of there being 600 Jews in
the place, but the above expression
shows that the School was purely
Christian. There is a panegyric
upon this 'Fons physicae, pugil
eucrasiae, cultrix medicinae', in the
medical poem of the Paris Physician Gilles of Corbeil, *c.* 1198, who
evidently learned his medicine

there. [See C. Vieillard, *Gilles de
Corbeil*, Paris, 1909, pp. 354–6,
from the 'de laudibus et virtutibus
compositorum medicaminum', bk.
ii, verses 469 *sqq.*; ed. L. Choulant,
Leipzig, 1826.] Another allusion
occurs in the *Archipoetae carmen
de itinere Salernitano* (J. Grimm,
*Gedichte des Mittelalters auf König
Fried. I*, ap. *Kleinere Schriften*, iii,
Berlin, 1866, p. 64):
'Laudibus eternum nullus negat
esse Salernum,
Illuc pro morbis totus circumfluit
orbis,
Nec debet sperni, fateor, doctrina
Salerni.'

CHAP. III. Renaissance of the eleventh century to begin with the introduction of Arabic translations of Aristotle. Works attributed
to Hippocrates, Galen, and other Greek physicians had been
translated into Latin as early as the sixth century;[1] and,
though these early translations are said to have disappeared,
the Graeco-Latin medical tradition was no more extinguished
by the ages of darkness which followed than Roman law was
extinguished in the north by the barbarian invasions. We
possess works of the medical writers of Salerno from the
early part of the eleventh century. The most important of
these early writers is Gariopontus, who wrote c. 1040. Their
writings exhibit not the slightest trace of Arabic influence.
Their medicine is neo-Latin, but the dominant influence is
not that of Galen, but the equally ancient though less enlightened system known as 'methodism', of which Caelius
Aurelianus is the chief representative. After the middle of
the eleventh century, however, there are evidences of a more
direct acquaintance with the writings of Hippocrates and
Galen, and from this time the system known as 'humorism'
becomes the established doctrine of the School. It is from
this period—the middle of the eleventh century, a generation
at least before Constantinus, and a generation at least before
the renaissance of the Roman law at Bologna—that we must
date the first medical renaissance. The Graeco-Roman medical
classics may not have been entirely unknown to the earlier
Salerno doctors, any more than Justinian had been unknown
in northern Italy before Irnerius. But it was at this period
that they began to be studied energetically and scientifically,
and their teaching to be applied with greater fidelity than heretofore. The smouldering sparks of scientific culture which had
survived from the old-world illumination were fanned into a
flame by the first breath of that mysterious new spirit which at
this time began to move upon the face of European civilization.

[1] Cassiodorus, *De Instit. divin.
litt.*, cap. xxxi (*Patrol. Lat.*
lxx. 1146). [For the medical
literature available in the early
Middle Ages cf. Singer, *From
Magic to Science*, pp. 140-1, and,
for Salernitan texts, *ibid.*, p. 148.
Historians of medicine would not
now speak so definitely of a Salernitan *doctrine* as Rashdall does in the
text; cf. Thorndike, i. 732 *sqq.* and
the note at the end of this chapter.]

How shall we explain the concentration of this revival of medical science in the city of Salerno, or (if that be too particular a question to be answered upon *a priori* or general grounds) why did it find its home in this part of Italy? The main cause must perhaps be sought in Roman times. It would seem that, after the full development of the schools, it was in Latin translations that the works of Hippocrates were habitually studied in what was henceforth styled the *Civitas Hippocratica*. But it cannot be doubted that the revival of medical science in the eleventh century was not unconnected with the survival[1] of the Greek language in this part of Italy, and the presumption is strengthened by the fact that the decline of the School after about the middle of the thirteenth century kept pace with the decline of the language. It should be remembered, moreover, that in the tenth century the Counts of Salerno usually acknowledged the Eastern Emperors, and that this part of Italy was in constant communication with Constantinople, the head-quarters alike of Greek culture and of Greek authority.[2]

Survival of Graeco-Latin medicine in southern Italy.

Survival of Greek language.

An incident in the life of the traveller Adelard of Bath confirms the view that the medical studies of the place were at least in part promoted by their contact with the Greek medical writers. Adelard in the course of his travels came to Salerno, and afterwards describes himself as listening (not, indeed, in Salerno, but in its immediate neighbourhood) to a 'Greek philosopher' discoursing upon 'medicine and the nature of things'. Among the subjects of the philosopher's inquiries was the cause of magnetic attraction, which Adelard is the first Western writer to mention.[3]

Adelard of Bath at Salerno.

[1] i.e. from the time of the Byzantine reconquest under Justinian.

[2] Giesebrecht, *Gesch. d. deutschen Kaiserzeit*, Brunswick, ed. 5, 1881, i. 374 *sq.* [Since Rashdall wrote, the importance of Sicily and South Italy as centres of Greek and Arabic learning, and the extent of communication with the Greek world, have been realized. See, especially, Haskins, *Studies in the History of Mediaeval Science*, pp.

141–2, 184 *sqq.*; also the quotation from Stephen of Antioch, early twelfth century, p. 133. In the preface to his second edition, p. xiii (1927), Professor Haskins notes an eleventh-century Greek medical manuscript from southern Italy with Arabic glosses; Paris, B.N. Suppl. Grec., MS. 1297.]

[3] *De eodem et diverso*: 'Et ego certe, cum a Salerno veniens in Grecia maiore, quendam philoso-

CHAP. III.   If we ask why it was at Salerno rather than elsewhere in
Salerno a southern Italy that the medical revival centred, the answer
health-
resort. may possibly be found in its renown as a health-resort, chiefly
due to the mildness of the climate, but partly also perhaps
to the mineral waters of the neighbourhood. As to the theory
which connects the rise of the School with the Benedictine
monastery of Monte Cassino, it is sufficient to say that Salerno
is eighty miles from Monte Cassino, and that the theory has
not a particle of historical foundation.[1]

But whatever theory we adopt as to the origin of the
Medical School, one thing is absolutely established by the
researches which began with the discovery of a volume of
Salerno *Codices* by Henschel at Breslau in 1837, and that is
that the School was in its origin, and long continued to be,
entirely independent of Oriental influences.

Constanti-   The first introduction of the Arabic influence at Salerno
nus Africa-
nus, is traditionally associated with the name of Constantinus
c. 1080. Africanus, one of those misty characters in the history of
medieval culture whom a reputation for profound knowledge
and Oriental travel has surrounded with a halo of half-
legendary romance. It is unnecessary to repeat the story[2] of

phum grecum qui pre ceteris artem
medicine naturasque rerum dissere-
bat sententiis pretemptarem' (ed.
H. Willner, Münster, 1903, p. 33).
The book was written before 1116
A.D., perhaps before 1109 (Jourdain,
Recherches sur des traduc. d'Aristote,
p. 258; Haskins, *op. cit.*, pp. 21, 22).

[1] If additional evidence is wanted,
it may be worth pointing out that
the poem in praise of Monte Cassino,
written by Alphanus, who became
Archbishop of Salerno in 1085,
contains no hint of any such connexion. The poem is published by
Ozanam, *Doc. inédits pour l'hist.
litt. de l'Italie*, p. 261. After all,
Benedictine monks were not 'University Extension Lecturers'. De
Renzi (i. 128) remarks that most
of the writers who have derived the
School of Salerno from Monte
Cassino did not know the distance

of Monte Cassino from Salerno:
the former did not belong to the
principality of Salerno but was
under the jurisdiction of the Counts
of Capua. [On the other hand,
medical manuscripts were copied
at Monte Cassino, and Constantine
the African, who settled at Monte
Cassino in the later eleventh century, must have exercised a strong
influence at Salerno; cf. Thorndike, *op. cit.* i. 757.]

[2] The half-legendary story of
Constantinus is told by Petrus
Diaconus, *Chron. Casin.* iii. 35,
ap. *M.G.H.*, *Scriptores*, vii. 728.
[There is an extensive literature on
Constantinus and his writings: see
the note at the end of this chapter;
also Haskins, *op. cit.*, pp. 132, 374,
with the authorities there mentioned, and Thorndike, ch. xxxii
(i. 742–59). The latest work is by

his wanderings in the East, his settlement at his native Tunis, CHAP. III. his enforced flight to Salerno, just before the advent of the Norman Robert Guiscard, and his eventual retirement from the world into the illustrious Benedictine Abbey of Monte Cassino, where, under the patronage of the famous Abbot Desiderius, afterwards Pope Victor III, he occupied himself for the remainder of his life in making Latin translations or compilations from Arabic or Greek medical writers. Whatever uncertainty may remain about the details of his history, there is no doubt that [Constantinus was a voluminous translator and writer on medical subjects. His most famous work was an adaptation of the art of medicine, written in the tenth century by an Arabic physician, Ali ben El-Abbas. This book, though much criticized by Constantinus's contemporaries, was well known throughout the Middle Ages as the *Pantegni*. But Constantinus was even more important because his translations, through the influence of Salerno, fixed the canon of the *ars medicinae*.] The zenith of the medical reputation of Salerno is marked in later legend by the visit of Robert, Duke of Normandy, who was believed to have come to the place to be cured of his wound after the *The Regi-* Crusade in 1099. The celebrated metrical treatise on medi- *men Sani-* *tatis Sa-* cine or hygienics, styled *Flos Medicinae Scholae Salernitanae,* *lerni.* or *Regimen Sanitatis Salerni* begins 'Anglorum regi scribit schola tota Salerni', and was thought to have been dedicated to him as 'King of the English' on this occasion.[1]

Rudolf Creutz in *Studien und Mitth. zur Geschichte des Benediktiner-Ordens*, new ser., xvi (1929), 1–44; xviii (1931), 25–40.]

[1] Of this curious production there had been (up to 1852) thirty-three translations (or new editions of translations) into German, fourteen into French, nine into English, nine into Italian, one into Czech, one into Polish, and one into Dutch. (De Renzi, *Coll. Salernitana*, i. 431.) Most of these belong to the sixteenth and seventeenth centuries, when the work was evidently still regarded in a serious

light, but it seems to be still popular in some quarters. A new English translation appeared at Philadelphia in 1870, a translation into Italian verse at Pavia in 1835, and the French translation of M. Daremberg as recently as 1880. Many still current pieces of proverbial medicine may be traced to this source (sometimes slightly altered): e.g. 'Sex horis dormire sat est juvenique senique Septem vix pigro, nulli concedimus octo'; and 'Post coenam stabis aut passus mille meabis.'

CHAP. III.   The opening of this work suggests that something like an
Organiza- organized school or college of doctors existed at Salerno.
tion.
Beyond that, we can really say next to nothing as to the
government or institutions of the School. Somewhat later
it had a *praepositus* at its head, afterwards called a *prior*.[1]
Nothing approaching a regular university ever existed there.
Certainly there was no university of students; while a mere
college of doctors in one faculty could present but a distant
resemblance to the magisterial or Parisian type of university
organization. Salerno in fact remains a completely isolated
factor in the academic polity of the Middle Ages. While its
position as a school of medicine was, for two centuries at
least, as unique as that of Paris in theology and that of
Bologna in law, while throughout the Middle Ages no school
of medicine except Montpellier rivalled its fame, it remained
without influence in the development of academic institutions: the constitution and organization even of the medical
faculties in other universities appear to have been quite uninfluenced by the traditions of this earliest home of medieval
medicine.

Edict of   It was not (so far as appears) till 1231 that Salerno obtained
Frederick
II, 1231. any official recognition, whether from Church or State. In
that year Frederick II, as King of Sicily, forbade either the
practice or teaching of medicine within his dominions without the Royal Licence, which was to be given after examination in the King's Court by the masters of Salerno and

It is printed in De Renzi's *Coll.
Salernitana*, i. 445; and there is an
important edition by Sir Alexander
Croke (Oxford, 1830). [The *Regimen* was in fact compiled later, and
was not generally known before the
middle of the thirteenth century:
see K. Sudhoff in *Archiv für Geschichte der Medizin*, 1915–16, ix.
1–9. For a bibliography see F. R.
Packard's edition of Sir John Harington's *The School of Salernum*,
London, 1922. Harington included a translation of the *Regimen*
in this work, 1609.]

[1] De Renzi, *loc. cit*. i. 226, 269,
274. A treatise of Gariopontus
bears the title *Gariopontus Salernitanus eiusque Socii*, which shows at
least a habit of co-operation among
the Salernese physicians though
not necessarily a regular college
(De Renzi, *loc. cit*. i. 115). It
should be observed that the *Scola
Salernitana* continued to receive
additions down to the time of
Arnald de Villanova, who played
the part of Pisistratus to this
medical Homer.

certain other royal officers.[1] These provisions show how far CHAP. III. the faculty of medicine at Salerno was from enjoying the position and privileges of the medical faculties elsewhere. In pursuance of the same paternal system the Emperor proceeded to issue an ordinance enforcing a period of medical study as well as a preliminary course of arts, and regulating a number of matters relating to the study and practice of medicine, elsewhere left to the free disposition of the faculties or the universities.[2]

As to the methods of graduation in use at Salerno in the *Mode of* earliest period we have no evidence, though we may presume *graduation.* that the college of doctors conducted both the licence and Inception of candidates for the mastership according to the system practised in the earliest days of Bologna.[3] After the above-mentioned edict of Frederick II in 1231, the candidate for a degree appeared in the Royal Court, produced letters

[1] 'Nisi Salerni primitus in conventu publico magistrorum iudicio comprobatus, cum testimonialibus literis de fide et sufficienti scientia tam magistrorum *quam ordinatorum nostrorum, ad presentiam nostram* vel, nobis a regno absentibus, ad illius presentiam qui vice nostra in regno remanserit [ordinatus accedat] et *a nobis vel ab eo* medendi licentiam consequatur.' Huillard-Bréholles, *Hist. Diplomatica Fred. II*, iv, Paris, 1854, p. 150. The examination of those who wanted to teach was also to be conducted 'in presentia nostrorum officialium et magistrorum artis eiusdem' (*ibid.*, p. 151). The provisions and the form of the *licentia medendi* given by Huillard-Bréholles (which does not even mention the masters of Salerno) show that these licences have nothing in common with the licences granted by the universities themselves. By an earlier Ordinance [ascribed in earlier editions and in one manuscript to King Roger] the intending physician had merely to present himself 'officialibus nostris et iudicibus' (*ibid.*, p. 149).

[2] The student was required to study three years 'in scientia logicali' (since 'nunquam sciri potest scientia medicine nisi de logica aliquid presciatur'), and five years in medicine, attending lectures on Hippocrates and Galen. He was also to practise for a year (like bachelors in other universities) 'cum consilio experti medici'. [The more elaborate statutes, of King Charles I, 16 Jan. 1280, distinguish in the residential qualifications between a candidate who was a *magister artium* and one who was not. In these statutes, also, the preliminary approval of the doctors of Salerno is definitely required; De Renzi, i. 361-2.] The physician was required to give advice *gratis* to the poor: to visit his patients '*ad minus* bis in die, et ad requisitionem infirmi semel in nocte'. He was not allowed to sell his own drugs ('nec ipse etiam habebit propriam stationem'). Huillard-Bréholles, iv. 235-6.

[3] [See, however, the additional note at the end of this chapter.]

testimonial from some of the doctors under whom he had studied, and was then examined in the presence of the Court, which, in the event of his success, drew up a *licence* or warrant to his own doctor to conduct his *conventio* or inception by tradition of the book in the presence of his colleagues,[1] as in other universities. Further explanation of this custom will be found in the chapters on Paris and Bologna.[2]

In the year 1224 the Emperor Frederick II opened a University at Naples,[3] and endeavoured to force all his subjects to study therein.[4] A faculty of medicine was at first included in the new university, but in 1231 this was implicitly suppressed (if it ever obtained a substantial existence) by the already-quoted decree which confined the right of examining in medicine to the Salerno doctors.[5] In spite of the monopoly which it enjoyed, the University of Naples[6] never was a success; and in 1253 the attempt to galvanize it into life was abandoned and an effort made to transfer all its faculties from Naples to Salerno, and to unite them with the old school of medicine in that place.[7] By 1258 this experiment also had failed, and the *status quo* was re-established. The other faculties moved back to Naples, and Salerno remained a school of medicine only. By this time, however, the European importance of the School of Salerno was passing away. So far from the rise of the fame of Salerno having been due to Oriental influences, it was these influences which brought about its fall. It was the increasing popularity of the Arabic

---

[1] See the diplomas in De Renzi, *Storia Doc.*, p. xcviii *sq.*

[2] See below, pp. 221 *sq.*, 283 *sq.*, 457 *sq.*

[3] See below, vol. ii, ch. vi, § 5.

[4] If the Charter of Frederick II (Huillard-Bréholles, ii. 452) be literally interpreted, even Salerno would have been included in the prohibition to study or teach anywhere else; but the professors mentioned in the Charter are professors of civil law only, and it seems improbable that Salerno was really affected. Ackermann (*Institutiones*,

p. 349) says, 'ita tamen, ut Salerno medicinae docendae facultas maneret'.

[5] It should be noticed, however, that there is no mention of Salerno in the Greek version. [Reprinted by Sudhoff from the edition of the *Constitutiones Regum Regni Utriusque Siciliae*, Naples, 1786, pp. 197, 198, in the *Mitth. zur Geschichte der Medizin*, 1914, xiii. 180–2.]

[6] See below, vol. ii, ch. vi, § 6.

[7] Huillard-Bréholles, ii. 447; Denifle, i. 236–7.

medicine in the thirteenth century, combined with the CHAP. III.
growth of medical faculties elsewhere—especially of the
medical schools at Montpellier and Bologna—which destroyed the popularity of the more conservative *Civitas Hippocratica.*

By the beginning of the fourteenth century the decline of The
Salerno was complete, and the Arabic medicine everywhere Arabic
medicine.
in full possession of the medical faculties. It is, however,
quite a mistake to assume (as is very frequently done) that
this new influence indicates a great advance. The medicine
of medieval Islam was based upon that of the Greek physicians as much as that of medieval Christendom; and what
was added to this traditional system by the Arabs themselves
or the physicians who practised in Arab countries—for Arabic
medicine was largely in the hands of Jews—was by no means
equal in importance to what they had received from the
Greeks. The most valuable Arabic contributions to medicine
were chiefly in the region of medical botany. The Arabs
added some new remedies to the medieval pharmacopeia, but
against their services in this respect must be set their extensive introduction of astrological and alchemistic fancies into
the theory and practice of medicine. On the whole, the thirteenth century represents a retrogression in medical theory,
though an advance in the region of surgery and anatomy.
But of this advance Salerno was not the centre.[1]

Additional Note to Chapter III

[Recent investigation, notably that of K. Sudhoff, enables us to
discuss the early history of Salerno and the significance of Constantinus the African in firmer detail and a better perspective. In the
tenth century the four streams of tradition, Greek, Latin, Arabic,

---

[1] The University of Salerno was
suppressed by a decree of Napoleon
I in 1811, Haeser, *loc. cit.*, p. 652.
[Rashdall added a paragraph, here
omitted, on the women doctors of
Salerno, who are now known to
have been mythical. On Trotula,
whose 'name passed long ago into
the fairy-tales as *Dame Trot*, and

has been known in every nursery
for four hundred years', see H. R.
Spitzner, *Die Salernitanische Gynä-
kologie und Geburtshilfe unter dem
Namen 'Trotula'* (Leipzig, 1921)
and *History*, x. 245. The compilations of one Trottus, a doctor of
Salerno, were referred to as the
Trotula.]

CHAP. III. and Jewish, which were to combine at Salerno, can be traced in the career of the Jew, Shabbethai ben Abraham ben Joel, or Donnolo, of Otranto (913–982); cf. C. Singer in *Essays presented to Sudhoff*, pp. 133–6. But dogmatic tradition was also active in the influential work of Herbrand of Chartres (Sudhoff, *Ausgewählte Abhandlungen*, pp. 30–3). As Giacosa remarks (*op. cit.*, p. xxi), the 'School' of Salerno at this time was a school of practitioners—like that 'Adamatus quidam medicus genere Salernitanus' who attended the dying Archbishop Adalbert at Goslar in 1072 (Sudhoff, in *Archiv*, 1915, ix. 356). The famous *passionarium* of Gariopontus in the eleventh century was a compilation with an earlier tradition behind it (*ibid.*, p. 352; for Gariopontus, cf. Giacosa, pp. xxvii *sqq.*). Constantinus the African, in Sudhoff's phrase, gave Salerno a tongue. His translations of the aphorisms of Hippocrates, the *ars parva* of Galen, the introduction to Galen by Hasein ben Ishak (*Johannitius* or Isaac), Philaretus on the pulse and Theophilus on urines, formed the *ars medicinae* of the Middle Ages, and, together with the *Viaticus* of Ibn al-Dschazzâr, and the *dietae universales* of Isaac, also translated by Constantinus, appear as the prescribed texts in the schools. They are found at Salerno at the end of the twelfth century, at Paris soon after, and in the Statutes of 1270, at Salerno again in 1280, and in library catalogues from the twelfth century, and their influence can be traced in the work of Gilles of Corbeil, who seems to have brought the learning of Salerno to Paris about 1200. See especially the important passage from an early commentary on Gilles of Corbeil, *de urinis*, edited and commented on by Sudhoff in the *Archiv für Gesch. d. Medizin*, 1928, xx. 51–62, where we get a picture both of the widespread influence of Salerno, *c.* 1200, and of an early examination of a candidate for the mastership there. This passage supplements the evidence given by the Constitution of Melfi in 1231, and helps us to connect the earlier organization of the School at Salerno with that implied by the Statutes of 1280 (De Renzi, i. 361–2). Other valuable essays by Sudhoff are on the library of Bishop Bruno of Hildesheim (*Archiv*, 1915, ix. 348–56), on Richard the Englishman, a commentator on Gilles of Corbeil, and a writer on anatomy (*ibid.*, 1927, xix. 209–39; cf. xx. 60, 61; and *Janus*, 1924, xxviii. 397–403), on anatomy at Salerno (*Archiv*, xx. 33–50) and various papers collected in Sudhoff's *Ausgewählte Abhandlungen* (=*Archiv*, 1929, xxi), especially on early medieval education in medicine (pp. 28–42) and Salerno (pp. 43–62). Although, as Rashdall says, the influence of Salerno (and, it may be added, of Paris) gave way later to that of Montpellier and Bologna, its significance in the twelfth and early thirteenth centuries as a centre of Greek and Arabic medicine, of surgery and anatomy, was very great. See, for the development of studies in medicine and surgery, the work of Stephen D'Irsay and the authorities there cited.]

CHAPTER IV
BOLOGNA

§ 1. IRNERIUS AND THE CIVIL LAW REVIVAL

The medieval sections of the work of DIPLOVATATIUS (fl. *c.* 1510), *De claris Iurisconsultis,* &c., still remain in manuscript, only extracts having been published by Sarti (see below) and others. [For his life and work see *Thomas Diplovatatius, De claris iuris consultis,* vol. i, edited by H. KANTOROWICZ and F. SCHULZ, Berlin and Leipzig, 1919 (Romanistische Beiträge zur Rechtsgeschichte, iii).] He was followed by G. N. ALIDOSI, *I dottori bolognesi di legge canon. e ciuile,* Bologna, 1620, and *I dott. bol. d. teol. filos. med. e d'arti liberali,* Bologna, 1623, and PANCIROLUS, *De claris Legum Interpretibus,* Venice, 1627 (republished with Jo. Fichardus, *Vitae recentiorum Iurisconsultorum,* and Marcus Mantua Bonavides, *Epitome Virorum illustrium qui vel docuerunt in scholis Iuris prudentiam,* &c., Leipzig, 1721), but both were superseded by the learned and critical work of SARTI (continued by FATTORINI), *De claris Archigymnasii Bononiensis Professoribus,* Bologna, I, pt. i, 1769; pt. ii, 1772. Of the new edition published at Bologna by C. ALBICINI and C. MALAGOLA there have appeared 1. i in 1888, 1. ii in 1889, II in 1896 (1 i. and ii correspond to 1. i of the original edition; wherever I have cited 1. ii of that edition I have added the date 1772. All other references are to the new edition.) Sarti may occasionally be supplemented by P. A. ORLANDI, *Notizie degli scrittori bolognesi,* Bologna, 1714, and G. FANTUZZI, *Notizie degli scrittori bolognesi,* Bologna, 1781. In spite of this wealth of Bolognese literary history, no systematic history of the university has appeared except the slight work of L. SCARABELLI, *Delle constituzione discipline e riforme dell'antico studio bolognese,* Piacenza, 1876. An earlier but valueless work by FORMAGLIARI († 1769) remains in manuscript at Bologna (Bibl. Mun. No. 5935), and other manuscript collections are mentioned in L. FRATI's very careful bibliographical work, *Opere della bibliografia bolognese,* &c., Bologna, 1888. The want of such a history is, however, nearly supplied by the notices and documents in Sarti, by the notices in TIRABOSCHI, *Storia della letteratura italiana,* Milan, 1822, vols. iii–vi, and by the full treatment which the University receives in SAVIGNY, *Geschichte des röm. Rechts im Mittelalter,* c. xxi, supplemented and corrected (as to the earliest period) by the researches of DENIFLE, *Die Entstehung der Universitäten des Mittelalters bis 1400* (Berlin, 1885, p. 132).

The following books on the history of the city contain frequent notices of the University: SIGONIUS, *Historia de rebus Bononiensibus,* Frankfurt, 1604; C. GHIRARDACCI, *Della historia di Bologna,* Bologna, pt. i, 1596; pt. ii, 1669 [new edition of the third part (1426–1509), by A. Sorbelli, in the new *Rerum Italicarum Scriptores,* xxiii, 11 fascicles, Città di Castello, 1915–32]. Rashdall had occasion to use only parts i and ii. Sorbelli gives a very full account of the whole work.] L. V. SAVIOLI, *Annali bolognesi,* Bassano, 1784–95. The Statutes of the city have been edited by FRATI, *Dei monumenti istorici pertinenti alle provincie della Romagna,* Ser. I, *Statuti,* vols. i–iii, Bologna, 1869–80. The little tract of GAGGI, *Collegii Bononiensis doctorum origo et dotes* (Bologna, 1710; unpaged), is chiefly valuable for its information as to the customs of the author's own time. [A. HESSEL, *Geschichte der Stadt Bologna von 1116 bis 1280,* Berlin, 1910.]

The Jurist Statutes of 1432 were printed in 1561 (*Statuta et privilegia almae universitatis Iuristarum Gymnasii Bononiensis*, Bologna); those of the Artists (*Philosophiae ac medicinae scholarium Bononiensis gymnasii statuta*, Bologna) in 1609. The Statutes of 1432 were the earliest then known to exist; but in 1887 DENIFLE published in the *Archiv für Literatur- und Kirchengeschichte*, iii. 195 *sq.* a large portion of the Statutes of 1317, with additions up to 1347, from a manuscript discovered by him in the Chapter Library of Pressburg in Hungary. These, together with the earliest extant Statutes of the other universities and of the doctoral colleges (hitherto unpublished), are printed in the magnificent volume edited by MALAGOLA, *Statuti delle università e dei collegi dello studio bolognese* (Bologna, 1888). [In 1932 Cardinal Fr. EHRLE published, with an important introduction, *I più antichi statuti della facoltà teologica dell'università di Bologna* (Universitatis Bononiensis Monumenta, i).] The Statutes and Registers of the German nation are published in *Acta Nationis Germanicae Univ. Bonon.*, Berlin, 1887 (a biographical index in G. C. KNOD, *Deutsche Studenten in Bologna 1289–1562*, Berlin, 1899); other documents in U. DALLARI, *I rotuli dei lettori legisti e artisti dello studio bolognese dal 1384 al 1799*, Bologna, 1888–91. [Seven rolls (1426–9, 1431–2, 1437) omitted by Dallari, have been edited by G. ZAOLI in *Studi e memorie*, iv (1920), 226–49. In 1909 the 'Commissione per la storia dell'Università di Bologna' began the publication of a great collection of documents under the title, *Chartularium studii Bononiensis*.]

A number of monographs were published in connexion with the Octocentenary of 1888. Of these, FORNASINI, *Lo studio bolognese* (Florence, 1887), is little better than a guide-book, and LEONHARD, *Die Universität Bologna im Mittelalter* (Leipzig, 1888), only professes to be a magazine article; CASSANI, *Dell'Antico studio di Bologna e sua origine* (Bologna, 1888), is especially valuable in relation to the early history of canon law studies at Bologna; L. CHIAPPELLI, *Lo studio bolognese* (Pistoia, 1888), contains some [investigations, often misleading] as to the Pre-Irnerian Jurisprudence; but the work to which I am most indebted is FITTING, *Die Anfänge der Rechtsschule zu Bologna*, Berlin u. Leipzig, 1888; RICCI, *I primordi dello studio di Bologna*, ed. 2, Bologna, 1888), prints the documents relating to Irnerius with some useful researches as to the *origines* of Bologna and Ravenna; MALAGOLA, *Monografie storiche sullo studio bolognese* (Bologna, 1888), contains interesting essays on detached points. [The most important later works are: F. SCHUPFER, 'Le origini della Università di Bologna', in *Atti d. R. Accademia dei Lincei*, 1889, a critical survey of recent views; N. TAMASSIA, *Odofredo*, Bologna, 1894; F. CAVAZZA, *Le scuole dell'antico studio bolognese*, Milan, 1896; A. GAUDENZI, *Appunti per servire alla storia dell'università di Bologna e dei suoi maestri*, Bologna, 1889, and *Lo studio di Bologna nei primi due secoli della sua esistenza*, Bologna, 1901, an inaugural address; G. MANACORDA, *Storia della scuola in Italia*, Milan, u.d., especially chapter vii (i. 187–252); *Studi e memorie per la storia dell'università di Bologna*, Bologna, 1907 onwards; PRINGSHEIM, 'Beryt und Bologna', in *Freiburger Festschrift für Lenel*, 1921.]

The study of the Italian universities in general was begun by MURATORI, *Antiquitates Italicae medii aevi*, iii (Milan, 1740), Diss. xliv, and carried on by Tiraboschi and Savigny in the works already named. Since then no work specially devoted to this subject has appeared which calls for notice except COPPI, *Le università italiane nel medio evo* (ed. 3, Florence,

1886), which is, however, an unsatisfactory piece of work. [See below,
vol. ii, p. 1.]

For the history of the Roman law in the Middle Ages SAVIGNY (*op. cit.*) is the primary authority. Among his predecessors I may mention Arthur DUCK, *De Usu et Authoritate Iuris Civilis Romanorum*, London, 1653, and BERRIAT-SAINT-PRIX, *Histoire du droit romain*, Paris, 1821, and among his successors, FICKER, *Forschungen zur Reichs- und Rechtsgeschichte Italiens*, 1868–74; FITTING in *Zeitschrift der Savigny-Stiftung für Rechtsgeschichte*, vol. vi, Röm. Abth. (1885), p. 94 *sq.*, and vol. vii. Röm. Abth., Heft 2, p. 1, and *Juristische Schriften des früheren Mittelalters*, Halle, 1876; FLACH, *Études critiques sur l'histoire du droit romain au moyen âge*, Paris, 1890; MUTHER, *Zur Geschichte der Rechtswissenschaft und der Universitäten*, Jena, 1876; CONRAT, *Die Quellen und Literatur des Römischen Rechts im früheren Mittelalter*, Leipzig, 1891. [C. CALISSE, *Storia del diritto italiano*, Florence, 1891, last edition of vol. i, *le Fonti*, Florence, 1930; A. PERTILE, *Storia del diritto italiano*, ed. 2, Turin, 1892–1902; and other works for which see the bibliography in the *Cambridge Medieval History*, v. 925. See also P. VINOGRADOFF, *Roman Law in Mediaeval Europe*, ed. 2, Oxford, 1929.]

[Since the first edition of this book appeared, much fine work has been done on the revival of the study of civil law, the subject of the following section. The most important works and studies are: E. BESTA, *L'opera d'Irnerio*, Turin, 1896; G. MENGOZZI, *Ricerche sull'attività della scuola di Pavia nell'alto medio evo*, Pavia, 1925; H. KANTOROWICZ, 'Ueber die Entstehung der Digestenvulgata', in the *Zeitschrift der Savigny-Stiftung*, Röm. Abth., xxx (1909), 183–271, xxxi (1910), 14–88, and separately; and especially EMIL SECKEL, *Das röm. Recht und seine Wissenschaft im Wandel der Jahrhunderte*, Berlin, 1921, and his essay, 'Die Anfänge der europäischen Judisprudenz', in *Zeits. der Sav.-Stift*. Röm. Abth. xlv (1925). For other work cf. VINOGRADOFF, *op. cit.*, p. 70.]

THE original impetus which imparted new life to the schools of Italy at the end of the tenth or the beginning of the eleventh century was, in its essence, the same spiritual force which manifested itself north of the Alps in the teaching of Roscellinus and Abelard. But in northern Italy that strange new birth of the world's energies took place under a totally different set of conditions and consequently gave rise to a movement in a totally different direction. In France the overthrow of Roman civilization by the barbarian conquest, followed by the ecclesiastical legislation of Charles the Great, had indissolubly associated education with the monasteries and the cathedrals. In Italy education was never as completely extinguished as had been the case in continental Europe north of the Alps. It was from the Italian deacon Peter of Pisa that Charles himself took his first lessons; it was from Italy that he obtained the first teachers whom he

Contrast between the Transalpine and Cisalpine Renaissance.

CHAP. IV, imported into Gaul.[1] Some of these teachers were undoubtedly
§ 1. ecclesiastics; for it was the ecclesiastical education of the
north that Charles had especially set himself to reform. But
it would appear that in Italy the educational traditions of the
old Roman world were by no means entirely broken off. The
Carolingian enactments respecting the cathedral and monastic
schools no doubt extended to Italy; but here they seem to
constitute no conspicuous landmark in the history of education.[2] Church schools of course existed,[3] and many of the

---

[1] [Eginhard, *Vita Karoli*, c. 25;
Alcuin in *M.G.H.*, *Epistolae Karo-
lini aevi*, ii. 458; G. Manacorda,
Storia della scuola in Italia, i. 42,
43.]

[2] Roger Bacon says as to his own
time: 'Atque domini legum Bononiae et per totam Italiam volunt
vocari magistri vel clerici, nec coro-
nam sicut clerici habent. Uxores
ducunt,' &c. *Opera ined.*, ed.
Brewer, p. 419.

[3] Indeed, the system of ecclesiastical education adopted by Charles
the Great seems to have been borrowed from Italy (Giesebrecht, *De
litterarum studiis apud Italos*, Berlin,
1845, p. 9). Later, in 826, Eugenius II ordered 'in universis epi-
scopiis subiectisque plebibus (i.e.
the Archipresbyteral Churches) et
aliis locis, in quibus necessitas oc-
currerit, omnis cura et diligentia
adhibeatur ut magistri et doctores
constituantur, qui studia literarum
liberaliumque artium habentes,
dogmata assidue doceantur' (Giesebrecht reads 'doceant'). *M.G.H.*,
Leges, II, add. p. 17. Only a year
before, schools—not apparently
ecclesiastical—had been established
in eight principal cities of Lombardy by Lothair, the smaller cities
being each assigned to one of these
centres; *Leges*, i. 249. Attempts were
made to compel even the ordinary
parish priests to establish schools
in their parishes. Atto of Vercelli
in the tenth century ordered that

'Presbyteri etiam per villas et vicos
scholas habeant'. *Capitulare*, c. 61
(*Patrol. Lat.* cxxxiv. 40). Rather-
ius, Bishop of Verona, declares that
he will not ordain any one who has
not been educated 'aut in civitate
nostra, aut in aliquo monasterio,
vel apud quemlibet sapientem'.
Synodica, 15 (*Patrol. Lat.* cxxxvi.
564). The last clause indicates a
freedom of private education hardly
recognized in the north. [For a
discussion of these and other texts
see A. Dresdner, *Kultur- und Sitten-
geschichte der italienischen Geist-
lichkeit im 10. und 11. Jahrhundert*,
Breslau, 1890, pp. 373 *sqq.* (ex-
cursus on the education of the
laity); G. Salvioli, *L'istruzione pub-
blica in Italia*, &c., Florence, 1912,
pp. 28–43; F. Novati, *Storia letteraria d'Italia: Le Origine*, Milan,
1926, pp. 126–9, and ch. v, *passim*;
Manacorda, *op. cit.* i. 41–69, a
chapter on Carolingian and papal
scholastic legislation in the ninth
century. Owing to the lack of
masters, Pope Leo IV, in a council
held at Rome in 853, modified the
requirements of Eugenius II.
Manacorda distinguishes between
the royal schools, the cathedral
schools, and the country schools,
the last of which were open to all,
and may have helped to prepare
the way for students in the royal
schools. Cf. also Margaret Deanesly in the *Cambridge Medieval
History*, v. 776, 777.]

famous Italian teachers of the Dark Ages were ecclesiastics.
But here the church schools enjoyed no monopoly. In the
cities of northern Italy the race of lay teachers seems never Lay education in Italy.
to have quite died out; and it is certain that when the revival
came, its most conspicuous effects were seen not in the church
schools but in the schools of independent lay masters. In
Italy we find no trace of the theory which looked upon
masters and scholars as *ipso facto* members of the ecclesiastical order,[1] nor were they subject in any greater degree than
other laymen to ecclesiastical supervision or jurisdiction.
Many teachers might receive the tonsure to secure the
valuable ecclesiastical immunities; but in the city-republics
of north Italy there were ecclesiastical disabilities as well as
ecclesiastical immunities; there were civil careers open to the
ambitious citizen for which the ecclesiastical status would
have been a disqualification.[2] Corresponding to the difference in the status of the teacher, there was a difference no
less marked in the class from which scholars were drawn. It
was customary for the Lombard nobility to give their sons
a literary education at a time when the knights and barons of
France or Germany were inclined to look upon reading and

---

[1] [Cf. below, p. 181 and iii. 397.
On the other hand Buoncompagno
undoubtedly included *magistri* and
scolares in the category of clerks,
e.g. in his 'Quinque tabulae saluta-
tionum', c. 1295. In his *Rhetorica
antiqua*, 'ordo quippe scolasticus
est ecclesie speculum,' &c. (B.M.
Cotton MS. Vit. C. viii, f. 103 v).
Again, in the regulations about
funerals which appear in the Consuetudines of Reggio (1242) *ecclesiastici et scholares* are mentioned
together (MS. Statuti, vol. i, f.
15 r). We owe this evidence to
Miss Helen Briggs. There was, of
course, a legal distinction between
the *clericus* who had only been
tonsured and the *clericus* in minor
orders; cf. Decretals of Gregory IX,
lib. iii, tit. i, c. 6; and a letter in the
Register of John Trillek, Bishop of
Hereford, 1345 (ed. Cant. and York

Society, p. 56): 'In scolis gramaticalibus Gloucestrie existens inter
alios parvulos inibi a non tuo episcopo et sine ipsius licencia speciali
ordinem psalmistatus sive primam
tonsuram per quam conferitur
ordo clericalis temere recepisti.']

[2] Thus while few of the civilians
were *clerici*, the humbler class of
teachers often took the tonsure to
escape taxation. A City Statute at
Bologna (Frati, ii. 102) directs the
Podestà to inquire 'omnes et singulos magistros qui sunt de civitate vel comitatu bon. qui doceant
pueros et omnes illos qui dicunt se
clericos vel conversos esse . . . et
non habeant clericam vel tonsuram, et faciant extimare bona
eorum'. The same statutes exclude
'clerici' from the office of Notary
or 'Tabellio'. *Ibid.*, p. 190.

CHAP. IV, writing as unmanly and almost degrading accomplishments
§ 1. fit only for priests or monks, and especially for priests or monks not too-well born.[1]

Its subject-matter. Connected with the wider diffusion of education south of the Alps was a certain difference in its subject-matter. In Italy as in France or Britain all education was held to be comprised in the seven liberal arts, and the ground covered by the seven liberal arts was much the same in all parts of Europe. But the relative importance of the different elements in this apparently comprehensive though really very meagre programme varied widely in accordance with the different bent and genius of north and south.[2] North of the Alps it was upon dialectic—and especially upon dialectic in its metaphysical and theological applications—that attention was concentrated. The famous teachers of the north from Scotus to Abelard, though most of them no doubt taught the whole of the narrow encyclopedia of their time, were known chiefly as dialecticians. And when the revival of intellectual activity came, it showed itself at once in a revival of dialectical activity, of speculation, of theological controversy. In Italy on the contrary grammar and rhetoric absorbed a large part of the attention almost monopolized in the north by theology and logic. Ozanam is right in declaring that people have exaggerated the abyss which separates the Middle Age and the Renaissance.[3] Throughout the Middle Ages the 'literary

[1] [This analysis requires some restatement. Although 'free' schools clearly existed in Italy in the early Middle Ages, the evidence for the existence of lay teachers is not so great as to justify sweeping generalizations. Manacorda goes too far, on the other hand, when he denies that laymen can be found in the teaching profession before the thirteenth century; see, for example, Davidsohn, *Geschichte von Florenz*, i. 807, note. Lay teaching developed with the growth of autonomous city life. See Manacorda, i. 129 *sqq.*, chapters on the 'free' school and lay masters.]

[2] It is possibly an indication of this difference that Charles the Great 'in discenda *grammatica* Petrum Pisanum diaconum senem audivit, in *caeteris disciplinis* Albinum cognomento Alcoinum, item diaconem, de Britannia', &c. Eginhard, *Vita Karoli*, c. 25. [L. Halphen points out in his edition of Eginhard (Paris, 1923, p. 74) that the reading, 'Albinum cognomento Alcoinum' is a slip, perhaps made by Eginhard himself, for 'Alcoinum cognomento Albinum'.]

[3] 'On a poussé trop loin le contraste, on a trop élargi l'abîme entre le moyen âge et la renaissance. Il

Paganism' which seems to cling to the very soil of Italy always CHAP. IV,
§ I. kept alive in the scholar's breast an attachment to the myths and poetry of antiquity, which occasionally assumed a character as really anti-Christian as the paganism of the fifteenth century and more avowedly so.[1] Moreover, in the Dark Ages grammar and rhetoric had a practical as well as a literary side. In Italy these arts were studied as aids to the composition of legal documents, as a preparation for the work of the notary and the pleader, rather than as the indispensable preliminary to the study of Scripture and the Fathers. Even logic was regarded rather as a sharpener of the wits and a discipline for the word-battles of the law-court than as the key to the mysteries of theology; while rhetoric was considered to include not merely instruction in the art of persuasion and of literary composition but at least a preliminary initiation into the science of positive law. The scholastic philosophy and theology of the later Middle Ages were the natural fruits of the seed sown in northern France, England, and Germany by the dialecticians of the Dark Ages. The revival of legal science which is associated with the name of Irnerius was the natural outcome of the educational traditions which the cities of north Italy had inherited from that old Roman world to which alike in spirit and in constitutional theory they had never wholly ceased to belong.

In truth, the differences between the two educational systems, if such they can be called, are all explained by the one great contrast which is presented by the social and

The contrast explained by the social condition of France and Italy respectively.

---

ne fallait pas méconnaître ce qu'il y eut de paganisme littéraire dans ces temps où l'on attribue à la foi chrétienne l'empire absolu des esprits et des consciences.' *Doc. inédits*, p. 28.

[1] Rodulphus Glaber relates an outburst of heresy under the year 1000 at Ravenna which seems to have amounted to an actual recrudescence of paganism, excited by one 'Vilgardus dictus, studio artis grammatice magis assiduus quam frequens, *sicut italicis mos*

semper fuit artes negligere ceteras, illam sectari'. Virgil, Horace, and Juvenal, or demons in the form of these poets, appeared to him in dreams and promised him a share of their glory, in consequence of which he 'cepit multa turgide docere fidei sacre contraria, dictaque poetarum per omnia credenda esse asserebat' (ed. Prou., Paris, 1886, p. 50). The heresy was only suppressed by much burning. As to the prominence of grammar in Italy, see Giesebrecht *passim*.

political conditions of the two regions. In northern France[1] all intellectual life was confined to the cloister or to schools which were merely dependencies of the cloister, because the governing class itself was composed of but two great orders —the military and the clerical—in the latter of which alone was there any demand for learning. In Italy, in place of a régime of pure feudalism tempered only by ecclesiastical influence, there had survived all through the darkest ages at least the memory of the old Roman municipal system, and with it at least the germ and the possibility of a free and vigorous municipal life. Hence, in Italy it was in the political sphere that the new eleventh-century activity first manifested itself; while the consequent or concomitant revival of culture took a correspondingly secular turn.

Continuity of municipal life in N. Italy. If the continued existence of the Roman Empire is the key to the history of medieval Europe at large, the continued existence (amid all social and political changes) of the Roman law is the key to the history of the Lombard cities and the Lombard schools. Beneath all changes of external government, the continuity of city life was never quite destroyed. Successive waves of conquest—Roman, West-Gothic, East-Gothic, Lombard, Frank—had swept over them without destroying their limited autonomy. The Goths had appropriated a share of the land, the Lombards a share of the produce: the castles of the invading hordes spread over the country. But within the walls of the towns at least the forms and the names of the Roman legal system maintained an unbroken continuity. It is true that Savigny exaggerated the extent of this continuity, and under-estimated the transformation which the whole political and judicial system underwent at the hands first of the Lombard, then of the Frankish, invaders.[2] But it is probable that the details of internal

---

[1] M. Thurot (*L'Organisation de l'enseignement dans l'Un. de Paris*, p. 3) remarks that the contrast ought strictly to be drawn between the countries north of the Loire on the one hand and southern France and Italy on the other. This is to a great extent true, though, as we shall see, the educational system of southern France stands in some respects midway between the Italian and the northern system.

[2] [Discussion of this subject lies outside the scope of this work.

administration, and certain that the private relations of the native citizens, continued to be regulated by Roman law or Roman tradition. Whatever changes were made in the magistracies, the Roman was still supposed to be judged according to Roman law, the Lombard according to Lombard law. In the period immediately after the barbarian invasions this state of things was more or less common to all parts of the Roman world. Eventually, however, the two races were everywhere fused. Where the barbarians formed a majority of the population, where the oppression and dispossession of the old inhabitants had been carried farthest, the law of the invaders prevailed, or rather the place of Roman and national law alike was taken by a multitude of varying local customs which had absorbed varying proportions of both the conflicting systems. Where the Roman element predominated, where the barbarian yoke was lighter and the Roman civilization more firmly established, there Roman law sooner or later asserted itself.[1] To a certain extent this was the case in southern Europe generally: the conditions of Burgundy and of the so-called *pays de droit écrit* partly resembled those of northern Italy. But in some respects the position of the Lombard towns was peculiar to themselves. In the first place the cities were here more numerous, more populous and prosperous as well as more independent than in any other part of Europe;[2] the Lombard invasion was a conquest rather

---

Since the appearance of the classic treatises of C. Hegel (1847) and J. Ficker (1868–74) the problem of the continuity of Italian city life has been examined from all sides, but especially in its legal and economic aspects. See, e.g., C. W. Previté-Orton in the *Cambridge Historical Journal*, i (1923), 14–19, and the bibliography in the *Cambridge Medieval History*, v. 862. A very penetrating analysis of the nature and causes of continuity can be read in Guido Mengozzi, *La città italiana nell'alto medio evo*, 2nd ed., Florence, 1931: see pp. 111, 311, &c.]

[1] Savigny, cc. ii and iii, §§ 49, 50.

[2] To account for their position we must go back to the early distinction between Italy and the provinces. The Italians were the *socii* of Rome: their *municipia* retained their autonomy and continued to elect their own magistrates. The provinces were conquered dependencies. Autonomy was at first granted to a few provincial cities as a rare and exceptional privilege: though eventually such privileges were widely extended in southern France and Spain—the countries whose civic life (and

than an immigration. Here the old municipal life died only to rise again with renewed vitality: the Romanized city-communities proved strong enough gradually to absorb a large part of the Germanic population, which passed into the position of a civic, instead of a feudal, aristocracy. And here eventually the towns were able with more or less of imperial assistance to throw off the yoke of the Lombard counts, except where the milder rule of their own elective bishops formed the stepping-stone to entire independence.

Causes which fostered the city autonomy. Several distinct chains of external circumstances combined with the social condition of the cities and the inherent vitality of their civic life to facilitate the development of the Lombard towns from mere municipalities into practically independent republics. The first of these was the absorption of the Lombardic kingship into the Holy Roman Empire, and the gradual transformation of that Empire into a Germanic monarchy whose possessors—except during an actual occupation of Italy by armed hosts—were without the power of permanently enforcing their high-sounding prerogatives. Thus when the cities were once emancipated from the rule of their counts, they found themselves practically without a political superior. The attempt of the Hohenstaufen to convert their nominal Italian monarchy into a real one was finally frustrated by the victory of the Lombard League at Legnano in 1176: the Treaty of Constance in 1183 secured the practical freedom of the cities. Another favourable circumstance was the long contest between the Emperors and the Popes. The co-operation of the Italian cities was of vast importance to both the contending parties, each of which was able to give some kind of constitutional sanction to any usurpation on the part of its allies which it might find it

---

consequently whose universities) approximated most closely to those of North Italy. Gallia Cisalpina ceased to be a *provincia* after 43 B.C. Some limitations were, indeed, placed upon the autonomy of the cities, but these were afterwards extended to other Italian cities. As to southern Italy, the absence of political life in the few large cities, the use of the Greek language, and above all the Norman and Saracen invasions, are the chief causes which explain its slight participation in the revival of Roman law.

expedient to tolerate. By engaging on one side or other of this great struggle the cities succeeded on the whole in maintaining an autonomy which often amounted to practical sovereignty. CHAP. IV, § 1.

The intellectual Renaissance of the twelfth century found the Italian cities just entering upon this struggle for independence: the intellectual Renaissance was indeed only another side of a political Renaissance. As the Lombard cities awoke to a consciousness of their recovered liberty, their energies were absorbed by a political life as engrossing, as interesting and dignified, as it had been in the cities of ancient Hellas. And thus a career was opening itself to men who were neither Churchmen nor soldiers. In such communities it cannot be a matter of surprise that the revival of intellectual activity took a political, or at least a civil, direction. Just as the demand of the cloisters north of the Alps for speculative knowledge—for knowledge for its own sake, knowledge apart from all relation to social life, manifested itself in a revival of metaphysical and theological speculation and was ultimately met by the rediscovery of the forgotten Aristotle; so in the commercial and political society of the Italian cities there arose a demand for fruitful knowledge, for science applied to the regulation of social life—for *civilization* in the strictest sense of the word. And this demand was met by a revived study of the long-neglected, but never wholly forgotten, monuments of Roman jurisprudence. It is only in such communities that in the heart of the Middle Ages the purely mundane science of law could have awakened the enthusiasm—the genuine intellectual enthusiasm—which attended its study in the early days of the School of Bologna: it is only in such communities that so democratic, so unhierarchical an institution as an autonomous university of students could have sprung into existence. Political character of the intellectual revival.

It must not be supposed, indeed, that the intellectual movement in northern Italy had no spiritual side, or that because men's minds were here little absorbed with metaphysical problems, their interests were purely material and utilitarian. On the contrary, the struggle between the Empire Spiritual side of the movement.

CHAP. IV, and the Papacy was essentially a battle of ideas. But the
§ 1.　　questions at issue assumed the form of constitutional questions. Both sides appealed in support of their claims to
antiquity and to authority rather than to abstract reason;
both sides derived large elements in their respective ideals
as well as the weapons with which they fought for them in
the legal literature of ancient Rome.

Alleged　　The old account of the revival of the Roman law repre-
discovery
of the sents that the Pisans, upon the capture of Amalfi in 1135,
Pandects
at Amalfi, discovered a manuscript of the Digest or Pandects of Jus-
1135. tinian, whereupon the Emperor Lothair II, with an intuitive
recognition of the value of the 'find', forthwith directed its
contents to be taught in the schools and enforced in the
tribunals. Since the time of Savigny at least[1] the baselessness
of this story has been generally recognized. It is nearly
certain that the celebrated manuscript in connexion with
which it is told, and which was removed to Florence (1406)
after the capture of Pisa, had been in that city long before
this event—according to the thirteenth-century jurist Odofredus, since the time of Justinian, when it was brought there
from Constantinople.[2] The story, as commonly told, is one
of those which are not merely not literally true, but which

[1] The fact was known to scholars
long before. See, e.g., Sarti, 1, pt. 1,
p. 3. The story finds a place in
Gibbon's narrative (*Decline and
Fall of the Rom. Emp.*, ch. xliv),
though he recognized that it was
'unknown to the twelfth century,
embellished by ignorant ages, and
suspected by rigid criticism'.

[2] The story of course breaks
down with the explosion of the
theory that the Pandects were unknown in North Italy till the
twelfth century. Moreover, it is
inconsistent with the probable date
of Irnerius's teaching. Nor is there
any evidence whatever of the existence of the law of Lothair II enforcing the use of the Roman law:
the Bologna text of the Pandects
shows the influence of other sources

than the Pisa MS.: finally, the
story about the seizure at Amalfi
rests on the statement of two
chroniclers of the fourteenth century. Savigny, c. xviii, § 35 *sq.*
The Pisa MS. is now in the Lauren-
tian Library at Florence. It forms
the basis of the text of the Pandects.
[The manuscript was certainly in
Pisa in the middle of the twelfth
century, when it was known to the
civilian Roger (d. 1170); see Kantorowicz, *op. cit.*, *Zeitschrift der Savigny-Stiftung*, Röm. Abth. xxx. 203
passim. Kantorowicz, who seeks to
give more precision to Mommsen's
analysis, argues in his first chapter
that the manuscript was written in
Byzantine Italy in the second half
of the sixth century by thirteen
scribes.]

possess what may be called the higher kind of historical falsity. It misrepresents the whole nature of the revival which we are studying, assuming as it does that the Roman law, or at least the Pandects, had been hitherto as unknown in medieval Europe as the laws of Manu. As a matter of fact, it may be broadly asserted that the Roman law never ceased through what are called the Dark Ages of European history to be (subject of course to changes incident to the altered political status of the Roman citizens) the law of the conquered races; while it powerfully affected and entered into the composition of the laws of the conquering tribes.

Most conspicuously, as might be expected from the political and social conditions, did the Roman law maintain its authority in the Lombard towns of northern Italy. Elsewhere other compilations (of which the most important was the *Breviarium*) were more frequently appealed to than the compilations of Justinian: in Italy the *Breviarium* was not introduced till Carolingian times, but, even if it was known, it did not supersede either the use or the authority of the Institutes and the Code.[1] There is abundant proof that these works were never entirely unknown from the fall of the Western Empire to the day of the alleged 'discovery'.[2] They were known of course only in the sense in which books are known in an illiterate age; that is to say, there were learned men here and there whose writings exhibit an acquaintance with them. It does not of course follow that the whole of the learned class or the whole of the lawyer-class were familiar with the original sources, or that every Lombard town possessed a complete library of texts. The Pandects were,

Con-tinuous use of Roman law in Italy.

---

[1] The *Breviarium* has been published by Hänel under the title of *Lex Romana Visigothorum* (Leipzig, 1847–9). The Theodosian Code was the basis of it.

[2] Savigny, c. xiv. [See Wretschko, preface to Mommsen's edition of the Theodosian Code, i (1905), pp. cccvii *sqq.* The continuous tradition or application of Roman law is one thing (cf. Brandileone, *Il diritto bizantino nell'Italia* *meridionale dall'VIII al XII secolo*, Bologna, 1886), the continuous study of the Pandects another. On this latter point opinion is nearly unanimous. So far no definite quotation from the Pandects, as distinct from casual allusion, has been traced between the letters of Gregory the Great (603) and 1076. For the bibliography of the discussion see Kantorowicz, *op. cit.* xxx. 183, 198 note.]

CHAP. IV, indeed, unknown or unstudied during the greater part of this
§ 1.   period, but their recovery dates from at least half a century
before the capture of Amalfi. Still, the Roman law was in
all the Lombard towns at least in part the recognized law of
the tribunals; and some knowledge of it was required for the
Tradi- exercise of public functions. This knowledge was obtained
tional
knowledge. in two ways. To a large extent no doubt the lawyer-class—
the *Iudices*, the *Advocati*, and the *Notarii*—acquired their
knowledge of law, not by attendance at professorial lectures
But law but (like our English lawyers) by tradition and practice.[1] But
also
taught in law was also taught in the schools. When we remember the
schools. enormous proportion of the intellectual energy of Europe
which had been concentrated on the study of law during the
latter days of the Roman Empire, it would have been ante-
cedently probable that, wherever any education at all survived, some elementary instruction in law would have formed
part of that education. And as a matter of fact there are many
distinct traces of the continuance of legal instruction in the
schools of the Dark Ages throughout Europe. In spite of
the rigid attachment of the English to their ancestral customs,
Roman law (no doubt in some extremely rudimentary form)
is said to have formed part of the curriculum of the School
of York in the days of Alcuin.[2] Even in the cloisters of
saintly Bec it seems probable that law was among the subjects
taught by Lanfranc, who afterwards played so important
a part in romanizing the law of the English Church;[3]

[1] Savigny (c. ix, § 42), though aware that Roman law was taught in the schools, laid most stress on the traditionary mode of transmission: Fitting, while rightly emphasizing the extent and importance of the school teaching, declares (*Die Rechtsschule zu Bologna*, p. 33) that Savigny's statement that law was learned by practice, would be no more true of the early medieval period than of our own. The evidence hardly warrants the assertion that the Italian lawyer of the tenth or eleventh century learned his law in the schools to the same extent as the German lawyer of the present day. Indeed, Fitting himself insists much on the literary and introductory character of the school law-teaching.

[2] For the rather slight evidence see Savigny, c. vi, § 135.

[3] This is an inference from Lanfranc's fame as a lawyer and the fact that the celebrated canonist Ivo of Chartres was his pupil. Robert of Torigni (*M.G.H.*, *Scriptores*, vi. 485) merely says that Ivo heard him 'de secularibus et divinis literis tractantem', and associates Lanfranc and Irnerius as joint dis-

and it may have been at Bec that the Abbot Theobald acquired that enthusiasm for the Roman law which led him as Archbishop of Canterbury to promote the study of the Roman law-texts, hitherto comparatively little known in England, among the clerks of his own household. But all that has been said as to the political and social condition of Italy would prepare us to find that it was especially here that law held its ground in the schools. That Irnerius was not in any sense whatever the first teacher of law in the medieval schools of Italy was strongly insisted upon by Savigny: he quotes for instance the statement of Lanfranc's biographer that the future archbishop studied at Pavia 'in the schools of the Liberal Arts and of the secular laws according to the custom of his country'.[1] Our conception of the extent and importance of this pre-Irnerian law-teaching as also of the pre-Irnerian law-literature has been considerably widened by later researches. The universality of this practice of learning law at school can be adequately illustrated only by the accumulation of passages, quoted by Savigny, Giesebrecht, Ozanam, Fitting, and others. If the evidence is not more abundant than it is, it is on

Law a part of rhetoric.

---

coverers of the Roman law-books; *ibid.*, p. 478 (an. 1032). The passage, in spite of the confusion of dates, is valuable as testifying to Lanfranc's high legal reputation. The opinions of Lanfranc are often cited by the commentators of the *Papiensis* (*M.G.H.*, *Leges*, iv, pp. xcv, xcvi). [Lanfranc introduced into England a canon-law book based upon the pseudo-Isidorian decretals: see Z. N. Brooke, *The English Church and the Papacy from the Conquest to the reign of John* (Cambridge, 1931); P. Fournier et G. le Bras, *Histoire des collections canoniques*, ii (Paris, 1932), 227–30. For Lanfranc at Pavia see N. Tamassia, in the *Mélanges Fitting* (1908), ii. 189–202; and cf. Vinogradoff, *op. cit.*, pp. 49–53; for legal studies at Bec, Pollock and

Maitland, *History of English Law*, i. 54–6, and A. J. Macdonald, *Lanfranc* (Oxford, 1926), p. 30. Macdonald points out that the possibility of confusion with other Lanfrancs in Pavia must not be overlooked, p. 7 n.]

[1] 'Nobili ortus parentela, ab annis puerilibus eruditus est in scholis liberalium artium et legum saecularium ad suae morem patriae. Adolescens orator veteranos adversantes in actionibus causarum frequenter revicit, torrente facundiae accurate dicendo. In ipsa aetate sententias depromere sapuit, quas gratanter iuris periti aut iudices vel praetores civitatis acceptabant. Meminit horum Papia.' Milo Crispin, *Vita Lanfranci*, c. v (*Patrol. Lat.* vol. cl, col. 39).

account of the complete amalgamation of law-studies with the ordinary educational curriculum. At least some rudiments of law were everywhere taught in the 'schools of the Liberal Arts' and by the masters of these arts. The old division of rhetoric into the three branches, 'demonstrative', 'deliberative', and 'judicial', allowed the introduction of law-studies under the last-mentioned category without requiring the addition of a new art to the sacred Seven.[1] The characteristics of this scholastic law-teaching may be inferred from its position as an element in the ordinary literary education. It must be remembered that the law-texts were written in what was becoming more and more a dead language even to Italians. Hence the close association of this law-instruction with grammar[2] as well as with rhetoric. Some linguistic culture was required to enable a Lombard youth to read the text of the Institutes, and more to enable him to draw a Latin deed; and if to the reading and writing of law Latin we add the explanation of the technical terms arising in the text-books, some rhetorical rules of pleading, and practice in their application by means of imaginary cases, we shall perhaps obtain a fair idea of what was involved in the ordinary grammatico-legal education of the schools before the time of Irnerius.

[1] 'Tria sunt genera causarum, quae recipere debet orator: demonstrativum, deliberativum, iudiciale.' Auctor ad Herennium, II. i. The metrical biographer of Adelbert VI, Archbishop of Mainz (1137–41), adopts this distinction in speaking of his hero's studies at Paris including rhetoric:

'iudiciale genus causae, quod abhorret egenus,
quod tunc tractatur, cum iudex ius meditatur.'

Bibl. Rer. Germ., ed. Jaffé, vol. iii, p. 590. [For full discussion of the study of law, as a branch of rhetoric, in the cathedral and monastic schools of Italy before the time of Irnerius, see Manacorda, op. cit. ii. 131–8, with the authorities there cited, from Cassiodorus onwards; and Emil Ott, 'Die Rhetorica ecclesiastica', &c., in Sitzungsberichte der K. Akad. d. Wissenschaften, Phil.-hist. Klasse, 1891, cxxv, Abh. viii (Vienna, 1892). F. Novati has emphasized the importance of legal study at Monte Cassino, in Rendiconti di R. Ist. Lomb. Lett. scienze ed arti, 1912, 2nd series, xiv. 95–114.]

[2] Thus the Elementarium doctrinae rudimentum (1053) of the Lombard, Papias (Milan, 1476, &c.), explains a large number of technical terms both legal and logical. Cf. Alcuin, Dial. de arte rhetorica (Halm, Rhetores lat. minores, p. 525 sq.).

When we turn from the schools to the literary remains of this period, we enter upon a more debatable region. By making the most of such scanty abridgements or epitomes as have come down to us and by assigning early dates in doubtful cases, Fitting and others have attempted to demonstrate the existence of a considerable jurisprudence,[1] not only in the age immediately preceding Irnerius but throughout the Dark Ages.[2] Most minds unbiased by enthusiasm for an *a priori* 'law of continuity' will probably be disposed to acquiesce in the conclusion of Flach, viz. that the earlier treatises and glosses[3] brought in evidence by the new school, where they do not date from the age of Justinian or a little later, are after all inconsiderable both in quantity and quality. They go to confirm Savigny's view of a continuous knowledge and practice of some parts of the Roman law throughout the Middle Ages, but they do little to remove a prevailing impression of the general ignorance of the earlier

[1] Fitting, *Die Rechtssch. zu Bol.*, p. 51, &c.; Chiappelli, *Lo studio bol.*, p. 45 *sq.*, 98 *sq.*, 125, and his edition of the celebrated Pistoian gloss, *La glossa pistoiese al codice giustinianeo*, Turin, 1885 (*Mem. della R. Acad. di Scienze di Torino*, Ser. ii, vol. xxxvii); Conrat, *Die Epitome exactis regibus* (Berlin, 1884). [Conrat, while he believed that there was a later period of slow evolution, mercilessly criticized Fitting's arguments.]

[2] [In his original note on this passage Rashdall was misled by Chiappelli, who worked from late printed editions of the glosses, which are full of misprints, and often misunderstood the terms used. In the glosses 'quidam' are contemporaries, 'veteres praeceptores' are Henricus de Bayla, a fairly recent civilian, not old authorities. The 'antiqua litera' was the vulgate text (used by Irnerius) as opposed to the 'litera Pisana', not 'a current text earlier than that bequeathed to the school of

Bologna by Irnerius', as Chiappelli supposed. The *sigle* noted by Chiappelli did not refer to unknown predecessors of Irnerius. See Pescatore, *Glossen des Irnerius*, 1888, pp. 27 *sqq.*; Seckel, *Paläographie der jur. Handschriften*, Weimar, 1925, p. 16; and Kantorowicz, *op. cit.*, § 5. On the whole subject cf. the paper of E. Genzmer, 'Die Justinianische Kodifikation und die Glossatoren', in *Atti del Congresso Internazionale di Diritto Romano*, Pavia, 1934, i. 347–430.] The idea that Irnerius was the first of the glossators dates from the time of Odofredus († 1265), who says: 'Sed dominus Yr. . . . fuit primus illuminator scientie nostre, et quia primus fuit qui fecit glosas in libris nostris, vocamus eum lucernam iuris.' In Dig. Vet. de iust. et iure L. ius civile (Lyons, 1550, i, f. 7 *a*). The statement is accepted by Savigny, c. xxiv, § 207.

[3] Flach, *Études critiques*, pp. 50, 102.

half of this period. On the other hand, the more important of these writings, such as the *Exceptiones Petri*[1] and the *Brachylogus*[2] cannot be shown to be earlier than the twelfth or at the earliest the end of the eleventh century—that is to say to the first dawn of the legal Renaissance. And here it may be admitted that the new school has done something to confirm and emphasize the important fact that the revival dates from considerably before the time of Irnerius; and though Fitting and his followers are disposed to exaggerate the 'scientific' character of the earliest products of the legal Renaissance, it is true also that Bologna was not the very earliest seat of this revival. In fact the law revival, in its commencement and its subsequent progress, exactly kept pace with the revival of dialectical activity north of the Alps; and the rise of the School of Bologna synchronizes almost exactly with the rise to pre-eminent importance of the schools of Paris. The scholastic movement did not begin in Paris and the civil law movement did not begin in Bologna; but though the movement may have been somewhat more gradual, and its earlier stages somewhat more important than has been commonly supposed, the latest researches do not detract very seriously from the epoch-making importance hitherto attached to the rise of the Bologna school.

[1] This epitome or introduction to the study of Roman law, known as the *Exceptiones legum Romanarum*, printed by Savigny in an appendix to his *Gesch. d. Röm. Rechts.*, is referred by Fitting (in the form in which it appears in the Tübingen MS.) to the School of Pavia and to *c.* 1063, but he regards it as a redaction of an early work belonging to the first half of the eleventh century. He identifies its author with Petrus de Ravenna, who appears with the title *Scholasticus, Scholasticissimus* or *Disertissimus* in various documents of 1021–37. Fitting, *Die Rechtssch. zu Bol.*, p. 60; *Ztschr. d. Sav.-Stift.* vii, Röm. Abth. Heft 2, pp. 42, 61 *sqq.* Cf. also Chiappelli, p. 78 *sq.* [It is now accepted as a product of legal studies in southern France or north Italy in the early twelfth century.]

[2] The *Brachylogus*, according to Fitting, was compiled at Orleans at the end of the eleventh or the beginning of the twelfth century. See Fitting, *Die Rechtssch. zu Bol.*, pp. 47, 67; and *Über die Heimat und das Alter des sog. Brach.* (Berlin, 1880). Its value is attested to by the twenty-three editions published between 1548 and 1829. [Conrat, *Geschichte*, pp. 550–82, attributes the *Brachylogus* to the twelfth century.]

Three places in Italy have been especially claimed as pre- CHAP. IV,
Bolognese schools of law: Rome, Pavia, and Ravenna.   § 1.

To the city of Rome, indeed, the term school can be Rome.
applied only in a somewhat vague and general sense. There
is no real evidence of any systematic or professorial teaching
of law at Rome during the Dark Ages over and above the
elementary school-teaching customary throughout Italy.[1]
Odofredus represents the *studium* of law as having been
transferred from Rome to Ravenna in consequence of 'the
wars in the March'—that is presumably after the great burning of Rome by the Normans in 1084. Elsewhere he tells us
that it was at this time that 'the books' of law were transferred
from the city of Rome to Ravenna.[2] Odofredus is not a very
valuable authority for the events of the eleventh century, but
we may probably recognize a certain element of truth in the
general statement that at about this time Rome was superseded by Ravenna as the centre of the best knowledge and
teaching of the Roman law which then existed in Italy.

The School of Pavia was famous from at least the beginning Pavia.
of the eleventh century. It was primarily a school of Lombard
law; but Roman law was studied with much earnestness
by the Lombard lawyers as a kind of universal code which
might be called in to supplement and elucidate the municipal
law of a particular nation.[3] The prominence of Roman law

[1] Fitting contends for a continued existence of the school
founded by Justinian down to the
time of Gregory VII. [For later
discussion see Kantorowicz, *op.
cit.* xxx. 252–5. Besta, in his life
of Irnerius, opposed the views of
Fitting, who suggested that Irnerius was at Rome in 1082. Fitting
was supported by F. Schupfer in
the *Atti d. R. Acc. dei Lincei*, mem.
d. Cl. d. scienze morale, series 5,
v (1897), 39. Kantorowicz shows
that the argument for a law
school at Rome rest upon mis-
understandings. For the schools
at Rome since the sixth century
see the references collected by
Manacorda, ii. 322, 323.]

[2] In Infortiatum, *ad L. Falcidiam* (Lyons, 1550, ii, f. 83). Cf.
below, p. 111, n. 1.
[3] Fitting, *Die Rechtssch. zu Bol.*,
p. 40. The fullest account of the
School of Pavia is given by Merkel,
Gesch. des Langobardenrechts, Berlin, 1850. Cf. also Boretius, praef.
ad Libr. Papiensem (*M.G.H.*,
Leges, iv, p. xcliii *sq.*). [Cf. Hazel-
tine in *Cam. Med. Hist.* v. 732, 733.
A. Solmi in his studies, especially
in the *Rendiconti del. R. Istituto
Lombardo*, lviii (1925), has dealt
with the evidence for the continuity
of the Schools of Pavia. G. Mengozzi, *Ricerche sull'attività della
scuola di Pavia nell'alto medio
evo* (Pavia, 1924), maintains the

at Pavia is shown by the fact that the school was resorted to by foreigners who could have had no object in studying the legal system of the Lombards.[1]

[Pavia was probably the main centre of legal studies in Italy before the rise of Bologna, although many scholars have given the chief place to Ravenna, whose schools, at which the poet Venantius Fortunatus studied in the sixth century,[2] would seem, in the eleventh century, to have been concerned with the study of law to more purpose than was the case elsewhere.[3]]

At Ravenna the old traditions of Roman jurisprudence

continuity of a school from Roman times, connected since the days of Theodoric with the royal palace. This school of grammar and rhetoric was from about 844 a true State school which became a creative centre of judicial teaching and action. Mengozzi points to the emergence of new juridical forms of action in the later ninth century.]

[1] In 1065 a monk of Marseilles writes a letter to his abbot in which he apologizes for having betaken himself to the study of law by alleging 'per totam fere Italiam scholares et maxime Provinciales necnon ipsius ordinis, de quo sum, quia plures [*lege* quamplures] legibus catervatim studium adhibentes incessanter aspicio'. Martène and Durand, *Ampl. Coll.* i, c. 470. He adds that he intends hereafter to go to Pavia 'ad exercendum ibi studium'. Later (1119–24) a French scholar is represented in a formulary-book as writing 'me exulem Papie studio legum—*vel* dialectice —alacrem'. Cf. Fitting, *Ztschr. d. Sav.-Stift.* vii, Röm. Abth. Heft 2, p. 66.

[2] 'Ravennae nutritus et doctus in arte Gramatica sive Rethorica seu etiam metrica clarissimus extitit.' Paul. Diacon. *Historia Langobardorum*, lib. ii, c. 13 in *M.G.H.*,

Scriptores rerum Langobardicarum, 1878, p. 79.

[3] See the account by Petrus Damianus of his disputation in 1045 with the Ravenna Jurists who took the anti-Church side on the question of the prohibited degrees, *De parentelae gradibus*, Opusc. viii (*Patrol. Lat.* cxlv. 191 *sq.*). Fitting considers that their opposition provoked the decree of the Lateran Council in 1063 (*Die Rechtss. zu Bol.*, p. 39). In 1080 the Ravennese Petrus Crassus addressed a legal disquisition in defence of the Emperor against Gregory VII which is highly esteemed by Fitting (p. 40), to Henry IV for use at the Council of Brixen. It is printed by Ficker, *Forschungen z. Reichs-u. Rechtsgesch. Ital.*, &c., Innsbruck, 1868, iv. 106. A slight monograph on the *Origini dello Studio ravennate* is published by Ricci, *Primordi dello St. d. Bol.*, p. 201 *sq.* Its scientific relations to Bologna are discussed by Tarlazzi, *Scuole d. dir. rom. in Rav. ed in Bol.* in *Atti e mem. della dep. d. sto. pat. per le prov. di Romagna*, Ser. III. iv. 29; Fitting, *op. cit.*, p. 38 *sq.*; Chiappelli, p. 38 *sq.*; Ficker, *op. cit.*, vol. i, Abth. i, p. 104 *sq.* [For later discussion on this point see Kantorowicz, *op. cit.* xxx. 193–4 notes, 255–6; and Genzmer, *op. cit.*, pp. 371 *sq.*]

had been kept alive alike by its earlier connexion with the new Rome and by its later connexion with the Holy Roman Empire. At Bologna—the point of junction between the Exarchate and the Lombard territory—these traditions came into contact with the new-born political life of the Lombard cities and with that development both of professional and of scholastic law-studies which was one of the outcomes of the Lombard political activity.[1] To a large extent the revival of legal science was common to all parts of northern Italy. But in the Lombard cities the Roman law had to contend for supremacy in the schools as well as in the courts with a rival Lombard jurisprudence: it was not unnatural that the Roman law should achieve its decisive victory in the most Roman of the Lombard towns.

Enough has been said to show the baselessness of the theory that Irnerius was the first teacher of the Roman law in medieval Italy. The traditional ideas of intellectual history seem to admit of no epochs or new departures except in immediate connexion with a great discovery or a great name. As a matter of fact, Irnerius 'discovered' nothing at all. 'Revival' is a term more applicable to the life-work of Irnerius. But his true position is rather at the culmination than at the beginning of the revival. So far his position in the great movement with which his name is associated may be compared to that of Abelard in the speculative movement north of the Alps. But the pre-eminence of Irnerius in historic fame over his predecessors, his contemporaries, and his immediate followers is perhaps less due to the personal greatness of the man than was the case with Abelard. What was the exact position of Irnerius in the development of medieval jurisprudence, we shall be better able to examine when we have collected together what is known of his immediate predecessors and of his own biography. We have seen

[1] Chiappelli, p. 132 *sq.* Ficker (ii, Abth. i, p. 139) traces the rise of the School of Bologna to an 'Anwendung der longobardischen Methode auf die Behandlung der römischen Rechtsquellen'. [Schup- fer's argument against the view of Tamassia on the Byzantine nature of the pre-Irnerian glosses tends strongly in the same direction; *Atti d. R. Acc. dei Lincei*, classe di scienze morali, 1889, pp. 202–26.]

CHAP. IV, that there was a medieval jurisprudence before the rise of
§ 1. the School of Bologna: it remains to show that there was
a law-school at Bologna before Irnerius.

Bologna a   At this point it becomes important to bear in mind what
school of
rhetoric has already been said as to the close connexion subsisting in
and the
arts. the early medieval schools between legal science and general
literary culture. The earliest scholastic fame of Bologna was
that of a school of the liberal arts; and it is very probable
that in that school what may be called the juristic side of
rhetoric early began to occupy the most prominent place.
At all events, by the year A.D. 1000 Bologna was already
sufficiently famous as a studium of arts to attract Guido,
afterwards Bishop of Acqui (1035–70) to its schools from a
region as distant as the neighbourhood of Genoa.[1] In about
the third quarter of the same century we hear of another
future bishop going to Bologna as a student of the liberal
arts.[2] Even after the career of Irnerius had closed, Bologna
was still famous primarily as a school of literature: law was
only one, though here no doubt the main, element in general
education.

John of   Nothing can more strikingly illustrate the importance of
Salisbury's
allusions Bologna as a school of the liberal arts than the fact that a
to
Bologna. famous teacher of Paris should have thought it worth while
to go to Bologna to study dialectic. Yet such appears to have
been the case. In one of those autobiographical fragments
which give so peculiar an interest to his writings, John of
Salisbury tells us that he studied dialectic for two years in
'the Mount' of Ste Geneviève under Alberic and Robert of
Melun (1136–8). Later on, one of these teachers went to

---

[1] 'Ab ineunte igitur aetate Guido memoratus . . . . studiorum causa Bononiam contendit. Ubi aliquot annis non minus sanctis moribus quam litterarum disciplinis incumbens socios et aemulatores sui in utroque studii honore devicit.' *Acta Sanctorum*, Jun., i. 229. [Cf. Besta, *Opera di Irnerio*, i. 51–2.]

[2] S. Bruno, Bishop of Segni († 1123). 'Voluntate parentum se Bononiam transferens, liberalium artium doctrinae vigilem curam exhibuit.' It is added that he studied both *trivium* and *quadrivium*, and afterwards, still apparently at Bologna, 'divinae paginae propensius operam dedit'. *Acta Sanctorum*, Jul. iv. 479. He had already been instructed 'singularibus disciplinis' in a monastery.

Bologna and 'unlearned what he had taught', after which he went back to Paris and 'untaught' the same to his pupils.[1] Though the dialectic of Bologna may well have been of a more practical and legal kind than the speculative dialectic of Paris, John of Salisbury does not seem to be conscious that they were two distinct sciences. How slowly the development of technical jurisprudence threw into the shade the ancient repute of Bologna as a school of the liberal arts may also be illustrated by the fact that even in 1158 Frederick I speaks of scholars of 'various arts' being attracted to the Lombard schools from all parts.[2]

In the older law-schools of the medieval world, and particularly at Bologna, the gulf which according to our ideas separates technical and legal from general education was bridged over by the existence of the rather curious art known as *dictamen*. *Dictamen* may be comprehensively described as the art of composition. It was specially occupied with the art of letter-writing, and included not only rules for private epistolary correspondence, but also more technical rules for the compilation of official briefs or bulls and other legal documents. In an age wherein reading and writing were the accomplishments of the few, while all business transactions of any solemnity or importance were carried on in a dead language, it is obvious that the connexion between grammar and law was indefinitely closer than it is according to modern ideas.[3] *Dictamen* may be described at pleasure as

Bologna famous for dictamen.

---

[1] 'Deinde . . . adhesi magistro Alberico, qui inter ceteros opinatissimus dialecticus enitebat. . . . Sic ferme toto biennio conuersatus in monte, artis huius preceptoribus usus sum Alberico et magistro Rodberto Meludensi . . . postea unus eorum, profectus Bononiam, dedidicit quod docuerat; siquidem et reversus dedocuit. An melius, iudicent qui ante et postea audierunt.' *Metalogicon*, lib. ii, c. 10 [ed. Webb, pp. 78, 79].

[2] See below, p. 143. As late as 1162 Bolognese law is still looked on as a department of general

'literary studies': 'Pollebat equidem tunc Bononia in litteralibus studiis pre cunctis Ytalie civitatibus quatuor legum columpnis inter ceteros magnifice radiantibus.' Acerbi Morenae *Continuatio*, &c. (*M.G.H., Scriptores*, xviii. 639.) [Cf. the reference by a poet, who wrote of the deeds of Frederick I in Italy, to Bologna as a centre to which scholars of *variae artes* flocked from all parts, in Monaci, *Gesta di Federico I in Italia*, Rome, 1887, p. 20.]

[3] By the Bologna City Statutes the 'Consules artis tabellionatus'

CHAP. IV, a branch of grammar or as a branch of law. For this art of
§ 1. *dictamen* Bologna possessed a special notoriety; the school
of *dictamen* was the cradle of the special school of law. That
Irnerius himself wrote a notarial form-book, as Sarti says,
cannot be accepted.[1] We possess a work entitled *Rationes
dictandi* written by the Bolognese Canon Hugo *c.* 1123.[2]
But the most famous Bolognese master of rhetoric and
dictamen was Buoncompagno, who lived as late as the
beginning of the thirteenth century. The fact that in 1215
his *Rhetorica Antiqua* was solemnly read before the professors
and students of canon and civil law[3] shows at once the

are to examine candidates for the
office of notary 'qualiter (sciunt)
latinare et dictare'. Frati, ii. 185,
188.

[1] Sarti, I. ii. 505.

[2] Edited by Rockinger in *Quellen
und Erörterungen zur bayerischen
und deutschen Geschichte*, ix. 49–94.
It is noteworthy that in the specimen letters which are given by the
writer there are allusions to the
scholastic fame of Bologna for
philosophy, medicine, and *dictamen*, none to the special teaching
of law.

[3] Sarti, I. ii. 602; Rockinger,
Ueber die ars dictandi in Italiam
(*Sitzungsberichte d. bayerisch. Akad.
zu München*, 1861, p. 134 *sq.*). The
Cedrus or treatise on *notaria* is
printed by Rockinger in *Quellen*,
&c., ix. 121 *sq.* It is observable as
we look through these treatises that
they become increasingly technical
in the later Middle Ages. Before
the middle of the thirteenth century *notaria* had become a distinct
art or faculty: Rolandino de'
Passeggeri, whose *Summa Notariae*
became the text-book of the art,
successfully asserted the monopoly
of the citizens to the right of teaching it in Bologna [see the agreement
of 1284 in Sarti, ii (ed. 1896), 205,
206]. According to Sarti (I. ii.
505–6), there were regular graduations in *notaria*. The notaries

formed a corpus or guild in the
days of Odofredus. Instruction in
notaria included the elements of
law, e.g. the institutes (*ibid.*).
[Cf. Manacorda, ii. 274–5; H.
Bresslau, *Handbuch der Urkundenlehre*, ed. 1912, i. 618–31, for the
Italian notaries. On the whole
question of the *ars dictaminis* in
Italy it is sufficient to refer to the
bibliography noted in Haskins,
Studies in Mediaeval Culture, pp.
2–8, *passim*, and his essay on the
early *artes dictandi* in Italy (*ibid.*,
pp. 170–92). The works of K.
Sutter and A. Gaudenzi on Buoncompagno should especially be
studied. It should not be overlooked that the *ars dictandi* acquired
such great importance in the twelfth
and thirteenth centuries as a preparation for the political position
acquired by many jurists and
notaries, i.e. as a training for public
life, the composition of state papers
and manifestoes (these involved the
use of the *cursus* or rhythmical
prose according to fixed rules) and
public speaking. See F. Novati,
Freschi e minii del dugento, Milan,
1908, pp. 299–308. As regards
the notarial art, the *societas* of
notaries was well established when
Ranieri of Perugia wrote his *ars
notaria* at its instance before 1218.
See his prologue in *Bibliotheca
Iuridica Medii Aevi*, ed. Gaudenzi,

importance attached to the art and the close connexion which
still subsisted between this branch of the old comprehensive
rhetoric and the rising professional school of law.

The principal source of the once universally accepted Pepo.
view of Irnerius as the sole originator of the law-revival at
Bologna is a celebrated passage of Odofredus in which he
speaks of Irnerius as the 'first who taught in that city'. Yet
Odofredus himself has preserved to us the name of one of
Irnerius's predecessors, Pepo, adding, however, that 'whatever
his knowledge may have been, he was a man of no name'.[1]

ii. 27. From the end of the eleventh century teachers of *dictamen* gave some instruction in the cognate art of *notaria*. The work of Irnerius may have been written when he was still a teacher of grammar; although in the later twelfth century *notaria* was probably a branch of law, the connexion with arts was never lost. Buoncompagno shows a fair knowledge of law, but his notarial works approach the subject mainly from the point of view of a *dictator*, and he was a famous *dictator* in Bologna and elsewhere from 1191 till after 1235. Rolandino of Padua, who became a notary, graduated in grammar in 1221 (see below, p. 147, n. 1). In the fourteenth century *notaria* seems to have been absorbed in arts, though doctors and students of the subject are still recognized in the Statutes of 1405. The golden days of *notaria* as a separate art or faculty were in the thirteenth century, owing to the work and teaching of Ranieri, whose *ars notaria* (written before 1218, and probably 1213–16) is a practical treatise of a legal character, and his successors Rolandino de' Passeggeri and Salathiel. An extant deed of sale, printed by Gaudenzi, was drawn up by Ramieri 'in scolis meis notarii iuris'; and Salathiel is styled 'doctor artis notarie' in a document of 1249 (*Chartul.* i. 55). It should

be noted that Salathiel in his *summa* refers to the celebrated jurist Odofredus as 'dominus meus'. In 1303, on the other hand, Giovanni di Bonandrea, a notary and head of the chancery of the commune, was, at the instance of the Rector, appointed lecturer in rhetoric (G. Zaccagnini in *Studi e memorie*, v. 151). Useful information may be found in Gaudenzi's article on the *Dettatori* in the *Bullettino*, vol. xiv; cf. the *Giornale storico della letteratura italiana*, 1915, vol. lxvi. For Salathiel cf. L. Sighinolfi in *Studi e memorie*, iv (1920), 67–149; for Giovanni di Bonandrea see Zaccagnini's article, *ibid.* v (1920), 147–204, which contains valuable information on the whole subject. Zaccagnini prints documents regarding the employment of *repetitores* (see below, p. 249) by doctors of *notaria*. We owe some of the substance of this note to Miss Helen Briggs.]

[1] 'Signori, Dominus Yrnerius qui fuit apud nos lucerna iuris, id est primus qui docuit in civitate ista, nam primo cepit studium esse in civitate ista in artibus: et cum studium esset destructum Rome, libri legales fuerunt deportati ad civitatem Ravenne, et de Ravenna ad civitatem istam. Quidam Dominus Pepo cepit auctoritate ṣua legere in legibus; tamen quidquid fuerit de scientia sua, nullius nominis fuit.

CHAP. IV,
§ I.

This contemptuous judgement of Odofredus is, however, hardly borne out by the scanty additional notices of Pepo which have come down to us.[1] One of the documents in which he appears as a 'legis doctor' and assessor to a feudal court[2] is said to exhibit as compared with others of the same or earlier dates a very superior legal skill and knowledge.[3] It is said that this is the earliest medieval document (A.D. 1076) in which the Digest is expressly cited as the ground of a legal decision,[4] and, if that be the case, it may reasonably be inferred that the revived study of the Digest which characterized the Bologna school dates not from Irnerius but from Pepo. Pepo is the only doctor of law who can be positively proved to have taught at Bologna, though allusions to other 'legis doctores' in Bolognese documents of about the same period may, or may not, be interpreted of actual teachers.[5]

His use of the Digest.

Sed Dominus Yr., dum doceret in artibus in civitate ista, cum fuerunt deportati libri legales, cepit per se studere in libris nostris, et studendo cepit docere in legibus, et ipse fuit maximi nominis; et fuit primus illuminator scientie nostre; et quia primus fuit qui fecit glossas in libris nostris, vocamus eum lucernam iuris.' Odofredus, in l. *Ius Civile*, Dig. Vet. *De iustitia et iure* (1550, i, f. 7).

[1] [Fitting, 'Pepo zu Bologna', in *Ztschr. d. Sav.-Stift.*, Röm. Abth. xxiii (1902), 31 *sqq*. Kantorowicz, *ibid*. xxxi. 29–34, throws doubt on the relevance of the 'scanty notices' of Pepo, and argues, against Fitting and Gaudenzi, that really nothing is known about Pepo.]

[2] 'In presentia Nordilli missi domine beatricis ductricis et marchionissae et iohannis uice comitis . . . in iudicio cum eis residentibus guillielmo iudice et pepone legis doctore', &c. Savioli, I. ii. 123; Ficker, *op. cit*. iv. 99; Ricci, No. iii; Muratori, *Ant. It*. iii, c. 889. Cf. Fitting, *Die Rechtssch. zu Bol.*, p. 84.

[3] What strikes the lay reader is the superiority of the Latinity to that of some other of the documents published by Ricci, which (if properly transcribed) are full of outrageous grammatical blunders such as are quite unparalleled in any legal documents of the later Middle Age which are known to me—another illustration of the fact that the 'revival of Roman law' was merely one side of a revival of general education and culture.

[4] 'His peractis supradictus Nordillus, predicte domine Beatricis missus, lege digestorum libris inserta considerata per quam copiam magistratus non habentibus restitutionem in integrum pretor pollicetur, restituit in integrum ecclesiam et monasterium sancti Michaelis,' &c.

[5] The earliest published by Ricci is a deed of 1067, witnessed by 'Albertus legis doctor' (Ricci, No. i). An 'Iginulfus legis doctor' occurs in *op. cit.*, No. iv. But Savigny (c. vi, § 136) warns us against inferring the existence of a law school from the mention of

The above-cited passage and one or two digressions in the garrulous Odofredus, together with a few allusions in documents or chronicles, constitute the whole of our authorities for the life and work of Irnerius. The one fact about his personal history which Odofredus tells us is that he was a master of the liberal arts,[1] and this is completely in accordance with all that we know of the character of his teaching and of the state of legal education at the time. Odofredus goes on to tell us that 'when the books of law were brought from Ravenna, he began to study in them by himself, and by studying to teach the laws, and he was a man of the greatest renown'. The literal truth of this account is quite out of the question. It is impossible to suppose that there were no law-texts at Bologna before the time of Irnerius. Indeed, Odofredus refutes himself, for he admits that before Irnerius a 'certain *dominus* Pepo began by his own authority to lecture in the laws'. If therefore there be any truth in this story of the importation of law-books from Ravenna, it must have taken place in the time of Pepo and not in that of Irnerius; and it is quite possible that the Digest at least may have been first introduced into Bologna from Ravenna in the time of Pepo.[2]

---

legis doctores, an expression which is sometimes a mere synonym of *iudex* or *causidicus.* This principle, not always sufficiently borne in mind by later inquirers, is unquestionably true of the earlier period, but it is not quite so clear of this period. [See also Kantorowicz, *op. cit.* xxxi. 20 *sqq.*, on the so-called pre-Irnerian doctors.]

[1] 'Et debetis scire vos, domini, sicut nos fuimus instructi a nostris maioribus, quod dominus Yr. fuit primus qui fuit ausus dirigere cor suum ad L. istam. Nam dominus Yr. erat magister in artibus, et studium fuit Ravenne, et collapsa ea fuit studium Bononie. Et dominus Yr. studuit per se sicut potuit; postea cepit docere in iure civili et ipse fecit primum formularium,

i.e. librum omnium instrumentorum: scripsit instrumentum emphyteuticum.' Odofred. in Codicem, *De SS. Eccl.* Auth. *Qui res* (iii, f. 17).

[2] It has indeed been established by the critical investigations of Mommsen that the texts of the Digest which were current in the Schools of Bologna were all derived from a descendant of the celebrated Pisa MS. which the later tradition supposed to have been captured at Amalfi. This descendant was corrected from an independent source. (*Digestorum Libri,* Praef., Berlin, 1870, p. lxiv *sq.*). [See Jolowicz, *Historical Introduction to the Study of Roman Law,* Cambridge, 1932, pp. 497 *sq.*]

CHAP. IV,
§ 1.
Extent of
Irnerius's
originality.

There is great probability in Odofredus's view that Irnerius was to a certain extent self-taught. It cannot, indeed, for a moment be supposed that Irnerius derived no assistance from any of those earlier law-books or glosses of which we have already spoken. In the scanty Irnerian glosses which have come down to us occur distinct allusions to the opinions previously expressed and to standing questions habitually discussed by his predecessors or contemporaries. If he had not heard of these discussions in the schools, he must have met them in books. The literary or grammatical character of the glosses ascribed to Irnerius makes it quite probable that his legal knowledge was originally the acquisition of a scholar without practical training or legal education beyond what was obtained by every young Italian of his time in the schools of the liberal arts;[1] the notion that he was as much without predecessors and without assistance in his legal studies as the Western scholar dealing with a newly discovered language, is only a part of the general misconception of an uncritical generation to which the history even of its own school before Irnerius was rapidly becoming a blank relieved only by a few flashes of confused and incoherent tradition.

Reasons
for
growth of
Bolognese
school.

When all deductions are made from the exaggerated position accorded by a later age to the traditional founder of the Bolognese school, there can be no doubt of the importance of the epoch which is associated with his name. Unquestionably it was his lectures that first raised Bologna to European fame. Can we in any way explain this sudden

---

[1] This is illustrated by the historically worthless story that Irnerius was led to the study of the civil law by a dispute as to the meaning of the word *as*. 'Nonne duo passeres asse veneunt? propter quod verbum venit Bonon. studium civile, sicut audivi a domino meo.' Hostiensis (Henricus de Segusia) *Comment. in Decretalium libros*, Venet. 1581, *De Testamentis*, iii, f. 73. Cf. also the remark of Odofredus: 'Or, segnori, plura non essent dicenda super lege ista, Dominus tamen Ir., qui laicus fuit, et magister fuit in civitate ista in legibus, antequam doceret in legibus, fecit unam glosam sophisticam, que est obscurior quam sit textus.' *In Codicem* l. ult. *de in int. rest. min.* (Lyons, 1550, iii, f. 101 *b*). So Odofredus in Dig. Vet. *De iustitia et iure*, L. *Manumissiones*: 'hic glossat dominus Yr. elegantissimis verbis' (i, f. 7 *a*). [But see above, p. 103, n. 2.]

emergence of Bologna into the position not merely of a great school of law but of *the* school of law *par excellence*? We have already dwelt upon the political and intellectual conditions which account for a great revival of the study of Roman law in northern Italy; can we account for its concentration in the city of Bologna? Much influence must of course be accorded to the genius of the man. The less it is admitted that there was any new departure involved in the subject or the method of his lectures, the more must they have owed their attractiveness to their own intrinsic merits. The more emphatically it is denied that his undoubtedly valuable glosses mark an entirely new beginning in the development of medieval law-literature, the more evident is it that Irnerius must have possessed powers as a teacher of which these scanty remains fail to give us any adequate idea. But the greatest of teachers is unable to raise a school even to temporary, much less to permanent, renown unless he appears at the right place and at the right moment—unless a concurrence of favourable circumstances second the personal attraction of the individual intellect. Even the career of Abelard was, as we have seen, only one of the causes which concurred to make Paris the intellectual centre of northern Europe; and Irnerius, on the most favourable estimate, does not belong to the same intellectual rank as Abelard. A passage of the chronicler, Burchard of Ursperg, supplies us with an important clue towards the solution of the problem. After speaking of the work of Gratian, he tells us that 'at the same time *dominus* Irnerius at the request of the Countess Matilda renewed the books of the laws, which had long been neglected, and, in accordance with the manner in which they had been compiled by the Emperor Justinian of divine memory, arranged them in divisions, adding perchance between the lines a few words here and there'.[1]

CHAP. IV, § 1.

Patronage of Matilda.

[1] 'Eisdem quoque temporibus dominus Wernerius libros legum, qui dudum neglecti fuerant nec quisquam in eis studuerat, ad petitionem Mathildae comitissae renovavit: et secundum quod olim a divae recordationis imperatore Iustiniano compilati fuerant, paucis forte verbis alicubi interpositis, eos distinxit, in quibus continentur instituta,' &c. *Abb. Ursperg. Chron.* (*M.G.H., Scriptores*, xxiii. 342).

The value to be assigned to a tradition of this kind, revealed to us nearly a century after the death of the persons to whom it relates, must depend entirely upon its accordance or non-accordance with the probabilities of the case and the facts known to us on more reliable evidence. Here there is considerable probability in favour of the chronicler's statement. The notion that Matilda founded the School of Bologna, in the sense in which later Emperors or Kings founded universities, is of course on the face of it untenable. It has grown largely no doubt out of this passage, but it is not really supported by its contents. There is nothing improbable in the statement that Matilda encouraged a Bologna master, already of some repute as a scholar and a teacher of the liberal arts, to apply himself to the study and editing of the Roman law-texts. And there were political reasons which sufficiently account for Matilda's wish to establish or foster a law-school at Bologna. Hitherto, as we have seen, Ravenna had been the centre of Italian jurisprudence: Ravennese jurists appear from the documents to have been constantly employed as advocates or assessors in the Italian law-courts. It is just after the accession of Matilda in 1075 that we first begin to meet the names of Bolognese doctors in Tuscan deeds; and after 1113 the Ravennese names disappear altogether.[1] Ravenna, the seat of the imperial jurisprudence, the inheritor of so many imperial traditions, warmly embraced the side of Henry IV in the great conflict with the Papacy; when a council was assembled at Brescia in 1080 for the election of an anti-Pope, it was in the Archbishop of Ravenna that the required anti-papal ecclesiastic was found. Hence it is easy to conceive that Matilda was anxious to enlist in her service a body of lawyers less unfavourable to the papal claims than the *causidici* of Ravenna; and the cause of Matilda was the cause of Italian liberty. The ultimate result of the anti-papal and anti-national attitude of Ravenna in this encounter was the ruin of its school of law. At that moment Bologna was ready to step into the vacant place; though the Bolognese doctors were not permanently faithful to the papal

[1] Fitting, *Die Rechtssch. zu Bol.*, p. 99 *sq.*

cause. If any further explanation is wanted for the super-session of Ravenna by Bologna as the head-quarters of Italian jurisprudence, it may be found in the final extinction of any schools there may have been at Rome by the Norman conquest of 1084, in the neighbourhood of Bologna to Ravenna, and its immense superiority in accessibility and position to the isolated and marsh-girt city on the Adriatic coastland. Bologna lay, as a forged university charter correctly states, 'at the intersection of four provinces—Lombardy, the March of Verona, the Romandiola, and Tuscany'.[1] To this day it is the point at which converge all the great lines of communication between the northern entrances to Italy and its centre: in that age there was no place better situated for a meeting-place between the students of Italy and students from beyond the Alps.

The facts and dates of Irnerius's life are all quite in accordance with the chronicler's statement as to his connexion with Matilda. Though the name (variously spelt as Irnerius, Yrnerius, Gernerius, Warnerius, Wernerius, Varnerius, Guarnerius or Garnerius[2]) is Teutonic, there is no reason to doubt the common account that he was a Bolognese citizen by birth.[3] His name first occurs among the *causidici* in a *placitum* of the Countess Matilda relating to property at Ferrara in 1113,[4] and as a *iudex* in various documents of the same kind under the Emperor Henry V ranging from 1116 to 1125. It was argued by Savigny that since Irnerius was in the imperial service from 1116 up to the time at which his name disappears from the documents, his work as a teacher must have been over before the beginning of that period. This contention can hardly be admitted, since it assumes that the position of a teacher was inconsistent with occasional employment of a judicial character.[5] A more important

Date of Irnerius's teaching.

---

[1] Muratori, *Ant. It.* iii, c. 22.

[2] Fitting, *Die Rechtssch. zu Bol.*, p. 89; documents in Ricci.

[3] This is expressly stated. He is habitually described as 'de Bononia' or 'Bononiensis'.

[4] 'Causidici quoque Varnerius de Bononia, Lambertus, et Alber-tus seu (*sic*) amicus.' Document in Savioli, I. ii. 151; Ricci, No. xvii; see also Ricci, Nos. xx–v, xxvii, xxviii, xxxi, xxxiv.

[5] Even non-legal teachers were often in request as assistants in legal business: e.g. 'Albertus gramaticus de sancto marino' is asso-

CHAP. IV, reason for throwing back the teaching of Irnerius to the very
§ 1.   beginning of the twelfth century or the end of the eleventh
is the early occurrence of the epithet 'learned' as applied to
Bologna and its law school. Thus in 1119 an anonymous
poet writes on the capture of Como:

Docta suas secum duxit Bononia leges.[1]

Again, with reference to the year 1127 the same poet has the
line:

Docta Bononia venit et huc cum legibus una.[2]

It should be observed, however, that there is here no allusion
to professorial teaching, but only to a reputation for legal
learning; and it is certain that whether or not they were
teachers, whether or not they had attended lectures on law,
the reputation of the Bologna lawyers was not in the first
instance created by Irnerius. While it is probable that he
had begun his work before the beginning of the century, even
this is not certain: still less is there any positive evidence for
placing the beginning of his career as a law teacher as early
as 1088—the year assumed by the octo-centenary celebration at Bologna.

It should also be mentioned that though the name of Irnerius
does not occur in the documents after 1125, it is probable
that he lived, and perhaps taught, to a somewhat later date.
The Ursperg chronicle speaks of him under the reign of
Lothair III (1125–38).[3] But the most weighty reason for
supposing that the scholastic career of Irnerius did not close
when he entered the service of the Emperor is that only on
that supposition can the 'Four Doctors' who come next to

---

ciated with the *causidici* in 1113
(Ricci, No. xviii).

[1] Muratori, *Ital. SS.* v. 418,
l. 211.

[2] *Ibid.*, p. 453, l. 1848. Early
Bologna coins have the legend
BONONIA MATER STUDIORUM, and
somewhat later BONONIA DOCET:
the ancient Seal of the City has the
words PETRUS UBIQUE PATER LE-
GUMQUE BONONIA MATER. Sarti
(1888), i. i. 10.

[3] *M.G.H., Scriptores*, xxiii. 342.

The work of Burchard of Ursperg
(† 1226) is believed to rest on the
earlier work of John of Cremona
(Fitting, *loc. cit.*, p. 96). On the
other hand, Robert of Torigni
speaks of 'Lanfrancus Papiensis et
Garnerius socius eius' ad an. 1032!
(*Scriptores*, vi. 478.) But so gross a
blunder can hardly count for much.
[For the life of Irnerius see
E. Besta, *L'opera d'Irnerio*, Turin,
1896, i. 40–76.]

Irnerius in the succession of great Bologna jurists have been CHAP. IV, his actual pupils, as they are stated to have been by a chron- § 1. icler of the next generation.[1] On the whole, then, it would appear that the teaching of Irnerius may be assigned roughly to the period 1100–30.

So far we have still left unmentioned the most striking Irnerius incident in the life of Irnerius which has come down to us. at Rome. On the election of Gelasius II in 1118 we find 'Master Irnerius of Bologna and many lawyers' taking a prominent part in the election of the anti-Pope Gregory VIII. They are represented by a contemporary chronicler as 'summoning the Roman people to the election of a Pope', while 'a certain reader in the pulpit of S. Peter's by a prolix lecture expounded the decrees relating to the substitution of a Pope'.[2] This is the one piece of contemporary testimony which really justifies the personal importance traditionally ascribed to the reputed founder of the School of Bologna. Whatever was the exact nature of his connexion with the Countess Matilda, this notice testifies to the completeness of his conversion to the imperial cause. It would be vain to speculate as to the relative shares which the ideas embodied in the imperial jurisprudence and the prizes of the imperial service had exercised upon the mind of the jurists. Certain it is that the early Bologna doctors were all staunch imperialists; and the patronage of the Emperors was at least an element in promoting the

---

[1] Otto Morena, ad an. 1158 (*M.G.H.*, *Scriptores*, xviii. 607). Moreover, Irnerius's fame would be hard to account for if he did not form a single teacher of repute among those who brought the School to the zenith of its fame. Of the illustrious 'four', Bulgarus died in 1166, Martinus before 1166, Jacobus in 1178, Hugo *c.* 1168. Fitting, *loc. cit.*, p. 103. [See Besta, i. 73–6. Besta's statement that Martinus refers to Irnerius as his master is erroneous; also, for Meijers in *Atti del Congresso internazionale di Diritto Romano*, (1934) i, 436 *sqq.*, has shown that the *Lectura*, on

which the evidence is based, was not written by Martin.]

[2] 'Magister Guarnerius de Bononia, et plures legis periti populum Romanum ad eligendum Papam convenit, et quidam expeditus lector in pulpito S. Petri per prolixam lectionem decreta Pontificum de substituendo Papa explicavit. Quibus perlectis et explicatis totus populus elegit in Papam quendam Episcopum Hispaniae qui ibi aderat cum Imperatore.' Landolfo di S. Paolo, 'Hist. Mediolanensis' (*M.G.H.*, *Scriptores*, xx. 40). [Cf. Besta, i. 66–72.]

CHAP. IV, growth and prosperity of the school. If such patronage may
§ 1. not have done much to increase the prestige of the school in
Italy, it may well have had its influence in attracting that
swarm of German students who had the largest share in
raising Bologna from the position of an Italian to that of a
European or cosmopolitan seat of learning.[1]

The We are now perhaps in a position to estimate the nature
Irnerian of the epoch in the history of medieval jurisprudence and
epoch, of medieval education which is represented by the name of
how far a
new de- of medieval education which is represented by the name of
parture. Irnerius. Most of the titles to fame traditionally claimed for
him rest, as we have seen, upon no historical basis. He was
not the rediscoverer of the Roman law, not even of the
Pandects. He was not the first medieval teacher of law, even
at Bologna. He was not the first of the glossators, possibly
not the first even of the Bolognese glossators. There is,
indeed, hardly any one respect in which Irnerius marks an
absolute new departure.

How, then, does the rise of the Bologna school constitute
an epoch? In attempting to answer the question it must be
premised that some of the changes which the Irnerian epoch
introduced began a generation before Irnerius himself, and
some were probably not completed till at least a generation
after him.

Study of (1) In the first place the rise of the School of Bologna is
Digest. marked by an increased prominence of the Digest—that is
to say, of far the bulkiest, most elaborate and most important
section of the *Corpus Iuris*. The Digest was practically
unknown before the time of Pepo.[2] Pepo was certainly

---

[1] Before the close of the thirteenth century (*c.* 1298) we find a
chronicler speaking of 'lo Studio
Bolognese, poco avanti in quella
città per Henrico instituito'. Rico-
bald. Ferrar. (Muratori, *Scriptores*,
ix. 371). There is probably a confusion between Henry IV and
Henry V.

[2] Thus it appears that so eminent
a canonist as Ivo of Chartres derived his extracts from the Pandects
only from an epitome, published by

Conrat from a British Museum
manuscript (*Der Pandekten- und
Institutionenauszug der brittischen
Dekretensammlung Quelle des Ivo*,
Berlin, 1887). Fitting (*loc. cit.*, p. 57)
refers to Mommsen's Preface to the
Digest (Berlin, 1868) as evidence
of the existence of 'Vorbolognesi-
schen Glossen' on the Digest; but
Mommsen himself (p. lxviii) places
these glosses (which appear to consist entirely in various readings),
'aut decimo aut quod magis credi-

acquainted with the 'Old Digest', but we do not know that the whole of that work was known at Bologna in his time; and the peculiar division of the Pandects into the Old and the New Digest with the detached parts known as the *Infortiatum* and the *Tres Partes* make it tolerably certain that they must have been introduced into the schools of Bologna in successive instalments.[1] It is quite probable therefore that the remaining parts of the Digest may have been first introduced by Irnerius.[2] The reputed founder of the Bologna school may therefore have been the first lecturer upon the *whole* Digest, and he may even have been the first glossator on any portion of it. What this change implies will be understood when it is remembered that the Institutes were a mere introductory text-book and the Code a compilation of imperial edicts—for the most part late imperial edicts—while the Digest was composed of the *responsa* of the jurists, and chiefly of the great classical jurists who made Roman law what it was. Without the Digest the study of Roman law was in a

derim undecimo saeculo aetate Irneriana'. The evidence which Fitting produces to show that the Digest was not unknown between the time of Gregory the Great and the middle of the eleventh century is of a very slender description. (See his art. in *Zeitschrift der Savigny-Stiftung*, Röm. Abth. vi. 112, 113.) [The early collections of canon law illustrate the use increasingly made of the Code and Institutes from the ninth century onwards. The *Authenticum* displaced the *Epitome Juliani*, by which the *novellae* had been known, in the middle of the eleventh century. See P. Fournier and G. le Bras, *Histoire des collections canoniques en Occident* (Paris, 1931–2), i. 118, 238; ii. 13, 30, 78 (for Ivo of Chartres). On the effects of the rediscovery of the Pandects see Fournier in the *Revue historique de droit français et étranger*, xli (1917), 129–80.]

[1] As Odofredus declares, In

Infort. *ad L. Falcidiam* (ii, f. 83).

[2] Fitting (*Die Rechtssch. zu Bol.*, pp. 94, 95) thinks 'dass sich Irnerius einzelne Stücke der Justinianischen Gesetzgebung, wie etwa das Infortiatum, erst aus Ravenna verschafft, und dass so vielleicht in der Erzählung des Odofredus doch ein Körnchen Wahrheit steckt'. Chiappelli (pp. 40–56) collects allusions to earlier comments on the Codex, Dig. Vetus and Dig. Nov., but there is only one not very convincing instance from the Dig. Vetus (p. 54), and the passages cited in the Dig. Nov. do not really prove the existence of pre-Irnerian glosses. He also notices (p. 96) that the *notulae*—short expository, grammatical or critical remarks—of the primitive type embedded in the Accursian gloss are found more frequently in the Institutes and Code than in the Pandects, and more frequently in the Dig. Vet. than in the Dig. Nov.

CHAP. IV,
§ 1.

worse position than the study of Aristotle when he was known only from the *Organon*, or of Plato when he was known only from the *Phaedo* and the *Timaeus*. The Digest alone adequately revealed the *spirit* of Roman law.[1]

A close, more technical and more professional study of texts.

(2) The emphasis now laid upon the Digest is only a detail in a more important change introduced into the spirit of medieval jurisprudence by the Bologna school. We have already insisted upon the literary character of the earlier legal literature. From another point of view it might be styled philosophical. In many of the countries in which Roman law was studied, it must be remembered that its enactments were merely called in to fill up gaps left by local laws or customs, to explain and to supplement in a more scientific and philosophical manner the inadequate provisions of the non-Roman or half-Roman codes or customs of the barbarian kingdoms.[2] At times, indeed, the Roman law-texts were studied almost purely as a literary exercise. Even where, as among the romanized inhabitants of the Italian cities, the old Roman law was still theoretically current in its integrity, it was looked upon to a large extent as a kind of higher natural law which owed its authority as much to its intrinsic reasonableness as to its express enactment. The very conflict of laws which in the Dark Ages prevailed among the mixed populations of the Lombard towns (where every one was supposed to be judged according to the law of his own race), tended to bestow this universal character upon the law which, by virtue largely of its intrinsic superiority, was gradually asserting its supremacy over all rival systems. Hence it was natural that the law-writers and law-teachers should be

[1] [Kantorowicz goes much farther than Fitting and most other scholars. He depreciates the alleged importance of Ravenna, and makes Irnerius responsible for the Bologna text of the Digest, derived indirectly from the Pisa MS. He tries to prove that the new division of the *Corpus Iuris* was made about 1080 by the scribe of the MS. on which Irnerius worked; *op. cit.*, especially xxx. 218, xxxi. 50 *sqq.* A convenient summary of the more conservative view and of the nature of the Bologna text and arrangement will be found in the *Cambridge Medieval History*, v. 734–6.]

[2] A Visigothic law (cited by Fitting) declares: 'Alienae gentis legibus ad exercitium utilitatis imbrui et permittimus et optamus; ad negotiorum vero discussionem et resultamus et prohibemus.' (*Rec. des historiens de France*, iv. 294.)

more anxious to extract from the texts before them a principle which seemed to accord with their ideas of equity and
natural justice than to interpret, in the spirit of the exegete
or the mere practitioner, the actual letter of the texts: the
doctors of the early Middle Age often wrote rather as
publicists, jurists, legislators than as mere lawyers; or, if they
wrote as lawyers, they wrote in the spirit of the old jurisconsults of the time when the *Responsa prudentum* were looked
upon as actual sources of law. At times they venture explicitly
to criticize the provisions of the code before them, and to
substitute rules of their own, as though fully on a level in
point of authority with the rule which they so superciliously
set aside. From the point of view of the jurist, the Irnerian
epoch represents the beginning of a more close, critical and
textual[1]—and at the same time more professional—study
of the original sources of the law.

(3) From the point of view of the historian of education, the epoch introduced by Irnerius marks the beginning of the systematic study of the whole *Corpus Iuris Civilis* as the regular curriculum of an ordinary legal education. Hitherto the ordinary text-books had been in parts of Europe the West-Gothic *Breviarium*, elsewhere the Institutes, together with the compilations or introductions composed by the older medieval teachers. It was at Bologna in all probability for the first time that lectures were delivered on all parts of the *Corpus*, and that attendance at such a complete course of lectures became the indispensable equipment of a properly trained civilian. The sections into which the law-texts are still divided are expressly ascribed to Irnerius by Odofredus.[2] How far the system of legal education—the division of lectures into ordinary and extraordinary, the 'repetitions', the disputations, and the examinations—which we find in operation in the later University of Bologna may be traced

Organization of legal study.

---

[1] This return to the letter of the imperial decrees no doubt tended to bring into prominence the source of their authority and so to empha-size the legislative prerogatives of the Roman Emperor, whether we regard this attachment of the Bologna school to the *littera scripta* as the cause or the effect of its imperialist proclivities.

[2] See above, p. 115 n., and below, p. 206.

CHAP. IV, back to the age of Irnerius, we have no materials for esti-
§ 1. mating. The examinations and the ceremonial of graduation
are in all probability not earlier than the generation of
Irnerius's disciples. But at all events we may safely declare
that the organization of legal education which extended itself
in time to all the universities of Europe and which has to a
large extent descended to modern universities, is the work
of the early School of Bologna and that this work of organization was begun by Irnerius.

(4) We are merely describing another side of the same
change when we trace back to Irnerius and his immediate
followers the differentiation of law-studies and law-students
from the faculty of the liberal arts.

Separation   If the whole *Corpus Iuris* was to be taught, it required the
of law
from undivided attention of its students; henceforth the student of
general
education. law had no leisure for other studies, and the student of arts
no longer ventured to meddle with so vast and so technical
a subject until mere school-education was over. There may,
indeed, have been special schools at which law was taught by
distinct teachers at such places as Pavia and Ravenna before
the rise of the Bologna school. But from this time the
distinction of the teachers and the students of law from other
teachers and students came to be much more sharply drawn
and extended itself to all universities and schools at which
law was taught at all. The change was not indeed quite complete in the time of Irnerius. In his day *dictamen* was still a
prominent element in a legal education, and *dictamen* included the art of literary composition as well as the technical
art of the notary. Even the notes of the 'glossators' who
followed Irnerius still retained something of the grammatical
or literary character which marked the expositions of the
founder of their school. But in the main it is true that from
the time of Irnerius law ceases to be a branch of rhetoric and
therefore an element in a liberal education; it becomes a
purely professional study for a special class of professional
students.

A new   (5) One consequence of this change—though we have little
class of
students. direct evidence on the subject—was no doubt the growth of

a class of students older and more independent than the students of the earlier Middle Age. In this fact—when taken in connexion with the lay character and higher social position already characteristic of the Italian student—we may trace the germ of that most characteristic institution of Bologna, the student-university. It was from the age of Irnerius, or at least very early in the century ushered in by his teaching, that men of mature age—men of good birth and good position—beneficed and dignified ecclesiastics[1] or sons of nobles—flocked from the remotest parts of Europe to the lecture-rooms of Bologna. Connected with this change in the position of the law-students was the rise of the law-doctor in southern Europe to a position of marked superiority to that of all other masters. Legal knowledge possessed then, as it still possesses, a political and commercial value to which no purely speculative knowledge can pretend. No teachers perhaps in the whole history of education had hitherto occupied quite so high a position in public estimation as the early doctors of Bologna; their rise to this position marks an epoch not only in the evolution of the university-system but in the development of the legal profession.

[1] See for instance the *Acta Nationis Germanicae*, where on an average about half the students matriculated are beneficed ecclesiastics, the great majority of them being dignitaries or canons. It must, however, be remembered that by canon law a boy of fourteen might be a canon of a cathedral church. Exceptional instances are mentioned of very young Bolognese students, such as Baldus who held a *repetitio* at 15 (Savigny, c. lv, § 66): parallels to which might be found in the Oxford of the last generation. Phillpotts, afterwards Bishop of Exeter, entered as a scholar of Corpus at 13, and Bethell (afterwards Lord Westbury) at Wadham at 14 in spite of the Warden's objection that they 'did not receive children'. The Statutes of Florence exclude from the right of voting students under 18. On the whole it appears that a majority of law-students in Italy were not younger than modern undergraduates, while the proportion of men considerably older was very much larger. It is curious, however, that the minimum age for the doctorate was lower than that at Paris. The Paris M.A. was required to be 20 (see below, p. 462); while in Italy (though the Statutes are silent) Petrus Anchoranus (ap. Middendorp., *Acad. Celebr.*, Cologne, 1602, p. 141) lays it down that a doctor must be at least 17 and of legitimate birth.

§ 2. GRATIAN AND THE CANON LAW

CHAP. IV, On the *Origines* of the canon law I have consulted chiefly F. MAASSEN,
§ 2. *Geschichte der Quellen und der Literatur des canonischen Rechts*, Gratz,
1870; J. F. VON SCHULTE, *Geschichte der Quellen und Literatur des Canonischen Rechts*, 3 vols., Stuttgart, 1875–80; E. FRIEDBERG, *Corpus Iuris
Canonici*, Leipzig, 1878–81; SARTI, *De claris Archigymnasii Bononiensis
Professoribus*, 1889, I. ii. 317 *sq.* [In view of the publication of the great
work of Paul FOURNIER and Gabriel LE BRAS, *Histoire des collections canoniques en Occident depuis les fausses décrétales jusqu'au décret de Gratien*,
2 vols., Paris, 1931–2, it is not necessary to summarize the extensive recent
literature. The authors give full bibliographical information. Special
reference, however, should be made to GHELLINCK's book already noted
(above, p. 26) and to G. LE BRAS's forthcoming work on Gratian. Cf.
S. D'IRSAY, *op. cit.* i. 87–90.]

The forged Decretals. THE movement which is associated with the name of Gratian played as large a part in the development of the university-system as the Irnerian revival of the civil law, and was destined to exercise perhaps an even more powerful influence over the course of European affairs. Twice in the course of its onward march the papal absolutism received a powerful impulse from literature: first from the publication of the pseudo-Isidorian Decretals in the ninth century, and now again in the middle of the twelfth from the publication of the *Decretum* of Gratian. By this comparison it is not intended to place the compiler of the *Decretum* on the moral level of the Isidorian forger. Though incorporating the pseudo-Isidorian and many other spurious documents, the *Decretum* Gradual codification of the canon law. was a perfectly *bona-fide* compilation. From a very early period attempts had been made to codify the mass of conciliar canons, papal rescripts, patristic *dicta*, and enactments of Christian Emperors, from which the law of the Church had to be gleaned.[1] And in the eleventh and twelfth centuries the improved method and completeness of these compilations

[1] An account of those which survive is given by Savigny (cap. xv, § 100 *sq.*); Schulte, i. 29 *sq.*; Friedberg, i. xlii *sq.* The earlier compilations consist simply of extracts from canons or Rescripts arranged in chronological order; but as early as the ninth century they begin to be arranged under the order of subjects, and these show the influence of the civil law in their arrangement, and also contain numerous extracts from the Institutes, &c. Cf. Maassen, p. 798 *sq.*

had fully kept pace with the advance of secular jurisprudence. CHAP. IV,
Among the more important predecessors of Gratian's work §2.
may be mentioned the *Decretum* of Burchard of Worms
(1008–12), the *Collectio Canonum* of Anselm of Lucca (*c.*
1083), and the work bearing the same title by Cardinal
Deusdedit (1083–7).[1] But the most complete of all these
earlier collections were the two compilations, known respectively as the *Decretum* and the *Panormia*, ascribed to Ivo, a
pupil of Lanfranc at Bec and afterwards Bishop of Chartres[2]
(1091–1116), a city famous for its school of classical literature almost before the dawn of Parisian science. In fact, the
Decretum of Gratian, which by its superior completeness and
arrangement rapidly supplanted all rivals, is little more than
a re-editing of the materials collected by a succession of
canonists.

The *Decretum* is one of those great text-books which, The *Decre-*
appearing just at the right time and in the right place, take *tum* of Gratian.
the world by storm. For in form it must be remembered that
the *Decretum* is a text-book and not a code. Its title is a
Concordantia discordantium Canonum. While its arrangement
is more distinctly juridical than the half-theological, half-
legal compilations which had preceded it, its method (unlike
theirs) is distinctly scholastic; and so far it may be considered Its
as an attempt to do for canon law what Peter the Lombard scholastic
method.
did a little later[3] for theology proper by the publication of the
Sentences. Both works are only fresh applications of the

---

[1] The two earliest collections of
importance are (1) an anonymous
Collectio Anselmo dedicata (882–
96), and (2) the *libri duo de synoda-*
libus causis (*c.* 906) by Regino,
Abbot of Prüm. [Fournier and
le Bras give careful description of
these works and of those mentioned
in the text, and show their relation
to the general developments and
influences in the history of canon
law.]

[2] The *Panormia* was printed at
Basel in 1499, and at Louvain in
1557. The *Decretum* was printed

at Louvain in 1541 and by Fron-
teau in Ivo's works, Paris, 1647.
Both are reprinted in *Patrol. Lat.*
clxi. [The *Decretum* was compiled
about 1094, and was quickly followed by its abridgement, the
Panormia. Fournier and le Bras,
op. cit. ii. 55–114.]

[3] So Friedberg (i, col. lxxiv),
though Schulte makes Gratian use
the Sentences. Denifle dates the
Lombard's work 1145–50 (*Archiv*,
i. 611). [The dates now accepted
are 1150–2.]

CHAP. IV, method inaugurated by Abelard. The mighty influence of
§ 2. the *Sic et Non* is as palpable in the *Decretum* as in the
Sentences. Gratian's method is to present the reader with
all the authorities alleged on both sides of every disputed
question in ecclesiastical law. The most exaggerated statements of views the most opposed to those of the compiler are
produced with all the freedom and ostensible impartiality
employed by scholastic theologians in stating the arguments
of the *advocatus diaboli*. Citations from laws or writers whose
authority the compiler would have disputed are given no less
than rulings of the most unquestionable validity: it is even
maintained that Gratian did not feel bound to exclude documents which he knew to be forged; his object being simply to
present the reader with the evidence actually alleged by the
conflicting parties. The compiler's object is to extract from
the conflict of opinions the doctrine which from its superior
authority, its more recent date, or its intrinsic reasonableness,
may be taken to be the ascertained law of the Church. Sometimes the writer's opinion is indicated in express words at the
beginning or end of the citations, at others (when the case is
clear) the authorities are left to speak for themselves.[1]

A text-book, not a code. Almost from its first publication the *Decretum* sprang into
the position of a recognized text-book both in the schools and
in the ecclesiastical courts. But a text-book the *Decretum*
always remained.[2] The authority due to the opinion of

---

[1] The *Decretum* is divided into
two parts. In the first the main
outlines of the law are collected.
The second is occupied with the
discussion of *causae* or imaginary
cases, each of which gives rise to
a number of *quaestiones* which are
discussed in a thoroughly scholastic
manner. [The connexion between
the work of Gratian and preceding
movements in theology and canon
law should be studied in J. de
Ghellinck's *Le Mouvement théologique du xiie siècle* (Paris, 1914) and
the same writer's article in the
Dictionnaire de théologie catholique,
vi, cols. 1731–51. Pending the

publication of G. le Bras, *Le
Décret de Gratien*, see Fournier et
le Bras, *op. cit.* ii. 314 *sqq.*]

[2] [This statement, though true
enough, requires some qualification. The *Decretum* was part of the
Corpus Iuris Canonici, was cited
by Popes, and was re-edited and
published by papal command,
without any marked distinction
from the later official collections
of Decretals, in the sixteenth
century. See the letter of Pope
Gregory XIII of 1 July 1580,
in Friedberg's edition of the *Decretum*, cols. lxxix–lxxxi.]

Gratian himself is the authority which in our own courts is ascribed to Bracton or Coke: his own comments—the *context* as they are technically called—are appealed to in the ecclesiastical courts, either as a witness to the common law or traditional practice of the Church or as the opinion of an eminent jurist, not as itself a binding authority. The several canons or other extracts which form the substance of the book derive no authority from their insertion in the *Decretum* or their adoption by its compiler that they would not have possessed independently of such insertion or adoption. Nevertheless it must be remembered that the authority of a text-book was in the Middle Ages something of which we have very little conception. To the medieval doctor the *littera scripta* was an end of all strife not only on matters of faith but on matters of science or speculation. The authority of Aristotle in philosophy and of Hippocrates in medicine was hardly less than that of S. Paul or S. Augustine in matters of theology. In a world habituated to this reliance on authority, it is obvious what an accretion of strength was brought to the cause which its compiler represented by the appearance and universal reception of such a text-book on what had hitherto been the chaotic and ill-defined field of ecclesiastical law. That cause was, it need hardly be said, the cause of papalism against imperialism, and what in that age was practically the same thing (at least in Italy), the cause of ecclesiastical immunity against civil authority. Wherever canon law was studied at all, it had henceforth to be studied in a work which placed the decrees of the Roman Pontiffs practically on a level in point of authority with the canons of general councils or the consensus of the most venerable Fathers. Individual doctors might differ from the views of Gratian, particular States or even particular Churches might refuse to accord to the decrees of the Roman Pontiff the reception which was given to them in the courts of Rome or the schools of Bologna, but nevertheless the eventual triumph of the *Decretum* is a monument of the victory, at least within the bosom of the Church, of the ideas for which Hildebrand contended against the Emperor Henry IV and S. Thomas

CHAP. IV, against our own Henry II. The ideas of national indepen-
§ 2.
dence and royal prerogative, such as had animated so many
of the English bishops in their opposition to Anselm and
Becket, disappeared from the minds of a generation of Churchmen whose education had been based upon the *Decretum* of
Gratian.

Life of   Of Gratian himself and his life almost nothing is known.
Gratian.
He was a monk in the Camaldunensian Monastery of S. Felix
in Bologna.[1] Lest mistaken inferences should be drawn from
this fact, it may be added that there is not the slightest trace
of any school of theology or of canon law in connexion
with that or any other monastery at Bologna.[2] Although
commonly styled *magister*, Gratian was not, so far as is
known, a teacher at all, but a solitary penman. It is natural
to conjecture that he may have been among the pupils of
Date of Irnerius, but of this we know nothing. The *Decretum* is
Decretum. traditionally stated to have been published in the year 1151,
but from examination of other works which appeared before
that date, it seems to be generally agreed that the *Decretum*
was completed at least as early as 1142.[3]

Oppor-   We have said that the *Decretum* owed no small part of its
tuneness of
its appear- success to its appearance at the right time and in the right
ance.   place. In point of time it came about twenty years after the
settlement of the long feud between the Papacy and the
Empire in the matter of Investitures by the Concordat of
Worms in 1122. It was this conflict—a conflict of antagon-

---

[1] Sarti, I. i. 331. There are some
traces of an earlier residence at
Classe (Ravenna), *ibid*. 332. The
canonist Huguccio, the master of
Innocent III, was also a monk of
S. Felix, according to Sarti (I. i.
372), but his evidence does not
seem to prove the statement.

[2] How far the schools of canon
law, before their definitive differentiation from theology, were connected with the cathedral, it is
more difficult to say. Bishop Lambert in 1065 gives an endowment
to the Church in which occur the
words 'Idcirco nostros canonicos

in studiis intentos esse decrevi-
mus'. Doc. ap. Sarti, I. i. 6.

[3] Schulte, i. 48. The traditional date 1151 rests upon the
authority of a gloss. Sarti, I. ii.
336. [The date 1140 or shortly
after is now generally accepted.
See especially the articles of P.
Fournier in *Revue d'histoire et de
littérature religieuse*, iii (1898), 97–
116, 253–80. Cf. also A. Gaudenzi's
discussion of the evidence suggested by the *forma appellationis*
(c. VI, q. vi. 31) in *Studi e
memorie*, i (1907), 67 *sqq*.).]

istic ideals of human society no less than of opposing armies CHAP. IV,
—which gave so great an impetus, which imparted such § 2.
intense interest and actuality, to the legal and canonical studies
of the Irnerian epoch. The outcome of that conflict was—
for the present at least—a modified victory to the Church
party. In theory, though not always in practice, the principle
of the Concordat of Worms remained the accepted principle
as to the relations between Church and State on this fundamental point throughout the Middle Ages. Thanks to
Gratian's method of antagonistic citation, the whole history
of the controversy, as well as its eventual settlement, could
be studied by the medieval Churchman in a single work. To
prove that the *Decretum* appeared at the right place, it is only Its in-
necessary to say that it appeared at Bologna. Bologna was the due to the
centre of the Investiture controversy in so far as it represents School of
an intellectual and not a merely physical antagonism. It was Bologna.
in the Bologna jurists that both parties found their intellectual
champions. Irnerius's application to the civil law seems to
have been partially inspired by the need which the Countess
Matilda experienced of learned defenders for the cause of
the Church and of testamentary freedom: afterwards Irnerius
and other Bologna jurists are found playing a leading part
on the imperialist side. At the Diet of Worms the solution
ultimately arrived at was chiefly the work of Lambert of
Fagnano, citizen and Archdeacon of Bologna, afterwards
Pope under the title of Honorius II.[1] Another great champion of the Church's cause was teaching theology—in which
canon law was then included—in the schools of Bologna
while Gratian was working in defence of the same cause in
his laborious cloister, Roland Bandinelli, afterwards Pope
Alexander III, whose *Summa* of canon law still survives.[2]

---

[1] The importance of Lambert *Magistri Rolandi*, Innsbruck, 1874.
in this controversy is pointed out [This work, more correctly called
by Cassani, p. 41 *sq.*; cf. Sarti, i. the *Stroma Rolandi*, is a summary
ii. 636–7. [The view that the of Gratian and was written not
settlement of 1122 was chiefly the later than 1148. For its significance
work of Lambert would hardly be cf. E. Portalié's article on Alexander
accepted now; cf. Hefele-Leclercq, III in *Dict. de théologie catholique*,
v. i. 614 n.] i. i (1920), col. 712; and on his
[2] Edited by Thaner, *Die Summa* career at Bologna see Ehrle, *I più*

CHAP. IV,
§ 2.

Little as we know of the Bologna schools of this epoch, there can be no doubt that these momentous questions of constitutional law in Church and State did much, both by the intellectual stimulus which they supplied and by the practical demand for trained lawyers which they created, to raise the law-schools of Bologna to their proud pre-eminence. It is easy to understand how welcome such a composition as the *Decretum* would be to the defenders of the papal cause; and, once accepted as the recognized text-book by Bologna, the prestige of the school secured the ecumenical reception of Gratian's work.

Relation of canon to civil law.

The connexion of the canon with the civil law is almost too vast a question to be touched upon here; but a few words as to the relation between the movement represented by Irnerius and the movement represented by Gratian are imperatively called for, to explain the position which these studies occupied in relation to each other and in relation to

(1) The civil a source of the canon law.

other university faculties at Bologna and elsewhere. The connexion between the formation of the *Corpus Iuris Canonici* and the old imperial jurisprudence of Rome may be regarded from three main points of view. In the first place the civil law may be regarded as one of the actual sources of the canon law. The civil law of Rome had entered into the composition of the law of the Christian Church at every stage of its formation. Its subtle and unrecognized influence upon the forms, institutions, and organization of the Christian Church—nay, in the West, even upon the very content of her theology—dates from the earliest days of Gentile Christianity. Every growth of systematic theology—at least in the Latin half of Christendom—deepened its influence. Then, in proportion as ecclesiastical bodies acquired property and became involved in complicated secular relations with one another and with non-ecclesiastical property-owners, a knowledge of law became increasingly necessary to ecclesiastical persons. The conversion of Constantine imparted of course an immense impetus to this tendency.[1] The laws of the

antichi statuti, &c., p. lxviii, with the authorities there cited.]

[1] 'Der Begriff eines Kirchen-rechts entstand in dem Momente, wo kirchliche Normen staatliche Anerkennung fanden.' Schulte, i. 32.

Christian Emperors became laws at once of the Church and of the State; the sanction of Christian Emperors gave the force of coercive jurisdiction to the rules of the Christian Society; the increasingly legal character of the Church's internal discipline tended to introduce the forms and procedure of the secular tribunals into the administration of the Christian Society and even into the relations of the individual conscience towards God. The extension of ecclesiastical jurisdiction to large classes of civil cases tended in the same direction. The barbarian conquests promoted still farther the fusion of law and theology. In an ignorant age the bishops and clergy became, if not the sole, certainly the most learned, depositaries of Roman jurisprudence. On the principle of personal law recognized by the barbarian rulers, the clergy in Italy were as Roman citizens entitled to claim the privilege of trial by Roman law; and, throughout the Middle Ages, the Roman law was recognized as more or less applicable to the transactions and property of ecclesiastics and ecclesiastical corporations in proportion as the immunity of ecclesiastics from the jurisdiction of the civil courts was recognized at all. The combined result of all these causes was that even before the appearance of the *Decretum*, the Roman law, whether by actual embodiment in canons or by practical recognition, already governed the forms and procedure of the ecclesiastical courts and supplied the principles of action wherever property or civil rights were concerned. In fact it may broadly be asserted that everything in the canon law was Roman which was not of directly Christian or of Jewish origin.

From another point of view the canon law, as embodied (2) The in the *Decretum* of Gratian, may be looked upon as an imita- law an tion of the civil law. It was the systematic study of the imitation compilations of Justinian in the schools of Bologna which civil. inspired the curialist monk with the ambition to create for the Church a code no less complete, no less imposing, and no less scientific than the code of the State; and this object could only be effected by means of a still further infusion of Roman law into the disciplinary system of the Western Church. Every fresh step in the development of the canon

CHAP. IV, law after Gratian brought with it a still further infiltration
§ 2. of legal ideas, so that ere long a study of the civil law
became an indispensable preliminary to the education of the
canonist, who became in consequence less and less of a
theologian, and more and more of a lawyer.

(3) The From a third point of view the *Decretum* may be said to
canon
law as a represent a reaction against the ideas associated with the
reaction
against the civil law. The influence of the revived study of the imperial
civil. codes in promoting the growth of imperialist ideas in Italy
may no doubt be exaggerated; but there can be no question
about the reality of that influence, at least in the eleventh
and twelfth centuries: we have already noticed the part
played both by the Ravennese and the Bolognese doctors in
opposition to the claims of the Papacy. The advantage which
the Empire derived from its possession of a venerable system
of law whose continuity was everywhere more or less completely admitted and in which the Emperor was recognized
as the fountain-head of all authority, suggested to the
partisans of the Papacy the idea of setting up an opposing
system of ecclesiastical polity in which the Pope should take
the place accorded by the civil code to the Holy Roman
Emperor. By the labours of successive compilers culminating
in the final work of Gratian, the canon law was for the first
time erected into a system distinct from theology on the one
hand and from the civil law on the other.

Differen- The importance of this change in the development of the
tiation of
canon university-system at Bologna needs no comment. We have
law from
theology. seen how Irnerius marks an epoch in the history of education
by the differentiation which he effected between the study
of law and the study of the liberal arts. With the name of
Gratian must in like manner be associated the differentiation
of canon law from general theology, of which it had been
hitherto but an ill-defined department.[1] There is abundant

---

[1] [Recent investigation has modified the view expressed in this
paragraph. The early connexion
between theology and canon law
was not close, and Gratian's book
was the culmination of a later
movement in which theology and
canon law combined. The influence of Abelard was considerable, but not so unique as Rashdall
suggests. See especially the works
already cited of Ghellinck, and

evidence that in the time of Gratian the study of theology was carried on with as much vigour and in the same spirit at Bologna as at Paris. The enemies of Abelard complained bitterly that Abelard's books had flown across the Alps. The earliest Bologna canonists were, as has been made more than ever evident by the researches of Heinrich Denifle, theologians as well. Roland, Ognibene, and Gandulph composed books of theological sentences,[1] as well as books on canon law; and the two last were, as theologians, avowed disciples of Abelard. Even Gratian himself (as we have seen) owed his method to the Abelardian influence. The civil law was hardly regarded as a proper study for ecclesiastical persons.[2] But after the time of Gratian all this was changed. The study of the *Decretum* called into existence a class of teachers and students distinct alike from the theologians on the one hand and from the civilians on the other, but ultimately in much closer relation with the latter than with the former.[3] In the middle of the twelfth century the study of theology was (it would seem) more or less closely connected with the cathedral. But by the following century a college of doctors in decrees has been developed side by side with the college of civil law, and no less independent of the cathedral and the bishop. The cathedral chair of theology no doubt remained, but from

Fournier and le Bras (e.g. ii. 317 *sqq.*), and cf. Ghellinck in *Dict. de théologie catholique*, VI. i (1925), cols. 1731–51, article on 'Gratian'.]

[1] All three collections exist in manuscripts discovered or first described by Denifle. See his interesting articles, in which ample extracts are given: *Archiv*, i. 402 *sq.*, 584 *sq.* *Die Sentenzen Rolands* are now edited by Gietl (Freiburg i. B., 1892).

[2] See Ep. viii of Peter of Blois (*Patrol. Lat.* ccvii. 22) 'ad quendam Priorem', apologizing because in an address to his convent 'quaedam interserui, quae potius philosophum gentilem et ethnicum, sicut asseris, sapiebant, quam Christianae fidei professorem'. The same writer, who had studied the civil law of Bologna, tries to defend himself by showing that 'Jeremias propheta quasi in iure civili fuerit eruditus'. Yet he confesses that 'res plena discriminis est in clericis usus legum' (Ep. xxvi, *ibid.*, c. 91). As to the later prohibition of the study to priests, beneficed clergy, and monks, see below, p. 322, n. 2. It was rendered entirely inoperative by wholesale dispensations.

[3] It was only gradually that the canon and civil law came to be studied by the same persons. Pascipoverus (fl. *c.* 1240–50) is said to have been the first 'Utriusque iuris professor': he wrote a 'Concordia iuris canonici cum civili'. Sarti, I. i. 173.

this period the study of theology proper ceased to have any special importance at Bologna. In the thirteenth century the theological instruction was here practically confined to the schools of the mendicant friars and had no organic connexion with the universities or doctoral colleges. Even the erection of a theological faculty at a later date, of which I shall speak hereafter, made practically little change in the academical system. The intellectual movement which culminated in the rise of the Bologna school of law was felt as powerfully by the Church as by the laity. Indeed, even in Italy, there were perhaps nearly as many clerks as laymen studying in the universities; but after the age of Gratian the studies even of ecclesiastics took a predominantly legal turn; speculative theology was abandoned in favour of the canon and even the civil law: while the estrangement of the canon law from theology kept pace with the increasing closeness of its union with the faculty of civil law.[1]

The canon law and the 'lay spirit' of Bologna. The contrast between the lay, democratic, student-universities of Italy and the hierarchically governed Church-schools of Paris and Oxford has been dwelt upon often enough. At times, however, a greater importance is given to the contrast than is warranted by the facts of the case. From a merely constitutional point of view, nothing can be more important than a correct apprehension of this fundamental distinction. But at times this constitutional difference is supposed to be a comprehensive key to the spirit of the respective universities. The spirit of Bologna is represented as free, enlightened, anti-papal, anti-clerical, revolutionary. Paris is regarded as the home of narrow bigotry, theological conservatism, and ecclesiastical despotism. Such a representation arises from the importation of modern ideas into a period in which they were quite unknown. Bologna owed its fame as much to the canon law as to the civil law; and that school of canon law originated, as we have seen, in the triumph of all that is represented by the name of Hildebrand. Even in the imperialist civilian of Bologna there was hardly

---

[1] Aegidius Fuscararius († 1289) is said to have been the first layman who taught canon law. Sarti, i. ii. 447.

anything in common with the modern anti-clerical. Of the spirit of intellectual revolt, of freedom of thought and audacity of speculation, there was far more in the earlier days of Paris than there ever was at Bologna. If we speak of the 'lay spirit' of Bologna in contrast with the clerical spirit of Paris, we shall be nearer the mark, but it must be distinctly understood that the lay spirit was not necessarily anti-clerical or irreligious, and that the clerical spirit of the north was by no means always ultra-orthodox or submissive, still less ultra-montane. The Bologna civilian is a representative of the lay spirit if by that is meant that his mind was entirely absorbed in the practical affairs of life to the exclusion of speculative questions; and hardly less might be said with truth of the Bologna canonist. In the eleventh and twelfth centuries, religion exercised at least as powerful an influence upon human affairs in Italy as it did in the north of Europe; but here even religious questions assumed a political shape. Bologna was absorbed with the questions about Investiture, about the relations of Papacy and Empire, Church and State, feudalism and civic liberty, while the schools of France were distracted by questions about the unity of intellect, about transubstantiation, about the reality of universals.

The publication of the *Decretum* was merely the basis of a vast superstructure. Its importance is, in fact, largely due to its having suggested to the Papacy a new method of imposing its will upon Christendom. In 1234 a compilation of five books of Decretals, selected for the most part from the previous Decretals or rescripts of himself and his predecessors,[1] was published by Gregory IX and dispatched to the Universities of Paris and Bologna with the command that they should be taught in the schools.[2] In 1298 there followed the *Liber Sextus* of Boniface VIII. The *Corpus Iuris Canonici* was completed by the addition of the *Clementines* prepared by Clement V and published by his successor John XXII in

TheDecretals of Gregory IX.

The Liber Sextus.

[1] Though partly (like the *Decretum*) derived from earlier materials —canons, Fathers, imperial laws, and Frankish capitularies. Friedberg, ii, cc. xi–xviii.

[2] Friedberg, ii, cc. x. 2. The Code was the work of the papal penitentiary Raymund de Pennaforte, and was really made from a number of previous collections.

CHAP. IV, 1317,[1] and an unofficial collection of later decrees extending
§ 2. down to the time of Sixtus IV and known as the *Extravagants*.[2] The Decretals of course occupy a different position
The *Extra-* in point of authority from the *Decretum*. The *Decretum* was
vagants. a text-book: the Decretals were a code. Even the Decretals
had to be modified in their practical operation by local custom
and by their varying relations to the temporal power,[3] while
in the Clementines and the Extravagants the exaltation of
papal and ecclesiastical authority was carried to such a pitch
that they conflicted with the secular laws of every country
in Europe.

The canon It is, indeed, sometimes much too broadly asserted that
law in the Roman canon law was only current in England in so
England. far as it was freely received by the Church of England and
embodied in her provincial constitutions.[4] Though there
were, no doubt, parts of it which remained practically in-

---

[1] There had been, however, a previous publication by Clement himself, but whether they were transmitted to the universities before Clement's death in 1314, and how far they were altered afterwards, is disputed. See Ehrle in *Archiv*, iv. 361; Friedberg, ii, cc. lvii–lxii; Denifle and Chatelain, *Chartularium Univ. Paris*. ii, No. 708 *et not.*, No. 754.

[2] These are divided into (1) the *Decretales Johannis XXI* (XXII), made soon after the publication of the Clementines, and (2) five books of *Extravagantes communes*. Their arrangement in the form in which they were generally current and were included in the official 'Roman edition' of Gregory XIII, is due to Jean Chappuis. Friedberg, ii, c. lxiv.

[3] The English courts, for instance, resisted the canon law requiring disputes as to rights of patronage to be decided solely by the ecclesiastical courts and the reservation of every civil suit in which an ecclesiastic was involved to the ecclesiastical courts; [and

also in the 'test case' of 'legitimatio per subsequens matrimonium'.]

[4] [Rashdall here referred to a passage in Stubbs, *Lectures in Medieval and Modern History*, Oxford, 1886, p. 305, which Stubbs modified in the 3rd edition (1900), p. 351. Rashdall proceeds:] Lyndwood's *Provinciale* is not 'the authoritative canon law of the realm' (*ibid.*, p. 356), but simply what it professes to be, a codified and annotated edition of the provincial constitutions, i.e. of such parts of the canon law as were peculiar to the English Church. It would be impossible to decide the simplest cases by the *Provinciale* alone (the important subject *De Iure Patronatus* is disposed of in three titles); and Lyndwood's notes habitually cite all parts of the canon law (including the earlier *Extravagants*) and the continental canonists as possessing as much authority in England as elsewhere, except where modified by the special custom which was usually due to lay pressure; e.g. a lay court is allowed to decide a disputed title to patronage.

operative, it is not disputed that, according to the law of the English Church (whatever the State might occasionally say to the contrary), an appeal lay from all inferior ecclesiastical tribunals to the Roman court, where the cases were of course decided by the canon law; and the law of a court of first instance cannot remain permanently and fundamentally different from the law of the appellate tribunal by whose decision it is bound, even had the acknowledged jurisdiction of Rome been limited to the cognizance of appeals, which was far from being the case.[1] It was the opposition of kings and parliaments and secular courts rather than any claim to spiritual independence on the part of the Anglican Church herself that put obstacles in the way of the complete realization in England (as in most other countries) of the Curialist ideal.

But, whether recognized or not in the courts, the whole of this marvellous jurisprudence of spiritual despotism was studied in the faculties of canon law throughout Europe; and the faculty of canon law was a faculty which every university in Europe possessed. By means of the happy thought of the Bolognese monk the Popes were enabled to convert the new-born universities—the offspring of that intellectual new-birth of Europe which might have been so formidable an enemy to papal pretensions—into so many engines for the propagation of ultramontane ideas. Even in their earlier days the universities often showed symptoms of an anti-papal spirit: at a later time they became the very hotbeds of ecclesiastical revolt. But it was never in the ranks of the canon lawyers that the Papacy found its most formidable opponents. At all periods of the Middle Age it was the canonists who filled the most important sees in Christendom; and herein lay one great cause of the failure of all academic attempts at Church reform. It was not so much the specific

Influence of the canon law.

---

[1] Professor Maitland referred the writer to Bracton, f. 412, where it is said that the Pope 'in spiritualibus super omnibus habeat ordinariam iurisdictionem'. [See F. W. Maitland, *Roman Canon Law in the* *Church of England*, London, 1898; and, for the eleventh and twelfth centuries, Z. N. Brooke, *The English Church and the Papacy*, Cambridge, 1931.]

doctrines taught by the *Corpus Iuris Canonici* that favoured papal usurpations and ecclesiastical abuses of all kinds as the habit of mind which its study created. In all ages the lawyers, invaluable as a conservative force, have been as a body greater enemies of reform than the priests. The worst corruption of the Middle Age lay in the transformation of the sacerdotal hierarchy into a hierarchy of lawyers.

And yet there is another side to the question. It may not be assumed that if the clergy of the later Middle Age had not become lawyers, they would have been devout theologians or earnest pastors. From the point of view of the Church no doubt the influence of the canon law stands almost wholly condemned to the modern mind; nor does the superiority of this ecclesiastical jurisprudence to that administered by the civil tribunals (wherever the Roman law was not in force), or its consequent extension to large departments of secular life, altogether destroy the impression that the development of the canon law was a retrograde movement—the most conspicuous triumph of that ecclesiastical reaction which to so large an extent managed to enlist the newly born intellectual forces of the twelfth century in its service. It is only when we turn to the indirect influence of the canon law upon the practice and procedure of the secular courts, and even upon the substance of the secular law in the less Romanized parts of Europe, that we must recognize in the canon law one of the great civilizing and humanizing influences of the later Middle Ages. It was chiefly through the canon law that the civil law transformed the jurisprudence of nearly the whole of continental Europe. Even so, its record is not wholly favourable: some growth of despotic power in King and Lord, some decay of rude Teutonic liberty, the historian —especially the German historian—has been wont to trace to the influence of Roman law, steadily increased by the growth of universities, especially during the fourteenth and fifteenth centuries. We have to take ourselves back to a state of society in which a judicial trial was a tournament and the ordeal an approved substitute for evidence, to realize what civilization owes to the canon law and the canonists with their elaborate system of written law, their judicial evidence, and their written procedure. Even the very chicanery of the ecclesiastical courts assisted the transfer of administration and judicature from the uneducated soldier to the highly educated man of peace. From this point of view the development of the canon law and its diffusion throughout Europe represent a very important stage in the triumph of mind over brute force.

So far I have spoken of Irnerius, of Gratian, and the School of Bologna; only by anticipation has there been any reference to the university the foundation of which is traditionally ascribed to Irnerius. This was perhaps the best way of emphasizing the fact that in the days of Irnerius no such thing as a university existed at all. When the university arose, and what in its origin the university was, must be investigated in the next section.

§ 3. THE *ORIGINES* OF THE JURIST UNIVERSITIES

THE passion for ascribing an immemorial antiquity to the place of one's education, which has hardly yet been killed by the progress of historical criticism, is a passion of very early growth in the history of the human mind. In the Middle Ages, indeed, men found it difficult to believe that an institution which had existed since a time 'whereof the memory of man goeth not to the contrary', had not existed from the remotest antiquity. When once the universities had sprung up it was found impossible to picture to the historical imagination a state of things in which there were no universities. Another inveterate prejudice of the human mind is the disposition to ascribe the origination of a great institution to a great man. Greek cities ascribed their origin to an eponymous hero; and, if tradition did not supply them with a name for him, they invented one. The medieval scholar, accustomed by the later practice to associate the origin of a university with a Charter of Foundation, was driven to postulate such a foundation where history recorded it not, and if the charter was not at hand, he forged one.

By the thirteenth century, and probably early in that century,[1] this familiar logical process had resulted in a legend which attributed the foundation of the University of Bologna to Theodosius II and in the concoction of a Charter of Foundation by that monarch bearing date A.D. 433. Unfortunately for the success of this patriotic effort, the zeal of the forgers somewhat overshot the mark. Two distinct charters were produced, both purporting to be issued by the

---

[1] The deeds are printed—one by Ughelli, *Italia Sacra* (1717), ii. 9, the other by Muratori, *Ant.* iii, c. 21. In these documents the authority of the archdeacon over the inceptions, first entrusted to that official in 1219 (see below, p. 221), is enforced as though it were still by no means beyond the reach of attack. The growth of this monstrous legend is elaborately traced by Chiappelli (cap. 1). The ἀπαρχή of the Theodosian legend seems to be an older tradition as to the foundation of the *city* by Theodosius I or Theodosius II. In 1306 the papal legate Ancaldo was petitioned to confirm the Theodosian privilege: the legate replied that he must first see the privilege. Ghirardacci, i. 525. The forgeries were then already in existence.

same Emperor in the same year. Possibly in consequence of
this contretemps, the Theodosian legend has never attained the same popularity or acceptance as the legends which make Charles the Great the Founder of Paris and Alfred the Founder of Oxford, the last of which still maintains a kind of underground existence in university calendars, in second-rate guide-books, and in popular histories of England. The early date of the legend is worth noticing as an illustration of the extremely small value which ought to be attached to scholastic traditions of this type even when they are not capable of the same historical confutation which is possible in this case. A further discussion of this and other inconsistent legends or traditions as to the origin of the university would be neither interesting nor instructive. All that is really known as to the origin of the school has been placed before the reader in a preceding section. So far there has been not the faintest trace of any even rudimentary organization similar to that of the later university. Irnerius and his contemporaries, so far as we know, were private and unauthorized teachers; neither they nor their scholars belonged to any institution or enjoyed any legal privilege whatever.[1] The first legal charter in which the school receives even an implicit recognition is a charter of the Emperor Frederick Barbarossa, known as the Authentic *Habita* and issued in 1158 at the Diet of Roncaglia, in which the doctors of Bologna played a very prominent part.

This privilege has often been treated as a kind of charter, Privilege of Frederick I, 1158. if not as an actual 'foundation', of the University of Bologna. But though there is no reason to doubt that this legislation was primarily intended for the benefit of the increasingly

---

[1] [This view is strongly opposed by Manacorda, who regards the ecclesiastical *licentia docendi* as the link at Bologna, as elsewhere, between the cathedral school of the past and the later universities. He thinks that the Canon Hugo of Bologna (*c.* 1125), who could teach how and when and where he wished, would have the licence, and that Irnerius, a *magister artium*, even if he were a layman, would have it also. See especially i. 198–204. V. Rossi, in his criticism of Manacorda, as strenuously upholds the opposite view, expressed in the text above; *Scritti di critica letteraria*, iii. 77–86. For the general significance of this discussion see above, p. 21.]

CHAP. IV, numerous body of law-students at Bologna, that city is not
§ 3. expressly mentioned in its provisions, and it is perfectly
arbitrary to limit its actual scope to the schools of that place.[1]
In any case this document does not recognize the existence
of a university whether of masters or of students at Bologna
or anywhere else. It is a general privilege conferred on
the student-class throughout the Lombard kingdom. This
charter does, however, constitute an important indication of
the growing importance and the independent position of the
doctors of law, and was no doubt procured by the interest of
the Bologna doctors. Its provisions were suggested by the
older privilege conferred by Justinian upon the scholars of
Berytus.[2] Besides taking the scholars under the especial
protection of the Emperor, it provides that in any legal proceedings against a scholar, the defendant is to have the option
of being cited before his own master or before the bishop.[3]

[1] As is done by Savigny (c.
xxi, § 63). This limitation is criticized by Denifle (i. 49 sq.), whose
view I have adopted. He there exa-
mines a story embodied in a Latin
poem (partly printed by Giesebrecht ap. *Sitzungsberiche d. bayer.
Akad. d. Wiss.* Phil.-Hist. Kl.,
1879, ii. 285), according to which
Frederick granted some such privilege to Bologna, on the petition of
the scholars in 1155. He comes
to the conclusion that the charter
meant is the Authentic *Habita* itself,
some copies of which bear no date,
and that the story grew out of the
fact of Frederick's having been near
Bologna in 1155. It is quite possible
that the privilege was asked for and
perhaps granted in 1155, but formally promulgated at the Diet in
1158 (as is suggested by Kaufmann,
Gesch. d. Deutschen Universitäten,
i. 164). On the part played by these
Bologna doctors at Roncaglia see
below, p. 259.

[2] The enforcement of the Em-
peror's regulations is entrusted at
Constantinople to the Prefect, at
Berytus to the *Praeses* of the pro-

vince, the Bishop and the 'legum
professores'.

[3] 'Verumtamen si eis litem super
aliquo negotio quispiam movere
presumpserit, huius rei optione
scolaribus data, eos coram domino
aut magistro suo vel ipsius civitatis episcopo, quibus hanc iuris-
dicionem dedimus, conveniant'
(*M.G.H., Constitutiones*, i (1893),
249). There has been much
needless discussion as to the meaning of 'dominus', but there can be
no doubt that it is a synonym for
'magister', though Malagola (*Monografie*, p. 39) still appears to
understand it of the Rector. The
use of this title (which was affected
only by the law-professors) shows
that the law-students were primarily in view; though the term
magister would include the teachers
of other faculties. Justinian had
entrusted a disciplinary jurisdiction over students and copyists at
the law-school of Berytus to the
professors in conjunction with the
Praeses of the province and the
Bishop. But it appears doubtful
whether this is extended to ordi-

Attempts were made at times to extend the first of these provisions to the scholars in the other parts of Europe, and in the Italian universities this pre-university charter was usually recognized as the basis of all the special privileges conferred on particular universities by the States in which they were situated. Whatever privileges were afterwards granted to the universities, whatever jurisdiction was conferred on their rectors, the jurisdiction of the bishop and the professors was usually, at least in theory, maintained. But after the rise of the universities the scholar was not allowed by their statutes to decline the jurisdiction of his own rector. Hence the choice of tribunal practically passed to the plaintiff, and was lost by the defendant scholar.[1] The jurisdiction of the professors was found difficult to enforce, and that of the bishop remained only in the case of scholars who were also clerks.

While the Authentic in no way recognizes the corporate existence of a college or guild of doctors, it does indirectly make it probable that some such society must have by this time sprung into existence.[2] In the days of Irnerius the teaching office could (so far as can be gathered) be assumed by any one who could get pupils: he required no licence or permission from any authority whatever, ecclesiastical, civil, or academical.[3] We can hardly, however, suppose that the

Indications of a society of masters.

nary criminal and civil proceedings. See the *Proaemium* to the Digest.

[1] *Stat.*, p. 12. [The Authentic *Habita*, whether the Emperor had the scholars of Bologna in mind or not, was approved by Pope Alexander III and was afterwards generally received, directly or indirectly. It defined a jurisdiction which, so far as the bishop was concerned, could be traced back to the Decretals of Pope Eugenius II. On the jurisdiction of the master, cf. the claim of the scholar of Reims, as given by Alexander III in a letter of 1170-2 (*Patrol. Lat.*, cc. 746). See Manacorda, i. 205-6, also pp. 195, 221.]

[2] I cannot understand the ground of Kaufmann's statement that at the time of the Authentic 'Es gab also damals wahrscheinlich schon landsmannschaftliche Verbindungen unter den Scholaren' (*Deutsch. Univ.* i. 166; cf. p. 184). These 'Verbindungen' he apparently regards as 'Anfänge von Korporationsbildung' (i. 184). It is quite possible that the beginnings of informal associations may be as early as 1158, but of this there is no evidence—least of all can it be inferred from the *Habita*.

[3] [He may have been required to have the ecclesiastical *licentia docendi*; see above, p. 143 note.]

Emperor would have conferred important judicial functions upon an independent body of self-constituted teachers like our modern 'professors' of music or of dancing. It is therefore probable that in Italy as in France at least some recognized course of study was demanded by custom before the pupil could become a master, and that he was required to obtain the approval of the existing body of masters and to enter upon the teaching office by some public, definite ceremonial, such as the later *Conventus* or inception. We may therefore consider it tolerably certain that at least the idea of a co-opting college or corporation of doctors dates in some shadowy form from before the year 1158; although the masters may not yet have proceeded to such definite manifestations of corporate existence as the making of written statutes, and the election of common officers. The guild was already in existence, but was merely, so to speak, a customary society, which existed in fact, though not on paper. Such an inference is strongly supported by the analogy of Paris, where we have positive evidence of the existence of a customary guild of masters, some ten or twenty years later, though it was not till fifty years after that that a single written statute existed, and not till a still later period that the guild was sufficiently organized to elect officers or use a common seal. At Bologna the first express evidence of the existence of such a society of masters comes in the year 1215, when we hear of Buoncompagno's new book being read before the 'University of Professors of the Civil and Canon Law';[1] but the whole

---

[1] The *Rhetorica Antiqua* of Buoncompagno, who says: 'Recitatus equidem fuit hic liber, approbatus et coronatus lauro Bononiae apud sanctum Johannem in monte in loco qui dicitur paradisus anno domini 1215 septimo Kal. April. coram universitate professorum iuris canonici et civilis et aliorum doctorum et scolarium multitudine numerosa.' Ap. Rockinger, *Sitzungsberichte der bay. Akad. zu München*, 1861, p. 135. The same writer, however, says: 'Tunc amici . . . ad Maiorem Ecclesiam deverunt (*sic*). Et ita fuit Magistrorum et Scholarium Universitas congregata' (ap. Sarti, ii. 32)—which might be held to indicate that some loose organization of *masters and scholars* preceded the formation of the student-universities. [This is the view of Gaudenzi (*Appunti*, p. 13) so far as the foreign students and professors are concerned. The foreign students, in the second half of the twelfth century, grouped themselves into nations, which

system of degrees which is known to have been fully estab-lished before 1219 implies the existence of such a society in a rudimentary form at a much earlier date. Taking the degree of doctor or master in its earliest form meant simply the being admitted or made free of the guild of teachers by receiving[1] the insignia of mastership.

In the account of Buoncompagno's recitation, to which I have already alluded, the professors of the civil and canon law are described as forming a single *universitas*.[2] What were the exact relations between the two classes at this time, we do not know; eventually there were two wholly distinct colleges—one of canon and one of civil law, each with a prior and other officers, and a code of statutes of its own. It is probable that the college of canon law was a later imitation of the civilian organization. In most other universities, how-ever, the doctors of civil and canon law were united in the same college or faculty, though the degrees were distinct.

early in the thirteenth century joined to form the university of ultramontane students. Cf. below, p. 155. For reference to a *consortium* of masters in 1201 and obser-vations on the subject-matter of this and the following notes see below, p. 232 (Additional Note).]

[1] It is probable that, originally, any master might admit any other person to the mastership, but that this right was controlled by the customs of the profession. It is possible that this state of things lasted longer in the arts schools than in the schools of law. Cf. the way in which Rolandino of Padua speaks of his graduation in 1221: 'apud ipsos Bononienses in sciencia litterali nutritus, in anno Domini M CC XXI illic a Boncompagno meo dompno et magistro, nacio-ne et eloquencia florentino, licet indignus, recepi officium magi-stratus.' *Chronica*, book ix, c. 4 in *M.G.H.*, *Scriptores*, xix. 120. [Now also edited by A. Bonardi in the new *Rerum Ital. Scriptores*, viii,

part i (Città di Castello, 1905), p. 135. Manacorda (i. 250) thinks that this refers, not to the licence to teach, but to the transmission of a school by a master to a pupil, his successor. In his *Rhetorica antiqua*, Buoncompagno describes a similar ceremony in his own career (before 1215; cf. above, pp. 110 and 146 n.). The passages are too concise to allow a convincing conclusion to be drawn. If they refer to the licence, they do not definitely preclude the co-operation of the archdeacon. There is a clear account of the transfer of a school at Paris in 1179 in Gerald of Wales, *De rebus a se gestis* (*Opera*, i. 48).]

[2] It is not implied that the mere use of the term *universitas* proves the existence of a formal guild: the term *universitas* might be used quite untechnically of any collec-tion of persons; but the passage seems to imply that the doctors of law were a recognized class or official body.

CHAP. IV, §3.

Two decades later than the Charter of Frederick I, we meet with another official recognition of the scholars, though it does not distinctly imply the existence of any academical organization. In 1189 a Bull of Clement III confirms an already existing legatine ordinance forbidding masters or scholars to offer to the landlord a higher rent for a house already inhabited by scholars.[1] At a very early date it became customary for the rents to be fixed by arbitrators or taxors, two of them appointed by the scholars, and two by the town. It is difficult to say whether the above-mentioned Bull implies the existence of this system,[2] but we find a similar system established in the very infancy of other universities and it obtained in some schools which never grew into universities at all.

Taxation of students' rents.

The University of Bologna has already been described as a university of students. And it is quite true that at Bologna it was the guild or rather guilds of students which eventually succeeded in getting into their own hands the real control of the *studium* in most of those matters which were at Paris settled by the masters alone. But it cannot be too clearly understood that the doctors of Bologna, probably at as early a date as the masters of Paris, formed a guild or guilds of their own, and that it was not till a later period than that with which we are now engaged that the control of strictly academical matters passed to the universities of students. It was a mere accident that the term university was appropriated by the student-guild, while the doctoral guilds were known as colleges. The students did no doubt at last succeed in reducing the masters to an almost incredible servitude. But there remained one function and one only over which the doctors to the last retained an exclusive control, and it is of the greatest importance that this should be clearly under-

The magisterial guild and the 'conventus'.

---

[1] Savioli, ii. ii. 160. So Decretal. Greg. IX. lib. iii, tit. xviii, c. 1.

[2] It is ordered that 'a te frater episcope et tuo quolibet successore hoc singulis annis in communi audientia magistrorum atque scholarium recitetur'. This implies that congregations of some kind were customary, but it also shows a very different relation existing between the masters and their scholars from that which we find a century later.

stood. Even the domineering student-guilds of Bologna left to the masters the indefeasible right which every professional guild possessed of examining into the qualifications of candidates for admission to the profession. The doctors examined the candidate, gave him licence to 'incept' or give his public probationary discourse, after which, if this further test was satisfactorily passed, he was received into the *collegium* of the doctors of civil or canon law, as the case might be, being presented by an existing member in the presence of the rest with the insignia of his office. Such in its essence was the idea of the 'conventus', 'principium', or 'inceptio'—the simple institution which formed the keystone of the whole university constitution. Unless its nature and meaning are thoroughly understood, the whole organization of medieval education will remain an unintelligible enigma. Postponing to a later date a detailed explanation of this part of the academic polity, we must now proceed to trace the *origines* of the student-universities.

The student-university which originated at Bologna forms The student-university. a wholly new departure in the history of education; the institution is as distinct from anything which preceded it as it is unlike any of the modern institutions which have nevertheless been developed out of it. It is not, however, difficult to explain the genesis of the new creation, if we bear in mind the character of the environment wherein it grew up. We have already contrasted the state of society in the Lombard towns with that which prevailed in the feudal monarchies of Europe. We have seen that traditions of education, and of legal education, survived among the noble families of Italy at a time when the French or Norman nobles were inclined to look upon reading and writing as rather effeminate luxuries, fit only for plebeian clerks. It is probable, if we may draw an inference from the state of things which we find established at a later date, that the teaching of Irnerius attracted somewhat older men and men of much greater wealth and social position than the boys who attended the arts schools of Paris. Into the Bologna lecture-rooms the idea of discipline never entered at all. The associations of

CHAP. IV, the school and of the cloister were alike absent. The professor
§ 3. was not originally the officer of any public institution: he was
simply a private-adventure lecturer—like the sophist of
ancient Greece or the rhetor of ancient Rome—whom a
number of independent gentlemen of all ages between seventeen and forty had hired to instruct them. If many of the
students were ecclesiastics, they were most of them already
beneficed—many of them archdeacons or dignitaries in
cathedral churches;[1] and they owed no ecclesiastical obedience
to their teachers. But even more important than the age and
status of the students was the political condition of the city
Fostered in which Irnerius and his successors taught. The conception
by the
political of citizenship prevalent in the Italian republics was much
and social nearer to the old Greek conception than that which prevails
environ-
ment. in modern states. Citizenship, which is with us little more
than an accident of domicile, was in ancient Athens or
medieval Bologna an hereditary possession of priceless value.
The citizens of one town had, in the absence of express agreement, no civil rights in another. There was one law for the
citizen; another, and a much harsher one, for the alien.[2]
Prolonged exile was a serious penalty, to which a body of

[1] The German students were probably more predominantly ecclesiastical than the Italian. In the
earlier period laymen predominate
even among the Germans, in the
later period they were mainly
either beneficed ecclesiastics or
else cadets of noble houses. See
the *Acta Nationis Germanicae*,
passim.

[2] The Town Statutes eventually
provided 'quod scolares sint cives
et tanquam cives ipsi habeantur, et
pro civibus reputentur, donec scolares fuerint, et res ipsorum tanquam civium defendantur . . . nec
possint ipsi tanquam forenses nec
eorum res detineri vel molestari
occasione represalie concesse contra
commune vel civitatem terre vel
castri, vel banni dictis terris castris
vel civitatibus dati, vel alicuius
debiti pecuniarii'. *Stat.*, p. 162.

It is of course certain that no
political rights whatever were conferred upon students: the provision
that they should be treated as citizens was necessary to secure them
the ordinary protection of the law.
Scholars who had resided over ten
years at Bologna were sometimes
granted actual citizenship; but then
they lost their rights in the university. Savigny, c. xxi, § 69,
note. That the grievances against
which the foreign student wanted
protection were not merely sentimental, we are reminded by the
frequent occurrence of a privilege
exempting scholars from torture
except in the presence of and with
the sanction of the Rectors. See,
e.g., *Stat. Fiorent.*, ed. Gherardi,
p. 109. So at Padua, *Stat. Artist.*,
f. xxxiii *b*.

young men of good position in their own cities, many of them old enough to be entering upon political life, would naturally submit with reluctance. The student-universities represent an attempt on the part of such men to create for themselves an artificial citizenship in place of the natural citizenship which they had temporarily renounced in the pursuit of knowledge or advancement; and the great importance of a *studium* to the commercial welfare of the city in which it was situated may explain the ultimate willingness of the munici-palities—though the concession was not made without a struggle—to recognize these student-communities.

Two other circumstances serve to explain the patience with which Bologna and other towns after her submitted to the erection of an 'imperium in imperio' within their own walls, and to confer an extensive civil, and sometimes even criminal, jurisdiction upon the elected officers of a student-club. The first is the prevalence of the conception of 'Personal Law'. For centuries Lombards and Romans had lived together under different codes of law and different magistrates. At an earlier date it had been quite common for even three or four men to live in the same town and yet to be in matters of private law members of as many distinct states; and respect for these personal rights had not entirely died out in the thirteenth century.[1] It remained in all its fullness as regards the clergy. This conception made it seem the less unnatural that alien-students should live under the jurisdiction of their own rectors, just as in eastern countries when there is a mixture of races foreigners are freely permitted to live under the jurisdiction of their own consuls or their own bishops. And then there is a fact which is, indeed, the most important clue to the origin of universities here and elsewhere. The university, whether of masters or of students, was only a particular kind of *guild*:[2] the rise of the universities is merely a wave of that great movement towards

Recognition of student-rights facilitated by the conception of personal law.

And by the contemporary guild movement.

---

[1] Savigny, c. iii, § 30 *sq.*

[2] As late as the middle of the fourteenth century this was still so fully realized in the Italian cities that we find at Florence the Statutes of the *universitas scholarium* subjected to the approval of the 'Approbatores Statutorum Artium (trades or crafts) comunis Floren-tie'. *Stat. Fiorent.*, p. 135.

CHAP. IV, association which began to sweep over the cities of Europe
§ 3. in the course of the eleventh century.

And the ruling ideas of the age made the guild a closer and more powerful association in an Italian city than it could be No in a modern state. In the first place, the Roman law con- charter required. ferred a legal existence upon 'collegia' or corporations of three persons or more, without any special authorization of the State. In some of the Italian cities the Guelf and Ghibelin party-clubs (at Bologna known as Lambertazzi and Geremei), overtly aiming at violent changes in the govern- ment of the city, were as much recognized legal corporations Influence as the guilds of merchants or craftsmen.[1] Moreover, while of oaths. the legal authority of modern clubs and other societies over their members is based for a most part upon a mere contract, in the Middle Ages it was based upon oath. And in the Middle Ages an oath meant a great deal more than it does in modern communities. Perjury was a mortal sin; and the oaths of obedience consequently enabled the guilds to subject disobedient members not only to public 'infamy' and to spiritual penalties at the hands of their confessors but even to proceedings *in salutem animae* in the ecclesiastical courts.[2]

---

[1] Ghirardacci, i. 248.

[2] In the Italian universities every offence prohibited by the Statutes is forbidden 'sub poena periurii'. Thus at Bologna, even absence from Congregation involved perjury unless the offender paid a price of five *solidi* within eight days (*Stat.*, p. 129). So at Paris the Rector, 'si dicti Scholares ipsas bursas solvere noluerint, et rebelles extiterint, contra ipsos procedere tenebitur tanquam periuros et infames' (Bulaeus, iv. 232). Whether this implied the promotion of an ecclesiastical suit or (as seems probable) simply a public notifica- tion of the fact, but such proceed- ings would have been quite in accordance with canon law. The German nation at Bologna pro- vides that the 'coercio' of the Bishop of Bologna or his vicar shall be brought to bear upon 'contra- dictores', but with the explanation 'quorum iurisdictioni circa exe- cucionem conservacionis predic- torum ordinamentorum ipsa nacio specialiter se subiecit'. *Acta Nat. Germ.*, p. 350. Here the right to promote a suit rests upon consent; but in Gloria, *Mon. della univ. di Padova* (1318–1405), ii. 223–7, are documents which seem to relate to suits before the Bishop concerning disputes in the college of arts where the jurisdiction is founded entirely upon the oaths taken by its members. So in London we find that the Bishop's Court 'enter- tained suits exactly analogous to those of the trades unions at the present day, turning on the question how far it is a breach of oath for the sworn member of a guild to impart the arts and mysteries of

The combined force of the social and the spiritual penalties thus wielded by the guilds was so enormous that in the Italian cities they often became more powerful than the State. At Bologna the revolution of 1228 gave them an important constitutional position; their magistrates were almost equal in authority to the magistrates of the republic and almost independent of their control.[1] In such a state of society, membership of a guild was essential to personal security. If the students had not formed themselves into guilds, if they had not insisted upon legal recognition and privilege for their officers, the position of scholars residing in a foreign city would have been wellnigh intolerable.[2]

To the professors and students who were citizens of Bologna these considerations of course did not apply. The State was not disposed to abandon any part of its jurisdiction over its own citizens, nor the universities to receive as citizens of the academic commonwealth students who were unable to give it an undivided allegiance. Bolognese students retained their natural citizenship: Bolognese professors were accorded a high position in the constitution of the republic.[3] Both alike were excluded from the scholastic guilds.

Citizens excluded from the universities.

Thus, by merely attending to the conditions or environment in which the law-universities grew up, the peculiar relations which subsisted in them between the students and the professors, and again between the Bolognese students and

The student-universities can be explained.

[1] his guild to outsiders' (Stubbs, *Lectures on Medieval and Modern History*, ed. 3, Oxford, 1900, p. 364). It may be observed that the dependence of university authority upon an oath secured for the Papacy an especial jurisdiction over them, even where (as in Italy) they were not wholly composed of ecclesiastics. As to the ecclesiastical jurisdiction in matters of oath or contract, cf. Fournier, *Les Officialités au moyen âge*, Paris, 1880, p. 86; and, for its importance in the development of English equity, Fry, *Specific Performance of Contracts*, London, 1892, p. 8 *sq.*

[1] The most convenient account of the Bologna constitution is given by Savigny, c. xx.

[2] M. Thurot well remarks that the University of Paris 'se constitua sous l'empire de cet esprit d'association qui produisait en même temps les villes Lombardes, les communes de France, et les corporations de métiers'. *De l'organisation de l'enseignement dans l'Un. de Paris*, p. 3.

[3] The Constitution of 1245 made them *ex officio* members of the *Credenza* or Council of 600. Savigny, *loc. cit.*

CHAP. IV, those from a distance, receive adequate explanation. Even
§ 3.   had we no knowledge of the actual history of the evolutionary
process, it would be unnecessary to look upon this constitutional phenomenon, as it has too often been looked upon,
with mere stupid astonishment, as a kind of historical *lusus
naturae*. Whatever surprise may be still felt at the appearance
upon the page of History of an institution so startling to
modern ideas as a student-university will be removed by an
examination of the actual facts, scanty as they are, which have
come down to us with respect to the early history of the
earliest student-guilds of Bologna.

The *two* law uni-versities.   From about the middle of the thirteenth century[1] the
organization of law-students at Bologna consisted of two
closely allied but distinct *universitates*—a *universitas citramontanorum* and a *universitas ultramontanorum*, each under
a rector of its own. We have no direct documentary evidence
of the state of the academic organization in the first half of

Elsewhere four uni-versities.   the century. But we have evidence that in the universities
which were established elsewhere by schisms or migrations
from Bologna there existed at the beginning of the century
not two universities but four. This was the case at Vicenza,
where a colony from Bologna established itself in A.D. 1204,
and in Vercelli which was colonized in 1228 from Padua,
itself an earlier colony of Bologna. To any one aware of the
servile fidelity with which the institutions of a mother-
university were reproduced in its daughters, the mere fact
that there were four universities at Vicenza and Vercelli
would be a sufficient proof that at one time there had been
four universities at Bologna also.[2] But we are not left entirely
to inference upon this fundamental point of our inquiry into
the origin of student-universities.

[1] The earliest evidence of the change is in a city statute of 1244. Frati, i. 367.

[2] Savigny conjectured that originally there were four universities at Bologna, c. xxi, § 616. When Kaufmann (i. 189) objects to De-nifle's inferences from the Bull of 1217, because by 1250 we hear of a single 'universitas' of scholars, he appears to forget that the term *universitas* does not necessarily imply a legal corporation, but may be applied to any collection of people. Kaufmann seems to me to exaggerate the solidarity of the student-body both before and after 1250.

In 1217 we hear of the 'Scholars from the City' (i.e. Rome), Campania, and Tuscany as forming either a separate society or more than one separate society; but in any case it is clear that they are not embraced in the same organization as the other Italian students. What was the exact distribution of the students at Bologna at this time, it is impossible to determine with absolute certainty. But it seems highly probable that originally the four universities were (1) Lombards, (2) Ultramontanes, (3) Tuscans, and (4) Romans, in which last university the Campanians may have been included.[1] This view is supported by two facts. First, in the later united Cismontane University there were, as is evident from the Statutes, three original *nationes*—the Lombards, Tuscans, and Romans, which were subdivided into smaller *consiliariae*[2] (bodies electing one or more councillors), while the Ultramontane University contained a much larger number

---

[1] Sarti, II (1772), p. 58. If this view be accepted, of course the 'scholares de urbe, Campania et de Tuscia' (notice the omission of the preposition before Campania) will represent *two* separate guilds, acting on this occasion in conjunction. The fact that a Bull is addressed to the three together does not, as Denifle assumes (i. 140), prove that they were embraced in one organization, any more than the existence of papal Bulls addressed to the masters and scholars of Bologna proves that the masters belonged to the universities or the students to the doctoral colleges, or the fact that Bulls were often addressed to the doctors of civil and canon law at Bologna proves that there was a single college for both faculties. Moreover, the earliest Statutes of the united universities *prove* the original distinctness of the Lombardi: 'De Citramontanis vero iuxta morem antiquum nacio Romanorum habeat sex (consiliarios), Tuschorum alios sex, reliquos

habeat nacio Lombardorum, quos per consciliarias sic dividimus, sicut *nacionis statutis est descriptum*. (*Stat.*, p. 16.) Denifle further assumes from the language of the Bull that this guild of the Romans, Campanians, and Tuscans had only just been formed (i. 140), and hence infers that the *universitas* originated with the Ultramontani. The fact is not improbable, but the language of the Bull seems to me to establish nothing as to the length of time (when the question is between one year and twenty-five) during which the guild or guilds had been formed. Honorius III speaks of the original motive of their formation, but so does the University of Paris fifty years after its first institution. See below, p. 302, n. 1. The amalgamation-theory is supported by the employment of the term *rector*, which was especially used to denote the head of a federation of guilds. See below, p. 162.

[2] *Stat.*, pp. 16, 68.

CHAP. IV, of nations—in 1265 fourteen[1]—each of which corresponded
§ 3. with a *consiliaria* of the Cismontane University. Whether
or not the united Ultramontane University arose by amalgamation from these smaller nations, its later constitution
bears no trace of having at any earlier period consisted of two
or three separate universities or nations, whereas this is
distinctly the case with the Cismontane University.[2] The
second reason for supposing that the four universities were
originally constituted as above, is that the University of
medicine and arts was to the last subdivided into four nations
only—Ultramontane, Lombard, Tuscan, and Roman.[3]

The various univer-sities probably arose at distinct periods. The fact that there were originally four distinct universities
and that we find one or more of them acting in independence
of the rest, makes it probable that they originated at distinct
periods; and it is highly probable that the final emergence of
two closely united universities is but the last stage of a process
of amalgamation by which the three societies of Cismontanes
and the numerous small Ultramontane nations had reduced
themselves to four large societies. The very distinct organization and exceptional privileges of the German nation[4] find

[1] [French (i.e. from the Île de
France), Picards, Burgundians,
Poitevins, natives of Touraine and
Maine, Normans, Catalans, Hun-
garians, Poles; and, *ex altera parte*,
Germans, Spaniards, Provençals,
English, Gascons. In this year
(1265) disputes about the method
of electing the Rector were settled,
and the Gascons, who had acted
with the Germans, Spanish, Provençals, and English against the
others, were joined with the
Poitevins in a single nation; Sarti,
II (1896), 18.]

[2] See above, p. 155, n. 1.

[3] *Stat.*, p. 215. Denifle (i. 139)
argues that since at Vicenza, Vercelli, and Padua, we find *one* university embracing all the Italians,
while at Bologna there was certainly more than one Italian university, there must once have been
more than four universities at

Bologna. I fail to follow the argument. The different distribution
of nationalities in these offshoots
of Bologna may have been due to
the composition of the seceding
bodies of students. In the migrations, both from Bologna and from
other universities, the *number* of
nations (four) was always preserved, but their composition varied.
His suggestion (*loc. cit.*) that the
larger universities may have arisen
by amalgamation from smaller
nations which after their union
remained as subdivisions of the
larger body, seems to me probable
as regards the Ultramontane nations only. Throughout Denifle
fails to recognize the marked distinction between the Ultramontane
nationes and the Cismontane consiliariae.

[4] In 1273 it is already claimed as
an ancient privilege 'quod nobiles

their most natural explanation in the supposition that it was the earliest of these national clubs and formed the nucleus round which other and younger bodies grouped themselves. Even in the fully developed academic constitution, the nations of the *Ultramontani* retained a much larger measure of individual corporate existence than either the three original nations of the *Citramontani* or the smaller *conciliariae* into which they were subdivided.[1]

But whatever uncertainty there may be as to the early history of these student-guilds, the one fact about them which is certain is fortunately the one fact which it is of fundamental importance to grasp. They originated with non-Bolognese students; and this circumstance is by itself a sufficient clue to their *raison d'être*. It is probable, indeed, that it was the German students who first felt the need of mutual protection and co-operation;[2] but at all events the guilds were formed by non-Bolognese students. The fact has been slightly obscured by the circumstance that the universities eventually succeeded in asserting *some* authority even over the Bolognese scholars, though to the last they remained exempt from the oath of obedience to the Rector, without a vote in the University Congregations, and ineligible for university offices. To the last they were not in the strict sense *members* of those corporations; originally they must have been

de Alamania non teneantur iurare rectori' (*Acta Nat. Germ.*, p. 349). The accounts of 1305 allude to written privileges (*ibid.*, p. 58), while a 'privilegium quod nobiles Almanni non tenentur iurare rectori' is included in an inventory taken in 1442 (*ibid.*, p. 189). The Statutes speak generally of privileges granted by the Emperor (*ibid.*, p. 13); but no actual charter appears to be preserved of earlier date than 1530, when Charles V wholly exempted the German nation from the rectorial jurisdiction, and subjected them to that of their own masters. At the same time the latter were created *ex officio* Counts of the Lateran, and

granted the power of making notaries and legitimating bastards (*ibid.*, p. 19 *sq.*). The nation retained its existence as a student-organization till the Revolution terminated its existence just, it would appear, as it was about to die by the less noble method of bankruptcy. (Malagola, *Monografie*, p. 286.)

[1] *Stat.*, p. 139.

[2] Cf. the words of Honorius III to the Tuscans and Campanians: 'Etsi multam honestatem, imo necessitatem, sicut asseritis, causa contineat, que vos ad contrahendam societatem induxit.' Sarti, II (1772), p. 58. This 'necessity' would be likely to be still earlier experienced by the Germans.

CHAP. IV, wholly exempt from their authority.[1] The reason of the
§ 3. exclusion is obvious. The Bolognese student no more wanted
to be protected by a university than a young Englishman
reading for the bar in London requires to be protected by
a consul. The very existence of the university was due to the
want of political status on the part of its members. In exactly
the same way we find foreign merchants[2] and other strangers
in an Italian town forming themselves into guilds for the
prevention of quarrels among themselves and the promotion
of their common interests.

Exclusion   In the same fact is found the explanation of the other
of pro-   characteristic peculiarity in the organization of the universi-
fessors. ties of the Italian type—the exclusion of the professors from
membership.[3] The earliest Bolognese professors were citizens of Bologna. Unlike Paris, whose political and commercial importance attracted student and teacher alike from
distant lands, Bologna owed her scholastic fame to the accident
(if it was an accident) that Irnerius and his first successors

[1] The earliest Bologna Statutes
assert the jurisdiction of the Rector
over the *Bononiensis* (*Stat.*, p. 12);
cf. the Statute of Lérida formed on
the model of Bologna in 1300: 'cum
te dicas civem Ilerdae, iurare non
cogeris universitatis statuta, licet
dum in hoc studio fueris ad eorum
observantiam tenearis.' Villanueva,
Viage Literario, xvi. 229. So at Pisa
and Florence the Rector must be
'forensis'. Citizens were forbidden
to take the oath to the Rector on
pain of confiscation and the ban by
a town statute of 1245 (Frati, ii.
29). Afterwards, a special oath
merely binding them not to injure
the University, &c., was imposed on
the Bolognese student (*Bononiensis
vel diocesanus*) and his name inserted in a 'matricula specialis'.
Stat., p. 128 (cf. p. 132: 'Com-
paternitatem cum bononiensi cive
vel diocesano nullus scolaris con-
trahat, nisi prius petita licentia et
obtenta a Rectore suo'). So they

paid modified dues to the university officials on taking their
degree, *ibid.*, p. 145.
[2] Especially German merchants.
Denifle, i. 136; Simonsfeld, *Der
Fondaco dei Tedeschi in Venedig*,
Stuttgart, 1887. So there were
universitates iudaeorum, e.g. at
Catania in Sicily before 1283
(*Documenti per servire alla storia
di Sicilia*, Palermo, vi. 28); so at
Messina (*ibid.*, p. 63), Syracuse
(*ibid.*, p. 78), Trapani (*ibid.*, p.
89), &c.
[3] [In the eyes of the law this was
not the case. For example, Miss
Helen Briggs has pointed to the
description of a master in the
faculty of medicine and arts,
Giovanni della Luna, a victim of
an assault in 1308: 'qui quidem
Johannes est de universitate scolarium studentium bononie' (Atti e
processi del podestà, vol. 578,
f. 28 *v*).]

happened to live, and therefore to teach, at Bologna.[1] Had the earliest teachers been foreigners, they might have occupied important positions in the university: as it was, the students had to choose their office-bearers from their own number. At first the professors were excluded not so much because they were professors as because they were citizens. But at a very early period in the development of the universities, we shall find the Bolognese doctors allying themselves with the city against the students in the selfish effort to exclude from the substantial privileges of the doctorate all but their own fellow citizens. The antagonism of interest thus created between the doctors and their pupils has much to do with the growth of the student domination. The doctors, as citizens and as laymen, were connected with the city in a way wholly foreign to the traditions of northern schools. It was through identifying themselves in the pursuit of a common pecuniary interest with the city rather than with the scholars that the doctors of Bologna sank into their strange and undignified servitude to their own pupils.

How entirely parallel to those of the non-scholastic guilds were the original purpose and organization of the student-universities is best illustrated by the statutes of the German nation[2] which have fortunately come down to us. The original idea of the universities became more or less obscured by the academical power which they eventually acquired. The smaller national associations naturally retained the more homely character of clubs for mutual protection, assistance, and recreation, and for the performance of those religious functions which in the Middle Ages supplied the sanction for every social bond and the excuse for every convivial gathering. In these statutes the object of the guild is declared to be the cultivation of 'fraternal charity, mutual association and amity, the consolation of the sick and support of the

---

[1] Thus the Bull of Honorius III in 1220 reminds the town 'quod ipsi gratuito ad studendum vestram preelegerint civitatem, que cum prius esset humilis, per eos ibidem congregatis divitiis fere super-gressa est civitates Provinciae universas'. Sarti, II (1772), p. 57.

[2] For the position of these subdivisions of the university see below, p. 182 *sq.*

CHAP. IV, needy, the conduct of funerals and the extirpation of rancour
§ 3. and quarrels, the attendance and escort of our *doctorandi* to
and from the place of examination, and the spiritual advantage of members'.[1] The statutes of any ordinary religious
guild or confraternity would define its objects in precisely
similar language. The statutes before us go on to provide
that the two proctors of the society shall visit sick members
and (if necessary) make a special collection for their benefit,
or apply the general funds of the guild to that purpose, or, if
they are not in need of assistance, at least alleviate their
sufferings by their 'cheerful presence'.[2] The same officials
are also required to adjust quarrels and to take measures, in
the interest of other members, for compelling students who
had left Bologna to satisfy their creditors.[3] But the liveliest
picture of the ordinary purposes of the guild is supplied by
its accounts from the year 1292—one of the earliest and com-
pletest series of university documents of the kind which have
come down to us.[4] The receipts are derived from entrance-
payments varying, according to means, from five to sixty
solidi or more, from fines, and from the occasional presents
of a newly mitred alumnus. The payments are chiefly devoted
to convivial and religious purposes, wine and spices upon the
great feasts either for the consumption of members[5] or the
payment of the officiating clergy[6] and singers, candles for
processions, charities to the poor, and other pious uses, such
as an occasional vestment or ornament for the Conventual
Church of S. Firmian habitually used by the guild. Sometimes, however, a larger drain is made upon the resources of
the society by the expenses attending the rescue of a com-

---

[1] 'Hec nostra congregatio, utilitatis tamen et publice et private
nequaquam expers credenda, presertim ex qua fraterna caritas, societatis amicitieque communicatio,
infirmorum consolatio et egenorum
subsidium, funerum deductio et
rancoris simultatumque extirpatio,
tum doctorandorum nostrorum in
locum et ex loco examinis comitiva
atque constipacio, bona spiritualia

resultarent.' *Acta Nat. Germ.*, p. 4.
[2] *Ibid.*, p. 6. [3] *Ibid.*, p. 7.
[4] *Ibid.*, p. 36 *sq.*
[5] The juxtaposition of the following is significant: 'Item, pro mal-
vasia (Malmsey) libras III. Item,
pro vitris fractis,' &c. *Ibid.*, p. 133.
[6] 'Item pro vino propinando
presbitero, qui nobis die illo missam cantavit ibidem, II solidos.'
Ibid., p. 36.

rade lying fettered in the bishop's prison.[1] These interesting
records enable us to realize the original purposes of the
larger universities of which the smaller national unions were
either the prototypes or the imitations,[2] though the former
may have been too large for the frequent convivialities and
fraternal intercourse of the smaller societies.

To appreciate the fact that the university was in its origin
nothing more than a guild of foreign students is the key to
the real origin and nature of the institution. It is also the
starting-point for an inquiry into the date at which these
societies began to be formed. It was not till towards the end
of the twelfth century that guilds of any kind, colleges of
arms and of arts (as they were called), came into existence
in the Italian cities.[3] The probabilities of the case would
suggest that some little interval would elapse between the
formation of the guilds of arms and arts and the imitation
of them by the scholars. The only direct evidence available
is derived from the silence of documents and other authorities
—particularly of the civilians who in their commentaries on
the title *De Collegiis* might be expected to allude to the existence of a kind of association the legitimacy or illegitimacy of

---

[1] *Ibid.*, p. 83. It was no doubt on some similar occasions that it was necessary to spend sixteen *denarii* in gratifications to the bishop's chaplains or other domestics to get an audience ('pro copia epi-scopi'). *Ibid.*, p. 76.

[2] Denifle (i. 153) makes the scholastic guilds originate with the Germans. This would to a large extent explain the exceptional privileges of the German nation; but the question turns in part upon the larger and very difficult question whether the guild was originally of Teutonic origin or a direct descendant of the Roman *collegia*. On this question I do not feel competent to enter.

[3] [The argument depends upon the interpretation of the evidence upon which earlier writers, e.g.

Savioli, followed by Denifle (i. 159), have relied for the assertion that a Lombard 'societas armorum' in 1174 was a guild in Bologna, and the first of the Italian local 'socie-tates armorum et artium'. Gau-denzi, who at first shared this view, afterwards argued that the evidence for 1174 had nothing to do with the later societies, which were formed in Bologna in the first half of the thirteenth century. They did not act as models for the scholastic organizations which took definite shape *c.* 1215, on the foundations laid in the twelfth century. See A. Gaudenzi, 'Gli statuti delle società delle armi del popolo di Bologna', in the *Bullettino del-l'Istituto storico italiano*, No. 8, 1889, pp. 7 *sqq.*, especially p. 27.]

CHAP. IV, which was a matter of considerable personal importance to
§ 3. themselves. Now the first of the long series of jurists who
comment upon the anomalous character of the *universitas
scholarium* is Bassianus, who, towards the close of the
twelfth century,[1] disputes the right of the scholars to elect
a rector. Thus the evidence all points to the conclusion that
the earliest *universitas* of students originated with the foreign
students of Bologna in the course of the last quarter of the
twelfth century. Farther than this it is hardly possible to
push the inquiry; though there is probability in Denifle's
opinion that the last decade of the century saw the birth of
the first university of students.[2]

Their evo- When, however, the spontaneous character of these
lution
spontane- student-societies is taken into consideration it will become
ous and evident that the process of growth may have spread over a
gradual.
considerable time. Such societies at first neither sought nor
obtained charters, privileges, or incorporation from king,
bishop, or municipality, any more than such permission
is required for the establishment of a debating-society or a
cricket-club among modern students. The university may,
indeed, have originated in a definite meeting of the students
from a particular country at a particular date; but it may
equally have grown out of informal gatherings or indignation-
meetings to concert measures for the release of an imprisoned
comrade or for the punishment of an extortionate landlord.
But we have no data for tracing the earlier stages of a process
which may be considered to have been completed when the
society proceeded to elect its first permanent rector. As to
the date at which this fundamental step was taken, we can
only say that it was before the close of the twelfth century.

Origin of The title of rector was one which only began to be applied
the rec-
torship. to various civic magistrates and officers of guilds after the
revival of Roman law-studies in the twelfth century. It was
a term commonly used as the Latin equivalent of the Italian

---

[1] As to the date of his life or
writings nothing appears to be
known except that he was a pupil
of Bulgarus. Sarti, 1. i. 89. [Cf.

Genzmer, *op. cit.* above, p. 103 n.]
[2] Denifle, i. 160. Cf. Savigny,
c. xxi, § 65. [But see above,
p. 161, n. 3.]

podestà, to denote the elected chief magistrate or dictator of CHAP. IV, a Lombard town.[1] It was also used of the head of a whole 3. federation of cities, or of the head of a single guild.[2] In the guilds the term rector is especially employed where the society was placed under the government of a single head, instead of (as was frequently the case) under a plurality of *consules* or other officers.[3] All the associations of the word suggest a concentration of corporate power in the hands of a single individual. From the guilds the expression was borrowed by the universities, as it had been borrowed by the guilds from the constitutions of the towns. The same was the case with the university *consiliarii*, who are first heard of in 1224.[4] In fact, the whole organization of the university was exactly parallel to that of the guilds, of which it formed merely a particular variety; while the organization of the guilds themselves was in Italy largely a reproduction of the municipal organization of the cities. The guild, whether of scholars or of the members of a political party or a particular trade, was a civic state in miniature, a *civitas in civitate*.

The jurisdiction of the rector was in the main derived from Nature of rectorial the statutes voluntarily enacted by the members, and from jurisdiction. that formidable oath of obedience to them and to himself, tion. on the significance of which we have already commented. At the same time the rectorship was from the first looked upon as something more than the mere presidency of a private

[1] Denifle, i. 147. Under the Empire *rector* had been one of the regular terms for the civil governor or *iudex ordinarius* of a province after Diocletian. Savigny, c. ii, § 25.

[2] Thus we hear of a *rector Societatum* in 1194 [referring to a leader of the Lombard and associated leagues; Gaudenzi, in *Bullettino*, No. 8 (1889), p. 12]; at Perugia in 1223 of 'Bailivi, Rectores vel Priores fraternitatum, societatum, familiarum seu quarumlibet artium' (Theiner, *Cod. Dipl. dom. temp. s. sedis*, i. 77); at Verona 'Prohibebo, quod nul-

lum misterium (ministerium) de civitate seu districtu Veronae habeat vel habere possit gastaldionem vel rectorem, nisi qui sit de suo misterio,' &c. (*Liber iuris civilis urbis Veronae script. 1228*, ed. Campagnola, 1728, p. 147). The last-mentioned statute probably originated in the twelfth century (see Denifle's note, i. 146).

[3] So Denifle, i. 146. But Accursius has a gloss on the passage of the Code quoted below: 'Pone in Campsoribus Bon. qui suos habent consules sive rectores' (ed. Contius, Paris, 1576, c. 559).

[4] Savioli, III. ii. 56.

society. According to the idea of the Roman law (at least as understood in the Middle Ages), every trade or profession had a kind of intrinsic right to form a *collegium* and elect magistrates of its own;[1] and the jurisdiction of these magistrates over its members in matters relating to the profession or trade was recognized by the town-governments even without any charter or express enactment as a legal, and not a merely consensual, jurisdiction. And the scholars, in setting up a *universitas* and electing a rector, undoubtedly claimed for themselves what were considered the natural or intrinsic privileges attaching to all recognized trades or professions. In general there seems to have been no unwillingness on the part of the Lombard towns to recognize to the full the jurisdiction of these student-guilds and their rectors, except on Opposition the part of one particular class. These were naturally the professors. professors of law themselves. A *universitas* of students at once offended their legal susceptibilities and infringed upon what they considered their professional prerogatives. They did not dispute the right of a profession or trade to be under the jurisdiction of a rector; but the students, they urged, did not form an independent trade or class by themselves. They were merely the pupils of the doctors of law. The right to elect a rector and to frame statutes binding at once upon the full members and the students of the profession belonged *de iure* to themselves, as it did *de facto* to their more fortunate brethren at Paris and elsewhere. The pupils of the doctors had no more right to form a *collegium* and elect magistrates than the apprentices of the smiths or the skinners.[2] The

Opposition of the professors.

---

[1] See the passage in the Code (iii, tit. xiii): 'Periniquum et temerarium esse perspicimus, eos qui professiones aliquas seu negotiationes exercere noscuntur, iudicum ad quos earum professionum seu negotiationum cura pertinet, iurisdictionem et praeceptionem declinare conari.'

[2] See for instance the words of Azo, Lecture in Cod. ad L. fin. C. *de iurisdict.* (iii. 13): ap. Denifle, i. 170: 'Ergo scolares, quia non exercent professionem sed sub exercentibus sunt discipuli, non possunt eligere consules, sicut nec discipuli pellipariorum. Magistri ergo possunt eligere consules, quia ipsi exercent professiones.' Savigny (c. xxi, § 65) continues the quotation: 'Sic et faciunt fabri, in terra ista, et alia corpora quia eligunt ministeriales suos sub quibus possunt conveniri.' This opinion is embodied in the Accursian gloss. Other instances are given by Denifle, i. 170 *sq.*

protests of the jurists, however, failed to check the growth of the institution. The university of students once formed was stronger than the handful of professors. Townsmen and professors alike stood in awe of a body which by the simple expedient of migration could destroy the trade of the former and the incomes of the latter. The jurists from the first recognize the *de facto* existence of the rectorial jurisdiction; and, after the fourteenth century, men who had grown up as students under the rectorial *régime* even attempted a theoretical justification of the anomaly.[1]

It must not be supposed that opposition to the professors formed any part of the original *raison d'être* of the universities. At first the universities no more claimed authority over the doctors or the control of strictly academical matters than the Union Societies of Oxford and Cambridge, or the militant and beer-drinking corps of a German university. The universities were formed for purposes of mutual protection and self-government, and had nothing to do with the *studium*, which was managed by the *collegia doctorum* as much as at Paris. The jealousy of the professors arose simply (so far as appears) from the fact that the students were attempting to do for themselves what the professors (on the analogy of the relations ordinarily subsisting between masters and their apprentices) claimed to do for them. But in process of time the universities did gradually acquire a complete control over the professors; and to a large extent usurped the powers elsewhere exercised by the professorial body. By means of the terrible power of 'boycotting', which they could bring into play against an offending professor or a student who adhered to a 'boycotted' professor, the student-clubs were masters of the situation.[2] And when the professors began

The universities originally claimed no academic authority.

---

[1] Cinus (ad *loc. cit.*) after giving his own opinion against the scholars, says: 'Quidam moderni dicunt contrarium, quia scolares exercent professionem, ut in Auth. *Habita*, et quia eorum universitas est licita, et sic possunt dare iurisdictionem, ut ff. [i.e. *Digest*] *quod cuiusque universitatis*' (Venice, 1493). So the earlier Odofredus († 1265) admits 'tamen per legem municipalem huius civitatis scholares creant rectores'. In Cod. ad *loc. cit.* (iii, f. 148 *a*).

[2] The statutes of the student-universities sometimes prescribe the measures to be taken against a contumacious professor. Thus at

CHAP. IV, § 3. The universities reduce the professors to subjection. to accept *salaria* from the universities themselves or from the towns which stood in awe of the universities in lieu of collecting fees from their scholars, they passed still more completely under the authority of the universities and their rectors. By these means the universities were able to compel the professors to take the oath of obedience to the rectors, which gave a certain legal sanction to their subjection. This subjection was well established by the end of the thirteenth century, as is evident from the statutes of Lérida; though the doctors still continued to assert their theoretical superiority to the universities.[1]

This subjection not undisputed. It must be remembered, indeed, that in the student-statutes we have merely the students' estimate of their own relations to the doctors. And we can no more assume that this was identical with the view taken by the doctors themselves than quotations from the writings of an ancient bishop can be taken to represent the views as to the limits of episcopal authority entertained by his presbyters or by the Church at large. Thus, while it is expressly provided by the student-statutes that they shall overrule all contradictory provisions in the statutes of the doctoral colleges,[2] the town

Parma penalties are provided against a scholar who attempts to graduate under a deprived doctor. (*Mem. e doc. per la storia della Un. di Parma*, Parma, 1888, vol. i, p. xxxix.) It should be remembered that 'privatio' meant *social excommunication* as well as mere refusal of official recognition. Thus the above-quoted statute of Parma provides that 'scholares teneantur eum vitare tanquam privatum omni commodo et honore Universitatis, et nullus scolaris ipsum admittat in societate nisi ottentum in Universitate fuerit, ut predicitur' (*loc. cit.*).

[1] 'In universitate ista Bononiensi doctores subsunt rectori. . . . Modo quaero, num quid doctores subsint universitati? Breviter dicendum est quod non: *nisi ex praerogativa consuetudinis vel iuramento*, quia iura-

verunt obedire rectori.' Bartolus († 1357), ad Auth. *Habita* (quoted by Savigny, c. xxi, § 70).

[2] 'Cassa et irrita et inania statuta et consuetudines decernimus que doctorum collegium habuerit vel observaverit seu habiturum servatum vel facturum de novo fuerit contra statuta universitatis nostre et scolasticam libertatem.' *Stat.*, p. 144. On the other hand, after the table of degree-fees, appears a clause respecting the statutes of the colleges. (*Ibid.*, p. 151.) The city enacted that their own statutes should prevail over those of the colleges, but the college-statutes over those of the universities. (*Stat.*, p. 156.) In one place in the university-statutes we find a clause 'secundum quod in statutis ipsius Collegii determinatum invenimus'.

statutes enact precisely the opposite. Moreover, it should be CHAP. IV,
§ 3. noticed that when the students seem to be most clearly usurping the functions of the doctoral body in defining the conditions precedent to degrees, their enactments are in the main identical with those found in the doctoral statutes: just as many of the provisions by which the students seem to be legislating for the city and its magistrates are mere embodiments of privileges conferred by the latter.[1] At the same time there can be no doubt that the real supremacy rested with the students; and the statutes of the colleges themselves in general adopted a sufficiently humble tone in their attitude towards the student-universities.

In so far as the claims of the student-corporations rested on anything more than usurpation and their undoubted right to pursue their studies elsewhere in the event of disagreement with the town-authorities,[2] their legal and constitutional basis would be found in the papal Bulls which from time to time confirmed the statutes of the universities, and subjected the impugners of them to ecclesiastical censures.[3] But little use seems practically to have been made of this papal privilege except as a weapon against the city in the earliest days of the university. The students seldom or never appealed, like the masters of Paris, to ecclesiastical authority for assistance in enforcing their own internal discipline.

There was, as we have seen, nothing in the university as an institution to arouse the jealousy or hostility of the magistrates or city of Bologna. That the students should have a *collegium* and be governed by a rector was completely in accordance with the political ideas of the time. The *universi-*

Papal
privileges.

Opposition
of the city.

---

[1] e.g. in the statute *De domibus in quibus habitant scolares non destruendis* (pp. 126, 153). The whole of the Fourth Book of University Statutes is a reproduction of town-statutes.

[2] Cf. the Statute of Florence as late as 1472 in *Stat. Fiorent.*, p. 24. The Rector is to insist on payment of the *salaria* by the City, 'Alias interdicat studium'.

[3] The first general confirmation dates from 1253. The Bull was addressed to the Archdeacon of Bologna and a Dominican friar. Sarti, II (1772), p. 124. Other ecclesiastics were from time to time appointed conservators of the privileges of the university, but their jurisdiction does not seem to have become so extensive as at Paris (Ghirardacci, i. 529; ii. 27, 66). Cf. below, ch. v, § 3.

CHAP. IV, *tates* met with no systematic opposition from the municipali-
§ 3. ties of the kind which we shall find the Parisian university of
masters experiencing at the hands of the Bishop, Chancellor,
and Church of Paris. The Bolognese government was quite
content to concede to the universities of students what it
conceded to other guilds. But in certain respects the universities demanded more than the city conceded to other
guilds. The guilds were composed of citizens, who never
thought of disputing the authority of the city-government,
and who could not put themselves beyond its jurisdiction
without losing both property and status. The universities
were composed of aliens, who refused to recognize the
authority of the State in which they lived when it conflicted
with the allegiance which they had sworn to their own artificial
commonwealth.[1] One matter was pre-eminently a subject of
contention between the city and university. The power of
secession was cherished by the university as its great instrument of warfare against all manner of enemies. The city
naturally wished to deprive it of this unfair advantage in its
controversies with itself and to render its own prosperity
independent of the goodwill of an alien corporation.

The first In the first collisions between town and gown at Bologna
migrations it was, however, the professors who were directly involved.
originate
with Long before the close of the twelfth century we find a ten-
professors. dency in the Bolognese professors to wander abroad, whether
in consequence of disputes with the town-authorities or
allured by prospects of more liberal remuneration elsewhere.
Thus Placentinus had left Bologna to establish schools first
at Mantua, afterwards at Montpellier, in the third or fourth
quarter of the twelfth century. And most of the numerous
law-schools which we find established in the Italian towns

[1] It was not merely in its relations with the city, as a whole, but in quarrels with individual citizens that the university could bring its powerful organization into play. Thus the Paduan *Statuta Arti-starum* (f. xxxiii *b*) denounce the punishment of 'interdictio' (i.e. from intercourse with scholars) against any one who cites a scholar before the city magistrates—the sentence to extend to the third generation of the offender's poster-ity. The same statutes (f. xxxii *b*) enact that if a householder refuses to execute repairs after fifteen days' notice, the tenant is to repair, and deduct the expense from the rent.

by the beginning of the thirteenth century had apparently been founded by similar secessions of doctors or students or both. The city was at last forced to bring to bear against the vagrant doctors the usual medieval method of prevention— making the suspected party swear that he would not commit the apprehended crime.[1] The first time that this measure was adopted was in the case of Pillius. Getting wind of a negotiation with the neighbouring town of Modena for the purchase of the doctor's services, the magistrates assembled all the professors of the school and compelled them to swear not to teach out of Bologna for the next two years. In spite of his oath, however, Pillius could not resist the renewed offers of Modena gold.[2] After this time such oaths appear to have been habitually exacted of the doctors;[3] and from 1227 to 1312 the oath was regularly enforced by the town statutes upon all doctors who intended to teach at Bologna.[4] At the beginning of the thirteenth century, however, the city found itself threatened with a much more formidable danger. Not merely individual professors, but whole bodies of students, dissatisfied with their treatment at Bologna, entered into negotiations with other towns for the transference of the *studium* to them. In 1204, after a secession of this kind to Vicenza, the city passed a statute prohibiting citizens from following the seceding scholars or from aiding and abetting similar secessions in future.[5] After the secession to Arezzo in

The student-migration to Vicenza, 1204.

---

[1] Sarti, I. i. 77, 78. Savigny (c. xxi, § 81) gives a list of the doctors who took the oath. Cf. Savioli, II. ii. 465. [Many texts of such oaths, re-edited from the *Registrum grossum* of Bologna, can be studied in the *Chartularium studii Bononiensis*, vol. i (1909). The earliest given is the oath of Lothair of Cremona, 1 Dec. 1189.]

[2] See extracts from Pillius in Sarti, I. i. 84. Savioli gives 1188 as the date of Pillius's flight, but he appears to be established in Modena before 1182. Savigny, c. xxii.

[3] Sarti, I. i. 84, 85.

[4] Frati, ii. 23. In 1312 the oath was abolished, but penalties for Doctors absconding during the time of their contract reappear in 1334. Savigny, c. xxi, § 81: Ghirardacci, i. 560, 561; ii. 11, 117.

[5] Frati, ii. 23. In 1211 we find a statute passed, which, without directly naming the scholastic universities, may possibly be directed against them, since in it citizens as well as strangers are forbidden to give a promise or oath 'de adiuvando unus alium'; the Societies of arms and arts being alone exempted from its provisions. Savioli, II. ii. 464. [Gaudenzi considers that the reference to the 'society of

CHAP. IV,
§ 3.
Secession
to Arezzo
in 1215
provokes
fresh
quarrels.
1215, in consequence of a great quarrel between the Lombards and the Tuscans,[1] or possibly in consequence of the measures which the city had adopted for the suppression of the tumults, the penalties of banishment and confiscation of goods were denounced against any scholar who should administer an oath to another binding him to leave the city if commanded to do so by him.[2] The *podestà* required the universities to incorporate the town statute with their own, by which means every student would be compelled to swear obedience to it. The 'scholars' especially aimed at were of course the rectors,[3] who must have been empowered either by a permanent statute or by some extraordinary resolution to demand such an oath as a means of securing a prompt and universal secession in the event of a request being refused or an injury going unpunished. One at least of the universities, if not all, appealed to the Pope, who, in accordance with what became the universal policy of the Holy See, warmly espoused the cause of the scholars; and in 1217 a Bull was issued by the new Pontiff, Honorius III—formerly Archdeacon of Bologna —urging or commanding the revocation of the obnoxious law, while the scholars were exhorted to leave the city rather than violate their oaths.[4] It would appear from subsequent documents that the papal intervention was unsuccessful, that the suppression of the rectorship took effect, and that the scholars, for non-compliance with the demands of the citizens, were placed under the ban of the city, by which they

---

arms' is a later interpolation: *Bullettino*, No. 8, p. 13.] At this time a clause was inserted into the doctors' oath pledging them not to aid and abet secessions of scholars. Sarti, I. ii. 70, 71.

[1] 'Ideo ego Rofredus Beneventanus iuris civilis professor ad preces et instantias sociorum meorum, nobilium de partibus Tusciae, cum essem in civitate scilicet arretina,' &c.—ap. Sarti, I. i. 139. Cf. *ibid.*, pp. 133, 134.

[2] 'Si quis scolaris vel alius aliquem scolarem aliquo modo vel ingenio astrinxerit ut ei possit

precipere de ducendo de civitate ista causa studii banniatur,' &c. Frati, ii. 25. Cf. Denifle, i. 161–2; Savigny, c. xxi, § 65. [A letter from the scholars to the Pope, given by Buoncompagno in his *Rhetorica antiqua*, suggests that the secession took place at the command of the papal legate during this time of dispute between the Pope and the Emperor Otto IV. See Gaudenzi in *Bullettino*, No. 14 (1898), pp. 108, 109.]

[3] Explicitly mentioned in the Bull of 1220. See below, p. 171.

[4] Sarti, II (1772), pp. 57, 58.

became 'infamous', lost their civil rights and were liable to the confiscation of all their goods. In fact it is probable that from 1217 to 1220, or at least for some time before the last-mentioned year,[1] there was a more or less complete dispersion of the *studium*. In 1220 a fresh papal remonstrance[2] induced the town to yield so far as to repeal the penal enactments against the scholars and their rectors, but it required that upon their accession to office the rectors should swear not to entertain any project for the removal of the *studium* from Bologna. The truce, if such it was, was of short duration, and in 1222 a great migration to Padua took place.[3] But in 1224 another papal Bull,[4] combined with the efforts of the Emperor Frederick II to destroy the *studium*,[5] seems practically to have resulted in the abandonment of the attempt to exact the suicidal oath from the rectors, though the statute requiring it remained on the city statute-book till 1288.[6] In the city statutes, printed as a supplement to the university statute of 1432, we still find the penalty of death denounced against any person whatever, whether citizen or stranger, who shall enter into a conspiracy for transferring the *studium*, as also against any citizen-doctor over the age of fifty who shall without permission of the city magistrates leave Bologna for the purpose of lecturing elsewhere. If the offender were a younger and therefore a less valuable professor, the milder penalty of 200 ducats is substituted.[7]

Migration to Padua, 1222.

A full account of the relations between the university and the city of Bologna in the thirteenth century would form one of the most interesting chapters in the history of universities. Unfortunately, the fragmentary and scattered details which

Recognition of rectorship.

---

[1] Savioli records these events under 1220, but the documents do not indicate that any fresh measures were taken in this year.

[2] Savioli, II. ii. 466. Cf. II. i. 395.

[3] See below, ch. vi, § 4.

[4] Savioli, III. ii. 56.

[5] See the Bull of Honorius III in 1227, requiring the Emperor to revoke his edicts against the Lombard league, 'et specialiter constitu-tionem factam de Studio et Studentibus Bononie'. Sarti, I. ii (1772), pp. 72–4.

[6] Denifle, i. 176.

[7] *Stat.*, p. 157. [A thirteenth-century statute to the same effect, but less drastic in its penalties, has been printed by Gaudenzi in 'Gli antichi statuti del comune di Bologna intorno allo studio', *Bullettino*, No. 6 (1888), pp. 122, 123.]

CHAP. IV, have been given are all which can be collected. It seems that
§ 3. a fairly satisfactory *modus vivendi* was effected between the
two bodies at about the middle of the thirteenth century, after
a great collision provoked by the execution of a scholar, and
also by the efforts of the Bolognese doctors to convert their
office into a lucrative monopoly.[1] Again the rectorate was
threatened; again the counter-threat of secession eventually
prevailed. The Statutes of 1245, while taking precautions
against the transference of the *studium* and still continuing
to prohibit oaths pledging the scholars to obey a rectorial
order for secession, fully recognize the right of the scholars
to elect rectors, though forbidding citizens to swear obedience
to them. Students are accorded the private or *civil* (though
of course not the *political*) rights of citizens; they are to be
allowed to make a will or receive property under a will, to
give evidence, and to do other 'legitimate acts'.[2] The Statutes
of 1289 confer still further privileges upon scholars: exceptional steps are taken for the protection of their person and
property, and the *podestà* is even directed to enforce the
rectorial sentences in civil disputes between scholars.[3] At
some time before 1432 the university appears to have succeeded in imposing upon the *podestà* a special oath to respect
and enforce the Statutes of the University: at all events the
rectors are required by the Statutes of the University to
demand such an oath.[4]

Migration   The last important collision between town and gown at
of 1321: Bologna took place in 1321, when, in consequence of the
Peace be-
tween execution of a scholar who had tried, with the aid of some
town and
gown. companions, to abduct a notary's daughter from her father's
house, the majority of the students, together with many
professors, seceded to Siena.[5] In the following year a recon-

[1] Savioli, III. i. 332.
[2] Frati, ii. 25–9.
[3] *Stat.*, p. 163.
[4] *Stat.*, p. 64. The statute was
introduced later than 1347. The
Town Statutes of 1244 required
the *podestà* to swear obedience to
all the town's provisions in favour
of the *studium*. Frati, i. 369.

[5] Ghirardacci, ii. 5, 6. [Ghirar-
dacci's highly coloured and inaccurate narrative is corrected by
F. Filippini, who shows the effect
of the incident on party feeling
in Bologna, and indirectly on academic developments in Florence as
well as at Bologna: *Studi e memorie*,
vi (1921), 107–85.]

ciliation was effected; the city compelled its *podestà* to receive discipline in the Dominican Church, and a chapel or church was built for the university by the grateful townsmen in memory of the event. The building was styled 'The Church of S. Mary of the Scholars in the Borgo of S. Mamolo', though spoken of in the statutes as the University Chapel.[1] The fact testifies to the vital importance of the university to the city,[2] and the consequent power wielded by the former.

Even for tracing the internal development of the university the materials are singularly scanty compared with those which we possess for the history of Paris. We know that a body of statutes received the papal approval in 1253. But the earliest complete collection of statutes dates only from 1432. Enough might even then have been gathered by inference from the statutes of daughter-universities to demolish the rash assumption of Savigny[3] that the bulk of these statutes had come down unaltered from the earliest days of the university. Denifle's discovery, in the Chapter Library of Pressburg in Hungary, of an earlier redaction of about half of this statute-book puts the matter beyond doubt. From the information supplied by these statutes themselves, it appears that they were originally drafted by the celebrated canonist Johannes Andreae, and published by the university in the

Scantiness of data: the statutes.

---

[1] Melloni, *Elenco delle chiese della città e diocesi di Bologna compilato nel MCCCLXVI* (Bologna, 1779, p. 18), and *Stat.*, pp. 16, 61 n. After 1529 the church was styled S. Maria delle Grazie: it is now suppressed. [This church, built in the Via San Mamolo, in the jurists' quarter of the Porta Procula, was popularly known as Santa Maria della Pace. See Cavazza, *Le scuole dell'antico studio bolognese*, 1896, pp. 223–5, and appendix of documents, No. 64.]

[2] The *Acta Nationis Germanicae* bear curious testimony to the frequency of secessions or migrations in the period immediately preceding this approximately permanent settlement. Under the year 1309

occur the words 'Nota, quod hic vacaverat natio tribus annis, quibus non fuit studium' (p. 59), and among the accounts of 1308 (*loc. cit.*) is an entry 'pro sacco, in quo portabantur res nacionis in discordia, II solidos'. Under 1312 (p. 65) is a payment 'pro instrumento cautionis, quam fecimus nacioni dum timore novitatum cederemus de Bononia'. There is a similar entry in 1316 (p. 72); while under 1321 and 1322 there are payments connected with the secession to Imola (pp. 79–80). On this last see Banchi, *Giornale storico degli archivi Toscani*, Anno V, 1861, p. 237.

[3] C. xxi, § 61.

year 1317. Additions were made to them in the years 1326, 1336, and 1346, and in the last-mentioned year they were subjected to a complete revision. The Pressburg MS. contains the form which was given to them in the academical year 1346–7.

Statutes
of 1317.
But a comparison of these statutes with those of various universities formed on the Bologna model in the period between 1317 and 1347 makes it clear that the changes introduced in 1347 were but slight. The re-editing consisted chiefly of additions, deciding moot points that had arisen in the interval, and which can generally be recognized by their interrupting the alphabetical arrangement of the original statutes. When, however, we turn to the only extant collection of university statutes believed to be copied from those of Bologna at an earlier date than 1317, we find little verbal coincidence with the collection of 1317. The university constitution in its main outlines—the rectoral jurisdiction, the nations and *consiliarii*, the student-supremacy over the professors[1] and other institutions to be more fully described in our next chapter—are all found faithfully anticipated in the statutes made for the University of Lérida in the year 1300.[2] But the actual statutes are expressed in a different style and language, and are very much less bulky and detailed than the Bologna code of 1317. It is from this epoch then that we must date the code of laws which continued with few modifications to govern the University of Bologna throughout our period.

In the following section I shall content myself with giving a sketch of the university-system as it is presented to us by the first collection of statutes which we possess in their integrity—the code of 1432. But the discovery of Denifle enables us to add that the account will in the main be applicable to the whole period between 1317 and 1432.[3]

---

[1] This supremacy was virtually recognized by Honorius III as early as 1224, where he speaks of the doctors 'qui . . . stare ut tenebantur sententiae rectorum con-
tempserunt'. Savioli, III. ii. 56.

[2] Published by Villanueva in *Viage literario a las iglesias de España*, xvi. 207.

[3] See below, § 6.

It may be convenient here to explain that there was at Bologna a wholly distinct university of students in medicine and arts, and a wholly distinct college of doctors in those faculties, which will be dealt with in detail hereafter. In the next two sections I am concerned only with the jurist organization.

§ 4. THE CONSTITUTION OF THE STUDENT-UNIVERSITIES

CHAP. IV,
§ 4.
Close
union of
the two
universi-
ties.
I⟶T will be noticed at once on comparing the extant statutes
with the state of things disclosed by the isolated documents
of earlier times that a great change has taken place in the
mutual relations of the separate universities. At the beginning
of the thirteenth century the four universities of jurists
appear as distinct as a number of separate trade-guilds.
Though the city legislation against the administration of
oaths pledging scholars to leave Bologna under certain circumstances was directed against all the universities, it was
(so far as appears) only by the non-Italian societies that it was
resisted; and other instances occur of independent action on
the part of particular universities. By the fourteenth century
the universities of jurists (now amalgamated into the two
Ultramontane and Cismontane universities), though remaining theoretically distinct bodies, are practically almost fused
into one. They have a common code of statutes; they hold
common congregations; the rector of either university is
empowered, in the absence or default of his colleague, to act
on his behalf;[1] they have even (it would seem) one common
seal.[2] Though they have no common head, the two universities have become practically as much one body as the four
nations of Paris.[3]

The jurisdiction of the rector was originally based upon
the statutes of the university and derived its sanction from
the penalties which the university as a private society had in

---

[1] *Stat.*, p. 63 *et passim*.

[2] *Stat.*, p. 127.

[3] It would seem that this state of
things came into existence at about
the close of the thirteenth century.
In 1273 the Ultramontanes in their
separate congregation discuss a
proposed alteration in their permanent statutes (*Acta Nat. Germ.*,
p. 349). In 1308 we read of a
'liber statutorum scholarium ultramontanorum et citramontanorum'
(*ibid.*, p. 350). In 1306 the Ultramontanes are said 'statuere et de-
clarare *ad hoc*' (*ibid.*, p. 352), but
its resolution related merely to an
internal dispute between its constituent nations and does not seem
to have involved any alteration in
its permanent statutes. Except
where the contrary appears from
the context, I shall employ the
term university to denote the combined universities of jurists.

its power to inflict on its own members, including the CHAP. IV, spiritual penalties in which transgressors were involved by § 4. their oaths of obedience. In accordance, however, with the prevalent ideas as to the authority of *collegia* and the inherent power of their members to elect consuls or rectors, the republic recognized the authority of the rectors over their students and directed its own magistrates to enforce their sentences. This applied, however, only in the first instance to cases in which both parties were members or public servants of the universities. But the universities claimed more than this. They claimed for the rectors an exclusive jurisdiction in all cases in which a scholar was involved either as plaintiff or defendant.[1] Such a demand the republic naturally resented, and there remained a permanent contradiction upon this point between the statutes of the university and those of the city.[2] Citizens may at times have elected to cite a scholar before the rector; but it is improbable that the rectors ever succeeded in getting their jurisdiction *in invitos* acknowledged where a citizen was defendant. The statutes of 1432 require the rector to demand of the *podestà* an oath to respect the privileges of the university and to enforce the rectorial sentences,[3] but in the practical application of this enactment there remained no doubt the old diversity of interpretation between the imponent and the taker of the oath; though, from the variations observable on this point in other

[1] Sometimes, but not always, the Italian university statutes admit the household (*familiares*) of scholars to their privileges, e.g. at Florence, *Stat.*, p. 22. So apparently at Bologna, *Stat.*, p. 163.

[2] Cf. *Stat.*, p. 57 with the extract from the town statutes, *ibid.*, p. 163. Such collisions between the town statutes and those of the scholars could probably be found in most Italian universities. Sometimes the universities expressly claim to override those of the town. Thus at Florence the rector is to bear arms 'non obstantibus . . . Statutis vel reformationibus Populi et comunis Florentie in contrarium loquentibus' (*Stat. Fiorent.*, p. 28). In 1366 we find the rectorial jurisdiction sanctioned by the city statutes with the express exception of the right to bear arms or 'ire de nocte' (*ibid.*, p. 149). In 1403, however, licences to bear arms might be granted to the *familiares* of the rector (*ibid.*, p. 181). At Ferrara the rector's house is to be a sanctuary for criminals (Borsetti, i. 379).

[3] 'Item mandabit sententias Rectorum vel alterius ipsorum esecutioni.' *Stat.*, p. 183.

CHAP. IV,
§ 4.

university statutes, it is probable that at Bologna itself there may have been fluctuations in the practical limits of the academical jurisdiction at different times.

The rector bound to exact penalties.

So completely was the rector's jurisdiction dependent upon the statutes that his functions were, in many cases, almost purely executive. When the statutes denounced deprivation or expulsion upon professor or student, the rectors had no discretion in inflicting it. The power of restoring a deprived doctor was reserved to the university itself.[1] Similarly when the amount of a fine was fixed by statute, it was regarded as a debt to the university incurred *ipso facto*. If the rector failed to collect it, he became himself indebted to the society to the same amount, and at the scrutiny held at the end of his term of office was required by the syndics appointed for that purpose to make good the deficiency.[2] All students—with a peculiar exception in favour of bishops and high dignitaries —were bound to give information if any breach of the statutes came under their notice.[3] At the *syndicatus* on the expiration of his office complaints might be made against the rector by professors or scholars, and the rector was personally liable in damages to individuals whom he had annoyed by excessive zeal just as he was liable to the society for his omissions.[4]

No criminal jurisdiction.

Criminal jurisdiction even over its own members—still less over citizens—the universities do not seem to have secured[5] until the fifteenth century, when it was conceded

[1] *Stat.*, p. 110.

[2] *Stat.*, pp. 60, 67 *sq.*, 149. This is one of the innumerable adaptations from Italian civic practice. The same method was adopted with the *podestà*.

[3] *Ibid.*

[4] For a most curious record of such a *syndicatus* see *Stat. Fiorent.*, pp. 425–38.

[5] 'Iurisdictionem ordinariam Rectores habeant in scolares in causis civilibus' (*Stat.*, p. 56). In a later addition (p. 181) there is an elaborate scale of fines for various forms of injury to the person or dignity of the rector, culminating

in the provision that any one who assaults that official 'cum armis et sanguinis effusione citra mortem vel mortale vulnus poenam manus et centum lib. bonon. incurrat'. But from the context it appears that the university was merely 'puniri curare et usque ad finem prosequi' before the city magistrates. In 1411 the rector's criminal jurisdiction over scholars is recognized by the city (*ibid.*, p. 168). So later (*ibid.*, p. 195): 'Et talis gerens se pro Bidello trudetur carceribus domini Potestatis per spacium trium dierum per Rectores Universitatis nostrae.' A privilege of

where both parties were scholars. In the late additions to the CHAP. IV,
§ 4. statutes of 1432 we find, moreover, a provision that a student shall not be arrested (except for treason) without the permission of the rector, that he shall not be dragged through the streets, and that he shall be admitted to bail when accused of carrying arms.[1]

There was, indeed, a large class of citizens on whom the Interdict. statutes did impose penalties. By a judicious employment of the mighty power of interdict or 'boycotting',[2] the university had acquired jurisdiction over the landlords of students' houses in matters affecting their relations with the students,[3] and over all classes of tradesmen or workmen engaged in the production of books.[4] With these exceptions the jurisdiction of the rector was confined to the members of the university; and even over students this jurisdiction was very strictly limited and defined by statute. The penalties which he could inflict consisted in ordinary cases of fines, or in serious cases of expulsion or 'privation', together with the power of pro-

---

Paul III in 1544 gave the rectors jurisdiction in all non-capital criminal cases in which a scholar was involved. *Stat. Iur. Bon.*, pp. 97, 98. Savigny (c. xxi, § 74) says that the right of the rectors to punish small offences was never contested, but gives no proof of such a right being recognized except in the case of offences against the statutes, which do not provide for the punishment of offences against the ordinary law. [Cavazza, p. 7, points out that very few actual cases of rectorial jurisdiction have survived in the records.]

[1] *Stat.*, p. 184.

[2] At Padua a person who violates the privilege of the university 'per scholas publicetur et comertio scholarium interdicatur'. *Stat. Artistarum*, f. xxxvi. The penalty of 'privatio' sometimes extended to the fifth generation. *Stat. Univ. Iur. Patavini Gymn.*, 1550, f. 51.

[3] The town recognizes the system

of joint-taxation (*Stat.*, p. 160), but it denies the university's right of *interdictio*, at least in certain cases (p. 161), while the university statutes denounce it against the 'hospites' of houses near which an outrage on a scholar is committed, even if the owner was not personally responsible (p. 124). Under the papal Bull authorizing the taxation (see above, p. 148) disputes about lodgings might be taken before the spiritual courts, but the university denounces perpetual interdiction against an interdicted landlord invoking their help (*Stat.*, p. 125).

[4] 'Scriptores, miniatores, correctores et miniorum repositores atque rasores librorum, ligatores, cartolarii et qui vivunt pro universitate scolarium.' *Stat.*, p. 59. The town statutes require that disputes between scholars and *scriptores* shall be settled by the *podestà* (*Stat.*, p. 162).

CHAP. IV, nouncing a student perjured. In the last two cases, the assent
§ 4. of a majority of the council was required. In the enforcement
of his civil penalties, the rector was dependent upon the
assistance of the *podestà* and his officers.[1]

The pro-   As has been already said, the jurisdiction conferred by the
fessorial
jurisdic- Authentic *Habita* upon the professors was always legally
tion.   recognized, however much out of harmony with the later
relations in other respects between the professors and their
domineering pupils. By the decree of Frederick I this jurisdiction extended apparently both to criminal and civil matters.
This interpretation of the law was, however, much disputed
by the citizens; and a great feud between the Lombards and
the Tuscans early in the thirteenth century, when (according
to the jurist Odofredus) there were 10,000 students at
Bologna, compelled them for a time to renounce a criminal
jurisdiction which they found themselves incapable of enforcing. This jurisdiction had been, however, nominally
resumed in the time of Odofredus († A.D. 1265), though it is
probable that it was very much of a dead letter.[2] At all events

---

[1] Cf. *Stat. Fiorent.*, p. 430, where a student complains that the rector 'misit pro familia domini Potestatis, uno mane, dum esset dominus Andreas in scolis ad audiendum, et eum de Studio ignominiose et vituperose capi fecit et duci ad Palatium et in carceribus detrudi', &c., for which excess of zeal the rector was heavily fined by the syndics.

[2] 'Sed per scholares et doctores renunciatum est Bononiae quantum ad criminales, et sic servatur exceptis clericis qui suo non potuerunt privilegio renunciare.' Accursius in Cod. iv, tit. 13 *Habita* Verb. *si litem* (ed. Contius, Paris, 1576, c. 750). 'Or, segnori, videtur quod hec constitutio quantum ad verba loquatur in civili et in criminali, nam vidi hoc in civitate ista tempore Domini Azonis quod scholares poterant declinare forum in causa criminali, et erant hic tunc

temporis bene x. millia scholarium. Sed scholares renuntiaverunt huic privilegio tempore Domini Azonis et fuit renuntiatum tali ratione, quia inter Lombardos et Tuscos fuit maxima discordia et maximum bellum, ita quod domini doctores non poterant se intromittere in puniendo eos; ... sed in civili bene habent adhuc suum hodie privilegium. Sed hodie reversum est ad pristinum statum: tamen deus velit quod non faciant sibi male adinvicem, nam per dominos doctores male puniuntur illa maleficia.' Odofredus, *Super Codicem* (iii, f. 204). Auth. *Habita*. He adds that the privilege applies only to *scholares qui studiorum causa peregrinantur*, hence not to *Bononienses*. Accursius (c. 1220) treats even the bishop's jurisdiction as obsolete 'quantum ad delicta'; *Authenticorum Collatio*, iii, tit. 4 (Paris, 1576, c. 133), though this must be

the professors would be entirely dependent upon the co-operation of the town authorities for the enforcement of any sentences that they might venture to pronounce. The right secured by the *Habita* of citing a scholar before the bishop was no doubt intended primarily for clerks, though originally the alternative appears to have been always open to a plaintiff-student; but in practice it was seldom claimed except by ecclesiastics. And at no time was either clerk or layman allowed to decline the rector's jurisdiction if cited before him by the other party.[1] As, however, the canon law forbade the exercise of any jurisdiction by a layman over a clerk, the university statute provided that the rector should be himself a clerk.[2] We shall have occasion again to speak of the medieval conception of *clericatus*, which is, indeed, of great importance in the appreciation of the relations between the universities and the church. Here it will be sufficient to say that any student could become a clerk and so acquire the immunities of an ecclesiastic by merely receiving the tonsure from a bishop, and adopting the clerical dress. The rector

CHAP. IV,
§ 4.

The rector a clerk.

---

understood with an exception in favour of *clerici*. Odofredus *ad Dig. Vetus* Const. *Omnem* (i, f. 4) assumes that even a lay scholar may still be cited before the bishop. The clerical privilege is enforced by Bull in 1252 (*Archiv f. Kirchengesch.* iv. 245). [The intervention of Pope Honorius III in the disputes between the scholars and the commune (above, pp. 170, 171), by confirming the student organization, assisted the development of rectorial jurisdiction at the expense of the masters. Passages in Odofredus show that the latter strongly preferred the Parisian system. They were naturally inclined to feel more sympathy with the commune during these early times of stress. See Tamassia, *Odofredo, passim*; and cf. Manacorda, i. 240 *sqq.*]

[1] *Stat.*, p. 57.
[2] The above explanation of the

proviso is clearly given by the jurist Baldus and adopted by Denifle, i. 87. Savigny (c. xxi, § 72), who never could understand what a *clericus* meant in the Middle Ages, rejects it, and says that *clericus* must mean merely 'scholar'. But compare the following statute of Ferrara (Borsetti, i. 367): 'Et si fieri posset, sit (Rector) qui promotus sit ad primos ordines ecclesiasticos, scilicet ad primam tonsuram et quatuor Ordines Minores et hoc quo convenitur (*lege* convenienter) Iudex competens Scholaribus fieri queat.' For the importance attached to the tonsure and clerical habit, cf. *Stat. Fiorent.*, p. 437, where it is pleaded in the archbishop's court that 'non potuit nec potest dictus magister Ieronimus gaudere aliquo privilegio clericali, et maxime quia iam diu ivit sine habitu et tonsura clericali'.

CHAP. IV, of a university of students was usually a beneficed ecclesiastic
§ 4. —a dean or archdeacon or canon for instance.[1] In such cases
he would have to be at least in minor orders; but he might
be a *clericus* without being even in minor orders.

The
nations.
We have already alluded to the subdivision of the two
universities into nations. In the earliest statutes we find the
Citramontanes divided into three nations only, the Romans,
the Tuscans, and the Lombards; but these are further subdivided into *consiliariae*, or smaller local divisions, each of
which elected one or two councillors.[2] By 1432, however,
these *consiliariae*, seventeen in number, are occasionally
spoken of as distinct nations, though traces of the earlier
arrangement still remained in the statute-book.[3] As early as
1265 the Ultramontanes were divided into fourteen nations.[4]

[1] Thus, at the time of the reformation of the statutes in 1432 we
find that both rectors are scholars
in canon law, one being Dean of
Troyes, the other provost of a collegiate church (*Stat.*, p. 47). At
Florence, in 1487, we find the
minimum age reduced to nineteen
(*Stat. Fiorent.*, p. 15).

[2] 'Statuimus quod consciliarii
sint numero triginta octo, scilicet
decem et novem ultramontani, et
totidem citramontani. De ultra-
montanis autem quod solitum est
servetur. De citramontanis vero
iuxta morem antiquum nacio Romanorum habeat sex, Thuscorum
alios sex, reliquos habeat nacio
Lombardorum, quos per consciliarias sic dividimus, sicut nacionis
statutis est descriptum.' *Stat.*,
p. 16.

[3] The above-cited words are repeated nearly *verbatim*, except that
the allusion to the statutes of the
nation disappears and the councillors are redistributed as follows:
'Natio Romanorum habeat octo,
Tuscorum sex, et natio Lombardorum quinque. Quas nationes per
consiliarias sic dividimus, videlicet: Nationes vero sunt decem
et septem, sex Romanorum, sex

Tuscorum et quinque Lombardorum. Romana continet sub se has
nationes: Nationem Romanorum,
nationem Abrucii et terre laboris,
apulie et calabrie, marchie infer-
ioris, marchie superioris, item
totius insule Sicilie. Natio Tuscorum habet sub se sex nationes,
scilicet Florentinam, pisanam et
lucanam, senensem, ducatum, ra-
venatem et venetorum. Natio
lombardorum quinque nationes,
cum vocibus contentis sub illis,
scilicet ianuensium, mediolanen-
sium, tessalonicam, longobardam
et celestinam' (*Stat.*, p. 68). Rome
and Sicily have each two councillors. So in *Stat.*, p. 50, the Ultramontane *consiliariae* are distinguished from the Cismontane
nations.

[4] Document in *Acta Nationis
Germ.*, p. 347. The nations are
Gaul, Picardy, Burgundy, Poitou,
Touraine and Maine, Normandy,
Catalonia, Hungary, Poland, Germany (Teothonici), Spain, Provence, England, Gascony. Poitou
and Gascony were merged and
assigned two councillors by the
agreement made in this year (*ibid.*,
p. 348).

In 1432 there were sixteen Ultramontane nations,[1] each electing one, or in a few cases two *consiliarii*.[2] In early times these
nations (which we have seen reason to believe were in reality
earlier than the two great federations into which they were
ultimately merged) were, like the nations of Paris, distinct
corporations with statutes, officers, and meetings of their
own. But (except in the case of the specially privileged
German nation) they here appear to have lost much of their
importance and autonomy, though they must have held congregations of their own for the election of *consiliarii*.[3]

It is obvious that so enormous a body as the whole body The *con-*
of law-students could not meet so frequently as the Parisian *siliarii.*
university of masters. Many matters therefore which were
at Paris dealt with by the university itself were at Bologna
left to the rectors and *consiliarii*, who jointly formed the
ordinary executive body of the university. The consent of
one rector and a majority of the councillors was necessary
to the calling of a congregation[4]—a provision which of course
gave them the initiative in all university legislation. Upon
the requisition of two councillors, the votes were taken by
ballot.[5] The concurrence of a majority of the council was, as
has been said, necessary before the rector could pronounce

---

[1] The names are now (*Stat.*, pp.
70, 71): (1) Gaul, (2) Portugal and
the Algarve, (3) Provence, (4) England, (5) Burgundy, (6) Savoy, (7)
Gascony and Auvergne, (8) Berry,
(9) Touraine, (10) Aragon and
Catalonia with Valencia and the
Majorcas (two councillors), (11)
Navarre, (12) Germany (two councillors), (13) Hungary, (14) Poland,
(15) Bohemia, (16) Flanders. The
statute speaks of nineteen Ultramontane councillors, but only
eighteen are accounted for.

[2] From the expressions 'habeat
unam vocem et unum concilia-
rium', 'habeat duas voces', &c.
(*Stat.*, p. 68), it would seem as if
the voting was by nations as at
Paris (below, p. 410 *sq.*), but the
statute *De modo partiti ponendi in*
Universitate proves the contrary
(*Stat.*, p. 130). Possibly the expression may be a survival.

[3] The statutes of 1432 limit the
'festivitates Nationum que non
sunt descripte inter festa universitatis' and abolish the 'officia pre-
positorum seu priorum Nationum
seu consiliariorum ultramontanorum per que etiam Rectorum
iurisdictio per tempora extitit
multum impedita' (*Stat.*, p. 139).
We know from the *Acta Nat. Germ.*
that the independent existence of
the specially privileged German
nation was quite unaffected by this
statute: how it affected other
nations we do not know.

[4] *Stat.*, p. 60.

[5] *Stat.*, p. 57.

CHAP. IV, the sentence of deprivation, or declare a doctor or scholar
§ 4.   perjured.[1]

Election   The rector was chosen biennially by that method of in-
of rector. direct election which bore so prominent a part in the constitutions of Italian republics. The electors were the ex-rectors,
the newly elected councillors, and an equal number of special
delegates. The voting was by ballot, a Dominican priest
acting as returning-officer.[2] The rector was required to be
a 'secular clerk, unmarried, wearing the clerical habit',[3] of
five years' standing in the study of law, and at least twenty-
four years of age.[4] The rector took precedence over all archbishops and bishops (except the Bishop of Bologna), and even
over cardinals.[5]

Rectorial   The expenses of the office must have been in proportion
expenses. to its dignity, the only salary attached to it being a moiety
of the fines exacted by its occupant.[6] The rector was expected
to live with a certain amount of state; he was bound, for
instance, by statute to keep at least two liveried servants.[7]
But the most serious expense was incurred in connexion with
the festivities of the installation day. If we may transfer to
Bologna the custom of Padua, the ceremony took place in the
cathedral, where, in presence of the assembled university, the
rector-elect was solemnly invested with the rectorial hood by
one of the doctors: after which he was escorted in triumph
by the whole body of students to his house, when a banquet,

[1] Stat., p. 50.

[2] Stat., pp. 49–51.

[3] 'Clericus non coniugatus, habitum deferens clericalem, ac nullius
religionis appareat.' Stat., p. 49.

[4] 'Qui . . . vigesimum quintum
sue etatis attigerit' (Stat., p. 49).
Savigny wrongly gives the minimum age as twenty-five (c. xxi,
§ 72).

[5] Stat. Iur. Bon., p. 90. The
legate and the vexilifer iusticie
are also placed above the rectors.
Cf. Ghirardacci, ii. 424.

[6] Stat., p. 60. It appears that it
had been at one time customary for
the university to grant a subventio

towards the rector's expenses. This
is forbidden by the statutes of 1432
(pp. 53, 54), unless the insufficiency
of the rector's purse is proved.
But later it appears that it was
customary to elect the rectors to
student-chairs of 100 librae—a
salary which was doubled when
the two rectorships were amalgamated, and largely increased in
the sixteenth century. Malagola,
Monografie, pp. 52, 53; Stat., p. 181.

[7] Stat., p. 256: the title rector
magnificus does not begin to be
used till the end of the fifteenth
century. Malagola, Monografie,
p. 47.

or at least wine and spices, awaited the constituents to whom CHAP. IV, he owed his exalted office.[1] It is worth mentioning as an § 4. illustration of the continuity of academic custom that this 'deductio' with the subsequent 'wine and spices' was prescribed not only by the statutes of universities which directly copied those of Bologna, but by the ancient customs both of Paris and of Oxford.[2] At the latter it is observed in a somewhat shrunken form at the inauguration of the vice-chancellor, and of the proctors. But in the Italian universities the festivities at the rectorial inauguration were on a much vaster scale than anything that could have been provided by a poor master of arts in a master-university. At Padua a tilt or tournament was held at which the new rector was required to provide two hundred spears and two hundred pairs of gloves for the use of combatants. The statutes of the Bologna university of arts and medicine forbade the rector to feast those who escort him home, to give a banquet to more than twelve persons on the day of his election, or to 'dance or make to dance with trumpets or without' for a month after that event.[3] In the terms of this prohibition we may probably read a picture of the rejoicings which were permitted in the case of the wealthier university of jurists. A still more curious and no less expensive feature of the entertainment as conducted in the sixteenth century was the custom of setting upon the newly elected rector, tearing his clothes off his back, and then requiring him to redeem the fragments at an exorbitant rate. The Statute of 1552, which was passed to restrain 'the too horrid and petulant mirth' of these occasions, does not venture to abolish the time-honoured 'vestium

---

[1] *Statuta Universitatis Iuristarum Patavini Gymnasii,* 1550, f. 11.

[2] Facciolati, *Syntagmata,* p. 17 sq.; *Stat. Iur. Pat., loc. cit.*

[3] 'Tripudiare aut tripudiari facere cum trombis vel sine vel cum aliis instrumentis, de nocte, cum dopleriis vel sine, directe vel indirecte.' *Stat.,* p. 221. What is to dance 'indirectly'? [Possibly 'by instigation'. *Tripudiare* here probably means tumultuous rejoicing.] The Artists' Statutes of 1486 at Padua (*Stat. Artistarum Achademiae Patavinae,* fol. 3 b, 4 a) require the rector to provide a *collatio* for the whole university, and to find at least 800 spears for the tournament, at which he awarded prizes compulsorily given by himself and the *doctores legentes.*

CHAP. IV,
§ 4.

laceratio'.[1] These are a few examples of the extortions to which the newly elected rector was exposed. The statutes of the various universities abound with regulations as to the number of servants that the rector shall keep, the value of his liveries,[2] the quality of the wine that he should provide at his installation banquet, and the like. Altogether, there is little cause for surprise that students eventually became as anxious to avoid the rectorship as English country gentlemen are to escape the burdensome honour of the shrievalty.

Acceptance compulsory.

The acceptance of the office by students of sufficient means was made compulsory, and elaborate precautions had to be taken to prevent those who had this unwelcome greatness thrust upon them from absconding before the expiration of their year of office. The rector was therefore not allowed to leave the city without the permission of his council, or without giving sufficient security for his return.[3]

Decay of the rectorship.

In the middle of the fourteenth century we already find an instance of the two jurist-rectorships being held by a single individual. Towards the end of the fifteenth century this arrangement became the rule instead of the exception. In the sixteenth century the difficulty of obtaining candidates able to perform such expensive duties, together with the growing hostility of governments to student-rectorships, led either to a great reduction in the splendour and dignity of the office, or to its permanent discharge by deputies—often professors —who were not expected to maintain the state invariably associated with the actual rectorship. At Bologna several instances of the appointment of a vice-rector occur in the later medieval period, and after 1580 this arrangement became

---

[1] 'Vestem quoque abripi atque etiam lacerari non prohibemus dummodo sciant hi qui lacerarunt nihil hinc exigi posse, &c. Qui vero integram detulerunt, contenti discedant pecunia eis danda per rectorem que non sit minoris summe scutorum sex in totum.' *Stat. Iur. Bon.* (1561), p. 103.

[2] So at Ferrara, where he is also to keep a horse 'vel mulam honorabilem'. Borsetti, i. 376. He is also to provide a 'collationem laudabilem' to appease the 'altercationes' that were wont to arise at rectorial elections, but it may be doubted whether the 'vinum dulce optimum' was the best means of securing that end.

[3] *Stat.*, p. 65. Cf. the elaborate statute *De excusatione electi*, p. 53.

permanent. After 1609 the rectorial duties were discharged by a deputy known as prior, elected by the students for a single month only.[1] In 1742 the rectorship was revived, but only to be conferred upon the cardinal-legate of Bologna. This arrangement is a sufficient indication of the practical extinction of the student-liberties: still in this their earliest home the whole student-constitution lasted in a shadowy form down to the Revolution.[2] In the university as in the state the sixteenth century everywhere (except to some extent in England) broke down the old medieval liberties as well as the medieval licences which those liberties had too often sheltered; but the last vestiges of them often lived on till they were swept away—only too ruthlessly—by that mightier revolution which was to bring back in a more advanced form the liberty which they had once enshrined.

The supreme governing body of the society was the Con- *Congregation.* gregation of the two universities, i.e. the whole body of students with the exception of poor men who lived 'at others' expense'.[3] The universities in their earliest days had no buildings of their own, and the fact is one which is of primary importance for the appreciation of the genius and history of the institution. Their power depended wholly upon the facility with which they could move from town to town; and when a university or a large section of it had decamped from the place, there were no effects left behind for the authorities to attach.[4] In the earliest days of the universities, the lecture-room or school was simply a hired apartment, or the private house of the doctor.[5] None of these schools of course were

---

[1] Malagola, *Monografie*, pp. 34, 133 *sq.* There was an isolated revival of the rectorship in 1604. *Ibid.*, pp. 60, 205.

[2] *Ibid.*, pp. 72, 205 *sq.* After many vicissitudes (*ibid.*, pp. 75–81) the rectorship is now re-established, but the rector is of course no longer elected by the students.

[3] 'Viventes sumptibus alienis . . . ut sunt socii doctorum bononiensium et scolarium bonon., repetitores et similes.' *Stat.*, p. 147.

[4] [Books were an important exception, as is shown by the measures taken to recover them; cf. Bianchi, in *Giornale storico degli archivi Toscani*, v. 237; and Filippini on the exodus of 1321 in *Studi e memorie*, vi. 116.]

[5] The will of Bonrecuperus Porrus († 1278) contains a clause: 'Et si decederet sine liberis legitimis masculis voluit et iussit ut domus ipsius testatoris in qua ipse moratur sic existat separata per

CHAP. IV, large enough to hold the entire body of students. For great
§ 4. solemnities, such as doctoral inceptions, the cathedral was
used. For ordinary congregations a convent or a church had
to be borrowed. At Bologna the usual place of meeting,
[before the separation of the jurists from the artists, was the
Benedictine church of San Procolo, where, indeed, the Ultramontane scholars met as late as 1265 for the election of a
rector. After the formation of the university of medicine and
arts, which used the Franciscan church, the jurists, Ultramontane and Cismontane, had their head-quarters in] the
great convent of S. Dominic (the burial-place of the Saint),
in the sacristy of which the common chest and seal of the
university were kept.[1] Attendance at these congregations
was compulsory. When a question was laid before the
assembly by the rectors, every member had the right of
speaking, but the rectors had the power of 'closure', and
might 'impose silence on too prolix speakers'.[2] The votes
were taken by ballot with black and white beans.[3]

murum a domo alia testatoris in qua morantur scholares et sunt schole', ap. Sarti, i. i. 215. So Sarti tells us that Odofredus 'scholas habuit peramplas in suis aedibus, quarum aliquando mentionem ingerit in commentariis ad Pandectas'. *Ibid.*, p. 166. [Cavazza, in his work *Le Scuole dell'antico studio bolognese*, Milan, 1896, has collected a wealth of information about these schools and their sites.]

[1] *Stat.*, pp. 127, 189. [Cavazza, pp. 210–22, and Appendix, no. 58. The jurists had an official building in the convent; in 1321, on the occasion of the disturbance caused by the execution of Giacomo da Valenza, the scholars required the *podestà* to make satisfaction at the convent 'in ecclesia vel capitulo vel domo universitatis'; *ibid.*, App., no. 64. We read also of] a 'statio universitatis' in which the rector sat and the notary had his office, but there is no evidence that it was actually the property of the uni-

versity. *Stat.*, pp. 81, 83. The rector held his court in the 'statio bidellorum generalium'—probably the same place. *Ibid.*, p. 85. [The *statutarii*, mentioned in the next paragraph of the text, sat in the 'statio bidellorum generalium'. The *stationarii* and *peciarii* did their academic business there. It was apparently in the middle of the city. Cavazza, pp. 124, 125. Cavazza prints an inquiry of 1368 (Appendix, no. 36) into some 'verba iniuriosa', said by a master of medicine 'in contrato porte nove in strata publica, coram statione medicorum, in qua redditur ius per rectorem medicorum in dicta capella', i.e. Sancti Salvatoris. The connexion is not clear, but an office or centre of some sort for the university of medicine and arts seems to be indicated.]

[2] 'Possint tamen Rectores nimium prolixis in sermone silentium imponere.' *Stat.*, p. 61.

[3] 'Priusquam ad fabas albas et

It must not be supposed that university legislation was to the students of Bologna the weekly employment that it has become to the resident M.A.s of Oxford and Cambridge. As in the old Greek and medieval Italian republics, the constitution provided most effectual checks against hasty or over-frequent legislation of a permanent character. The statutes could only be altered once every twenty years, when eight *statutarii* were appointed to conduct the revision and to publish the new code, which passed into law without any further confirmation by the university. In the intervals between these revisions, changes could only be made by the unanimous consent of the university upon a proposal already approved, first by the rectors and councillors, and then by a body of twenty-four members of the university named by them. A still more self-denying ordinance was the provision that in this case the consent of the doctors was also necessary.[1]

One of the most curious parts of the university system was the institution of *peciarii*.[2] The *peciarii* were six in number. Their duty was to supervise the *stationarii* or keepers of book-stalls. The stationer was compelled periodically to submit his manuscripts to the inspection of this board, and the stationer was liable to a fine of five Bologna *solidi* for every incorrect copy which he produced. Students who might detect clerical errors in their books were bound on pain of perjury to give information against the stationer; and both doctors and students were bound at all times to lend their books to the *peciarii* for the purpose of collation. The actual

nigras perveniatur.' *Stat.*, p. 61; cf. p. 130. At the beginning of every congregation four *consiliarii* were chosen who with the rectors determined the form in which the question should be put ('forma partiti'). *Stat.*, p. 60.

[1] *Stat.*, pp. 76–8.

[2] The following regulations are from *Stat.*, pp. 75, 76. [On the significance of this system of super-vision, especially of the production of the *exemplar* or officially ap-proved 'original' of a book, see

J. A. Destrez, 'La *pecia* dans les manuscrits du moyen âge', in *Revue des sciences philosophiques et théologiques*, xiii (1924), 182–97. Cf. also the city statutes, printed by Gaudenzi, in *Bullettino*, no. 6, p. 123. Stationers were forbidden to dispose of their *exempla*, 'ut portentur ad studium alterius civitatis vel terre', and were to sell copies for no more than the usual prices. See also L. Frati, 'Gli stazionari bolognesi nel medio evo', in *Archivio storico itali-ano*, ser. 5, vol. xlv, 1910.]

CHAP. IV, correction of the manuscripts was carried out by the *corre-*
§ 4.   *ctores peciarum*. The stationer's primary business was to let
out books on hire to scholars, the rate of hire being determined by the university statutes.[1] So far the regulations are
mainly applicable to books produced by the writers in the
stationers' employment. But a very large proportion of the
book-trade in the Middle Ages was a second-hand trade.
Books were dearer, but much more durable, than at the
present day. In the sale of second-hand books, however, the
stationer was not allowed to reap the enormous profits made
possible by the modern system. He occupied the position
not so much of a trader as of an agent acting on behalf of the
owner, and was remunerated by a fixed commission which
was defrayed half by the buyer and half by the seller.[2] In the
sale of new books he likewise, it would appear, served as a
middleman between the buyer and the writers. A continual
supply of fresh scholastic literature was ensured by the
provision that every doctor, after holding a 'disputatio' or
'repetitio' should, on pain of a fine of ten golden ducats, write
out his argument and deliver it to the general bedel of the
university, by whom it was transmitted to the stationers for
publication.[3] Some similar regulation in our own universities
might be found a more effectual stimulus to research than
much 'endowment' and many 'visitatorial boards'. The
stationarii were subject to a number of other minute regulations, most of which we shall find substantially reproduced
at Paris, with a view of securing an adequate supply and
keeping down the prices. Paternal government was in this
matter carried so far that books above a certain value might
only be sold in presence of the university notary.[4]

[1] Six *denarii* were paid for the
loan of a *quaestio* (for how long
does not appear), and the stationer
might demand a 'pignus' of twice
the value. (*Stat.*, p. 76.) A list of
prices for the hire of books is given
in *Stat.*, p. 91 *sq.* A complete
Digest costs 30 *solidi*, the Institutes
2*s*. [The catalogue of books of the
stationarii, given in the early

statutes (*Stat.*, pp. 32–5) and
previously edited by Sarti and
Savigny, has been re-edited with
full commentary by B. Brugi in
Studi e memorie, v (1920), 3–44.]
[2] Six *denarii* on each *libra* up to
60, afterwards four. *Stat.*, p. 89.
[3] *Stat.*, p. 109.
[4] *Stat.*, p. 87. In Fournier, *Stat.
et priv. des univ. françaises*, i, No.

Of the remaining university officials the most important were the taxors, who, jointly with arbitrators appointed by the city, fixed the rents of houses used by scholars. Five years' 'interdiction to scholars' was the penalty of refusal to abide by the decision of the arbitrators or any other infringement of the regulations of the university.[1] This system of taxation was, as has been seen, very early recognized by papal authority. Traces of it are found in other places even before the rise of the universities, and it soon became universal in all university towns whether of the Parisian or of the Bologna type. Landlords were not the only class of citizens against whose exactions the universities sought to protect their members. Both the university and the town statutes provide Merchants. for the appointment by the university of four licensed merchants or money-lenders or (as they might be no less correctly termed) pawnbrokers, who were privileged to lend money to students.[2]

The other officials employed by the university but not Other officials. selected from the student-body were the two *massarii* or treasurers,[3] the *notarius*,[4] the *syndicus* or common advocate (a lawyer who also acted as legal assessor to the rectors[5]), and the *bidelli generales*[6] (one for each university). The functions of the first three pretty well explain themselves.

150, is a contract for the sale of a book as elaborate as a conveyance of a landed estate.

[1] *Stat.*, pp. 121 *sqq.*, 160. Four *proxenetae* were also appointed by the universities to assist students in finding lodgings and the employment of other intermediaries was forbidden. *Ibid.*, p. 123. [The city statutes, *c.* 1270–80, gave protection to 'hospitia et domus in quibus habitant scolares'; ed. Gaudenzi, *op. cit.*, pp. 123, 124, 126.]

[2] *Stat.*, p. 64, *De electione mercatorum*. The nature of their functions is explained in the town statute (*Stat.*, p. 161), which exempts from military service 'quatuor mercatores vel feneratores qui mutuent eis pecuniam'. [Cf. sta-

tutes of *c.* 1270–80, where it is laid down that the money-lenders are to be 'forenses, qui sint de parte Ecclesie seu guefi'; ed. Gaudenzi, *op. cit.*, p. 127.] So at Florence, a *faenerator* is to be elected 'cum quo paciscatur de salario usurarum; qui Scholaribus mutuet sub usuris, pro minori quantitate lucri quam alii feneratores mutuent, tempore opportuno'. *Stat. Fiorent.*, p. 34. Scholars were here forbidden to borrow from other money-lenders.

[3] *Stat.*, pp. 19, 20.

[4] *Stat.*, p. 79 *sq.* He kept the *matricula*, and recorded the acts of the university.

[5] *Stat.*, p. 79.

[6] *Stat.*, p. 84 *et passim*.

CHAP. IV, The duties of the bedels were fairly analogous to those of the
§ 4. venerable and picturesque functionaries who bear the same
name in our own universities, except that they performed
some of the duties now entrusted to the clerk of the schools
and others which have fallen into desuetude. Thus, besides
preceding the rectors on public occasions, collecting the votes
in Congregation, and so on, the bedels went the round of
the schools, to read statutes and decrees of Congregation,
announcements of lectures by students, lists of books which
the *stationarii* or individual students had on sale and other
matters of general interest. He was remunerated by a special
collecta to which all students were required to contribute the
customary amount.

Antiquity of bedels. The bedelship is among the most ancient of academical
offices—perhaps as ancient as the rectorship. It is found in all
medieval universities without exception. In fact, an allusion
to a *bidellus*[1] is in general (though not invariably) a sufficiently
trustworthy indication that a school is really a university or
studium generale. It is interesting to observe that in spite of
the decay of most that is medieval in the continental universities the bedels of Bologna and the other Italian universities
still appear upon public occasions with the ponderous maces
which they have borne from medieval times, and which retain
almost exactly the form familiar to Oxonian or Cantabrigian
eyes.

Special bedels. Besides the general or university bedels, each doctor had
a 'special bedel' of his own, who looked after his school,
opened and shut the door, swept it out twice a month,
strewed the floor with straw in winter and carried his doctor's
books to the school. He was remunerated by a *collecta* from
his master's pupils. Both the special and general bedels preceded the rectors at funerals or other university processions.[2]

Few dis-ciplinary statutes. The statutes of the student-universities naturally do not
regulate the private life of students with the same detail as
the college statutes or even the later university statutes of

---

[1] Often spelt *pedellus*, whence
the *pedel* of the German universities. It is derived of course from
pedum (a stick).

[2] *Stat.*, pp. 84, 85. Cf. *Stat.
Fiorent.*, pp. 68, 81, 96.

Paris and Oxford. The students of Bologna lived in their own houses and entirely after their own fashion. The usual practice was not to take lodgings in a citizen's house like the modern extra-collegiate student, but for parties of students (*socii*) to hire the whole house together and make their own arrangements as to servants, furniture[1] and the like.[2] To live in a townsman's house (*ad contubernia* or *ad cameram*) was the exception.[3] The principal disciplinary regulations which we do find relate to two subjects—the wearing of arms and the practice of gambling: quarrelling and gambling were no doubt the most prevalent, or at all events the most trouble-some, vices among Italian students. The wearing of arms at Congregation is prohibited; but, mindful that without them the life of a student would not always be safe, the statutes allow any one who fears his enemy's stiletto privately to inform the rector and so obtain leave of absence.[4] The statutes against gambling are extremely strict. 'With a view of obviating the loss of money' attendant upon the practice, it is made an offence even to watch a game of dice played in public. Students are forbidden to enter or to keep gaming-houses, and the latter prohibition is expressly extended to doctors.[5] There is also a very curious provision that a student was not even to play in his own house during the three months

---

[1] What this furniture was may be gathered from a statute of the college of Spain at Bologna: 'Cameram quoque unusquisque predictorum fulcitam habeat ex-pensu collegii lectisternio uno, matalatio uel cultra, coopterorio plumari et linteaminibus de tela grossa, archobanco, studio (a desk) et paleis pro lecto necessariis.' He is allowed to buy additional furni-ture at his own expense. MS. *Stat.*, f. 13 *b*. (See below, p. 199, n. 4.)

[2] At Lérida the bedel is required to introduce the new-comer to a suitable *societas*. *Stat.* ap. Villa-nueva, *Viage literario*, xvi. 223. So at Bologna a student 'going down' is required to deliver his key not to the landlord but to his 'socii'. *Stat.*, p. 125.

[3] *Statuta Iuristarum Patavini Gymnasii*, 1550, f. 119. If the analogy of Paris may be trusted it was customary only with the poor-est students. (Cf. below, p. 475.)

[4] *Stat.*, pp. 130, 131.

[5] *Stat.*, p. 133 (*De ludo taxil-lorum*). There is, however, an exception in favour of playing 'ad scacos (chess) vel ad tabulas causa recreationis'. [A distinction was made between games of chance and games of skill.] The pro-visions against professorial gamb-ling were not uncalled for: 'Joannes Bassianus . . . nonnumquam pannis exutus, nudus remanebat in alea.' Guil. de Pastrengo, ap. Sarti, I. i. 90.

CHAP. IV, before 'going down' for good or (as it was technically styled)
§ 4.   'going home a wise man', or again for one month after taking
his degree.[1] Was the legislator anxious to provide against the
exceptional temptations to frivolity and dissipation which the
close of an academic career brought with it, or was he influenced by a merely prudential desire to protect the remaining students against irrecoverable debts of honour? In the
Student-University of Lérida scholars are forbidden to entertain or be entertained by actors or professional jesters, except
at Christmas, Easter, and Whitsuntide, or at the Inceptions:[2]
even at these times they might only provide them with food,
but not with money, in return for their professional services.
The thrifty students of Lérida are also forbidden to ride to
the schools or to keep a horse, though a mule is allowed. The
statutes even prescribe the number of courses to which they
might entertain their friends, and the maximum price of their
clothes.[3] At Bologna the regulations, so far as extant, were
less inquisitorial.

Academi-   The statutes relating to costume must be regarded more
cal dress. in the light of sumptuary regulations than as a requirement
of 'academical dress'. The 'cappa' or other outer garment
was required to be of 'statutable or black' stuff,[4] the penalty

[1] 'Adiicientes quod nullus doc-
torari volens, vel sapiens recedere
infra duos menses ante suum re-
cessum vel conventum audeat
ludum in hospitio suo tenere, vel
aliis ludentibus consentire nec
etiam post doctoratum per men-
sem.' *Stat.*, p. 133.

[2] 'Mimis, joculatoribus, istrioni-
bus, militibus qui dicuntur sal-
vatges, caeterisque truffatoribus,
&c.' Villanueva, *Viage Literario*,
xvi. 230. [For *milites* in this sense,
Dr. Coulton refers us to Salimbene
(*M.G.H.*, *Scriptores*, xxxii. 53,
354, &c.).] The clause as to the
rectorial and doctoral inaugura-
tions was repealed in the following
year, *loc. cit.*, p. 233.

[3] *Ibid.*, pp. 233, 234.

[4] 'Damnosis scolarium sumpti-

bus providere cupientes, statuimus
quod nullus scolaris . . . emat per
se vel per alium pannum alium
quam qui vulgariter vocatur pannus
de statuto vel de panno coloris
nigri, quem pannum pro habitu
superiori, cappa, tabardo vel ga-
bano vel consimili veste consueta
pro tunc longiore veste inferiori et
clausa a lateribus ac etiam fibulata
seu maspillata anterius circa col-
lum portare teneantur infra civitatem sub poena trium librarum
bonon.' (*Stat.*, pp. 132, 133.) It
is difficult to explain the contradiction between the insistence in
this statute upon *black*, and the
fact that in the medieval illumination reproduced in *Acta Nationis
Germanicae* the majority of the
students are represented as coming

for the violation of this statute being much higher than the ineffectual Oxford five shillings. Hoods were not limited to graduates, but a miniver hood was the especial distinction of rectors and professors. The former were required to wear their hoods whenever they appeared in public, but in summer were allowed to exchange them for cooler hoods of silk.[1] On state occasions at least, the doctors of all faculties wore robes of purple and miniver, while the rectors were robed in scarlet or scarlet and gold.

If the discipline which the free and independent students of Bologna imposed upon themselves exhibits few indications of extraordinary strictness, the same cannot be said of the discipline which they imposed upon their subjects—the professors. Whatever view, as a matter of constitutional theory, the doctors might take of their relations with the students, it is certain that while the latter were in no way bound to obedience to the prior or college of the doctors, the doctors were compelled, under pain of a ban which would have deprived them of pupils and income, to swear obedience to the students' rector,[2] and to obey any other regulations which the universities might think fit to impose upon them.

Bondage of the professors.

to the proctor to be sworn attired in long *red* gowns. Was this a privilege of the German nation or of nobles? The statute at Florence simply requires 'omnes de uno eodemque colore panni'. (*Stat. Fior.*, p. 97.) The form of both the doctoral and student *cappa* may be seen in the beautiful tombs of the doctors which form the most characteristic feature of the Bologna churches. There is usually a recumbent effigy of the doctor above, while below he is represented as lecturing (seated) to his students sitting at slightly sloping desks or narrow tables, very much like those of a modern lecture-room. Some of the college statutes, even in Italy, insist on the 'clericalem habitum'. (Facciolati, *Fasti*, p. xx.)

[1] *Stat.*, p. 55. At Padua the rector of the artists is to wear a robe of scarlet silk in summer, and a scarlet robe of some thicker material (*de grana*) in winter (*Stat. Artist. Pat.* f. iii *b*, iv *a*), while the rector of the jurists wears robes embroidered with gold as well as fur. (Colle, *Storia dello studio di Padova*, i. 104; Malagola, *Monografie*, p. 87.) Later we hear of a rectorial hood of gold brocade. *Ibid.*, p. 62. In the time of Gaggi, doctors of divinity wore the *Almutium violaceum* (a tippet) and doctors of the other faculties had the privilege 'uti varris (ermine) et torque aurea'. In processions of the college, the bedels carried gold maces before them.

[2] *Stat.*, p. 99. A doctor, neglecting to take the oath, 'non possit eo anno facere collectam suam et ultra hoc Rectorum arbitrio puniatur'. *Ibid.*, p. 100.

While not entitled to a vote in the university Congregation, the professor was liable to 'privatio' or expulsion from a society to whose privileges he had never been admitted.[1] At any moment his lectures might be interrupted by the entrance of the bedel to serve a summons on the professor to appear before the rector, or to read a rectorial proclamation to the students or a new statute of the student-university to which his consent had not been asked but to which his obedience was none the less required. A scholar was, indeed, obliged as the condition of enjoying the privileges of 'scholarity' to attend lecture at least three times a week; but a professor requiring leave of absence even for a single day was compelled to obtain it first from his own pupils and then from the rectors and *consiliarii*; and if he proposed to leave the town, he was required to deposit a sum of money by way of security for his return.[2] He is expressly forbidden 'to create holidays at his pleasure';[3] and his scholars are bound on pain of perjury to give information against a truant doctor.[4] By the city-regulations, moreover, for each day on which he failed to secure an audience of five for an ordinary lecture, or three for an extraordinary one, he was treated as absent and incurred the appointed fine accordingly.[5]

Punctuality is enforced with extreme rigour. The professor was obliged to begin his lecture when the bells of S. Peter's began to ring for mass, under a penalty of 20 *solidi* for each offence,[6] though he has the privilege of beginning at an earlier hour if he pleases; while he is forbidden to continue his lecture one minute after the bell has begun to ring for tierce. To secure the observance of this statute a more effectual means is adopted even than that of fining the doctor: his pupils are required under a penalty of 10 *solidi* to leave the lecture-room as soon as the bell begins.

Punctuality enforced upon professors.

---

[1] A ban which sometimes extended even to the descendants of the offender.

[2] *Stat.*, p. 109.

[3] 'Nec festa pro libito faciant.' A penalty of 40s. is provided 'pena periurii non obstante'. *Ibid.*, p. 101.

[4] *Ibid.*, p. 110.

[5] 'Punctetur perinde ac si eo die non legisset.' Dallari, i, p. xxii.

[6] 'Nec audea[n]t tardare ad veniendum post pulsationem dicte campane ad scolas pena XX solidorum.' *Stat.*, p. 105.

Even in the actual conduct of his lectures the doctor is CHAP. IV,
§ 4. regulated with the precision of a soldier on parade or a reader in a French public library. He is fined if he skips a chapter or decretal: he is forbidden to postpone a difficulty to the end of the lecture lest such a liberty should be abused as a pretext for evading it altogether. In medieval as in modern times lecturers had a tendency to spend a disproportionate time over the earlier portions of a book, and so leave none for the rest. With a view to checking this practice, an expedient was adopted at Bologna which became universal in the law-universities of southern Europe.[1] The law-texts were divided into portions known as *puncta*; and the doctor was required to have reached each *punctum* by a specified date. At the beginning of the academical year he was bound to deposit the sum of 10 Bologna pounds with a banker, who promised to deliver it up at the demand of the rectors: for every day that the doctor was behind time, a certain sum was deducted from his deposit by order of these officials. With a view to enforcing obedience to this and other statutes on the part of the doctors, a committee of students (*Denunciatores Doctorum*) was appointed by the rectors to observe their conduct, and report their irregularities to the rector.[2]

Mode of lecturing prescribed by statute.

Compelled servare puncta.

The colleges which played so large a part in the development of the northern universities were comparatively unimportant in Bologna and the other Italian universities. They were as a rule smaller foundations than the colleges of Paris and Oxford, and they remained to the last (what all colleges were originally intended to be) eleemosynary institutions for

Colleges.

---

[1] This provision occurs only in the earlier statutes (p. 42), but the institution is implied in the later statutes (pp. 78, 79). The meaning of the expression 'ut puncta per eos bene serventur' has to be inferred from the statutes of other universities. [For the examination for the licence in theology at Bologna, the dean of the faculty assigned 'puncta, id est duas libris Sententiarum distinctiones'; *I più antichi*

statuti, ed. Ehrle, p. 34.]

[2] *Stat.*, pp. 23, 78, 79. The stakeholder was known as the *Depositarius* (Dallari, i, p. xxiv). The students profess to be actuated by anxiety for their masters' spiritual welfare. The statute begins 'Christiano cuique sed precipue sacre legis doctoribus periculosum noscentes esse periurium' (*Stat.*, p. 78).

CHAP. IV, the help of poor students, boarding-houses, and not places
§ 4.
Coll. of of education. A small College of Avignon was founded in
Avignon, Bologna in 1267 by Zoen Tencararius, Bishop of Avignon,
1267. for eight students, three of whom were to be canons of his
cathedral;[1] but it does not seem clear whether its members
originally lived in community, or merely received pensions:
in any case the property of the scholars was held in trust for
Coll. of them by the Bishop of Avignon. The College of Brescia was
Brescia. founded by Guglielmo da Brescia, Archdeacon of Bologna, in
1326,[2] and the College of Reggio by the physician, Guido
College Bagnoli of Reggio, in 1362.[3] But the first college, on a scale
of Spain,
1367. at all approaching that with which we are familiar in the
English universities, was the College of Spain, founded by

[1] Sarti, I. ii (1888), 416; I. ii
(1772), 118–23. [In 1436 Pope
Eugenius IV incorporated the
Avignon with the Gregorian college; *Chart. Studii Bonon.* i. 89–91,
No. 85.]
[2] [See P. Guerrini, 'Guglielmo
da Brescia e il collegio bresciano
in Bologna', in *Studi e memorie*,
vii (1922), 58–116, where the
statutes are given. In 1436 and
1437 Eugenius IV merged both the
College of Avignon and the College
of Brescia in the *Collegium Gregorianum* founded by Gregory XI
in 1371 (*Chartul. Studii Bonon.* i,
Nos. 84, 86). The Gregorian
college deserved more attention
than Rashdall gave to it, for
Gregory XI's statutes, prescribed
at Avignon, 18 Dec. 1372, are very
full and precise. They were printed
in Ghirardacci (ii. 308 *sqq.*) and
have in recent years, since the first
edition of this book, been twice
edited, first by G. Zaoli in the
Studi e memorie, iii (1912), 163–88,
and again, from more manuscripts,
in the *Chartul. Studii Bonon.*
ii (1913), 289–313. The college
was located in a palace acquired
from the heirs of Giovanni Pepoli,
and was generously endowed.

The foundation was to consist of
thirty jurists, half civilian and
half canonists, of whom twenty
were to be Frenchmen from the
diocese of Limoges. The rector was
to be French. The statutes correspond in many respects to those
of the College of Spain, and illustrate the various points discussed
by Rashdall in this section. The
regulations for chapel and library
are especially dealed. Zaoli gives
a summary of the history of the
college from 1371 to 1474. In spite
of the care of Pope Martin V and
the absorption of the Colleges of
Avignon and Brescia in 1436–7 it
never recovered from the effects
of the Great Schism and the depredations of Pope John XXIII. Its
revenues were at last diverted to
assist the school of the Dominicans
at Bologna and to various other
purposes; see Zaoli, *op. cit.*, pp.
122–34. Zaoli also prints a list of
the books collected by Gregory XI
for the college (*ibid.*, pp. 134–8).
For the various letters of Gregory
XI relating to the foundations and
interests of the college see *Chartul.*
ii. 243–6.]
[3] Malagola, Pref. to *Stat.*, p. xiii.

the will of the great Spanish cardinal, Egidio Albornoz (once CHAP. IV,
§ 4. Archbishop of Toledo, but compelled to fly from the tyranny of Peter the Cruel, and afterwards papal legate at Bologna), who died in 1367.[1] This college appears to have been the model of many others in Italy and Spain. In the sixteenth century we may infer from the privileges which the university conferred upon its rector, that it had acquired some faint shadow of the prestige enjoyed by the Sorbonne and the College of Navarre at Paris or at Oxford by the foundations of Wykeham and Wolsey. The College of Spain may be taken as a type of the college-constitution in universities of the Bologna type.[2] A short account of its organization and arrangement may therefore be worth giving.

In the statutes as revised by papal delegates in 1377 it is Statutes
of 1377. provided that the college shall consist of thirty scholars— eight in theology, eighteen in canon law, and four in medicine. The scholars held their places for seven years, except in the case of a theologian or medical student who wished to stay up and lecture as a doctor. The scholarships were divided among the numerous Spanish dioceses in which the founder had held preferment. The patronage was vested in the bishops and chapters of those dioceses together with two members of the Albornoz family, i.e. the head of the house and any member of it who was a prelate, or if more than one were prelates, then the superior or senior prelate. The qualification for election was poverty,[3] and competent grounding, 'at least in grammar'. In the case of the theologians and medical students, logic was also required, and if they had not heard philosophy before, their first three years of residence

---

[1] Ghirardacci, ii. 285 *sqq.* Savigny in his list mentions this college twice over under different names (c. xxi, § 72).

[2] The printed statutes are of the sixteenth century; no earlier statutes were known to be extant. In 1889, however, I found that the statutes of 1377 were contained in MS. No. 5383 of the Phillipps Library at Cheltenham (catalogued as 'Statuta Bononiensia'). Their provisions are materially different from the printed edition. [Four years earlier, in 1373, the disorder rampant in the new society had led to a papal commission of inquiry given by Pope Gregory XI to the Bishop of Cuenca; *Chart. Studii Bonon.* ii. 322, No. 280.]

[3] i.e. his income (unless he were rector) must not be 'ultra summam quinquaginta florenorum auri Bononiensium'. *MS. Stat.*, f. 5 *b*.

CHAP. IV, were to be devoted mainly to that faculty.[1] An entrance
§ 4. examination was held, and the college was at liberty to reject
nominees who failed to satisfy these requirements. Every
scholar received daily a pound of moderate beef or veal or
other good meat with some 'competent dish', the larger part
at dinner, the smaller at supper.[2] Wine, salt, and bread were
at discretion; but the wine was to be watered in accordance
with the rector's orders.[3] A portion of the allowance for meat
might be applied by the rector to the purchase of salt meat
or fruit. We may charitably hope that the college availed
itself of this provision on feast-days and on the Sunday before
Lent, when the above-mentioned 'portions' of meat were
doubled. On fast-days the ordinary allowance was to be spent
on fish and eggs. At a 'congruous time' (not further defined)
after dinner and supper respectively, the college reassembled
for 'collation', when drink was 'competently' administered
to every one.[4] Besides commons, each scholar received
every autumn a new scholastic 'cappa, sufficiently furred
with sheep-skin', and another without fur, and with a hood
of the same stuff and colour as the cope,[5] at the beginning

---

[1] The printed statutes add that the scholars must be 'Ancient Christians'—a provision redolent of the Moorish wars and the fanaticism which they engendered.

[2] 'Carnium castratinarum uel uitilinarum mediocrum uel aliarum bonarum . . . cum aliquo ferculo competenti.' *MS. Stat.*, f. 12 b.

[3] 'De uino autem Rectoris arbitrio temperato, panem, et sal habeant in prandio et in cena quantum uoluerint et conueniat honestati', *loc. cit.*

[4] 'Post prandium uero et post cenam quolibet die hora congrua signo campane in modum cibali ad iussum Rectoris uel eius uices gerentis pulsato, ad collacionem conueniant et prebeatur potus cuilibet competenter.' *MS. Stat.*, f. 13 a.

[5] 'Una capa scolastica et noua et foderata suficienter pellibus pe-

cudis, ut studentes Bononienses habere communiter consueuerint'; the other to be 'sine foderatura de panno statuti coloris eiusdem et capuceum de competenti panno eiusdem eciam coloris, ualoris quinque solidorum' (f. 13 a). The printed statutes (Bonon. 1558, f. xviii) order that scholars 'utentur veste ex panno nigro ... talaris sit et manicata, qua forma nunc doctores, olim cum hoc primum in Collegio fuit institutum etiam scholastici Bononienses uti videbantur, et focali quod dicitur caputeus ex hyacinthino panno qui morellus vulgo nuncupatur . . . quibus vestibus et focali semper uti debeant, quocumque sive ad scholas sive per urbem iuerint et quacunque hora diei'. It is obvious that the form of the dress has considerably altered since the fourteenth century. A black gown with a cherry-

of May; and there was an annual allowance of twelve Bologna pounds for candles, breeches, shoes, and other necessaries. Poor scholars of the founder's kin have a peremptory claim to a vacant scholarship; while any scholar of the Albornoz family residing in Bologna becomes the 'protector' of the college with certain visitatorial powers, and the right to a seat in the college 'chapter'. If he is twenty years of age, these powers are to be exercised on his own responsibility; if under twenty, he is to act by the advice of his tutor, but may none the less be present at college meetings to gain experience.

So far the regulations of the College of Spain are of very much the same character as those of medieval college statutes in our own magisterially-ruled universities. When we come, however, to those respecting the mode of internal government, all is changed. The Bologna college is governed as democratically as the Bologna university. Scholars under eighteen years of age are, indeed (as was the case in many universities), to have no vote, though they might be present at chapters. But the rector is to be elected annually by ballot; like the rector of the university he is to be at least twenty-four years of age and a clerk. He is assisted by *consiliarii* elected in the same way; but in important matters such as the alienation of property, the consent of the whole college is necessary. In fact the constitution of the college is the university constitution in miniature. But though establishing this system of popular government, the cardinal-founder was not of opinion that democracy necessarily meant weak government or no government at all. The discipline prescribed by the statutes is decidedly stricter than that contemplated by the Oxonian or Parisian statutes of the same period. There was a chapel served by four chaplains; two masses were to be said daily, one before and one after the 'ordinary' lecture, and presence at one or other of these was to be compulsory, besides attendance at Matins and Vespers on holidays and at Vespers on Vigils. Daily attendance at lecture is enforced by fines. The

Democratic constitution of the college.

Strict discipline.

coloured silk scarf (by way of 'focale') is still worn by students of the college on state occasions. [1895.]

monastic silence and Bible-reading are observed in hall.[1]
Lateness in returning to college at night is visited by a day's
'penitence on bread and water', a second offence by three
days' bread and water, and a third entails expulsion. A
chaplain who stays out of college for a night loses half his
year's salary, besides being condemned to three days' bread
and water. A nocturnal exodus by the window involves
immediate expulsion. For an assault on a brother-scholar,
the penalty was no less than five days in the stocks and one
day's penance on bread and water to be eaten sitting on the
floor of the hall.[2] For an assault resulting in effusion of blood
or for assisting in the quarrels of others, the penalty is
doubled. The punishment of·the stocks is not mentioned in
English or Parisian colleges till the sixteenth century, though
these colleges contained boys much younger than were
usually to be found in the College of Spain. It may be added
that women are warned off the premises—including even the
chapel—in language as ferociously ungallant as could be
culled from the statutes of the rudest northern discipli-
narian.[3]

The col-
lege sur-
vives.
The College of Spain still flourishes upon its ancient site
in sumptuously adorned buildings of the sixteenth century,
whose quadrangle, chapel, hall, and students' rooms still
testify to the continuance on a small scale (there are only five
or six students) of the college life with which we are familiar
in the English universities. Indeed, the College of Spain
reproduces the medieval type far more faithfully than any
English college; for all its members are graduates in arts,
none of them teachers, but all students in law. The college
is now under the control of the Spanish Government, which

---

[1] It is, however, expressly provided that scholars may be either
clērici or *laici*.

[2] 'Quinque diebus stent in cipo
ligneo saltem cum uno pede et die
qua extrahentur in pane et aqua
coram omnibus in terra peniteant'
(*MS. Stat.*, f. 27 a).

[3] 'Et quia mulier est caput pec-
cati, arma diaboli, expulsio para-
disi et corrupcio legis antique et
propterea omnis eius conuersacio
sit diligencius euictanda, interdici-
mus', &c. (*MS. Stat.*, f. 20 a). [Cf.
Cart. de l'univ. de Montpellier, i
(1890), 511.] Dancing is forbidden
'quia secundum sanctorum patrum
sentenciam in coreis diabolus faci-
lius illaqueat homines' (*loc. cit.*
27 b).

sends to it candidates for the diplomatic service who have CHAP. IV,
§ 4. taken the B.A. degree in a Spanish university [1895].[1]

The colleges continued to be exceptionally few at Bologna— Later
colleges. fewer even than in other Italian universities—throughout the medieval period. The names of only two others are recorded as founded before 1500[2]—the *Collegium Gregorianum* founded by Gregory XI in 1371, and the *Collegium Ancaranum* founded by Pietro d'Ancarano, doctor of decrees, in 1414.[3] It was only in the fervour of the Catholic reaction that Bologna began to be a city of colleges. One explanation of the paucity of the Bologna colleges is no doubt to be found in the selfish policy pursued by the Bologna Government towards foreign students who were here deprived of all chance of a career as teachers. One of the numerous seventeenth-century colleges—the little house founded by John Jacobs for Flemish students in 1650[4]—still survives to assist the more magnificent College of Spain in bearing testimony to ·the cosmopolitanism of the old medieval universities. Thus at Bologna, all but alone among continental universities, in one of the two great original homes of university life, there survive specimens of the true medieval college, reduced to smaller dimensions than of old, but retaining more completely the old form and purpose of a medieval college than the more famous but more altered foundations which form the especial glory of our English universities.

[1] [For further information see J. Miret y Sanz, 'Escolars catalans al estudi de Bolonia en la xiii centuria', in *Bol. Acad. Buenas Letras*, Barcelona, viii (1915), 137 *sqq.*; J. Beneto Pérez, 'La tradición española en Bolonia', in *Revista de Archivos*, i (1929), 174–84 (before Albornoz); F. Filippini, *Il cardinale Egidio Albornoz*, Bologna, 1934.]

[2] See the statutes in Ghirardacci, ii. 308 *sq.* Here also we find the students' lecture-fees paid out of the foundation.

[3] Orlandi, *Notizia*, p. 89. Cf. Ghirardacci, ii. 603; *Stat.*, p. 200. [For the *Collegium Gregorianum* see above, p. 198, n. 2.]

[4] *Statuta servanda a Iuvenibus Belgis qui admissi fuerint in Collegium Jacobs Bononiae fundatum an. 1650 sub titulis SS. Trin. Reformata*, A.D. 1829, &c.

§ 5. THE ORGANIZATION OF THE *STUDIUM*

CHAP. IV,
§ 5.
The guild
of doctors
acquires a
monopoly. WE have seen reason to believe that the guilds of doctors were in their origin somewhat more ancient than the guilds of foreign students. By some process which we are quite unable to trace the old liberty of teaching, in which the School of Bologna originated, came to an end. In the teaching profession, as in so many others, trades-unionism ultimately triumphed over liberty of contract, and the right of teaching became practically, if not theoretically, restricted to those who had been made free of the teaching guild.[1] The degree was in its origin nothing more than a qualification to teach. But when, in consequence of the general advance of civilization and enlightenment which marked the twelfth century, the services of learned men came to be in general request, it was natural that this certificate of competency should be valued for other than teaching purposes. In the course of the twelfth century the style of master came to be regarded as a title of honour which it was not beneath the dignity of a bishop or a cardinal to prefix to his name. If we
may judge from the number of persons who enjoyed this designation in the second half of the century, we may infer that it had already become pretty common for a 'degree' to be taken—to use the modern expression—by persons who had no intention of devoting themselves, or at least of permanently devoting themselves, to the work of teaching. We may presume that this was the case at Bologna as well as at Paris, though the masters of the civil or canon law were never so numerous as the Parisian masters of arts. But at Bologna the distinction between simple 'graduates', who had no intention of permanently devoting themselves to the teacher's office, and actually teaching doctors, was from an early period much more sharply drawn than at Paris and Oxford. The number of actual teachers of law at Bologna was always comparatively small: enormous crowds attended

[1] The liberty of private teachers may perhaps be considered to have been legally terminated by the Bull of Honorius III, in 1219. See below, p. 221.

the lectures of a single professor; the teacher's chair was here a coveted and lucrative prize. At Paris, in consequence of the multiplication of masters of arts, the remuneration that could be got by teaching was small, and a difficulty was experienced in getting a sufficient supply of teachers. Hence it was left open to any one to teach who chose, and it was even necessary to compel graduates to reside and teach for a time to ensure a sufficient number of lecturers. At Bologna, on the contrary, the distinction between the *magistri* or *doctores legentes* and the *non-legentes* was fundamental. The teaching doctors of Bologna very soon passed into something like the position of a modern professoriate, and the rights of the doctor or master as such fell more and more into abeyance. The various steps of this process must now be investigated, so far as the scanty data at our disposal admit. As to the use of these alternative titles, it may be observed that at Bologna the title most affected was doctor, rather than professor or master. At first the title master was used by other faculties than the legal, but eventually the term doctor became universal. A scholar would speak of his master as 'dominus meus'; but the mere use of the term 'dominus' does not imply a master: in Italy, as a title, it connotes nobility or one of its equivalents, and would therefore be applied to a man of rank whether he was a master or a student.[1] It is characteristic of the different relations in which the master stood to his class at Bologna that the Parisian term 'regens' is here rarely used.

Teaching confined to an inner circle of doctors.

Before, however, the successive changes in the position of the teaching body can be understood, it is absolutely necessary to explain a distinction between two classes of lectures which originated at Bologna, and which afterwards spread, with more or less modification, to all the universities of Europe. The lectures were divided into 'ordinary' and 'extraordinary'. Ordinary lectures were those given in the morning: extraordinary lectures in the afternoon. Originally this distinction of time corresponded with a distinction between what were considered

'Ordinary' and 'Extra-ordinary' lectures.

[1] [Cf. for usage in the Midi, R. Limouzin-Lamothe, *La Commune de Toulouse* (Toulouse, 1932), p. 58. In the vernacular *dominus* = mes- ser, ser. So we have Ser Brunetto Latini, but *not* Ser Dante Alighieri. The priest in the thirteenth and fourteenth centuries was 'il sera'.]

CHAP. IV, the more essential and the less essential of the law-texts. The
§ 5. ordinary books of the civil law were the first part of the Pandects
technically known as the *Digestum Vetus* and the Code: the
extraordinary books were the two remaining parts of the Pandects known respectively as the *Infortiatum*[1] and the *Digestum Novum*, together with the collection of smaller text-books known as the *Volumen* or *Volumen Parvum*, which included the *Institutiones* and the *Authentica* (i.e. the Latin translation of Justinian's Novels), the Lombard *Liber Feudorum*, and a detached fragment of the Code known as the *Tres Libri*.

Origin of this distinction. This distinction between the various parts of the Digest is purely arbitrary. The *Infortiatum*, though its ending corresponds with a natural transition in the subject-matter, begins in the middle of a book. It is obvious on the face of it that the division must have originated in an accidental separation of some archetypal manuscript—probably of the original Bologna copy of the great Pisa codex. According to a tradition which has already been alluded to, Irnerius began his work as a teacher by lecturing on a manuscript of the Old Digest, which was the first to arrive from Ravenna; while the *Infortiatum* came to Bologna later and the *Digestum Novum* (we may presume) last of all.[2] The distinction must in any case have originated in some accidental circumstance of the kind; and the matter is only noticed here because it seems probable that the distinction between ordinary and extraordinary books originated in the same historical fact.[3]

---

[1] The *Dig. Vetus* extends from the beginning to the end of lib. xxiv, tit. ii, the *Infortiatum* thence to the end of lib. xxxviii, tit. iii, the rest of the Pandects being the *Dig. Nov.* There is an extremely arbitrary section known as the *Tres Partes* (beginning in the middle of a paragraph), so called from its commencement at the words *Tres Partes* in L. *Querebatur*, 82. D. *ad L. Falcidiam*. The *Tres Partes* is sometimes treated as part of the *Infortiatum*, sometimes as a distinct portion.

[2] See above, pp. 115, 123. Of

the various explanations of 'Infortiatum' Mommsen accepts the view 'Id est auctum'; he sanctions the above explanation of the division. *Digest. Libri*, 1866, i, Praef., p. lxxii. [See, however, the previously cited articles of Kantorowicz, above, pp. 89, 122 n. 1.]

[3] [A statement in Buoncompagno's *Rhetorica nova* that Cicero's Rhetoric 'iudicio studentium est cassata, quia numquam ordinarie legitur', suggests that by the early years of the thirteenth century, the distinction was between lectures stipulated by the will of the uni-

The ordinary are not intrinsically more important than the extraordinary, but they must have formed the main or exclusive subject of the doctoral lectures in the early days of the school, the *Infortiatum* and the *Digestum Novum* being successively introduced at a later period. In the schools of the canon law the ordinary books were the *Decretum* and the five books of Decretals published by Gregory IX, the Clementines and Extravagants being extraordinary.[1]

Ordinary lectures were reserved to doctors, but extra- ordinary lectures on certain limited portions of the law-texts might be given also by scholars of a certain standing, after being 'admitted to read' such lectures by the rector. By delivering such a course of lectures a scholar became a bachelor. The term was at first probably a popular term applied to any senior student who was shortly intending to proceed to the doctorate: eventually it obtained the more definite and technical meaning already mentioned.[2]

versity of students, and lectures voluntarily given by the teachers. For the former the teacher would be paid, for the latter he would depend upon casual offerings. Odofredo, in the well-known passage given below, p. 269 n., points to a tendency of this kind. See the discussion in Manacorda, i. 250–4. In the later part of the thirteenth century the city of Bologna paid a fixed stipend, 'ultra collectam a scholaribus ordinatam', to the professors of law 'qui de cetero legent ordinarie de mane': *Bullettino*, No. 6, pp. 136, 137. Later, in order to keep teachers of repute, salaries were raised, in some cases to 200 li. bon. and we find salaries paid for extraordinary lectures, *ibid.*, pp. 135, 136 (*c*. 1334). Cf. a deed of 1374, by which a doctor of decrees appoints proctors to receive on his behalf 'libras.1.pro anno presenti lecture extraordinarie decreti per eum lecti in Bononia' (*Chart. Studii Bonon.* iv. 136, No. 211).]

[1] *Stat.*, p. 159. At Paris only the *Decredum* was ordinary, which was

no doubt once the case at Bologna. See below, chap. v, § 4. Kaufmann (i. 214), on the authority of Odofredus ('licet insolitum sit quaerere a dominis sive doctoribus in mane de eo quod legant in mane, peto veniam'), holds that questions might be asked at extraordinary and not at ordinary lectures. This is not impossible, but I do not feel sure that the distinction is not one between the lectures proper and the afternoon *repetitiones* on the morning lecture. The lectures of Odofredus on the *Infortiatum* certainly show no difference in style or manner from those on the *Dig. Vet.* Hugolinus makes it the duty of the student 'socium quaerentem pati cum benignitate' (ap. Savigny, *loc. cit.*).

[2] [Cf. city statutes, *Bullettino*, No. 6, p. 125: 'dicimus etiam quod scolares cives qui extraordinarie scolaribus legunt . . . excusentur ab exercitibus et cavalcatis'.] Many absurd definitions of the word *Baccalaurius* or (according to the earlier spelling) *Baccalarius* have

We are now in a position to trace the process by which the simple doctorate was gradually shorn of its prerogatives and degraded from an office—carrying with it the full rights of teaching, of membership in the doctoral college, and of control over the extension of those rights to others—into a mere honorary distinction or 'degree'. This revolution was the effect of three distinct changes:

Doctors originally dependent upon fees.

(1) We know in reality very little of the teaching system of the university—or indeed of any other parts of its organization—in the thirteenth century. But enough evidence has come down to us to make it clear that the teacher was absolutely dependent for support upon his *collecta*, i.e. the fees paid to him by his pupils.[1] The ordinary practice was for a professor to employ a couple of scholars to negotiate with the other students as to how much each was to pay; but at times a large body of students would make their own terms with the professor, and divide the cost among themselves. The amount of the honoraria was not even approximately fixed by custom, and at times we find learned professors of the highest reputation haggling with their scholars over these payments in a highly sophist-like and undignified manner.[2] Thus, for

been given. The actual etymology of the word seems to be doubtful; but there can be no doubt that the general meaning of the word *Bachelier* at the time when it came to be applied—first in common usage, and eventually as a formal designation—to students authorized to teach by way of preparation for the mastership, was 'a young man', with the special sense of apprentice or assistant (e.g. the landless man who worked for a *colonus*). 'En réalité,' says M. Thurot (*L'Organisation de l'enseignement dans l'Un. de Paris*, p. 137), 'ce terme signifiait apprentissage.' We everywhere meet with the institution of the baccalaureate or pupil-teachership before the name occurs in formal documents. It probably arose as a slang term: cf. the list of students 'qui legunt extraordinarie et *vul-*

gariter Bachalarii vocantur', in a document of 1297, ap. Sarti, I. ii (1772), p. 105. At Paris we likewise find the *institution* before the name. See below, p. 450.

[1] Ghirardacci (i. 77) speaks of 'molti Dottore da publico stipendiati' in 1150, but produces no evidence.

[2] 'Anno MCCLXIX die Iovis XIII exeunt. April. Albertus qu. (*sc.* quondam) dn. Odofredi doct. leg. fuit confessus recepisse a dn. Viviano . . . scholare bonon. quinquaginta libras bonon. quas in solidum cum mag. Gorlano suo fratre ei dare tenebatur ex instrumento manu Ugolini qu. Ugolini Presbiteri notar. Item xxxvi libr. bonon. pro parte sua et dicto suo fratri contingente de debito quadringentarum libr. bonon. quas in solidum cum pluribus scholaribus

instance, we find the eminent jurist Odofredus announcing at the termination of a course of lectures, that next year he would give no afternoon lectures at all, because he had not found the scholars good pay-masters: 'they want to learn', he pathetically explains, 'but not to pay. All want to learn, but no one will pay the price.'[1] The introduction of the system of *salaria* paid by the State seems to have arisen elsewhere than in Bologna. The neighbouring towns in their

Fees partially superseded by salaria.

dicto dn. Odofredo dare tenebantur ratione collectae ex instrum. Mich. Vinciguerrae notar. *Ex Memor. Com. Bonon.* ap. Sarti, I. i. 166. 'Bene scitis quod cum doctores faciunt collectam, doctor non quaerit a scholaribus, sed eligit duos scholares, ut scrutentur voluntates scholarium: promittunt scholares per illos. Mali scholares nolunt solvere quia dicunt, quod per procuratorem non quaeritur actio domino.' Odofredus in l. *Si procuratori*: Dig. *De verb. obligat.* ap. Sarti, I. i. 167. And the doctor is much concerned to prove that he has a right of action against 'bad scholars' who would not pay. Franciscus Accursius obtained absolution for himself and his late father for having lent money to students in hopes of obtaining 'maiores collectas' [see the letter of remission issued by Nicholas IV, 31 Aug. 1291 in Sarti, ii (1896), 70], and from the words of Odofredus— 'contra doctores qui mutuant pecunias scholaribus ut audiant eos'—it would seem that this was a frequent practice (ad L. *Omnia omnino crimina* Dig. *de off praef. urbis,* t. i, f. 27 *b*). So another doctor leaves a sum of money to the poor 'ex questu, quem feci in Scholis, quia multis et variis modis peccatur in Scholaribus habendis' (Sarti, I. ii. 1772, p. 76). We find doctors (not of law) sub-letting their 'schools and scholars' in a very curious fashion (Sarti, I (1769), i. 245; ii. 110, 131). Franciscus Accursius

gives two chalices to a Minorite church on behalf of the souls of the scholars, 'a quibus aliquid iniuste percepit tam Laicorum quam Clericorum dantium de bonis eorum propriis eidem non secundum dictum'. Sarti, I. ii (1772), 95. Sometimes there is a contract for board and lodging as well as instruction: 'An. MCCLXVIII Mag. Gerardus de Cremona Doctor Grammaticae promittit Adamaro Tebaldi de Villa S. Attredii docere eum in scientia Grammatice et dare sibi libros quos legerit in Scholis et victum in duodena secundum quod alii Scholares habuerint et dare cameram a festo S. Michaelis ad omnem annum pro pretio lib. xxiii. Bonon. de quibus habuit lib. x.' Ex *Memor. Com. Bonon.* ap. Sarti (1769), I. i. 511. So 'aliquem ex Scholaribus intrinsecus abitantibus in dictis Scholis cum dicto Mag. Petro', *op. cit.* I. ii. 110.

[1] Odofredus in *Dig. Vet.* (ad L. fin. D. *de divortiis*), ii, f. 192, 'Et dico vobis quod in anno sequenti intendo docere ordinarie bene et legaliter, sicut unquam feci; extraordinarie non credo legere; quia scholares non sunt boni pagatores; quia volunt scire, sed nolunt solvere, iuxta illud; "Scire volunt omnes: mercedem solvere nemo". Non habeo vobis plura dicere: eatis cum benedictione Domini.' In the preceding sentences Odofredus alludes to the custom of attending a Mass of the Holy Ghost after the completion of every 'book' in lecture.

eagerness to rival the academical fame of Bologna, would make overtures to a Bologna doctor, and invite him to come and lecture in their midst; and afterwards, when the great scholastic migrations began, the universities through their rectors would make a contract with the town selected, in which, together with facilities for the hiring of houses, exemptions from taxation, immunities from the ordinary courts and the like, the payment of certain *stipendia* to the professors was stipulated for. Eventually the Bolognese Republic found it necessary to imitate the liberality of its neighbours. The first recorded instance of such a payment occurs in 1280, when the Spanish canonist Garsias agreed to lecture for one year at a salary of 150 *librae*.[1] The contract was originally made by the students, but at their petition the republic undertook the payment, and in 1289 two permanent chairs were endowed with salaries of 150 and 100 *librae* respectively per annum.[2] The election of the professor was annual

and was left to the students, which must have been, at all events, an excellent system for keeping the teacher up to the mark.[3] The chairs were at first few in number, poorly endowed, and conferred only on strangers (*forenses*), no such measures being necessary to keep Bologna citizens from straying abroad in search of higher pay. Gradually, however, the number and amount of the *salaria* were increased; and as the power of the purse thus passed from the students to the city, the control of the former over the elections was gradually withdrawn, and the nomination appropriated by the State.[4]

---

[1] Sarti, I. i. 481. The first *civis* who received a *stipendium*—a small one of fifty *librae*—was Joannes Passavantius, in 1289, *loc. cit.*, p. 498.

[2] The first doctors elected were the canonist Altigradus de Lendinaria and the better-known civilian Dinus. Sarti, I. i. 255, 491. In 1297 Guildinus de Patralata is offered 500 *librae*. *Ibid.*, p. 495. In 1305 the number salaried has risen to seven besides six (in various faculties) appointed by the council. Ghirardacci, i. 504.

[3] ['Concessum est universitati scolarium forensium studii civitatis Bononie iuris canonici et civilis, et eciam universitati scolarium forensium siencie medicine sibi eligere et habere infrascriptos doctores seu lectores ad legendum in studio civitatis Bononie' . . . (here follow the number of chairs and the salaries) 'que sallaria solvi debeant per commune Bononie et de avere communis Bononie', &c.; city statute in *Bullettino*, No. 6, p. 135.]

[4] At first it seems clear that the *salaria* did not supersede the *col-*

In 1381 we find as many as twenty-three salaried doctors CHAP. IV,
of law, receiving payments varying from 100 to 620 *librae*,[1]   § 5.
the total grant for all faculties amounting to 63,670 *librae*.
At this time the fact that one of the twenty-one salaried
law professors had been elected by the university is mentioned as something exceptional.[2] The appointment of the *The Refor-*
matores.

lectae (Sarti, I. i. 256 [and above, p. 206, n. 1]); afterwards the practice seems to have varied. The canonist Hostiensis (*Summa in decretal.* tit. *de magistris*, n. 7, Lyons, 1597, f. 288 *b*) had raised the question 'utrum a scholaribus collectam facere vel levare possit?' and answers, 'quod sic, si non percipiat salarium de publico', or if the master is poor. On the other hand we find a Bolognese student, Wardus de Clusio, in 1324–5, paying 'Domino meo Ray. Doctori pro suo salario . . . unum florenum. Item dedi Domino Belviso' (evidently a bachelor) 'pro bancis et domo . . . decem solidos'. Clossius, *Codicum MSS. Dig. vet. descriptio.* Weimar (1818), 8, pp. 16–18 (Savigny, xxi, § 94). The contracts with Garsias certainly allowed him 'collectas facere' (Sarti, I. ii (1772), 131). At Padua, by the town statute of 1283 (Facciolati, *Fasti*, p. vi), salaried doctors are forbidden to charge anything except 'pro aedium pensione'; but we hear of a *collecta* in the later statutes, f. 15 *b*. At Lérida in A.D. 1300 the payment to the salaried Decretist is 'ad minus tempore collectae viginti turonenses argenti' (*Stat.* ap. Villanueva, *Viage Literario*, xvi. 220, 221). At Florence there were some 'Doctores ordinarie legentes' who received a *collecta* limited to one florin a head per annum; others were forbidden to take anything. (*Stat. Fiorent.*, pp. 65, 66.) So at Perugia (*Doc. per la storia dell'univ. di P.*, p. 52), though here *cives* were exempted from the *collecta*. At Bologna a non-doctor

'extraordinarie legens' is forbidden to demand fees (*Stat.*, p. 111), which may be thought to imply that doctors might receive them, but possibly not the salaried doctors. In 1437 Eugenius IV assigned a particular tax—the 'datum gabellae grossae mercantiarum'—to the payment of the salaria (Bull of Pius V, ap. Gaggi). Kaufmann's inference from the passage of Odofredus (quoted above, p. 207, n. 1), that 'die Scholaren hatten die ausserordentliche Vorlesung eines Professors frei, dessen ordinaria sie hörten und bezahlten' (i. 209), is unwarranted. Odofredus merely states that he did not find his afternoon lectures pay sufficiently to make it worth his while to continue them. [See above, p. 209, note. For recent discussion of the subject of fees see Gaines Post, 'Masters' Salaries and Student-Fees in Mediaeval Universities', in *Speculum*, vii (1932), 181–98, especially pp. 192, 193; and G. Zaccagnini, *La vita dei maestri e degli scolari nello Studio di Bologna nei secoli XIII e XIV*, Geneva, 1926.]

[1] Ghirardacci, ii. 389, 390. The year before the university had itself attracted the civilian Guido da Suzzaro by the offer of 300 *librae*, Sarti, I. i. 185.

[2] Ghirardacci, ii. 389. The canonists and medicals still retained a larger share in the elections. The statutes of the College of Spain provide: 'Hec autem in canonistis et medicis qui solent per suas uniuersitates eligi locum uolumus obtinere.' *MS. Stat.*, f. 6 *b*.

doctors and the general management of the *studium* in its
relations to the State were eventually entrusted to a board
known as the 'Reformatores Studii'.[1] In the course of the
fourteenth and fifteenth centuries such a body (under that or
some similar name[2]) was established by the city government
or prince in all Italian universities, and the real control of the
university more and more passed to this body of external
governors, which by the sixteenth or seventeenth century
succeeded in destroying the student autonomy or reducing it
to a shadow. After the full establishment of the papal domination in Bologna a supreme control was exercised over the
university by the legate and the 'Sixteen'.[3]

Restriction
of right
of promo-
tion.
(2) The 'right of promotion', i.e. of taking part in the
admission of other doctors, which had originally no doubt
(if we may trust the analogy of Paris and the probabilities of
the case) been enjoyed by all doctors, came to be restricted
to a small inner circle, who were limited in number and who
filled up the vacancies in their body by co-optation.[4] By the

[1] Dallari, i. xix. Earlier we find
the elections made 'per dominos
Antianos . . . et per collegia dominorum Confaloniorum et Massario-
rum artium civitatis Bononie'.

[2] Such as 'Gubernatores Studii' or
'Tractatores Studii'. In the smaller
studia the universities were from
the first more closely dependent on
the State, of which they were the
creatures, than at Bologna or Padua.

[3] The consent of the legate was
required for an additional holiday.
Dallari, i, p. xxiii. An official was
appointed to keep an eye on the
professors, and inform the reformers as to their attendance, &c.
[A good example of the system is
the activity of the sixteen *reformatores* in restoring the status and
protecting the immunities of the
doctors and students in 1416;
G. Zaoli, 'Lo studio bolognese
e papa Martino V', in *Studi e
memorie*, iii (1912), 111 *sqq.*].

[4] The process by which this
change was effected is far from
clear; but it would seem as if at
first the attempt was made to exclude even from the honorary
doctorate all Bolognese citizens
except relatives of doctors. Sarti,
I. i. 291, 300. At all times the
number of Bolognese citizens who
might be promoted was limited.
Stat., p. 386. In part the exclusion
was perhaps accounted for by the
efforts of the dominant political
party to exclude their opponents.
Cf. Ghirardacci, i. 327. It is clear
that by 1304 the college was already limited to Bolognese, since
in that year the city and university
united to force it to admit new
members. Ghirardacci, i. 464. It
would appear that at present *all*
Bolognese doctors became *ipso
facto* members of the college. [The
process of admission to a college
of doctors can be studied in proceedings of the colleges of medicine, arts, and theology (1380–6)
in the *Chartularium*, iv. 153, 194–5,
198, 199, 210–11. These documents

earliest extant statutes of the civil law college (published in 1397) their number is fixed at sixteen,[1] together with three supernumeraries who possessed the right of voting in all matters except graduations (in which they could only participate during the absence of any of the sixteen), and who succeeded to vacancies as they occurred. The college of canon law in 1460 consisted of twelve members, to which three supernumeraries were added in 1466.[2]

(3) Membership of the college and admission to the most valuable salaried chairs were alike restricted to Bologna citizens.[3] Both these restrictions probably had their origin in the fact that Irnerius and the other doctors who made the fame of the school were citizens of Bologna, and this original nucleus of Bolognese professors was assisted by all the resources at the disposal of the republic in the patriotic effort to reserve for their own countrymen the substantial emoluments, while they freely distributed to strangers the honorary distinctions, of their world-famous *studium*. Attempts to narrow the teaching body had been made before the year 1259, but in that year the doctors were compelled to swear (no doubt under pressure from the students) that they would not prevent external doctors duly elected by the universities from filling a chair at Bologna.[4] Eventually, however, the city enacted that ordinary lectures on ordinary books should be reserved to Bolognese citizens;[5] and

give an admirable idea of the small numbers, procedure, method of voting, &c. The colleges met in the cathedral, generally in the sacristy.]

[1] *Stat.*, pp. 370, 371. [See Ehrle's introduction to *I più antichi statuti della facoltà teologica*, pp. xl–lvii, for the development of this closed corporation of hereditary interests. He points out the influence of the political troubles of Bologna, e.g. in 1334.]

[2] *Stat.*, pp. 336, 353.

[3] 'Vere et naturaliter cives civitatis Bononie origine propria, paterna et avita.' Statute of civil law college in 1397 (*Stat.*, p. 370; cf. p. 391).

[4] 'E si decretò finalmente, che a qualsivoglia straniero invitato per via legittima degli studenti sarebbe libero al presentarsi, ed ascendere col favor loro le cattedre,' Savioli, III. i. 333. They also swore 'non ricevessero dagli alunni compenso alcuno per dichiararli capaci del magistero' (*ibid.*).

[5] *Stat.*, p. 159 (cf. p. 391). In canon law the restriction was extended to extraordinary books if read at ordinary hours, *Stat.*, p. 337. There were, however, as late as 1347, four chairs—two ordinary and two extraordinary—to which the universities elected; and to two

CHAP. IV, also that admission to the colleges should be similarly
§ 5.   restricted.[1]

Efforts to   So long as the doctors limited their efforts to creating a
make the
profes-   monopoly for the Bolognese, their interests were identical
soriate
hereditary.   with those of the city and were accordingly supported by the
municipal authorities. It appears, however, that from the
first the ultimate object of the professorial clique was to
reserve the substantial endowments of the *studium* to
members of their own families. The preferential right of
sons of doctors to succeed to vacant chairs is expressly
claimed by the jurist Accursius.[2] In 1295, however, we find
the city interfering to prevent the faculty promoting their
own sons or nephews;[3] and similar interpositions compelled
the doctors to admit outsiders in 1299[4] and 1304.[5] At the
date of the earliest statutes of the civil law college (1397)
the privileges of doctoral families are found to be much
restricted. As a general rule, only one Bolognese citizen
might be promoted to the doctorate in any one year; but sons,
brothers, and nephews of doctors are exempted from this
provision.[6] On the whole then it appears that the actual
monopoly of the doctoral families was destroyed, but there
can be no doubt that from about the middle of the thirteenth
century the professoriate of Bologna became largely hereditary. The effects of this restriction upon the prosperity of
the school we shall see hereafter; but the most fervent

of these (one ordinary and one extraordinary) 'forenses' alone might be
nominated, *Stat.*, pp. 36, 37. This
statute disappears before 1432.

[1] *Stat.*, pp. 336, 370.

[2] In Codicem L. 4. *de adv. div.
iudic.* (ed. Contius, cc. 353, 354).

[3] At this time it appears to have
been necessary for the faculty to
obtain leave from the city authorities before carrying out a promotion of Bologna citizens: on this
occasion leave was granted on condition that the new doctors should
be 'della parte della Chiesa, e de'
Gieremei di Bologna . . . o non
fossero figliuoli, fratelli, o nepoti

di detti dottori'. Ghirardacci, i.
327. Not all the professors were on
the Guelf side. When the city
imposed differential taxes upon
the Lambertazzi party, the descendants of the Accursii were specially
exempted on petition of the universities. Sarti, I. ii (1772), 76.

[4] Alidosi, pp. 223, 224.

[5] Fantuzzi, *Scritt. Bologn.* ii. 48,
49, 331.

[6] *Stat.*, p. 386. There is no
similar provision in the statutes of
the decretist college published in
1460. The earlier canonists were
unmarried ecclesiastics.

believer in hereditary institutions will hardly augur well of CHAP. IV, the experiment of an hereditary professoriate. § 5.

From the nature of the case this limitation to citizens could *Collegia in other* not be imitated in new and struggling universities. The *universities* object of Bologna was to reap the full pecuniary benefit of an *ties.* established prestige; towns which had a reputation to create, were anxious to entice doctors from other cities. All the universities organized on the Bologna model had a limited college or 'faculty of promotion', but it was not always restricted to citizens,[1] while in some cases citizens were actually excluded from the salaried chairs.[2]

A very peculiar and anomalous feature of the Bologna The student constitution as it is presented to us in the statutes of 1432 chairs. now demands a word of explanation. This anomalous feature is the existence of six salaried chairs for which only students or bachelors were eligible. Its origin must be sought in the events of the year 1338. In that year, Bologna, having expelled the legate, had fallen under the power of Taddeo Pepoli. Its tyrant siding with the Ghibelines, the city was laid under an interdict, a sentence which forbade the legal continuance of the *studium*. A body of the students, however, seceded to Castel S. Pietro and there elected six of their own number to take the place of the silent or scattered professors.[3] Upon the return of the seceders, the city found it advisable to allow the chairs to continue, perhaps as a solatium for the loss of the university's right to elect to the regular professorships.[4] In the course of time, however, it

[1] At Florence this restriction at one time existed, but was modified in 1404 and repealed in 1417. *Stat. Fiorent.*, pp. 182, 195.

[2] e.g. at Florence in 1392, *ibid.*, p. 172.

[3] 'De mense Aprilis Dominus Raynerius de Forlivio Doctor Legum, et sex Scolares electi ad legendum et tenendum Studium in Castro S. Petri propter interdictum Studii, iverunt ad dictum Castrum, dicta occasione, et multi Scholares iverunt ad intrandum ibi.' (Matt. de Griffonibus, *Me-* *moriale Historicum*, ap. Muratori, SS. xviii, c. 163). Cf. *Stat.*, p. 95. [A letter, printed by Cavazza, *Le scuole*, App., No. 52, gives a good picture of the life of the students in Castel S. Pietro. A certain Francesco Marchi, *notarius scolarium*, writes to the chancellor of Taddeo Pepoli. He had accompanied the son and nephew of Pepoli.]

[4] The origin of these chairs explains the fact that one of them, though held by a student, was 'ordinary'. *Stat.*, p. 95 *sq.*

CHAP. IV,
§ 5.

was found that these elections led to serious encounters in the streets between armed supporters of the rival candidates, to infinite perjury, and to the election of undeserving and illiterate candidates, perhaps popular athletes or the like. Henceforth the lot was substituted for election,[1] a remedy which might have been considered worse than the disease, had not the chance of delivering one of these lectures been looked upon as more valuable than the privilege of listening to them.[2]

The student's career: matriculation.

I must now try to give the reader some connected account of the career of a law-student at Bologna, from the time of his matriculation to his graduation. 'Matriculation' it should be observed, i.e. the placing the name of the student upon the *matricula* or list of members of the university, was originally peculiar to the student-universities; because only in them was the student a full member of the university. At Paris and Oxford only the masters were really members of the corporation: consequently there was no *matricula* of students. At matriculation, the student took his oath of obedience to the rector[3] and at the same time (it goes without saying) paid a fee—at Bologna amounting to twelve *solidi*.[4]

Hours of lecture.

It is difficult to reproduce the time-table of a medieval institution, since the time of day was more frequently indicated by the hour at which the bells rang for such a service at such a church than by the clock or the sun-dial. At Bologna there appear to have been three lecture-hours daily. The first and most important lecture of the day—the 'ordinary' lecture—began at the hour of the 'morning bell' for mass at S. Peter's and lasted till the bell began to ring for tierce (presumably about 9 a.m.). It must therefore have lasted at least two hours and possibly longer.[5] In the afternoon there might be two lectures of two hours and one-

---

[1] *Stat.*, p. 188 *sq.*

[2] By the city-regulations of 1475 students are required to 'prove their poverty' by two witnesses before becoming candidates. Dallari, i, p. xxiii.

[3] *Stat.*, p. 128.

[4] *Stat.*, p. 73.

[5] By the city-regulations of 1475

the salaried doctors are required to lecture for one or two hours 'secundum quod disponunt statuta Universitatis predicte'. Dallari, i, p. xxii. At Padua the doctor must lecture for two hours (*Stat. Iur. Pat.*, f. 76 *b*). Students are forbidden 'bancas pulsare' to enforce an earlier termination.

and-a-half hours respectively, the time being 2–4[1] p.m. and 4–5.30 in winter, 1.30–3 p.m. and 3.30–5 p.m. in summer. The period from tierce till 1.30 or 2 p.m. was thus left vacant for dinner and siesta; but it is probable that extraordinary lectures might be given after tierce. Other university statutes provide for a lecture at this time in addition to the two hours or two-and-a-half hours' lecture in the morning.[2] It should be observed that there was this difference between the two legal faculties as to the distinction between ordinary and extraordinary lectures. In civil law the ordinary books were reserved for the ordinary hours: in canon law, since the bulk of the ordinary books far exceeded that of the extraordinary, extraordinary lectures might be given on ordinary books. The books were divided among the doctors in such a way that all the texts should be lectured on annually (if the *studium* had sufficient doctors) or at least once in two or four years.[3]

The place of the lectures was originally the private Lecture-house of the doctor, or a school rented for that purpose. rooms. In the case of an exceptionally popular professor whose audiences could not be crowded into any ordinary room, a public building or an open space in the city was borrowed for the purpose. There is a tradition that Irnerius himself lectured from the open-air pulpit in the corner of the great square in front of the venerable Basilica of S. Stephen;[4]

[1] 'In hora vigesima intrent scolas, et in eis legendo stent usque ad vigesimamsecundam horam.' *Stat.*, p. 105.

[2] e.g. at Ferrara. Borsetti, *Hist. Gym. Ferrar.* i. 434.

[3] *Stat.*, p. 104 *sq*. Cf. Borsetti, i. 433; Fabroni, *Acad. Pisan. Hist.*, i. 122.

[4] The tradition perhaps arose from the statement of Odofredus ad L. *Si duas*, Dig. *De excusat.* (ap. Sarti, i. i. 86) that 'scholares voluerunt quod dominus Azo legeret in platea S. Stephani'. [In 1294 Giovanni di Bonandrea lectured in the Palazzo dei Notari (see

G. Zaccagnini in *Studi e memorie*, v. 145 *sq*.); and his successor—so it is stated at his election—'ultra intendit legere super palatio honorabilis cetus notariorum vel aliquo alio famoso et publico loco' (Riformazioni for 1321). That exceptional public discussions may in early times have taken place in the piazza of S. Stephen is suggested by a passage in the *Rettorica* of Buoncompagno (Gaudenzi, in *Bullettino*, xiv. 102); but the answer of Azo to the request of his students —that the piazza lay outside the bounds of the old *regia civitas*, i.e. east of the Aposa—shows why no

and Albericus is recorded to have lectured in the Palazzo Pubblico.[1] It was not till the fifteenth century that the universities generally began to build or acquire handsome and permanent buildings of their own, instead of leaving their professors to lecture in their private houses or hired schools. The Archiginnasio of Bologna, now the Biblioteca Comunale, dates only from the sixteenth century.[2]

A good idea of the nature of a Bolognese law-lecture—or indeed (allowing for the difference of subject-matter) of a lecture in any faculty in any medieval university—is given by the following account of the plan of a course of lectures ascribed to Odofredus, which is quoted by Savigny:[3]

Manner of
lecturing.
'First, I shall give you summaries of each title before I proceed to the text; secondly, I shall give you as clear and explicit a statement as I can of the purport of each Law (included in the title); thirdly, I shall read the text with a view to correcting it; fourthly, I shall briefly repeat the contents of the Law; fifthly, I shall solve apparent contradictions, adding any general principles of Law (to be extracted from the passage), commonly called "Brocardica", and any distinctions or subtle and useful problems (*quaestiones*) arising out of the Law with their solutions, as far as the Divine Providence shall enable me. And if any Law shall seem deserving, by reason of its celebrity or difficulty, of a Repetition, I shall reserve it for an evening Repetition.'

Glosses.
In the above account there is, however, no mention of a very important feature of all medieval lectures—the reading of the 'glosses'. By the Bologna statutes the doctor is required to read the 'glosses' immediately after the text.[5] The 'dicta-

---

schools are found there. See Cavazza, pp. 40–3.]

[1] The tradition is preserved by Odofredus in Dig. vetus L. 2 *de fide instrum.* (Lyons, 1557, ii, f. 165 *b*). [See Cavazza, p. 50.]

[2] In the fifteenth century we find salaries voted to doctors of arts 'dummodo legat in scholis consuetis artistarum' (Dallari, i. 46). But I can find nothing else about these schools. [The evidence, such

as it is, has been collected by Cavazza in his important work. For the Archiginnasio and the discussions which preceded its building, 1561–3, see *ibid.*, pp. 230–78.]

[3] c. xxiii, § 204. [This *Proemium* was in fact written by a pupil of Odofredus, Petrus Peregrossi, who taught at Orleans. See Meijers in *Tijdschrift voor Rechtsgeschiedenis*, i (1921), 462–4.]

[5] *Stat.*, p. 105.

tion' of lectures in the 'ordinary' hours was strictly forbidden;[1] and the extant lectures of Bologna doctors are thoroughly familiar and conversational in style. The 'repetitiones' alluded to by Odofredus consisted in a more detailed and elaborate discussion of some particular question arising out of a recent lecture. Any doctor might give a repetition in extraordinary hours whenever he pleased; but the salaried doctors were required to arrange by rotation among themselves for a repetition every week on some day on which no ordinary lectures were given.[2] In Lent repetitions were suspended and disputations took their place.[3] At these disputations, the doctor maintained a thesis against all comers. The rectors presided and determined the order of precedence when two rose at once. The precedence was settled by degree or standing, but nobles who sat on the front bench at lecture took precedence over all but doctors.[4] The students' disputations, which were presided over by a doctor, took place on holidays.[5]

Holidays were of frequent occurrence. To obviate the inconveniences arising from the caprices of the ecclesiastical calendar, it was prudently provided that there should be a holiday on every Thursday when no festival recognized by the university occurred during the week; but on such days repetitions and disputations might be held. While doctors were peremptorily forbidden to lecture on saints' days, students, whose lectures there was of course no moral or legal obligation to attend, were allowed to lecture whenever they would. The scholastic year opened with a Mass of the Holy Ghost[6] in the Dominican Church on the morrow of S. Luke, i.e. 19 October, while the Long Vacation, unlike the luxurious

Repetitions.

Disputations.

Holidays.

---

[1] *Ibid.* At Padua the Doctor 'post horam lectionis teneatur summarium lectionis, vel questionis disputate, dictare' (*Stat. Iur. Patav.*, ff. 79, 80), also to answer questions handed to him in writing (f. 77); and in 1474 he is required 'ad se reducendum post lectionem ad conferendum et ad circulos more artistarum' (*ibid.*, ff. 78, 79). These 'circuli' seem to have been informal disputations or discussions among the students presided over by a doctor. [2] *Stat.*, p. 106.
[3] *Stat.*, p. 107.
[4] *Stat.*, p. 108.
[5] Dallari, i, p. xxiii.
[6] Which the friars were required to say 'sine nota prolixa'. *Stat.*, p. 101. [The earliest notice of a meeting of the University of Jurists in San Domenico comes from 1290. See Cavazza, pp. 215–17, and cf. above, p. 188, n. 1].

recess of Oxford and Paris, did not begin till 7 September.[1] There was a vacation of ten days at Christmas, a fortnight at Easter, and three days at the carnival, which was afterwards extended to three weeks.[2] Bologna also enjoyed two days' holiday at Whitsuntide, in place of the short vacation allowed at the beginning of May in other Italian universities for medical purposes.[3]

Bachelor-ship.　After five years' study a student of civil law might be admitted by the rector[4] to lecture on a single title of the civil or canon law, or on a whole book after six years. A canonist could simply lecture on a single title after four years of 'hearing', or on a whole decretal after five years. The licence of the rector to 'read' a title or book or rather the completion of such a course of lectures made a man a bachelor. Bachelors admitted to read a whole book or decretal might give a repetition.[5] They might lecture twice a week.[6] Before presenting himself for admission to the doctorate, a bachelor must have given a course of lectures or at least a repetition, must have completed eight[7] or at least seven years of study in civil law or six years for the degree in canon law. But time spent in the study of one Law was accepted in reduction of the time necessary for graduation in the other, and it was possible to

---

[1] In the time of Odofredus the Long Vacation seems to have begun earlier, and to have lasted a little longer. Savigny, c. xxi, § 92.

[2] *Stat. Iur. Bon.*, p. 106.

[3] Borsetti, *Hist. Gym. Ferrar.* i. 418, 419. Fabroni, *Hist. Acad. Pisan.* i. 446. At Ferrara the May Vacation is described as 'pro potionibus sumendis more solito'; at Pisa it is more bluntly styled 'vacatio purgationum'. At Pisa there was also a week at Midsummer.

[4] Elsewhere the admission to bachelors' degrees belonged to the masters, very rarely to the chancellor. So at Vienna, 'Ordinamus quod ad solos Doctores et non ad alios spectet ... Baccalarios creare.' Kink, *Gesch. d. k. Univ. zu Wien*, ii. 136. The candidate having held

a 'repetition', and responded to opponents, was solemnly admitted by a doctor (*ibid.*, p. 146).

A bachelor was originally simply a student allowed to teach in a masters' school—a pupil teacher. Thus it is said of S. Richard, Bishop of Chichester, who studied at Bologna in the early years of the thirteenth century, that 'mellea Canonum fluenta sic hausit, quod Magister suus, infirmitate detentus, ad lectiones suas vice sua continuandas, prae omnibus discipulis suis dictum Richardum elegit'. *Acta Sanctorum*, April, i. 278.

[5] *Stat.*, p. 111.

[6] *Stat.*, p. 112.

[7] So by the Civil Law College Statutes, p. 382. The university Statute of 1432 adds 'vel ad minus per septem annos' (p. 113).

become a doctor of both civil and canon law (*Doctor utrius-*
que iuris) in ten years.[1] Bachelor-lectures were apparently
looked upon rather in the light of academical exercises for the
lecturers than as means of instruction for the pupils. It was
sometimes necessary for an ambitious student who was
anxious to have an audience to bribe scholars to come and
sit under him by gifts or loans of money.[2] No examination
or formal test was ever required at Bologna for the baccalaureate, which was altogether much less of a distinct 'degree'
and of much less importance than it eventually became in the
academical system of Paris or Oxford.[3]

In the earliest period the masters of Bologna had enjoyed
the same freedom as any other professional guild in admitting
or rejecting candidates for membership. They alone conducted the examinations, and conferred in their own name Licence
the licence to teach; and the student thus licensed became doctorate.
an actual doctor by receiving the 'book', the symbol of his
office, from an existing member of the guild. This unfettered
liberty of the Bologna doctors was, however, out of harmony
with hierarchical ideas: it was contrary to the general principle of canon law which claimed for the Church a certain
control over education; and it was contrary to the analogy of
the schools north of the Alps, particularly of the great University of Paris, where the *licentia docendi* had always been
obtained from the chancellor of the cathedral church. Accord- Honorius
ingly, in 1219 Honorius III, himself a former Archdeacon the au-
of Bologna, enjoined that no promotion to the doctorate the arch-
should take place without the consent of the Archdeacon of deacon,
Bologna,[4] who was probably the head of the chapter school[5]

---

[1] According to the Statute of
1432 (p. 113).

[2] Sarti, I. i. 231.

[3] On this point Kaufmann (i.
361 *sq.*) has some good remarks.
When he makes the bachelorship
more of a distinct degree at Oxford
than at Paris, the remark is only
true in respect of the bachelorship
of arts, which perhaps gained additional importance from the fact that
here alone was it conferred by the

chancellor. As to the explanation
of this peculiarity of Oxford, see
below, ch. xiv, § 1.

[4] Doc. in Sarti, I. ii (1772), 59.
[See Additional Note at the end of
this section, below, p. 231, for a
comment on the Bull and on
Rashdall's argument.]

[5] It would seem that the archdeacon was occasionally called
'Cancellarius', and already exercised a kind of honorary and in-

as well as of the chapter itself. The innovation was accepted without opposition, perhaps on account of the accident that the archdeacon's stall was at the time filled by a distinguished Bolognese canonist, Gratia Aretinus.[1] In 1270 an attempt was made on the part of the doctors to throw off the yoke,[2] but, with this exception, the relations between the archdeacon on the one hand, and the doctors and the university on the other, present a striking contrast to the chronic hostility which prevailed between the chancellor and university at Paris. The comparatively wealthy students of Bologna were less disposed to resent the pecuniary exactions of the archdeacon, and enforced them by their statutes. The archdeacon on the other hand, content with an accession of dignity and an enormous increase of income, does not appear after 1270 to have seriously attempted to interfere with the actual conduct of the examinations over which he presided.

Importance of the change. It is hardly necessary to comment on the importance of the Bull of Honorius III in the history of the university system throughout Europe. By that bull and the imitation of its provisions in favour of other schools the universities throughout Europe were, so to speak, brought within the ecclesiastical system. Graduation ceased to imply the mere admission into a private society of teachers, and bestowed a definite legal status in the eyes of Church and State alike. The gulf which had hitherto separated the free lay system of education in Italy from the ecclesiastical system of northern Europe was to some extent (more, it is true, in form than in substance) bridged over. By the assimilation of the degree-system in the two great schools of Europe, an archetypal organization

formal presidency over the *studium*. Cf. the words of Buoncompagno, who, in 1235, read his *Rhetorica novissima* 'in praesentia venerabilis fratris Henrici Bononiensium episcopi, magistri Tancredi archidiaconi *et cancellarii*, capituli et cleri, et in presentia doctorum et scolarium', &c. (ap. Rockinger in *Sitzungsberichte d. bay. Akad. zu München*, 1861, p. 136). In the Church of Bologna the archdeacon ranked next to the bishop. See *Stat.*, p. 417.

[1] Savigny (c. xxi, § 83) thinks that the right was meant to be a personal concession to the then archdeacon, but the document does not prove this.

[2] See the 'compromise' referring the dispute (which had led, as usual, to a scene in church) to the arbitration of the bishop, in Sarti, ii (1896), 56, 57; Savioli, III. ii. 433.

was established which supplied a norm for all younger universities. It came to be a recognized requirement of every university organization that it should have an official duly commissioned by public authority to confer the licence. And a further step was taken in the same direction in 1292, when a Bull of Nicholas IV conferred on all doctors licensed by the Archdeacon of Bologna the right to teach not only in Bologna but throughout the whole world.[1] Henceforth the universities passed from merely local into ecumenical organizations: the doctorate became an order of intellectual nobility with as distinct and definite a place in the hierarchical system of medieval Christendom as the priesthood or the knighthood. The archdeacon henceforth occupied the same relation to the University of Bologna that the chancellor of the cathedral occupied towards the University of Paris; and in course of time it became usual to speak of the Archdeacon of Bologna and the officials charged with similar functions elsewhere as chancellors of their respective universities: in a Bull of 1464 this phraseology even receives the sanction of papal authority.[2] By this time the term 'universitas' or rather 'universitas studii' was coming to be usual as a synonym of *studium* or *studium generale*. But originally it should be remembered that the archdeacon or chancellor was not an official, or even *ex officio* a member, of either the university of students or the doctoral colleges. He was rather an external representative

The archdeacon eventually styled chancellor.

[1] The Bull is also noticeable as recognizing the doctorate as a permanent rank which a man retained even when he had ceased to teach: 'ut quicumque ex Universitate vestra apud Civitatem predictam per Archidiaconum Bononien., vel eius Vicarium, prout est ibidem hactenus observatum, examinatus et approbatus fuerit, et docendi ab eo licentiam obtinuerit in Iure Canonico, vel Civili, ex tunc absque examinatione, vel approbatione publica, vel privata, aliquo vel alio novo privilegio regendi atque docendi ubique locorum extra Civitatem Bononien. predictam liberam habeat facultatem, nec a quoquam valeat prohiberi, et sive velit legere sive non, in facultatibus prelibatis, pro Doctore nihilominus habeatur.' Sarti, I. ii (1772), 59, 60. The privilege was confined to the Faculties of Canon and Civil Law, yet it was never disputed that Bologna was a *Studium Generale* in Arts and Medicine also.

[2] 'Universitatem Studii Bononie, cui archidiaconatum ipsum pro tempore obtinens, ut illius maior Cancellarius, preesse dignoscitur.' (*Stat.*, p. 417.) In the same Bull he is styled 'caput et Cancellarius Universitatis dicti studii'. [It is clear that, in some periods if not usually, the place of the arch-

of the church's authority over the *studium*.[1] The only jurisdiction which he exercised in connexion with the school,
besides that of presiding over the promotions, was that of
absolving for assaults on clerks, an offence for which absolution was by canon law reserved to the Holy See. The
faculty for this purpose was conferred upon the archdeacon
by a Bull of Honorius III at the same time as the right of
promotion.[2]

Process of
gradua-
tion. The account which must now be given of the graduation
ceremony at Bologna relates to the period in which it was
presided over by the archdeacon. Of the earlier procedure
we know nothing; but in all probability the main outlines
of the ceremony were already established before the introduction of the archidiaconal presidency. The process of
graduation consisted of two parts: (1) the private examination, (2) the public examination or *conventus*.

The
private
examina-
tion. The private examination was the real test of competence,
the so-called public examination being in practice a mere
ceremony. Before admission to each of these tests the candidate was presented by the *consiliarius* of his nation to the
rector for permission to enter it, and swore that he had complied with all the statutable conditions, that he would give
no more than the statutable fees or entertainments to the
rector himself, the doctor or his fellow-students, and that he
would obey the rector. Within a period of eight days before
the examination the candidate was presented by 'his own'
doctor or by some other doctor or by two doctors to the archdeacon,[3] the presenting doctor being required to have satis-

deacon could be taken by persons
who represented the bishop and the
chapter. Such persons normally
presided over the private and public
examinations in the later fourteenth
century. A member of the college
of doctors could be selected, e.g.
Lorenzo Pini in 1376 (*Chartularium*,
iv. 104). The position is defined
in an undertaking by the 'vicarii
domini episcopi et capituli *ad quos
spectat archidiaconatum officii* (*sic*)'
that they would not proceed with
examinations without the *conscien-*

tia of the doctors in medicine and
arts; *ibid.*, pp. 100–1, 30 May
1371.]
[1] If a doctor of the College of
Canon Law received this appointment he ceased to be a member of
it, unless dispensed by a unanimous vote. *Stat.*, p. 343.
[2] Doc. in Sarti, I. ii (1772), 59.
[3] [Or, in later times, to the prior
of the college of doctors. In 1385
a Hungarian was presented to the
prior of the college of canonists
who fixed the day of examination.

fied himself by private examination of his presentee's fitness. CHAP. IV,
Early on the morning of the examination, after attending a §5.
Mass of the Holy Ghost, the candidate appeared before the
assembled college and was assigned by one of the doctors
present two passages (*puncta*) in the civil or canon law as
the case might be.[1] He then retired to his house to study
the passages, in doing which it would appear that he had the
assistance of the presenting doctor.[2] Later in the day the
doctors were summoned to the cathedral or some other
public building[3] by the archdeacon, who presided over but
took no active part in the ensuing examination. The candidate was then introduced to the archdeacon and doctors by
the presenting doctor or *promotor* as he was styled. The

The candidate took an oath that
he had no degree elsewhere and
would not seek to gain admission
to the college, &c.; *Chartularium*,
iv. 200–1.]

[1] It will not be necessary to give
a separate reference for every detail
of the above account: I may refer
generally to the University Statutes,
pp. 116–19, and those of the colleges, pp. 344–6, 383–6, and Gaggi.
For the elucidation of the somewhat perplexing statute *De punctis
in privata examinatione*, the Statutes of Montpellier (*Cartulaire*,
i. 314 *sq.*, cf. also p. 389 *sq.*) and
other universities, are almost indispensable, e.g. the *Stat. Varia Civ.
Placentiae*, pp. 565–8; Fabroni,
Acad. Pisan. Hist. i. 431, 457, which
show the universality of this system
of *punctorum assignatio*. At Bologna
it dates from before 1289. See the
doc. in Sarti, I. ii (1772), 106. It
also obtained in the Medical School
of Montpellier: Astruc, p. 86; and
in the law faculty at Vienna: Kink,
Gesch. d. k. Univ. zu Wien, ii. 147.
So at Cologne, where the candidate
was allowed eight hours' study and
to give his lecture in the evening;
Bianco, *Die alte Univ. Köln*, i. Anl.
p. 53. Something like a survival of
this system is said to be found at

Salamanca (see Graux, *Notices
Bibliographiques*, Paris, 1884, p.
335), and Coimbra, where candidates are required to lecture on
three questions chosen by lot from
a large number, and to meet objections, answer questions, &c., three
hours' preparation being allowed.

[2] 'Et die extimationis [*leg.* ex-
aminationis] ipsius scholaris teneatur dictus doctor presentans ire ad
domum dicti scholaris et eum iterum examinare et ipsum audire
super legibus eidem in punctis
assignatis.' *Stat.*, p. 384. In the
time of Gaggi, the candidate was
still further assisted by knowing
that one of a limited number of
puncta was sure to be set, and was
coached in the preparation of his
apparently written exposition.

[3] The statutes seem to contemplate that the ceremony took place
in the cathedral. [Cf. Cavazza,
pp. 202–10. In the later fourteenth
century the private examination or
scrutinium usually took place in a
doctor's house or in the bishop's
palace, the public examination or
laureate in the cathedral. The
colleges seem to have transacted
all public business in the cathedral.
See *Chartularium*, iv, *passim*.]

CHAP. IV, prior of the college then administered a number of oaths in
§ 5. which the candidate promised respect to that body and solemnly renounced all the rights of which the college had succeeded in robbing all doctors not included in its ranks. The candidate then gave a lecture or exposition of the two prepared passages: after which he was examined upon them by two of the doctors appointed by the college.[1] Other doctors might ask supplementary questions of law (which they were required to swear that they had not previously communicated to the candidate) arising more indirectly out of the passages selected, or might suggest objections to the answers.[2] With a tender regard for the feelings of their comrades at this 'rigorous and tremendous examination' (as they style it) the students by their statutes required the examiner to treat the examinee 'as his own son'. The examination concluded, the votes of the doctors present were taken by ballot and the candidate's fate determined by the majority, the decision being announced by the archdeacon.[3]

Relation of licence to doctorate. A candidate who had passed the private, and had been admitted to the public examination, became a licentiate. Normally and naturally the licentiate proceeded to the ceremony which made him a full doctor after a very short interval; but the expense of this step sometimes compelled candidates to postpone it, while others (in spite of statutory prohibition) went off and took it at a cheaper university.[4] On

Public examination.

[1] By the Statutes of Padua (*Stat. Iur. Patav.*, f. 94), the 'puncta' were to be taken from the first 'utilis materia' which occurred after the place at which the book was casually opened.

[2] The function of the examining doctors is only distinguished from that of the rest by the university statutes. In the college statutes of 1387 all the doctors in turn are to argue with the candidate (*Stat.*, p. 385).

[3] [The *Chartularium*, vol. iv, contains many notarial descriptions of examinations and voting; e.g., pp. 80–102 *passim*. Occasionally unanimity was marred, as in a

medical examination in 1369, where one doctor suggested that the candidate study for a further year, 'quia respondet aparenter et non existenter'; p. 82, no. civ.]

[4] The Paduan statutes allow a licentiate of Bologna to receive the insignia at Padua. *Stat. Iur. Patav.*, f. 95 b. In the sixteenth century, however, when Padua had far surpassed Bologna in scientific prestige, the Paduan charges were higher than Bologna. Ferrara was much cheaper [because the number of doctors there, each of whom might demand the customary gift of gloves, &c., was smaller]. A student of this period, George

the day of the *conventus*, or public examination,[1] the love of pageantry characteristic of the medieval and especially of the Italian mind was allowed the amplest gratification. Shortly before the day appointed the candidate had ridden round the city to invite public officials or private friends to the ceremony or to the ensuing banquet, preceded by the bedels of the archdeacon and of the promotor or promotors. The statutes, indeed, forbade on this occasion the blowing of trumpets or other instruments, but on the actual day of the *conventus* no such sumptuary limitation was imposed. On that day the candidate was accompanied to the cathedral by the presenting doctor, and by his 'socii' or fellow-students lodging in the same house with him. The idea of the 'conventus', or 'public examination', was essentially the same as that of the ceremony known as the 'principium' or 'inceptio' in the northern universities. That idea was derived from the principle of the Roman law according to which a man was invested with the *de facto* possession of his office by an actual and solemn performance of its functions. At the same time and by the same act the new doctor was recognized by his

Wagner, thus writes: 'Laurea, seu doctoratus gradus, ut vocant, Patavii sine maximo sumptu suscipi non potest: nam collegio Doctorum amplius 43 sc. numerantur et subductis aliis impensis sumptus fere ad 50 sc. excurrunt. Bononiae paulo minus numeratur, Senis circiter 34 sc., Ferrariae vix ultra 28, sed haec urbs, nec literis nec studiosorum frequentia celebris, vulgo miserorum refugium vocatur, qui suae inscitiae conscii alibi alliam rigorosi examinis, ut dicunt, subire non audent. Qui Patavii et Bononiae insigniuntur, apud Italos in precio, sed nec contemnuntur Doctores Senonenses ob Academiae quondam florentissimae et professorum qui eam illustrarunt auctoritatem.'—ap. *Nuovi Documenti reguardanti la Nazione Alemanna nello Studio di Bologna*, ed. Luschin von Ebengreuth, Modena, 1884. There are two important articles by the same writer on the German students at Bologna in *Sitzungsberichte d. Kais. Akad. d. Wissenschaften.*. Ph.-Hist. Cl. B. 118, 124.

[1] Kaufmann (i. 364) well points out that there was a certain difference between the licence of Paris and that of Bologna. At Bologna the licence conferred at the *Privata* was merely a licence to proceed to the *Publica*; at Paris the actual *licentia docendi*, which at Bologna was only given in the *Publica*, was authorized. Hence at Bologna the archdeacon presided at both functions: whereas at Paris the chancellor (except in the faculty of theology) took no part in the subsequent inception. It should be added that the *Publica* is occasionally described as a *Principium* in universities of the Bologna type.

colleagues and received into the teaching guild or brother-hood, though at Bologna (as has been explained), by the period with which we are dealing, that admission had ceased to carry with it a practical right to the full exercise of the doctor's teaching functions.

The cere-monial. Arrived at the cathedral, the licentiate delivered a speech and read a thesis on some point of law, which he defended against opponents who were selected from among the students, the candidates thus playing for the first time the part of a doctor in a university disputation. He was then presented by his promotor to the archdeacon, who made a compli-mentary oration, and concluded by solemnly conferring the licence to teach the civil, canon, or both laws as the case might be, by the authority of the Pope and in the name of the Holy Trinity. In pursuance of the licence thus con-ferred, he was then invested by the promotor with the *insignia* of the teaching office, each no doubt with some appropriate formula.[1] He was seated in the magisterial chair or *cathedra*. He was handed the open book—one of the law texts which it was his function to expound. A gold ring was placed upon his finger, whether in token of his espousal to science, or in indication of the doctor's claim to be the equal of knights, and the magisterial *biretta* placed upon his head: after which the promotor left him with a paternal embrace, a kiss, and a benediction.[2] The ceremony concluded, both

[1] [The details can now be studied in the notarial acts. The various rites were undertaken by different doctors, e.g. *Chartularium*, iv. 81 and *passim*. The presentation of the book, accompanied by the master's blessing, was the essential act; cf. the city statutes in *Bullettino*, vi. 124: no one can become a doctor, 'nec aliquis doctor legum debeat *eidem examinato dare librum ut legat cum sui licentia*, nisi prius corporaliter iuraverit', &c. Some-times the book is described as *liber clausus et apertus*.]

[2] 'Cum paterna benedictione conferri pacis osculum consuetum;

in nomine Patris et Filii et Spiritus Sancti, amen.' *Stat. Fiorent.*, p. 439, where the ring is explained, 'in signum desponsationis utrius-que scientie, canonice scilicet et civilis'. At Padua we find the ring described as 'signaculum fidei quam debent sacris iussionibus profes-sores'. Gloria, *Mem. di Padova*, 1318–1405, ii. 267. In the medical faculty at Montpellier the doctor was also invested with a golden girdle; Astruc, *Mém. de la Fac. de Méd. à Mont.*, p. 88. At Valladolid, the Doctorand 'gradum sibi con-ferri humiliter deprecetur, et Patri-nus ipsum Cancellarium oratione

universities were required to escort him in triumph through the town, surrounded no doubt by a mounted cavalcade of personal friends or wealthier students, and preceded by the three university pipers and the four university trumpeters.[1]

A fuller knowledge of the customs and ritual of the Italian guilds would perhaps reveal a tolerably close analogy between these ceremonies of the *conventus* and those by which other guilds of merchants, professional men or craftsmen, received a new member into their brotherhood. In obedience to an inveterate instinct of human nature, members so admitted, while welcomed with effusive cordiality, were also expected to pay their footing. The earliest custom was no doubt to send presents of robes to the doctors, bedels, and other officials taking part in the ceremony; but by the date of our statutes these presents were commuted into money payments, though a fixed quantity of cloth of a certain specified colour might still be substituted for some of them; and in addition to the regular fees there were also some customary presents— a cap, gloves, and a present of sweetmeats to each of the doctors and to the archdeacon, while the prior of the college claimed a ring.[2] But the greatest expense of all was the

quadam ad illud faciendum, et dandum sibi facultatem ac potestatem insignia tribuendi, exoret, et mox Cancellarius conferat gradum, quo dato novus Doctor Thronum conscendat', &c. See *Estatutos, &c. de Valladolid*, 1651, p. 33, where the whole ceremony is minutely described. Here the new doctor kisses the chancellor and every doctor present. The ceremony in Spain included investiture with gloves, a golden cincture, and golden spurs ('non tantum in signum nobilitatis equestris, sed ut magis ac magis per assiduum studium continuumque laborem ad honorem conservandum exciteris'), and finally with the sword ('ut . . . officium et munus tibi concessum tuendi Regem, Legem, et Patriam accurate adimpleas'). See the formulae in use at Alcalá, ap. de la

Fuente, *Hist. de las Universidades en España*, ii. 620. Cf. *Cartulaire de l'Un. de Montpellier*, i. 373: 'dicunt quod unus doctor non potest incedere comode sine uno scutifero.' Charles V conferred on the college at Bologna the right of conferring actual knighthood upon doctors, while the doctors of the college were themselves *ipso facto* knights and counts of the Lateran. At the same time the college received the widely diffused imperial privilege of legitimating bastards. Gaggi, *ad init.*

[1] In the case of poorer students it would seem that these ceremonies were dispensed with. See the stat. *de recipiente librum in secreto* (p. 119).

[2] So at Pisa, the candidate is required to send each doctor a box full of comfits, of 1 lb. weight (*Scatulam unam refertam libra una*

CHAP. IV,
§ 5.
Banquet.

banquet which the new doctor was expected to give to his colleagues and university friends. Even more magnificent entertainments, such as tilts or tournaments, were at times provided by wealthier students.[1] At some of the Spanish universities the incepting doctors were required to provide a bull-fight for the amusement of the university. The immense scale on which these inception rejoicings were carried out may best be estimated from the fact that the Council of Vienne in 1311 passed a canon limiting the expense of such entertainments to '3000 *solidi* tournois'.[2] It should be added that besides the legitimate expenses of graduation, bribery was by no means unknown in the Bologna examinations.[3]

confectorum); Fabroni, *Acad. Pisan. Hist.*, i. 477. At Bologna the archdeacon received 12 *lib.* 10s. from each candidate at each examination (*Stat.*, p. 150), the university 30s., each doctor 40s. at the private and 20s. at the public examination, the presenting doctors 10 or 12 ducats. A host of minor officials of the universities, the doctors, and the archdeacon, had also to be remembered. One poor student annually received the doctorate *gratis* (pp. 181, 348). There were also certain exemptions for sons or brothers of doctors; and for all citizens the fees were much lower; *Stat.*, p. 145. Many of these expenses depended partly upon the inclinations of the donor. Thus the statutes of the Spanish College forbid the provision of refreshments for the examiners: 'Panis uero uel uinum in dicto priuato examine uel in disputacionibus uel repeticionibus per eos fiendis . . . de bonis Collegii alicui nullatenus errogetur: ymo eciam de proprio facere reprobamus, quia tales uanitates et pompe nedum in pauperibus scolaribus set eciam in diuiditibus (*sic*) sunt per sapientes et uiros laudabiles reprobate et per statuta uniuersalia (?) studii bonoñ. prohibite'; *MS. Stat.*, f. 6 *b*. A statute of Toulouse, on the other

hand, makes compulsory a payment of 8 *grossi* to the Capitoul's jesters or mummers ('quatuor mymis dominorum de capitulo eadem die, si dicti domini veniant ad aulam'); besides a payment to the three ordinary *mimi*; Fournier, *Stat. des Univ. Franc.* i, No. 772. [A solemn modification of the statutes by the colleges of medicine and arts in 1387 compelled the successful candidate to give each doctor in the college a pair of gloves, whose price, size, and material were carefully defined; *Chartularium*, iv. 262.]

[1] These are forbidden by the Statutes: 'Nullus autem scolaris, in alicuius civis vel forensis scolaris publica, se pro chorea vel brigata seu hastiludio faciendis vestire audeat vel tunc eques hastiludere'; and the Doctorand is to swear 'quod die qua equitat invitando pro publica recipienda non faciat hastiludere seu brigardare'. (*Stat.*, p. 116.)

[2] 'Tria millia Turonensium argenteorum' or 'circa 500 librae Bononienses'. Clem. 2. *de magistris*. See Savigny's note, c. xxi, § 82.

[3] The Jurist Francis Accursius took the precaution to get a Papal absolution for the 'munera' which he and his father had received from L. Faminando. Sarti, i. ii. 96.

In our English universities, conservative as they are in many things, every trace of the ceremony of inception has at length unhappily disappeared; only the preliminary ceremonial of the licence survives. Fragments of the old ritual survive in different parts of Europe. In the Scottish universities doctors are created by *birettatio*: at Bologna honorary doctors are still invested with the *anulus*. Still more of the full medieval ceremonial survives in the Spanish peninsula, and at Coimbra doctors of law or medicine are said even now to enter upon their office with the full medieval pageantry of book and ring, *cathedra*, *biretta*, and *osculum pacis*.[1]

Additional Note

[Much discussion has centred on the interpretation of the famous bull addressed by Honorius III to Archdeacon Gratia in 1219 (cf. above, p. 221). The Bull says: 'Cum sepe contingat ut in civitate Bononie minus docti ad discendi regimen assumantur, . . . duximus statuendum ut nullus ulterius in civitate predicta ad docendi regimen assumatur nisi a te obtenta licentia examinatione quoque prehabita diligenti.' Most scholars have regarded this injunction as a turning-point in the history of Bologna and as originating the control of the archdeacon over the licence to teach. Rashdall emphatically adopted this view and refers (p. 221) to the previous 'unfettered liberty' of the doctors. Manacorda, on the other hand (i. 208, 246), points out with some justice that the last words in the passage quoted, providing for a rigorous examination, express the intention of the Pope, who, in his reference to the grant of the licence, was simply repeating the canonical injunctions of his predecessors (cf. above, p. 22). He argues that episcopal authority must have been required in the eleventh and twelfth centuries at Bologna as everywhere else, before any authorized teacher, such as canon Hugo, could teach. And he fails to find any evidence for systematic examination before 1219. The development of powerful colleges of doctors was a later development, and Pope Honorius did not introduce anything revolutionary, but merely sought to remedy tendencies to laxity in the testing of the candidates and the granting of the licence.

Although Manacorda's further argument, that the schools of

---

[1] Some of these ceremonies survive (I am informed) in Spain, but not the kiss; as to Coimbra, see *Notice Historique de l'Un. d. C.*, p. 172. Oxford still retained the creation of doctors, by the cap, ring, kiss, &c., in 1654; *Diary of John Evelyn*, ed. Austin Dobson (1906), ii. 76. The ceremonial has also been revived at Louvain, see below, ch. ix, § 9 [1895].

CHAP. IV, Bologna grew out of the cathedral school, is not convincing, we are
§ 5. justified, in view of the canonical tradition of the episcopal jurisdiction over scholars recognized by the Authentica *Habita* of
Frederick I (above, p. 143) in concluding that the masters in the
twelfth century were not altogether free from ecclesiastical authority.
The Bull of Honorius III emphasized this authority. On the other
hand, there is good evidence to show that, as we should expect, the
masters had acquired an organization of their own before 1200,
conducted some kind of examination and recommended, if they did
not grant, the licence to teach. In his *Liber de obsidione Anconae*
(1201) Buoncompagno tells how Ugolino Gosia refused the office of
podestà at Ancona, on the ground of his moral obligations to his
colleagues in the schools: 'militavi siquidem sub senatoribus sapien-
tie, iuris videlicet peritis, addiscendo iura civilia ut patrum vestigia
imitarer; et nondum elapso unius anni spatio, *promerui de ipsorum
beneplacito et assensu in cathedra residere, ac illorum consortio aggre-
gari*, qui sunt candelabra lucentia, et quorum scientia mundus
regitur et illustratur: unde non decet me studium relinquere in-
choatum' (ed. Gaudenzi, in *Bullettino dell'Istituto storico italiano*,
xv (1895), 193, cf. *ibid.*, xiv. 94–5). Descriptions of examinations
conducted by the masters of Salerno about this time are much
more explicit. On the other hand, as Ehrle has pointed out (*I più
antichi statuti*, &c., pp. xlii, xliii), the existence of an *organized*
college of doctors cannot be proved for any period before the middle
of the fourteenth century, though such a college doubtless existed
earlier. It was of the nature of an examining body, what Savigny
called a *Promotionsfakultat*, which acquired other powers and
excluded many of the regent doctors, notably the *forenses*. The
earliest and most casual form of it is suggested in the well-known
references by Odofredus to the *antiqui doctores* of 1179, who 'con-
venissent in ecclesia S. Petri pro quadam examinatione'.

The very close connexion between the cathedral, the episcopal
household, and the colleges of doctors in the various faculties is
made very clear for the fourteenth century by the acts of four
notaries of the episcopal curia, published in the *Chartularium Studii
Bononiensis*, vol. iv (1919). References to several of these acts have
been inserted in the preceding pages.]

§ 6. THE UNIVERSITIES OF MEDICINE, ARTS, AND THEOLOGY

ONE of the most striking differences between the academical system of Bologna and that of the northern universities lies in the mutual relations of the various faculties. In the organization which originated under the very peculiar circumstances of Paris, but which has eventually spread over Europe, the doctors and students of all faculties are embraced in a single body and subject to a common head and a common government. In ancient Bologna there was absolutely no constitutional connexion between the faculty of law on the one hand and that of arts and medicine on the other, except the fact that the students of each faculty obtained their degrees from the same chancellor, the archdeacon of Bologna. The student universities with which we have been hitherto engaged were composed of law-students only, the colleges composed solely of doctors of civil and canon law. The organization of the law-students and the law-professors attained a developed form far earlier than that of the students and doctors of medicine or the liberal arts. The doctors of arts were no doubt from an early period sufficiently organized to conduct graduations very much after the same fashion as the doctors of law.[1] But the students long remained without any recognized organization of their own. In the thirteenth century, indeed, if we may trust to the analogies of Padua and Lérida, the jurist rectors with characteristic insolence claimed jurisdiction over the students of other faculties.[2] The necessities of the struggle by which the latter eventually won

Marginal notes: CHAP. IV, § 6. Entire separation of law from arts and medicine. — Students of arts and medicine originally subject to law universities.

---

[1] [Manacorda, i. 274 sq., inclines to the date c. 1250. Miss H. Briggs has called our attention to a passage in Buoncompagno, *Rhetorica Antiqua*, which appears to suggest some form of graduation conferred on him with ceremony before 1215 '[me] in presentia scolarium purpuravit considerans merita scientie non personam'.]

[2] As to Padua see below, chap. vi, § 4. At Lérida, the statutes (A.D. 1300) provide that 'quamvis scolares cives civitatis istius, necnon phisici et artistae, et alii multi non sint de stricto corpore universitatis studii nostri quantum ad ordinationes sive statuta condenda, debent tamen Rectoris subesse iudicio et universitatis statuta servare'. Villanueva, *Viage Literario*, xvi. 226.

their independence may partly account for the curious fact that the medical students were members of the same university as the students of the liberal arts, including even the mere schoolboy grammarians. But since there was a similar relation between the doctors of the two faculties, the explanation must also be sought in the close relations of the two branches of study which obtained in Italy.

We have seen that the law-school of Bologna was itself only an outgrowth of a more ancient and very famous school of rhetoric and grammar. Rhetoric and grammar always remained important subjects of instruction in Italy; throughout the Middle Ages they were far better and more thoroughly taught than in northern Europe, where the new Aristotle and its attendant scholasticism threw all literary studies into the shade. But after the rise of the law-school at Bologna, rhetoric and grammar came to be looked upon mainly as a schoolboy preparation for the higher professional studies; and the importance of their professors who, unlike the lawyers, were entirely dependent upon teaching for an income, was proportionately diminished. Logic was also regarded as a useful discipline for the future lawyer; but the new Aristotle—the study of physics, metaphysics, and moral philosophy—was in no way an essential or usual preliminary to a legal education: nor were these speculative studies or the degrees to which they led ever able in Italy to attain anything approaching the importance which they occupied in the less materially-minded universities of northern Europe.

But there was another study whose practical value commended it not less strongly to the utilitarian sympathies of Italian citizens than the study of law, and that was the study of medicine. Its development in northern Italy was somewhat later than the law-revival; and its practice, though almost as lucrative, never led to the same political or ecclesiastical distinction as a legal career. The status of the medical doctors and the medical universities of Bologna always remained inferior to that of the jurists. Nevertheless Bologna occupies a very important place in the history of medieval medicine —a position second only to that of Salerno and Montpellier.

Margin notes: Rhetoric and grammar important but preparatory. Unimportance of philosophy. Except as a preparation for medicine.

And the study of medicine according to medieval notions CHAP. IV,
§ 6. was closely bound up with the study of the Aristotelian physiology, and consequently with the whole of the Aristotelian philosophy. Aristotle, regarded in northern Europe chiefly as the basis of speculative philosophy and as the indispensable propaedeutic for the scholastic theologian, was in Italy studied largely as constituting the scientific basis of medicine. Hence the intimate connexion in all Italian universities between medicine and arts.

The names of physicians are of frequent occurrence in Bologna documents from the beginning of the eleventh century, and from about the end of it some of these bear the title of *Magister*.[1] At the beginning of the thirteenth century we hear of a *Medicus Vulnerum*, Hugh of Lucca being induced by an offer of 600 *librae* to come to Bologna as a public surgeon—a sort of military surgeon and police surgeon combined;[2] his son Theodoric and many other members of his family were also eminent surgeons.[3] Some of the early physicians were ecclesiastics,[4] others laymen. But at first the profession seems to have had little connexion with the regular academical schools. It is not till the second half of the century that teachers of medicine assumed the title of doctor or

Growth of medical school at Bologna.

---

[1] The first recorded *medicus* styled *magister* is said to be Jacobus Britonoriensis. Sarti, I. ii. 527.

[2] In 1214. Sarti, I. ii. 531; ii. 146. Cf. the city statute in Frati, i. 47, which provides that in cases of violence 'a magistro deutisalvi (*misread* dentisalvi) medico vel a magistro ugone de lucha vel ab aliquo alio medico plagarum quesitum fuerit', &c. Ozanam (*Docs. inédits*, p. 5) notices the numerous lay physicians mentioned in the archives of Lucca (Brunetti, *Codice dipl. Toscano*, No. 68 *sq.*) between the eighth and eleventh centuries. Lucca no doubt received the Arabic medicine from Spain or southern France. Brunus came from Calabria (Raige-Delorme and

Dechambre, *Dict. Encyc. des Sciences Méd*. Art. Bruno), another channel of communication with the East. All the early Bologna physicians and surgeons came from other towns.

[3] Sarti, I. ii. 537 *sq.*

[4] The prohibition of the study to the priests, monks, and beneficed clergy (see the Decretals of Gregory IX, lib. iii, tit. l, cc. 3, 9, 10, texts of 1163, 1215, 1219) shows its growing importance, but did little to check the practice denounced, since dispensations were freely granted. Theodoric, though a friar, was allowed to make a fortune by the exercise of his art, which he appears to have practised even after becoming a bishop. Sarti, I. ii. 537–41.

CHAP. IV, professor,[1] that graduations can be shown to have taken place[2]
§ 6.   and the school to have been organized after the fashion already
established in the schools of law and arts. It was, it would
appear, at about this time that the study of medicine, hitherto
pursued at Bologna empirically and traditionally, began to
be undertaken by men philosophically trained in the schools
of the liberal arts and to be based upon the writings of the
classical physicians and their Arabian imitators or corrupters.
The foundation of a scientific school of medicine at Bologna is
generally associated with the name of Taddeo di Alderotto of
Florence, who began to teach in that city about the year 1260.[3]

Gradua-   It was no doubt in consequence of this revolution that the
tion in College of Doctors in Medicine and Arts, and the university
arts and
medicine.

[1] From 1222 we begin to find a
class styled *Medici Physici*—a title
used apparently to distinguish the
scientific physicians alike from the
ordinary empirical practitioners and
from the *Medici Vulnerum* or Surgeons (Sarti, I. ii. 520, 555): the
title *Medicinae* or *Physicae Professor* or *Doctor* begins to be used
about the middle of the century
(*ibid.*, pp. 463, 464) and implies a
distinct imitation of the titles
assumed by the *Doctores Legum*.
In the *Rationes dictandi* of Hugo
Bononiensis is a letter from a
master to his scholars in which he
wishes them 'Ypocratis prudentiam et tullianam eloquentiam'.
Rockinger, *Quellen zur bayer. u.
deutschen Gesch.* ix, Abt. i, p. 63.

[2] One of the first academically
trained physicians who taught at
Bologna was Nicholas of Farnham,
who, after teaching at Paris and
Oxford in arts, professed medicine
(*rexerat*) at Bologna (Mat. Paris,
Chron. Maj. ed. Luard, iv. 86;
Sarti, I. i. 535), and became Bp.
of Durham in 1241 [see *D.N.B.*,
s.v. Nicholas of Farnham]. It does
not follow that there was a separate
graduation in medicine. As to
graduation in arts see above,
p. 146.

[3] 'Haec potissima Thaddaei laus
fuit quod primus ex nostris Medicinam cum Philosophia arctissimo
foedere coniunxisse visus sit.'
(Sarti, I. ii. 555.) Marvellous
stories are told of his wealth and
professional exactions. He received
3,000 *librae* to attend a patient at
Modena (see the contract in Sarti,
II (1772), 153); and would not
go to Rome to attend the Pope for
less than 100 golden ducats *per
diem* (Villani, *Vite d'uomini illustri
Fiorentini*, Florence, 1826, p. 24).
His bequests of books (Sarti, I. ii.
559; I. ii (1772), 158) suggest that
this teaching was largely based on
Avicenna, but he at times consults
the original Greek as well as the
Arabic versions of the Greek physicians; he is even said to have made
a translation of the Nicomachean
Ethics into Tuscan—a translation
which is severely criticized by
Dante (*Convivio*, I. x. 10). Special
privileges were granted to his
scholars by the City in 1283. Sarti,
I. ii. 557. [Dante mentions him also
in *Parad.* xii. 83. See for Taddeo,
F. Pucinotti, *Storia della medicina*,
Leghorn, 1885, II. i. 289 *sqq.*, and
G. Pinto, *Taddeo da Firenze o la
medicina in Bologna nel XIII secolo*,
Rome, 1888.]

of students in the same faculties, began to acquire a fresh importance, if not their first definite organization. Graduation in arts was certainly practised before 1221,[1] that is to say regular inceptions took place, and so at least in a rudimentary form some guild or college of doctors must have existed. But we have no proof of the existence of a distinct medical graduation till the days of Thaddeus,[2] though in each case the custom of inception probably dates in some form or other from a much earlier period. The first evidence of the existence of an organized joint-college of doctors of medicine and arts and of a joint-university of students is supplied (as is so often the case in university history) by a daughter-university—that of Padua, where Rolandinus read his book before the assembled masters and students in 1262.[3] Whether the medical University of Bologna at this time had no rector at all or whether the medical rector was subject (as was certainly the case at Padua) to the over-lordship of the jurist rectors, it is certain that the medical university did not at first enjoy the same legal recognition and privilege as the universities and rectors of the jurists. In 1295 we find the jurists successfully opposing the pretensions of the medical university to elect an independent rector like themselves, and it was not till 1316 that the independent jurisdiction of the medical rector was explicitly recognized by the city and the rival jurist-corporations.[4]

The College of Arts and Medicine.

The student university and rector.

---

[1] See the passage quoted above, p. 146 n.

[2] Gulielmus Brixiensis 'a Padua recedens conventum suscepit in Medicinis Bononiae sub Magistro Tatheo, Medico praecipuo tunc ibidem'. Engelbertus Abbas, ap. Pez, *Thes. Anecd. Nov.* 1721, i, c. 430.

[3] *Chron.* xii. 19 ap. Muratori, SS. viii, c. 360 (cf. below, chap. vi, § 4). The first express mention of the *Collegium Magistrorum* (of Arts and Medicine) at Bologna appears to occur in 1292. Sarti, i. ii. 558; i. ii (1772), 155. [A useful summary may be found in Ehrle, *I più antichi statuti della facoltà teologica*

dell'università di Bologna, pp. xxxviii, xxxix.]

[4] Ghirardacci, i. 329, 588. [The city statutes, so often cited (*Bullettino*, vi), had recognized the equality of the medical students some years before 1295: 'statuimus quod scolares forenses qui audiunt vel audient in futuro fisicam a magistro Thadeo et aliis doctoribus fisice, gaudeant omnibus et singulis privillegiis quibus gaudent scolares qui student vel studebunt in civitate bononie in iure civili vel canonico ex forma alicuius statuti vel reformationis vel ordinamenti communis vel populi bononie.']

CHAP. IV, § 6.

Constitution like that of jurist college and university.

The medical college and university, when once their constitution was developed, were mere imitations of the corresponding institutions among the jurists. The exact parallelism which exists between the two organizations will make it unnecessary to do more than notice a few points on which the account already given of the jurist organization is inapplicable. The medical university claimed to embrace every student in medicine, surgery, 'notaria', philosophy, astrology, logic, rhetoric or grammar residing in the city of Bologna, and to exercise jurisdiction over the teachers of all those faculties. It is, indeed, obvious from the language of the statutes, as well as probable from the nature of the case, that there were many more or less irregular schoolmasters who with their pupils neglected to take the oaths to the rector and get themselves put upon the *matricula*. But the constitutional right of the university to control the humbler order of masters and scholars does not appear to have been contested. It imposed few restrictions and conferred important privileges.

Only the medical students had votes in congregation.

Although scholars in all the above-mentioned subjects were subject to the rectorial jurisdiction and the university statutes, and entitled to university privileges and protection, only the students of medicine were full citizens of the academical republic: they alone were 'scholars of the university' and entitled to vote in Congregation; the rest were only *subditi* or subjects of the university.[1] But students of a certain standing in any faculty were allowed to take part with those of the superior faculties who had passed through the inferior in the election of their own professors, except in the case of students of grammar. Moreover, all above the grammarians were qualified to vote in the rectorial elections except the students of rhetoric, who were only allowed to elect twelve representatives to vote with the students of medicine and the higher arts.[2]

[1] *Stat.*, pp. 287, 288. At Florence a curious and invidious distinction is drawn between the medical student and the artist. The former's oath in a civil dispute is to be taken 'usque ad quantitatem unius floreni auri'; the artist's only to a smaller amount. *Stat. Fiorent.*, p. 23.

[2] *Stat.*, pp. 305, 306. In 1378 a dictinction was drawn between medical students who lived at their

The relations between the professors and the students are
exactly the same as those contemplated by the jurist statutes. Even the schoolboys possessed, it would seem, at least theoretically, the same rights against their schoolmasters as the students of medicine or philosophy, except that the statutes which conferred them were made by their older brethren, the students of medicine. But the power of the medical student-university does not seem quite so entirely beyond question as the power of the universities of jurists. The statutes occasionally admit that they are not always implicitly obeyed, and complain somewhat querulously of the 'arrogance' of masters who defied the university and the extreme penalty which it had the power to inflict, i.e. 'privation'.[1] The only way in which the university could enforce its privation upon a non-salaried doctor was by threatening his scholars with a like penalty if they refused to leave their deprived instructor; but since the scholars of arts had not the full privileges of membership in the guild, it is clear that the hardship of exclusion must have been rather sentimental than substantial.

The medical statutes claim for the students the right to elect to all chairs salaried by the municipality, though here they are directly contradicted by the counter-claim of the magisterial college. So far as historical records go, the students succeeded in enforcing their pretensions.[2] Salaries appear to have been first extended to other faculties than law in 1305, when they were bestowed upon doctors in grammar, physics, and 'notaria'.[3] In 1321 we hear of Giovanni di Antonio del Virgilio being appointed with a 'large salary' to lecture

own expense and those who lived at the expense of others (i.e. on charity or as dependants or servants). But by an agreement arrived at in 1379 an elaborate system of indirect election to the rectorship is prescribed, so as to give a preponderating weight to the students of independent means. Ghirardacci, ii. 377. It is curious that the statute of 1378 should be so early

disturbed. At Padua 'nullus nisi qui pervenerit ad quartum decimum aetatis suae annum' was allowed to vote. Priests, regulars, and 'famuli' or 'mercenarii' were also excluded. *Stat. Artist. Patav.*, f. 1 *b*.

[1] *Stat.*, p. 256.
[2] See above, p. 211, note 2.
[3] Ghirardacci, i. 504.

CHAP. IV,
§ 6.

upon Virgil, Statius, Lucan, and Ovid, an indication of the enormously higher position occupied by classical studies in the Italian as compared with the northern universities; and at about the same time a salaried professor of rhetoric lectured on Cicero.[1] Soon afterwards salaries of 100 or 50 *librae* were voted to professors of philosophy, of astrology, of medical practice, of natural philosophy.[2] At a later time the salaries, as in the case of the legal faculties, increased in number and amount; but it would appear that here also the appointment to the majority of them was eventually lost by the students.[3] The highest salaries paid in medicine were nearly, but not quite, equal to the salaries enjoyed by eminent doctors of law; and were generally higher than the salaries for arts. The fees payable to doctors of the various faculties, whether salaried or otherwise, were limited by statute. The lecturer in logic might charge anything up to 40 *solidi Bononienses*, the doctor of grammar up to 30. The latter, however, might add to his profits by taking boarders; though there was no obligation for the grammarian any more than for any other scholar to reside in a house kept by a master.[4] The fee for the medical lecture was, strange to say, lower than that for the lecture on grammar, being limited to 20 *solidi*,[5] probably because the medical doctor addressed a large audience, while the grammar-boy required 'individual attention'. In philosophy the fees were fixed not by the

Lecture fees.

[1] *Ibid.* ii. 17, 18, 19. [Giovanni del Virgilio was Dante's friend. The document of appointment (16 Nov. 1321) is in G. Albini, *Dantis Eclogae, Io. de Virgilio Carmen et Ecl. responsiva*, Florence, 1903, p. x, n. 2. In 1325 Giovanni experienced some difficulty in getting his salary of 40 *li*. Some extracts from the documents, which record a vote in the council at Bologna (422 for, 22 against, payment), in G. Albini, *Lectura Dantis: Le opere minori*, Florence, 1906, pp. 281–2. These correct Ghirardacci, ii. 59. Biographical information about Giovanni will be found

in G. Lidonnici, 'La corrispondenza poetica di Giovanni del Virgilio con Dante e Il Mussato', &c., in *Giornale Dantesco*, xxi (1913), 232–5.]

[2] *Ibid.* ii. 56 [see *Bullettino*, vi. 135].

[3] In 1383 it is specially mentioned that two of the twenty chairs in medicine and arts were filled by student-election. *Ibid.* ii. 398; Dallari, i. 45.

[4] *Stat.*, pp. 248, 249.

[5] *Stat.*, p. 253. For reserved seats ('si fuerit scholaris in bancha Rectoris vel in banchis anteriori-bus') a florin might be charged.

year but by the course, varying from 40 *solidi* for the *De* CHAP. IV,
Animalibus to five for the *Oeconomica*.[1] § 6.

Next to the entire separation of the legal faculty on the Relation of
one hand from the faculties of arts and medicine on the other, to philo-
the most distinctive peculiarity of the Italian university- sophical
system was the relation in which the professors of the various doctors.
sciences represented by the medical university stood towards
each other. In the northern universities medicine ranked
with theology and law (though the lowest of the three) as a
'superior faculty'; all masters of arts, whether they actually
taught philosophy or logic or grammar, possessed equal
rights as members of the faculty of arts. Grammar was hardly
a faculty at all. Some of the universities claimed authority
over the grammar schools; in some there was even a ceremony of graduation in grammar.[2] But the master of grammar
had no rights in the university. At Bologna a much more
complicated system prevailed. There was a *collegium*, composed—like the colleges of canon and civil law—of a
limited number of Bolognese citizens, which possessed an
exclusive right of examining candidates for the doctorate in
all the faculties embraced in the medical university.[3] This
college consisted, it would appear, only of doctors in medicine or full doctors in arts, i.e. those who had graduated in
all the liberal arts;[4] though those who were masters of arts
only, of course, took no part in the medical examinations, and

[1] *Stat.*, p. 252 (for extraordinary
lectures only).

[2] See below, vol. ii, ch. xiv.

[3] See the statutes of the college
(dated 1378), *Stat.*, p. 425 *sq.*

[4] *Stat.*, pp. 257, 445. The
medici and the *artistae* are spoken
of as the two 'membra' of the
college: the doctors of arts are
apparently included in the number
above given, but the relation
between the two bodies is somewhat obscure. [The 'prior medicorum' and the 'prior artistarum'
head the short list of masters, 'predicti omnes representantes et fa-
cientes totum colegium medicorum
et artistarum, congregati subtus

confessium ecclesie bononiensis',
on 13 June 1387 (*Chartularium
Studii Bononiensis*, iv. 212). The
existence of a prior of the artists
suggests that a separate college of
artists also existed, at any rate for
examinations. Bologna, like Florence, had its 'quinque collegia
doctorum', i.e. canonists, civilians,
physicians, philosophers or artists,
theologians; cf. Ehrle, *op. cit.*,
p. lv.] In the lists of the Paduan
College (Gloria, *Monumenti della
Univ. di Padova, 1318–1405*, i.
78 *sq.*) there are doctors of medicine only, doctors of medicine and
arts, and a few of arts only.

CHAP. IV, had not the full rights of the medical doctors. But besides
§ 6. this complete graduation in all the liberal arts, it was
possible at Bologna to graduate in, and obtain authority to
teach, some of the subjects embraced in the arts' curriculum
without taking up or being examined in the rest. We thus
hear of doctors of philosophy, of astrology, of logic, of
rhetoric, and of grammar, the subjects being enumerated in
what appears to have been considered their relative dignity.[1]

Gradua-
tion not
essential
for teach-
ing in-
ferior
arts.

It should be added that, though graduation in the lower
arts was recognized, it was not essential. Though the university claimed to extend both its privileges and its control
to the humblest schoolmaster in the city, the monopoly of
graduates extended only to the higher faculties and arts; the
teacher of grammar or surgery was not required to have
graduated in the university, but merely to have put his name
upon its *matricula*.[2]

Astrology.

Two of the subordinate subjects which fell within the
jurisdiction of the medical university demand special notice
—astrology and surgery.[3] Bologna did not become important as a school of medicine till the close of the thirteenth
century, when the power of Salerno had begun to decline,
and the popularity of the Arab medical writers was at its
height. The effect of the new influence—in so far as it was
really Arabic and not a revival of Greek medicine and surgery
in an Arabic dress—was on the whole distinctly detrimental
to the progress of medical science. It contaminated the quasi-
scientific medicine of Hippocrates and Galen with a mass of
astrological superstition: it was considered necessary for the

[1] *Stat.*, pp. 287, 488, 489, &c.
According to Sarti, actual degrees
were given in 'notaria', but this
does not appear from the statutes,
though we hear of scholars in that
art.

[2] *Stat.*, p. 254.

[3] [Rashdall here had a paragraph,
which we omit, on the place of
Italy in the revival of medieval
science. His references to Adelard
of Bath and Leonard of Pisa were
either incorrect or out of relation

to the main development in Spain
and Sicily as this has since been
established. Moreover, the part of
Bologna in the revival of Greek
studies and the infiltration of
Arabic science was slight. On the
whole subject see the excellent
introduction in Haskins, *Studies in
Medieval Science*, and the pregnant
observations on the nature of
Italian science in Duhem, *Le
Système du monde*, iv (1916), 184–8.]

physician to ascertain what would be his patient's critical days and to modify his treatment according to the aspect of the heavens.[1] We have already seen that astrology was one of the regular studies of Bologna: there was a salaried professor of astrology, one of whose duties was to supply 'judgements' gratis for the benefit of inquiring students.[2] The position of an astrological professor in a medieval university must have been a delicate one; for the scientific prediction of future events which might be practised and taught by ecclesiastic or layman under the patronage of the Church shaded off into the necromancy and the materialistic fatalism on which the Church had no mercy. The most distinguished occupant of the astrologer's chair at Bologna—the prince of medieval astrologers—Cecco d'Ascoli, ended his days at the stake in 1327, a victim of the Florentine Inquisition.[3]

Although the astrological bias of Bologna was not an improvement from a medical point of view, we must not despise the illusions through and by means of which all truth has to be reached. It was at Bologna, it would appear, that Copernicus, though a student of canon law, began the calculations which founded modern astronomy,[4] and the university has also claimed as one of its sons the Cardinal Nicholas of Cusa,[5] one of those anticipators who herald the

Astrology injurious to medicine, but not unfruitful.

---

[1] 'Oportet Medicum de necessitate scire ac considerare naturas stellarum et earum coniunctiones, ad hoc ut diversarum aegritudinum et dierum creticorum habeat notiones, quoniam alterabilis est equidem ipsa natura secundum aspectus et coniunctiones corporum superiorum.... Medicus sine Astrologia est quasi oculus qui non est in potentia ad operationem.' Cecco d'Ascoli ap. Sarti, i. ii. 523. [See Thorndike, *History of Magic*, &c., ii. 948–68.]

[2] *Stat.*, p. 264.

[3] [See Thorndike, *History of Magic and Experimental Science*, ii. 949–68. The still more significant Guido Bonatti, who lived in the later part of the thirteenth

century, is said to have been a professor at Bologna; *ibid.* ii. 825 *sqq.* On the whole matter cf. Haskins, *op. cit.*, pp. 256–8, and especially Duhem's chapter on Italian astronomy, *op. cit.* iv. 188 *sqq.* Here also Bologna did not take a leading part in Italy.]

[4] See the interesting monograph of Malagola (*Monografie*, p. 367 *sq.*).

[5] [Nicholas of Cusa passed from the School of the Brethren of the Common Life at Deventer to the universities of Heidelberg (1416) and Padua (1417). He became a doctor of canon law at Padua in 1423. See E. Vansteeberghe, *Le cardinal Nicholas de Cues*, Paris, 1920.]

approach of every great scientific revolution. In the department of medicine it was only or chiefly on account of its
increased attention to surgery that the fourteenth century
represents a period of progress; and in the history of medieval
surgery Bologna holds an important and very distinguished
place. There were surgical writers at Bologna as early as the
second half of the thirteenth century whose works continued
in sufficient circulation to be included among the earliest
productions of the Venetian press and to be often reprinted
up to the middle of the seventeenth century.[1] The theoretical
part of these books was based upon the Arabic authors who
derived them for the most part from the late Greek writer
Paul of Aegina; but it is the especial glory of the Bolognese
medical school that it was the earliest home of real anatomical
inquiry. It was one of the first schools at which the old
Dissection. religious prejudice against dissection succumbed to the
advance of the scientific spirit.[2] Dissection was practised at

[1] Among these were Theodoric
of Lucca, whose work was, however, largely based upon the earliest
Paduan teacher Brunus, and the
more important Gulielmus de Sali-
ceto (1215–80). Gui de Chauliac,
the famous fourteenth-century surgeon of Montpellier, speaks of
these two surgeons as the chief
representatives of the school 'qui
indifferenter omnia vulnera cum
vino exsiccabant', a treatment based
upon the Galenian doctrine that
'siccum vero sano est propinquius,
humidum vero non sano'. There
were, however, at Bologna representatives of the older Salerno
school, which treated wounds on
the principle that 'Laxa bona,
cruda vero mala' (a Hippocratic
maxim); of these the most important was Roland of Parma (a pupil
of the Salernitan Roger), who was
the first Bolognese writer on
surgery. (Sarti, I. ii. 536 *sq.*;
Raige Delorme et Dechambre, *Dict.
encycl. des sciences méd.*, art.
'Bruno'.) The 'Chirurgia Magna'
of Brunus and the 'Chirurgia' of

Theodoric and of Roland were
published with the 'Chirurgia' of
Gui de Chauliac at Venice, in 1497,
&c. It is a curious fact that the
Bishop-Physician Theodoric paid
special attention to veterinary surgery: he wrote a *mulomedicina* and
a *de cura accipitrum*. (Sarti, I. ii.
544.)

[2] Not, however, without a struggle: 'Ante hunc (Mundinum) ob-
soleta quasi erat secandorum hu-
manorum cadaverum consuetudo
nimirum contra Graecorum bar-
baram immanemque feritatem atque
audaciam publico supplicio con-
demnatos avide impetrantium, ut
in seditionem quasi concitatis, lex
tandem iniuncta infamiae paena
vetavit, ne quis exuviis denudata
cadavera imposterum ferro scin-
dere et ut exta videret, auserit
aperire.' Gulielminus, *De claris
Bononiae Anatomicis Oratio*, Bologna, 1737. For further information see the elaborate work of
Medici, *Compendio storico della
scuola anatom. di. Bol.* (Bologna,
1857), p. 8 *sq.* [Much curious

Bologna at least as early as the time of Thaddeus of Florence (1223–1303), who established a practical method; and the later statutes make provision for somewhat more frequent 'anatomies' than were customary in other universities even in the south of Europe.[1] Mondino da Luzzi (1276–1328) sometimes styled the father of modern anatomy, was one of the earliest teachers of surgery at Bologna, and his 'Anatomia' remained the standard text-book on the subject for more than two centuries. It was the ordinary practice in the Italian universities for a medical doctor to read the relative parts of this treatise while the professor of surgery performed the dissection and another doctor pointed out to the students the various bones or muscles as they were named by the reader.[2] By the statutes of Florence food and wine and spices were to be provided to keep up the spirits of professors and students during this unwonted ordeal.[3] The importance of surgery in Italy as compared with its neglect in the northern universities is indicated by the different position occupied by its teachers. Not only was surgery taught by doctors of medicine, but the latter were allowed to engage in surgical practice, an employment which was looked upon by the doctors of Paris as a degrading manual craft, entirely beneath the dignity of a sage learned in all the wisdom of Aristotle and Galen.[4] At the same time the mere surgeon who was not also a physician was in an inferior position. Examinations in surgery were held by the medical faculty, and licences to

information of a miscellaneous kind has been collected by G. Martinotti, 'L'insegnamento dell'anatomia in Bologna prima del secolo XIX', in *Studi e memorie*, ii (1911), 3–146. In a later paper he traces the history of the effect of the decretal *De sepulturis* of Boniface VIII (1299), who was erroneously supposed to have legislated against dissection (*ibid.*, pp. 162 *sqq.*).]

[1] It was arranged that every medical student of over two years' standing should be able to attend an 'Anatomy' once a year, twenty students being admitted to see the anatomy of each man, thirty of each woman. *Stat.*, p. 289. Some other universities had to be content with the body of a single criminal *per annum* for the whole body of students.

[2] e.g. at Padua (Facciolati, *Fasti*, p. xlviii: *Stat. Artist.* f. xxvii *b*). The method is described in some university statutes, and depicted in the woodcuts prefixed to many early editions of the old medical writers.

[3] *Stat. Fiorent.*, p. 74.

[4] *Stat.*, p. 444.

CHAP. IV, practise granted to those who passed them; but such qualified
§ 6. surgeons did not apparently rank as doctors of surgery.[1]

The medi- The subjects in which the medical student was examined
cal curri- for his degree were simply the 'Liber Tegni' (i.e. τέχνη
culum. ἰατρική) of Galen and the 'Aphorisms' of Hippocrates, on
each of which the candidate was required to give one 'lectio'.[2]
The custom dates perhaps from a period previous to the
introduction of the Arabian medicine; it may be presumed
that in the ensuing discussion the candidate might be required
to show a knowledge of the other books lectured on in the
schools. Among these the 'Canon' of Avicenna had the first
place; but they included also other works of Galen and
Hippocrates besides those above mentioned, and the medical
treatise of Averroës, the famous *Colliget* or *Correctorium*.[3]
The two *lectiones* of candidates for the examination in
surgery were upon a part of Avicenna and upon the 'Surgery'
of Brunus.[4] Among the books lectured on appear also the
'Surgery' of Galen and the seventh book of the 'Almansor'
of Rhazes.[5]

For the degree of doctor in medicine the candidate was

[1] *Stat.*, pp. 442, 443. What was
the exact position of the 'Doctor
Cirurgiae' is not at all clear. In the
College Statutes of 1378 (p. 443) we
hear of 'promoveri ad examen
Cirurgiae' as if it was possible to
take a degree in surgery only; on
the other hand, in the college
Statutes of 1395 (p. 471) it is
ordered 'quod nullus possit audeat
vel presumat legere in scientia
medicine Bononie, tam in physica
quam in cirusia, nisi fuerit doctoratus in eadem scientia medicine,
videlicet in physica'. The student-
statutes (p. 254), after laying it
down that no one who is not 'con-
ventuatus' may teach at Bologna,
adds 'salvo quod legentes in gramatica vel Cyrurgia non teneantur
ad predicta, nisi esset pro utilitate
Universitatis scholarium'. In Gloria,
Mon. d. Padova, 1318–1405 (ii.
289), is a diploma conferring 'auc-

toritatem ubique legendi . . . in
eadem facultate cyrugie'. It is
clear, therefore, that there were
degrees in surgery only, but that
at Bologna the *doctor legens* in
surgery was required to be also
M.D. At Padua no one was
allowed to practise surgery who
was not either *doctor cyrurgiae*, or
a student of three years' standing
who had 'seen' a doctor practising
for one year. *Stat. Art. Patav.*,
f. xxvii *b*.

[2] *Stat.*, p. 439.

[3] 'Legatur de libro *coliget* [i.e.
Kitab al Kollijât] primo prohe-
mium', &c. *Stat.*, p. 275 *et not.*

[4] 'Pro prima lectione super tercia
parte fen quarti canonis Avicenne,
et pro secunda lectione super
prima parte cirugie Bruni.' *Stat.*,
p. 443. ['Fen' is 'section'; see
Ducange, *s.v.*]

[5] *Stat.*, p. 247.

required to be twenty years of age, of five years' standing CHAP. IV,
in the study of medicine, and 'sufficient in arts'. If he had § 6.
been licensed in arts, four years' study of medicine sufficed.
He must also have lectured on some medical 'tractate or book'
as a bachelor, and have responded or disputed at least twice
in the schools.[1] The medical statutes of some universities
further require that as a bachelor he should practise for a year
under the supervision of 'some famous doctor'.[2]

The subject-matter of the arts course was so exactly the Course in
same as that of Paris that it will be best to consider in detail philosophy.
the medieval philosophical curriculum when we come to
deal with the university which was its headquarters. It will
be enough to say here that in the Italian universities parts
only of the Aristotelian treatises[3] were lectured on instead of
the whole; while the actual examination was limited to still

[1] *Stat.*, p. 433.

[2] e.g. at Padua, *Stat. Artist.*
f. xxix *a*: cf. a statute of Angers,
'Nullus non graduatus praesumat
ordinare seu administrare quamcun-
que medicinam digestivam, laxa-
tivam, *seu etiam confortativam*, nec
alias quovis modo infirmum visitare, causa cure, excepta prima
vice, nisi cum Doctore vel Licen-
tiato, si aliqui fuerint praesentes'.
*Statuts des quatre facultés de l'Un.
d'Angers*, Angers, 1878, p. 38.
Here the bachelor was either non-
existent or not reckoned a 'graduate'. [Cf. Fournier, *Statuts*, i. 409.]

[3] *Stat.*, p. 274. The Paduan
artist-statutes of 1486 (*Stat. Artist.*,
f. xxxiii *bis*) introduce a number of
text-books by recent writers, mostly
Paduan teachers: 'deputati ad
sophistariam teneantur legere logicam pauli ueneti questiones strodi
cum dubiis pauli pergulensis et pro
tertia lectione regulas seu sophismata tisberi.' Ralph Strode, fellow
of Merton College, Oxford, the
anti-Wycliffite, and Chaucer's 'philosophical Strode', wrote logical
works which were printed in 1488
and 1507 with commentaries by

Italian logicians. (*D.N.B.*, s.v.;
Ueberweg-Geyer, p. 603.) Paul of
Pergolae was a Venetian philosopher contemporary with Paul of
Venice. M. Hauréau, *Dict. des
sciences phil.*, *ad voc.*, questions
whether the 'Dubia' ascribed to
Paul of Pergolae is not really the
work of the better-known Paul of
Venice. The above allusion seems
to show the doubt to be unnecessary. Tisberus is the Oxonian
Heytisbury, as to whom see Poole
in *D.N.B.* [On his and other Oxford influence on Italy and the
study of logic see Duhem in the
Bulletin Italien, xii (1912).] At this
time it is observable that both in
the theological and the philosophical faculties (as in so many German
universities), there were separate
sets of lectures for Thomists and
Scotists; the Paduan statute (*loc.
cit.*) provides: 'Volumus quod
deputati ad legendum theologiam
unus legat secundum uiam sancti
thomae alter secundum uiam scoti.
Et similiter deputati ad metha-
phisicam.' Scotus was himself
much influenced by the Averroistic
philosophy.

smaller portions.[1] Moreover, the course seems to have been got through in a much shorter time—four years instead of a real or nominal seven. But, while the Italian universities never rivalled the scholastic fame of Paris, rhetoric, mathematics, and astrology flourished more vigorously in the Italian universities than in the north. In the former subject the text-books at Bologna were the *De Inventione* of Cicero and the treatise *Ad Herennium* then attributed to the same writer,[2] or the compendium of it compiled by the Friar Guidotto of Bologna.

Astrology and mathematics. Astrology was so interpreted as to include mathematics.[3] The subjects prescribed were:

(1) A work on arithmetic styled *Algorismi de minutis et integris*.

(2) Euclid, with the Commentary of the thirteenth-century geometrician, Johannes Campanus of Novara.[4]

(3) The tables of Alfonso X, King of Castile, with the 'Canons' [of John of Saxony].

(4) The *Theorica Planetarum* [? of Gerard of Cremona, or Campanus of Novara's free translation of Ptolemy's *Almagesta*].

(5) The *Canones super tabulis de lineriis*, i.e. rules for the use of astronomical tables to determine the motions of the heavenly bodies, by John of Linières or Lignières of Amiens (fl. A.D. 1330).

(6) The *Tractatus astrolabii* of Messahala or Maschallah [a Jewish astrologer of the ninth century].

---

[1] 'Qui examinari voluerit in artibus omnibus simul, ordine servato supradicti statuti, prima die recipiat poncta pro prima lectione in libro metaphysice et pro 2ª lectione in matematicis in libro sp[h]ere; in 2ª vero die pro prima lectione in loyca in libro posteriorum, pro secunda lectione in gramatica in prisiano minori.' *Stat.*, p. 489. At Florence the whole of the *Organon* was read, to which was added the *Tractatus* and *Fallaciae* of Thomas Aquinas (*Stat. Fiorent.*, p. 65).

[2] The latter was styled the *Retorica vetus*, the former the *Retorica nova*. *Stat.*, p. 488 *et not.*

[3] There was a chair of arithmetic whose occupant was required 'omnem mensuram terre et muri et generaliter cuiuslibet laborerii communis Bononie mensurare et agrimensare, et etiam omnes rationes communis Bononie male visas et chalculatas revidere et refformare'. Dallari, i. 5.

[4] See below, vol. iii, p. 249, notes.

(7) Alcabitius [fl. *c.* A.D. 850: probably his *Isagoge* to judicial astrology, translated by Gerard of Cremona].

(8) The *Quadripartitum* and the *Centiloquium* of Ptolemy with the Commentary of Haly, which were works upon judicial astrology.

(9) A certain *Tractatus Quadrantis.* [On the use of the quadrant.]

(10) A work on astrological medicine or medical astrology, which bore the title, very characteristic of the Arabs and their followers, *de urina non visa* [by William of England].[1]

(11) Portions of the *Canon* of Avicenna.[2]

Characteristic of the arts course at Bologna was the promi- nence of the *Repetitiones*. A *Repetitio* in medicine and arts was apparently somewhat different from the exercise so called in the law-schools. It was, as a rule, not given by the master himself but by a 'repetitor' who attended the lecture and then repeated it to the students afterwards and catechized them upon it.[3] Every doctor teaching logic was obliged to have a 'repetitor generalis' attached to his chair;[4] besides these official 'repetitores' there were 'repetitores speciales' who may be considered the private tutors or 'coaches' of the period.[5] The 'repetitores' at Bologna occupied to some extent the position of the bachelors in the northern universities.[6] Although students of a certain standing in all faculties could be admitted to give extraordinary lectures by the rector, and by so doing become bachelors,[7] the bachelorship possessed

Repetitions and repetitores.

---

[1] [Written in 1219; see Thorndike, ii. 486.]

[2] *Stat.*, p. 276. I am indebted to Malagola for some of the above explanations. According to Boncompagni (*Della vita e delle op. di Gherardo Cremona*, Rome, 1851) the *Theorica planetarum* is the work of Gerardus Cremonensis of Sabbioneta (thirteenth cent.), not of the earlier Gerardus Cremonensis the translator of the medical works of Avicenna, &c.

[3] 'Teneatur etiam repetere lectiones, scilicet de mane et in nonis usque ad pascha, et examinare de sero.' *Stat.*, p. 253.

[4] *Stat.*, p. 251.

[5] *Stat.*, p. 253.

[6] But the *repetitores* were more decidedly attached to the particular master than bachelors: they were in fact in the position of assistant-masters in the school of their chief. See the curious deed of scholastic partnership in Sarti, I. ii (1772), 11.

[7] *Stat.*, p. 272. Nothing seems to be said of 'Responsions', or any preliminary examination in the statutes, but at Padua we find a student supplicating 'quod possit acedere ad examen—absque

CHAP. IV, §6. much less importance in the Bolognese schools of arts and medicine, than in the Schools of Paris or even in the Law-School of Bologna.

Theology in thirteenth century left to friars. The last peculiarity of the Italian universities which has to be noticed was the absence, in their earliest days, of a theological faculty. Ecclesiastics attended the universities as much in Italy as in France; but in Italy, after the rise of the canon law, the study of theology proper was completely overshadowed by the practical studies of law and medicine. Many of the greatest schoolmen were Italians by birth; but theology rarely flourished on Italian soil. Just as among secular studies the practical and the literary prevailed over the speculative, so in Italy ecclesiastical studies flourished chiefly in their practical, their social, their political applications. For secular Churchmen canon law took the place of theology. Pure theology was abandoned to the regulars, that is, for the most part, to the mendicant friars, who taught and studied not, as in France, in universities where they had to hold their own against scholastically trained seculars, but in purely conventual schools. Here too it may be said that the practical interest was predominant; unlike the speculative secular doctors of Paris and Oxford, the friars studied as a preparation for the work of the preacher and the confessor. While the seculars were fighting for the rights of the Church against the Empire or the municipalities, the friar alone sought to bring other weapons to bear upon the souls of men than those of excommunication and interdict.

No theological faculty till 1364. Throughout the thirteenth and the first half of the fourteenth century, the Italian schools of theology had no official relations with the universities of the *studia* in which they were placed.[1] The policy of the Popes preserved for Paris

responsione questionum et lecturis librorum'; Gloria, *Mon. d. Padova, 1318–1405*, ii. 267. So *ibid.*, p. 273, and the *Statuta Artistarum* of 1465 (f. xxviii) provide 'Rector autem in Baccalariis ab ipso creandis ex auctoritate qua fungitur antequam illi gradum Baccalariatus conferat in eius presentia super duobus punctis sibi asignatis, per duos idoneos Doctores Legentes quos ipse Rector elegerit, diligenter examinari faciat, quibus si approbatus fuerit illi gradum Bacalariatus conferat, et privelegium per notarium nostrum fieri mandet'.

[1] They were no doubt open to such secular students as chose to

and the English universities their practical monopoly of theological graduation. Friars might prepare themselves for their theological degrees wholly or partially in other convent schools, but they had to go to Paris to graduate.[1] Bologna obtained its theological faculty from Innocent VI, in 1360, and it was inaugurated in 1364.[2] A little later, the Schism altered the relations between Paris and the Papacy; and the Roman Popes sought to weaken the great School of the Avignon obedience by granting Bulls to authorize theological graduation both in the existing and in the newly created universities; while after the Schism the same policy was continued by the Pontiffs of reunited Christendom who had discovered at Pisa, at Constance, and at Basel, that Paris was now a rival rather than a supporter of the papal autocracy. But the establishment of these faculties of theology in southern Europe made little real change in the constitution of the *studia*.[3] Theology was still taught and studied almost exclusively by the mendicants.[4] The college of theological doctors was wholly independent alike of the student-universities and of the other colleges. On the other hand its doctors naturally stood in a closer relation to the chancellor, who was in this case the Bishop of Bologna.[5] The arch-

---

attend them, but these were probably few. We hear that S. Richard, Bishop of Chichester, *c.* 1241 'ad Theologiam se contulit Aurelianis in domo Fratrum Praedicatorum addiscendam'. *Acta Sanctorum*, April, i. 279. For another case at Padua see Pez, *Thes. Anecd. Noviss.* i, c. 43. See above, p. 6, n. 1. [For the study of theology in cathedral and other schools in Italy cf. Manacorda, ii. 123–6; for Bologna before 1364 see Ehrle, *op. cit.*, pp. lxvi–cviii.]

[1] Papal Bulls were frequently granted to exempt friars from all or part of the requisite residence and exercises.

[2] [See Additional Note at the end of this section.]

[3] [Ehrle, *op. cit.*, pp. lxi–vi, col-lects, from the scattered references in Denifle, the main facts in the history of theological faculties.]

[4] [See Additional Note.] That a secular could become a doctor and teacher at Bologna is shown by the provisions of the statutes of the College of Spain (*MS. Stat.*, f. 6 *b*). The printed Statutes of 1536 provide for a permanent chair of theology in the college (ff. xxi *b*, xxii *a*).

[5] At Padua the dean and college of theology could not make statutes without the consent of the bishop. Gloria, *Mon. di Padova, 1318–1405*, i. 83; so the bishop admits to the bachelorship ('ad lecturam libri sententiarum'); Gloria, ii. 151. [A vice-chancellor sometimes presided over the meetings of the college, e.g. in 1388, *Chartularium*, iv. 152.]

CHAP. IV, deacon had nothing to do with the licensing of theological
§ 6. doctors.

In the following chapter we shall see how important in their effect upon the history of Italian culture were the purely constitutional relations of the various faculties to one another —the predominance of law-studies, the separation of theology from the secular arts-schools, the close alliance between the faculties of arts and medicine. Rather perhaps we ought to say that these constitutional arrangements are but the external counterpart and concomitant of deeply seated tendencies of the north Italian genius.

Additional Note on the Faculty of Theology

[Since Rashdall wrote the foregoing chapter, the activities of the colleges of doctors or professors have been fully illustrated in print by the publication of the fourth volume of the *Chartularium*, which contains notarial acts of the fourteenth century. The foundation and statutes of the theological faculty have been explained by Cardinal F. Ehrle in *I più antichi statuti della facoltà teologica dell'università di Bologna* (Bologna, 1932). The establishment of a faculty of theology, to follow the example of the privileges granted by Pope Clement VI to Florence in 1349, was sought by the commune on its submission to the Papacy in 1360, after a long period of revolt. Pope Innocent VI granted the request on 30 June 1360 at Avignon, and the faculty was solemnly inaugurated on 2 June 1364. The statutes were declared by nine 'founders', all of whom were drawn from the religious orders, eight being friars and one a Cluniac. The Statutes of 1364 survive in the register of the faculty begun in 1440, and a later body of statutes as they existed in 1426 were compiled for the use of Vienna and survives in a manuscript of the University of Vienna. Paris was taken as the model, and as Denifle, who used the official text, realized, the Bolognese statutes help to explain the Parisian system. (Cf. the observations of A. G. Little, *Eng. Hist. Rev.* xlviii (1933), 290.) The 'congregatio magistrorum' or college of doctors met under the presidency of the dean in the sacristy of the cathedral (see the judgements printed by Ehrle, pp. 88, 89). The members of the college, which was less of a closed corporation than the colleges of other faculties (*Statutes*, c. 2, p. 10) were a 'universitas magistrorum', who had taken the oath to the bishop or his vicegerent. They elected the dean, who was to be a senior master, 'regens regentias universitati incorporatas'. He was to hold office for six months and be succeeded by another 'senior et regens'. All incorporated *regentia* or *scola* had to comprise an 'ordinarium bachalarium' under the master. The dean was to

summon the masters once a month or when business required a CHAP. IV,
meeting (c. 33, p. 14). A religious, to qualify for the mastership, § 6.
must have studied six years in a *studium theologicum* (of his order)
and three years in a *studium generale*, and have obtained his licence
at Bologna (pp. 26, 27); a secular must be a master of arts who had
studied theology for five years (p. 17). In fact nearly all the Bolognese doctors from 1364 to 1500 (see the matriculation lists in Ehrle,
pp. 102–27) were members of the religious orders. Of the 447 the
great majority were friars, Austinians, Minorites, Preachers, Carmelites, &c. During this period of 136 years, only twenty-four seculars
appear on the lists (including the later Pope Gregory XII) and only
four monks (including Master William Selling of England in 1466 and
Master Thomas Hampton, *Anglicus*, in 1499). The faculty can never
have been very large in medieval times, and further discussion of
the statutes can be more suitably made with reference to Paris.

   Even in this limited circle, theological controversy soon appeared.
Ugolino di Malabranca of Orvieto, one of the nine organizers of the
faculty, and afterwards General of the Augustinian Hermits (1368)
and titular Patriarch of Constantinople (1371), felt constrained to
write a tract, *De uno et trino*, against certain of his colleagues who
were teaching Joachimite errors; see J. Rousset, 'Hugolin d'Orvieto:
une controverse à la faculté de théologie de Bologne au XIVᵉ siècle',
in *Mélanges d'archéologie et d'histoire de l'école française de Rome*,
xlvii (1930), 63–91.]

§ 7. THE PLACE OF BOLOGNA IN THE HISTORY OF CULTURE

CHAP. IV,
§ 7.
The great
age of
medieval
jurispru-
dence. IN many respects the work of the School of Bologna represents the most brilliant achievement of the intellect of medieval Europe.[1] The medieval mind had, indeed, a certain natural affinity for the study and development of an already existing body of law. The limitations of its knowledge of the past and of the material universe were not, to any appreciable extent, a bar to the mastery of a science which concerns itself simply with the business and the relations of everyday life. The jurist received his Justinian on authority as the theologian received the canonical and Patristic writings, or the philosopher his Aristotle, while he had the advantage of receiving it in the original language. It had only to be understood, to be interpreted, developed, and applied. The very tendencies which led men of immense natural powers so far astray in the spheres of theology, of philosophy, and still more of natural science, gave a right direction to the interpretation of authoritatively prescribed codes of law. An almost superstitious reverence for the *littera scripta*; a disposition to push a principle to its extreme logical consequences, and an equally strong disposition to harmonize it at all costs with a seemingly contradictory principle; a passion for classification, for definition and minute distinction, a genius for subtlety—these, when associated with good sense and ordinary knowledge of affairs, are at least some of the characteristics of a great legal intellect. Moreover, the exercises which were of such doubtful utility in other branches of knowledge formed an excellent course of legal education. The practice of incessant disputation produced a dexterity in devising or meeting arguments and a readiness in applying acquired knowledge, of comparatively little value to the student of history or physical science, but indispensable to the advocate and even to the

---

[1] In the following account of the medieval jurists I rely mainly on Savigny, though I have tried to correct and supplement him by later authorities.

judge. While it fostered an indifference to the truth of things fatal to progress in theology or philosophy, it gave the pleader the indispensable faculty of supporting a bad case with good, and a good case with the best possible, arguments.[1]

In estimating the place of the civil law in the history of medieval culture we must carefully distinguish between its cultivation as a science and its pursuit as a profession. During the most brilliant period of its cultivation as a science its professors were almost all congregated in Bologna itself. That period embraces the century and a half after its revival by Irnerius. It was in the hands of the 'Glossators'—of Irnerius, of the famous 'Four Doctors' of whom we shall have more to say hereafter, of Rogerius, Placentinus, Azo, and Hugolinus—that the most real progress was made. The works of these men are, perhaps, the only productions of medieval learning to which the modern professor of any science whatever may turn, not merely for the sake of their historical interest, not merely in the hope of finding ideas of a suggestive value, but with some possibility of finding a solution of the doubts, difficulties, and problems which still beset the modern student. *The glossators.*

One important part of the work of the school of the glossators was the formation of a sound text. In no other department of knowledge did the medieval mind show itself capable of judicious textual criticism. The jurists of Bologna made frequent pilgrimages to Pisa to consult the celebrated 'Florentine' Codex[2] of the Pandects. By diligent collation of this and other manuscripts there was gradually formed what was known as the *Textus Ordinarius* or Vulgate of the civil law, the text which was henceforth so jealously guarded by the *peciarii* of the universities and which has formed the basis of all subsequent editions down to quite modern times. *Textual criticism.*

Good sense and knowledge of affairs were, it has been said, conditions of progress in the study of law. It was just during *Democratic revolution: decline of the school.*

---

[1] It is interesting to observe that the old 'Moots' or arguments by students under the presidency of a bencher have recently been revived in the English Inns of Court [1895].

[2] So called since its removal to Florence, after the Florentine conquest of Pisa.

the period when the jurists of Bologna were most conspicuous as statesmen in a free republic that their labours produced really valuable results. Before the middle of the thirteenth century there occurred at Bologna, as in most of the other Lombard republics, a great democratic revolution. The chief power in the State passed out of the hands of the aristocracies into the hands of the people;[1] and in the popular governments the jurists enjoyed a less commanding position.[2] The doctors more and more degenerated as teachers into mere legal schoolmen, as jurisconsults into mere practitioners. The use or abuse of the forms of dialectic, the imitation of the subtleties, the intricacies, the interminable elaboration of the philosophers exercised a malign influence upon their work. Jurisprudence—like every other department of human knowledge (including even grammar and medicine[3])—became scholastic; while the formation of a semi-hereditary professoriate tended to the extinction of originality and genius in the School of Bologna. And to these causes of the decline of the science ought perhaps to be added the innate tendency of medieval learning to a sort of crystallization. Reverence for authority was harmless when the only authorities were the original sources of law. When the same reverence was extended to the glosses as had before been bestowed on the text, progress was at an end. The gloss of Accursius exercised upon the civil law the same narrowing influence which the 'Sentences' of Peter the Lombard had on theology.[4] This

The Accursian gloss.

---

[1] i.e. as in ancient Athens, the citizens, not the actual population. See Symonds's *The Age of the Despots*, London, 1875, p. 131.

[2] Thus Odofredus complains that 'Quando plebeii huius civitatis volunt facere sua statuta non plus vocarent prudentes quam tot asinos et ideo ipsi faciunt talia statuta que nec habent Latinum nec sententiam'. Ad. leg. *Lex est*, Dig., *de orig. iur.* (ii, f. 10).

[3] Well pointed out by Kaufmann, *Gesch. d. deutschen Un.* i. 25, 73 *sq.*

[4] [Accursius, a Florentine from Bagnolo, south of Florence, began his studies at Bologna, *c.* 1200. His gloss was finished in 1228, according to K. Neumeyer, but he taught for about forty years, 1213–53, and, like his son Francesco after him, became a rich citizen of Bologna with a palace, as well as his *aula* in the middle of the city. Davidsohn has shown that his last years were spent in Florence, where he died 1263–4 as *judex et assessor* of the Podestà (*Forschungen zur Geschichte von Florenz*, iv (1908), 537). On the life and work of Accursius see especially H. Kantorowicz in the

gloss was a selection, and as we are assured by Savigny not CHAP. IV, altogether an intelligent selection, of the glosses of previous § 7. writers. Yet a century later the professors had come to busy themselves more with this gloss than with the text. Instead of trying really to develop the meaning of the text, they aimed at a tediously exhaustive recapitulation and criticism of all the glosses and comments they could collect. In short, they lost sight of the end and aim of their work, which consequently became more and more stagnant and pedantic.[1]

The mere mass of matter accumulated by his predecessors Multiplication of commentaries. must have weighed upon the unfortunate professor of a later age, crushed his originality, and narrowed the sphere within which originality could be exercised. The truth is that the exigencies of academic lecturing upon text-books tend of themselves to produce a vast quantity of unnecessary commentation.[2] Where much has been well said, it is hard to say anything fresh that is both original and important: comments must perforce be either unoriginal or superfluous. No doubt comments, analyses, paraphrases, illustrations, applications, which are of no permanent value, may be useful simply as a means of impressing the substance of an author upon the mind of pupils. Lectures of this character are not commonly, in modern times, given to the world. In the Middle Ages, however, when it was possible to produce a dozen copies of a book at the same proportionate cost as to produce a hundred

Rivista di storia del diritto italiano, ii (1929), 35 *sq.*, 193 *sq.*, where references to other works may be found.]

[1] A fifteenth-century writer complains: 'Scribunt nostri doctores moderni lecturas novas, in quibus non glossant glossas, sed glossarum glossas. Et hodie in lecturis suis transponuntur iam dicta. Quod enim unus in una lege ponit, alius ponit in alia per eadem verba, vel paulo distantia'; ap. Sarti, I. i. 155.

[2] Thus the sixteenth century jurist Alciatus (*Opera*, Frankfurt, iv. 1617, c. 866) notices the contrast between the glossators and the fourteenth-century doctors who 'diffusius omnia attigerunt . . . non usque adeo tamen, ut omnia in unum locum congererent: dumtaxat vacationum diebus aliquam legem iterum interpretandam accipiebant quam diffusius disputarent, ideoque Repetitiones dixerunt: et hodie omnes repetitiones sunt nihilque plerisque dictum videtur, si quidquam omissum fuerit, quod commodius in alium locum reservetur. Unde efficitur ut singulis annis paucas admodum leges interpretemur.'

CHAP. IV,
§ 7.
or a thousand, the temptation to the publication of lectures was greater. To this cause we may perhaps owe the publication of large quantities of matter contrasting unfavourably with the terseness, the freshness, the good Latinity, the close contact with the original texts which impress the modern student of the older medieval jurists.

The most famous jurists.
It must not be supposed that the estimate which has been given of the relative importance of the earlier and the later medieval jurists corresponds with the reputation which they enjoyed in the Middle Ages themselves. The greatest legal reputations of the Middle Ages were made in the period which begins with Accursius. In the estimate of the later medieval world, the greatest authorities (next to Accursius himself) were such men as Odofredus, Dinus, Cinus, Bartolus, Baldus, and Jason;[1] and it is to no small extent the very success of these men (especially of the Bartolists) in adapting the Roman law to the needs and the customary practice of their own time that diminishes their value as scientific commentators.[2] Nor must it be supposed from what has been said as to the altered position of the Bologna jurists after the democratic revolution that lawyers and law-professors no longer played an important part in public life; but their influence was of a different kind. The effect of the study of Roman law upon the progress of imperialistic ideas has sometimes been exaggerated. It is chiefly in the earliest period that this influence can be traced. In the later Middle Age as many civilians were Guelph as Ghibelline. But it is a fact that the most famous of the early glossators were

Political influence of the earliest jurists.

[1] Savigny's somewhat enthusiastic admiration of the glossators may be qualified by the remarks of Berriat-Saint-Prix (p. 286 sq.), who, however, has no higher estimate of their successors, the Bartolists. The great disqualification of all medieval interpreters was of course their inadequate knowledge of classical antiquity.

[2] [On the other hand, this work gave them, and notably Bartolus, their great importance in the history of political thought and private international law. See the illuminating essay of Cecil N. S. Woolf, *Bartolus of Sassoferrato*, Cambridge, 1913. In this chapter Rashdall has omitted to treat of the development of the *Corpus Iuris* from this point of view and of the later widespread reception of Roman law; for a good introduction see P. Vinogradoff, *Roman Law in Mediaeval Europe*, ed. 2, Oxford, 1929.]

imperialists, and in their case it is perhaps no mere fancy to connect their politics with a bias derived from their special studies. Irnerius, as has been mentioned, played an important part in the imperial service. The four doctors, the most celebrated of his immediate successors—Bulgarus, Martinus, Jacobus, and Hugo—were prominent imperialist politicians, and the two former were intimate friends and advisers of Frederick Barbarossa. It was (according to the common but uncertain tradition) by the advice of the four doctors that the celebrated attempt was made to reimpose the neglected 'regalian rights' upon the Lombard towns, at the Diet of Roncaglia in 1158. The doctors, if they did not answer as Roman lawyers, certainly answered as lawyers.[1] They earned the undying hatred of their fellow citizens as traitors to the liberty of their country.

From this period the position of the great professors as Influence of later Bolognese statesmen was no doubt altered, but jurists were jurists. still in request both in Bologna and other Italian cities as judges and magistrates, as assessors or ambassadors, or simply as consulting lawyers.[2] A large and very lucrative part of the business of the great law-doctors consisted in giving 'consultations' whether to private inquirers or to princes and cities on matters of public and constitutional law. In truth, if the purely scientific and the purely political greatness of the Bologna School belongs pre-eminently to its earliest period, it was at a much later period that its influence was most widely diffused, though it was an influence now exerted

---

[1] Ghirardacci, i. 80; Sarti, i. i (1888), 37: Savigny, cc. 24 and 28, points out that these rights were founded on Lombard, not on Roman, law, and vehemently defends the counsel of the doctors. Perhaps, while disposed to deny altogether the imperialistic tendency of the study of the civil law, the great jurist is really illustrating its effect upon his own mind.

[2] Study at a university was usually required by the Italian cities as a qualification for judicial posts. Cf. the statute of Bologna in 1158 (Frati, i. 119): 'Nullus possit esse Iudex Comunis, nec vocari ad aliquod dandum consilium, nisi ipse studuerit in scolis V. annis in legibus.' So in France, 'Nemo in Gallia admittitur in Iudicem aut Advocatum nisi in utroque aut altero iure Doctor aut Licentiatus fuerit, iis solum Dignitatum porta in Curiis Galliae supremis aperta est sicut et apud reliquas nationes (paucissimis exceptis) soli iuris Romani Consulti Iudicem et Advocatorum munera exercent.' Duck, *De usu Iur. Civ.*, f. 102 *b*.

CHAP. IV, indirectly through a multitude of daughter-universities whose
§ 7. professors often eclipsed the reputation of their Alma Mater.
The great work of the universities—in southern Europe at
least—was the training of educated lawyers: the influence of
Bologna and of the universities generally meant the influence
of the lawyer-class upon social and political life. To estimate
the extent and value of that influence would lead us too far
astray from our immediate subject. We must be content to
state in general terms that wherever the civil law was more
or less recognized as the law of the secular courts—in Italy,
southern France, Spain, Germany, and (at a later date)
Scotland—the men who aimed at being advocates and judges
went to the universities, just as lawyers and country gentlemen alike went to the London Inns of Court in the days
when the inns were in fact what they were sometimes expressly called, a university of English law.[1]   And the universities were almost as much the nurseries of practical
lawyers in many countries governed by customary law, as
for instance in the French *pays de droit coutumier*, in which
the civil law was used to explain and to supplement a local
custom often itself in part of Roman origin. Even where the
civil law commanded least respect in the secular courts, its
study was still indispensable to the canonist. The study of the
civil law was indeed forbidden to priests by Honorius III.[2]
The canonist accordingly who looked forward to an ecclesiastical career usually went through the course of civil law
or at least spent some years in its study before taking Holy
Orders and entering upon the proper studies of his own profession, though it was easy for an individual or even for a
whole university to obtain dispensation from the prohibition.[3]
While the science of civil law rapidly degenerated and the

[1] [e.g. by Holinshed, *Chronicles* (ed. 1807), i. 249.]

[2] Savigny speaks as if this prohi-bition was altogether inoperative, at least at Montpellier. But it was fully respected at Oxford and Cam-bridge, as is evident from the pro-visions as to orders in the statutes of Trinity Hall and New College.

It is possible that Savigny forgets that in the Middle Ages a canonry or a rectory might often be held by a deacon or a clerk in minor orders.

[3] These bulls were often granted for a term of years, such a course being the more remunerative to the Holy See.

civilians no longer held the place they had once occupied as CHAP. IV, Italian statesmen, the importance of the profession of the § 7. canon law continued to increase, until it reached the zenith of its influence in the days of the Avignon Papacy, though here also the period of scientific progress had ceased. Distinction in canon law at the universities and practice at the Bar of the ecclesiastical courts constituted the great avenue to fame and preferment.

In the fifteenth century Roman law began to attract atten- The study tion as a branch of Roman literature, and to be studied by of Law and the Politian and others in its connexion with Roman history and Renaissance. antiquities; but the scientific and historical study of Roman law made little progress till the time of Alciatus and Cujas. The history of this later revival is a part of the history of the Renaissance. And if in Italy the Renaissance was contemporary with the Middle Age of northern Europe, it closes the Middle Age of Italy, and we must abstain from entering upon the origins of the mighty movement which was destined, after a long struggle, to extinguish scholasticism beneath a torrent of execration and contempt, and to destroy or transform throughout Europe that medieval university system which it is our present object to sketch.

It was through the civil and canon law that the School The canon of Bologna exercised its most powerful, at least its widest, law. influence over the course of human affairs. It would, however, be a great mistake to look upon Bologna as purely a school of law. We have, indeed, seen that from the time when canon law became fully differentiated from theology, no secular studium of theology of any importance existed at Bologna. In the academic organization a faculty of theology Neglect of had no place till 1364. The consequences of this constitu- theology. tional peculiarity were of the highest importance. From the Schools of Bologna strictly theological speculation was practically banished, and with it all the heresy, all the religious thought, all the religious life to which speculation gives rise. The prominence of legal studies in the south of Europe and of theology in the north is a fact of decisive importance in determining the destinies of the Western Church. In the

Middle Ages theology was, if not the foe of the Papacy, at least a very dangerous and suspected ally. The Latin Church received her laws from Rome, her theology from Paris and Oxford. It was only in the hands of the Dominican friars—and not quite always even then—that theology could be reckoned upon as a safe ally of papal pretensions. Wherever theology was studied by seculars—in France, in England, and in Germany—revolt came sooner or later. It was not by theology so much as by law—by her inheritance of those traditions of imperial jurisprudence which had subtly wound themselves round the common faith of Europe—that Rome established her spiritual monarchy. The canonist was by his profession a champion of the power which had created his class. No canonist (with the doubtful exception of Cranmer) ever headed a reform-party or inaugurated a religious movement, and no religious movement was ever originated or fostered in an Italian university.

Specula-
tion finds
a refuge in
the schools
of medi-
cine.
On the other hand, the speculative thought which at Paris was cultivated in the schools both of theology and of philosophy by philosophically trained ecclesiastics, was in Italy abandoned to schools of philosophy taught by laymen and chiefly attended by future physicians. In Italy medicine was a more distinct and a more flourishing profession than in northern Europe; medical men were not as a rule ecclesiastics; and the faculties were quite independent, in so far as any profession was independent, of ecclesiastical authority. The popularity of the Arabic medicine carried with it the popularity of Arabic astrology and Arabic philosophy. And the philosophy of Averroës, the most famous of the Arabs, was (in a popular if not in a strictly philosophical sense) a system of Pantheism, and a Pantheism of a materialistic rather than a spiritualistic complexion. In theological Paris, as we shall see, Averroism was for a time a source of serious alarm. But long before the close of the thirteenth century the triumph
Influence
of Aver-
roism in
Italy.
of the orthodox monotheism in the Parisian schools was complete. Averroës was remembered chiefly as the commentator, and was regarded indeed (his theological errors duly excepted) as one of the accredited expositors of the accredited

philosophy of the Church.[1] But Averroës, the champion of the 'Unity of Active Intellect' and all the heresies and infidelities associated with that pantheistic theory, ceased after the thirteenth century to have any formidable influence over the thought of Paris. In Italy it was far otherwise. To the schools of arts and medicine in Italy Averroës was not merely 'the commentator'. The authority ascribed to his characteristic doctrines equalled that attributed throughout Europe to Aristotle himself: here the Averroistic Aristotle wellnigh superseded not merely the actual Aristotle but the Aristotle of Albert and of Aquinas. To the Italian mind of the Middle Ages Averroës presented himself, as he does in the poetry of Dante and the painting of Andrea da Firenze, as the incarnation of all heresy.[2] Some of the foremost leaders of Averroistic thought both in and out of Italy were friars or churchmen:[3] some

[1] See below, p. 369. The statute there cited must qualify what Renan (*Averroès*, p. 425) says as to the neglect even of the comments of Averroës in France. At Paris in the fourteenth century Averroistic influences were felt almost exclusively (1) among the Franciscans, (2) in the English nation, i.e. not in the dominant school; and even here they produced no irreligious movement.

[2] [Dante placed 'Averroìs che'l gran comento feo' in the noble castle in Limbo among the souls whose only fault was that they had not been baptized into the true faith (*Inf.* iv. 144). He placed the famous Averroist Siger of Brabant in Paradise, and stamped his doctrine with approval:
'Che, leggendo nel vico degli strami,
Sillogizzò invidiosi veri.'
(*Paradiso*, x. 137–8.)]

[3] Two Oxford doctors, the Carmelite John of Baconthorp, known as *Averroistarum princeps*, and Walter Burley, were much influenced by Averroës, but their own influence was much greater in Italy than in England. Renan,

Averroès, p. 318 *sq.* Two of the leaders of Italian Averroism were friars, the Servite Urbano of Bologna, and the Augustinian Paul of Venice. The first denied the most dangerous Averroistic doctrine of the Unity of Intellect, the latter maintained it in its most uncompromising form. *Ibid.*, pp. 343–47. [For further information on the Averroists see the bibliographical notes in Ueberweg-Geyer, pp. 612–18. On Walter Burley, who was not, as stated above, an Averroist, see the remarks of C. Michalski in his paper 'la physique nouvelle et les différents courants philosophiques au xiv⁰ siècle' (from the *Bulletin de l'Académie polonaise des sciences et des lettres*: Classe d'hist. et de philos.: Cracow, 1928), p. 27 *sq.* The significance of the movement described by Renan and summarized here by Rashdall should be considered in the light of philosophic scepticism in Europe generally, of the uncritical nature of Italian science, and the vigour of Thomist philosophy in the Dominican schools of theology and elsewhere.

made distinctions and attempted to minimize the heterodoxy
of the Averroistic theses; others saved themselves, sincerely
or insincerely, by the convenient assumption that what was
philosophically true might be theologically false. And in
some cases the reserve was quite sincerely made. The
authority of Averroës stood almost as high with Savonarola
and with Cajetan as with the most heterodox of the lay
Averroists.[1] But there cannot be the smallest doubt that
under the name of Averroism a thinly veiled materialism
which treated the most fundamental doctrines of Christianity
with no more respect than the myths of paganism became
fashionable among the cultivated physicians and so to a large
extent in cultivated Italian lay society—and not always in lay
society only—particularly in that north-east corner of Italy
which included Bologna, her twin-sister the Venetian University of Padua, and gorgeous, materialistic, worldly Venice
herself. The philosophical scepticism of the Renaissance
period was, indeed, very largely due to the working of the old
leaven of Averroism which had long been fermenting beneath
the superficial orthodoxy of medieval Italy. The new leaven
of humanism and the purer Hellenistic philosophy which
humanism brought with it encountered a no less strenuous
opposition from the lay, sceptical, materialistic scholasticism
of the south than from the clerical, orthodox, metaphysical
scholasticism of the north.[2]

Depen-
dence of
the Aver-
roists on
authority.
We need not go back to the Middle Ages to find that the
adherents of a dominant philosophy—even a negative philosophy—are quite as prone to an immovable conservatism and
a bigoted attachment to the tradition of a school as the
adherents of a dominant theology. But it is, indeed, characteristic of the Middle Ages that an unreasonable subservience

Some of the leading Thomists in
Paris were Italians; cf. J. Koch's
article in Ueberweg-Geyer, pp.
538–41.]
    [1] Renan, *Averroès*, pp. 350, 351.
    [2] Petrarch, in particular, main-
tained a furious polemic against the
Averroists and the Physicians. He
even refuses to be cured on Arab

principles, or by drugs with Arabic
names. See his *Contra medicum
quendam invect.* (*Opp.* Basel, 1559,
p. 1093, &c.; Renan, *Averroès*,
p. 329 *sq.*) [See Valeria Benetti-
Brunelli, *Le origini italiane della
scuola umanistica*, Milan, 1919, pp.
228–36.]

to authority was carried quite as far among the sceptics as CHAP. IV, § 7. among the orthodox; they differed only in the choice of authorities. To the Italian physician—sceptical in religion, but capable of enormous superstition in an astrological direction—Averroës was as infallible whether in medicine or in metaphysics as was the Bible in matters of faith and Aristotle in matters of philosophy to the Parisian ecclesiastic. But though the deference to authority is now less avowed, it would be easy to illustrate from every period in the history of modern philosophy the truth of the statement that authority counts for quite as much in the formation of philosophic as it does in the formation of theological opinion.

Indeed, in the Italian schools of philosophy, scholasticism Persistence of scholasticism in Italy. offered a perceptibly more vigorous resistance to the encroachments of humanism than was the case elsewhere. The reign of scholasticism lasted longest in the country where the reaction against it first began. In the school of Padua an Averroistic scholasticism of the driest and most pedantic type lasted in a tolerably vigorous condition far into the seventeenth century,[1] even after the reign of scholasticism had been substantially overthrown in the schools of Paris, of Germany, and of England, by Ramus, by Descartes, by the humanists, and by the Reformation.[2]

---

[1] According to Berriat-Saint-Prix (p. 315), exactly the same phenomenon is exhibited by the history of Italian jurisprudence. The humanism which had produced the school of Alciatus and Cujas in France did not extinguish the legal scholasticism of the Bartolist type till the middle of the seventeenth century or later.

[2] The mode of thought characteristic of the school of Padua was really in full vogue in the fourteenth century, though the period in which the school stands out with the strongest individuality—because in greater contrast with other schools—was later. [See J. R. Charbonnel, *La Pensée italienne au*

xvie siècle et le courant libertin, Paris, 1919, especially pp. 192–201.] It is usually considered to have been founded by Gaetano of Tiena (1387–1465). (Renan, *Averroès*, p. 347.) Renan treats Peter of Abano (writing in 1303) as its real founder. (*Ibid.* 326.) In justification of the whole of the preceding paragraph, I must be content to refer generally to the same admirable work, which should be read by any one who wishes to realize the seething mass of free speculation which really underlay the smooth surface of medieval orthodoxy. His estimate requires, however, some qualification. See below, p. 362 *sq.*

CHAP. IV, §7.

Tenacity of educational tradition.

This curious fact illustrates the extreme tenacity of educational traditions. A philosophy, a mode of thought, a habit of mind, may live on in the lecture-rooms of professors for a century after it has been abandoned by the thinkers, the men of letters, and the men of the world. The contrast which we have drawn between the history of scholasticism in Italy and its history in northern Europe also illustrates another important truth in the history of education, i.e. the close connexion between great educational reforms and religious movements. The rapidity with which humanism conquered in the schools of Italy and Germany was due to its association with the cause of the Reformation. It was not till the counter-Reformation had raised up a body of educational reformers in Catholic Europe that humanism triumphed over scholasticism in the schools of the laity and considerably limited its dominion in the schools of the clergy.

Downfall of scholasticism completed by positive science.

One other influence ought to be mentioned as completing the downfall of scholasticism in its last stronghold, and that is the progress of positive science. Italy was not more decidedly the earliest home of humanism than she was the earliest home of modern science. And here too—here even more perhaps than on its literary side—the course of the movement was determined by the traditions of Italian education in the Middle Ages.[1] It was astrology-loving Italy that produced Galileo: it was the University of Mundinus that produced Galvani: it was a continuation of a medieval tradition that made Montpellier and Padua the centres of European medicine in the sixteenth and seventeenth centuries. The Renaissance was no doubt from one point of view a reaction against the ideas and tendencies of the Middle Ages; but the direction which a reaction assumes is determined by the direction of the forces against which it reacts: the reformer is as much indebted to his environment as the conservative. The Renaissance was none the less indebted to the traditions of classical education, of medical and legal study, of student-

[1] [But see below, p. 492, on the relation between the philosophical and physical studies at Paris and the beginning of modern science in Italy.]

freedom, of municipal patronage, of lay teaching and lay speculative culture, which we have found to be characteristic of the Italian university-system, because it was a reaction against many of the traditions of which the universities, even in Italy, were the depositaries.

The Renaissance undoubtedly made its influence felt in the schools long before the period which has been chosen as a *terminus ad quem*; but it was not till the sixteenth—even if we should not say the seventeenth—century that it succeeded in revolutionizing that medieval system of education which it has been our business to study. The Renaissance lies beyond our province. It will be enough to have pointed out to what a large extent the peculiarities of the Italian system contributed to pave the way for that movement and to make Italy its earliest home. Enough has already been said to show how decided, all through the medieval period, was the predominance in Italian education of human and practical, of linguistic and literary interests as compared with the theological and speculative tendencies of Parisian and Teutonic culture. In the arts schools of Italy the study of antiquity, the half-regretful looking back to antiquity, never quite died out. The schools of Italy could no more escape from the traditions of the old Roman culture than the architects of her churches and her palaces could avoid the unconscious influence of classical art even when most vehemently striving after the ideals of the ruder but more vigorous north. The revival of Roman Law studies in the eleventh century was itself but one phase of the return to antiquity which I have ventured to call the first Renaissance; and throughout the Middle Ages the schools of Roman Law, in spite of their invasion by the methods and traditions of scholasticism, were training the Italian mind for that second return to antiquity which is known as the Renaissance *par excellence*. The more deeply the history of the Italian Middle Age is studied, the more shall we discover to justify the striking saying of Ozanam that in Italy the night which intervened between the intellectual daylight of antiquity and the dawn of the Renaissance was but 'une de ces nuits lumineuses où les

Influence of Renaissance: continuity of intellectual life in Italy.

dernières clartés du soir se prolongent jusqu'aux premières blancheurs du matin'.[1]

For the limits which I have imposed upon myself there is a double justification. In the first place, although in Italy the earlier phases of the movement lie within our chronological limits, it would be unsatisfactory to attempt to trace its beginnings and suddenly to break off at some arbitrarily selected date: it is best to deal with the history of the Italian universities in the fourteenth and fifteenth centuries only in so far as they still belonged to the medieval world. In the second place, although the progress of the Renaissance may be traced in the foundation or increased importance of chairs for rhetoric or poetry or Dante or classical literature in the universities of arts, yet in the main humanism was not primarily in Italy a university movement. Its earliest home was rather in courts or princely houses, in cultivated social circles or dilettante 'academies' than in the schools—in Tuscany rather than in Lombardy—in artistic, dreamy, Platonic Florence than in stately, scientific, scholastic Bologna.[2]

[1] *Doc. inédits*, p. 78.

[2] [A full annotation of this section would have required us to touch upon nearly every aspect of medieval Italian thought. Cf. the Introduction to this volume and the observations in vol. ii, pp. 1, 2. In his paper, noted above (p. 103, note), E. Genzmer has dealt with the work of the earlier glossators and given a useful introduction to the extensive literature.]

CHAPTER V
PARIS

§ 1. THE ORIGINS OF THE UNIVERSITY

The earliest historical account of the University of Paris is a little black-letter quarto by Robertus GOULET (*Compendium recenter editum de multiplici Paris. Univ. magnificentia*, Paris, 1517 [translation by Robert B. Burke (University of Pennsylvania Press, 1928)]), which is more valuable as a contemporary sketch of the University than for its historical information. BELLE-FOREST (*La Cosmographie Universelle*, Paris, 1675, i. 187 *sq.*) gives a somewhat fuller historical sketch of the University and colleges. PASQUIER made valuable critical researches into the early history of the University, rejecting the Carolingian myth, but mistakenly dating the existence of the University from the charter of Philip Augustus in 1200. (*Les Recherches de la France*, Paris, 1596, &c.) The first systematic historian of the University is HEMERAEUS (*De Academia Parisiensi*, Paris, 1637), who gives a fairly correct account of the evolution of the University out of the episcopal school. Caesar Egassius BULAEUS (du Boulay), in his six enormous folio volumes, *Historia Universitatis Parisiensis a Carolo M. ad nostra tempora*, 1665–73, gathered together an immense mass of material for its history, but his own view of its origin is as completely mythical as anything in the first decade of Livy, while his inaccuracies and inconsistencies are only equalled by his tedious prolixity. He was perhaps the stupidest man that ever wrote a valuable book. (He also published an *Abrégé de l'histoire de l'Univ. de Paris*, no date.) The later historians of the University have done little but copy his conclusions with a little more common sense, but no original research. The most important are CREVIER (*Histoire de l'Université de Paris, depuis son origine jusqu'en l'année 1660*, Paris, 1761) and DUBARLE (*Histoire de l'Université depuis son origine jusqu'à nos jours*, Paris, 1829). RICHOMME, *Histoire de l'Université de Paris* (Paris, 1840), is a slighter work of the same type. The only English book on the subject is an Oxford prize essay by T. RALEIGH (*The University of Paris*, 1873).

Meanwhile, the most valuable contribution ever made (till quite recently) to the history of this or any other university had been lying unpublished (on account of its unpatriotic view of the date of the University) and unstudied in the MS. presses of the Sorbonne. This anonymous work is entitled *Universitas Parisiensis eiusque Facultatum quatuor Origo vera*, and is usually spoken of as the MS. refutation of du Boulay, who is throughout styled the 'Fabulator' and attacked with the characteristic bitterness of the seventeenth-century scholar. Two copies of it exist, one at the Sorbonne, the other in the Bibliothèque Nationale (Cod. Lat. 9949). I have used the latter. There is also in the Bibl. Nat. (Cod. Lat. 9943–8) a MS. history of the University by RICHER, of no particular value, but far more enlightened than those of du Boulay and his adherents. THUROT's essay, *De l'organisation de l'enseignement dans l'Université de Paris au moyen âge*, Paris and Besançon, 1850, gave a fairly accurate picture of the educational system in the developed University, but hardly touched the question of origins, the critical treatment of which begins with the appearance

CHAP. V,
§ 1.

of DENIFLE's great work in 1885. Ch. Brechillet JOURDAIN had, however, done good service by his *Index Chronologicus Chartarum pertinentium ad historiam Universitatis Parisiensis*, Paris, 1862, which printed in full many important documents omitted by Bulaeus. But this collection is now superseded by the magnificent *Chartularium Universitatis Parisiensis*, edited by DENIFLE and CHATELAIN, four volumes (Paris, 1889–97) with two volumes of an *Auctarium*, containing the earlier Proctors' books of the English Nation (Paris, 1894–7). [Other volumes of the *Chartularium*, including one on the colleges, and of the *Auctarium* are in course of preparation.]

Notices and documents relating to the University occur in many of the older books, of which it will be enough to mention DUBOIS, *Historia Ecclesiae Parisiensis*, Paris, 1690–1710; SAUVAL, *Histoire et Recherches des Antiquités de la Ville de Paris*, Paris, 1724; DU BREUL, *Théâtres des Antiquités de Paris*, ed. 2, Paris, 1639 (1st ed. 1612); FÉLIBIEN, *Histoire de la Ville de Paris*, ed. Lobineau, Paris, 1725; D'ARGENTRÉ, *Collectio Iudiciorum de Novis Erroribus*, Paris, 1728–36; GUÉRARD, *Cartulaire de l'Église de Notre-Dame de Paris* (in *Docs. inédits pour l'hist. de France*), Paris, 1855, &c.; JAILLOT, *Recherches Critiques sur la Ville de Paris*, 1772–5.

Other works bearing on special departments of the subject are LAUNOI, *De varia Aristotelis in Academia Parisiensi fortuna*, Paris, 1653, &c., and the tractates of DU BOULAY, *Remarques sur la dignité, rang, préséance, autorité, et jurisdiction du Recteur de l'Un. de Paris*, Paris, 1668; *Factum ou Remarques sur l'élection des Officiers de l'Université*, Paris, 1668; *Remarques sur les bedeaux de l'Université*, Paris, 1670; *Recueil des Priviléges de l'Université de Paris*, Paris, 1674 [Anon.]; *Mémoires historiques sur les Bénéfices qui sont à la présentation de l'Université de Paris*, Paris, 1675 [Anon.]; *Fondation de l'Université de Paris par l'Empereur Charlemagne, de la propriété et seigneurie du Pré-aux-Clercs*, 1675, 4to [this last I have not seen; only one copy is said to exist]; *De patronis quatuor Nationum*, Paris, 1662; *Défense des droits de l'Université*, Paris, 1637. The very rare *Mémoire touchant la seigneurie du Pré-aux-Clercs, appartenante à l'Université de Paris* (Paris, 1694 and 1737), by POURCHOT, based on the above work of du Boulay, has been reprinted by FOURNIER (Marcel) in *Variétés Historiques et Littéraires*, Paris, 1856, iv. 87. FILESACUS, *Statutorum Sacrae Facultatis Theologiae Parisiensis origo prisca*, Paris, 1620, I have not seen. BUDINSZKY, *Die Universität Paris und die Fremden an derselben im Mittelalter*, Berlin, 1876, is a useful piece of work, as is DELALAIN, *Étude sur le Libraire Parisien du xiiie au xve siècle*, Paris, 1891. HALMAGRAND, *Origine de l'Université*, Paris, 1845, and DESMAZE, *L'Université de Paris, 1200–1875*, Paris, 1876, are of no value. PÉRIES, *La Faculté de Droit dans l'ancienne Université de Paris*, Paris, 1890, is a substantial and learned piece of research; CORLIEU, *L'ancienne Faculté de Médecine de Paris*, Paris, 1877, a slight but interesting work, is chiefly concerned with post-medieval times. SPIRGATIS, *Personalverzeichniss d. Paris. Univ. von 1464*, Leipzig, 1888, is useful on the question of the numbers at Paris. Some paragraphs in the following chapter are reproduced from the author's art. in the *Eng. Hist. Review*, 1886, p. 69, on 'The *Origines* of the University of Paris'. The art. by FERET, 'Les Origines de l'Université de Paris' in *Rev. des Questions Historiques*, lii, 1893, 337–90, is quite uncritical, and ignores all recent research.

For a full bibliography see CHATELAIN, *Essai d'une Bibliographie de*

l'ancienne Université de Paris in *Revue des Bibliothèques*, i (1891); and for CHAP. V,
books on French education generally, below, vol. ii, chap. viii. §1.

[The extensive literature which has appeared since 1895 deals in the
main with particular aspects of academic history in Paris, and will be
noticed as occasion arises. We may mention here A. LUCHAIRE, *L'Université de Paris sous Philippe Auguste* (Paris, 1899); L. HALPHEN, 'Les
débuts de l'université de Paris', in *Studi medievali*, new series, ii (1929),
134–9, and 'Les Universités au xiiie siècle' (articles reprinted from the
Revue Historique, clxvii (1931), 37 pp.); J. BONNEROT, 'L'Ancienne Université de Paris, centre international d'études', in the *Bulletin of the
International Committee of Historical Sciences*, i, pt. v (1928), pp. 662–82,
valuable for its account of the archives and matriculation lists of the
University. Cf. E. CHATELAIN on the Cartulary of the English Nation
(in *Mémoires de la Société de l'Histoire de Paris*, xviii, 1891, 73–100) and
H. OMONT on the more recently discovered Cartulary of the French
Nation (*ibid.*, xli, 1914, 1–130). A general account of the University may be
found in Stephen D'IRSAY, *Histoire des Universités*, i. 53–74 and *passim*.]

I. *The Rise of the University*

THE myth which attributes the foundation of the Uni- The Caro-
versity of Paris to Charles the Great is one which ought Palace
long since to have ceased to be mentioned by serious histo- not at
rians even for the purpose of refutation. There is not the Paris.
slightest ground for localizing the Palatine Schools of Charles
the Great or Charles the Bald, the School of Alcuin or the
School of Scotus, in the city of Lutetia Parisiorum. These
schools were probably migratory and followed the person of
the sovereign, like our ancient courts of Law, in his progresses
through his dominions. In so far as they had any fixed abode
we should have to look for it rather at Aachen than at Paris.
The assumption of an identity between the schools of the
Palace and the later church schools of Paris is in truth only
an outgrowth of that inveterate historical misconception, dear
to the heart of the French nation, which represents the
founder of the Germano-Roman Empire as a French king
with his capital and his court at Paris.[1]

The sole historical connexion between the Palatine Schools Real
of Charles the Great or Charles the Bald[2] and the later the Carolingian

[1] 'On ne voit pas même que, ville de Paris.' Hauréau, *Charle-* reform in
durant tout le cours de son long *magne et sa cour*, p. 172. education.
règne, ce prince, qui visita tant de [2] The Bull printed by Bulaeus
villes, habita tant de palais, ait (i. 184) in which Nicholas I is repre-
séjourné quelques heures dans la sented as speaking of John the Scot

University of Paris is to be found in that revival of the episcopal and monastic schools throughout the Frankish Empire of which enough has already been said. Before the time of Charles the Great the British Isles could boast of far more famous schools than any that were to be found in continental Europe. The call of Alcuin from York to the Palace School marks the transference of the primacy of letters from Britain to France. And some of the features which characterized the Parisian university system may really be traced to the work of Charles. In the first place there is its intensely ecclesiastical character—the system of supervision by ecclesiastical authorities and the complete identification of the scholastic with the clerical order. Moreover, the educational tradition which was inherited by the School of Paris was one ultimately derived from the Schools of Alcuin and John the Scot. But this educational tradition was not transmitted by any single school. All through the dark ages that intervened between Charles the Great and the twelfth century, there were at least a few monasteries and perhaps one or two cathedrals where the fame of some great teacher drew students from distant regions, and where some ray of enthusiasm, some spark of controversial fire, infused a little life into the dull conglomerate of old-world learning and traditional theology which made up the education of this dismal period. The historians of the University of Paris have amused themselves with tracing the long scholastic pedigree of master and scholar—the academical succession, so to speak—which connects Alcuin with Abelard.[1] But it is only in this somewhat imaginative sense that the smallest connexion can be established between

---

as living 'Parisius in Studio cuius Capital iam olim fuisse perhibetur' is obviously interpolated. Part of it (which may be genuine) is given by William of Malmesbury, *De gestis pontificum* (ed. Hamilton, p. 393), Symeon of Durham (ed. Arnold, ii. 116), and Hoveden (ed. Stubbs, i. 47, &c.), but without the allusions to Paris. Cf. Poole, *Illustrations*, p. 56, n. 3. Bulaeus, in i. 183, gives this version as well

as his own, but includes part of Hoveden's text in the letter. The words are also omitted in the collection of Nicholas I's letters. (*Patrol. Lat.* cxix, c. 1119.)

[1] Thus Rabanus was the pupil of Alcuin at Tours; at Fulda Rabanus taught Servatus Lupus of Ferrières, whose pupil Heiricus was the master of Remigius, &c. (*MS. Refut.*, f. 181.)

Charles and the great French university. In the age of Charles CHAP. V,
the Great or of Charles the Bald nothing whatever is heard   § 1.
of the schools of Paris. Tours and Fulda and Reims were
famous places of education before Paris could claim a single
important master or a single distinguished scholar.[1]

The first school at Paris which is actually known to history The
is the School of Remigius of Auxerre at the end of the ninth Remigius
century. But the utmost diligence of an investigator full of at Paris.
the most infatuated belief in the unfathomable antiquity of
his Alma Mater has only succeeded in discovering two or
three names of masters or scholars recorded to have taught
or studied at Paris in the ninth or tenth centuries—Remigius' Early
pupil, Odo, afterwards Abbot of Cluny[2] (A.D. 912–42), Abbo, at Paris.

---

[1] These assertions may perhaps
surprise the reader who, glancing
over Du Boulay's colossal work,
finds one folio volume devoted to
the history of the University before
A.D. 1000, another to the period
between A.D. 1000 and A.D. 1200, of
which the first 550 pages refer to
the first of the two centuries thus
embraced, i.e. to the period during
which practically nothing is known
of the state of the schools of Paris.
But the preliminary dissertation on
'the Academies of the Druids' will
have warned the reader not to take
Du Boulay *au sérieux*. The first
writer whom our author can adduce
in support of the connexion of the
University with Alcuin is Helin-
andus († A.D. 1227), who says that
Alcuin 'Studium de Roma Parisius
transtulit' (Bulaeus, i. 110); but
the passage which he quotes must
be an insertion, since it does not
occur in the printed edition. See
Tissier, *Biblioth. Cisterc.* vii (Paris,
1669), 100: *Patrol. Lat.* ccxii, c.
833 *sq*. In the fifteenth century a
papal legate gravely ascribes the
foundation of schools at Paris to
Bede, whom he declares to have
stopped there on his way to Rome
(Bulaeus, i. 113). A number of
similar absurdities are critically

examined by Launoi, *De Scholis
Celebrioribus*, pp. 1–26.

[2] 'Nono decimo aetatis suae anno
apud beatum Martinum Turonis
est tonsus, ibique grammaticae artis
liberalibus studiis educatus. Deinde
apud Parisium dialectica musicaque
a Remigio doctissimo viro est instructus, et tricesimo ortus sui
anno Burgundiam petiit,' &c. *Vita
scripta a Joanne monacho eius disci-
pulo*; ap. *Patrol. Lat.* cxxxiii, c.
45. 'His diebus abiit Parisius, ibique dialecticam sancti Augustini
Deodato filio suo missam perlegit,
et Martianum in liberalibus artibus frequenter lectitavit: praecep-
torem quippe in his omnibus
habuit Remigium; quo peracto
Turonicam remeavit,' *ibid*. c. 52.
Another biographer says, 'His
diebus honestus juvenis succensus
amore discendi, Parisium [? Pari-
sius] adiit primam sedis regiae civitatem. Ibi Remigius Autissiodo-
rensis, vir praedicabilis, et thesau-
ros scientiae tunc temporis plures
habens, moderandis et regendis
studiis insudabat. Florescebant
sub eo studia, quae obsoluerant
iam per tempus, quia tunc primum
ex eius magisterio nascerentur.'
Ibid., cc. 89, 90. The anonymous
Refuter of Bulaeus indeed (f. 179)

CHAP. v, the Scholasticus of Fleury[1] († A.D. 1004), and one Hucbald
§ 1.   of Liége[2] who (some time between A.D. 972 and 1008) taught
in the schools of Ste Geneviève. Nor do the names become
more frequent till after the middle of the following century,
when we find the schools of Paris attracting a few scholars
from a distance, such as the Englishman Stephen Harding,[3]
afterwards Abbot of Citeaux, and the Breton Robert de
Arbrisselle.[4] Of course there would be no reason, even had
the allusions been fewer than they are, to doubt that there
were schools in the monasteries of Paris, just as there were
in all other monasteries, at least from the reign of Hugh
Capet, when the cessation of the Viking ravages and the
substitution of regular abbots for the lay usurpers of the
'iron age' began to make learned leisure once more a possibility. But it is abundantly clear that Paris was not at this

suggests that the story of Remigius
of Auxerre having taught at Paris
is due to some confusion between
S. Germain of Auxerre, of which
Remigius was a monk, and the
monastery of S. Germain-des-Prés
at Paris; but this is a somewhat
hazardous conjecture.

[1] 'Parisius atque Remis ad eos
qui philosophiam profitebantur
profectus, aliquantulum quidem
in astronomia, sed non quantum
cupierat, apud eos profecit. Inde
Aurelianis regressus', &c. *Vita
auctore Aimoino Monacho* (his
pupil), ap. *Patrol. Lat.* cxxxix, c.
390.

[2] 'Quid dicam de Hupaldo, qui,
dum adolescentulus a scolari disciplina hinc (i.e. from Liége) aufu-
gisset, Parisius venit, canonicis
sanctae Genovefae virginis adhesit,
in brevi multo (*sic*) scholarium in-
struxit.' (Bulaeus, i. 314, reads
'multarum scholarum institutor
fuit': the true reading is perhaps
'multorum scholarium institutor
fuit'.) Ubi cum aliquamdiu mora-
retur, interim videlicet cum a
domno Notkero episcopo nescire-
tur, tandem canonica episcopalis

sententiae executione compulsus
est redire.' Anselmi Leodiensis,
Gesta Episcoporum Leodiensium, ap.
Patrol. Lat. cxxxix, c. 1094. Notker
was Bishop from A.D. 972 to 1008.

[3] 'Ex Anglia studiorum caussa
primum Scotiam, inde in Gal-
liam Parisios transfretaverat.' *Acta
Sanctorum*, April, ii. 493.

[4] 'Et quoniam Francia tum flore-
bat in scholaribus emolumentis
copiosior, fines paternos, tanquam
exsul et fugitivus, exivit, Franciam
adiit et urbem quae Parisius dicitur
intravit, litterarum disciplinam,
quam unice sibi postulaverat, pro
voto commodam reperit, ibique
assiduus lector insidere coepit.'
Vita auctore Baldrico (a contemporary), ap. *Patrol. Lat.* clxii, c.
1047. Of the scores of names
massed together by Bulaeus in his
Catalogus Illustrium Academicorum
(i. 542–649) this is the only one for
whose connexion with Paris he produces a respectable authority. In
some few cases a very late writer is
cited, in most none at all. Crevier
(i. 69) mentions a few names as
belonging to the eleventh century,
but without citing authorities.

period even one among the great educational centres of
Europe; Remigius was the only master of any note who is
recorded to have taught there, and his connexion with Paris,
if historical, seems to have been of very short duration. It is
not till quite the end of the eleventh century that anything
like a stream of scholastic pilgrimage begins to flow towards
Paris. The authors of the *Histoire Littéraire de la France* have
spoken of the School of Remigius as the 'first cradle of the
University of Paris'.[1] But the School of Remigius was no
doubt connected with a Monastery—probably that of Saint
Germain-des-Prés[2]—and the university schools were essentially secular. The only secular school that we hear of before
the end of the eleventh century is the School of Ste Geneviève, which in the following century passed into the hands
of the Canons Regular, and which at first had no organic connexion with the University. The University was an out- The uni-
growth of the Cathedral School of Paris,[3] and this school did outgrowth
not attain the very smallest repute till towards the close of the of the
eleventh century. The transference of educational activity school.
from the monks to the secular clergy constituted (as has been
remarked) the great educational revolution of that century.
In this change we may already discern the germs of the university movement.[4] In this sense we shall be right in finding

[1] *Hist. Lit.* vi. 100.
[2] In the continuation of the
history of Aimoinus of Fleury
(*Rec. des historiens de France*, xi.
275), Remigius and Abbo are said
to have been successive 'deans' of
the monastery under Count Robert
who 'Abbatis nomen assumpsit'.
[3] A curious relic of this connexion was the right of canons of
Paris to teach theology and canon
law without the authority of the
University. It was not till 1384
that it was definitely decided that
a canon must be a doctor of canon
law before being appointed to one
of the chapter schools. See *Chartul.*
iii, Nos. 1486-9.
[4] In this change the zeal of
Monastic Reformers probably co-

operated with the improvement of
the cathedral schools. Cf. Petrus
Damianus, *Opusc.* 36, c. 16, ap.
Patrol. Lat. cxlv, c. 621. [On this
subject cf. U. Berlière's bibliographical note in his *L'Ordre monastique des origines au xiie siècle*
(3rd ed., 1924), p. 177; and Manacorda, i. 110.] The Benedictine
Reform of 1336 forbids seculars to
be taught with the Monks, and
it is evident that there were not at
this time any 'exterior schools'.
Wilkins, *Concilia*, ii. 594. [On the
other hand, the Benedictine General
Chapters, at least in England,
tended, through the appointment
of proctors by abbots, to become
assemblies of graduates, i.e. monks
who had graduated in Oxford or

the cradle of the University, not indeed in the School of Remigius, but in the School of William of Champeaux, the first known master of the cathedral school, and the first Parisian teacher who left his mark upon the development of the scholastic philosophy. It was not till the time of William that Paris even began to rival the scholastic fame of Bec or of Tours, of Chartres or of Reims. But half a century later Paris had fairly surpassed its rivals. It was the teaching of William's great pupil and opponent Abelard that first attracted students from all parts of Europe and laid the foundation of that unique prestige which the schools of Paris retained throughout the medieval period.[1]

The schools of Paris in the time of Abelard. The less imaginative historians of the University of Paris have generally been contented with tracing its origin to the teaching of Abelard. And it was undoubtedly to the intellectual movement of which Abelard is the most conspicuous representative that the rise of the University must ultimately be ascribed. But there was nothing in the organization of the schools wherein Abelard taught to distinguish them from any other cathedral schools which might for a time be rendered famous by the teaching of some illustrious master. In the age of Abelard there were three great churches at Paris more or less famous for their schools. In the first place there was the cathedral, whose schools were presided over by William of Champeaux. Then, on the left bank of the Seine, there was the Collegiate Church of Ste Geneviève; and there was the Church of the Canons Regular of S. Victor's, where a school for external scholars was started by William after his retirement from the world. S. Victor's became the headquarters of the old traditional or positive theology, and produced the chief opponents of the rising dialectical or 'scholastic' theology—mystics like Adam and Hugh and Walter of S. Victor. Hence the school played no part in the development of the University: it had ceased to exist, or ceased to attract secular students, before the first traces of a university organi-

No university at this time.

Cambridge from the Benedictine colleges (W. A. Pantin, in *Trans. R. Hist. Soc.*, 4th ser. x (1927),
221, 222).]
[1] [For comments on this view see above, p. 62.]

zation begin to appear.[1] With both the secular schools of Paris Abelard was at one time or other connected. It was during the period at which he taught 'the liberal Arts' at Ste Geneviève that his teaching attracted the greatest crowds. For a time the 'Mount' of Ste Geneviève became the most famous place of education in Europe. But the external schools of Ste Geneviève appear to have declined, though not to have totally disappeared, by the end of the century. In 1147 the church passed from its secular chapter to a body of Canons Regular imported from S. Victor's and S. Martin-des-champs;[2] and though there are certainly traces of external schools in the 'Mount' after this date, the change was no doubt calculated to drive away secular masters. Before the beginning of the following century the cathedral seems to be the only centre of education for seculars in Paris:[3] it is from the Chancellor of Notre Dame alone that the masters obtain their licences: it is not till the second or third decade of the century that we again find the masters of arts attempting to cross the river and teach under the authority of the Abbot of Ste Geneviève. Denifle's repudiation of the old view that the University arose from a junction between the arts schools of Ste Geneviève and the theological schools of Notre Dame goes slightly beyond the evidence, but in the main he is unquestionably right in contending that it was the

[1] It had quite disappeared by 1237, *Chartul.* i, No. 111. In 1309 the university recognized the abbot and convent as 'boni et etiam legitimi scolares Parisienses in facultate theologica studentes', *Chartul.* ii, No. 675: Bulaeus, v. 208. [Rashdall does some injustice to the place of the abbey of S. Victor, and notably of the work of its greatest son, Hugh of S. Victor, in the history of scholasticism. See Grabmann, *Gesch. d. schol. Methode*, ii. 229–90; Fourier-Bonnard, *Hist. de l'abbaye royale et de l'ordre des chanoines réguliers de Saint-Victor de Paris* (Paris, 1904), vol. i; G. Paré, &c., *La Renaissance du xiie siècle*, especially pp. 218 *sqq.*]

[2] See documents in Bulaeus, ii. 216, 228–30; *Rec. des histor. de France*, xiii. 183, 291, xv. 503–5, 949–51; *Acta Sanctorum*, April, i. 617 *sq.*; Feret, *L'Abbaye de Sainte-Geneviève*, Paris, 1883, i. 101 *sq.*

[3] This is strongly supported by a rhetorical description of Paris in a letter of Gui de Bazoches (A.D. 1175–90) which declares that 'in hac insula perpetuam sibi mansionem septem pepigere sorores, artes videlicet liberales', without any reference to the schools of Ste Geneviève, though he dwells upon the glories of the 'duo suburbia' on the two banks. *Chartul.* i, Introd., No. 54.

CHAP. V, cathedral schools which eventually developed into the
§ 1.   university.[1]

Certain   It was the fame of Abelard which first drew to the streets
scholastic
traditions of Paris the hordes of students whose presence involved that
date from multiplication of masters by whom the university was ulti-
Abelard's
time. mately formed. In that sense, and in that sense only, the
origin of the University of Paris may be connected with the
name and age of Abelard. Of a university or a recognized
society of masters we hear nothing; nay, the existence of such
an institution was impossible at a time when the single master
of the cloister school seems to have been as a rule the only
recognized master in or around each particular church. At
the same time we do find in the schools of this period some
slight traces of a traditional discipline and organization, of a
kind of scholastic common-law which formed the basis of the
later academic polity.

Origin   Education in France since its revival under Charles the
of the
licence. Great had been so completely confined in practice to the
cathedrals and monasteries that no express legislation was

---

[1] See Denifle, i. 656 *sq.* He declares that all trace of external or
secular schools at Ste Geneviève
is lost after 1147. But Giraldus
Cambrensis (ed. Brewer, i. 93) tells
us that his old master Willelmus de
Monte obtained his name 'quoniam
in monte S. Genovefae Parisius
legerat'. Now this William died
Chancellor of Lincoln in 1213 (Le
Neve, *Fasti Eccles. Ang.*, Oxford,
ed. T. D. Hardy, 1854, ii. 91); and
Giraldus was born in 1147, so
that there must have been secular
schools at Ste Geneviève at least as
late as 1165 or 1170. Nor do the
letters of Stephen of Tournai,
Abbot of Ste Geneviève 1176–91,
seem to me to prove Denifle's case.
The Abbot refuses the request of
the Archbishop of Lund, who has
asked that his nephew should study
in the secular schools: 'Quod autem
de ipso nobis per litteras vestras
intimatis vel in monte vel Parisius

ad secularium scolas et venditores
verborum mittendo . . . non admit-
timus.' (*Lettres*, ed. Desilve, p.
109; *a.* 1185–8. *Chartul.* i, Introd., No. 42.) The nephew was
residing in the convent, and was
therefore not allowed to go to secular schools, but the words distinctly imply that there were secular schools 'in monte' as well as in
the city proper. It is impossible to
say whether there were any schools
left at Ste Geneviève at the beginning of the thirteenth century; but
it is plain that at this time the
cathedral 'Parvis' was the centre
of such schools. This is one of the
points upon which Denifle has
been criticized by Kaufmann,
Zeitschr. der Savigny-Stiftung, vii.
124 *sq.*; but the latter fails to see
the substantial truth of Denifle's
main contention—that all Paris
masters were originally licensed by
the cathedral chancellor

needed to establish the necessity of the church's sanction to the teacher.[1] In the days when a church normally possessed no more than one authorized master, this master might or might not, it would appear, be a member of the capitular body, according to circumstances. Any member of the church from the bishop or abbot downwards who was capable of teaching would gather other scholars around him. If none of the canons were competent to teach, they would hire the services of some wandering scholar. From the eleventh century onwards, however, we find a tendency to make the master of the schools, as he was called, a regular member of the cathedral body.[2] This was done in one of two ways. Either the new dignity of *scholasticus* or *magister scholarum*[3] was created, or the duty of presiding over the schools was annexed to some already existing office—often in southern Europe to that of *magiscola*, *primicerius* or *precentor*,[4] in northern Europe more frequently to that of chancellor. The

[1] In face of the difficulty which Abelard constantly experienced in lecturing at Paris, I cannot imagine what Kaufmann (*Deutsch. Univ.* i. 246) can mean by saying that the works of Giraldus Cambrensis and Stephen of Tournai show 'dass die Pariser Lehrer in den letzten Jahrzehnten des 12. Jahrhunderts noch in ähnlicher Unabhängigkeit neben einander standen wie zur Zeit Abälards, dass es keine überwachende Behörde und keine bindende Regel gab'. Stephen of Tournai's later complaints of the extreme youth and profane audacity of the masters (*Lettres*, ed. Desilve, pp. 344, 345) do not show that no authority was recognized at this time but only that the authority was not efficient. Kaufmann's whole view of the 'Lehrfreiheit' of the early Middle Ages as regards the north of Europe seems to me opposed to all the evidence, though no doubt there may have been exceptions and irregularities in the application of the general principle of ecclesiastical control.

[2] For instances of such arrangements see *Hist. Lit.* ix. 31 *sq.* The Council of Lateran in 1179 required that in every cathedral 'magistro qui clericos eiusdem ecclesie et scholares pauperes gratis doceat, competens aliquod beneficium prebeatur'. *Chartul.* i, Introd., No. 12. But it seems probable that by this time the duties of the titular *magister scholarum* were limited to supervision and that the benefice was intended for an actual working master; the matter is, however, an obscure one. Cf. Joly, pp. 173, 174. The Fourth Lateran Council repeats the injunction, adding that every Metropolitan Church should have also a 'Theologus'. (Mansi, xxii, c. 999.)

[3] Instances of both will be found below in the chapters on the French and Spanish universities. In Narbonne and Gascony we find the title *capischola*; Joly, pp. 160, 166.

[4] So also at Metz. *Hist. Lit.* vii. 28. For other cases see below, vol. ii, ch. viii, § 5.

CHAP. V, original duties of the chancellor were analogous to those of
§ 1. a royal chancellor, i.e. to keep the chapter seal and to draw up
the letters and documents which required sealing; and, as
this function demanded an amount of learning which was
not a matter of course in those days, it was natural enough
that the supervision of the schools, and again the care of the
library, should be entrusted to the same functionary.[1] But
while a definite ecclesiastical status was thus given to the
head of the capitular school, a tendency was also at work
which made him less and less of a teacher himself. Wherever
the number of scholars required it, he would naturally appoint others to teach under his direction. If he still taught
theology himself, he would delegate the teaching of grammar
and dialectic to others;[2] and in the course of time the elementary instruction of the choir-boys and other poor scholars
seems usually to have been delegated to a regular paid master
who taught under the supervision of the nominal head of the
schools. But with the rapid spread of education in the twelfth
century there also grew up round the more famous churches

[1] Thus an agreement between the chapter of Paris and the chancellor drawn up in 1215 (*Chartul.* i, No. 21) contains the following clause: 'Libros quidem Parisiensis Ecclesie sine cantu corrigere, ligare et in bono statu tenebitur conservare, et talem instituere Magistrum in Claustro qui sufficiens sit ad Scholarum regimen, et ad officium quod debet facere in Ecclesia, et ad litteras capituli, si opus fuerit, faciendas.' Cf. the very similar statute of S. Paul's, London; *Registrum Stat. et Consuetud. Eccl. Cath. S. Paul. Lond.*, ed. Simpson, 1873, p. 23. At Paris the supervision of the schools by the chancellor may be traced at least from 1120. Guérard, i. 28, 142. As some confusion exists on this subject in the minds of some English writers, it may be well to point out that the chancellor of the church is a quite different officer from the chancellor of the diocese, a title applied by modern English usage to the bishop's 'official'. [In the thirteenth century the chancellor of a bishop was distinct from both the chancellor of the cathedral and the official.]

[2] Cf. the statute of the Metropolitan Church of York: 'Cancellarius (qui antiquitus Magister Scolarum dicebatur) Magister in Theologia esse debet, et iuxta Ecclesiam actualiter legere, et ad ipsum pertinet Scholas Grammaticales conferre. Sed Scholae Eboracenses, alicui Regenti in artibus . . . qui secundum antiquam consuetudinem Ecclesiae ipsas habebit per triennium.' *Brit. Mus. Addit. MS.* (Cole) 5884, f. 63. So at London, while the chancellor appoints the grammar master, he is bound to teach theology 'per se vel substitutum ab eo ydoneum'; *Chartul. Univ. Paris.* ii, No. 791. Cf. Simpson, *loc. cit.*, p. 413 *sq.*

an increasing number of masters anxious to obtain permission to teach scholars who could afford to pay something for their education. Hence it became usual for the *scholasticus* or chancellor to grant a formal permission to other masters to open schools for their own profit in the neighbourhood of the church. In 1138 we find a council at London forbidding the growing practice of selling such permissions.[1] By a decretal of Alexander III[2] and a little later at the Third Council of Lateran in 1179 a still more important step was taken. Not only were the presiding masters of the church schools forbidden to take any fee or reward for granting the *licentia docendi* (as the permission to teach had come to be called) but they were absolutely required to grant such a licence to every properly qualified applicant.[3] The chancellor thus ceased to be the holder of a lucrative educational monopoly, and became merely a judge of the fitness of the candidates for the teaching

---

[1] 'Sancimus praeterea, ut si magistri scholarum aliis scholas suas locaverint *legendas* pro precio, ecclesiasticae vindictae subiaceant' (Mansi, *Concilia*, xxi, c. 514). Bulaeus reads 'tenendas' (ii. 155), but the expression 'tenere scholas' is unusual if not unparalleled: read 'regendas'. Crevier is inaccurate in saying that this council as well as the Lateran Council of 1179 'ordonnent aux maitres des Écoles d'accorder la *license* à tous ceux qui en sont dignes' (i. 256). It merely forbids the sale of the permission, and it should be noticed that the technical expression *licentia docendi* does not occur till the time of Alexander III. A comparison between the language of the two canons throws much light on the growth of the system.

[2] 'Sub anathematis interminatione hoc inhibere curetis ne qui dignitate illa, si dignitas dici potest, fungentes, pro prestanda licentia docendi alios ab aliquo quidquam amodo exigere audeant vel extorquere; sed eis districte precipiatis,

ut quicunque viri idonei et litterati voluerint regere studia litterarum, sine molestia et exactione qualibet scolas regere patiantur, ne scientia de cetero pretio videatur exponi, que singulis gratis debet impendi.' *Chartul.*, Introd., No. 4. The custom of taking fees was, however, so inveterate, that the Chancellor of Paris obtained a decretal enjoining respect for his vested interests. *Ibid.*, No. 8.

[3] 'Pro licentia vero docendi, nullus omnino pretium exigat, vel sub obtentu alicuius consuetudinis ab eis qui docent, aliquid querat, nec docere quemquam, qui sit idoneus, petita licentia interdicat. Qui autem contra hoc venire presumpserit, ab ecclesiastico fiat beneficio alienus. Dignum quippe esse videtur, ut in Ecclesia Dei fructum sui laboris non habeat, qui cupiditate animi dum vendit docendi licentiam, ecclesiasticum profectum nititur impedire.' *Chartul.*, Introd., No. 12; Mansi, xxii, c. 228; Decretals of Gregory IX, lib. v, tit. v, c. 2.

office or, as we might say, an ecclesiastical superintendent of education.[1]

The control of the chancellor on the one hand, and the right of the competent teacher to a gratuitous licence on the other, formed the basis of the French educational system. The control of the chancellor distinguished it from the early Italian system: without the corresponding right, a university of masters could never have grown up at all.[2]

[1] Specht lays it down that the authority of the *scholasticus* extended to schools of the whole diocese; and cites the case of Aschaffenburg (*Gesch. des Unterrichtswesens in Deutschland*, Stuttgart, 1885, pp. 187, 188). This was certainly the case in some places, e.g. at Noyon, *Chartul.* i, No. 322, and Amiens (Darsy, *Les Écoles et les collèges du dioc. d'A.*, Amiens, 1881, pp. 20, 181); but sometimes it only extended to the city, e.g. in London, where to the chancellor of S. Paul's 'subsunt scolares in civitate morantes, exceptis scolaribus scolarum de Arcubus et Sancti Martini, qui se privilegiatos in hiis et aliis esse contendunt'; *Registrum S. Paul.*, ed. Simpson, p. 23. [The chancellor of Lincoln Cathedral had the duty 'scolas theologie regere', and 'quod omnes scolas in *comitatu* lincolnie pro suo conferat arbitrio, exceptis illis que sunt in prebendis'; Bradshaw and Wordsworth, *Lincoln Cathedral Statutes*, i. 284, 285. For other exceptional cases see Gaines Post in *Haskins Anniversary Essays*, p. 256, note.] It must not be assumed that because a municipality sometimes supported a school and nominated the master he could dispense with the chancellor's licence. See *Extracts from Council Reg. of Aberdeen* (Spalding Club), i. 5, 37. The theory of Mr. Mullinger (*Cambridge*, i. 78) that the conferment of the licence originally rested with the teachers is inconsistent with all

our data as to Paris: it is possible that it was the case under the very peculiar circumstances of Oxford and Cambridge. Mr. Mullinger misses what seems to me the keystone of the whole constitutional structure, i.e. the distinction between the licence conferred by the bishop's representative and the *magisterium* conferred by the university.

[2] [These conclusions should be modified in the light of the penetrating examination made of the legislation of Alexander III by Gaines Post, 'Alexander III, the *licentia docendi* and the rise of the Universities', in *Haskins Anniversary Essays* (Boston, 1929), pp. 255–77. The object of Alexander III was to prevent simony, maintain the freedom of the licence and the right of poor students to free instruction, and generally to control the chancellors in cathedral churches and diocesan schools. His action directly attacked the chancellor of Notre Dame at Paris, although in fact the chancellor, who was at this time more than a 'superintendent of education', continued to charge for the licence, but only indirectly affected the growing corporation of masters, who were not yet authorized to take part in the grant of the licence. Their share, whether by examining students or presenting them, was a matter of custom and not yet clearly established. They became a *de facto* university apart from

The right to the licence once established, there was nothing CHAP. V, to prevent the multiplication of masters in connexion with § 1. any famous church school. Wherever scholars congregated Masters united by round some famous teacher, the number would increase of a body of customs those who were ambitious of becoming teachers themselves. formed guilds. And, wherever teachers multiplied, there naturally in that age of association grew up certain professional customs and unwritten laws which in some cases ere long crystallized into statutes of an organized guild or university.

That nobody should set up as a teacher without having Germs of the inception. been himself for an adequate period taught by some duly authorized master was almost too obvious a principle to need formal enactment.[1] That he should not enter upon the work of teaching without his former master's sanction and approval was an almost equally natural piece of professional etiquette. In the time of Abelard we see these principles, if not firmly established, at least on their way towards recognition. We have seen how, when the famous dialectician became ambitious of distinguishing himself as a theologian, it was considered necessary for him to put himself under a master before he could teach in another faculty, as it would have been called in later times; and, when after an incomplete period of study

papal intervention. Alexander's action, on the other hand, although he 'had no university consciousness', did help to bring the chancellor of the later university under papal control, just as the Bull of Honorius III *super speculam* (1219), which secured the income from their prebends for five years to promising students sent from a cathedral chapter to study in a higher faculty of theology, helped the teachers of theology in Paris and elsewhere (Cf. Gaines Post, 'Masters' Salaries and Student-Fees' in *Speculum*, vii (1932), 181–98, especially pp. 182–6). On the whole question of the chancellor or *magiscola* and papal legislation see Manacorda, i. 65 *sq*.]

[1] It seems that a period of five

to seven years was expected at an early period. Nigellus Wireker, in his *Speculum Stultorum* (*Satirical Poets of the 12th Century*, ed. Wright, 1872, i. 9, 10), speaks of the 'asinus, qui Parisius scholas frequentat . . . quia discedens nomen urbis non poterat retinere in qua moram fecerat septennem'. In the Life (written *c.* A.D. 950) of Aicardus, who lived as early as the seventh century, we read 'Quinquennio transacto visum illi fuit magistrum fore et inter primores conscholasticos residere' (Mabillon, *A. SS. Ord. S. Ben.*, Venice, 1733, ii. 916)—an expression which points to something like an inception about A.D. 950. It cannot of course be relied upon as evidence for the seventh century.

he ventured without his master's permission to begin the lectures on Ezekiel, this unauthorized assumption of the magisterial office was treated not merely as a scandalous exhibition of immodesty, but as an actual ecclesiastical offence. He was compelled to leave Laon,[1] and at the Council of Soissons his conduct on this occasion was made the subject of a distinct article of charge, the accusation being not that he had taught without the licence of the Church—though even this would have been unlawful—but that he had begun to teach 'without a master'.[2] Then too the opening of his course on Ezekiel seems to be spoken of as a kind of formal and public inaugural lecture, or what would have been called in later times an 'inception', though, since no master presided over it, it was an irregular one. How far the inception was already accompanied by those ceremonies which were afterwards an essential part of it, we cannot tell. It is possible that some of them may be of great antiquity : it is just possible that some of them may have descended by some vague tradition from the philosophical and rhetorical schools of the old Roman world. We have already seen the establishment of a very similar institution in Italy; the idea of the 'principium' or 'inceptio' was essentially the same as that of the Italian 'conventus'.[3] A clear understanding of this idea is absolutely essential to appreciate the constitutional theory of the Parisian university. It was out of this custom that the university of masters ultimately grew.

Idea of the inception.   The idea of the inception involved two elements. It was,

---

[1] For a curiously parallel story cf. Martène, *Thesaurus Anecdot.* iii. 1714.

[2] 'Quod sine magistro ad magisterium divinae lectionis accedere praesumpsisset,' Bulaeus, ii. 66. In the words 'Quod nec Rom. pontificis nec ecclesiae auctoritate commendatus legere publice praesumpseram' from Abelard's *Hist. Calam.*, Bulaeus (i. 284, ii. 67, 669) relies upon a corrupt text. Cousin reads *commendatum* (*sc.* libellum) for *commendatus*. The notion that the chancellor conferred the licence in the name of the Pope is much later. See Denifle, i. 765. It is tempting to see the germs of the baccalaureate in the position occupied by Abelard when he taught in the school of another master.

[3] The Paris term 'principium' is often applied to the Bologna 'conventus' or 'conventatio'; more rarely the Paris licence examination is styled 'privatum examen', and the inception 'publicum examen'.

on the one hand, the formal entrance of a newly licensed CHAP. V,
teacher upon his functions by the actual performance of its   § 1.
duties—a ceremony which, according to the ideas of the
Roman law, was essential to the actual investiture of an
official with his office.[1] On the other hand, it was the recognition of the new-comer by his old master and other members
of the profession—his incorporation into the society of
teachers.[2] The new master had a cap placed upon his head,
which is sometimes explained as the old Roman ceremony
of manumission or emancipation from the subjection of pupil-
lage. But the biretta[3] was also a badge of the mastership,
which with the other insignia of his office—the ring and the
open book—he received from his former master, who further
conferred upon him a kiss and a benediction. Then, seated
in the magisterial cathedra, he gave an exhibition of his professional capacity by delivering an inaugural lecture or holding an inaugural disputation. The idea that a new-comer
should 'pay his footing' seems almost a primitive instinct of
human nature. It formed an essential part of inception that
the 'inceptor' should entertain at a banquet the whole or a

[1] For similar customs in the merchant guild see Gross, *The Gild-Merchant*, Oxford, 1890, i. 33, 34.
[2] Compare the reading of the Gospel by the newly ordained deacon. In the Roman Church the newly ordained priests stand for the rest of the office in a circle round the altar and are 'concelebrant' with the bishop (cf. Hatch, *Organization of the Early Christian Churches*, London, 1882, pp. 131, 132). A relic of the last usage survives in the neglected Anglican rubric which requires the newly ordained priests to 'remain in the same place where Hands were laid upon them, until such time as they have received the Communion'. The tradition of the insignia of the various orders—which in the case of the minor orders constitutes the whole of ordination—is another point of analogy between the cere-monies of graduation and those of ordination. On a lower level an excellent illustration of the idea is supplied by the investiture of the grammar-master with a birch with which he proceeded to flog a boy. See below, chap. xiv. Another analogy is supplied by the cere-mony with which a Scottish judge takes possession of his office. After presenting his patent to his col-leagues, he tries two cases and reports his decision on them before being sworn in as a member of the 'college of justice'. There was anciently a somewhat similar pro-bation for serjeants-at-law in Eng-land. See Pulling, *Order of the Coif*, London, 1884, p. 8.
[3] The 'biretta' was always re-garded as the most important of the insignia of the office. Bachelors taught uncovered.

considerable number of his new colleagues. Presents of gloves or gowns had also to be made; and gradually contributions in money to the funds of the society were exacted in addition to the presents to its individual members—an exaction which has ever since been the inseparable accompaniment of degree-taking even in those universities in which all other formalities are most generously dispensed with. The whole affair was originally nothing but a piece of unauthorized buffoonery—hardly more dignified or important perhaps than those sometimes brutal and sometimes silly student initiations which the masters of later times tried to stamp out by every possible penalty, and which still linger on in bad schools and in the artistic *ateliers* of modern Paris.[1]

The university or guild of masters grew out of inception.

Out of this custom, however, the idea of a guild or corporation of teachers in all probability arose, as perhaps other guilds may have arisen from similar initiations. Gradually, and probably by imperceptible steps, the ceremony passed from a mere jollification or exhibition of good-fellowship into the solemn and formal admission of a new master into an organized and ultimately all-powerful corporation of teachers. And the trades union of teachers rapidly succeeded in acquiring a monopoly of the trade. 'Inception' became as

[1] It is not impossible that the magisterial initiation was partly copied from the student initiation, which was certainly of great antiquity. See the passages cited by Conringius, *Op.* v. 447, 448. Gregory Nazienzen gives an elaborate account of his τελετή at Athens, which he describes as παιδιὰ σπουδῇ σύμμικτος. *Or.* xliii, ed. *Patrol. Graeca*, xxxvi, cc. 515, 516. Photius, on the authority of Olympiodorus, declares that in the fifth century no one was allowed to teach (εἰς τὸν σοφιστικὸν θρόνον ἀναχθῆναι) at Athens ᾧ μὴ τῶν σοφιστῶν ἡ γνώμη ἐπέτρεπε καὶ αἱ κατὰ τοὺς σοφιστικοὺς νόμους τελεταὶ ἐβεβαίουν τὸ ἀξίωμα. The new master went to the bath, where he and his friends had to force an entrance against a body of students who made a στάσις and tried to keep them out. He then came out wearing the τρίβων, was escorted home in solemn procession, δαπάνας σιτιανοὺς φανερὰς εἰς τοὺς τῶν διατριβῶν προστάτας τοὺς λεγομένους Ἀκρωμίτας, *ibid.* ciii. 269. The parallel to the later inception is curiously exact. An edict of Justinian forbids practical jokes—an integral part of the τελετή—on freshmen in the law schools (Digest. *Proaem.*). In medieval Paris frequent statutes were passed against the exaction of money from *bejauni* (=*becs-jaunes*, yellow-bills), i.e. unfledged birds (Bulaeus, iv. 266; *Chartul.* ii, No. 1032). In the fifteenth century the practice of initiating *bejauni* passed into the brutal ceremony of *depositio*, as to which see below, ch. xiv (vol. iii, p. 379).

necessary to the teacher as the chancellor's licence. The CHAP. V,
'licentiate' was not regarded as a full 'master' or 'doctor' till § 1.
he had 'incepted'.

Another great institution which was a development of the Analogy
same idea was the institution of chivalry. The original con- of knight-hood.
ception of knighthood was the solemn reception of the novice
into the brotherhood of arms. The blessing of the priest was
required by the knight bachelor as the scholastic bachelor
required the licence of the chancellor; but it was by the
touch of the veteran's sword that the candidate received
his actual initiation into the brotherhood of arms, as it
was through the veteran master's act that the licentiate
became a full member of the brotherhood of teaching. Both
of these great institutions arose from the transference to
the military and the scholastic life respectively of one of
the most characteristic social and political ideas of the age
—the idea of a guild or sworn brotherhood of persons
following a common occupation. In the later ceremonies
attending the bestowing of degrees there are many traces
of the idea that graduation formed a sort of intellectual
knighthood. In some of the Spanish universities the new
doctor was actually invested with a sword: in all universities the ring formed one of the insignia of the doctorate, and at Vienna the preliminary bath of the candidate for
knighthood appears to have been imitated by candidates for
degrees.[1]

In the age immediately succeeding the years of Abelard's Multi-plication
teaching Paris leapt almost at one bound into a unique of masters at Paris.

[1] Such at least is the only explanation I can give of the words of
the statute: 'Quod nullus baccalariorum aut scolarium finito examine
pro baccalariatu aut magisterio aliquem inuitet ad balneum ante suam
determinationem aut incepcionem
preter examinatores, cum quibus
balneetur in eodem balneo, si saltem pro tunc sibi placeat balneari,
sub pena retardacionis, &c.... quod
nullus licentiatus post suam incepcionem exponat in balneo ultra 30
denarios ultra hoc, quod placet sibi
pro magistro, qui eum promovit,'
&c. (Kink, *Gesch. d. kais. Univ.
Wien*, I. ii. 55.) It is obvious from
these last words that for internal
application some liquid more expensive than water was provided; and
it is just possible that the 'bath'
was wholly metaphorical, but the
explanation given in the text is
the more probable. Cf. p. 228,
above.

position in the scholastic world. The cathedral or abbey-schools, however numerous their students, had owed their celebrity entirely to one or two illustrious teachers. Paris became a city of teachers—the first city of teachers the medieval world had known. Here then were the materials for the formation of a university. In that age of guilds we may almost say that the formation of a teaching-guild in some form or other was inevitable. At what precise date the body of teachers loosely bound together by a professional etiquette assumed something like the form of an organized society we cannot exactly determine. Any precise date that might be given would be essentially misleading. The university was not made but grew. We can only notice the few recorded facts which throw light on the process of development, culminating (as we shall see) at the beginning of the thirteenth century in the reduction of the hitherto unwritten customs of the profession to a code of regular statutes or by-laws.

A statute of the bishop and chapter in 1127[1] ordering that none but members of the cathedral body should lodge in the cloister seems to mark the beginning of the process by which a *studium generale* was evolved out of the mere cloister school. Before long we find the teachers too numerous to be accommodated within the cloister or even in the island round the cathedral walls. And now we hear of masters licensed by the Chancellor of Notre Dame teaching in houses built upon the bridges of the Seine.[2] At about the same time

---

[1] Bulaeus, ii. 666; Guérard, i. 339. This regulation was, however, relaxed in the case of young men of royal or illustrious birth, who were frequently admitted to board with the canons (Bulaeus, iii. 307; *Chartul*. i, No. 283). S. Louis was one of the band, as well as his brother Philip, afterwards archdeacon in the same church. Other instances are given in the *Hist. Lit*. ix. 62. At the end of the century the cathedral schools were moved from the cloister of the cathedral or the adjoining episcopal palace to the

'parvis' between the palace and the Hôtel-Dieu. The special cathedral school for the cathedral 'clerks' was of course quite distinct from the schools which now began to multiply around it. In the time of Bishop Maurice (1160–96), a statute of the bishop and chapter ordained 'ne quis canonicorum domos claustrales alicui scolari conduceret aut etiam commodaret'. *Chartul*. i, Introd., No. 55.

[2] One of John of Salisbury's masters was known as Adam de Parvo Ponte, from his school on

—towards the middle of the century—we can trace in the CHAP. V, writings of John of Salisbury a multiplication of masters both § 1. round the cathedral and in the Mount of Ste Geneviève.[1] The absurd story which represents Gratian as having deliberately 'invented' academical degrees and Peter the Lombard as having transferred the system to Paris may be accepted as fixing roughly the period at which the honours of the master's chair began to be sought by those who had no intention of devoting themselves, or at least of permanently devoting themselves, to the profession of teaching. The consequences Especially masters of of this rising passion for 'degrees' were particularly important arts. to the faculty of arts. We have seen how in the days of John of Salisbury 'grammar' and rhetoric were taught and studied as earnestly as theology. The teachers were mature scholars who looked upon teaching as their life's work. The students studied for long periods. After the middle of the century the passion for graduation together with the absorbing enthusiasm for the scholastic philosophy and theology caused the usual course of study in the Latin language to be reduced to a minimum. The mastership in the philosophical faculty became the natural goal of every student's ambition and the usual if not essential preliminary to study in the higher faculties. Hence the enormous multiplication of masters, and especially of very young masters, which was one of the immediate causes of the growth of the university.[2]

the Petit-Pont. He was afterwards Bishop of S. Asaph (*Hist. Lit.* ix. 62). There were also a Jean de Petit-Pont and an Adam de Grand-Pont who taught at Paris later in the century (*ibid.*, p. 75); also a Pierre de Petit-Pont (*ibid.*, p. 78). A letter of Gui de Bazoches (1175–90) declares that 'Pons . . . Parvus aut pretereuntibus, aut spatiantibus, aut disputantibus logicis dedicatus est'. *Chartul.* i, Introd., No. 54.

[1] [For the early masters and their dates see R. L. Poole, 'The Masters of the Schools of Paris and Chartres in John of Salisbury's time',

E.H.R. xxxv (1920), 321–42; reprinted in his *Studies in Chronology and History* (Oxford, 1934), pp. 223–47; cf. C. C. J. Webb, *John of Salisbury* (1932), pp. 5–10.]

[2] [Cf. John of Salisbury, *Metalogicon* (i. 24, 25), ed. Webb, pp. 57, 58 on the contrast between the method of Bernard of Chartres and later pratice (*c.* 1159) when professors undertake to teach the whole of philosophy in two or three years. 'Isti hesterni pueri, magistri hodierni.' Gerald of Wales gloried in this rapidity. See also the letter of Stephen of Tournai, quoted below, p. 303, n. 1]. Cf. *Carmina Burana*

CHAP. V,
§ 1.
Early
scholastic
privileges.

In the second half of the twelfth century we meet with increasingly frequent recognition of scholars as a distinct and privileged class. The privileges of the scholars in northern Europe rested upon a somewhat different basis to the privileges bestowed upon students in the Italian universities. In the Italian towns scholars were recognized as a class distinct alike from the clergy and from the ordinary lay population: their privileges were obtained for the most part by treaty with the citizens. In France all students and still more all masters in the church schools were assumed as a matter of course to be clerks, and enjoyed—like a host of other persons connected however remotely with the service of the church —the immunities of clerkship as fully as persons actually in orders. Hence the Parisian scholar's privilege of trial in the ecclesiastical courts originates in no explicit grant of any secular or ecclesiastical authority. It existed long before the rise of the university. After the grant of the special privilege of trial by their own masters to the students of Bologna by Frederick I, some attempts were, indeed, made to introduce the same principle into France. Thus in the case of a quarrel at Reims, Alexander III ordered that the townspeople should allow scholars to be tried by their own masters,[1] and the

---

(ed. Schmeller, Breslau, ed. 2, 1883), p. 40:

> 'Sed retroactis seculis
> vix licuit discipulis
> tandem "nonagenarium"
> quiescere post studium.
>
> At nunc decennes pueri
> decusso iugo liberi
> se nunc magistros iactitant,
> cęci cęcos pręcipitant.'

So again:

> 'Iam fit magister artium
> qui nescit quotas partium
>   de vero fundamento:
> habere nomen appetit
> rem vero nec curat nec scit,
>   examine contento.
>
> Iam fiant baccalaurei
> pro munere denarii

>   quam plures idiotae:
> in artibus, ab [? et] aliis
> egregiis scientiis
>   sunt bestiae promotae.'

Du Méril, *Poésies populaires du moyen âge*, Paris, 1847, p. 153.
But of this poem the date is unfortunately doubtful.

[1] 'Prohibeatis omnibus ne prefatos scolares contra libertatem eorum in aliquo molestare audeant vel gravare, quandiu coram magistro suo parati sunt iustitie stare.' *Chartul.* i, Introd., No. 5. Two points are to be remarked in this document: (1) that the principle is claimed as an old custom; (2) that it holds good as against ecclesiastical censure as well as civil justice. The appeal to Rome had

earliest papal statutes of Paris—those of 1215—appear to CHAP. V, § 1.
recognize the same privilege. But the youth, number, and
legal inexperience of the masters of arts must have made a
system which eventually broke down even at Bologna wholly
unworkable at Paris, and the master's jurisdiction was rapidly
superseded by the ordinary ecclesiastical courts and by the
extraordinary academical tribunals which the growth of the
universities called into existence in the course of the following
century.[1] Another remarkable privilege was possibly granted
to the masters and scholars of Paris before the close of
the twelfth century. Louis VII is said to have authorized the
masters to suspend their lectures as a means of protest in the
event of an outrage being committed upon a master or scholar
as a means of compelling the authorities to grant redress.[2]

arisen in consequence of the conduct of a certain 'J. Presbyter de
burgo S. Remigii' who had been
derided by certain scholars when
publicly dancing on a Sunday.
Provoked by this he first assaulted
the scholars and broke the windows
and doors of their schools, and then
(without applying to archbishop or
official) promulgated sentence of
excommunication against them! So
at Salisbury, where no university
existed, there was a dispute between
the sub-dean and the chancellor in
1278 for ecclesiastical jurisdiction
'in scholasticos in ciuitate Saris-
buriensi studiorum causa commorantes'. See Caius, *De Antiq.
Cant.* (1574), p. 110. [Cf. Leach,
Schools of Medieval England, pp.
165, 178. It should be remembered
that Frederick I recognized the
authority of the bishop. The
masters, apart from the recognized
ecclesiastical authority, would have
a moral disciplinary authority of
a paternal character. Cf. the
decree of the legate Guala (below,
p. 304, note) and Langton's commentary on Exodus xxi. 35, 36, summarized in *Theology*, xvii (1928),
90.]

[1] The Bull of Celestine III in
1194 (*Chartul.* i, Introd., No.
15), directing that 'causas seculares',
or (according to another reading)
'pecuniarias' of 'clerici Parisius
commorantes' should be tried by
canon law is usually quoted as the
foundation of the ecclesiastical
privilege of the scholars. But (1)
this privilege appears to have been
covered by the general principle
above explained. (2) The Bull is
not specially applicable to scholars.
(3) The true explanation of it would
seem to lie in the secular jurisdiction of the Bishop of Paris. Causes
of laymen would of course be tried
by the ordinary law; but a doubt
would arise as to the *law* to be
applied to the civil cases in which
ecclesiastics were either plaintiffs
or defendants. This is made particularly clear by the concluding
words 'nec permittatis iuri scripto
consuetudinem prevalere'. See
Bulaeus, ii. 498; Denifle, i. 679;
Chartul. i, Introd., No. 15, note.

[2] This rests on the authority of
William the Breton, *De Gestis
Philippi Augusti*, in *Rec. des
historiens de France*, xvii. 82 (cf.
p. 395).

CHAP. V, The text of this privilege, if it ever assumed a documentary
§ 1. form, is not preserved; but, so far as appears, there was
nothing in it to constitute a recognition of the university or
corporation of masters as such.

First   So far we have heard nothing of a university in the strict
trace
of uni- sense of the word. One passage, and one only, in all the
versity,
c. 1170. chronicles and documents of the period supplies us with
positive evidence of the existence of a guild of masters at
Paris before the beginning of the thirteenth century. In the
life of Johannes de Cella, Abbot of S. Alban's, by his pupil
Matthew Paris, we are told that the subject of the biography
was, as a young man, a student at Paris and was there admitted into the 'fellowship of the elect masters'.[1] The Abbot
died 'full of days' in 1214. He may therefore be assumed
to have become a master not much later than A.D. 1170 or
1175. At about that date then the society of masters had some
kind of existence, however indefinite, inchoate, and rudimentary. The complete silence of John of Salisbury, whose
works are full of reminiscences of student life at Paris, and
the whole account which he gives of his own career as student
and teacher, forbid us to place the first beginnings of the
university earlier than the middle of the century. It is therefore a fairly safe inference that the period 1150–70—probably
the latter years of that period—saw the birth of the University
of Paris. We must beware, however, of exaggerating the
extent and definiteness of the association implied by the use
of such expressions as society or university. They prove little
more than the fact that it was customary for a master, after
being licensed by the chancellor, to be formally initiated into
the society of his fellow masters. They point to the existence of

---

[1] 'Hic in iuventute scolarum Parisiensium frequentator assiduus ad electorum consortium magistrorum meruit attingere.' *Gesta Abbatum Mon. S. Alb.*, ed. Riley, London, 1867, i. 217. [*Consortium* is, of course, Matthew Paris's word and reflects the thought of the thirteenth century. The word was first applied to the masters of Paris by Innocent III in 1208–9: *Chartul.* i, No. 8; cf. Gaines Post in *Speculum*, ix. 423, n. 9.] Bulaeus indeed (ii. 489, 490) represents the university as sending a legate to the Pope in 1192, but his authority does not neessarily imply corporate or official action. Cf. Stephen of Tournai, *Lettres*, ed. Desilve, p. 295.

meetings of the masters for the celebration of these inceptions, and probably also for disputation and perhaps upon rare emergencies to concert measures for the vindication of an injured colleague or student, for the punishment by expulsion or professional excommunication of a breach of professional etiquette, or for the pursuit of some similar common object. But two facts are a sufficient indication of the amorphous and merely customary character of the bond which held together the guild into which the masters of Paris were spontaneously, and perhaps almost unconsciously, constituting themselves. Till *circa* A.D. 1208 the university had no written statutes, and till a considerably later period no head or presiding officer.[1]

---

[1] Innocent IV, on the authority of the civil law, lays it down that 'adesse collegii non exigitur, quod ibi sit praelatus'. Decret. 3. De praebend. *Cum non* (Venice, 1578, p. 147). To say with Denifle (i. 129) that the chancellor was to some extent ('gewissermassen') *caput generale* of the university seems to me essentially misleading. He may have been *caput* of the *studium*, but he was not even *ex officio* member of the *universitas*. [Rashdall here added a note on the word *magistrari* as suggesting a system of graduation. He cited Girald. Camb. *Speculum Ecclesiae*, in *Opera*, iv. 3 (where, as Mr. R. Hunt has pointed out to us, the correct reading, preserved by Twyne and Wood, is *massati*, not *magistrati*: cf. the *Gemma ecclesiastica*, ii. 37 in *Opera*, ii. 349), *Rec. des histor. de France*, xiv. 443D, and Innocent III 'magisterii honore insignitum', *Patrol. Lat.* cciv, p. xvii note. These passages do not seem to imply any academic formalities apart from the grant of the licence by the chancellor, whose authority over the masters in the twelfth century Rashdall unduly minimizes; cf. above, p. 282, and G. Lacombe, *La Vie et les œuvres de Prévostin* (Kain, 1927), pp. 40, 41. In the following sections, however, the position of the chancellor is more correctly described, though with some disregard for chronology. A passage in the *De rebus a se gestis* of Girald. Camb. (*Opera*, i. 48) illustrates both the absence of a definite system and the growth of academic terminology. Gerald studied canon law for three years and refers to his 'preceptor in ea facultate'. When Matthaeus Andegavensis, 'quem in legibus et decretis tunc audiebat', was summoned by Alexander III to the Lateran Council, 1179, 'a sociis in auditorio suo licentiam accipiens, quatinus magistrum Giraldum loco ipsius auditorem et preceptorem haberent cum multa ipsius commendatione monuit attentius et suadendo consuluit. Quod cum *scolares* omnes appeterent et postularent,' &c. Here a master, with the consent of his pupils, offers his *scola* to a young and popular teacher. Presumably Matthaeus was the preceptor previously mentioned. Gerald had obtained the licence to teach in arts after three years' study during a previous period in Paris (*Opera*, i. 23). He may have acted as the 'clericus et prepositus' to Matthaeus. Cf. Powicke, *Stephen Langton* (Oxford, 1928), pp. 28, 29.]

The evidence for these assertions will appear in the sequel. For the present it will be enough to clear the ground for its reception. The two great problems connected with the early history of the university are the origin of the four nations and the origin of the rectorship. The solution of these problems has been hitherto impeded by a gross misinterpretation of two important pieces of documentary evidence. In the first place, an episode in the history of Thomas Becket's quarrel with Henry II has been, by all the historians of the university before Denifle, relied upon as proving the existence of the 'nations' at that time. Henry offered to submit his quarrel to the arbitration of 'scholars of different provinces, examining the matter with equal scales',[1] or (as the Archbishop himself says) of 'Parisian scholars'.[2] It is natural enough that to minds preoccupied with the antiquity of their *alma mater* the former passage, when interpreted by the latter, should have appeared incontrovertible proof of the existence of the 'nations', and even of the practice of voting by nations in or about A.D. 1169. But in reality the words imply no more than a proposal to submit the matter to the arbitration of learned men from the Parisian schools, chosen from different nationalities to secure impartiality. With equally little ground an allusion has been found to the rectorship in the celebrated charter granted to the scholars of Paris by Philip Augustus in A.D. 1200.

No nations or rector in twelfth century.

Riot of A.D. 1200. The occasion of this first extant charter of privileges was the fatal issue of the first recorded 'town and gown' disturbance at Paris. The riot began in a tavern. The servant of a noble German student (a bishop-elect of Liège)[3] was assaulted, whereupon a concourse of his fellow countrymen took place; the host was severely beaten, and (according to the usual

---

[1] 'Scholaribus diversarum provinciarum aequa lance negotium examinantibus.' Ralph de Diceto, *Op. Hist.*, ed Stubbs, 1876, i. 337, and Matt. Paris, *Chron. Mai.*, ed. Luard, ii. 1874, p. 263.

[2] 'Paratum esse stare iudicio curiae Domini sui Regis Franco-rum vel iudicio Ecclesiae Gallicanae aut Scholarium Parisiensium.' *Materials for the Hist. of Thomas Becket*, ed. Robertson, vii. 164; *Chartul.* i, Introd., No. 21.

[3] Henricus de Jacea, Archdeacon of Liège. Hoveden, *Chronica*, ed. Stubbs, iv (1871), 120, 121 and note.

formula of medieval chroniclers on such occasions) 'left half-
dead'. The Provost of Paris at the head of an armed band
of citizens in return attacked a hall or hostel (*hospitium*) of
students of the same nationality. In the fight which thereupon
ensued, several students were killed, including the Elect of
Liège himself. The masters appealed to the King for redress,
which—from fear, it is said, lest the masters should withdraw
from the city altogether—was granted with no niggard hand.
The Provost was sentenced by the King to perpetual imprisonment, subject however to a curious proviso. The accused
was to be allowed if he pleased to go through the ordeal by
water or by fire: if convicted by the ordeal, his punishment
was to be aggravated to hanging; if acquitted, it was to be
commuted to banishment from Paris. The houses of the
offenders who had fled justice were destroyed; those who
were caught were sentenced to the same fate as the Provost,
unless they could prevail upon the injured scholars to inter-
cede for them. The scholars relented so far as to ask to be
allowed, in lieu of all other satisfaction, to flog them 'after
the manner of scholars', in their schools.[1] But this request
was refused as detrimental to the royal prerogative. The
charter now granted secured that any scholars arrested by the
royal officers should forthwith be handed over to the ecclesiastical judge. The burghers of Paris were required to swear
to respect the privileges of scholars, and to give information
unsolicited against any one whom they might see maltreating
a scholar. The provost was also on admission to his office to
swear to respect the scholastic privileges in presence of the
assembled scholars in one of the churches of Paris. This was
the origin of the position of the provost of Paris as 'Conservator of the royal Privileges of the University'. Cases in
which the defendant was accused of violating any privileges
granted to them by the King came to be tried in the court
over which the provost presided, the Châtelet. For the
further protection of the clerks, it was ordered that trial by

[1] 'Ut praepositus ille et com-   The Provost escaped the grim alter-
plices sui more scholarium in   native by breaking his neck in an
scholis flagellati, essent quieti et   attempt to escape from prison.
facultatibus suis restituti,' *loc. cit.*

CHAP. V, battle or ordeal should be refused to prisoners charged with
§ 1. assault on a scholar. Then follows a clause which protects
from arrest by the hands of secular justice the *capitale
Parisiensium scholarium*.[1] Bulaeus and his followers (including
even Savigny) have interpreted these words of the rector,

[1] The clause runs as follows:
'In capitale Parisiensium scolarium pro nullo forifacto iustitia
nostra manum mittet; sed si visum
fuerit illud esse arrestandum per
iustitiam ecclesiasticam arresta-
bitur et arrestatum custodietur, ut
de illo capitali fiat quod per Ecclesiam fuerit legitime iudicatum.' ·
(Bulaeus, iii. 2, text corrected by
Denifle, i. 7; *Chartul*. i, No.
1.) Hemeraeus (p. 95) understands the chancellor to be meant.
I had already conjectured from the
meaning of cognate words in Du
Cange that *capitale* must mean
'chattels', when I came upon the
French translation of the provost's
oath, in which the provisions of
each of the clauses in the charter are
given in succession. It runs, 'Vous
jurerez qu'en chastel des écoliers
ne ferez mettre main' (Jourdain,
p. 66).

I may add the following remarks:
(1) The use of *capitale* either for
'head' or 'regent master' is unex-
ampled. (2) The continued use of
the neuter for a person would be
unparalleled. (3) The clause would
be mere surplusage, since masters
as well as scholars have been already
privileged from arrest. (4) For the
quite common use of *arrestare* of
the sequestration of property cf.
Jourdain, Nos. 371, 551 (*arrestari
bóna*), Bulaeus, iii. 469. (5) Provision is made for the case where
the *iustitia ecclesiastica* cannot be
found in the case of a scholar, not
in the case of the arrest of the
capitale. The reason on my view
is obvious. The case could not be
so urgent where only property was
concerned as to require a tem-

porary detention by the secular
arm. According to the other interpretations a privilege is conferred
on the 'scholar' which is withheld
from the rector or master.

M. Jourdain's own view is that
'haec verba non ipsum rectorem
sed aliquem e magistris aperte de-
clarant' (p. 66, note), and to this
view Denifle, though not without
hesitation, subscribes. M. Jourdain (No. 274, p. 47) relies upon a
passage contained in the pleadings
of the university against the chancellor. A doctor of medicine had
upset the water in which he had
been steeping his herbs upon the
watch in the street below. The
officers entered the house, and
after nearly killing him by their
violence carried him off to the
King's prison. The university
contended that its privileges had
been violated by the arrest and imprisonment in two distinct ways:
'quod de quocumque esset scholari
non debuisset fieri, sicut in privilegio regis continetur', and because
'iustitia laycalis in capitale scholarium, quantum ad illam iniuriam,
manum imposuit, quod tamen per
privilegium regale fieri non debuit
similiter'. According to M. Jourdain's interpretation there is hardly
any distinction between the two
breaches of privilege complained
of. It is easy to suppose that the
doctor's property had been seized
by the guard even if the forcible
entry was not construed as an
attachment of property by lay
justice.

Denifle replied *ex cathedra* that
'arrestare capitale, letzteres im
Sinne von "Vermögen" genom-

whose office the former at least believed to date from the
times of Alcuin and Erigena. Recent writers have strangely understood the *capitale* to mean 'a regent master', but without offering any explanation of so strange a mode of expression. Even Denifle has here missed or rather rejected the true explanation. The word *capitale* merely means 'chattels' or property, which, like the persons of the scholars, was protected from sequestration except by process of the ecclesiastical court. It is obvious that the correction of these two blunders involves a re-writing of the whole constitutional history of the university during the first half-century of its existence. As the charter of Philip Augustus has sometimes been treated as a kind of deed of foundation, or at least as the

men, kennt das Mittelalter nicht'. (*Hist. Jahrbuch*, x, 1889, p. 372, note.) With all deference I submit that it is enough to show that each word can bear the sense assigned. If we may have 'arrestare bona' (which is habitual), why not 'arrestare capitale', since 'capitale' undoubtedly has the same meaning as the commoner 'catallum'? At all events it is clear that this meaning was assigned to 'capitale' by the medieval translator, who presumably knew medieval Latin as well as Denifle himself. The argument from usage is the less valuable since 'capitale' was obviously a comparatively rare form which suggested different interpretations within a century after the date. It should be stated that the thirteenth-century Phillipps MS. (No. 76, f. 54 *b*) translates: 'Vous jurrès que en le chevetaine des escoliers de Paris pour nul forfait vous ne mettrès main, ne ne ferès mettre'; and this reading has been adopted by Denifle (*Chartul.* i, No. 67). But over 'chevetaine' is written in an early hand 'chateils' (as also in the copy followed by Bulaeus, *Recueil des priv. de l'Un. de P.*, p. 277)—a fact which Denifle omits to chronicle; and (as he tells us)

the Vatican codex renders: 'Qu'en l'enqueste des escoliers ne ferés mettre main.' I must observe that the reading of the Phillipps MS. can give no support to Denifle: if it is worth anything, it makes for the old view which interprets it of the rector. But Denifle knows that in 1200 there was no rector; and he himself thinks that the translation was made *circa* 1231, i.e. just when the rectorship was rising into importance, when a scholar of Paris would have been as eager to see additional tribute to the dignity and antiquity of the office as Bulaeus was 400 years later. Under these circumstances it cannot be doubted that 'chateils' or 'chastel' represents the wording of the oath which the provost actually took. My view of the matter has been accepted by Kaufmann. [Cf. the words of the oath of 1364–6: 'Comme il aient de privilege royal que votre justice pour nul forfait d'escolier ne mecte main es biens de l'escolier, mes seulement soient arrestés et gardés par la justice de l'eglise' (*Chartul.* iii, No. 1324). Luchaire (in Lavisse, *Hist. de France*, III. i. 339) translates: 'Le trésor ou *capital* de l'Université', where *trésor* is right, *l'Université* wrong.]

CHAP. V, first recognition of the university, it may be added that the
§ I. privileges which it bestows are bestowed upon scholars simply
as such. There is no official recognition of the university, its
officers or members; except in so far as it recognizes the
existence of assemblies of scholars by requiring the provost's
oath to be taken before them.[1] The conferment of these
privileges no more implies the existence of a university than
the exemption of chemists or dissenting ministers from jury
service by act of parliament implies the existence of guilds
or corporations composed of members of those classes of the
community.

II. Development of the University from 1210 to 1249: Origin of the Four Nations

The uni-
versity a
corporation
in germ.
We have seen that the bare existence of a university of
masters can be traced from about the year 1170.[2] It was not,
however, till some years after the beginning of the thirteenth
century that the society assumed anything like the form of a
legal corporation or obtained in its corporate capacity recognition and privilege from the civil and ecclesiastical authorities.

[1] [In the first edition Rashdall, without justification, translated *scolares* in the charter of 1200 as 'masters', when reference is made to gatherings of scholars. There are good grounds to believe that in the early days assemblies of scholars, which might even have developed in imitation of the institutions of Bologna, had conditions in Paris been favourable, caused some embarrassment to the chancellor and masters. Thus the chancellor, Philip (de Grève ? 1218–36), contrasts past and present in one of his sermons: 'In the old days, when each master taught for himself and the name of University was unknown, lectures and disputations were more frequent and there was more zeal for study. But now that you are united into a University, lectures are rare, things are hurried, and little is learned, the time taken from lectures being spent in meetings and discussions. In these assemblies, while the older heads are deliberating and legislating, the younger spend their time hatching the most abominable schemes and planning their nocturnal raids.' Haskins, *Mediaeval Culture*, p. 61.]

[2] [Gaines Post, in his important article, 'Parisian Masters as a Corporation 1200–1246' (*Speculum*, ix, 1934, pp. 421–45), has put the subject of this section on a new footing by his careful investigation of the documents in the light of contemporary thought and practice. His main contention, as against Halphen, is that, if regard is paid to contemporary ideas, especially those expressed by the canonists, the university of masters was a 'legal corporation, fully recognized by the highest ecclesiastical authority, by 1215 at the latest', p. 444.]

Four steps would seem to have been pre-eminently neces- sary to give to mere customary meetings of masters for the initiation of new members or similar purposes the character of a definite and legally recognized corporation: (1) the reduction of their unwritten customs to the form of written statutes or by-laws, (2) the recognition or (if authoritative recognition was unnecessary) the exercise of the right to sue and be sued as a corporation, (3) the appointment of perma- nent common officers, (4) the use of a common seal. We must now briefly investigate the date at which each of these stages in the development of the university was reached.

The first two steps were taken considerably before the two latter and at about the same period, i.e. about the year 1210. The actual text of the earliest statutes is lost; but there is a Bull of Innocent III of about the last-mentioned date which sanctions the restitution to the society of a master who had been expelled for a breach of them. From this document it appears that they were three in number.[1] The

[1] 'Ex litteris vestre devotionis accepimus, quod cum quidam mo- derni doctores liberalium artium a maiorum suorum vestigiis in tribus presertim articulis deviarent, habitu videlicet inhonesto, in lectionum et disputationum ordine non servato, et pio usu in celebrandis exequiis decedentium clericorum iam quasi penitus negligenter omisso, vos cupientes vestre consulere hone- stati octo ex vobis iuratos ad hoc unanimiter elegistis, ut super dictis articulis de prudentium virorum consilio bona fide statuerent, quod foret expediens et honestum ad illud imposterum observandum vos iuramento interposito communiter astringendo, excepto dumtaxat magistro G., qui iurare renuens et formidans fideiussoriam pro se tan- tum optulit cautionem. Fuit in- super ad cautelam a vobis fide prestita protinus constitutum, ut si quisquam magistrorum adversus alios duceret resistendum et primo, secundo tertiove commonitus infra triduum universitati parere con- tempneret magistrorum, ex tunc beneficio societatis eorum in magi- stralibus privaretur.' Bulaeus, iii. 60; *Chartul.* i, No. 8. The Bull is undated, but appears in the Vatican Register between the years 1210 and 1211. Denifle dates it 1208-9. [The Bull was included in the un- official 'Compilatio Tertia' and, later, in the official Decretals of Gregory IX, lib. i, tit. ii, c. 11, and was freely glossed by the com- mentators; *inter alia*, it was re- quested as illustrating the right of corporations to make statutes; see the quotations in Gaines Post, *op. cit.*, pp. 427-8, note.] At about this date the university took some kind of corporate part in the condemna- tion of Amaury of Bène; see William the Breton in *Rec. des histor. de France*, xvii. 83; but the words 'compellitur ab Universi- tate confiteri', &c., are suspicious, since *ab Universitate* is omitted by Vincent of Beauvais, who repro-

CHAP. v, first dealt with the dress of masters, no doubt prescribing the
§ 1.   'round black cope reaching to the heels at least when new',
mentioned in one of the earliest extant statutes;[1] the second
enforced the observance of 'the accustomed order in lectures
and disputations'; the third required 'attendance at the
funerals of deceased masters'. From the extreme simplicity
of these regulations, and the fact that their enactment is
spoken of as something new, it is sufficiently evident that
they were the first ever formally made by the society—the
first reduction to a written form of the established but hitherto
unwritten customs of the profession. They are also interesting
on account of their close analogy with the statutes of the
ordinary guilds or religious confraternities of the Middle
Ages, with which attendance at funerals and the obtaining of
prayers for deceased members was likewise a primary object.[2]
Sometimes too their members wore a common livery. This first
step towards the consolidation or crystallization of the hitherto
fluid organization must therefore have been taken in the year
1209 or not much later. A modern mind, accustomed to look
for very definite expressions of corporate existence, might indeed be disposed to assign the 'foundation' of the university
to the decade 1200–10 rather than to the years 1160–70: such
a conception would, however, be thoroughly anachronistic.

Recog-   At about the same date the university acquired a definite
nized   recognition of its existence as a legal corporation. A Bull of
as a
corpora- Innocent III (himself a Parisian master) empowers the society
tion.   to elect a proctor, i.e. a syndic or common *procurator ad litem*,
to represent it in the Papal Court.[3] By this permission the

duces the rest almost *verbatim*
(*Speculum*, Douai, ed. 1624, iv.
1221).

[1] 'Nullus magistrorum legentium in artibus habeat capam nisi
rotundam, nigram et talarem, saltem dum nova est. Pallio autem
bene potest uti.' Bulaeus, iii. 82;
Chartul. i, No. 20. [Cf. Tancred's
gloss ad v. *inhonesto* (Bull of Innocent III, *Chartul.* i, No. 8),
'forte capas manicatas portando,
cum doctores consueverint capas

clausas deferre', in Leipzig Uni-
versitätsbibliothek MS. 968, f.
164 r, communicated to us by Mr.
Gaines Post.] The 'Confirmatio
Statutorum' which Bulaeus (iii. 52)
ascribes to Innocent III really
belongs to Innocent IV, and the
date is 1246–7. See Jourdain,
p. 116; *Chartul.* i, No. 169.

[2] See Toulmin Smith, *English
Gilds*, 1870, *passim.*

[3] Denifle, no doubt rightly, connects the Bull with the suit of

society acquired, in modern legal phraseology, the right 'to sue and be sued' as a corporation. It must not, however, be supposed that according to the ideas of the thirteenth century any charter from either Pope or King was conceived to be indispensable to enable a private society to acquire a legal corporate existence. Whether owing to the predominance of ideas ultimately derived from the Roman law,[1] or simply from the mere absence of a clearly defined conception of a corporation as a distinct legal personality, we find that the growth of corporations of all kinds was at this period gradual and spontaneous.[2] The borough, the guild-merchant, the ordinary social or religious guild, all came into existence, held corporate property, and exercised other attributes of

No charter necessary.

1210–11 (i. 86); but in his *Chartul.* i, No. 24, places it vaguely between 1210–16.

[1] For the ideas of medieval civilians as to freedom of association see Denifle, i. 191, 192, 169–75. They would seem to be to a certain extent inconsistent with the true interpretation of the Roman law in imperial times (see Mommsen, *De Collegiis et Sodaliciis Romanorum*, Kiel, 1843, p. 72 *sq.*). But still the idea seems always to have been that unauthorized *Collegia* were forbidden, not that *a priori* special legislation was necessary to create artificial or fictitious persons. It must be remembered that the Roman law had everywhere some recognition in relation to the clergy (see Savigny, *Gesch. des Röm. Rechts im Mittelalter*, cap. 15). Thus we find bishops incorporating colleges of priest-vicars (see e.g. Freeman, *Cathedral Church of Wells*, 1870, p. 137 *sq.*). So in 1347 the Chancellor of Oxford incorporates the barber-surgeons (Wood, *Hist. and Antiq. of Oxford*, ed. Gutch, i. 443, 444), who enjoyed the privilege of the university. But there is no necessity to appeal to the conceptions of the Roman law. As to the spontaneous origin of

English Guilds and Boroughs, see the excellent treatment of the subject in Gross, *The Gild Merchant*, Oxford, 1890, i. 33 *sq.*

[2] [Freedom and frequency of association, the *post hoc* recognition or the creation of associations, even the provision of facilities 'ad agendum et respondendum' (see below) and the possession of a seal should be sharply distinguished from the conception of a fictitious and distinct legal personality. Innocent IV had not yet coined the phrase *persona ficta*, and when he did he taught that the corporation could commit neither sin, crime nor tort. The Church led the way in framing a theory of personality before the legal consequences of the theory were worked out. Hence the university, in Bologna and Paris, was accepted as a 'corporation', acting with *consensus communis*, before it acquired corporate freedom from excommunication. It was 'legal', was exempt from the episcopal right to authorize corporations, and could act in the courts through a proctor before it acquired 'personality'. In short it both reflected and helped to shape juristic descriptions of the *collegium licitum*.]

CHAP. V, corporate personality without any formal charter or legal
§ 1. incorporation. Charters and formal privileges were for the
most part granted to confirm or extend a corporate existence
already *de facto* established. A sovereign or other superior
authority might and often did deny to a particular class or
community the right to form a particular kind of corporation
or to claim particular corporate privileges; but there was no
idea that for the mere holding of common property a definite
act of legal incorporation was necessary. That notion is an
invention of later jurists, and is responsible for a great deal
of bad history.[1]

Thus Innocent expressly recognizes the inherent right
of the masters to a corporate existence, both in the Bull
authorizing them to appoint a proctor[2] and in the Bull

[1] The best account of the origin
of the university as a voluntary
society is that given by the masters
themselves in their letter to the
prelates of Christendom in 1253–4
(Bulaeus, iii. 255; *Chartul.* i, No.
230): 'Magistri reverendi vita et
doctrina clarissimi, mente religiosi,
omnes tamen degentes in habitu
seculari, qui processu temporis
crescente numero auditorum, sicut
oportuit, ampliati, ut liberius et
tranquillius vacare possent studio
litterali, si quodam essent iuris
specialis vinculo sociati, corpus
collegii sive universitatis cum multis privilegiis et indultis ab utroque
principe sunt adepti.' In the controversy with the Mendicants they
even denied the right of the Pope
to meddle with the university, *qua*
university, at all: '1. Quia secundum iuris civilis ordinationem nullus ad societatem compelli debet,
cum societas voluntate firmetur.
2. Authoritas Apostolica non se
extendit nisi ad ea quae ad Cathedram pertinent. Ad Cathedram
autem non pertinet studentium
societas, sed collatio Beneficiorum,
administratio sacramentorum et
alia huiusmodi.' (Abstract in
Bulaeus, iii. 649.) When the

university attempted, in later times,
to subject the chancellor to its
regulations in the conferment of the
licence, it was by virtue of his personal oath of obedience as a member of the university. A curious
illustration of the medieval view
of freedom of association is quoted
by Sarti from Manni, *Degli antichi
Sigilli*, xii (Florence, 1742), 117.
When the Pisans were defeated by
Genoa in 1284, a large body of
Pisan captives were kept in prison
for eighteen years, and assumed the
right of using a common seal which
bore the legend, 'SIGILLUM UNI-
VERSITATIS CARCERATORUM JANUAE
DETENTORUM.' State-authorization
is here of course out of the question.

[2] The date is 1210–16. 'Scolaribus Parisiensibus. Quia in causis,
que contra vos et pro vobis moven-
tur, interdum vestra universitas ad
agendum et respondendum com-
mode interesse non potest, postu-
lastis a nobis, ut procuratorem
instituere super hoc vobis de nostra
permissione liceret. Licet igitur
de iure communi hoc facere valeatis,
instituendi tamen procuratorem
super his auctoritate presentium
vobis concedimus facultatem.'
Bulaeus, iii. 23; *Chartul.* i, No. 24.

sanctioning the readmission of the expelled master. In the latter case the Pope was called upon to dispense with the obligation of the oath which the masters had taken to refuse their *consortium* to all offenders against the statutes. In the former the necessity for appointing a proctor arose from the suit with which the society was engaged against the chancellor and church of Paris, to whom the claims of the new organization seemed inconsistent with the allegiance of the individual masters to the chancellor. Hence to secure from the pope the recognition of their proctors was to win half their case.

In taking the momentous step—for such it proved in its ultimate consequence—of passing written statutes, it is not impossible that the nascent society was influenced by the example of the student-universities of Bologna.[1] It is true that the existence of the Parisian Society of Masters becomes traceable in a rudimentary form considerably before we have express evidence of the existence of the earliest student-university at Bologna. But in the more congenial atmosphere of Italian city-life, these societies rapidly attained a higher stage of development and organization than the looser association of masters which had grown up around the cloister-school of Paris. Though the Italian universities were universities of students, the Parisian masters formed a body numerous enough to imitate their organization. It must be remembered that the great mass of the masters at Paris were masters of arts—men not much older than the Italian law-

Influence of Bologna.

[This Bull was inserted in the 'Compilatio Quarta' and, later, in the Decretals of Gregory IX, lib. i, tit. xxxviii, c. 7. The address 'Scolaribus Parisiensibus', which may possibly not be original, seems to have caused some confusion to the canonists. Gaines Post (*op. cit.*, p. 434, n. 3) gives reasons for the view, taken by Rashdall without comment, that the Bull was intended for the masters.]

[1] The statutes were made by a committee of *eight*, which suggests the eight *statutarii* of Bologna. See above, p. 189. The statutes of

1215 required that a master should be at least twenty (see below, p. 462), and it is probable that the regulation was not uncalled for. Cf. the complaints of Stephen of Tournai a quarter of a century earlier: 'Facultates quas liberales appellant, amissa libertate pristina, in tantam servitutem devocantur, ut comatuli adolescentes earum magisteria impudenter usurpent, et in cathedra seniorum sedeant imberbes; et qui nondum norunt esse discipuli, laborant ut nominentur magistri.' *Lettres* (ed. Desilve), p. 345; *Chartul.* i, Introd., No. 48.

CHAP. v, students, and many of them actually students in the higher
§ 1. faculties as well as masters in the lower. When we come to
deal with the formation of the nations and the appointment
of their officers, the influence of the institutions of Bologna
on those of Paris will be still more obvious.

Development of university due to struggle with the chancellor. Both these steps towards a legal incorporation of the university are unmistakably connected with the great struggle which was now beginning against the Chancellor of the Cathedral Church of Paris.[1] It was perhaps some invasion of the unwritten customs of their order by a licentiate forced upon them by the chancellor that suggested their reduction to writing and the exaction of the oath to observe them. It was still more certainly the appeal of the masters to Rome against the tyranny of that official which called for the appointment of a common proctor. It was in fact the necessity of mutual support and united opposition to the chancellor which called into existence the university-organization if not the university itself. A clear understanding of the original relations between the chancellor and the masters is essential to any intelligent appreciation either of the process of the university's growth or of the complex constitutional system in which that process finally resulted.

Original position of the chancellor. The control which the chancellor exercised over the masters before the rise of the university and in the first few decades after its emergence, was not limited, as in later times, to the conferring of the licence. He could not only grant or refuse the licence at his own discretion in the first instance: he could deprive a master of his licence or a scholar of his 'scholarity', with its attendant ecclesiastical privileges, for adequate cause. He was an ecclesiastical judge as well as the head of the schools. He claimed to be the *iudex ordinarius* of scholars, though his jurisdiction was not exclusive of that

---

[1] As to its earlier stages, we only know that in 1208 the Cardinal-legate Guala ordered that scholars should not be excommunicated till after two admonitions, (1) 'generaliter ... per magistros', (2) 'nominatim ... in scolis'. Since the injunction begins 'volentes ... magistris et scolaribus deferre, eatenus erga ipsos rigorem, si quis est, nostre constitutionis duximus temperandum,' it is clear that an earlier legatine decree has been lost. *Chartul.* i, No. 7. (In Hemeraeus, p. 93, the decree is mistakenly attributed to Walo, Bishop of Paris, in 1108.)

of the ordinary bishop's court.[1] He enforced his judgements CHAP. V, by excommunication and possessed a special prison for the § 1. confinement of refractory clerks. Besides enforcing the ordinary ecclesiastical law, he claimed, at least with the concurrence of the bishop and chapter, the right of issuing ordinances or regulations for the government and discipline of the masters and scholars. But in spite of the large extent of his powers over the masters as individuals, or rather just because of those powers, the chancellor had no position whatever in the university as such. As chancellor, he was not even member of it.[2] Though it was probably from an early period customary for the chancellor to ascertain from the masters the qualifications of a candidate for the mastership, the masters could not force the chancellor to grant a licence, nor could the chancellor compel the masters to admit to their association one whom he had licensed, but who had not complied with the regulations or customs of the society. In their power of recognizing or refusing to recognize the inception of a new member[3] and of requiring a new master to swear to obey the rules of their society as a condition of his admission to professional association, the masters possessed an equivalent to the chancellor's control over the licence. This right, which in its essence was nothing more or less than the power wielded by all professional associations, of refusing to associate with professional brethren guilty of unprofessional conduct, served as the *point d'appui* for their resistance to the chancellor. Originally formed for the purpose of self-protection rather than of aggression, the university soon

The chancellor not an officer of the university.

---

[1] It should be remembered that in the Middle Ages the chapter or capitular officers everywhere exercised actual spiritual jurisdiction, enforced by excommunication, over the inferior members of the cathedral body. The cantor was the ordinary superior of the singers, the chancellor of the scholars. Cf. above, p. 291 n.

[2] So in 1386 the university alleges 'que comme chancelier il n'est pas membre de l'université,

mais comme maistre en arts', Bulaeus, iv. 609.

[3] This is well illustrated by a statute of the faculty of medicine in 1270 enacting that 'quicumque bachelarius recipiet licenciam contra consuetudinem facultatis, vel magister qui hoc procuraret, ipso facto esset privatus in sempiternum societate magistrorum et omni actu scolastico predicte facultatis'. Bulaeus, iii. 398; *Chartul.* i, No. 433.

aimed like other trade unions at acquiring a monopoly. The university could not prevent a licentiate from teaching, but they could refuse to dispute with a licentiate who would not submit to their regulations, and they could refuse to present for the licence or to admit to their own guild a scholar who persisted in attending the lectures of a master whom they had deprived of their *consortium*.[1] By these means the admission to the university by inception was rendered practically as essential to the teacher as the chancellor's licence. The licentiate was not reckoned a full master till he had been received into the society by a public and duly authorized inception.

Originally the chancellor and the university were thus quite independent of one another.[2] Each party tried by the use of its unquestionable prerogative to nullify in practice the equally unquestionable prerogative of the other. Had the parties been left to fight the matter out without interference,

---

[1] Thus in the statute of the faculty of theology against the Dominicans, the masters declare 'Quod si aliquis contra dictas eorum ordinationes venire presumpserit, ei societatem suam tam in principiis quam aliis penitus denegabunt' (Bulaeus, iii. 245; *Chartul*. i, No. 200); and in 1253 the university resolves that no master shall hold or be present at the inception of a bachelor who has not taken the oath to the statutes, adding 'Nec idem bachelarius si alio modo inceperit, magister a nobis aliquatenus habeatur'. Bulaeus, iii. 252, 253; *Chartul*. i, No. 219.

[2] [Rashdall is here too emphatic. The absence of any but customary relations before 1212 and the growth of a spirit of corporate independence among the masters do not prove that the chancellor was not regarded as head of the university in the later twelfth century. Some light on the position of the chancellor is thrown by the sermons of Prévostin of Cremona, the famous *Prepositinus*, who was chancellor during the years 1206–9, when the quarrel was beginning. He was much disturbed by the bad behaviour of some of the scholars and by the conduct, as teachers, of the theologians, whom he elsewhere describes as *magistri nostri*; see G. Lacombe, *op. cit*. 39–42. He was succeeded by Jean de Chandelle (*ibid*., p. 44). The exaction from the chancellor of an oath of residence at this time, and the limitation by Innocent III of the number of teaching masters of theology to eight (1207), were inspired, as Lacombe suggests, by the same intention, the desire to maintain order and regularity in the academic life. It is worthy of note that, when John Garland urged a return to the classics in the teaching of grammar in Paris, he appealed to the chancellor, Odo of Châteauroux (*Morale Scolarium*, c. xiv, ed. Paetow, pp. 221–4, especially the gloss on line 371).]

the legal weapons at the disposal of the chancellor might have strangled the rising society in its birth or reduced it to dependence upon himself. Coercion might have proved a match for 'boycotting'. As it was, the interference of the papal authority turned the scale. Except where the claims of the still more favoured orders of friars introduced a new factor into the dispute, the university gained in the end, though not without temporary rebuffs, by every appeal to the Roman Court. But in so doing, it naturally lost to a great extent its own autonomy. It entered into the ecclesiastical system (as the merchant-guilds entered into the political system by their acquisition of a share in the town-government[1]), and became as completely subject to ecclesiastical regulation as the monasteries or the chapters.

The relation of the chancellor to the university may thus Illustra- be compared with that of the Crown to the extinct Serjeants' tions. Inn. The Crown alone could make a man a serjeant-at-law just as the chancellor alone could make a licentiate; but, though the appointment by the Crown in the one case and the chancellor's licence in the other was the condition of eligibility, it was by the free election of his professional brethren that the new-comer entered the professional society. The presentation of rings by the newly admitted serjeant to his colleagues[2] was one of the last relics of those customary presents of hats, gloves, gowns and the like by the new member of a guild in which the more prosaic degree-fees of modern universities have their origin.

The 'Circuit Mess' at the English Bar illustrates the enormous power which may be wielded by a society which has no legal or corporate existence. A barrister expelled therefrom for breach of professional etiquette retains his legal position, but he is effectually incapacitated from practice, since no member of the mess will hold a brief with him, even if a solicitor should be found bold enough to give him one.

---

[1] It must not, indeed, be supposed that the guild merchant was identical with, or in any way superseded, the municipality proper. For the true relation between them see Gross, *The Gild Merchant*, i. 61–105.

[2] Pulling. *The Order of the Coif*, p. 245.

CHAP. V,
§ 1.
Suit
between
chancellor
and uni-
versity,
ante 1212. A Bull of the year 1212 makes it evident that a suit between the chancellor and the university had been proceeding for some time past. It was addressed by Innocent III to the bishop, dean, and archdeacon of Troyes and required them to compel the chancellor by ecclesiastical censure to redress the grievances of the masters.[1] The matters in dispute were referred to arbitration and the decision of the arbitrators enforced by the apostolical delegates in a formal sentence[2] which is of capital importance for the light which it throws upon the beginnings of the university. The chancellor had, it appears, required the masters to take an oath of obedience to himself. Had he succeeded in the attempt, either the university could not have continued to exist or the chancellor's position in it would have become even more powerful than that of the chancellor of Oxford in the days when he was really the bishop's officer and before the masters had succeeded in making him merely the executor of their own decrees. He would have become himself (like our Oxford chancellor) the head of the masters' guild; and there would have been no

room for the growth of the rectorship. As it was, the papacy, with that unerring instinct which marks its earlier history, sided with the power of the future, the university of masters, and against the efforts of a local hierarchy to keep education in leading-strings. The obligations of the oaths already taken were relaxed and the exaction of such oaths in future forbidden.[3] The chancellor was required to grant the licence gratuitously; and further, he was enjoined (without prejudice to his right of licensing at his own discretion) to grant the licence to all candidates recommended by a majority of the masters in any of the superior faculties of theology, civil or canon law, or medicine, or by six selected masters in the faculty of arts: the six examining masters being chosen three by the faculty and three by the chancellor.[4] Moreover,

[1] Jourdain, No. 13; *Chartul.* i, No. 14. Jourdain wrongly dates this and the next-mentioned document 1210.

[2] Jourdain, No. 15; *Chartul.* i, No. 16.

[3] 'Quod Cancellarius sacramenta fidelitatis vel obedientie vel aliam obligationem aliquam pro licentia legendi danda non exiget ab aliquo lecturo Parisius, et etiam relaxabuntur prestita iuramenta.'

[4] This regulation was, however, only of temporary force, 'quamdiu

the chancellor had grossly abused his judicial power. He CHAP. V, § 1. had imprisoned scholars for very trifling offences and had exacted fines by way of penance which were appropriated to his own benefit—a mode of ecclesiastical discipline which was in universal employment where the sins of the laity were concerned, but which was unusual in dealing with the privileged clerical order. Henceforth the chancellor was not to imprison pending trial when the offence charged was a slight one; in any case he was to allow the accused to be discharged on finding sufficient bail, and he was not to impose a pecuniary penance on a scholar under any circumstances whatever, though he might award damages to the injured party.

Three years later, most of these provisions were embodied Curzon's statutes, 1215. in a permanent Code of Statutes imposed upon the university by the cardinal, Robert Curzon, or de Courçon. At the same time the right of the university to make statutes for its own government and to administer oaths of obedience to them was recognized, but only in the following cases—'on occasion of the murder or mutilation of a scholar or of grievous injury to a scholar, if justice is refused, for taxing the rents of *hospitia*, concerning dress, concerning burial, concerning lectures and disputations', and with the proviso 'that the *Studium* be not thereby dissolved or destroyed'.[1] The clause relating to the 'taxation' of *hospitia* no doubt shows that the custom of fixing the rents of houses in the occupation of scholars by a joint board of scholars and burghers was already in existence.

The support of the Holy See was, however, unable to The conflict continues. prevent the renewal of the attempts of the bishop and chancellor to stifle the newly born university. The old grievances remained unredressed—the grant or refusal of the licence without consultation of the masters, the vexatious

videlicet predictus cancellarius cancellariam tenebit'. A curious difference is noticeable as to the way in which the masters of the different faculties were to bear testimony to the fitness of candidates. The doctors of law and theology were to give it 'in verbo veritatis'; the *phisici* were required 'dare fidem'; the masters of arts were only to be believed 'fide corporaliter prestita'.

[1] Bulaeus, iii. 81, 82; *Chartul.* i, No. 20. Note how the threat of migration, here as at Bologna, is the great instrument of academic warfare.

CHAP, V,
§ 1.

imprisonments, the pecuniary penances and so on; and fresh subjects of dispute were added to them. The oppression of the chancellor called forth fresh efforts after corporate autonomy, and these efforts in turn became offences which called down upon the masters fresh measures of ecclesiastical vengeance, necessitating renewed appeals to Rome.

The struggle necessitates common seal and officers.

It was in the conduct of this continued litigation that the university first experienced the want of the two important attributes of corporate existence which were still lacking to it. The support of its legal representatives at the Roman court compelled the university to borrow money, and a seal was wanted to affix to the bond for its repayment;[1] while officers were required to collect the money and direct the legal proceedings.

Effort of chancellor and cathedral to crush the university, 1219–22.

From Bulls of the years 1219[2] and 1222[3] it is evident that the bishop and chancellor were straining every nerve to suppress the formidable organization which threatened to destroy the authority of the ancient Church of Paris over the masters and scholars who were multiplying beneath her shadow. An old ordinance or proclamation against 'conspiracies' was furbished up, and the university was excommunicated *en masse* for disobedience to it. The language of the Bulls[4] makes it quite plain that the acts of the conspiracy were simply the passing of statutes by the masters

[1] See the Bull of Alexander IV in 1259 ordering payment of a debt incurred 'thirty years and more before' to certain Florentine merchants 'prout in litteris compositionis eiusdem Universitatis sigillo sigillatis plenius continetur'. Jourdain, No. 184; *Chartul.* i, No. 330.

[2] *Chartul.* i, Nos. 30, 31.

[3] *Chartul.* i, No. 45. Stephen Langton, Cardinal and Archbishop of Canterbury, and others had been appointed delegates by a Bull now printed by Denifle, *Chartul.* i, No. 41.

[4] 'Dilecti filii magistri et scolares Parisienses nobis graviter sunt conquesti, quod venerabilis frater noster . . . Parisiensis episcopus excommunicationis sententiam ab

O. bone memorie predecessore suo, et O. Hostiensi episcopo quondam apostolice sedis legato latam de conspirationibus et coniurationibus scolarium minime faciendis iam dudum innovans eos qui, circa statum scolarium sine consensu ipsius vel capituli seu cancellarii Parisiensis conspirationem, coniurationem, constitutionem, seu aliquam obligationem iuramento, fide vel pena vallatam facere attemptarent, pro sue voluntatis arbitrio, simili vinculo innodavit et ipsorum insuper pedibus laqueos excommunicationis expandens in illos qui noverint scolares arma portantes ac de nocte incedentes, nisi eos infra certum tempus ipsi vel eius officiali seu cancellario

for the government of themselves and their scholars and the CHAP. v, administration of oaths to observe them. The Church of Paris § 1. claimed that no such 'constitutions' should be passed without the consent of the bishop, chapter, or chancellor. When the university respectfully inquired whether the prohibition applied to all constitutions or only to unlawful constitutions, they were expressly told that it applied to all constitutions, 'lawful or unlawful, good or bad'.[1] It is obvious that the very existence of the university was at stake.

The definitive sentence of the Holy See upon the points Papal at issue has not come down to us,[2] but there can be no doubt decisions. from the sequel that Honorius III and Gregory IX continued in the main the policy initiated by Innocent III of supporting the claims of the new society. The Bulls of 1219 and 1222 are of an interlocutory character, though the first of them decides an important point in favour of the scholars by ordering the instant abolition of the chancellor's prison, and forbidding the wholesale excommunication of the university without the special licence of the Holy See.[3] It is in these Nations Bulls that we find the first traces of the existence of nations and their and their officers. It appears that the *scolares* had elected a proctors. leader or leaders 'according to their nations' for the avenging of injuries'. [The nature of these officials and their connexion with contemporary events are very obscure. They are mentioned only in a document of 1222 in which their election is forbidden. The context[4] suggests that they were

---

nuntiarent, similem sententiam fulminavit,' &c. *Chartul.* i, No. 30.

[1] 'Quesierunt interpretationem . . . utrum videlicet intelligerent generaliter tam de constitutione licita utili et honesta, quam de illicita erronea et iniusta, quibus respondentibus, quod intelligebant generaliter de omni licita vel illicita, bona vel mala,' &c. *Chartul.* i, No. 31.

[2] If the document of 1219 in *Chartul.* i, No. 33 refers to this matter, the dispute must have broken out again before 1222. Cf. Bulaeus, iii. 130; *Chartul.* i, No. 58.

[3] See the Bull of 1219; *Chartul.* i, No. 31. The immunity of the university as a whole from excommunication without the special licence of the Holy See is re-enacted in 1222 (*Chartul.* i, No. 45. M. Thurot (p. 12) makes the astounding assertion that Honorius III forbade the excommunication of '*aucun membre* de l'université sans l'autorisation du St.-Siège'. So Malden (p. 30), and others.

[4] 'Magistri etiam a magistro vel scolari penam pecuniariam per tempus non exigent supradictum, nec scolares interim secundum

CHAP. V, elected by 'scholars' as distinct from masters, and reveal an
§ I. early form of organization by 'nations' which came to nothing. They are not called 'proctors', but, if they actually were elected by the masters], it is possible that they were identical with the proctors, whom the masters had appointed to direct from Paris the suits pending at Rome against the chancellor, and to collect money for that purpose.[1]

Rectors or proctors.
In the year 1222 the election of such officials is prohibited *pendente lite*. We hear no more of them again till 1231 or (since the text is there doubtful) 1237, when the institution appears thoroughly established. A Bull issued in the latter year forbids the unauthorized excommunication not merely of the masters and scholars, but of their 'rector or proctor', or other person when acting officially on their behalf.[2] It is

nationes suas sibi quemquam preficient ad iniurias ulciscendas.' *Chartul*, i, No. 45. (Bull of Honorius III, May 1222.)

[1] 'Porro, cum ad prosecutionem appellationis predicte foret nuntius ad sedem apostolicam destinandus, et sine collecta universitas (*sc.* a corporation) non haberet expensas, magistri liberalium artium fide interposita se ac suos discipulos astrincxerunt ad servandum quod super hoc a suis procuratoribus contingeret ordinari' (Bulaeus, iii. 94; *Chartul*. i, No. 31). From the Bull of 1260 (Jourdain, No. 134) it appears that these *procuratores* were four in number. We have possibly an earlier trace of the custom of appointing four representatives upon such occasions, and so perhaps of the nations, in Innocent III's Bull of 1208–9. The master who had been expelled for breach of the statutes 'in quatuor vestrum iuramento interposito compromisit, illorum dictum pro bono pacis se gratum et ratum pariter habiturum.' Bulaeus, iii. 60; *Chartul*. i, No. 8. [On the other hand, it is more likely that the proctors mentioned by the Pope in 1219

were simply persons, elected to act for the masters and scholars in the conduct of the case in Paris. This would be the natural meaning. The Pope nowhere forbade the election of such in so many words. Cf. the words 'usus sigille scolarium *preterquam in hiis, que ad officium procurationis in hac causa pertinent*, suspendatur'. The levying of fines by the masters, the appointment of proctors, the use of a seal, illustrate corporate developments, but may have had nothing to do with the rise of 'nations'. Gaines Post, inclines to agree with Rashdall; *op. cit.*, p. 429, note 1.]

[2] 'Ut nullus contra universitatem magistrorum vel scolarium seu rectorem vel procuratorem eorum aut quemquam alium pro Universitatis vel facto vel occasione,' &c. Such is the reading of Jourdain, No. 49, for the document of 1237. Denifle, in his *Entstehung d. Univ.* i. 112, gave 'rectorum' (upon the unsatisfactoriness of which Kaufmann has commented in his *Gesch. d. Deutsch. Univ.* i. 270). Denifle has since accepted 'rectorem' as the true reading in 1237 (*Archiv*, iii. 627 and *Chartul*. i, No.

possible that rector and proctor are here alternative titles for the same official.[1] But whether this was so or not, it is quite clear that when the first appointment of these officials took place, there was only one official to each nation and no general head of the whole body. At a later date the term proctor was appropriated to the heads of the several nations: while a common head of all four nations was elected with the style of rector. We may conjecture that the term *procurator* was first employed in view of the temporary, representative, and financial character of the official:[2] while the analogy of the four Bologna rectors may have suggested that of rector as a name for the national officers, as they passed from temporary into permanent delegates, until the election of a common head by the united nations required a distinction between the two titles. At the same time, a trace of their original character remained in the short tenure of both offices, which were at

113); in the document of 1231, printed for the first time in *Chartul.* i, No. 95, he gives 'rectorum' as the reading of his manuscript (the Vatican Register). If this is the true reading, 'rectorum' must of course = 'regentium'. There is much uncertainty about the text of these successive renewals; see Jourdain, pp. 11 *b*, 14 *a*; Denifle, i. 113, 114; *Chartul.* i, No. 162 note.

[1] There are some slight indications of such a use of terms: (1) William of S. Amour referring to the year 1256 says that he was not then (as he had been earlier) 'procurator scholarium vel rector de collegio eorum'. (*Opera*, Constance, 1632, p. 94.) The two titles here seem to be alternative titles for the same office, though it is just possible (with Denifle) to take rector in the sense of regent: (2) In 1264 we hear of the Seal-Chest being opened 'presentibus rectoribus et procuratoribus'. *Chartul.* i, No. 405. (3) In 1254, the Pope, retaining the older phraseology, clearly uses the term 'rectores artistarum' to include the four proc-

tors as well as *the* rector. *Chartul.* i, Nos. 338, 342. (4) At Vercelli, in 1228, the heads of three nations are spoken of respectively as *rector*, *procurator*, and *provincialis*, but at other times collectively as *rectores* (see below, vol. ii, c. ii, §§ 4, 5). (5) At Oxford and Cambridge the proctors were called 'rectores sive procuratores'. Whence could such a usage be derived except from Paris? But see below, vol. iii, c. xii, § 2. The term *procurator* was commonly used of any legal agent or attorney, but especially of a financial agent. In continental colleges it is the common equivalent of our 'bursar'. It is the ordinary Latin of our 'churchwarden'.

[2] From the town statutes at Bologna it appears that a guild, the '*homines artis lanae*', were governed by 'castaldi et *procuratores*'. (Frati, ii. 72.) So the 'Company of Merchants of Alnwick' was governed by an alderman and proctors. Gross, *Gild Merchant*, i. 130. Rector was also a name for guild-officers. See above, p. 163.

first held for periods of only a month or six weeks and afterwards for three months.[1]

The first document in which the rector and proctors are clearly distinguished from one another is a statute of the faculty of arts in 1245,[2] which visits offenders with expulsion till 'satisfaction shall have been made to the rector and proctors on behalf of the university' (sc. *universitas artistarum*) 'to the full and at their pleasure'. In the same year a statute of the whole university orders that scholars who take a house which has been interdicted to scholars by the university are to be expelled after monition by the rector or a servant sent by him, or in like manner by the proctors or a messenger sent by them.[3] It is now clear that the term rector has come to be reserved for the head of the whole body of artists, the term proctor alone being applied to the heads of the nations, while in 1249[4] we meet with an agreement between the four nations as to the mode in which this new officer—the common head of the four nations—should be elected by the four proctors. It should be added that the bedels or 'common servants of the scholars', i.e. of the university or nations, make their appearance at about the same time as the proctorships in their earliest form.[5]

[1] From 1279. Bulaeus, iii. 444; *Chartul.* i, No. 492.

[2] 'Quousque pro qualitate et quantitate delicti vel transgressionis mandati Universitatis rectori et procuratoribus pro Universitate fuerit ad plenum et pro ipsorum voluntate satisfactum' (Feb. 1244–5), Bulaeus, iii. 195; *Chartul.* i, No. 137.

[3] 'Per rectorem vel servientem ab eo missum, vel per procuratores similiter.' Bulaeus, iii. 195; *Chartul.* i, No. 136.

[4] Bulaeus, iii. 222; *Chartul.* i, No. 187. It appears that at this time there were two rectors, one presiding over the French nation only, the other over the remaining three nations. Whether this arrangement, closely parallel to the later Bologna constitution, had

lasted some time, or whether the agreement was merely designed to settle a disputed election, cannot be determined; but it seems to be treated as irregular and exceptional. The one thing that comes out clearly is that the *single* rectorship is much later than the four national headships, by whatever name called. It is worth noticing that Gregory IX in 1231 gave the administration of the goods of intestate scholars to 'episcopus et unus de magistris quem ad hoc Universitas ordinaverit'. (*Chartul.* i, No. 79.) This suggests that a single representative of the masters was already appointed for some purposes. This very enactment may have had something to do with the growth of the single rectorship.

[5] *Chartul.* i, No. 28 (dated by

We see, then, that the nation-organization came into CHAP. V,
§ 1. existence at some time before 1222, that it was for a time suspended by papal authority, but that by 1231 it seems to have obtained a fully recognized legal existence; while at some time between 1222 and 1249[1] the common rectorship was instituted by the united nations. Like the formation of statutes, the appointment of the common proctor, and the use of the common seal, the new organization is clearly connected with the great war against the chancellor. It is true that the suit against the chancellor was instituted in the name of the whole university, whereas the rectorship was a development within the body of artists, but the masters of arts formed by far the most numerous body of masters; the masters of the superior faculties who were left outside the new organization were in fact a mere handful.[2] And it is probable that it was the masters of arts and their pupils who were particularly interested in resisting the oppression of the ecclesiastical authorities. It was not the elderly and dignified doctor of divinity, but the young master of arts and his still younger pupils who would be most in danger of having their heads broken in a tavern brawl, or being lodged in the chancellor's prison for breaking other people's heads, and who would have needed the assistance of powerful organization for the 'avenging of injuries'. It is probable, therefore, that the suit at Rome was practically carried on mainly by the faculty of arts and at their expense.[3]

The nations composed only of masters of arts.

Denifle *circa* 1218). [Here, as later, Rashdall gives an inadequate idea of the organization of the nations under their dominating officials, the proctors. He sees the proctor throughout with the rector in mind. For a detailed description of the election, duties, rights, tenure of office, of the proctors, and of their control of the procedure of summoning and directing the congregations of the nations, see Boyce, pp. 41–53. He summarizes (pp. 50, 51) from the *Auctarium* (i. 631) an illuminating dispute in 1382 between the rector and the proctor of the English nation about the latter's right to summon meetings of the nation.]

[1] Probably after 1237. See above, p. 312.

[2] In 1207 Innocent III limited the theological chairs to eight. (Bulaeus, iii. 36; *Chartul*. i, No. 5.) In 1289 there were about 120 regent masters of arts (Jourdain, No. 274, p. 45 *a*; *Chartul*. i, No. 515).

[3] [In the first edition Rashdall took for granted that the masters of arts had elected the officers to avenge injuries, who were forbidden by the Pope in 1222. But the

CHAP. V,   The peculiar relation which must at this time have existed
§ 1.   between the legal corporation of masters of all faculties and
Composi-
tion of the more popular and informal nation-organization which
four   had grown up within it is well illustrated by a papal Bull of
nations.
1259[1] ordering the payment of debts contracted by the society
'thirty years and more before'. The suit is distinctly spoken
of as the suit of the whole university; the bond for the repayment of the money was sealed with the university seal; the
Bull itself is directed to the whole body of masters.[2] But it
appears that the money had been borrowed by four proctors
whom we can hardly avoid identifying with the proctors of
the nations; and the order for the repayment is in a special
manner addressed to the rector, though it was not till much
later that it became the habitual practice to address official
communications to the 'rector, masters, and scholars'. The
small proportion which the masters of the superior faculties
bore to the whole body, together with the fact that but for the
rector the university was still an acephalous corporation, is
almost a sufficient explanation of the curious circumstance
that the rector of the inferior faculty of arts rapidly became
the real head of the whole society. The probable history of

Bull refers to *scolares* and it is exceedingly difficult, if not impossible, to be sure when this word means 'masters and scholars' or 'scholars who are not masters'. The word *scolares* might exceptionally be used, as in the address of the Bull of Innocent III (*Chartul.* i, No. 24; see above, p. 302 n.), for the body of masters acting on behalf of the whole university, or as equivalent to 'masters and scholars' where the scholars might comprise masters of arts studying as scholars in higher faculties, or, lastly, for the young students in arts. The context may or may not help to decide what meaning is intended. Until the organization of the 'universitas magistrorum et scolarium' is defined in the second half of the thirteenth century, it is safer not to interpret, as stages in a single pro-

cess, incidents which may well have expressed different interests, had no effective outcome, or had no clear relation with each other. Cf. above, p. 298, n. 1.]

[1] Jourdain, No. 184; *Chartul.* i, No. 330.

[2] Moreover, in 1218 it appears that though only masters of arts and their scholars had been excommunicated, 'in omni facultate silet Parisius vox doctrine'. (*Chartul.* i, No. 31; Bulaeus, iii. 94.) When John of S. Victor says 'tota universitas quatuor Nationum decrevit quod a lectionibus cessarent' (Bulaeus, iii. 564), there is no reason with Denifle (i. 83) to make the expression an anachronism. It is quite probable that the nations of arts took the lead in all these movements.

the relations between the university and the faculty of arts during this transition period is that, in consequence of its superior numbers, organization, and activity, the affairs of the university were passing more and more into the hands of the faculty of arts. The doctors of the superior faculties were called in to give their assent to what had been already settled upon by the masters of arts. Since the superior faculties had as yet perhaps no heads of their own, the position of the rector in such 'general congregations' must have been from the first virtually that of a presiding officer.

It is impossible to fix the exact date at which the practice of voting by faculties in the university and by nations in the faculty of arts came into vogue, but a circumstance in the anti-chancellor movement which has hitherto been passed over helps to explain its origin. In one only of the main issues between chancellor and university does the papacy seem to have failed to support its protégé. The Bull addressed to Archbishop Langton and his colleagues in 1221, while referring the other points at issue to the discretion of the delegates, contains a peremptory order to break a seal which the masters had recently made for themselves.[1] How far this order was obeyed, we know not; but in 1225 a university seal —the same or a successor—was, upon the complaint of the chapter, solemnly broken by the papal legate, Romano, Cardinal of S. Angelo, and the university peremptorily forbidden to make another. The sentence provoked an attack by a mob of masters and scholars armed with swords and sticks upon the legate's house: the doors had been already broken when the cardinal was preserved from further outrage by the timely arrival of the soldiers of the king.[2] It was not till 1246 that the right of common seal was conceded;[3]

The common seal broken, c. 1225.

[1] *Chartul.* i, No. 41. The chapter had also complained of the masters unreasonably 'iuramentum non solum super observatione factarum (constitutionum) sed etiam faciendarum decetero exigentes penis gravibus constitutis'; and on this point also the Pope here seems to decide against the

masters in advance.

[2] *Chron. Turonense*, ap. Martène, *Ampliss. Collectio*, v, c. 1067. At the ensuing Council of Bourges, some eighty masters appeared and received absolution for this assault.

[3] *Chartul.* i, No. 165. [See, for the history of the seal, Gaines Post, *op. cit.*, pp. 438–43.]

CHAP. V,
§ 1.
but meanwhile it is very possible that the prohibition had already been evaded by the formation of four separate seals for the four nations, which were used to signify the assent of the faculty of arts whether to its own deeds or those of the whole university.[1] It is obvious that this measure, necessitated by the action of the legate, would have the effect of consolidating the nations and emphasizing the fourfold division of the faculty of arts. Henceforth, in fact, the faculty of arts ceased to exist except as a federation of the four independent nations; and since the seals could not be used without the consent of the nations to which they severally belonged, separate deliberations would be necessary whenever a document had to be sealed.[2]

Relation of nations to university.
It remains to state the actual constitution of these nations. They were named from the nationalities which predominated in each of them at the time of their formation, namely, the French, the Normans, the Picards, and the English.[3]

---

[1] The first extant document which bore these seals is the agreement as to the election of rector in 1249 (see above, p. 314). That the seals were made to evade the prohibition of a university seal is supported by the fact that as late as 1283–4 the chancellor 'asserit se a facultate gravatum esse, inserendo ibi quedam de sigillis quibus utuntur quatuor nationes facultatis predicte'. (Jourdain, No. 274; *Chartul*. i, No. 515.)

[2] It was distinctly ordered in 1266 by the papal legate that 'fiant in licitis casibus ipsius facultatis statuta . . . communi et expresso cuiuslibet nationis interveniente consensu'. *Chartul*. i, No. 409.

[3] It is not easy to indicate briefly the differences between my view of the origin of the nations and Denifle's. (1) He holds (following the *Anon. Refut.*, p. 325 *sq*.) that the nations were an organization of *scholars*, in which the masters of arts were included as scholars of the superior faculties (i. 84, 88, 97);

but, as he admits that those below M.A. had no voice in the assemblies (p. 102), and as the university itself is constantly spoken of as a body of *scholars*, the distinction seems to rest on a somewhat slender basis. I admit that the nations were formed for a different purpose from the faculties, though I see no reason to believe that after the nations were once formed any distinction was in practice maintained between the faculty of arts and the collective nations, or that when once the rectorship was established, the rector did not preside in all meetings of the masters of arts for whatever purpose assembled. (2) He holds that the nations were formed for purposes of discipline among the scholars (i. 104). This view seems to me unfounded and anachronistic. The discipline of scholars, in so far as such a thing existed, was left to their own masters. I believe that the primary purpose of the organization was (*a*) 'ad iniurias ulciscendas' by legal process and otherwise,

Picardy was held to include the whole of the Low Countries.[1] The more distant regions were divided between the English and French nations, the French embracing all the Latin races, the English including the Germans and all inhabitants of the north and east of Europe. It is clear that the classification is to a certain extent arbitrary,[2] and in later times constituted a very unequal division of the academic population, the French nation often outnumbering the other three. But at the beginning of the thirteenth century it is quite possible that it represented as fair a division of the countries from which the bulk of Parisian students came as could be effected consistently with the preservation of the number four. This number was in all probability adopted in imitation of the practice of the early Italian universities. If it gave the strictly French members of the university somewhat less influence than the rest, that also was in accordance with Bolognese ideas.

The French nation was, however, far from submitting unquestioningly to this preponderance of the foreign element in the faculty. More than once we find the faculty of arts

Frequency of schism.

(b) to elect officers for this purpose and for collecting and administering funds with the same object. See above, p. 312. In 1251 we find the English nation prescribing the studies of candidates for 'determination' (*Chartul.* i, No. 201). Both the nations and their officers are found performing precisely the same functions as were discharged by the other faculties in relation to their own studies. [We cannot but think that Rashdall complicated his narrative by identifying with the later proctors of the nations the earlier proctors appointed to represent the *universitas* at the papal court in definite cases. (See above, p. 312, n. 1.) Also he identified too closely the nations with the faculty of arts. The fullest, general treatment of the nations is still that of Alexander Budinszky, who studied at Paris (from 1871) and in 1876 published

his *Die Universität Paris und die Fremden an derselben in Mittelalter*. The documents in the *Chartularium* and its *Auctarium* have to be supplemented by the registers and accounts still in manuscript; cf. Jean Bonnerot in *Bulletin of the International Committee of Historical Sciences*, i, pt. v (July 1928), pp. 677–80. The best detailed account of the organization into nations is in G. C. Boyce, *The English-German Nation in the University of Paris* (Saint Catherine Press, Bruges, 1927), with a good bibliography.]

[1] In 1358 the Meuse was fixed upon as the boundary between 'Picardy' and France. Bulaeus, iv. 346.

[2] If this is his meaning, Denifle (i. 95) rightly contrasts the 'artificial' nations of Paris with the 'natural' nations of Bologna.

CHAP. V, temporarily splitting up into two bodies—the French electing
§ I. a rector of their own and the other three nations another
rector.[1] In the year 1266 the liability of the university to
such schisms had been so signally manifested that, upon an
appeal to the papal legate, a dissentient nation was accorded
a constitutional right to secede from the other nations and
elect a rector of its own, provided that it succeeded in satis-
fying a board of arbitrators consisting of the three senior
theologians and the four senior canonists in the university of
the reasonableness of its grievances.[2]

Provinces. 　At a much later period these nations were subdivided into
provinces or tribes, which had regular deans at their head,
and in some cases the officers of the nation were chosen from
the provinces or tribes in regular succession and the votes
of the national congregations were taken by provinces.[3]

[1] This was the case when the
Statute of 1249, prescribing the
mode of electing a rector, was introduced. See above p. 314, n. 4.

[2] Cf. the statute in *Chartul*. i,
No. 409; Bulaeus, iii. 375. The
fact that there were often two
rectors at Paris is not without importance in suggesting a possible
source of two 'Rectores sive Procuratores' at Oxford and Cambridge. See below, vol. iii, c.
xii, § ii.

[3] Thus the French nation was
divided into five 'provinces' corresponding with the five ecclesiastical provinces of France which
were subdivided into 'dioceses'.
We hear of 'magistri de quinque
provinciis consuetis nostre nationis'
in 1327. Bulaeus, iv. 213; *Chartul*.
ii, No. 871. The German nation
(as the English was usually called
after about 1440) was divided at
first into an English and a non-
English province, afterwards into
three 'tribes', viz. (1) *Altorum
Almanorum*, (2) *Bassorum Almanorum*, (3) *Insularium* or *Scotorum*.
[In the middle of the fourteenth century we hear also of a 'Provincia

Sueciae et Daciae'; and the English-
German nation appears undivided
under a 'provisor' (*Auctarium*, i,
pp. xviii, xix, &c.)] Picardy was
also at one time divided into two
sections of five dioceses each. Bulaeus, iii. 558 *sq.*; Thurot, pp. 19,
20. The Norman nation seems to
have been divided into seven 'epi-
scopatus' as early as 1275. Bulaeus,
iii. 314 *sq.*; *Chartul*. i, No. 460.
The internal arrangements of the
nations as to the mode of voting
and election to national offices
varied considerably in different
nations and at different periods. It
does not seem worth while to enter
into further detail. Sometimes we
find elaborate processes of indirect
election, in which the first nomina-
tor was elected by lot ('per inven-
tionem nigre fabe'). *Chartul*. ii,
No. 997. The provinces had at
times separate funds, meetings, and
festivals. [Boyce, *op. cit.*, p. 30,
shows that the movement to change
the name of the English nation
began in 1367; cf. *Auctarium*,
i. 529, 815, 816. 'The first use of
Alemania as a title of the nation
occurred in August 1400, but it was

III. *The Faculties and the Rectorship*

Such an account as our data permit has now been given *The superior faculties left outside the nations.* of the origin of the celebrated four nations at Paris. We have seen that a new organization has risen within the university, composed not of all its members, but of the most numerous section of it—the masters of arts. We have seen how from the first the officers of the federated nations had begun to act as the officers and representatives not only of the faculty of arts but of the whole university of masters. The faculty of arts had thus attained the full attributes of a corporation or group of corporations with seals, officers, and common funds, at a time when the university proper was still in an acephalous and half-organized condition, and when the doctors of the superior faculties, who were left outside the nations, possessed hardly any separate organization at all. The eventual predominance of the faculty of arts and of its head, the rector, in the whole university, was rendered almost inevitable by this state of things. In order, however, to trace in detail the complicated history of the relations between the faculties, it will be necessary to go back to the origin of the distinction between the different classes of teachers in the schools of the Middle Ages.

We have seen how clearly the distinction between two main branches of study—theology and arts—was recognized in the time of Abelard. The teaching of the civil law was introduced into Paris soon after the revival of that study under Irnerius at Bologna; and the study of the canon law was *Canon law, c. 1177.* fully established when Giraldus Cambrensis studied and taught in the Parisian schools about 1177.[1] Indeed, although the legal fame of Paris was never comparable with that of Bologna, Daniel of Morley, who visited its schools at about this period, speaks of law as the most prominent study of the place.[2] Medicine was certainly taught in Paris at about the *Medicine.*

not until 1442–3 that it was customarily employed.']

[1] *Opera*, i. 44 *sq.*

[2] Daniel of Morley (in Norfolk) visited Paris, *c.* 1170–90, and gives an amusing account of seeing 'quos-

dam bestiales in scholis gravi authoritate sedes occupare, habentes coram se scamna duo vel tria, et desuper codices importabiles aureis litteris Ulpiani traditiones representantes, necnon et tenentes stilos

CHAP. V, same time. A medical school in a great capital could not be
§ 1. without a certain importance, but the Parisian School of
Medicine always stood far below those of Salerno and Montpellier. Alexander Neckam, who studied at Paris some time
between 1175 and 1195, thus sums up the studies of his time:

The four
faculties.

Hic florent artes, coelestis pagina regnat,
Stant leges, lucet ius: medicina viget.[1]

Civil law forbidden, 1219. Such were the four 'faculties' recognized by the medieval
universities. It should be added that the study of the civil
law was forbidden in 1219 by Honorius III,[2] not (as is
sometimes represented) in a narrow spirit of hostility to legal
or to secular studies in general, but because it threatened to
extinguish the study of theology in the one great theological
school of Europe.[3] It is probable that the Pope's zeal for the

plumbeos in manibus, cum quibus asteriscos et obelos in libris suis quadam reverentia depingebant'. Printed by Prof. Holland in *Collectanea* (Oxf. Hist. Soc.), ii. 171. [For Daniel of Morley see Thorndike, *History of Magic and Experimental Science*, ii. 171 *sqq.*, with a copious bibliography; cf. Haskins, *Studies in Mediaeval Science*, pp. 126, 127.]

[1] *De laudibus divinae sapientiae*, ed. Wright, 1863, p. 452. [A much more important description of Parisian studies at this time is Neckam's list of text-books (1179–94), edited by Haskins from a Caius College manuscript, with an introduction, *Studies*, pp. 356–76.]

[2] Bulaeus, iii. 96; *Chartul.* i, No. 32. At the same time its study was forbidden to priests, regulars, and beneficed clerks. It was afterwards explained that the last restriction did not extend to mere parochial cures; while universities and whole orders frequently obtained dispensations. No general dispensation appears to have been given for Paris. [For the decretal *Super specula* see M. Fournier in *Nouvelle revue historique de droit français et étranger*, 1890, pp. 115–18; A. Tardif, *ibid.*, 1880, pp. 291–4;

A. Luchaire, *La Société française au temps de Philippe-Auguste* (Paris, 1903), pp. 109, 110; and E. Chenon in *Mélanges Fitting*, i (Montpellier, 1907), pp. 198–201. An ordinance of Philip the Fair shows that Philip Augustus was instrumental in procuring the Bull, in order to emphasize the validity and independence of the customary law of France. The motive alleged was the desire to encourage the study of theology.]

[3] There can be no doubt that the civil law continued to be studied and quoted by the canonists of Paris; and the education of a Parisian canonist usually included a study of the civil law at another university. The evidence collected by Péries (pp. 99–108) fails to prove that formal and avowed lectures in civil law were ever given at Paris after 1219, still less that degrees were ever taken in that faculty. The only exception is an allusion to 'Bachelarii decretales et leges legentes' in 1251 (*Chartul.* i, No. 197), which need not imply more than that a certain instruction in civil law was mixed with that of canon law in extraordinary lectures. Much of the later evi-

theological fame of Paris was seconded by the French king's suspicion of a legal system which endangered the supremacy of the customary law of his country in the courts of his capital. After this change the four faculties of Paris were theology, canon law or decrees, medicine, and arts[1]—the three former being styled the superior faculties as contra-distinguished to the inferior faculty of arts, whose course was regarded more or less as a preparation for the other three. In what relation did the professors of these four faculties stand to one another in the earliest days of the Parisian guild of masters?

From the beginning of the thirteenth century the docu-ments show that the society or university included masters of three faculties, theology, law, and arts; the masters of medicine are not yet mentioned as a distinct element.[2] And in the earliest corporate act on the part of the university itself which is preserved to us—the deed by which in 1221 that body transfers its rights over the Place S. Jacques to the newly arrived Dominican order as a site for their convent—it appears distinctly that the members of all these faculties were included in the same magisterial corporation. The consideration for which the university sold its property was to be a right of burial for masters 'of whatever faculty'[3] in

Theology always distinguished from arts.

dence produced by Péries tends the other way. [On the other hand, it is clear that dispensations in favour of those *leges legentes* at Paris could be obtained (cf. Fitting on a *disputatio* held at Angers, in *Nouvelle revue hist. de droit*, 1905, pp. 724, 725). Paetow, arguing from passages in the satires of Henry d'Andeli and John Garland, contends that Péries was quite right; see his edition of the *Morale Scolarium*, p. 157, note to line 107. The passages are not very convincing. For the erroneous use made by Péries of the Bull of Innocent VI, August 1358 (*Chartul.* iii, No. 1242), see Denifle's note *ad hoc*.]

[1] Jourdain, No. 15; *Chartul.* i, No. 16. Denifle (i. 70) well remarks that 'die Promotionsfrage war in Paris der erste Schritt zur Facul-tätenbildung'.

[2] 'Universis doctoribus sacre pagine decretorum et liberalium artium Parisius commorantibus.' (*Chartul.* i, No. 8.) This was the usual order of precedence, though at Oxford the medical doctors have now acquired equality with the lawyers. Where there was a faculty of civil law, its doctors ranked between the decretists and the medicals. The licentiates and bachelors of superior faculties ranked among themselves in the same order; bachelors of theology (at least *Baccalaurei formati*) ranked above regent masters of arts, but not so bachelors of the other superior faculties.

[3] 'Pro quolibet magistro, cuius-cumque facultatis fuerit de nostris.' Bulaeus, iii. 106; *Chartul.* i, No. 42.

CHAP. V,
§ 1.
the Church of the Order together with certain masses and 'whole psalters', and it is added that, if the deceased is a theologian, he is to be buried in the chapter-house, if 'of another Faculty'[1] in the cloister. The document bears the seals of the individual doctors of theology and of them alone: the theologians are not merely members but representatives of the university.[2]

The superior faculties always distinct corporations within the university.
As soon as the masters of theology and canon law became at all numerous, they must have held meetings of their own apart from those of the masters of arts. The artists could not have taken part in the inception of a theological master, in a theological disputation, or in the discussion of a case of heresy submitted to them by the bishop of the diocese. The agreement of 1213 recognizes the right of each faculty—including the medical doctors (who are here for the first time mentioned in connexion with the university)—to testify to the qualifications of candidates to the licence in its own department, and this right practically involved the regulation of the studies and the discipline of the students.

Voting by faculties.
At the same time it does not follow that, when the united university of masters met in general congregation, they voted by faculties in the manner which afterwards obtained. It is, however, probable that in so far as anything like 'voting' took place in these primitive assemblies, the consent of all faculties would have been practically necessary to make a resolution or statute binding upon all. It would have been a matter of little importance to the theologian to be denied the

---

[1] 'Alterius facultatis.' The distinction between 'alter' and 'alius' was habitually neglected in the Middle Ages.

[2] According to Denifle (i. 71) the *word* faculty is first found in the sense of a distinct branch of learning in connexion with Paris in a Bull of Honorius III addressed to the scholars of Paris in 1219. But Giraldus Cambrensis, in his celebrated description of Oxford, speaks of ' doctores diversarum facultatum' as early as *circa* 1184

(see *Opera*, i. 73) [also, i. 48, 'praeceptor in ea facultate' of Paris. The word was used by Boethius of disciplinary instruction in dialectic, and is frequently found in a more technical sense in twelfth-century writers; cf. Ueberweg-Geyer, p. 352.] Its use for a body of teachers in a particular subject grew out of the earlier usage by imperceptible stages. Cf. the use of ' facultas nostra' in Bulaeus, iii. 280; *Chartul.* i, No. 246.

fellowship or *consortium* of the artists, if he were still admitted to the disputations, discussions, and inceptions of his theological brethren. But we really know nothing of the procedure of university congregations before the growth of the rectorship.

We have already traced the process by which the nations of artists and their officers grew up within the university, and to a large extent superseded it in the conduct of what was strictly speaking the business of the whole body. We have seen that though the rector was technically the rector of the artists only, he was from the first employed in the collection of money for university purposes, in the conduct of university litigation, and in the execution of university decrees. He was from the first the representative or agent of the whole university: he rapidly rose to the position of its *Head*, though still elected only by the faculty of arts. This predominance of the 'inferior' faculty of arts in the University of Paris is explained in exactly the same way as the predominance of the 'lower' house in the British Parliament. The licentiates, bachelors, and students of the superior faculties remained subject to the authority of the nations[1] (though their studies and exercises were regulated by the several colleges of doctors); so that the power of the purse lay almost exclusively with the rector and masters of the faculty of arts.[2]

Impor-tance of rector founded on power of the purse.

[1] If M.A. they had votes as regent or non-regent masters. If B.A. they were 'iurati facultatis Artium'. The authority of the masters of arts over the bachelors of the superior faculties who were not B.A. or M.A. is rather a constitutional anomaly, but, when once established, would be sanctioned by the oath to obey the customs of the university.

[2] The old theory—that of Du Boulay and Crevier—was that the masters of the superior faculties were originally included in the nations, and that the faculties did not, so to speak, emerge out of them till after the mendicant controversy. This view is inconsistent with all the facts; and with it goes

the boast, [if it was intended in this sense], that the university was 'founded in Arts'. It is possible, however, that though the theologians and canonists were from the first members of the university, they were considered to be so as ex-masters of arts, and that admission to the university was originally obtained only by inception in arts. Filesacus, the historian of the theological faculty, declares that in the time of Philip Augustus there were no inceptions in the theological faculty (ap. Conringius, v. 455). If this was so, it would go far to explain the confusion introduced into the whole system by the mendicant doctors, who had not graduated in arts.

CHAP. V,
§ 1.
His posi-
tion in
general
congrega-
tions. If it should still appear strange that when the four faculties met together they should have been presided over by the head of the lowest of them, it must be remembered that (if we may infer the earliest mode of proceeding from the later practice) there was no actual debate in the meetings of the whole university. When the affair had been laid before the congregation by the rector, the matter was debated by the respective faculties and nations, and the assent of each faculty and nation signified by the respective presiding officers. The proceedings thus resolved themselves into a sort of conference between these officials, which could be conducted without any of them asserting a formal superiority over the rest. But it is clear that in such conferences the representative of the great mass of the university must have been from the first the most conspicuous and important figure. The internal organization of the superior faculties developed itself much more slowly than that of the artists. As soon as there were separate meetings of these faculties, the senior doctor must have enjoyed the right of convoking them and presiding in them, but it is not till 1264 that we actually hear of 'deans' of the superior faculties.[1] It is not till 1252 that we hear of one of the superior faculties making written statutes of its own;[2] nor till about 1270 that the faculties of law and medicine acquired corporate seals.[3] At first the deans appear to act rather side by side with the rector than in obedience to his authority; though from the first the initiative and superior

Deans.

Statutes
and seals
of superior
faculties.

The
rector
and the
deans.

---

[1] In 1265 there is a dispute between the chancellor, who claims to be the sole head of the faculty, and the theologians, who claim that 'hactenus pacifice observata consuetudine Parisius sit obtentum ut antiquior ex eisdem magistris in actu regendi nomen decani habeat inter eos et ipsis indicat festa per nuntium proprium, et alia faciat que ad suum noscuntur officium pertinere.' *Chartul*. i, No. 399. In 1267 we find deans of the other two superior faculties. Jourdain, No. 216; *Chartul*. i, No. 416. The deanship of medicine had become elective by 1338 (*Chartul*. ii, No. 1017). The deanship of canon law was also elective; that of theology was always held by the senior secular doctor.

[2] Bulaeus, iii. 245; *Chartul*. i, No. 200.

[3] The step is complained of as an innovation by the ever-jealous chancellor, *circa* 1271 in the case of law, in 1274 in the case of medicine, *Chartul*. i, Nos. 446, 451. [In 1359 the faculty of theology claimed that it had had a seal for a long time: *Chartul*. iii, No. 1246, p. 62.]

importance of the rector is plain enough. During the heat of the great conflict with the mendicants (1250–60) which contributed so much to develop the importance of the rectorship, we hear of no disputes on this head. When the tie of a common enmity was removed, the superior faculties seem to have awaked to the fact that they were falling under the authority of an official not elected by themselves. Hence perhaps the attempts to increase their own corporate solidarity by separate statutes, seals and officers. At about the same time (1279) we find a dispute arising between the faculty of arts on the one hand and the faculties of canon law and medicine on the other as to the manner in which the latter should be summoned to general congregations.[1] The superior faculties contended that the rector was bound to wait in person upon the deans, who would in turn summon their respective societies. The rector, on the other hand, maintained that he was at liberty to send a bedel with the summons. A little later (1283–4) we find the theologians contending that the rector could only summon them through their dean 'by way of supplication and request'.[2] In both cases the rector eventually carried the day. The dean of theology continued for some time longer to maintain a claim to be consulted before the day was fixed for a general congregation; but both incidents testify to the fact that the rector's right to summon all the faculties was by this time practically undisputed. They no doubt point back to a time when 'general congregations' were summoned rather by arrangement between the rector and deans than by the previous summons of the former.

We have seen that as early as 1244—that is to say, as early as we have any certain evidence of the existence of a single rector—he is employed in the execution of the university decrees. In 1255 he is styled by the secular masters of all faculties 'Rector of our University'.[3] In 1259 he is addressed by the Pope as 'Rector of the University' and required to

Gradual emergence of rector into head of the university.

[1] Bulaeus, iii. 445; *Chartul.* i, Nos. 490, 493.

[2] 'Supplicando et rogando.' Jourdain, No. 274 (p. 49 *b*); *Char-* tul. i, No. 515.

[3] Bulaeus, iii. 257; *Chartul.* i, No. 230.

enforce payment of a debt incurred in the name of the whole university.[1] In 1276 a deed runs in the name of the deans of canon law and medicine and the rector and proctors of the nations (mentioned in that order) 'by the assent and consent of all the masters regent at Paris in the aforesaid faculties and in arts'.[2] The eight masters of theology assent as individuals, their names being recited at the end of the deed. In 1289 we find the rector mentioned before the 'deans of faculties, the proctors of the nations and the masters of the four faculties'.[3] It has seemed worth while to enumerate these facts because they will enable the reader to observe for himself the gradual steps by which the rector emerged from an undefined initiative or presidency to an acknowledged headship of the whole university. It is really impossible to say at what exact date the rector may be considered to have attained this position. He was from the first the executive officer, and the only executive officer, of the whole university. By about the decade 1280–90 he had unquestionably attained the presidency if not the formal headship of the whole society, and the faculty of arts was already endeavouring to convert that presidency into a formal and acknowledged headship. It was not, as we shall see, until the middle of the following century that these efforts were crowned with entire success. One of the means by which the faculty endeavoured to effect their object is of especial interest and constitutional importance.

The oath *ad quem-cumque statum*, *c.* 1256. The oath administered to a bachelor of the faculty of arts upon his determination had at first bound him to obey the rector only 'as long as he should profess the faculty of arts'.[4] About the year 1256 or earlier it would seem that this last clause was omitted; and the oath to 'obey the liberties and honest customs of the faculty' was supplemented by the words 'to whatever state you shall come'.[5] Sooner or later similar

[1] Jourdain, No. 184; *Chartul.* i, No. 330.

[2] Jourdain, No. 216; *Chartul.* i, No. 416.

[3] *Chartul.* ii, No. 559.

[4] 'Item eidem iniungatur, quod per totam quadragesimam et dein-

ceps, quamdiu facultatem arcium profitebitur in illis studendo vel regendo, mandato rectoris et procuratoris pareat in licitis et honestis.' (1252) *Chartul.* i, No. 201.

[5] 'Item iurabitis, quod libertates singulas facultatis et consuetudines

words were added to an explicit oath of obedience to the rector, thus making the subjection of every member of the faculty of arts to that official permanent and unalterable.[1] As at least the vast majority of the secular masters of all faculties had taken the oath,[2] the ingenious change practically secured the supremacy of the rector over the whole university. If in a certain technical sense the rector was still the head of the artists only, the members of the superior faculties were henceforth extraordinary or non-regent members of the faculty of arts. Hence there could be no question about the rector's right to summon them to congregations, to enforce against them the decrees of the whole university, and to declare them 'perjured and rebels' if they disobeyed. The new oath supplied a much-needed connecting link between the four faculties. In time it even made possible the establishment of the principle that a majority of the faculties had the right to override the opposition of one of them. The rector, after hearing the decision of the several faculties, pronounced in accordance with the decision of the majority; in other words, he commanded every individual member of the university to obey the decision of the whole body. Hence the almost superstitious importance attached to his rectorial 'conclusion', which was deemed essential to the legal validity of any resolution of the university.[3] The oath of

facultatis honestas et totius universitatis privilegia deffendetis, ad quemcumque statum deveneritis.' *Chartul.* i, No. 501. This document is of *circa* 1280.

[1] *Chartul.* ii, App., No. 1675, p. 674.

[2] It was by no means the habitual practice of canonists to take the M.A., but most of them would probably have studied arts up to B.A. [Although in the middle of the fourteenth century masters in medicine were nearly always masters in arts, the obligation to have been licensed in arts was not clearly stated until 1426, when Pope Martin V granted a petition from the faculty of medicine to this effect

(*Chartul.* iv, No. 2274). Hence the necessity of the oath exacted from masters of the higher faculties who had not passed through arts (*ibid.* ii, p. 685). Cf. E. Wickersheimer, *Commentaires de la faculté de médecine*, pp. xviii, xix. Although a medical student could not simultaneously study or teach in the faculty of arts, a rector of the university, during his period of office, might actually be studying for the degree in a higher faculty.]

[3] A very curious light is thrown upon the nature of the bond which connected the superior faculties with the parent body, of which, as I have endeavoured to show, they were offshoots, by a deed of

obedience to the rector was the key-stone of the academic constitution.[1]

composition between the faculty of arts and the theologians in 1341. The rector having on one occasion sent a written summons to congregation to the dean of theology by a deputy, the latter refused to summon his faculty. Thereupon the faculty of arts—not the university—expelled the dean from their society on the ground that he had acted 'contra iura et libertates rectorie et per consequens facultatis artium predicte, contra etiam iuramentum ab ipso magistro Symone dicte facultati artium olim prestitum temere veniendo'. And the dean on his part expressly admitted 'quia a magnis temporibus et per magna tempora fuerat et erat iuratus dicte facultatis artium'; and supplicated the faculty 'si iniuste esset privatus, facere sibi iustitiam; et in casu dubii, facere sibi gratiam, et ipsum dicte facultati artium reunire' (Bulaeus, iv. 268; *Chartul.* ii, No. 1051). So in 1451 at a congregation of the faculty of arts, we read that 'vocati fuerunt et comparuerunt multi magistri de singulis facultatibus superioribus singularum nacionum *ad consulendum*' (Bulaeus, v. 560; [*Chartul.* iv, No. 2681]. So on another occasion when a difficulty was experienced in getting a representative of the theological faculty to go on an embassy to the king, the university 'volebat in crastino Facultatem Artium Praeclaram congregari apud S. Julianum Pauperem solemniter per D. Rectorem, processuram contra eosdem Magistros nostros (a technical name for doctors of divinity) quorum uterque erat Magister Artium, omnibus viis et modis possibilibus, etiam usque ad privationem inclusive ipsorum Magistrorum nostrorum tanquam periurorum, si praedictam Ambassiatam recusarent accipere.'

Bulaeus, v. 583.

Denifle holds that the rector was not recognized as the head of the faculty of arts till 1274 (pp. 110, 119, 120), or as the head of the university till the middle of the fourteenth century. I have not space to examine his arguments in detail, but the contention rests mainly on the fact that the rector's name is not mentioned in the enacting clause of the statutes of the faculty till 1274, or in those of the university till 1338 (pp. 109, 110). Denifle relies upon the analogy of Oxford and other universities; but, though there was never any doubt as to the chancellor being head of the University of Oxford, the statutes, &c., by no means uniformly run in the name of the chancellor and university. Besides, in 1309 Clement V does speak of a suit as being the suit of the rector and university (Jourdain, No. 385); and in 1327 a statute is 'facta per venerabilem et discretum virum magistrum Joannem Buridam rectorem Universitatis supradicte'. (Bulaeus, iv. 212; *Chartul.* ii, No. 870.) Denifle further alleges (p. 121) that the rector cannot have been considered head of the university in 1283 or 1284, since the faculty of arts at that time declares that the Pope was head of the university. This is inaccurate. What the faculty says is that 'Parisiensis universitas non credit nec confitetur *secundum suum rectorem* habere caput aliud a vestra Sanctitate' (Jourdain, No. 274), or according to Denifle's reading, 'supra suum rectorem' (*Chartul.* i, p. 618). The words distinctly imply that the rector was head of the university. What they deny is the head-

For note 1 see p. 331.

From this time at least, there could be no doubt about the rector's position as virtual head of the whole corporation. As a constitutional technicality it might be maintained, and ship of the chancellor. Moreover, it is useless for Denifle to explain that in 1261 'rector universitatis' means 'rector universitatis arti-starum', when as early as 1255 we find the secular masters of all faculties speaking of the rector as 'rectorem universitatis nostre'. Another good instance of his recognition occurs in 1278, when the king enjoined that the candidate selected by the university for a chaplaincy in its gift should be presented by the rector (*Chartul.* i, No. 482). Father Denifle hardly realized that the question whether the rector was or was not 'head' of the university is one which might have been answered differently by different persons at the same time. I admit that the rector's headship was not formally placed beyond dispute till the middle of the fourteenth century. But Denifle's treatment of the subject obscures the fact that his *virtual* headship was established, and his *formal* headship persistently asserted by the faculty of arts, at a much earlier date. [The documents published in the third volume of the *Chartularium* (Nos. 1246, 1504–22) illustrate the nature of the controversy in the fourteenth century. Early in 1359 the faculty of theology protested against the claim of the artists that the rector was *caput aut superior* of the university and set out facts alleged to prove the contrary (No. 1246). In 1385 Pope Clement VII instituted an inquiry into the charges brought by the university against the chancellor, John Blanchart. The main charge against the chancellor was his arbitrary and venal use of his powers in granting the licence, but inciden-tally his claim to be head of the university was resisted. The claim turned on questions of precedence, on his right to refuse to attend congregations when summoned by the rector, &c. (e.g. pp. 408, 419). A Franciscan who, at the end of a sermon, said 'Orate pro Universi-tate et pro cancellario, qui est caput Universitatis', was forced to retract publicly (No. 1300). The chancellor complained, on the other hand, that a newly licensed doctor of decrees had 'determined' that the chancellor, by refusing to obey the rector, was a heretic (pp. 409, 410). For examples of letters addressed to the chancellor as head of the university, cf. Nos. 1610 (1378), 1692 (1394) with Denifle's notes; see also the note on p. 366. For further comment on the disputes of 1385–6 see below, p. 400 n.]

Denifle's contention that the rector was not head of the faculty of arts, but only of the nations, till 1274, rests on the same inadequate ground as his contention with respect to the university—i.e. that his name does not appear in the acts of the faculty. The fact that, when the university proclaimed its own dissolution in 1255, it sealed the deed with the seals of the four nations, 'utpote ab universitatis Collegio separati', at most goes to establish a distinction between the nations and the university, not between the nations and the faculty of arts (below, p. 384).

---

[1] It was probably on this account that we find it alleged that the faculty of arts can expel from the university, while the superior faculties cannot expel even from their own 'consortium' without the consent of the university. *Chartul.* ii, No. 930.

no doubt was maintained, by the theological faculty and
especially by the sworn enemies of the faculty of arts, the
Dominican theologians, that the rector was not the head of the
university, as it was maintained in more recent times by
the learned Dominican who has thrown so much light upon
the history of the medieval universities. The fact that the
precedence of the rector at ecclesiastical functions was till
the middle of the following century disputed by the dean of
theology—often, it must be remembered, a bishop or archbishop—proves little against his virtual headship. An officer
who summons the meetings of a society, whom every member
of the society is bound to obey, and who executes its decrees,
is for practical purposes the head or at least the president of
that society. In the English House of Lords the royal dukes
and the Archbishop of Canterbury take precedence of the
Lord Chancellor; but he is the unquestioned president of
that House, though his very limited powers in that capacity
supply but an incomplete analogy to the rector's importance
in the university congregations.[1]

Depen-
dence of
theologi-
cal faculty
on the
chan-
cellor.
Another circumstance which tends to explain the facility
with which the faculty of arts managed to thrust their rector
into the position of head of the whole university is the
peculiarly close relation in which the most important and,
in a sense, most ancient of the superior faculties stood to the
chancellor. As late as 1264 the chancellor is found claiming
to be *ex officio* dean of the theological faculty,[2] and, though
this claim is denied by the masters, it is certain that there

---

[1] [Cardinal Ehrle recently re-
examined the problems discussed
by Denifle and Rashdall (*I più
antichi statuti della facoltà teologica
dell'università di Bologna*, pp. clx–
lxxi). He inclines to the view
that the headship of the rector,
both in the faculty of arts and in
the university was definitely secured
later than Denifle admitted and
much later than Rashdall urged.
This view seems to be based
upon his distinction between the
faculty as a whole and the nations,
and between the acts of the faculty
and the acts of the rector. This
distinction, so far as it goes, is
sound, but Ehrle seems to deduce
too much from it and from varieties
of phrasing in academic documents.
The oath *ad quemcumque statum*
referred explicitly to the faculty,
and it is impossible to distinguish
between the acts of the faculty and
those of the nations acting together.
Ehrle was perhaps unconsciously influenced by the system at Bologna.]

[2] *Chartul.* i, No. 399.

must have been a time when they had no head other than the chancellor. The chancellor was himself originally chief theological teacher of the cathedral school; and not only the chancellor but the canons of Paris long retained the right of teaching theology and canon law without any authorization from the faculties.[1] The chancellor was thus the natural head of the theological faculty in its relations to the bishop of the diocese and to the Church at large. The earliest recorded instances of the corporate action of the theological faculty are occasions on which it was formally asked for its decision on a theological question, or when its members were called upon to meet as the assessors of the bishop in a trial for heresy.[2] On such occasions, even after the university had completely shaken off the yoke of the capitular official, and the theological faculty had acquired a dean of its own, the chancellor continued to preside over the deliberations of the theological doctors. But it was clearly impossible for the chancellor to act as the head and representative of the faculty in its relations with the masters of the other faculties. Of the guild of masters, the chancellor was not necessarily even a member; much of the early corporate activity of both faculty and university directly grew out of resistance to his pretensions. Thus the faculty was for a time left without a head at all in its relations to the other masters; and even when a dean of theology was appointed his position was weakened by the rival claims of the chancellor.

It was this extra-academical position of the chancellor which prevented him becoming, like the chancellor of Oxford,

The extra-academical chancellorship explains anomalous position.

[1] Thus the canons of Paris are specially exempted from the privileges conferred upon other masters and scholars by the charter of Philip Augustus in 1200, on the ground that they have special privileges of their own as canons. *Chartul*. i, No. 1. Their position as canons of course originally gave them no rights in the university. [Clement VII allowed that one canon, being a doctor of decrees might retain regency by lecturing in the cloister of Notre Dame instead of the 'Clo Brunel'. See the documents of the suit between the chapter and the university in 1384 (*Chartul*. iii, Nos. 1486–9).]

[2] For early instances see *Chartul*. i, Nos. 16, 21; [cf. Powicke, *Stephen Langton*, p. 62]. We find the theological doctors acting as the assessors of the bishop in a case of heresy in 1240–1. (Jourdain, No. 59; *Chartul*. i, No. 128.)

the head of the magisterial guild.[1] At the same time the close connexion between the chancellor and the theological faculty long prevented the latter acquiring a head who might have taken that position in the university organization which would naturally have been accorded to the head of what always ranked as the first among the faculties of Paris. The position in which that faculty was placed by its peculiar relations with the extra-academic chancellor thus explains that singular and otherwise unintelligible feature of the Parisian constitution by which the headship of the whole university was vested in an officer elected exclusively by and from the 'inferior' faculty of arts.

IV. *The Great Dispersion and the Papal Privileges*

Profit-
able mis-
fortunes. The university, as we have already seen and we shall have frequent occasion to observe, lived upon its misfortunes. The 'town and gown' disturbance of 1200 procured its first chapter from the Crown: the oppression of the chancellor produced its first batch of papal privileges. The third era in the growth of its privileges is introduced like the first by a tavern brawl; but this time the quarrel brought it into collision not merely with the citizens or the chapter, but with the monarchy itself. Its eventful triumph over court and capital united shows that a new force had been introduced into the political system of Europe—that a new order had arisen who were to share the influence hitherto monopolized by nobles and priests.

Carnival
Riot of
1228–9. During the carnival of 1228–9 some students were taking the air in a suburban region known as the Bourg of S. Marcel, when they entered a tavern and 'by chance found good and sweet wine there'.[2] A dispute arose with the landlord over

---

[1] In 1385 the university resolved 'quod ipse Cancellarius Parisiensis nec est caput Universitatis *nec alicuius Facultatis*'. Bulaeus, *Remarques sur la dignité, &c., du recteur*, pp. 7, 8. [Du Boulay was referring to the disputes of 1385–6; see above, p. 331 n. One of the chancellor's witnesses testified that 'in Universitate . . . fuit aliquociens

tractatum quod si cancellarius vellet fateri rectorem esse maiorem et quod deberet precedere eum, et fateri quod male fecerat quia precesserat eum in sede, dimitteretur in pace'; *Chartul.* iii, p. 419.]

[2] 'Invenerunt ibi casu vinum optimum in taberna quadam et ad bibendum suave.' Matt. Paris, *Hist. Mai.*, ed. Luard, iii. 166, 167.

the reckoning. From words the disputants rapidly proceeded to blows—to pulling of ears and tearing of hair.[1] The worsted inn-keeper called in his neighbours, who compelled the clerks to retire severely beaten. The next day they returned with strong reinforcements of gownsmen armed with swords and sticks, who broke into the tavern, avenged their comrades on the host and his neighbours, set the taps running, and then 'flown with insolence and wine' sallied forth into the streets to amuse themselves at the expense of peaceable citizens, men and women alike. So the clerks continued to disport themselves until the tables were once more turned in favour of 'town' by the appearance on the scene of the provost and his satellites—the savage police of a savage city. The Prior of S. Marcel had complained to the papal legate and to the bishop, who had urged upon the regent, Blanche of Castille, the instant suppression of the riot. The Queen 'with female impulsiveness' (as Matthew Paris has it) rashly ordered the provost and the mercenary body-guard (*ruptarii*) to punish the authors of the outrages. The soldiers fell upon the offenders or (if we may trust our historian) a party of perfectly innocent students engaged in their holiday games outside the walls; and several of them were killed in the ensuing mêlée. The masters, availing themselves of the singular mode Suspension of lectures. of protest expressly conceded to them by royal authority, suspended their lectures. But complaints to the bishop and legate were alike in vain. We may judge of the strength of the feeling against the university on the part of the bishop and Church of Paris by the fact that in an age when under ordinary circumstances the slightest insult to a 'clerk' was thought adequate cause for wholesale excommunication or interdict, the murder of a number of students by a brutal soldiery was welcomed by their official superiors as tending to the humiliation of the upstart university. The Court was much under clerical influence, and was particularly attached to the special enemies of the university, the canons of Paris. And in this one instance the legate took the same side: it was but four years since he had been mobbed

[1] 'Alapas dare et capillos laniare.' Matt. Paris, *loc. cit.*

CHAP. V, on account of his conduct in the matter of the university
§ 1. seal.[1]

Dispersion   Finding the 'cessation' ineffectual, the masters on the
of 1229. Easter Monday following[2] proceeded to a more extreme
remedy. They resolved that, if justice were not done them
within a month, they would dissolve the university for a
period of six years, and would not return even at the expiration of that period unless satisfactory redress had been
granted in the interval.[3] And the masters were as good as
their word. The great mass of the masters and scholars left
Paris. Many of them no doubt accepted the pressing invitation of Henry III of England, crossed the channel, and
reinforced the rising universities of Oxford and Cambridge.[4]
Others retired to the smaller *studia generalia* or cathedral
schools of France—Toulouse, Orleans, Reims, and especially
Angers, which perhaps dates its existence as a university
from this dispersion. Here they could pursue their studies

[1] The fullest account of the affair is given by Matt. Paris, *Hist. Mai.* iii. 166–8. Bernard Gui says: 'Anno Domini . . . MCCXXIX facta fuit Parisius inter scolares dissensio, quam mox secuta est ad tempus multipharia dispersio. Alii quidem Remis, alii Andegavis, alii Aurelianis, alii vero in Angliam, alii in Italiam vel Hispaniam; sive in alias mundi provincias, causa studii sunt profecti. Multi quoque magistri et scolares Tholosam venerunt et rexerunt ibidem' (*Rec. des historiens de France*, xxi. 695). So Alberic of Trois Fontaines, *Chron.* (*M.G.H., Scriptores*, xxiii. 923): 'Guerra pessima nimis et crudelis orta est Parisiis intrante quadragesima inter clericos et laycos satis pro nichilo . . . Paucis remanentibus in civitate, exierunt omnes alii, maxime eminentiores magistri.' Cf. also *Chron. Simonis Montisfortis*, ap. Duchesne, *Hist. Franc. SS.* v. 778; *Annales Monast.* (Dunstable), ed. Luard, iii. 117; *Chronicon Fiscamnense* (*Patrol. Lat.* cxlvii, cc. 482, 483); John de Oxenedes,

Chronica, ed. Ellis, 1859, p. 157. It would appear from the *Annales Stadenses, M.G.H., Scriptores SS.* xvi. 360, that the chief migration was to Angers: 'ita ut studium in Andegaviam transferretur'. So Matt. Paris, *loc. cit.*: 'Quorum tamen maxima pars civitatem Andegavensium metropolitanam ad doctrinam elegit universalem'; and below, p. 374, n. 4. According to Ralph of Coggeshall, 320 clerks were thrown into the Seine (ed. Stevenson, London, 1875, p. 192). Cf. *Rec. des historiens de France*, xx. 546, xxi. 3, 214, 599, 695, 764. [For the evidence of sermons see Haskins, *Studies in Mediaeval Culture*, pp. 61, 62, note.]

[2] April 16, 1229.
[3] Jourdain, No. 30; *Chartul.* i, No. 62.
[4] Bulaeus, iii. 133; *Chartul.* i, No. 64. An invitation was also received from the Duke of Brittany to transfer the *studium* to Nantes. John of S. Victor, ap. Bulaeum, iii. 555.

at their own discretion, without interference from either civil CHAP. V,
or ecclesiastical authority. The prestige of the Paris masters § 1.
was so high that at Angers they could even venture to grant
licences on their own authority, without the sanction of
bishop or chancellor.[1]

Though the individual legate was hostile to the university, Gregory IX inter- venes.
his master, Pope Gregory IX, showed no signs of abandoning
his protégé; he peremptorily required the King and the
Queen-mother to punish the offenders, and recalled the
obnoxious legate, Romano, Cardinal of S. Angelo.[2] What
redress exactly was granted to the masters, or when, we are
not able precisely to say.[3] At last, however, the Court was
seriously alarmed at the loss of the prestige and of the commercial prosperity which the capital derived from its scholastic
population. It would appear that the dispersion continued
throughout the years 1229 and 1230. During the whole of this
interval, and for some time afterwards, the agents of the
university were busily engaged at the Roman Court extracting
Bulls and privileges on behalf of their clients.[4] It is not till The re- turn, 1231.
the beginning of 1231 that we find the masters and scholars
at work again in their old quarters. The heroic remedy of a
dispersion had not been applied in vain. Not only the
particular grievance which had immediately provoked it, but
others which had no doubt contributed to the disaster now
met with effectual redress. To the month of April 1231
belong Bulls for the punishment of the outrages at S. Marcel,

[1] The licences afterwards received an *ex post facto* validation by
papal Bull. Bulaeus, iii. 146; *Chartul.* i, No. 89. [See J. C. Russell
in *Colorado College Publications*,
Dec. 1927, pp. 47–9.]

[2] Bulaeus, iii. 135; *Chartul.* i,
No. 71.

[3] 'Tandem procurantibus dis-
cretis personis, elaboratum est, ut
factis quibusdam pro tempore exi-
gentibus utrobique culpis, pax est
clero et civibus reformata, et scolarium universitas revocata.' Matt.
Paris, *Hist. Mai.* iii. 169. The date
is given more exactly by Alberic

(*loc. cit.*): 'tandem infra triennium
reversi sunt quicumque voluerunt,
omnibus seditionibus pacificatis'.

[4] It appears that one master,
William of Auxerre, was accredited
by the King (*Chartul.* i, No. 74) at
the command of the Pope; Alexander, and afterwards Geoffrey of
Poitou, were dispatched by the
masters at Angers (*ibid.*, Nos. 75,
88, 90). The various privileges to
be mentioned are marked with the
name of the masters at whose
instance they were granted: many
of them bear the name of William,
the King's envoy.

CHAP. V, Bulls requiring the King to enforce the privilege of Philip
§ I.   Augustus and to allow the rents of the scholars' halls or
hostels to be 'taxed' (as at Bologna) by two masters and two
burghers; Bulls to the Abbot of S. Germain-des-Prés and to
the Bishop requiring respect for the university privileges
within their secular jurisdictions;[1] most important of all,
the great Charter of Privilege which Father Denifle justly
The Parens called the *Magna Charta* of the university. By the Bull *Parens
Scien- Scientiarum* the university received apostolical sanction for
tiarum; restraints its great engine of welfare, the right of suspending lectures,
on chan- cellor. in case satisfaction for an outrage were refused after fifteen
days' notice, and for its authority to make statutes and
punish the breach of them by exclusion from the society.[2]
At the same time a new set of shackles was forged for the
chancellor, and even on some points for the bishop himself.
Every new chancellor is to be required before installation
to swear to be impartial in the conduct of examinations, and
not to reveal the votes of the examining masters. The bishop
is required to be moderate in the exercise of his jurisdiction
over scholars; he is forbidden to have innocent scholars
arrested instead of the guilty (a significant indication of the
way in which godly discipline had heretofore been administered at Paris), to imprison for debt or to impose pecuniary
penances. The chancellor is forbidden to have a prison at all;
scholars are to be imprisoned in the bishop's prison only,
and bail is to be allowed in all cases.[3] The effect of this
measure would seem to be to destroy the chancellor's criminal
jurisdiction altogether. How far he still retained a civil and
spiritual jurisdiction would appear to have remained a matter
of dispute till late in the century,[4] after which almost all traces

[1] Bulaeus, iii. 144 *sq.*; *Chartul.*
i, Nos. 81–8.

[2] Bulaeus, iii. 140; *Chartul.* i,
No. 79. Denifle (i. 73) declares
that this Bull recognizes the power
of *each faculty* to make statutes.
But of this I see no trace: the power
is conferred 'vobis', i.e. on the
masters generally. Cf. also *Chartul.*
i, No. 61.

[3] 'Quod si forte tale crimen com-
miserit quod incarceratione sit opus,
episcopus culpabilem in carcere
detinebit, cancellario habere proprium carcerem penitus interdicto.'

[4] From the long indictment
against the chancellor, Philip de
Thori, in 1283–4 (Jourdain, No.
274; *Chartul.* i, No. 515), it appears that scholars were still in the

of his strictly judicial authority disappear except in so far as is implied by the exercise of certain faculties entrusted to him from time to time by special delegation from the Holy See.[1] Of these the most important was the power of absolving scholars who had incurred *ipso facto* excommunication for violence upon clerks. This being a *casus papalis*, it would otherwise have been necessary for every boy who inflicted a scratch upon another in the course of his academical career, to undertake a journey to Rome before he could get absolution. The disciplinary power of depriving a master of his licence would seem to have remained in theory but to have gradually become obsolete, though the chancellor retained the right of depriving scholars of 'scholarity' with its attendant privileges for carrying arms or the like, and of excommunicating 'vagabond, truant and incorrigible scholars'.[2]

In regard to the most important of all the matters in dispute between the masters and the chancellor, the conferment of the licence, the Bull of Gregory IX seems somewhat less favourable to the masters than the statutes already in force. The chancellor is merely bound to consult the masters before conferring a licence, and to swear upon admission to his office to exercise his powers 'in good faith according to his

The licence.

---

habit of citing one another before the chancellor, but that the university had forbidden the practice. They deny his jurisdiction, and contend that 'cancellarius Parisiensis non est iudex ordinarius scolarium, nec delegatus; et ideo unus de ipsis non debebat facere alterum convenire coram cancellario, nec conveniri coram eodem'. Among the almost equally formidable array of grievances presented against another chancellor in 1290 (Jourdain, No. 302; *Chartul.* ii, No. 569) we find no allegation of judicial usurpation or oppression. Hence we may perhaps assume that the chancellor's jurisdiction began to fall into desuetude at about this time.

[1] e.g. by Innocent IV in 1252

(Bulaeus, iii. 244; *Chartul.* i, No. 215). So he is required to enforce the papal regulations as to the taxation of halls by Innocent IV in 1244 (Bulaeus, iii. 196; *Chartul.* i, No. 138); and 1252 (Jourdain, No. 92; *Chartul.* i, No. 203). But this power was of course derived entirely from the special delegation of the Holy See, and was conferred only for a term of years. At other times we find other ecclesiastics not specially connected with the university entrusted with similar powers, e.g. the Abbot of S. Victor in 1212 (Bulaeus, iii. 63; *Chartul.* i, No. 15), or the Prior of the Cistercian House at Paris in 1262–3 (Bulaeus, iii. 370; *Chartul.* i, No. 379, &c.).

[2] Goulet, f. viii *b*. He is silent as to the power to unlicense masters.

CHAP. V, conscience', whereas formerly he was bound to grant a licence
§ 1. whenever it was demanded by a majority of the faculty or examiners.[1] The previous statutes are neither expressly confirmed
nor expressly repealed; and the ambiguity in which the matter
was left naturally gave ample scope for misconception and
litigation. The issue between the chancellor and the university
was not finally fought out till towards the close of the century.

The Chan-   It was a fact of immense importance to the university in
cellor of
Ste Gene- these struggles with the chancellor of Paris that there was
viève. another source from which the masters could obtain their
licentia docendi. Whether or not any continuity can be established with the schools of the 'Mount' which were so flourishing in the days of Abelard and his successors, is a somewhat
doubtful point. There can, however, be no doubt that at the
end of the twelfth century the schools of the masters were for
the most part situated in the narrow and overcrowded island
round the cathedral,[2] and (even if there were masters teaching
at Ste Geneviève) there is no trace of any other licence than
that of the cathedral chancellor. Early in the thirteenth century, however, masters began to recross the river, and to open
schools in the southern suburb recently enclosed within the
city-walls by Philip Augustus and only now beginning to be
built over. By this measure they placed themselves outside
the jurisdiction of the cathedral chancellor, who accordingly
attempted to bind the masters by oath to teach only 'between
the two bridges'.[3] This imposition was forbidden in 1227 by

[1] Jourdain, No. 15; *Chartul.* i,
No. 16. It is true that this restriction was only laid upon the chancellor then in office. In 1331–3
there was a great quarrel between
the chancellor and the faculty of
medicine, in the course of which
the chancellor's official excommunicated the masters. *Chartul.*
ii, Nos. 930, 930 *a*, &c. This was
evidently at that time an unwonted
exercise of authority. The masters
do not categorically deny his jurisdiction, but contend that if he has
any, he has it 'tanquam subdictus
. . . Parisiensi (episcopo)', to whom

they appeal. On the other side it
is alleged that the punishment of
offences 'circa actum scolasticum'
belongs to him, 'tam de iure quam
de consuetudine, stilo *et privilegiis
sedis apostolice*' (*loc. cit.*, Nos. 931,
932). It appears that he still
demanded an oath to respect the
privileges of his office (No. 937),
though the faculty deny his right
to do so. No permanent settlement
of the matters in dispute seems to
have been arrived at.

[2] See above, p. 277.

[3] 'Ad regendum inter duos pon-
tes.' Bulaeus, iii. 124–5; *Chartul.*

Gregory IX, who recognized the right of the abbot and canons of Ste Geneviève to license masters of theology, canon law and arts to teach within their jurisdiction.[1] As a matter of fact, however, the permission was never taken advantage of except by the faculty of arts.[2] The arts schools gradually transferred themselves to the *Rue du Fouarre* (*Vicus Stramineus*), so called from the straw-strewn floors of the schools —in the region which is still known as the *Quartier Latin*, and is still the haunt of Parisian students. Candidates for the licence in arts could now obtain it either at the cathedral or at the abbey. If attempts at extortion were made by the cathedral, they had the remedy in their own hands. The faculty could even (in the event of a dispute with the chancellor of Paris), direct all its students to apply for licences only at Ste Geneviève.[3] At first the licences at Ste Geneviève were granted by the abbot; in 1255 we find an abbey chancellorship established,[4] in imitation of the office so called at Notre Dame, the chancellor being a canon nominated by the abbot with the approval of the faculty. The existence of *two* chancellors ought by itself to have prevented English writers from identifying the position of the cathedral chancellor (whom they persist, in defiance of medieval usage, in styling 'Chancellor of the University')[5] with that of the chancellor of Oxford or Cambridge.

i, No. 55. Denifle identifies this oath with the oath of obedience to the chancellor, of which we hear so much from 1210 onwards.

[1] Bulaeus, i. 274; *Chartul.* i, No. 55. The Pope had already recognized *pendente lite* the rights of licentiates of Ste Geneviève in 1222: 'nec episcopus et officialis ac cancellarius memorati licentiatos ab . . . abbate Sancte Genovefe quin ubi consueverint libere incipere valeant interim molestabunt.' *Chartul.* i, No. 45.

[2] Bulaeus (iii. 464) declares that licences in the superior faculties were granted by Ste Geneviève during the quarrel with the Parisian chancellor in 1281–4, but seems to be unsupported by the documents. The cathedral chancellor's jealousy of Ste Geneviève is illustrated by the mutual recriminations in the suit of 1283–4 (Jourdain, p. 44 *b*, 45 *a*; *Chartul.* i, No. 515). The Chancellor of Paris alleges 'quod vix potest aliquis obtinere licentiam ex parte Sancte Genovephe, nisi pecunia mediante' —a libel for which the faculty of arts lay the damages at 1,000 golden marks.

[3] Bulaeus, iii. 501; *Chartul.* ii, No. 579.

[4] Bulaeus, iii. 293; *Chartul.* i, No. 260.

[5] In the Middle Ages he is always 'Cancellarius ecclesiae Parisiensis' or 'Cancellarius B. Mariae' or 'Cancellarius Parisiensis'.

CHAP. V,   We have already several times noticed by anticipation the
§ 1.   influence of the great dispute with the mendicants upon the
development and consolidation of the university constitution.
The history of this conflict is of so much importance in itself
and throws so much light upon the real nature and constitutional theory of the university that it demands a section to
itself. But before we leave this period of our history it may
be well to mention the grant of a privilege which became
henceforth *the* characteristic university privilege, not only
of Paris but of all universities which were in any degree
Ius non influenced by Parisian usage—the *ius non trahi extra* by
trahi extra. which (in order to prevent the interruption of studies)
students were exempted from citation to ecclesiastical courts
at a distance from Paris.[1] This privilege the university
obtained in 1245 from Innocent IV in so far as regards
ecclesiastical jurisdiction;[2] and it was afterwards granted by
the King in respect of civil matters.[3]

The con-   A year later the Pope entrusted to the Archbishop of Reims
servator and the Bishop and Dean of Senlis a general power of
apostolic. protecting the university from molestation and securing
respect for privilege by ecclesiastical censure.[4] In these Bulls
of Innocent IV must be sought the origin of the very extensive
jurisdiction rapidly accumulated by the apostolic conservator.
Though in form a temporary and extraordinary commission
(like the *conservatorium* commonly attached to all papal Bulls
of privilege), the business which the exemption of the university from other tribunals and the protection of its extensive
privileges brought before the conservator was so great that
a regular 'Court of Conservation' sat periodically in the

---

[1] i.e. by papal delegates under
apostolic letters, 'nisi expressam
de indulgentia huiusmodi fecerint
mentionem'. *Chartul.* i, No. 142.
[The editors wrongly describe this
privilege as the *privilegium fori*,
which exempted from secular jurisdiction and had been obtained by
the masters and scholars of Paris
from Philip Augustus in 1200; see
above, p. 295, and M.-M. Davy,

'La situation juridique des étudiants', &c., in *Revue d'histoire de
l'église de France*, xvii. 299, 310 *sq.*]
[2] *Chartul.* i, No. 142.
[3] See below, p. 418.
[4] *Chartul.* i, No. 163. The Bull
ran only for seven years, but was
renewed from time to time. For
the growth of the jurisdiction cf.
ibid., Nos. 377, 391.

Mathurine Convent, which ere long developed such a host of extortionate officials that the university was forced to seek protection against its own protectors and procure Bulls from Rome to rectify the abuses of this tribunal.[1] The university, or rather the faculty of arts, later obtained the right of electing the conservator, though by law or custom obliged to elect the bishop of one of three sees in the neighbourhood of Paris— Meaux, Senlis, and Beauvais.[2]

[1] Bulaeus, iv. 206; *Chartul*. iii, No. 841.

[2] There is an allusion to the election of a conservator by the nations in 1266 (Bulaeus, iii. 378; *Chartul.* i, No. 407), [but this does not appear to have been usual; for in 1362 the university petitioned Urban V to concede 'certos conservatores' to protect the masters and scholars against the 'officiales Parisienses' who disregarded the privilege granted by Gregory IX. The Pope appointed the Bishop of Senlis for five years; *Chartul*. iii, No. 1261]. Later, we find the university electing one or other of the three Bishops of Meaux, Senlis, and Beauvais. *Ibid.*, 653, 654, 778; *Remarques sur la dignité du recteur*, p. 17.

§ 2. THE MENDICANTS AND THE UNIVERSITY

CHAP. V,
§ 2.

The *Scriptores Ordinis Predicatorum* (Paris, 1719; new edition by R. Coulon, Paris, 1909–13) of QUÉTIF and ECHARD is here of great value; also *Chronica Fr. Salimbene de Adam Ordinis Minorum*, ed. O. Holder-Egger, 1913 (in *Mon. Germ. Hist.*). Great light is thrown upon the subject, and indeed upon many other points of university history, by the letters of the second master-general of the Dominicans, Jordan of Saxony (ed. B. ALTANER, in *Quellen und Forschungen zur Gesch. d. Dominikanerordens in Deutschland*, no. 20, 1925 and 1927). The writings of WILLIAM OF SAINT-AMOUR I have consulted in the edition printed at Constance in 1632. The case of the mendicants is stated by THOMAS AQUINAS, *Contra impugnantes religionem* (*Opera*, Antwerp, 1612, xvii. 127), and BONAVEN-TURA (*Opera*, Rome, 1688, vii. 373 *sq.*). The edition of ALBERTUS MAGNUS which I have cited is that printed at Lyons in 1657.

[On no part of the ground covered by Rashdall has so much new work been done during the last forty years as on the development of philosophical and theological thought in Paris, the organization of the schools of the mendicant orders, and the disputes between seculars and mendicants in the thirteenth century. It would be quite impossible here to attempt to cover this ground. Fortunately good guides exist.

Rashdall's emphasis on the mendicants should be studied in the light of recent work upon the intense activity of teachers as a whole, both by secular clergy and by religious from *c.* 1200 onwards. Here the best guide is UEBERWEG-GEYER, with the bibliographies, pp. 358, 447, 728 *sqq.* P. MANDONNET's classic *Siger de Brabant et l'averroïsme latin au xiii siècle* (Louvain, pt. i, étude critique, 1911; pt. ii, textes inédits, 1908) was outstanding in the growth of the new learning. Much of it is indicated in P. GLORIEUX, *Répertoire des maîtres en théologie de Paris au xiii* siècle (Paris, 1933). As an example of the work now being done, we may mention F. PELSTER's essay in *Scholastik*, v (1930), 46–78, and O. LOTTIN's paper in *Recherches de théologie ancienne et médiévale*, v (1933), 79–95.

For work on the Franciscans and Dominicans and other mendicant orders see the bibliography in the *Cambridge Medieval History*, vi. 960–7. Here the outstanding publication has been the volumes of the *Monumenta Ordinis Fratrum Predicatorum Historica*, edited by B. M. REICHERT (Rome, 1897–1904). A good introduction to the subject is Mandonnet's paper, 'La Crise scolaire au début du xiiie siècle et la fondation de l'ordre des Frères-Prêcheurs', in *Rev. d'hist. ecclésiastique*, xv (1914), 34–49.

Bibliographical notes on particular points will be added as occasion arises.]

I. *The Intellectual Revolution*

Educational activity passes from the monks to the secular clergy.

IN the age which preceded the rise of the universities the monks were the great educators of Europe. A revival of monastic life—a return to some nearer approach to the old Benedictine ideal—was one of the signs of that great revival of ecclesiastical activity which the twelfth century ushered in.

But it was in the nature of things that every revival of monasticism should carry in itself the seeds of renewed corruption. A revival of monastic life meant an increase of wealth, of influence and of ecclesiastical independence for the great convents. By the twelfth century the old Benedictine and Cluniac monasteries had for the most part sunk into rich corporations of celibate landed proprietors, whose highest ambition was the aggrandizement of the house to which they belonged. Even the reforms initiated by Bernard and Norbert were transitory: the new orders of Cîteaux and Prémontré,[1] though they professed a stricter asceticism and more primitive simplicity than the ordinary Benedictine houses, had no prominent intellectual or educational aims. On the contrary the tendency of the monastic reformers of the twelfth century was distinctly hostile to the more intellectual side of the old monastic ideal. The 'external' schools which the Carolingian age had introduced were found to interfere with the discipline of the cloister; and in the course of the twelfth century the monasteries ceased to be, to any considerable extent, places of higher education for the secular clergy. Anselm of Bec was the last of the great monastic teachers.[2] Among the many educational changes of the century none is more important than the transference of educational activity from the regular to the secular clergy. It was, as we have seen, the cathedral schools which formed in northern Europe the germ of the universities. To those who are fond of speculating on the 'might have beens' of history, it were an interesting question to ask what would have been the consequences to the intellectual development of Europe had the university faculties of theology remained as exclusively in the hands of the secular clergy as was the case at the beginning of the thirteenth century.

Just at this crisis in the intellectual history of Europe two *New monastic ideal of Francis and Dominic.*

[1] Technically the Premonstratensians were canons regular, not monks, but the canon regular, as much as the monks, belonged to the old class of religious grouped together as *possessionati*.

[2] Unless, indeed, we except the School of S. Victor. But the canons regular of S. Victor did not (after this period) teach seculars. See above, p. 276.

great minds, S. Francis and S. Dominic, conceived almost independently and almost simultaneously a wholly new ideal of monastic perfection.[1] The educational and social usefulness of the older orders had been, it may be said, almost accidental. Study or labour was enjoined upon the monk rather as a means of fighting against the evil passions of his own heart than as a means of bringing the world into subjection to the Gospel or to the Church. Monks had become teachers only because there were no other teachers to be had: monasteries had become houses of learning only because learning had become impossible outside them: it was inevitable that the intellectual light which the monasteries communicated should wane with the diffusion of intellectual light in the outside world. Every advance of civilization diminished the value of the monasteries as civilizing agencies. The ideal of the new monastic orders in the twelfth century was a still more emphatically non-social ideal than that of their predecessors. The spiritual benefit of the surrounding population may have been no part of the Benedictine founder's aim, though it often happened that the foundation of a monastery was the foundation of a town. The Cistercians deliberately turned their backs upon the towns and villages in search of more absolute seclusion from the world which they professed to forsake. To the friars preacher and the friars minor on the other hand was assigned not a wilderness to be turned by patient labour into a retreat in which some foretaste of the repose and the worship of Heaven might be enjoyed by souls weary of earth, but a world to be christianized. To the mendicants the calm, monotonous round of solemn service was but a Attitude subordinate object: the end of their existence was the salvation towards education. of souls. Like the great modern order which, when their methods had in their turn become antiquated, succeeded to their influence by a still further departure from the old

---

[1] S. Dominic was himself a Premonstratensian, and his brethren were long regarded as canons regular; but this does not much affect his originality. See Denifle, *Archiv*, i. 169. Still the regular canons were a link between the monks and the friars. [See G. R. Galbraith, *The Constitution of the Dominican Order* (Manchester, 1925), pp. 21–34.]

monastic routine, the mendicant orders early perceived the necessity of getting a hold upon the centres of education. With the Dominicans, indeed, this was a primary object: the immediate purpose of their foundation was resistance to the Albigensian heresy: they aimed at obtaining influence upon the more educated and more powerful classes. Hence it was natural that Dominic should have looked to the universities as the most suitable recruiting-ground for his order: to secure for his preachers the highest theological training that the age afforded was an essential element of the new monastic ideal. Hence the headquarters of the Dominicans in Italy were fixed at Bologna, in France at Paris, where a colony was established from their first foundation in 1217; in England their first convent was at Oxford.[1] These central houses from the first assumed the form of colleges[2] and a Dominican convent was ere long established in every important university town. Jordan of Saxony, the second master of the order, passed his Lent alternately at Bologna and Paris, preaching to students;[3] at other times he travelled from one university to another, holding missions and enrolling new members. He is never so happy as when he can report the 'capture' of 'famous masters' or 'good bachelors'.[4] To get into their own hands the theological teaching of the universities themselves formed, indeed, no part of their original design, but, when circumstances suggested the attempt, the Dominicans were not slow to avail themselves of the opportunity.

The Dominicans have their head-quarters in universities.

The Franciscan ideal was a less intellectual one. Their founder was a simple and unintellectual layman: he would

Franciscans imitate Dominicans.

---

[1] [At the first general chapter of the order in 1220 it was decided that the general chapter should meet alternately at Bologna and at Paris. There appears to be some doubt whether Oxford or London should be regarded as the first English house: Galbraith, *op. cit.*, pp. 36, 66.]

[2] Thus in 1220 Honorius III speaks of 'dilectos filios fratres ordinis Predicatorum, in sacra pagina studentes apud Parisius'. *Chartul.*

i, No. 36.

[3] 'Frequentabat . . . civitates in quibus vigebat studium; unde Quadragesimam uno anno Parisius, alio Bononie sepe faciebat.' So again 'se totum dabat ad attrahendas personas bonas ad ordinem, et ideo morabatur quasi semper in locis in quibus erant scholares, et praecipue Parisius'. *Vitae Fratrum*, ed. Reichert, pp. 108, 529.

[4] [*Epistolae*, ed. Altaner, pp. 25, 36, 50, 51.]

have been content that his disciples should have been the same. To him secular if not even theological learning was one of the vanities upon which the fisher of men must turn his back. But, though the Franciscans laboured largely among the neglected poor of crowded and pestilential cities, they too found it practically necessary to go to the universities for recruits and to secure some theological education for their members. In 1230 the first Franciscan convent was established at Paris,[1] and rivalry with the Dominicans soon made the Minorite friends of the poor almost as conspicuous for intellectual activity as the Dominican champions of the faith. Other mendicant orders—Carmelites, Austin Friars, and some others of less importance—likewise established convents at Paris and sent their novices to the theological schools, but, although they were to play an increasingly important part in the life of the university,[2] the intellectual history of Europe for the next two hundred years is especially bound up with the divergent theological tendencies of the two great orders of S. Dominic and S. Francis.

[1] [This statement is misleading. The first Franciscans had been sent by S. Francis himself in 1219 and were in or near the city early in 1220 (see letter of Pope Honorius III in *Chartul.* i, No. 37). At first they lived in a house at Saint-Denis. Their new convent at Vauvert collapsed in 1229 just after the brothers had taken possession. In 1230 they established themselves in a group of houses at Paris belonging to S. Germain-des-Prés. In 1234 S. Louis bought these buildings and a large piece of land, and offered both to the friars. In 1236 Pope Gregory IX confirmed them in possession. See H. Felder, *Geschichte der wissenschaftlichen Studien im Franziskanerorden* (Freiburg-i.-B., 1904), pp. 168–74.]

[2] The four orders above-mentioned had convents in all scholastic centres, but the two last were always of secondary importance. The Augustinians were, indeed, more important in the history of scholasticism in Italy, their great theological luminary being Giles of Rome (*Egidius Romanus*), who, however, taught at Paris. The Carmelites possessed considerable influence in England, which produced their *Doctor Ordinis*, John Baconthorp. [A good introduction to the literature on the academic activities at Paris and Bologna of the Hermits of S. Augustine, the Carmelites and, as should be added, the Servites, may be found in Ehrle, *I più antichi statuti*, pp. xciv–civ; cf. Ueberweg-Geyer, pp. 543–8, 617. Both Carmelites and Augustinians played an important part in the university in the fourteenth century. For the former see B. Xiberta's papers in the *Analecta Ordinis Carmelitarum*, since 1922.]

In spite of their general similarity in aim and constitution, the two orders preserved in a marvellous degree the stamp impressed upon them by the genius and character of their respective founders. The Dominican mind and the Franciscan mind were each of them as clearly marked, as clearly distinguished from all other ecclesiastical types, and as clearly the reflection of a founder's individuality as the Jesuit mind has been for the last three hundred years. With the Dominican love of souls there was always mingled a fiery zeal for conservative orthodoxy—an orthodoxy which the more emotional temper and more democratic sympathies of the Franciscan constantly threatened. The main lines of Dominican orthodoxy in philosophy and theology were laid down early in their history, and the order has remained to this day faithful, as far as external pressure has permitted, to the teaching of its great doctors.[1] Franciscanism all through the Middle Ages was the fruitful parent of new philosophies and new social movements, of new orthodoxies and of new heresies.[2] At the beginning of the thirteenth century, however, we find the two orders united in the effort to crush or rather to control the prevalent rationalism. We have seen the alarm which the Abelardian spirit of inquiry and discussion inspired in men like S. Bernard. But by the time at which we have now arrived the relations between theology and philosophy were very different from what they had been in the time of Bernard. The movement which is associated with the name of Abelard was of purely Western, purely Latin, purely Christian origin. Aristotle's chief contribution to the contest

Marginal notes: CHAP. V, § 2. Contrast between the two orders.

The theological situation.

---

[1] Repeated statutes were passed by the chapters general, from those of Milan 1278 onwards, enjoining increasingly strict adherence to Thomist principles. In 1315 a bachelor at Florence was silenced for two years and given ten days' bread and water for 'determining' against the Thomist doctrine. *Chartul. Univ. Paris.* ii, No. 717, note. Cf. No. 676, &c. [*Monumenta Ord. Praed.*, ed. Reichert, i. 199, 204, 235; ii. 38, 64;

see Ehrle on Thomas Sutton in *Festschrift Georg von Hertling*, 1913, p. 438 *sq.*]

[2] [From the point of view of academic history this generalization is too sweeping. With the exception of a few ultra-nominalists, the Franciscans held in general to the Augustinian tradition. The movement of the Spirituals was not widespread and did not much affect the universities.]

CHAP. V, was the dialectical weapons with which it was fought. It is
§ 2. true that, in addition to the *Categories* and the *De Interpretatione*, which had been regularly taught in the Church's schools
since the time of Charles the Great, Abelard knew the *de
sophisticis elenchis*, the *Prior Analytics*, and perhaps the
Posterior Analytics; and in the course of his lifetime, the
whole of the *Organon*, long since translated by Boethius,
came again into general use in new translations by James of
Venice[1] and others; but there was nothing in the *Organon*
to excite the alarm of churchmen who did not disapprove of
dialectic altogether.[2] The heresies which alarmed S. Bernard
and the mystics of S. Victor's were the outgrowth of a
spontaneous revival of intellectual activity within the bosom
of the Church herself. But the most daring heretics of the
twelfth century never dreamed of assailing the essential truths
of Christianity or even the authority of the Bible or the
formulae of the Church. Abelard's pupils and successors
became the orthodox prelates and scholastics of the next
generation. John of Salisbury, the best representative of
the twelfth-century classicism, was the sturdiest of churchmen, the counsellor and apologist of Becket himself. By
the end of the century, indeed, the alarm with which the
mere application of dialectic to theology had been at first
regarded had pretty well subsided. On the whole the Church
had adopted and absorbed into herself the intellectual movement of the age; the scholastic method in the treatment of
theology had triumphed.

Introduc-   At the beginning of the thirteenth century an entirely new
tion of
the new intellectual influence was introduced into the schools of the
Aristotle. West. In order to understand the nature of that influence
Aristotle in and the channel by which it reached the schools of Paris, we
the East. must recall for a moment the strange fortunes of Greek culture

---

[1] *Circa* 1128; Jourdain, *Recherches*, p. 58. Gilbert de la Porrée (†1154) cites the *Prior Analytics*: John of Salisbury had the
whole *Organon* before him. [See
Haskins, *Studies in the History of
Mediaeval Science*, pp. 225 *sqq.*]

[2] [We have modified Rashdall's
original statements, but even so
this judgement probably fails to do
justice to the influence of the 'new
logic'; cf. Geyer, in the *Philos.
Jahrbuch*, xxx (1917), 25–43.]

in the east. At the decline of the Eastern Empire the pro-
verb 'Graecia capta ferum victorem cepit' received a fresh
illustration. The despised and persecuted Nestorians formed
the connecting link by which Hellenic science and Hellenic
philosophy were transmitted from the conquerors to the
conquered. Upon the accession of the Abbasid dynasty to
the Caliphate in A.D. 750, learned Nestorians were summoned
to court. By them Greek books were translated into Arabic
from the original or from Syriac translations,[1] and the
foundations laid of Arabic science and philosophy. In the
ninth century the School of Bagdad began to flourish, just
when the schools of Christendom were falling into decay in
the West, and into decrepitude in the East. The newly
awakened Moslem intellect busied itself at first chiefly with
mathematics and medical science; afterwards Aristotle threw
his spell upon it, and an immense system of orientalized
Aristotelianism was the result. From the east Moslem
learning was carried to Spain; and from Spain Aristotle re-
entered northern Europe once more, and revolutionized the
intellectual life of Christendom far more completely than he
had revolutionized the intellectual life of Islam.

During the course of the twelfth century a struggle had The
been going on in the bosom of Islam between the philosophers philo-
and the theologians (*Motékallémin*). It was just at the moment sophy.
when, through the favour of the Caliph Almansor, the theologians had succeeded in crushing the philosophers, that the
torch of Aristotelian thought was handed on to Christendom.
The history of Arabic philosophy, which had never succeeded
in touching the religious life of the people, or leaving a
permanent stamp upon the religion of Mohammed, ends [so
far as it became known in the west] with the death of Averroës
in 1198. The history of Christian Aristotelianism and of the
new scholastic theology which was based upon it begins
just when the history of Arabic Aristotelianism comes abruptly

---

[1] Usually direct. Jourdain, *Re-*   Syriac (*Averroès*, p. 51). [See, for
cherches, p. 86. Renan, however,   recent work, M. Horten in Ueber-
declares that the translations used   weg-Geyer, pp. 291 *sqq.*]
by Averroës were based on the

CHAP. V, to a close. At a much earlier date the peripatetic philosophy
§ 2. in its orientalized form had spread from the mosque to the
synagogue, and with far more profound and lasting results;
Jewish the fact is of importance for our present inquiry inasmuch
philo-
sophy. as the Jews played a large part in the transmission of the
Graeco-Arabic philosophy from Islam to Christendom.
Among the Arabs Averroës was persecuted as a heretic during
his lifetime, and was remembered only as a physician or a
jurist after his death. With a large section of the Jewish
community Moses Maimonides obtained an authority second
only to that of his namesake, the founder of Judaism; in the
synagogue the philosophers on the whole succeeded in
holding their own against the theologians. The intellectual
life of medieval Judaism was long based upon a philosophy,
the natural tendencies of which were as frankly opposed to
orthodox theism as those of its Arabian sources, though here
much greater concessions were made to effect a harmony
between the philosophical and the religious creed.[1] The
destiny of the orientalized Aristotle in the Christian Church
was to be a very different one alike from his triumph among
the Jews and from his extinction among the Arabs.[2]

[1] [In his notes to the first edition
Rashdall referred to the conflict
between the Jewish philosophers
and theologians, especially in the
south of France in the thirteenth
century, and pointed out that
Renan, in his *Averroès* (cf. also *Hist.
litt. de la France*, xxvii. 647 *sq*.), had
exaggerated the 'naturalistic' element in the teaching of Maimonides, and misunderstood his attitude to the Averroistic doctrine of
the eternity of the world. On all
these matters see now Ueberweg-
Geyer, pp. 325–42, and Duhem,
Le Système du monde, v. 170–232.
The mutual influences of Jewish
and Christian thought upon each
other were more subtle and far-
reaching than was once supposed.]
[2] The council which condemned Amauri de Bène (below,
p. 355) speaks of 'libri Aristotelis

de naturali philosophia' and the
'Commentaries' thereon (Martène,
Thes. Nov. Anecdot. iv, c. 166). M.
Jourdain's opinion (*Recherches*, p.
197) that the works of Avicenna and
Algazel are meant is based upon
the character of the doctrines
ascribed to Amauri and David de
Dinant. He even thinks that the
study of the true Aristotle was pursued largely with a view to find
weapons to combat the pseudo-
Aristotelian philosophy of the
Arabs. Roger Bacon, however
(*Op. Tertium*, ed. Brewer, p. 28),
distinctly says that the council
'damnaverunt et excommunica-
verunt libros Naturalis et Metaphy-
sicae Aristotelis qui nunc ab omnibus recipiuntur pro sana et utili
doctrina'. In any case there was
clearly much confusion between
the genuine Aristotle and the inter-

Soon after the beginning of the thirteenth century the CHAP. V, § 2. Translations from the Arabic. new Aristotle began to make its appearance in the schools of Paris. Before the middle of the same century Avicenna's (†A.D. 1037) paraphrases or adaptations of the various Aristotelian treatises—works composed on the same subjects, with the same titles, preserving the same order of treatment, and embodying the doctrine of Aristotle interpreted in accordance with the views of the author—had been translated into Latin at Toledo by a band of translators, headed by John Avendeath (*Johannes Hispanus*) and the Archdeacon Dominic Gondisalvi, in the employment of Raymund, Archbishop of Toledo. And it has been maintained, though without sufficient ground, that the first works bearing the name of Aristotle which reached the schools of Paris were these translated paraphrases of Avicenna, and not actual translations. But many of the early translations of Aristotle were made from the Arabic.[1] Aristotle thus came to Paris in an orientalized dress; and that was not all. He was accompanied or followed by Arabic commentators and by independent works of Arabian philosophers, some of which at first claimed the sanction of Aristotle's name. Now the Arabic interpretation of Aristotle as exhibited by Avicenna and more decidedly by Averroës, taking the direction first imparted to peripatetic thought by the commentator Alexander of Aphrodisias, emphasized and developed precisely the most anti-Christian elements in the teaching of the philosopher—the eternity of matter, the unity of the 'active intellect', the negation of individual immortality. The Neoplatonic element is still

pretations and even writings fathered on him by the Arabs. As late as *c*. 1220 Giraldus Cambrensis speaks of an intellectual revolution created by 'Libri quidam, *tanquam Aristotelis* intitulati, Toletanis Hispaniae finibus nuper inventi et translati' (*Opera*, iv. 9). So Robert of Auxerre (*Mon. Germ. Scriptores*, xxvi. 276), who adds that the prohibition to read the works of Aristotle was for three years only. William the Breton says that in

1209 'legebantur Parisiis libelli quidam ab Aristotele, ut dicebantur, compositi, qui docebant metaphysicam, delati de novo a Constantinopoli et a graeco in latinum translati' (*Rec. des historiens de France*, xvii. 84). Denifle (*Chartul.* i, No. 11, note) appears to have no doubt that the actual works of Aristotle were meant by the Paris Council of 1210.

[1] See below, pp. 358 *sqq*.

CHAP. V,
§ 2.

more explicit in a famous Arabic or Jewish compilation known as the *Liber de Causis*,[1] which was translated in the twelfth century and was accepted under the name of Aristotle.

Scepticism at Paris.

The result of these importations was an outbreak of speculation of a much bolder character than any that had been known in the twelfth century. To about this period belongs the celebrated legend of the Parisian master, Simon of Tournai. Intoxicated with the applause which greeted his dialectical defence of the doctrine of the Trinity—conducted 'so lucidly, so elegantly, so catholicly'—the doctor announced that if he pleased he could demolish with equal plausibility the faith which he had that day maintained. His audacity is said to have been rebuked by an immediate stroke of paralysis, which deprived him at once of speech and of memory. With difficulty did the famous doctor in time relearn from his own child his *Credo* and his *Paternoster*.[2] In the earlier years of the thirteenth century Paris was, indeed, the scene of an outburst of free-thought which at one time threatened to pass far beyond the limits of the schools. About the year 1204

Amauri de Bène.

Amauri de Bène, a theological doctor of Paris, died of chagrin

[1] Albert the Great tells us that the book was compiled by David the Jew from the (pseudo-) Aristotelian epistle, *De Principio Universi*, 'multa adiungens de dictis Avicennae et Alpharabii' (*Opp.* v. 563 sq.). Thomas Aquinas rightly regards it as a compilation from the Neoplatonist Proclus. [The Arabic text was edited by Bardenhewer (Freiburg-i.-B., 1882). The Latin translation was probably made by Gerard of Cremona. See Ueberweg-Geyer, p. 303, Duhem, *op. cit.* iv. 329–47. The so-called *Theologia* of Aristotle, to which Rashdall also referred in the first edition as known in a Latin translation, was not translated until 1519, although some scholars have professed to find references to it in S. Thomas and other writers. See Grabmann, *Aristotelesübersetzungen*, pp. 245–7, and cf. Ueberweg-Geyer, p. 302.]

[2] The story is told by Matt. Paris, *sub anno* 1201 (*Chron. Mai.* ii. 476, 477), who says he heard of the miracle from an eye-witness, Nicholas (of Farnham), afterwards Bishop of Durham. Stories of this type are very common. One illustrates the antagonism which existed at the time between the religious and the scholastic spirit of the age— an antagonism not yet bridged over by the work of the Angelical doctor. A master of arts named Silo is said to have promised in life to appear to his favourite pupil after his death. He appeared 'cum cappa de purgamento, tota de sophismatibus descripta et flammâ ignis tota confecta'. He declared that this was given him 'pro gloria quam in sophismatibus habui'. The scholar became a Cistercian (Bulaeus, ii. 393).

at an enforced retractation. He was accused of teaching a CHAP. V, doctrine which sounds innocent enough to modern ears—the § 2. doctrine that every believer should regard himself as a member of Christ. But the pantheistic character of his teaching, —[the identity of the creator and the created]—and the still more unorthodox and anti-sacerdotal interpretation given to it by his followers, did not come to light till after his death.[1] At a synod held in Paris in 1210, in which the masters of the university took part, the works of one David of Dinant were condemned to the flames.[2] At the same time the body of Amauri was ordered to be dug up and buried in unconsecrated ground, and a posthumous excommunication

[1] This is the account of the sect given by Caesarius of Heisterbach (*Mirac. et Hist. Mem.*, Dist. v, *c.* 22, ed. Strange, pp. 304, 305): 'Dicebant non aliter esse corpus Christi in pane altaris, quam in alio pane et in qualibet re, sicque Deum locutum fuisse in Ovidio, sicut in Augustino: negabant resurrectionem corporum, dicentes nihil esse paradisum, neque infernum, sed qui haberet cognitionem Dei in se, quam ipsi habebant, haberet in se paradisum: qui vero peccatum mortale, haberet infernum in se sicut dentem putridum in ore.' But, according to this monastic scribbler, there was another and less edifying side to this Spiritualism. 'Si aliquis in spiritu est sancto, aiebant, et faciat fornicationem vel aliqua alia pollutione polluatur, non est ei peccatum.' As, however, the sentence of the council is silent as to any such doctrine, it must be regarded as a libel. There can be no doubt, however, that the movement had a naturalistic as well as a religious side. In the present century we have seen a very parallel instance of a highly speculative and essentially naturalistic philosophy clothing itself in the phrases of a high-flown spiritualism or even of orthodox piety, and not revealing its true character

till the second generation. We are beginning to understand the real drift of Hegelianism even in England. [1895.]

[2] [Many attempts have been made to discover the exact nature and the sources of the views ascribed to Amauri and to David of Dinant, but it is still uncertain whence they derived them and how they were related to each other. For a summary and bibliographies see Ueberweg-Geyer, pp. 250–2, 706–7; cf. Duhem, *op. cit.* v. 244–60, and especially G. Théry, *Autour du décret de 1210: David de Dinant* (Kain, 1925), and Mlle G. C. C. Capelle, *Amaury de Bène: étude sur son panthéisme formel* (Kain, 1932). Father Théry (p. 83) is disposed to stress the influence of the *Metaphysics* and *Physics* of Aristotle. Cf. G. H. Luquet, *Aristote et l'université de Paris* (Paris, 1904), pp. 20–7, who suggests that the *Metaphysics* were included in the *libri naturales* condemned in 1210. The discussion turns mainly on the passages in which the later scholastics and the chronicler Martin of Poland refer to the heretics. The decrees of 1210 are in the *Chartul.* i, Nos. 11, 12. The condemnation of Amauri was repeated at the Fourth Lateran Council in 1215.]

CHAP. V, launched against him. A batch of persons infected with the
§ 2. heresy—priests and clerks from the schools, as well as a
goldsmith from the neighbouring Grand-Pont—were handed
over to the secular arm, some for the stake, others for per-
The New petual imprisonment. At the same time the 'books of Aristotle
Aristotle
forbidden. upon Natural Philosophy, and his Commentaries' were forbidden to be read at Paris publicly or privately for a period of
three years. [The works aimed at were probably the *Physics*, the
De Anima and, perhaps, parts of the *Metaphysics*, all of which
Sources of had become known in Latin translations by this time.] It is
heresies.
difficult to define with precision the part which was played
in the generation of heresy by the new Aristotle. Renan
was inclined to see in this Parisian heresy in the main a wave
of the great popular Catharistic movement,[1] which was
rapidly undermining Catholicism in Provence and the neighbouring countries. Again, in so far as the movement was
philosophical as well as mystical, it was at one time supposed
that the revived influence of Johannes Scotus is more clearly
discernible than that of the *Liber de Causis* and other pseudo-
Aristotelian writings.[2] In the works of David of Dinant,
however, the only heretic who seems to have been important
from a strictly philosophical point of view, the influence of
Alexander of Aphrodisias has been found. [All these explanations are very doubtful.] The thought of the time exhibits a
strange fusion of popular mysticism of a more or less Christian
character with a speculative Averroism which showed a
tendency to assume pantheistic or even materialistic forms
which would have been repudiated by the Arabian master
himself. But from whatever sources the heresies derived their
inspiration, their outbreak goes far to explain the alarm with
which the advent of the Aristotelian writings was at first

[1] Renan, *Averroès*, p. 223. [This
is denied by Théry (*op. cit.*, p. 83),
who also considers that David was
not much influenced by Johannes
Scotus Erigena. David was not
an Amalrician, and was not under
the influence of Alexander Aphrodisias (*ibid.*, pp. 47, 52–73), as Jourdain suggested (*Mém. de l'acad.*

d'inscriptions, xxvi. 1867, 493, 497).
For his connexion with Averroës
see note below, p. 357, n. 1.]
[2] See especially the Bull in *Chartul.* i, No. 50, ordering search for
the *perifisis* (περὶ φύσεως, i.e. περὶ
φύσεων μερισμοῦ), and Denifle's important note.

regarded. The rapidity with which Aristotle and even his Arabic commentators lived down these suspicions is one of the most remarkable facts in the intellectual history of the Middle Ages.[1]

In 1215 a body of statutes was drawn up for the guidance of the masters of Paris by the papal legate de Courçon. *Measures against Aristotle.* Lectures on the physical and metaphysical books of Aristotle[2] (the latter now mentioned for the first time) were forbidden, and an oath not to read the works of David and certain other heretics was enforced on all candidates for the licence in arts. Among these was one Mauritius Hispanus who is plausibly identified with Averroës himself.[3] The prohibition of the books condemned by the Council of Paris was renewed by Gregory IX in 1231 with the significant reservation 'until they shall have been examined and purged from all heresy'.[4] The theologians seem quickly to have satisfied themselves

---

[1] [It would seem that the influence of Averroës in its early stages should be connected with the interest shown in the natural science of Aristotle (cf. A. Birkenmajer, *Le rôle joué par les médecins et les naturalistes dans la réception d'Aristote au xii⁰ et xiii⁰ siècles*, Warsaw, 1930). Michael Scot, for example, in his *Questiones Nicolai peripatetici*, written while he was in Spain (*c.* 1217) 'took shelter in anonymity in order to preach strong Averroism' (Haskins, *Mediaeval Science*, p. 279). A work 'epistola Averroys super questione de generatione animalium', a fragment of Averroës's commentary on the twelfth book of the *Metaphysics*, is in Vienna MS. 2302. Now this particular book of the *Metaphysics* had an early and separate circulation (R. de Vaux, 'La première entrée d'Averroës chez les Latins', in *Revue des sciences philosophiques et théologiques*, xxii, 1933). A different work with a similar title, 'tractatus Adverrois de generatione animalium', has been ascribed by

Birkenmajer to David of Dinant himself: see *Revue néo-scolastique de philosophie*, xxxv (1933), 220–9.]

[2] [The context shows that the words, 'non legantur libri Aristotelis *de methafisica et de naturali philosophia*, nec *summe* de eisdem', should be interpreted in this way. *Legere* has its technical meaning.]

[3] Bulaeus, iii. 82; *Chartul.* i, No. 20. Denifle shows that Albert the Great distinguishes Mauritius and Averroës (*Chartul.* i, No. 20, note). This is not decisive [and Mandonnet identifies him with Averroës, *Siger de Brabant*, i. 17, but, as M. Bouyges has shown in a careful if inconclusive analysis of the evidence (*Rev. d'hist. ecclésiastique*, 1933, xxix. 637–58), the identity of Maurice is still quite uncertain.]

[4] Bulaeus, iii. 142; *Chartul.* i, No. 79. At this time Gregory IX directed the absolution of offenders against the decree of the council and appointed a commission for the examination of the books (*Chartul.* i, Nos. 86, 87). [Cf. also the papal letters of 1288 (No. 59).]

CHAP. V, as to the innocuous character of the suspected work or to have
§ 2. learned the art of distinguishing the genuine Aristotle from
spurious imitations. William of Auvergne, a Parisian doctor
who became Bishop of Paris in 1228 and was still writing in
1248, makes free use of the suspected books, and labours to
refute the heresies which had been deduced from them; and
Toleration in 1255 we find nearly the whole range of the Aristotelian
of Aris- writings prescribed by a statute of the faculty of arts as text-
totle. books for the lectures of its masters.[1]

Early Among the early translators from the Arabic were Gerard
Arab- of Cremona, Hermann the German, and Michael Scot,
Latin whose half-magical reputation still testifies to the air of
transla-
tions. mystery and dark suspicion which surrounded the labours
of these pioneers of the later scholasticism. In this way the
eight books of the *Physics*, the nineteen books of the *De
Historia Animalium*, the *De Caelo et Mundo*, the spurious
De Plantis, and the *Meteorica* became known in northern
Europe. But while the Arabic Aristotle was thus re-entering
northern Europe from the south, another chain of events was
Direct bringing him back from the East in his original Greek. [In
transla-
tions from north and south Italy and Sicily translators from the original
the Greek. Greek had been active since the first half of the twelfth
century. And, although it is easy to exaggerate its influence]
the Latin conquest of Constantinople in 1204 threw open the
original home of Greek philosophy to Latin scholars. Latin
ecclesiastics accompanied the crusading host: others were
settled in Greek towns as bishops of the latinized sees. Some
of these men made good use of their opportunities as translators, or collectors of manuscripts which were afterwards
translated by others.[2] In this way the *De Anima* had already

[1] Bulaeus, iii. 280; *Chartul*. i,
No. 246. [In 1252 the English
nation prescribed the *De Anima*
(*ibid*., No. 201). Although Urban
IV in 1263 renewed the prohibition,
it was not effective after 1231. It
was not applied at Toulouse till
1245. See Ueberweg-Geyer, pp.
350, 351, and Mandonnet, *op. cit.*
i. 18, 22 and *passim*.]

[2] The best known of them is per-

haps John of Basingstoke, who was
taught Greek by a learned daughter
of the Archbishop of Athens (who
predicted pestilences and eclipses)
and assisted Robert Grosseteste in
his efforts to procure manuscripts
and translations (Matt. Paris, *Hist.
Mai*. v. 284, 286 *sq.*; Jourdain,
Recherches, p. 63). At about this
time Frederick II is said to have
dispatched his famous letter to the

become known to William of Auvergne in Graeco-Latin translations before the Arab-Latin version of Michael Scot reached the Schools of Paris. The *Rhetoric* and the collection of small treatises known as the *Parva Naturalia*, the *De Coloribus*, the *De Lineis Insecabilibus*, part at least of the *Metaphysics*, and the first three books of the *Nicomachean Ethics*, together with the *Politics* and the *Magna moralia*, were known from the first in translations from the original Greek; though the earliest complete version of the *Ethics* was Arab-Latin. In the case of many of the Aristotelian treatises the direct and indirect versions were long current side by side. The earliest Graeco-Latin translations were slavishly literal word-for-word reproductions of the original Greek; but they were less unintelligible than translations which at times bristled with Arabic words in Latin letters; for the medieval translators (like the authors of the Septuagint), when unable to construe a word in the original, cut the knot by simply transliterating it. It is true that the Graeco-Latin translators not unfrequently resorted to a similar expedient, but some at least of the Arab-Latin versions laboured under the further defect of having passed through even more than one language in the process of translation. The paraphrase of Avicenna and the commentaries of Averroës were alike made not from the original Greek but from the Syriac; and the nominal translator—the Latin ecclesiastic who gave his name to the work—was commonly as ignorant of the Arabic as he was of the original Greek. The version was produced by the collaboration of a Western who knew no Arabic and a

masters of Bologna and of Paris (ap. Jourdain, *Recherches*, p. 156), sending them some rare translations of Aristotle and other Greek writers, composed under his orders; but since these were logical and mathematical books, their introduction has not much bearing upon the history of Aristotle at Paris. It should be observed that some of the manuscripts of the above letter have the name Manfred instead of Frederick. Jourdain decides for Frederick (*loc. cit.*, p. 164); but cf. Roger Bacon, *Opus Tertium* (*Opera*, ed. Brewer, p. 91), and *Chartul.* i, No. 394, with Denifle's note. [Most recent scholars assign the letter to Manfred and connect it 'with the translation of the *Magna moralia* and various pseudo-Aristotelian treatises made by his direction'; Haskins, *Studies in Mediaeval Science*, pp. 261–2, note, with references.]

CHAP. v, Saracen or a converted Jew who knew no Greek, the Spanish
§ 2. or other vernacular language serving as the medium of communication between the translator and his animate dictionary.[1] However this may have been, the Arab-Latin versions, as we have seen, were not the only means of transmission. Some of the versions direct from the Greek were still earlier in the field; and the later Graeco-Latin versions were somewhat superior to the earlier. Thomas Aquinas endeavoured to procure better translations from the original Greek, and his efforts were seconded by Pope Urban IV. Special translations or special revisions of the existing Graeco-Latin translations were prepared for his use by a Dominican William of Moerbeke, Archbishop of Corinth. To him at least the common tradition of the Middle Ages ascribes the 'translatio nova' of the books of *Natural* and *Moral Philosophy*, which, in spite of many imperfections, held its place in the schools as a kind of authorized version of Aristotle till the dawn of the new learning.[2]

[1] [This vivacious generalization should not be taken literally. Both Gerard of Cremona and Michael Scot understood Arabic, and so did Dominic Gondissalvi before them.]

[2] [The results of investigation into the reception of Aristotle prior to 1916 were brought together and extended by M. Grabmann in his *Forschungen über die lateinischen Aristotelesübersetzungen des XIII. Jahrhunderts* (Münster, 1916). Since this date much more detailed work has been done; cf. Ueberweg-Geyer, pp. 343–50, 728; S. D. Wingate, *The Mediaeval Latin Versions of the Aristotelian Scientific Corpus* (London, 1931). The Union of Academies has in hand, as the first part of a projected 'Corpus Philosophorum Medii Aevi', an edition of the medieval translations of Aristotle, of which the first volume will be G. Lacombe's survey and catalogue of the manuscripts, some 1,800 in number. The result of this intense activity has been to modify considerably some of the traditional views, although some problems are still unsolved. Unknown versions have come to light, Aristotelian writings once thought to have first been known in the west in the thirteenth century are now known to have been known in the twelfth (e.g. the *Posterior Analytics*), and the relation between earlier versions and the translations of the Fleming, William of Moerbeke (c. 1215–86, Archbishop of Corinth 1277), are being elucidated. In particular, largely owing to the work of Haskins, the twelfth-century translations direct from the Greek have been given due weight. Rashdall's emphasis on the influence of the crusade of 1204 is as unnecessary as the old view which ascribed humanism to the capture of Constantinople by the Turks in 1453; see Haskins, *Studies in Mediaeval Science*, p. 149 and chapters ix, xi, xviii.]

To a large extent no doubt the suppression of independent CHAP. V,
speculation was due to the vigorous exertions of the ecclesi- § 2.

It is necessary to distinguish between the appearance of an early version and the use which was made of it. Some versions seem to have had little or no currency. But such studies as those of Haskins on Neckam's list of text-books (1190–1200; *op. cit.*, pp. 357 *sqq.*, especially 367–8), Cl. Baeumker on Alfred of Sareshel (*Alfredus Anglicus*), Miss Wingate on the *De Plantis*, and many other scholars on the scholastics from William of Auvergne and Grosseteste onwards, help to date approximately the effective entrance of the particular books of Aristotle into the schools. For the 'new logic', i.e. *Analytics Topics, Elenchi*, which, in the translation now generally accepted as that of Boethius, became known in the first half of the twelfth century, see Haskins, *op. cit.* c., xi. Haskins discussed at Toledo a translation of the *Posterior Analytics* from the Greek, different from that of Boethius, and distinct from the lost translation of James of Venice (*c.* 1128), but earlier than the translation from the Arabic made by Gerard of Cremona, who died in 1187.

The earliest translation of the *Metaphysics* from the Greek, known at Salerno *c.* 1175, covered three and a half books and survives in ten manuscripts. Birkenmajer thinks that the so-called *translatio vetus* resulted from this and from another translation, now known as the *media*, of Books i–x, xii–xiv, *c.* 1210–30. Of this last, first noticed by F. Pelster, ten manuscripts are known. The so-called *Metaphysica nova* was made from the Arabic, perhaps by Michael Scot (but cf. Haskins, i. 279, and S. H. Thomson in *The New Scholasticism*, vii (1933), 221), in the first quarter of the century

and was accompanied by the commentary of Averroës. Like the *media*, it contained 13 books, excluding Book XI. William of Moerbeke's translation from the Greek contained all 14 books. Although S. Thomas in 1270 said that the last two books were not translated, they appear in various combinations of translations earlier.

A twelfth-century translation of two books of the *Physics* survives in a Vatican manuscript. Haskins (pp. 224–5) ascribes it to the early years of the thirteenth century, but it is now regarded as earlier. (For knowledge of the *Physics* cf. Haskins, pp. 38, 92 and *passim*.) The translation from the Greek current in the Middle Ages was made at the end of the twelfth century and was revised by William of Moerbeke. Gerard of Cremona (before 1181) and Michael Scot translated the work from the Arabic; the latter with the commentary of Averroës.

The *De Caelo* was known in Sicily *c.* 1160 (Haskins, p. 162), but the current versions were from the Arabic (Gerard of Cremona and Michael Scot, with Averroës, 1210–30). William of Moerbeke's translation from the Greek was influenced by another ascribed to Grosseteste (Vatican MS. Lat. 2088).

The *De Generatione* was translated from the Greek by Henricus Aristippus in Sicily (before 1162) and revised by Alfred of Sareshel. Gerard of Cremona and Michael Scot translated from the Arabic. The later translation (Books I–III) from the Greek was a revision of the earlier. It is possible also that Moerbeke's translation of the *Meteorology* had a predecessor, in addition to Gerard's version from the Arabic, and that of Book IV

CHAP. V, astical and civil authorities. The burning of the Almaricians
§ 2.
Suppres-
sion of
heresy.
in 1210, and the ruthless suppression of the not wholly unconnected though much more popular and more distinctly religious movements in the south of France, taught the daring speculators of the schools a lesson which could not easily be forgotten. Above all, the establishment of the Inquisition, wherever it got a firm hold, placed medieval orthodoxy beyond the reach of open attack for another three centuries. Averroistic free-thought smouldered on in a more disguised and more purely speculative form, occasionally bursting forth into a short-lived flame which called for ecclesiastical extinction. The favourite device of disputants in the arts schools was to take refuge under cover of the convenient distinction (very prominent in Averroës himself) between philosophical and theological truth: what was true in philosophy might be false in theology and vice versa. At times this distinction no doubt represented a really divided state of the thinker's mind; but an examination of the heretical doctrines condemned in 1270[1]

Pantheistic
errors of
1270 and
1277.

by Aristippus from the Greek. Michael Scot translated the *De Animalibus* from the Arabic, and Moerbeke from the Greek.

The *De Anima* was translated from the Greek in the twelfth century, from the Arabic, with Averroës, by Michael Scot. Moerbeke revised the former. A translation of the *Parva Naturalia* cited by Alfred of Sareshel, who may have himself translated some of them (Haskins, p. 128 n.), has been found in several manuscripts in Austria and Italy (*De Iuventute, De Respiratione, De Morte*).

The *Ethics, Politics, Economics, Poetics, Rhetoric*, pseudo-Aristotle and Greek commentators were translated in the thirteenth century, the translations (as in the case of the *Ethics*) sometimes depending to some extent on earlier versions from the Greek, of which fragments survive.

Two important matters, the way in which the new Aristotle was first

brought into wider circulation, and, secondly, the range of writings, genuine or not, regarded as Aristotle's in the Middle Ages, have been examined in two valuable papers by A. Birkenmayer: *Le rôle joué par les médecins et les naturalistes dans la réception d'Aristote au xii⁰ et xiii⁰ siècles*, 15 pp., Warsaw, 1930 (from the volume 'Pologne au vi⁰ Congrès International des sciences historiques'), and *Classement des ouvrages attribués à Aristote par le moyen âge latin*, 21 pp., Cracow, 1932 (Union Académique Internationale).

We were much assisted in the compilation of this note by the late Monsignor Lacombe.]

[1] Among these errors were the following (Bulaeus, iii. 397; *Chartul*. i, No. 432):
'Quod omnia que hic in inferioribus aguntur subsunt necessitati corporum celestium' (a clear indication of the source of the distinctly theological errors which follow).

and of the still more explicit errors enumerated in 1277[1] leaves no doubt that the introduction of the new philosophy into the medieval schools was attended by a real outburst of pantheistic thought, at times bordering (as pantheism always will border) on pure materialism, and even to a recrudescence of paganism in ethics.[2] After this date, however, the heresies condemned at Paris become less and less destructive. This result was due (as has been said) partly to the steadily continued pressure of a vigilant authority, partly to the natural evaporation of the excitement and unsettlement which attended the first introduction of the new ideas. But the most effectual counteractive of the dangerous influence of Averroistic Aristotelianism was supplied by the development of a great system of orthodox Aristotelianism. The work had been begun by the cautious Alexander of Hales, the first doctor of the Franciscan Order.[3] In the domain of logic he

Heresy counter-acted by orthodox Aristotelianism.

Alexander of Hales.

'Quod mundus est eternus.

'Quod nunquam fuit primus homo.

'Quod anima post mortem separata non patitur ab igne corporeo.

'Quod Deus non cognoscit alia a se.'

[1] 'Dicunt enim', complains the Bishop of Paris in 1277 (Bulaeus, iii. 433; *Chartul*. i, No. 473), 'ea esse vera secundum philosophiam, sed non secundum fidem catholicam, quasi sint due contrarie veritates, et quasi contra veritatem sacre scripture sit veritas in dictis gentilium dampnatorum.' Among the errors condemned on this occasion were the denial of the Trinity, of the Immortality of the Soul, and of the Creation, &c. These 219 propositions exhibit a curious mixture of Aristotelian and Platonic notions with the Oriental astrology which had been infused into the ancient philosophies by the media through which they had reached the Parisian thinker. [See especially Mandonnet, *Siger de Brabant*, for the significance of the movement, in which the condemnations

of 1270 and 1277 are the outstanding episodes. He points out (i. 198, 199) that the disputes cut across the nations, in spite of the contemporary struggle between nations over the election of Alberic as Reims as rector. For its human interest as well as for the development of medieval logic and method, the history of the life and times of Siger is now seen to have far more importance in development at Paris than was realized when Rashdall wrote. For the literature up to 1928 see Ueberweg-Geyer, pp. 445 *sqq.*, 757–8.]

[2] See the 'errores de vitiis et virtutibus' in Bulaeus, iii. 442; *Chartul*. i, No. 473, p. 553.

[3] [There is not much reliance upon Aristotle in the works of Alexander. The 'system' was due to Albert the Great and Aquinas, although they had forerunners. See especially Ehrle's papers on Augustinianism and Aristotelianism in Denifle and Ehrle's *Archiv*, v (1898), 603–35, and *Xenia Thomistica*, iii (1925), 517–88.]

CHAP. V, began what may be called the rehabilitation of realism, the
§ 2.　cruder forms of which had been discredited by the criticism
of Roscellinus and Abelard. But he was in the main a theologian, not a philosopher.[1] He was the first great medieval
theologian who was free to use the whole of the newly imported Aristotelian writings, and who set the example of
employing them in the defence and exposition of the Catholic
Faith. But in the main the construction of a Catholic philosophy and an Aristotelian theology was the work not of the
Franciscans but of the Dominicans. Although on the actual
question of universals a very moderate realistic position was
now taken up, the general tendency of Franciscan philosophy
as seen in the writings of Alexander of Hales, of his successor
Jean de la Rochelle, and still more markedly of the mystic
Bonaventura (1221–74), was towards a Platonic or Arabic
interpretation of the master whom all medieval schools alike
acknowledged: the Franciscan School from the first maintained within its bosom the germs which were to attain their
most luxuriant growth in the multiplied 'entities' of Scotism.
The most unquestionably orthodox and at the same time
The great most genuinely Aristotelian system of the Middle Ages was
Domini-
can the creation of the two Dominicans, Albert the Great (1193–
School. 1280) and his more famous if not greater pupil Thomas of
Aquino (1225 or 1227–74), who respectively taught in the
convent of their order at Paris between 1243 and 1248 and
1252–9.[2] If the larger part of their literary labours was
carried on elsewhere, the Dominican convent at Paris was
the most influential centre from which their teaching diffused

---

[1] His ponderous *Summa Theologiae* ('quae est plusquam pondus
unius equi', as Roger Bacon has it,
Opp. Ined., ed Brewer, i. 326) was
completed after his death in 1245.

[2] [Mandonnet has argued that
Albert was born in 1206 (*Revue
Thomiste*, xiv (1931), 233–56; but
H. C. Scheeben, in his *Albert der
Grosse: Zur Chronologie seines
Lebens* (Quellen und Forschungen
zur Gesch. des Dominikanerordens
in Deutschland, No. 27, 1931),

holds to 1193 and dates his teaching
in Paris, 1243–8; cf. also his reply
to Mandonnet in *Divus Thomas*, x
(1932), 363–77. St. Thomas Aquinas probably studied under Albert
at Cologne after 1248. He was in
Paris during most of the years
1252–9, and again from January
1269 to Easter 1272. See the summary in Ueberweg-Geyer, pp. 423–
4, 744. For the literature about
Albert the Great up to 1928, *ibid.*,
pp. 403–4, 739, 740.]

itself through Europe. It was Paris, with the Dominican order and papal authority behind it, that made the theology of S. Thomas the basis of theological discipline and speculation. Just as the Jesuits in later times turned the universal desire for the new learning, hitherto associated with the new religion, into an instrument for attaching men to their order and their creed, the Dominicans conceived and executed the idea of pressing not merely (as of old) the Aristotelian logic but the whole Aristotelian philosophy into the service of the Church.

Albert continued the system of loose paraphrase or adapta- *Albert the Great.* tion adopted by Avicenna.[1] In this way the whole of the Aristotelian philosophy was for the first time presented to the world in a Christian dress. This mode of presentation gave opportunity for the discussion, criticism, or modification of the principles of his author as well as of other writers on the same subjects: the twenty-one folio volumes of Albert are a perfect encyclopaedia both of the knowledge and of the polemics of his time. Aquinas in his purely philosophical *Thomas Aquinas.* treatises adopted Averroës's method of comment on the actual text of Aristotle; while, as a theologian, he composed independent treatises so superior in form, method, and relative good sense, that they have nearly doomed to oblivion the more cumbrous and discursive works of the predecessor from whom, nevertheless, the basis of his doctrine was derived. The Italian imparted form, system, even style (if the term may be applied to a language which had now become as technical as the language of law or of physical science), to the rough masses of thought heaped up by the ruder genius of the Teuton. The unimpeachable orthodoxy of the two Dominicans finally dissipated alike the prejudice against the scholastic method which had filled the minds of strict Churchmen in the days of S. Bernard or Walter of S. Victor, and the better-founded alarm excited by the introduction of the Arabian and Aristotelian philosophy at the beginning *Effects of their work.* of the thirteenth century. It was from this time and from this time only (though the change had been prepared in the region

[1] Except in his work on the *Politics*, which is a regular commentary.

of pure theology by Peter the Lombard) that the scholastic philosophy became distinguished by that servile deference to authority with which it has been in modern times too indiscriminately reproached. And the discovery of the new Aristotle was by itself calculated to check the originality and speculative freedom which, in the paucity of books, had characterized the active minds of the twelfth century. The tendency of the sceptics was to transfer to Aristotle or Averroës the authority which the orthodox had attributed to the Bible and the Fathers of the Church. The theologians made peace between the contending factions by placing Aristotle and the Fathers side by side, and referring as reverentially to the one as to the other, except on the few fundamental points upon which the former could not be interpreted into harmony with the latter. The scholastic form of argument which attained its full development in Aquinas—a chain of authorities and syllogisms in defence of one thesis, another series for the opposite view, a conclusion in harmony with Augustine or Aristotle as the case might be, and a reply to the opposing arguments by means of ingenious distinction or reconciliation —afforded exceptional facilities for the harmonious combination of orthodoxy and intellectuality. The scholastics showed the Latin Churchman how to be ingenious, startling, brilliant, even destructive, without suspicion of heresy. Bernard would have been shocked at the idea of inventing or even of fairly stating objections to the Catholic Faith. By the time of Aquinas it was felt that the better the imaginary opponents' case could be stated, the more credit there was in refuting it. The scholar's intellectual enjoyment of thirty ingenious arguments against the Immortality of the Soul was not diminished by the thirty-six equally ingenious arguments with which the attack would immediately be met.[1] In scholastic disputation —now as freely practised in the cloister of the ascetic mendicants as in the arts-schools of the profane and audacious seculars—restless intellectual activity found an innocent outlet, love of controversy and speculation an innocent gratification;

[1] This is the mode of argument adopted by Albert the Great in his *De Unitate Intellectus* (*Opp.* v. 218).

and into love of controversy and speculation the real ardour for truth and knowledge which distinguished the age of Berengar and the age of Abelard had for the most part degenerated.

In logic Albert and his greater pupil were moderate realists —the latter so moderate that it is possible for a nominalistic admirer like Hauréau to contend with some plausibility that he may be called nominalist with as much truth as realist. With Aquinas the reality of the universal *ante rem* was acknowledged, but only as an idea in the Divine Mind: the universal *post rem* was admitted to be an abstraction from the particulars; the universal *in re* became, as with Aristotle, as with Gilbert de la Porrée in the preceding century, a form inseparably immanent in matter.[1] Enough of realistic doctrine was preserved to harmonize with the teaching of the Platonically minded Fathers, and with the recognition of the substantial existence of the body and blood of Christ beneath the *species* of bread and wine; on the other hand, good sense was no longer shocked by the idea of universals with a real existence apart from and before the particulars, nor was theism or morality endangered by positions which tended to reduce all realities to one. But in the age of Aquinas the old quarrel of realism versus nominalism which had absorbed the speculative energies of the preceding century was thrown into the shade, or rather it was merged in wider and more fundamental issues, by the discovery of the Aristotelian writings. Logic had now become merely the basis of a vast encyclopaedia of science. Albert and Aquinas wrote upon psychology, metaphysics, physics, physiology, natural history, morals. These subjects had to be treated directly from a purely scientific point of view; while their theological applications opened a wholly new region of thought to the theologian proper. The Dominicans neither maintained, with the obscurantists and the mystics, that religious truth lay entirely beyond the domain of logic and of reason, nor, with rationalists like Erigena or Abelard, did they attempt either to establish

The Thomistic philosophy.

---

[1] [Students of Thomism would not now agree that S. Thomas identified the universal *in re* with Form. It is the constituent reality (*essentia*) distinct from that which gives it actuality or being.]

or to criticize the most mysterious doctrines of the Church by *a priori* reasoning. By Albert and Aquinas a clear line was—perhaps for the first time—drawn between the provinces of natural and of revealed religion, between the truths which reason could establish for herself and the region in which she could only examine the credentials and demonstrate the self-consistency or rationality or at most probability of

Attitude towards reason. what is placed before it by authority. It is hardly too much to say that the lines laid down by S. Thomas as to the attitude of reason towards revelation are, amid all change of belief as to the actual content of revelation, the lines in which, as much in the Protestant as in the medieval or modern Roman Churches, the main current of religious thought has moved ever since. Hitherto philosophy had been either an avowed foe to theology or a dangerous and suspected ally. By the genius of the great Dominicans all that was Christian or not unchristian in Aristotle was woven into the very substance and texture of what was henceforth more and more to grow into the accredited theology of the Catholic Church. The contents of whole treatises of the pagan philosopher—including even his great treatise on ethics—are embodied in the *Summa Theologiae* of Aquinas, still the great classic of the seminaries. To that marvellous structure — strangely compounded of solid thought, massive reasoning, baseless subtlety, childish credulity, lightest fancy—Aristotle has contributed assuredly not less than S. Augustine.

Concilia-tion of religion and philo-sophy. The work which Aquinas did for the Church of his day —the fusion of the highest speculative thought of the time with its profoundest spiritual convictions, the reconciliation of the new truths of the present with the kernel of truth embodied in the traditional creed—is a task which will have to be done again and again as the human mind continues progressive and religion remains a vital force with it. It will have to be done in a different spirit, by different methods, and with very different results from those of the *Summa*. But in one respect the work of Aquinas is built on the solid foundation upon which all such efforts must repose—the grand conviction that religion is rational and that reason is divine, that all knowledge and all truth, from whatever source derived, must be capable of harmonious adjustment. Of that conviction—not often so intensely held as by the best minds of the thirteenth century—the *Summa Theologiae* remains a magnificent monument, still on some points not wholly useless as a help to the rationalization of Christian belief.[1]

It is a striking fact that the authority which his Dominican advocates thus secured for the great pagan philosopher extended itself also in a measure to the Moslem disciples by whom he had been first introduced to Latin Christendom. Though Averroism was still practically a synonym for freethought, a distinction was drawn between Averroës the thinker and Averroës the commentator. Averroës became almost as much the authoritative commentator as Aristotle was the authoritative philosopher. The oath not to read the works of 'Mauritius' continued to be administered to inceptors in arts; but when, about the middle of the fourteenth century, nominalism, the defiant foe alike of Aristotle and of Averroës, began to rear its head again, the university, in sublime ignorance of its inconsistency (if Mauritius was indeed identical with Averroës), required the candidate almost in the same breath to adjure Mauritius and to swear to teach no doctrine inconsistent with that of 'Aristotle and his commentator Averroës'.[2] Under cover of this commentatorial fame,

[1] [We leave these characteristic pages as they were written, but it is hardly necessary to remind readers of this work that, while the main facts and their relative significance generally remain, the whole study of the growth of thought in Paris and elsewhere during the thirteenth century has been greatly enlarged and modified since 1895. Rashdall naturally wrote under the influence of Hauréau. Some references to the new learning, as it affects the history of universities and especially of scholastic method, are given elsewhere, as occasion arises. The most convenient guide is B. Geyer's edition of Ueberweg, frequently cited in this volume. Cf. also the excellent sketch of F. Ehrle, *Die Scholastik und ihre Aufgaben in unsere Zeit*, ed. 2, Freiburg-i.-B., 1933. As detailed investigation proceeds, the amount of freedom in theological and philosophical discussion is seen to have been greater than Rashdall allowed.]

[2] Bulaeus, iv. 273; *Chartul.* ii, App., p. 680. So a statute of Heidelberg requires the inceptor to swear 'quod textum Aristotelis et sui commentatoris . . . firmiter et tamquam authenticum observabit'. Hautz, *Gesch.* ii. 352, where the extraordinary explanation is given, 'wahrscheinlich Porphyrius'.

CHAP. V, Averroës had still a great part to play in the schools of medieval
§ 2.   Christendom.

II. *The Constitutional Struggle*

[For the literature see UEBERWEG-GEYER, pp. 728, 729. Some of the
literary texts, with selections from William of Saint-Amour, have been
edited by M. BIERBAUM, *Bettelorden und Weltgeistlichkeit an der Universität Paris* (Münster, 1920). The chief studies are: MANDONNET, 'De
l'incorporation des Dominicains dans l'ancienne Université de Paris', in
Revue Thomiste, iv (1896), 135 *sq.*; M. PERROD, *Maître Guillaume de S.
Amour: l'Université de Paris et l'ordres mendiants au xiiie siècle* (Paris,
1895, revised as 'Études sur la vie et sur les œuvres de Guillaume de S.
Amour' in *Mémoires de la société d'émulation du Jura*, 1902, pp. 61–252);
F. X. SEPPELT, 'Der Kampf der Bettelorden an der Universität Paris in der
Mitte des 13. Jahrhunderts' in *Kirchengeschicht. Abhandlungen* (Breslau,
iii. 1905, 197–241, vi. 1908, 73–140); A. VAN DEN WIJNGAERT, 'Querelles
du clergé séculier et régulier et des ordres mendiants a l'Université de
Paris au xiiie siècle', in *France franciscaine*, 1922, 1923; F. EHRLE, 'S.
Domenico; le origini del primo studio generale del suo ordine a Parigi',
in *Miscellanea Dominicana*, 1923, pp. 85–134. Cf. E. JALLONGHI in *La
scuola cattolica*, Milan, xlv (1917), 488–502, xlvi (1918), 103–23, 177–87.
CHRISTINE THOUZELLIER, 'La place du *De Periculis* de Guilluame de
Saint-Amour dans les polémiques universitaires du xiiie siècle' (*Revue
historique*, clvi, 1927, 69–83).

   On the organization of study in the orders see C. DOUAIS, *Essai sur
l'organisation des études dans l'ordre des Frères Prêcheurs au xiiie et xvi^e
siècle* (Paris, 1884); H. FELDER, *Geschichte der wissenschaftlichen Studien
im Franziskanerorden bis um die Mitte des 13. Jahrhunderts* (1904); F.
EHRLE's introduction to *I più antichi statuti della facoltà teologica della
università di Bologna* (1932). Cf. B. VOGT in *Franziskanische Studien*, ix
(1933), 137–57, and H. SPETTMANN, *ibid.* x (1934), 95–103.]

Such were the effects which followed the introduction
into the Parisian Schools, nearly at the same time, of a new
philosophy of non-Christian origin and of a new order
pledged to the defence of the Christian Faith. We must now
go back to the early days of the movement whose progress has
been sketched, and trace the relations between the new orders
and the great educational organization of secular clerks which
was just beginning to be known as the University of Paris.
The influence which the coming of the friars exercised upon
the constitutional development of the university was not less
important than its effects upon the intellectual life of the
university and of the world which looked to that university
as to its intellectual centre.

The training of theologically educated preachers was (as we have seen) an essential part of Dominic's original design. [In the course of the century after the foundation of his order, an educational system, comprehensive, elastic, perfectly adapted to its needs, set always under the firm control of the chapters and heads of the widespread organization, was gradually devised. The basis of the system was the conventual school, which in some degree was open to external students. In this the Bible, the *Sentences* of the Lombard and subsidiary texts, including the *Historia Scolastica*, were studied. The constitutions of 1228 enacted that no priory was to be founded unless it could be provided with a *lector*, who was to have studied theology for four years. In each province special *scolae provinciales* were established in certain convents, and beyond these were the *studia generalia* to which students from various provinces could be sent or 'assigned'. In course of time the early concentration upon theology was followed by the recognition of other studies, although alchemy, medicine, and the civil and canon law would seem never to have been permitted in the curriculum. For the study of logic and the more advanced physical and metaphysical subjects represented in the works of Aristotle, the priories of the various provinces were grouped about *studia artium* and *studia naturalium*. This development can be traced from the middle of the century. Early in the fourteenth century the growing sense of the need for more Biblical study as the foundation of theology led to the establishment of special *studia bibliae*, while the missionary policy of the order gave rise to special *studia arabica*, *graeca* and *hebraica*. It is important to realize that in the Dominican schools, except the last named, the *curricula* were similar to those of the universities and the qualifications of the teachers parallel to, but not dependent upon, those required by the universities. From one point of view the order, whose will was expressed through the provincial and general chapters and by the minister general, was a university distributed in the convents and especially in the provincial and general *studia*. This fact gave its strength to the position of the order in its relations

CHAP. V, with the corporations of masters in the universities.[1] The
§ 2. *lector* in a Dominican school had not necessarily, though if
he were a theologian he had generally, been a student in a
university. His greatest work was, as often as not, the outcome of lectures given in the schools of the order. Thus
many of the biblical commentaries of S. Thomas and his
philosophical writings came from the years when he was
teaching in the convents and provincial *studia* of the Roman
province. His *Questiones disputatae* resulted from disputations held at Anagni, Rome, and Viterbo between 1259 and
1268.[2] On the other hand, it was the policy of the order from
the first to establish its *studia generalia* so far as was practicable in university towns, and it was to the students in the
university that the order naturally turned for its most
promising recruits. A *studium generale* already existed in the
convent at Paris in 1228.

In these early days the coming of the friars would seem
to have caused no concern.] On their first advent, not the
slightest hostility was shown by the university as a body to the
new order: it was from the university in part that the friars
obtained, in exchange for certain masses and funeral services,
the site of their famous convent, hitherto occupied by the
Hospital of Saint-Jacques.[3] The great dispersion of 1229,

[1] [Similarly, Franciscan lecturers
on theology 'in houses of their
Order not situated in university
towns required . . . no licence from
any authority outside the Order.
Those appointed to lecture "in
places where a University flourishes"
had to conform to the laws and customs of the University'; A. G.
Little, who refers to papal letters of
1257 and 1265, 'The Franciscan
School at Oxford in the Thirteenth
Century', in *Archivum Franciscanum Historicum*, xix (1926), 821–
2. Cf. the constitutions of Benedict XII for the Cistercians, *Chartul.* ii, No. 992 (1335).]

[2] [See the various articles of
Mandonnet in the *Revue Thomiste*
for 1909, 1918, 1926, and 1928.

The constitutions of 1228 are
edited in the *Analecta Ordinis
Praedicatorum*, 1895–6, pp. 621–
47. The general development, described by Douais, Ehrle and others,
can be traced in the *acta* of the
general chapters (*Monumenta*, ed.
Reichert, iii (1898), iv (1899), viii
(1900), and in the chronicles and
the works of Humbert de Romanis,
ed. Berthier (Rome, 1888). The
whole subject is intricate and far
too large to be fully discussed here.
We have been much helped by an
unpublished essay, 'On the Dominican Organization of Studies in
the Middle Ages', written by Miss
Mary C. Rixon.]

[3] The hospital was the gift of
the secular doctor, Jean de Barastre,

however, entirely changed the relations between the· friars and the university. Although there is no truth in the accusation that the friars had contributed to that event by poisoning the minds of the court against the secular masters,[1] they were not disposed to relinquish their studies and incur the hostility of their royal patrons in a quarrel that was none of theirs. On the contrary they availed themselves of the opportunity to start an independent theological school of their own, or rather to throw open to secular scholars a school which they had long possessed, and which in 1229 and 1230 was taught by Roland of Cremona, a friar of the order.[2] Upon the return of the university, there seems to have been at first no disposition on the part of their secular rivals to disturb the *status quo*. But an unexpected event tempted the friars to venture on a still further innovation. John of S. Giles, a secular master, under whom Roland of Cremona had incepted in theology, was invited to preach *ad clerum* in the Dominican Church.[3] He preached on the beauty of voluntary poverty. In the

Dominican Schools at dispersion of 1229.

A second Dominican doctor.

Dean of S. Quentin, whom Honorius III had given to them as their theological teacher [*Chartul.* i, No. 44]; but the university surrendered in favour of the preachers certain rights over the ground. Thus one of the witnesses at S. Dominic's process of canonization says: 'data fuit ei et sociis suis a magistro Joanne decano S. Quintini tunc regente in theologia Parisius et ab universitate magistrorum et scholarium Parisiensium ecclesia S. Jacobi posita in porta Aurelianensi, ubi steterunt et fecerunt conventum.' Echard, i. 50. (Cf. *Chartul.* i, No. 43.) The university's deed of gift is printed in Bulaeus, iii. 105, *Chartul.* i, No. 42. [For the hospital and its transference to the friars preacher cf. Marcel Poëte, *Une Vie de cité, Paris*, i (Paris, 1924), 178 *sq.*]

[1] As to their influence with the Queen, Jordanus says in 1227, 'ipsa regina tenerrime diligit fratres, que mecum ore proprio satis fami-

liariter loquebatur'. Ep. No. 17; *Chartul.* i, No. 52. Cf. Poëte, *op. cit.* i. 179.

[2] [F. Ehrle, 'S. Domenico; le origini del primo studio generale del suo ordine a Parigi e la somma teologica del primo maestro Rolando da Cremona', in *Miscellanea Dominicana*, Rome, 1923, pp. 85–134. A list of Dominican masters at Paris, compiled by Stephen of Salanhac and Bernard Gui, has survived and was printed by Denifle, *Archiv für Litteratur- und Kirchengeschichte*, ii. 204 *sq.*]

[3] Trivet (ed. Hog, p. 211), Echard (i. 100) and several modern writers make this incident occur at the General Chapter of the Dominican Order held in 1228. But this view appears to be inconsistent with the chronology. [Mandonnet (*Revue Thomiste*, 1896, p. 156 *sq.*) considers that John was preaching an ordinary university sermon. On John of S. Giles see also Ehrle, *op. cit.*, p. 9.]

CHAP. V,
§ 2.

midst of his discourse he stopped, and, 'that he might con-firm his words by his own example, descended from the pulpit, received the habit of the friars, and therein returned and finished his discourse'. The scholars were eager for the famous doctor to continue his lectures; but the order was not inclined to silence their master in his favour. Henceforth there were two regular schools of theology in the Convent of S. Jacques.

Constitutional position of friar doctors.

At about the same time another Englishman, Alexander of Hales, entered the Franciscan convent, and continued there the lectures which he had begun as a secular.[1] The example was followed by other religious orders,[2] and the university now began to awake to the irregularity of the whole proceeding; particular exception was taken to the erection of the second Dominican chair. It is, indeed, difficult to say how far the mendicant doctors had been admitted to their degrees with the usual formalities. The first Dominican doctor had certainly been licensed by the chancellor and had incepted under John of S. Giles, apparently before that doctor's entrance into the order; but, as the majority of the secular doctors had dispersed, he could hardly have been regularly admitted to their 'consortium'.[3] The second Dominican doctor had graduated as a secular, but his continued teaching in the convent of the order is expressly said to have been 'without the consent of the chancellor'.[4] This

---

[1] Trivet, *loc. cit.*; Echard, i. 101. [Alexander probably joined the Franciscans in 1231; Felder, pp. 178 *sqq.*]

[2] By 1254 the 'Clarevallenses', Praemonstratensians, the order 'De Valle Scholarium', and the Trinitarians or Mathurines had regular colleges and theological *cathedrae* at Paris, besides unattached mendicant doctors. Bulaeus, iii. 255; *Chartul.* i, No. 230. The Carmelites and Austin Friars acquired Houses in Paris about 1260. *Ibid.*, Nos. 358, 358*a*, 360.

[3] [The *admissio ad consortium* was not strictly necessary, as the

chancellor could still grant the licence at his discretion; *Chartul.* i, No. 16; cf. above, p. 308. There is no evidence that the Dominican and other masters among the regulars had not been duly licensed.]

[4] See the letter of 1254 to the prelates of Christendom (Bulaeus, iii. 255; *Chartul.* i, No. 230.): 'translata maiori parte studii Parisiensis Andegavis, in illa paucitate scolarium, que remansit Parisius . . . conniventibus episcopo et cancellario Parisiensibus, qui tunc erant, in absentia magistrorum sollempne magisterium et unam magistralem cathedram sunt adepti.

anomalous state of things continued for twenty years after
the great dispersion. During this period of peace we are not
able positively to determine exactly how the theological faculty
was constituted or what share the mendicant doctors had in
the congregations, disputations and other privileges of the
university. A good deal of friction there must no doubt have
been before matters came to an open breach ;[1] but there is not
sufficient evidence of any official resistance of the university

Deinde . . . *per eandem cathedram multiplicatis sibi doctoribus* successive preter voluntatem cancellarii, qui tunc erat, maioribus nostris, qui nondum aliis regularium scholasticorum conventibus arctabantur, dissimulantibus, per seipsos secundam cathedram erexerunt'. The position is thus interpreted by the Catalogue of Dominican *Lectores* at Paris (*Archiv*, ii. 204): '(1) frater Rotlandus Lombardus Cremonensis qui fuit primus licentiatus Parisius de ordine predicatorum. (2) frater Joannes de Sancto Aegidio, Anglicus, qui intravit ordinem predicatorum magister existens. Sub eo incepit prefatus frater Rotlandus.' [Hugh of S. Cher incepted under Roland, whom he succeeded in 1231; *ibid.*, n. 3. Thomas of Cantimpré, *De apibus*, Book I, c. 19, refers to Hugh as the second master.] Trivet (p. 212) in speaking of John of S. Giles says: 'Occasione eius habuerunt Fratres duas scholas infra septa sua, resumente eo lectiones suas post ordinis ingressum ad importunam instantiam auditorum.' [Rashdall in the first edition interpreted the university's statements in 1254 to mean that the licence of the chancellor was withheld from holders of the second chair and that the mendicant masters were not incorporated. They suggest rather that the chancellor and masters connived at developments without formal approval. The mendicant masters certainly

took part in meetings of the theological masters: *Chartul*. i, Nos. 108, 178; in the former case (1235–8) three Dominicans are described as determining a matter submitted by the bishop to a *convocatio* of all the masters of theology held in the Dominican convent. The statute of 1252 (*ibid.*, No. 200; see below, p. 377) was intended to limit the practice. For the further history of the conflict see the authorities given above. The chronicles of William de Nangis (in the *Rec. des historiens de France*, xx), Matthew Paris and others supplement the documents.] Several of the poems of the *trouveur* Rutebeuf (*Œuvres*, ed. Tubinal, Paris, 1839, i. 151 *sq*.) relate to this conflict; they side strongly with the scholars, and testify to the strength of the feeling in their favour and the importance of William of S. Amour.

[1] Richerius (*M.G.H., Scriptores*, xxv. 327) thus states a side of the controversy which is not very distinctly indicated by the official documents: 'de dificicione questionum et magistrorum legentium approbatione . . . nam predicatores dicebant ab eis questionum diffiniciones debere proferri, quia potior sciencia in personis Ordinis ipsorum vigeret . . . Clerici vero e contra asserebant se antiquitus Magistros et difinitores habuisse, qui scholarum et scholarium Rectores extiterant'.

CHAP. V, to the mendicant claims before 1250.[1] The difficulty which
§ 2. arose in that year was one of the friars' own making, though
Bull on
behalf of it was no doubt eagerly seized upon by the jealous seculars as
friar doc-
tors, 1250. a pretext for refusing to increase the number of the regular
doctors. While the desire for promotion to the magisterial
chair was not thought incompatible with the humility and
unworldliness professed by the orders, it was considered
inconsistent with their rule to ask for such an honour. [In
1250 the chancellor, whatever his previous practice may have
been, was availing himself of his discretionary right to refrain
from licensing any scholars who did not apply for the licence.
Pope Innocent IV accordingly enjoined] the chancellor to
confer the licence upon as many religious as, after examination,
he should 'according to his conscience' consider qualified,
even if they had scrupled to ask for the honour.[2] The rights
of the other theological doctors were entirely ignored. It
now became necessary for the society to assert the right to
refuse to recognize the inception of a doctor who had been
Theologi- licensed without its consent. The theologians accordingly,
cal statute
against in 1251–2, passed a formal statute against the mendicants—the
Domini-
cans,
1251–2.

[1] Wadding (*Annales Minorum*, iii. 371) speaks of papal injunctions c. 1244 to admit the regulars to the full rights enjoyed by the secular doctors; and the previous historians of the university have accepted the statement. But, as the researches of Denifle have failed to discover any trace of Bulls on this subject of the date specified, we may safely accept his suggestion (*Chartul.* i, No. 191 note) that the Bull of 1250 has been mistakenly referred to an earlier date. Cf. *Mém. de la soc. de l'hist. de Paris et de l'Île de France*, x. 246.

[2] Bulaeus, iii. 223; *Chartul.* i, No. 191. [The wording of the Bull (30 May 1250) suggests that the chancellor's policy was not traditional. With regard to the refusal to seek the licence, Miss Rixon has pointed out that neither the Rule of S. Augustine nor the Dominican constitutions enjoins it, and that S. Thomas, in his *Contra impugnantes Deum* (c. 2), maintained that the licence to teach conferred an obligation, not an honour. Whatever the cause of the scruples of the religious may have been, the origin of the dispute between the university and the mendicants must be sought rather in the facts mentioned by Thomas of Cantimpré and Richer (see note above), facts which in their turn are due to the emergence of a strongly organized and efficient system of Dominican education. The Bull of 1250 applied *praecipue* to regulars generally and had no particular reference to the mendicants. In 1254 (*Chartul.* i, No. 230) the university alleged that the friars had disregarded the evangelical precept, 'ne vocemini magistri'.]

first formal statute (so far as we know) ever enacted by the theologians or any other of the superior faculties. It was ordered that 'no Religious not having a College at Paris' should be admitted to the Society of Masters,[1] that each religious college should in future be content with one master and one school, and that no bachelor should be promoted to a chair unless he had already lectured in the schools of an actually regent master, i.e. a master recognized as such by the faculty. Any master refusing to assent to this statute was 'deprived of the society of the masters'.

We know nothing of the progress of events for more than a year. It seems clear that, the decree of the theological faculty notwithstanding, the mendicants, even the second Dominican doctor, were admitted to general congregations of the university.[2] But in the year 1252-3 an event occurred which gave the seculars the opportunity of renewing the contest. The affair was very much like the incident which produced the dispersion of 1229. Lent in the Middle Ages, whether through an unseemly prolongation of carnival disorder or through the reaction of youthful spirits against enforced abstinence, was as fruitful a source of crime as the Ramadan in Turkey: nearly all the great university riots took place at this season. In the present year a scholar was killed by the provost's officers in a street-brawl: others had been outrageously ill treated and imprisoned in defiance of the scholastic privilege. The university decreed a 'Cessation of

[1] 'Ut de cetero religiosus aliquis non habens collegium et cui est a iure publice docere prohibitum, ad eorum societatem nullatenus admittatur', Bulaeus, iii. 245; *Chartul.* i, No. 200. The Bull of 1255 in reciting this prohibition inserts the word 'Parisius' after 'collegium'. Bulaeus, iii. 283; *Chartul.* i, No. 247. To appreciate the situation, it should be remembered that the mendicant system was to change their *lectores* frequently. [Thus, when Roland went to Toulouse, in 1230, he was succeeded by Hugh of S. Cher (*Archiv,*

ii. 173, 174). For the *lectores*, teaching in convents outside universities, see above, p. 372.]

[2] Otherwise they could hardly have been subsequently expelled. It is clear that they attended the congregations at some period later than the publication of 'The Perils of the Last Times' from the complaint of the masters that they had libelled its author as well as the Pope 'in Congregationibus nostris'. (Bulaeus, iii. 290; *Chartul.* i, No. 256.) [In 1255 (*ibid.*, No. 249) Alexander IV ordered their reinstatement.]

Lectures'; the two Dominican doctors and the one Franciscan[1] refused to obey it, and, since obedience to duly ordered cessations was enjoined under ecclesiastical penalties, appealed to Rome against the decision of the university. The cessation proving ineffectual, the university agreed that all its masters should take an oath to insist on obtaining justice. Again the three friars refused compliance: whereupon they were expelled from the 'consortium' or company of the masters, and the scholars forbidden to go to their lectures. A tardy redress for the outrage was at length obtained through the intervention of the King's brother, Alfonse, Count of Poitiers and Toulouse. Two of the offenders were convicted, dragged through the streets at the heels of horses, and finally hanged. But, though the immediate cause of complaint was removed, the friars—or at least the two Dominicans—were not re-admitted.

The affair had brought out more clearly than ever the fact that the friars were claiming to enjoy the privileges of membership of the masters' college while they refused to submit to its authority. The university accordingly determined to bring matters to a head. In April 1253 a statute was passed by the whole university enacting that henceforth no master of any faculty should be admitted to the 'College of Masters or fellowship of the University' unless he should first have sworn in full congregation, or at least in the presence of three masters of his own faculty specially deputed for the purpose, to obey the statutes of the university, to keep its secrets, and further to observe a 'cessation' when ordered by the university.[2] The secular masters of the superior faculties would have taken such an oath to the statutes on inception in the faculty of arts; but the friar doctors, having never graduated in arts, would have hitherto escaped it. The erection of the second chair, however, and the attitude taken up by the two Dominicans and the Franciscan in the matter of the cessation

The university demands an oath of obedience.

---

[1] [Felder at one time maintained that, for some years, the Franciscans also had two regent masters. This was disputed by Seppelt, and Felder withdrew his suggestion in 1911, *Études franciscaines*, xxv. 598–613.]

[2] Bulaeus, iii. 250; *Chartul.* i, No. 219.

determined the secular masters to insist on their rights, and to compel the intruders to acknowledge the authority of the university if they wished to enjoy its rights and privileges. The exact extent of the authority claimed by the university should be clearly understood. No one denied the right of a friar duly licensed by the chancellor to teach theology to members of his own order or to others. What the masters asserted was the hitherto unquestioned right of the university to impose its own regulations upon its own members, to refuse professional association to masters who did not choose to comply with them, and to exclude from their society the pupils of such unrecognized extra-university masters.[1] The question which was thus really at stake was the autonomy of the society. It had in truth already parted with its voluntary character too far by its acceptance of papal statutes and privileges to claim to be treated purely as a private club. And by the issue of the present controversy it was placed beyond dispute that henceforth the university was as much a part of the ecclesiastical system, as much subject to papal regulation, as the older capitular body whose authority it had by papal favour nearly succeeded in shaking off.

The oath of obedience to the statutes was, to an extent which it is hard for us to realize,[2] a matter of vital importance to the universities. Their whole power over their members,

---

[1] Cf. the words of the Bull of 1255, 'eos beneficio societatis in magistralibus privavistis ipsosque privatos publice nunciantes iniunxistis districte, ut scolares lectiones eorum decetero non audirent.' (Bulaeus, iii. 282; *Chartul.* i, No. 247.) In the letter of 1255 (Bulaeus, iii. 290; *Chartul.* i, No. 256) the masters expressly declare that they do not want to prevent them 'quominus tot scolas habeant et scolares, sive de secularibus sive de regularibus, quot habere volunt et possunt, nec quominus privilegiis nostris omnibus tam ipsi quam eorum auditores gaudeant'. They only demand 'ut nos ex una parte civitatis patiantur pacifice et quiete, nec ad domos aut scolas nostras seu etiam ad conventus nostros, in quibus magistri non nisi rogati conveniunt, sicut nec consuetum extitit, nobis invitis se ingerant violenter'.

[2] [It might perhaps be suggested that Rashdall's insistence in this paragraph on the peculiar sanctity attached in the Middle Ages to an oath, more appropriately applies to the frequency with which oaths were exacted, and to their enforcement 'in foro externo', than to any serious difference between medieval and modern ethical theory about the seriousness of perjury.]

CHAP. V, their very existence depended upon the sanction of this oath.
§ 2.   The obligation of such oaths, according to the notions of the
time, could not be neutralized by the claims of conflicting
duties or obligations. They were (subject to the papal power
of dispensation) absolute, irrevocable, eternal. An oath,
according to medieval notions, was no mere appeal to the
conscience, no mere solemn recognition of an already
existing duty. Whatever the nature of the act to which
the oath pledged the deponent, the violation of it placed him
in a state of mortal sin, and doomed him to eternal perdition
should he die unabsolved. A good illustration of the un-
bounded claims which the academical oath was supposed to
give the university over its members is afforded by an incident
which occurred about a century after the period with which
we are dealing. The Bishop of Paris had, with a severity
very unusual in dealing with the sins of the clergy, imprisoned
as well as excommunicated a scholar convicted of rape, and
imposed upon him a fine of 500 livres as a condition of absolution. The university asserted, though the Bishop denied, that
the privileges of the university forbade the imposition of a
pecuniary penance upon a scholar under any circumstances
whatever, and the Bishop had sworn to maintain these
privileges upon his admission to the degree of doctor in
canon law. They accordingly placarded the walls of the
Bishop's cathedral city with broadsheets proclaiming him
a perjurer. The bishop was powerless to resent the insult,
and was forced to go to Avignon for a papal Bull absolving
him from the obligation of his oath so far as it affected the
discharge of his episcopal duties.[1] A century later still, we
find the university affecting, on the strength of the same all-
powerful oath, to dictate to its graduates in the King's Privy
Council the advice which they should give to the King on
matters of public policy.[2]

But we must return to the events of the thirteenth century.
The statute of the university requiring the oath under penalty
of expulsion was drawn up shortly before Easter, 1253—the

[1] Bulaeus, iv. 226; *Chartul*. ii,
Nos. 899, 903.

[2] Monstrelet, *Chronique*, Paris,
1857, ii. 106.

Easter immediately following the cessation. Though not finally sealed till September, its contents appear to have been at once published and acted upon. The friars were solemnly expelled and proclaimed excommunicate as having disobeyed statutes to which papal authority had been annexed. The order promptly procured papal Bulls requiring the university to readmit them to 'fellowship' (*consortium*) and to suspend all statutes against them pending the decision of their appeal to the Holy See.[1] The Bulls were entrusted for execution to two bishops, who in the heat of summer had doubtless no inclination for a visit to Paris and appointed as their sub-delegate one of the traditional enemies of the university— the Chapter of Paris, who with indecent alacrity (as the uni- versity complained), without admonition, citation, or other formality, had the whole body of masters and scholars solemnly 'suspended from their office or privilege one Sunday morning during Mass in all the churches, in the presence of all the laity to the grave scandal of us and of all the clergy'. The Bull and the ecclesiastical censures notwithstanding, the university persisted in its course, and, that the unwary fresh-men might be warned against attending the schools or sermons of the expelled and excommunicated brethren, once more at the beginning of the October term the bedels were sent round the schools to proclaim the academical ban. They even made an attempt to publish the edict in the schools of the friars themselves, when the university officers were attacked and maltreated 'even to the effusion of blood' by the sturdy young friars, who seldom had such a chance of letting off their somewhat pent-up spirits in so holy a cause. The bedels reported what had happened to the rector, who came to publish the edict in person but met with no better reception. The papal legate vainly endeavoured to mediate. The masters paid no more respect to the 'suspension' than was implied in appealing against it. The friars remained expelled, the seculars impenitent.[2]

---

[1] *Chartul.* i, Nos. 222, 223, 225, 226; Bulaeus, iii. 254.

[2] The above narrative is chiefly from the university circular letter mentioned in the next paragraph.

CHAP. V,
§ 2.
University's En-cyclical
Letter,
1254.

At the beginning of the following year (1254) the masters unfolded their grievances in a letter to the prelates of Christendom,[1] which throws much light upon the real grounds of the quarrel. There were, it appears, at the time fifteen doctors of divinity at Paris. Of these, three were canons of Notre Dame, and taught (in accordance with the ancient privileges of the chapter) without any authorization from the university. Of the rest, nine were regulars of various orders.[2] The masters naturally complained that secular students were virtually deprived of the principal inducement to study—the hope of themselves occupying the professorial chair. Even apart from the limitation of the number of the theological doctors to eight which had been enacted by Innocent III,[3] the theological students were not numerous enough to supply fees, or even audiences, for an unlimited number of teachers. And the mendicant doctors, being maintained in part or entirely by the contributions of the charitable, must have competed at an advantage with the seculars, even had not such teachers as Albert the Great and S. Thomas Aquinas been among the number of the former.[4]

The enemies of the university were powerful. The Court was much under the influence of the friars. The party of the

[1] Bulaeus, iii. 255–8; *Chartul.* i, No. 230. (4 Feb. 1254.)

[2] [This figure depends upon the accuracy of the statement made by the university that it possessed only three secular regent masters at this time, i.e. in addition to the three canons of Notre Dame. Denifle could find trace at most of seven chairs possessed by the six religious orders, Cistercian, Premonstratensian, Austin Canons, Trinitarian, Franciscan, Dominican, and it is not clear that each order had a chair. But the real point was that the friars were so popular that there were not enough scholars to go round.]

[3] Bulaeus, iii. 36; *Chartul.* i, No. 5. The regulation had been relaxed in favour of the mendicants (*ibid.*, No. 27).

[4] Thomas of Cantimpré puts the inferior teaching powers of the secular masters down to heavy feeding and the excessive vacations which their luxurious habits compelled them to give. 'Videbant enim scholares quod magistri seculares, sicut viri diuitiarum, dormierunt somnum suum, ducebantque in bonis dies suos. Et cum vespere multiplicitate ferculorum obruerentur et potuum, et postea vigilare non possent, nec studere, et per hoc nihil inuenire in manibus quod proferrent, sequenti mane solemnem diem constituebant auditoribus in condensis (*sic*) et sic per ineptas vacationes, quibus sua clerici inaniter expendere se dolebant, optato priuabantur studio.' *De Apibus* (Douai, 1627), p. 181.

seculars had the disadvantage, like the Jansenists of a later CHAP. V,
day, of fighting the King's Confessor, who was invariably §2.
chosen from the ranks of their opponents. At first, indeed,
there was some hope of obtaining at all events a compromise
through the favour of Innocent IV, who had, except in this
matter, shown himself disposed to favour the seculars and to
repress the usurpations of the friars. The death of Innocent
IV in 1254, just after issuing a Bull withdrawing the extraordinary privileges of the mendicants,[1] destroyed the last
hope of a settlement favourable to the university. Alexander
IV at once reversed the policy of his predecessor. The Bulls
which Innocent had issued to restrain mendicant encroachments upon the rights of ordinaries and curates were promptly
revoked;[2] and a few months later, in April 1255, appeared
the celebrated Bull *Quasi lignum vitae*, which decided the Bull *Quasi*
matters in dispute, on almost every point, in favour of the *lignum*
vitae de-
mendicants.[3] The expulsion of the Dominicans was annulled. cides for
friars,
The chancellor was directed to grant the licence to as many 1255.
duly qualified candidates as after examination (by himself
alone) he should think fit, thus implicitly conceding the second
Dominican chair. The friars were indeed to obey a cessation,
but only when voted by a two-thirds majority of the masters
in each faculty. This put it in the power of the mendicant
theologians to stop a cessation whenever they pleased, as
more than a third of the theological faculty at any one time
were sure to be friars. Finally all sentences of expulsion or
deprivation were quashed by apostolical authority, and the
university required peremptorily to readmit the two Dominican doctors[4] into full membership. The execution of the Bull

[1] In preaching, hearing confessions and burying the dead;
Bulaeus, iii. 270; *Chartul.* i, No.
240.

[2] Bulaeus, iii. 273; *Chartul.* i,
No. 244.

[3] Bulaeus, iii. 282; *Chartul.* i,
No. 247 (April 1255).

[4] In 1253 the university is
directed to readmit both Minorites
and Preachers (Bulaeus, iii. 254;
Chartul. i, No. 222). In 1255

(Bulaeus, iii. 286; *Chartul.* i, No.
249) only the two Dominicans,
Bonushomo and Helias, are mentioned. We should naturally infer
(cf. *Chartul.*, p. 258, note) that the
minorites had made their peace
with the university [and that this
was actually the case is proved by
the declaration of the general of the
order, John of Parma, related by
Salimbene under the year 1253
(*M.G.H., Scriptores*, xxxii. 299)];

CHAP. V, was entrusted to the Bishops of Orleans and Auxerre;[1] and
§ 2. upon the refusal of the university to obey, its members were
Wholesale excommunicated *en masse* by the two prelates.
excom-
munica- The masters now resolved upon a very curious manœuvre,
tion. which illustrates with great clearness the real nature of the
University institution whose very existence was attacked by the mendicant
dissolves privileges. In spite of the papal recognition, in spite of
itself.
statutes and the privileges bestowed upon it by both the
crown and Holy See, the society was still, like the English
inns of court, which enjoy nevertheless legal privileges at
least as extensive as those of the Paris Society of Masters,
ostensibly a 'voluntary society', and, unlike the inns of court,
a voluntary society almost unencumbered with property.
The masters contended that the society could be dissolved
in the way in which it was originally formed. They accordingly sought to evade the papal restrictions upon their liberty
of association as well as the excommunication launched
against its members by proclaiming the dissolution of their
society. At the end of the long vacation the individual
masters and scholars who returned to Paris addressed a letter
to the Pope, formally declaring the dissolution of the university, and renouncing all papal and other corporate privileges
and immunities whatsoever. The existence of the nations
was, however, considered to be unaffected by the dissolution
of the university itself and the document bore the seals of
these four bodies.[2] The masters did not want, they declared,

but in 1256, in the first of the series of submissions to the *Quasi lignum*, we find the penitents promise to receive the Franciscan Bonaventura as well as the Dominican Thomas Aquinas (Bulaeus, iii. 315; *Chartul.* i, No. 293). [Pelster has pointed out that Bonaventura, unlike Thomas, was already a master in theology, and that, in his case, the order for his reception implies that some new occasion of conflict had arisen; *Zeitschrift für Kath. Theologie*, xlviii (1929), 525.]

[1] Bulaeus, iii. 286; *Chartul.* i, No. 248.

[2] The letter begins 'singuli magistri et scolares omnium facultatum, reliquie dispersionis Parisiensis studii, preter Universitatis collegium Parisius commorantes'. It concludes, 'Nos autem magistri et auditores omnium facultatum, magistris fratribus et eorum auditoribus duntaxat exceptis, quoniam sigillum commune non habemus utpote ab Universitatis collegio separati, sigillis quatuor nationum ab antiquo Parisius distinctarum in hac littera usi sumus.' (Bulaeus, iii. 288–92; *Chartul.* i, No. 256.) The Domi-

to prevent the friars from having as many schools and as CHAP. V,
many scholars, whether secular or regular, as they pleased. § 2.
All that they wanted was the right to exclude these unwelcome
intruders from the schools which they held in their own
hired houses and the congregations conducted in convents
lent by friendly bodies. The friars, it was suggested, had
already shown that they were quite capable of getting on
without the enforced association of the seculars, since they
had of late been holding their own inceptions apart from the
rest of the university under the protection of an armed guard
placed at their service by their royal patron. Such were
the circumstances under which the prince of the schoolmen, Thomas Aquinas, was admitted to his degree in the
university of which he was for ever afterwards regarded by
Dominican and secular alike as the most distinguished
ornament.[1]

An important underplot had been going on by the side of 'The
the main action. The seculars were trying to procure the Perils of
the Last
condemnation of a work emanating from the fanatical section Times'
and the
of the Franciscan Order, among which the apocalyptic 'Introduction to the
speculations put forth by the Abbot Joachim had taken a new Eternal
and more startling form. This work, styled an 'Introduction Gospel'.
to the Eternal Gospel', and written by Gerard of Borgo San
Donnino, a lector in theology at the Franciscan convent
in Paris, was selling in large numbers (it would appear in
a French translation) under the very eyes of the masters
of Paris on the 'Parvis' of Notre Dame.[2] The friars

nican General Humbert adds that
'novam quamdam societatem,
nomine universitatis verbo tenus
extincto, pariter inierunt ad sedem
apostolicam appellantes' (Chartul.
i, No. 273)—an evasion to which
the Pope replies by declaring that
by the name of 'university' is meant
'omnes magistros et scolares commorantes Parisius, cuiuscumque
societatis seu congregationis existant'. (Chartul. i, No. 262.)

[1] Chartul. i, Nos. 279, 280.
[2] See the Roman de la Rose, ed.

Francisque-Michel, Paris, 1864, ii.
35 sq. [In addition to the Chartularium and the papers by Denifle
and Ehrle in the Archiv, see the
works of Bierbaum and others
noted above, p. 370. A good introduction, with bibliography, may be
read in D. Douie, The Nature and
Effect of the Theory of the Fraticelli
(Manchester, 1932), especially pp.
7, 8, 22 sqq. For a discussion of the
latest literature cf. G. la Piana,
'Joachim of Flora: a critical survey',
in Speculum, vii (1932), 257 sq.]

CHAP. V, retaliated by getting up an agitation against a work entitled
§ 2. 'The Perils of the Last Times', attributed to William of
S. Amour, the leading spirit among the secular masters—a
violent attack upon religious mendicancy which sought to
represent the friars as the 'ungodly men' whose advent the
Apostle had foretold as the immediate sign of the coming of
Antichrist and of the end of the world.[1]

The 'In- The Franciscan brochure seemed to erect S. Francis into
troduc- a position as much superior to Christ's as the position of
tion' con-
demned. Christ was to that of Abraham: it attacked the Pope and
hierarchy with prophetic vehemence, if also with prophetic
vagueness, and announced the speedy advent of a reign of
universal poverty, wherein the true ideal of the Gospel should
be for the first time realized, and the secular clergy superseded
by bare-footed mendicants. Such a work was naturally not
likely to find much favour with popes and cardinals. But,
though the majority even of the Franciscans had no sympathy
with these ideas, the orthodoxy of the whole order and even
of the other mendicant orders was undoubtedly compromised
by the book, especially as it was believed to represent the
views of the Franciscan General, John of Parma. The consequence was that the book was condemned, but with all the
leniency possible under the circumstances, the burning being
conducted privately and without *éclat*.[2]

[1] Special emphasis was laid upon the obvious applicability of the texts, *Ex iis sunt qui penetrant domos*, and *Coaceruant sibi magistros*. The writer's general conclusion is: 'Ergo nos sumus in ultima aetate huius mundi; et ista aetas iam plus durauit quam aliae, quae currunt per millenarium annorum; quia ista durauit per 1255 annos; verisimile ergo est, quod nos sumus prope finem mundi; ergo propinquiores sumus periculis nouissimorum temporum; quae futura sunt ante aduentum Antichristi.' *Opera*, p. 37. It is interesting to observe that the two parties were agreed as to the mysterious significance of the year 1260. (See Apoc. xi. 3, xii. 6.)

Denifle points out that Christian of Beauvais (another of the representatives of the university) also indulged in Chiliastic speculations. (*Chartul.* i, No. 280, note.)

[2] The errors found or alleged to be found in the *Introductorium* are given in *Chartul.* i, No. 243; the condemnation, *ibid.*, Nos. 257, 258, 277; Bulaeus, iii. 292, 293, 302. The second of these Bulls enjoins the Bishop of Paris 'quod sic prudenter, sic caute, sic provide in apostolici super hoc mandati executione procedas, quod dicti fratres nullum ex hoc opprobrium nullamque infamiam incurrere valeant sive notam'.

Very different was the fate of 'The Perils of the Last Times'. The first accusations against William of S. Amour seem to have been based not upon the contents of this book but upon pulpit utterances against the mendicants. He was cited to appear before the Bishop of Paris by a papal chaplain. But on the day appointed for the hearing, intimidated by the storm which the attack upon their champion had awakened among the secular clergy, the promoter did not venture to appear; and the Bishop of Paris, no friend to the scholars but still a secular, was obliged to admit the accused to canonical purgation in the presence of a great assemblage of four thousand clerks.[1] After the final breach with the mendicants, William of S. Amour was cited to answer charges of contumacy contained in 'The Perils of the Last Times' before an assembly of prelates belonging to the provinces of Sens and Rouen. The accused availed himself of the thin veil of anonymity which he had thrown over the objects of his attack. They had been assailed in general terms as 'false prophets' and the like, so that he was able to plead that the libel was not meant for the Dominicans. The prelates and the university were in favour of a council.[2] But the friars distrusted a tribunal composed mainly or entirely of secular prelates and members of the old religious orders. The pious but friar-ridden king was persuaded to send the book to Rome with a request for the decision of the Holy Father upon its orthodoxy. With splendid audacity the university resolved to send as its proctors to the Roman Court the accused himself, whose excommunication, banishment, imprisonment, had already been commanded by the Pope,[3] together with three other theologians, accompanied, according to Matthew Paris, by the rector of the university[4] and another master of arts to represent the inferior faculty. For once the

---

[1] Bulaeus, iii. 290; *Chartul.* i, No. 255.

[2] Bulaeus, iii. 309; *Chartul.* i, No. 287.

[3] Bulaeus, iii. 306; *Chartul.* i, No. 282.

[4] So Matthew Paris styles him. *Chron. Mai.* v. 599. [The rector was John Sackville, an Englishman; see Powicke, in *Essays in Mediaeval History presented to T.F. Tout* (Manchester, 1925), p. 122, and *The Medieval Books of Merton College*, p. 154, note. Alexander IV mentions only two doctors, *Chartul.* i, No. 320.]

CHAP. V, proceedings of the Roman tribunals were not dilatory. The
§ 2. proctors did not leave Paris before August 1256. By the
beginning of October the affair had been committed to the
decision of a commission including the Dominican Cardinal
Hugh of S. Cher,[1] their report had been accepted, and the
Bull of condemnation issued. The language of the book about
religious mendicancy and its implied though unavowed contempt for the authority of the sovereign pontiff were condemned as scandalous and pernicious, but not (the historians
of the university are careful to remark) as heretical. William
was saying what wellnigh every French secular clergyman
in France was thinking.[2] But, as might have been anticipated,
obstacles were placed in the way of the return of the ringleaders in the anti-mendicant conspiracy to the scene of their
crime and their influence. The other envoys of the university
soon gave in their submission:[3] it is a curious indication of
the hold which mendicancy had got over the religious feelings
of the time, that one of these stalwart champions of the secular
clergy on his death-bed desired that he might be buried in
the Church of the Dominican Convent at Paris.[4] William of
S. Amour, a man endowed with more than the pugnacity if
with less than the piety of a Wyclif or a Huss, alone remained
firm, and refused at all costs to associate with the friars. With
difficulty was he allowed to leave Anagni, and then only on
condition of banishment from France and perpetual suspension from preaching and teaching.[5] S. Louis was at last
reluctantly compelled to supplicate the Pope that he might
be allowed the papal permission to recall a French subject
to his own dominions.[6] But the Pope was inflexible; and

[1] A famous commentator and
theologian, and author or at least
beginner of the first great Biblical
Concordance.

[2] [For the sentiments of the
French clergy see *Chartul.* i, Nos.
268, 295, 387.]

[3] Bulaeus, iii. 308, 315, 316, 344;
Chartul. i, Nos. 293, 317, 320.

[4] Thomas of Cantimpré, *De
Apibus*, p. 179.

[5] Bulaeus, iii. 342, 343; *Chartul.*

i, Nos. 314, 315, 318.

[6] Jourdain, Nos. 166, 168; *Chartul.* i, Nos. 355, 356, 357. [The
King's part is not very easy to
follow. On his return from the
Crusade he convoked an assembly
of secular clergy from the provinces
of Sens and Reims (1255). According to Rutebeuf (Jubinal edition,
i. 75), he promised William of S.
Amour protection against exile,
but in obedience to the Pope he

the darling of the university retired impenitent to his native CHAP. V, soil in Franche-Comté.[1]

It is difficult to construct from our documents a consecu- The struggle in tive narrative of events at Paris during these troubled years. Paris. It must be remembered that what the Pope enjoined was not merely an official recognition of the friars' doctorate but a cordial and friendly reception of the unwelcome intruders by every individual master and scholar. 'Boycotting' is notoriously an offence with which it is difficult for the most resolute authority to deal: it was only by slow degrees that the implacable pontiff could secure respect for his commands. We have seen that the decree of dissolution was finally promulgated in October 1255; the general excommunication already mentioned followed in December of the same year; and deprivation was threatened against the ringleaders if they refused to receive the friars within fifteen days.[2] A reiterated appeal to Rome and an abortive attempt at compromise suspended the execution of the sentences for some months longer.[3] Meanwhile a pathetic letter of the Dominican General, Humbert,[4] gives us a lively picture of the kind of treatment the friars of Paris had had to put up with during that winter of strife. The masters had forbidden their pupils to approach the mendicant convents for any cause whatever, to receive a friar into their own houses, to confess to him, to give him alms, or to attend his sermons. And in practice the 'boycotting' passed, as is its wont, into intimidation and violence. The friars were victorious in the battle of the law-courts, but they still had to face the rough battle of the streets. They were treated as 'blacklegs' are treated in a great strike. It was dangerous for a friar to be seen abroad: it was not only

supported the papal decree of banishment by a royal one. Later, at the request of the masters, he asked that William might be allowed to return.]

[1] *Hist. Litt.* xx. 752; *Opp.*, Ep. Introd., p. 63; this was apparently in 1260. [Du Boulay, iii. 368, followed by later writers, says that he returned to Paris in 1272, but there

is no evidence. William was still in exile in 1270-1, and died in 1272, probably at Saint-Amour.]

[2] Bulaeus, iii. 294; *Chartul.* i, No. 262.

[3] Bulaeus, iii. 296; *Chartul.* i, Nos. 268, 280, 284.

[4] *Chartul.* i, No. 273; cf. the letters of Alexander IV; *ibid.*, Nos. 272, 275.

the clerks they had to fear, but a section, at all events, of the lay mob was equally hostile. No sooner was a friar caught sight of (Humbert complained) than he was surrounded by the human swarms that poured forth from every house and hostel in the narrow street, 'hurrying as if to a spectacle'. Instantly the air was full of 'the tumult of shoutings, the barking of dogs, the roaring of bears, the hissing of serpents', and every sort of insulting exclamation. Filthy rushes and straw off the floors of those unsavoury dwellings were poured upon the cowled heads from above; mud, stones, sometimes blows greeted them from below. Arrows had been shot against the convent, which had henceforth to be guarded night and day by royal troops. When every allowance is made for the exuberance of medieval rhetoric and the tendency of a friar, with the evangelical blessing on the persecuted ever in his ears, to make the most of his own or his brethren's sufferings, there can be no doubt that the friars whose lot it was to beg their bread from door to door in the Quartier Latin during the winter of 1255–6 must have had a decidedly hard time.

Gradual collapse of secular resistance. Bulls commanding the readmission of the mendicants and denouncing every possible penalty upon transgressors now follow one another in bewildering profusion. From the way in which these Bulls succeed one another it is evident that, entrusted as they were to secular prelates who secretly sympathized with the university, they must have been very tardily and partially executed, and such execution as they obtained must have been attended with very partial success. In December 1256 the two chancellors were forbidden to license candidates without exacting a formal acceptance of the *Quasi lignum*:[1] so that from this date onwards there must have existed an official university (so to speak) which admitted the mendicants to their company on formal occasions, though the majority of the masters may have long held aloof and

[1] Bulaeus, iii. 334; *Chartul.* i, Nos. 298, 299; repeated in March 1257, *ibid.*, Nos. 303, 304. In Dec. 1255 the chancellors had been ordered not to admit any who would not observe the *Quasi lignum*, but without apparently requiring a formal pledge. *Ibid.*, Nos. 259, 260.

adhered to the schismatical society which they had set up in place of the old and professedly dissolved university of the papal privileges. In all probability the neck of the rebellion was broken after the discomfiture of S. Amour and his colleagues on their last journey to Italy in the summer of 1257. But the surrender of the seculars, so far as we can judge, did not take place at any one definite moment; their opposition was broken down by slow degrees, as individual after individual, with his eyes fixed on preferment, deserted the strikers, joined the official university, and obtained absolution. But, even after formal and official resistance had ceased, the opposition to the mendicants was long kept up by private annoyance and unofficial exclusiveness.[1] It was not till September 1257, two years after the solemn expulsion of the friars, that the Bishop of Paris received powers from the Holy See to absolve those who had submitted to the apostolic injunctions:[2] it was not till the April of the following year that the Pope is able to declare that something like peace was established,[3] though in that very Bull he is still obliged to denounce those who attempted to keep alive the feud by private avoidance. It is followed by a succession of fulminations against those who still refused to treat the mendicants with the cordiality exacted by apostolical authority and persisted in hiding their treasured copy of that storehouse of anti-mendicant libel, 'The Perils of the Last Times', or in singing and circulating 'indecent songs' against the friars, while at the same time the numerous submissions of individual

---

[1] See e.g. a Bull of 1259 (*Chartul*. i, No. 342), in which the Pope denounces a bedel of the university who had circulated a 'libellus famosus' among the congregation when Thomas Aquinas was preaching. Verily the treatment of Thomas Aquinas by the University of Paris is a notable example of building the sepulchres of the prophets! (See the petition of the faculty of arts that his body might be buried among them. *Ibid.*, No. 447.) Another Bull of the same year enables us to see the 'ingeniose adinventiones' that the masters resorted to in order to repel the 'consortium' of the friars. Since the friars could not for fear of spiritual penalties ('spirituales plage') take any part in the movement for the recall of William of S. Amour, they were accustomed to bring the matter on at every congregation, so that the friars had to retire; *ibid.*, No. 343.

[2] Cf. *ibid.*, No. 319.

[3] *Ibid.*, No. 331.

CHAP. V.
§ 2.

masters and faculties for the absolution of less prominent penitents attest the gradual victory of the friars.[1]

Death of
Alexander
IV, 1261.

With the accession of the Parisian canonist Urban IV in 1261, documents of this kind come suddenly to an end and Bulls of privilege and protection take their place. It is therefore reasonable to conclude that the friars, now that they had lost their great patron, quietly submitted to the restrictions which we find practically imposed upon the regulars at a later date. These restrictions were as follows:

Restric-
tions on
friars.

(1) While the university as such had received the regulars, the faculty of arts refused to admit them or their pupils to membership. The exclusion of all regulars from the ranks of the faculty remained a permanent feature of the academic constitution.[2]

(2) No religious college was allowed to have more than *one*, or in the case of the Dominicans *two*, doctors acting as

---

[1] [The Act printed by Bulaeus (iii. 356), readmitting the Dominicans but relegating them to the lowest place among the theological doctors, does not belong to 1259, but to the time of a later quarrel about the doctrine of the Immaculate Conception (Denifle, i. 67). Humbert de Romanis, writing from Toulouse in 1258, stated that the tribulations of the friars were ended; *Monumenta*, ed. Reichert, v. 46.]

[2] *Chartul.* i, No. 501, oath of inceptor in arts, *c.* 1280. Regulars were also excluded from the faculty of medicine. The older orders were admitted to the faculty of canon law in 1337–9. Bulaeus, iv. 253, 315; *Chartul.* ii, Nos. 1002, 1018. [Rashdall thought that Alexander IV had ordered the faculty of arts as such to admit regulars, and that the foundation by the Dominicans of their *studia artium* was the result of their failure to be admitted at Paris. Neither conclusion seems to be justified. The papal Bull of June 1259 (*Chartul.* i, No. 342) bids the Bishop of Paris command the 'rectoribus et artistis ac *aliis*

magistris et scolaribus Parisius commorantibus' to admit the Dominican to their *consortium*. The friars had never shown any desire to enter the faculty of arts, and at this time were only beginning to organize their *studia artium*, and to depart from the spirit of the constitution of 1228 which forbade secular study. Again, although the order by the general chapter for the establishment of a *studium artium* in every province was not made until 1259 (*Monumenta*, iii. 99), the process had begun at least by 1250, before the disputes at Paris began. At Oxford in 1311 the Dominicans protested against a tendency requiring their theological students to have taken a degree in arts: see below, vol. iii, pp. 70–4, and as early as 1253 the Franciscan master, Adam Marsh, had protested against a statute of a similar tendency, occasioned by the petition of Friar Thomas of York to be allowed to incept in theology; see *Monumenta Franciscana*, ed. Brewer, i. 346–9, and the comments of A. G. Little in *Archiv. Franc. Hist.* xix. 823–4.]

regents and sitting at the same time in the general congrega- CHAP. V,
§ 2. tion of the university.[1]

(3) Though as a matter of canonical or university law, there was no objection to a secular attending the theological lectures of the friar doctors, it seems probable that in practice their lecture-rooms were henceforth attended chiefly by members of their respective orders.[2] At all events the most valuable privilege of the doctorate was secured by the custom that secular students should incept only 'under' secular doctors.[3]

Technically the mendicants had triumphed: practically the university had by stolid persistence, by the tremendous power of organized combination and by the death of its great ponti- fical enemy, secured for ever a large part of what it had all along been contending for. By 1318 the university had grown strong enough to impose once more upon the friars the oath of obedience to the statutes, and this time they had quietly to submit to the demand which had created such a storm of opposition sixty years before.[4]

Friars'
victory
partial and
short-
lived.

The controversy left permanent effects upon the subsequent organization, and still more upon the tone and temper of the university. We may trace its influence in three main directions:

(1) We have already said something about the effect of the *Quasi lignum* upon the separate organization of the faculties. It is no doubt a mistake to suppose (with Du Boulay) that the theological doctors were before this date

Constitu-
tional
results.

---

[1] A larger number were often summoned to congregations of the faculty of theology for the dis- cussion of theological questions.

[2] This aspect of the question lost its importance as doctors ceased to lecture. For biblical lectures seculars certainly resorted to friar bachelors, but for lectures on the Sentences they probably as a rule went to a secular; but on this point I have come across no definite information.

[3] [This was probably the case,

but we do not know any evidence for Rashdall's statement. The famous oath of the masters of arts on inception, cited by Rashdall in the text of the first edition, has nothing to do with attendance at lectures: 'Item stabitis cum magi- stris secularibus . . . toto tempore vite vestre ad quemcumque statum deveneritis' (*Chartul.* i, No. 501).]

[4] Bulaeus, iv. 181; *Chartul.* ii, No. 776.

included in the nations. There were meetings of the theological faculty almost as early as there were formal meetings of the whole university; and even the practice of voting by faculties had perhaps grown up by a process of spontaneous development.[1] But, however this may be, the *Quasi lignum*, by requiring a two-thirds majority in each faculty to legalize a 'cessation', sanctioned and stereotyped the practice.[2] In the earlier part of the thirteenth century the theological faculty appears rather as a separate organization whose members were also members of the university than as a distinct member of a federal body. The necessities of the anti-mendicant campaign, however, compelled the theologians at once to reduce their customs to the form of written statutes and closely to ally themselves with the rest of the university, especially with its most powerful factor, the faculty of arts. It is in the course of this controversy that the university for the first time distinctly claims to legislate, not merely for the theologians as individual members of the larger society, but for the theological faculty as such. The process of welding the faculties into the university-system was completed in 1281, when a university statute formally lays down the principle that the acts (*facta*) of the faculties are the acts of the university.[3]

(2) In yet another way the mendicant affair contributed to the consolidation of the university. The university was first compelled to borrow money for the purposes of its litigation with the chancellor, and we have seen reason to believe that it was this financial necessity which more than anything else contributed to the growth of the rectorate and the four proctorships. The expenses of the mendicant suit must have been much heavier.[4] It was now that the financial

---

[1] In 1277 we find a statute passed 'per totam Universitatem, quatuor facultatibus hoc volentibus'. Bulaeus, iii. 432; *Chartul.* i, No. 478.

[2] The Dominican friars of Oxford contended that the two-thirds majority was required not only for a cessation, but for every other pur-

pose. *Collectanea* (Oxf. Hist. Soc.), ii. 221. Of this I find no other trace.

[3] Bulaeus, iii. 456; *Chartul.* i, No. 505.

[4] The collection is thus described by the friar Thomas of Cantimpré: 'Nequitiae primordialis actores (*leg.* auctores), simplices

system of the university may be supposed to have grown up— the system of levies of one or more *bursae* (i.e. the sworn amount of his weekly board) upon each member of it, by means of which a system of proportionate taxation was secured. Regular payments were exacted at determination and inception[1] while special calls were made on all students when circumstances required, and the payment of such contributions was enforced by papal privilege.[2] The constitutional importance of this financial system has already been explained.

(3) But still more important than its constitutional results were the effects of the controversy upon the theological tone and temper of the university. Till now there had been no reason whatever for any hostile feeling against the papacy on the part of the university. The university in so far as it was anything more than a private society was as much the privileged creature of the Holy See as the mendicant orders themselves: so far from the university having any special tenderness for the rights of bishops and secular prelates, we have seen that it was in its origin an organized rebellion against episcopal authority. The alliance between the Holy See and the mendicants sowed the seeds of Gallicanism in the university which was to be its stronghold.

Uniuersitatis scholares sibi velut unum corpus miris astutiis adunarunt, ut in multis librarum milibus eos roderent placitantes; ut sic in dictos ordines crudelius deseuirent, et id quod per se non poterant, non sufficiente pecunia, in euacuatione bursarum innocentiae puerilis, multorum copiis obtinerent.' *De Apibus*, p. 182.

[1] 'Item antequam bursam unam talem vel tantam, quam ponit fide corporali prestita super hoc, ad opus Universitatis persolverit et ad opus nascionis aliam, eidem determinandi licentia non largiatur.' *Chartul.* i, No. 201. On Inception:

'Dabit tres bursas unam Universitati, aliam nascioni, tertiam bedellis, quas solvet procuratori sue nascionis.' *Ibid.*, No. 202 (*c.* A.D. 1252). [This early reference to the *bursa* disposes of Richer's statement that the scholastic meaning came from the weekly payments made on Fridays by students of the Sorbonne (Ch. Jourdain, *Mém. de la soc. de l'histoire de Paris*, i (1874), 170, 171). Cf. the gloss in the Bruges manuscript of John Garland's *Morale Scolarium* (ed. Paetow, Berkeley, California, 1927, p. 213, n. 261).]

[2] *Chartul.* i, Nos. 352, 376, &c.

Additional Note

[The story of the relations between the university and the friars does not end here, although it becomes increasingly involved in wider disputes about the privileges and views of the mendicant orders. The university was an inevitable centre of the discussions to which these disputes gave rise, while on at least one occasion the academic status of the theological teachers of the orders was called in question (from 1442 onwards). The hot dispute about Thomistic doctrines, which culminated in the decrees of Stephen Tempier, Bishop of Paris, in 1277 (cf. below, vol. iii, p. 251, and the bibliographical notes in Ueberweg-Geyer, p. 764), cannot be regarded as an attack upon the mendicants, for these were fiercely divided, even within the Dominican Order. This dispute belongs rather to the history of the attempt, led by S. Thomas, to reconcile orthodoxy with Aristotelian doctrine as against the Averroistic teaching of the secular Siger de Brabant and his followers. But the struggle of the bishops against the privileges of the friars in preaching, confession and the like, stirred feeling in the university. See the accounts of the discussions of 1286 and 1287 in the *Chartularium*, ii, Nos. 539, 543. The secular masters who took the lead against the friars were connected, moreover, by a continuous stream of discussion, with their predecessors of 1254; for the disputations and pamphlet warfare about the problem of evangelical poverty had not ceased. A famous Franciscan tract *Manus quae contra omnipotentem tenditur* (1256–7), variously ascribed to Bertrand of Bayonne and Thomas of York, became a centre of controversy, in which Gerard of Abbeville, Nicholas of Lisieux, and others took part on the secular side, S. Thomas and many others on the side of the friars. (See Bierbaum, *op. cit.*; Douie, *op. cit.*; Ueberweg-Geyer, p. 729.) The storm about privileges, allayed for a time by Pope Boniface VIII (see A. G. Little, 'Measures taken by the Prelates of France against the Friars', in *Miscellanea Fr. Ehrle*, iii. 49–66), broke out again in the early fourteenth century, and now centred mainly round the teaching of John of Pouilli, a secular who denied the papal right to grant privileges to the friars on the ground that the jurisdiction of bishops and priests was given immediately by God (see *Hist. litt. de la France*, xxxiv. 220–81; J. Koch, 'Der Prozess gegen den Magister Johannes de Polliaco und seine Vorgeschichte', in *Recherches de théologie ancienne et médiévale*, v (1933), 391–422; Glorieux, *La Littérature quodlibetique de 1260 à 1320* (Kain, 1925), pp. 223–8; J. G. Sikes, 'John de Pouilli and Peter de la Palu', in *Eng. Hist. Rev.* xlix (1934), 219–40). John of Pouilli, who was a famous master at Paris, was forced to submit. His teaching was condemned in the year of his death (1321) by John XXII in the Bull *Vas electionis* (*Chartul.* ii, No. 798). This Bull was a useful weapon during subsequent efforts by the papacy to maintain its control over the university and to keep the balance even between the

seculars and the regulars. In the later fourteenth and early
fifteenth centuries the Dominicans, owing to their support of
the Thomist view on the Immaculate Conception of the Virgin,
were in difficulties and had to submit (see below, pp. 550-1). But
in 1409, when the secular masters had won their battle on this
ground, Alexander V renewed the condemnation of John of
Pouilli's views, and insisted upon a strict observance of Boniface
VIII's Bull, *Super cathedram*, defining the privileges of the friars
(*Chartul.* iv, No. 1868). The strong efforts of the masters to get
John XXIII to revoke Alexander's Bull involved the friars in
disputes between 1410 and 1417 (*ibid.*, Nos. 1877, 1887, 1917, 1965,
2037-8, 2086). Again, during an intermittent conflict (1442-57)
about the 'lecturers' of the mendicant orders, Eugenius IV in 1447
and Nicholas V in 1448 again renewed the condemnation of the
errors of John of Pouilly (*ibid.*, Nos. 2620, 2636).

The dispute which began in 1442 turned on the standing of
lecturers sent to Paris by the superiors of the four chief orders of
friars to lecture on the Sentences. It had been the practice, maintained by numerous acts of the Popes in favour of particular
teachers, to admit these members of the orders to begin their course
although they had not resided in the university as the statutes
required. Opposition to this practice led to a Bull of Eugenius IV,
March 1442 (*Chartul.* iv, No. 2562), ordering the admission of the
lecturers, if found suitable by the faculty of theology, and the admission of one in each order to the doctorate at the end of the course. The
university replied by insisting on four years' residence before the
doctorate by students who belonged to the French province, and
on an oath from every friar bachelor and master that he would not
avail himself of the papal bull and would work for its revocation
(*ibid.*, No. 2570). The conditions of residence imposed also cut
across the Dominican course of teaching. In this dispute the masters
on the whole held their own (cf. *ibid.*, Nos. 2559, 2567, 2577, 2585,
2636, 2690). But Calixtus III, when he annulled the action of his
predecessors, gave the orders the right, if required, to confer the
degrees (*Bull. Ord. Praedicatorum*, iii. 362, 365). This privilege
was really a stage in the gradual separation of the orders from the
universities (cf. the privileges to the Franciscans, 1376-1429;
Bulaeus, iv. 448; v. 389).

The latter part of this note is based upon the work of Miss Rixon.]

§ 3. THE CONSTITUTION AND PRIVILEGES OF THE UNIVERSITY

CHAP. V, § 3.
Comple-
tion of the
constitu-
tional
develop-
ment. BY the end of the thirteenth century the university constitution had attained the form which in its main features lasted till the close of our period. The penultimate decade of the century is marked by the last important conflict in that long struggle with the chancellor to which the university corporation owes, if not its very existence, at least much of its importance and many features of its organization. From the mutual recriminations of the parties in the papal Court[1] it Conflict
with the
chancel-
lor, Philip
de Thori,
1280–90. appears that the chancellor, Philip de Thori, had renewed the illegal demand of an oath to respect the liberties of the Church of Paris. He had licensed a princely candidate (the brother of the King of Aragon) without the consent of the masters. In some cases he had dispensed with the conditions, in respect of time, age, and study, required by the university; in others he had arbitrarily rejected bachelors who presented themselves for the licence. Moreover, he had disobeyed the papal Bulls relating to the appointment of examiners. When the chancellor was required to examine with the assistance of six masters of the university, it was intended (the university alleged) that they should be regent masters: instead of which the chancellor had appointed old non-regents who 'are ignorant of modern opinions and have forgotten the old ones'.[2] The chancellor replied by contending that the masters had in a variety of ways exceeded their powers, and infringed upon those of his office. There is a general accusation of making statutes to the prejudice of the bishop and Church of Paris. More specifically the chancellor contended that the masters had resisted his judicial authority by forbidding scholars to cite one another before him: they had compelled students to go to Ste Geneviève to be examined instead of to the 'Examination of S. Mary', and they had enforced determination as a condition of the licence. But most presump-

---

[1] Jourdain, Nos. 266, 274; *Chartul*. i, Nos. 503, 515.

[2] 'Nesciunt opiniones modernas et amiserunt antiquas.'

tuous of all, they had dared to cite him through the bedel—
him, the 'Head of the University' (as he contended but the
masters denied)—to attend congregation not (as he alleged
was the custom) 'by way of supplication and request' (*supplicando et rogando*) but peremptorily and *sub poena* in his quality
of a doctor of theology, and upon his refusal had actually
suspended him from lecturing, and forbidden scholars to
attend his sermons. In the course of the conflict the university even advanced to a pitch of audacity beyond this. On
this one occasion and this only, in the whole course of its
history,[1] the university presumed altogether to dispense with
the aid of the Chancellor of Paris, and to elect a chancellor of
their own to bestow the licence. We do not possess the final
judgement of the Holy See upon all the points at issue, but on
these two last points the rights of the chancellor were peremptorily vindicated. He was exempted from compulsory
attendance at congregation, and the licences granted by the
university were quashed or invalidated.[2]

In 1290 we have a fresh batch of complaints against Philip Suit against Chancellor Bertrand of S. Denis.
de Thori's successor, Bertrand of S. Denis. He had persisted
in rejecting duly qualified candidates in the teeth of the
examiners' verdict. Before the unfortunate candidates could
get the answer to the first question out of their mouths,[3] the
chancellor, 'carried away by the whirlwind of his impatience
and captiousness', had driven them from his presence with
insult and abuse, 'vilely and irrationally expelling them from
the examination'. At other times when bachelors had presented themselves to him in the church or cloister requesting

---

[1] 'Scholares Parisienses institue-
runt quemdam Cancellarium propria authoritate, contra libertatem
Ecclesiae Parisiensis'. *Chron. Roth-
omagen.* ap. Hemeraeum, p. 79. In
1482 the theological faculty, in-
censed at the appointment of a
canonist instead of a theologian to
the chancellor's stall, conducted the
Birettatio of certain licentiates
without the chancellor, but did not,
it would seem, attempt to license.
Bulaeus, v. 749 *sq.*; Hemeraeus,

p. 84. A B.D. had been appointed
chancellor in 1387 and a licentiate
of decrees in 1433: Hemeraeus,
pp. 134, 136 With these exceptions the chancellor had always
been D.D.
[2] Bulaeus, iii. 464; *Chartul.* i,
Nos. 516, 528.
[3] 'Antequam possent in unius
argumenti repetitione vel solutione
a vobis audiri.' Jourdain, No. 302;
Chartul. ii, No. 569.

CHAP. V, admission to the examination, he had refused to examine them
§ 3.   at all, and had so far forgotten himself as to call them 'stinking
asses'. Amid a host of minor irregularities, he had carried on
an extensive traffic in licences, allowing passes in the chancellor's examination to be sold by laymen, women, actors, or
servants of his household. In some cases the licence had been
given without the examiners even having the opportunity of
setting eyes on the candidates. Here again there is at present
an hiatus in our documents. We possess neither the chancellor's reply nor the judgement of the Holy See. On the
majority of the questions at issue between the university and
the chancellor, there can be no doubt that in the long run,
whether by virtue of papal decision or by the irresistible
Loss of growth of custom, the university gained the day. From this
the chan-
cellor's time the strictly judicial authority of the chancellor fell into
judicial
power. desuetude: he ceased to be, if he had ever been, the *iudex
ordinarius* of scholars.[1] He even ceased to have any real
control over the grant or refusal of licences, except in so far
as he retained the nomination of the examiners in arts.[2] His

---

[1] But see above, p. 339.

[2] There was an occasional attempt of the chancellor to shake off
the fetters imposed upon him by
the examiners. The last attempt
which I have noticed to license
against the opinion of the examiners
occurred in 1385. A mass of pleadings, depositions of witnesses, &c.,
in the suit, are printed in *Chartul.*
iii, Nos. 1504–22. It is alleged
on behalf of the university that the
chancellor took money-bribes of all
amounts up to 100 *franci aurei* and
presents of silver cups, 'jocalia',
furred garments, knives, fowls,
wine, dinners, and the like. On
one occasion certain nobles had
positively been refused the licence
because they had not sent the chancellor 'vestes cum furraturis more
nobilium'. On another, when the
candidate had already paid eight
francs, the chancellor observing
that one remained in his purse,
exclaimed 'adhuc illum! adhuc

illum!' Other candidates had been
compelled to give pledges which
were to be redeemed after licence
—an obligation which in one case
was escaped by an 'egregious beat-
ing' inflicted on the sub-chancellor.
The evidence of the witnesses is
largely hearsay; but the chancellor
himself pleads that by custom he
was entitled to a 'denarius aureus'
from every decretist, two from each
M.D., and ten from each theologian, while the artists gave presents
to his 'famuli'. He represents that
these sums were given 'libera et
spontanea voluntate, sine exac-
cione quacumque', but from the
admissions of his own witnesses it
is clear that degrees were not to be
had without payment (in spite of
the papal prohibition), the only
dispute being as to the amount of
the bribe and as to the degree of
compulsion exercised. There appear to have been various opinions
as to the chancellor's power to

position remained one of great dignity, though more and more overshadowed by the growing pretensions of the rector; but its substantial power was gone. Only his mysterious prerogative of conferring the licence was left him, and that remained henceforth almost as sacred and incommunicable as the bishop's power of conferring orders; though, as already explained, his powers were as regards the faculty of arts shared by his upstart rival, the Chancellor of Ste Geneviève.[1]

In order to appreciate the peculiar sanctity which attached *The ius ubique docendi.* to the chancellor's barren prerogative, it is necessary to bear in mind the change which we have already noticed as taking place in the course of the thirteenth century with respect to what may be called the constitutional theory of university institutions. We have seen that in its origin the university was nothing more than a private society: the schools in connexion with which it grew up were nothing more than a development of the episcopal School of Paris: the 'licence' no more than an episcopal permission to teach in a particular city or diocese. The extraordinary prestige of Paris and Bologna—and in a subordinate degree a few other *studia*, most of which had imitated more or less closely the organization of Paris or Bologna—had practically given to their

license without the assent of the masters: one witness held that he was bound to accept the 'depositions' as to 'scientia', but might use his own judgement as to 'mores'. It is clear that the suit was promoted by the faculty of arts—largely at the instigation of d'Ailly, who (as Denifle suggests) wanted the chancellorship himself, in consequence of a renewal of the dispute with the rector for precedence at the inception-banquet, and that the chancellor's irregularities might otherwise have been winked at. Still, though there may have been exaggeration, the case against the chancellor is a fairly strong one. The matter was terminated by the resignation of the then chancellor, John Blanchart, at Rome—no doubt by some arrangement satis-

factory both to the Holy See and himself (1386). I have perhaps exaggerated the unimportance of the chancellor at this period; but it is clear from the admission of Blanchart's own witnesses that he was attempting to revive prerogatives which had long lain comparatively dormant. The attempt to demand certain oaths objected to by the university (i.e. probably of obedience to the chancellor or respect for his rights) and to extort fees or promises was renewed by the next chancellor, Jean de Guignecourt, in 1389 (*ibid.*, Nos. 1550–5), but we hear no more of interference with the examiners.

[1] The chancellorship of Paris was in the gift of the bishop but was often 'reserved'. *Chartul.* ii, No. 592, &c.

CHAP. V,
§ 3.
licences an ecumenical prestige and validity. It was little more than a recognition of an accomplished fact when in 1292 Nicholas IV conferred on the licentiates of Paris the prerogative of teaching in all other schools and universities throughout the world, without any additional examination.[1] Henceforth the chancellor conferred the licence in the name not of the bishop but of the Pope—a circumstance which has largely contributed to blind historians to the recognition of his original position as head of the episcopal school.

Increasing importance of rectorship:
In proportion as the practical importance of the chancellorship declined, that of the rectorship increased. The rector, as has been already said, was elected by the proctors or four other representatives or 'intrants'[2] of the four nations, who were shut up after the manner of the sacred college at papal

Mode of election.
elections in a 'conclave' after the solemn singing of the *Veni Creator*. They were required to complete the election before a lighted taper had burnt itself out.[3] Though a peculiar sanctity was supposed to attach itself to this method of election, known as the 'way of the Holy Spirit', the solemnity of the proceeding was not always sufficient to prevent the 'intrants' coming to blows in their seclusion.[4] If an election had not been made by the expiration of the time, fresh 'intrants' were elected; and if a majority were not secured in this way, the ex-rector was called in to give a casting vote.[5]

Conflicts with the dean of theology.
By the end of the thirteenth century we have seen that the rector had attained a virtual presidency but not an acknowledged headship of the whole university of four

---

[1] *Chartul*. ii, No. 578. [See above, pp. 10 *sqq*. A similar Bull in favour of Bologna had been issued by Nicholas IV in Aug. 1291; *Registres de Nicolas IV*, No. 5861.]

[2] [*Chartul*. i, No. 187 (1249), and the decisions of the papal legate, Simon de Brie, afterwards Pope Martin IV in 1266 and 1279, *ibid*., Nos. 406, 492. Rashdall passes over the disputes between the nations which led to these statutes.] The practice in this re-spect seems later to have varied at different times and in different nations. Cf. Bulaeus, iv. 246 (*Chartul*. ii, No. 989), v. 530, 877, &c.

[3] Bulaeus, iii. 451 (cf. v. 530, 554); *Chartul*. ii, No. 554. [a. 1289, professing to be a confirmation by the masters of the faculty of the statutes of Cardinal Simon.]

[4] Bulaeus, v. 550; *Remarques sur la dignité du recteur*, p. 11.

[5] Bulaeus, iii. 451; *Chartul*. ii, No. 554.

faculties: another half a century secured his triumph over CHAP. V, all rivals. The dispute as to the mode of summoning the § 3. dean and faculty of theology was settled in 1341 by a compromise: it was ordered that the rector or a master of arts deputed by him should personally wait upon the dean, but if the dean were not at home, a written summons might be left for him.[1] In 1339 and 1347 there were disputes between the two officials for precedence in church: here victory was secured for the rector by the superior numbers and athletic prowess of the young masters of arts and their younger pupils. On the last occasion the dean of theology, though an archbishop and papal legate, was forcibly expelled from the rector's chair of state in the choir of S. Germain-des-Prés.[2] Even after this (in 1353) the faculties of theology and canon law opposed the dispatch of a letter in the name of the 'Rector and University';[3] but in 1358 the innovation received the sanction of the Pope, who addressed a Bull to the 'Rector and Masters of the University'.[4]

His position in the university itself being secured, the The rector's prece- dence. rector entered upon a series of disputes with the highest ecclesiastical dignitaries for precedence at royal funerals and other public processions. For a time the difficulty was met

---

[1] Bulaeus, iv. 267 sq.; Chartul. ii, No. 1051. [See, for the claims to summon 'per bidellum', ibid., No. 602, a. 1297.]

[2] Crevier, ii. 386, 389; Jourdain, No. 613; Chartul. ii, No. 1145; cf. No. 1143.

[3] Bulaeus, iv. 329; Chartul. ii, No. 1143.

[4] Bulaeus, iv. 359. [Chartul. iii, No. 1239. Ehrle, however, points out variants in usage (op. cit., p. clxx, n.).] An instrument of the theological faculty cited by the Anon. Refut. (p. 356) says that the faculty of arts elects a rector 'non ut regat Universitatem, nec praeferatur, sed Rectorem, id est, rerum Actorem aut procuratorem negotiorum Universitatis, cuius mandata et deliberata per eam idem Rector vel Actor et procurator ac etiam merus exequutor et minister habet et debet exequi etiam per proprium iuramentum'. This would have been denied by the artists who long required bachelors to swear 'quod Decretum factum et ordinatum per Facultatem Artium de praepositione Rectoris in Actibus communibus Universitatis inviolabiliter observabitis, ad quemcunque statum deveneritis'. Bulaeus, Remarques sur la dignité du R., p. 40. [In 1359 the theological faculty claimed that any master in a superior faculty ranked higher than the rector, who could be, and once had been, deposed by the university (Chartul. iii, No. 1246). Cf. above, p. 331 n.]

CHAP. V, by allowing an academical and a capitular dignitary to walk
§ 3. side by side, while the Bishop of Paris brought up the rear
in solitary grandeur. This arrangement brought the rector
to the side of the Dean of Notre Dame; but ere long we find
the ambitious functionary falling back to the side of the
bishop, and, after a riot or two, he succeeded in securing
that position.[1] The ex-rector, Du Boulay, records with a glow
of official and antiquarian pride the numerous occasions on
which some plebeian and moneyless rector of the artists took
precedence of bishops, cardinals, archbishops, papal nuncios,
ambassadors, and peers of France.[2]

Dignity of the rectorship representative rather than personal. A very mistaken impression will, however, be given of the
real importance of the office if it is compared to the Oxford
or Cambridge chancellorship. Its dignity was mainly sym-
bolic and representative. It was held that at first only for a
month or six weeks, afterwards for three months.[3] The rector,
while appearing in state with his eight bedels[4] at the head of
the university, rarely spoke in its name—a function usually
entrusted to some eloquent 'orator' chosen for the occasion
from the theological doctors, just as a municipal deputation
is headed by the mayor, but finds its mouthpiece in the more
intellectually qualified recorder. Moreover, unlike the
chancellor of Oxford, the rector had scarcely any judicial
powers, except those which he derived from the statutes.
Consequently, his jurisdiction extended only to members or
'clients' of the university.[5] His punishments (except in so

[1] Bulaeus, vi. 402. It should be observed, however, that in purely university processions the rector still walked with the dean of theology. Goulet, f. xiii [E.T. p. 79]; Bulaeus, Remarques sur la dignité du R., pp. 67–88.
[2] Bulaeus, i. 269, 270; iv. 585; v. 543; Remarques sur la dignité du R., p. 41.
[3] From 1266; Chartul. i, No. 409. The proctorship remained a monthly office, but a proctor was more often than not re-elected for another month or more. Bulaeus, v. 631, and registers, passim. [Cf.

Boyce, The English-German Nation, p. 44.]
[4] We are told by Bulaeus (iii. 561) that each nation elected two bedels who walked before its proctor with silver maces, but these appear to have also attended the rector. The superior faculties had bedels of their own.
[5] In the seventeenth century it would appear, from the Recueil des priviléges de l'Un. de P., pp. 1–9, that the 'greater part' of personal actions were triable by the rector's tribunal, while 'real' causes went to the royal conservator. [The

far as he could indirectly call in the aid of spiritual terrors by CHAP. V,
pronouncing a contumacious master to be a 'perjured' person) § 3.
were purely academical—fine, suspension, and expulsion.

No continuous records of proceedings before the rector's The
court appear to be preserved, and we are therefore left some- court.
what in the dark as to the exact sphere of its jurisdiction. Its
ordinary business, we may suppose, consisted in the hearing
of disputes about the rent of hostels,[1] and of complaints
against members of the trades carried on under the supervision
of the university, in the granting of certificates of scholarity,
the initiation of measures for procuring the release of an
imprisoned or the satisfaction of an injured scholar, the
settlement of disputes and the trial of strictly personal actions
between masters and scholars, and above all the punishment
of offences against the statutes. In the exercise of this jurisdiction, the rector was assisted by the proctors who formed
the permanent 'deputies' or (as they were afterwards called)
'tribunal' of the faculty of arts.[2] From the decision of a
nation or its proctor there was an appeal to the whole faculty
of arts or its officers. From the decision of the rector and Appeals.
proctors, or from one of the superior faculties, there was an
appeal to the whole university, which heard the case by means
of specially appointed deputies.[3] In the post-medieval period

university, acting apparently for
the bishop, seems to have had
administration of the estates of
deceased scholars (cf. *Chartul.* ii,
No. 663, a. 1308), but, according to
a document issued by the theological faculty in 1359, the rector
had no part in the distribution of
the goods (*ibid.* iii, No. 1246.).]

[1] Jourdain, No. 551; *Chartul.* ii,
No. 803.

[2] Bulaeus, iv. 128, 211, 218;
Chartul. ii, Nos. 803, 870, 881.
Crevier (ii. 309) attempts to find
the tribunal of the university in
this document; I see no express
evidence that when the deputies of
the university are mentioned in
medieval times, the rector, proctors,
and deans are invariably meant.

[3] Bulaeus, iii. 594-6, iv. 172;
Sur la dign. du R., pp. 98 *sq.*, 119 *sq.*;
Chartul. ii, No. 721; Jourdain, No.
741. The legality of any appeal to
the university was not beyond dispute. See Bulaeus, vi. 22 *sq.* It was
a moot point whether the rector
and proctors ought to be present
with the 'deputies' in hearing
appeals from themselves. Thus in
1366 we hear of the dean of decrees
wanting to retire because they
refused to withdraw on such an
occasion. The rector ordered him
to sit down 'primo simpliciter,
secundario sub iuramento'. The
lawyer replied with true medieval
boyishness, 'Non curo de preceptis
vestris plus quam de uno obolo'.
Upon the matter being referred to

CHAP. V, the rector, proctors, and deans formed a permanent board of
§ 3.   deputies or 'tribunal' of the whole university, which eventually
succeeded to a large extent in ousting the popular congregation from the government of the university. From about
the middle of the seventeenth century the 'tribunal' of the
university at Paris, though more popular in its constitution,
passed into something like the position of the old, oligarchic
'Hebdomadal Board' of Oxford.[1]

No uni-   Each of the faculties and nations constituting the university
versity
buildings. had some church or convent which was usually borrowed for
its meetings; but the place of meeting was not invariable, and
neither the university nor its constituent bodies assembled in
a building of its own. The great medieval universities (as
distinct from their colleges) were poor corporations. Neither
Paris nor Oxford possessed any endowments whatever, except
a few legacies devoted to special purposes, such as a bene-
faction for poor scholars, or the patronage of a few chaplaincies
or other benefices.[2] In this poverty lay the real strength of
the universities, upon occasions of collision with the spiritual
and temporal authorities: just as their wealth was the weakness of the great ecclesiastics in their struggles with the
secular arm. If a university 'seceded' or 'dispersed',· there
were no temporalities which could be sequestrated; it took
all its property—the fees of its students—with it. Wherever
there were rooms to be hired for schools, and churches and
convents to be borrowed for congregations, a university could
soon make itself at home. At Paris it is not till the beginning
of the fourteenth century that it becomes clear that the nations
even undertook to rent the schools in their corporate capa-

the university the dean apologized,
but three nations and the faculty of
medicine ('quibus accessit Rector')
against the two remaining faculties
and one nation held that the proctors should sit: 'Et fuerat eatenus
indecisa controversia.' Bulaeus, iv.
387, 388 [in part, in *Chartul.* iii,
No. 1322].
    [1] Bulaeus, iii. 577, 578; Dubarle,
i. 352.

[2] The benefices (other than
chaplaincies) to which the university presented were (1) SS. Cosmas
and Damianus, (2) S. Andreas de
arcubus, (3) S. Germanus Vetus;
all in Paris. Bulaeus, iii. 612 *sq.*
[In 1362 the university petitioned
Urban V to protect their 'pauca
beneficia' from external collation
(*Chartul.* iii, No. 1261.)]

city;[1] and it was still later that the nations and faculties began
to acquire schools of their own.[2] The only property which
in the early part of our period belonged to the university or
rather to the faculty of arts as a whole was the Pré-aux-clercs
—a sort of university play-ground outside the walls,[3] the
freehold of which it had acquired by custom, or by usurpation
from the neighbouring monks of S. Germain, with whom
the masters and scholars were engaged in incessant litigations
and a succession of murderous affrays.[4] Each nation borrowed
a church for its national Mass. The university sermons took
place in the churches of the Franciscans and Dominicans, or
at times in the chapel of the College of Navarre.[5] To the

[1] Bulaeus, iv. 100, 187, 213, 224; Chartul. ii, Nos. 655, 793, 897. It is at about this time (1329) that we find the first certain evidence of the concentration of the arts schools in the Rue du Fouarre.

[2] [The 'liber procuratorum nationis Anglicanae', now printed in the Auctarium, enables us to trace the property in schools owned by the English Nation in the Rue du Fouarre and its vicinity. The evidence begins in 1364; cf. Boyce, op. cit., p. 118.] In 1415 the faculty of decrees built two large schools in the region long appropriated to the schools of the faculty—the Clos Bruneau. The Musée de Cluny still preserves a block of stone inscribed 'Scole secūde facultatis Decretorum'. Péries, pp. 50, 51.

[3] [In July 1365, after a special meeting of congregation, 'quoddam bladum quod fuerat a quodam laico . . . seminatum' on the Pré-aux-clercs was dug up and destroyed in the presence of the rector and a number of doctors and masters; Chartul. iii, No. 1310.]

[4] [Just as the conflict between the nations in 1266 led to a definition of the organization of the faculty of arts, so these disputes helped to develop the corporate sense of the university; cf. R. Poupardin on the

conflicts of 1266 and 1278, with documents, in the Bulletin de la société de l'histoire de Paris, xxxvi (1909); xl (1913).]

[5] [See Haskins, Studies in Mediaeval Culture, c. ii, with bibliographical notes; M. M. Davy, Les Sermons universitaires parisiens, Paris, 1931.] 'Sermones in Scholis' appear among the writings of the twelfth century. In the fourteenth century there was a sermon in the morning and a collatio or 'conference' in the afternoon of every Sunday or holiday. The preacher in the afternoon (at least if a regular) was required to take the same subject as that of the morning sermon whether he himself or another had preached it. Bulaeus, iv. 181, 278, 427 (Chartul. ii, Nos. 774, 1057). Statutes relating to the conduct of students, e.g. the statute against bullying freshmen (Bulaeus, iv. 267; Chartul. ii, No. 1057), and notices of many kinds were published at university sermons. On one occasion we find that a decayed and deserted college was ordered to be put up to public auction (subhastari) from the university pulpit, 'secundum morem et consuetudinem in casu simili hactenus observatos'. Bulaeus, iv. 368. (Possibly only the announcement of the sale was so made.) [Cf. Chartul. iii,

last-mentioned chapel was transferred in the course of the fourteenth century the chest containing the archives of the university, hitherto kept at the Mathurine Convent, and the seal-chest, which had previously been deposited at the Abbey of Ste Geneviève. In the early days of the university general congregations were commonly held in the Church of S. Julien-le-Pauvre. Later on, that Church came to be appropriated to the congregations of the faculty of arts;[1] and the university itself met sometimes at the Dominican or Franciscan Convent, sometimes (on occasions of special importance when a large attendance was expected) in the more ample chapter-house of the Bernardines or Cistercians, but most commonly in the mean little refectory of the Mathurine or Trinitarian Convent.[2]

Composition of the general congregation.
Before explaining the procedure of these 'general congregations', it may be well to recapitulate what has already been said as to their constitution. The university consisted of four faculties—the three superior faculties of theology, decrees, and medicine, and the inferior faculty of arts. The faculty of arts was subdivided into four 'nations'—France, Picardy, Normandy, and England. Each faculty was presided over by a dean: each nation by a proctor. The rector had come, at least by the middle of the fourteenth century, to be the incontestable head of the university, as well as of the united faculty of arts. Each of these sections of the university was a corporation in itself, with its own head, receiver, bedels, common seal,[3] congregations, statutes, &c. But all scholars and graduates of the superior faculties except the masters remained under the jurisdiction of the nations and their

No. 1246, in the document of 1359 already cited, referring to scenes in 1347 (above, p. 331 n.): 'in quadam missa in Sancto Germano de Pratis, *ubi tunc erat universitas*'.]

[1] *Chartul.* i, No. 485. [Congregations of the faculty are sometimes held at the Mathurine Convent or elsewhere; cf. *ibid.* ii, No. 570.]

[2] Bulaeus, iii. 486, iv. 223–4, v. 606. The full title of the last-men-

tioned order was the 'Ordo fratrum SS. Trinitatis de redemptione captivorum', founded about 1197 by John de Matha. [The convent at Paris was near the Church of S. Mathurinus. For the meetings of congregation cf. also *Chartul.* iii, Index, p. 768.]

[3] Except the faculty of theology, which long used the chancellor's seal.

officers.[1] The general congregation was composed of the united masters of all the faculties. The university was originally composed exclusively of regents, i.e. masters actually engaged in teaching in the schools; and, in the faculties of arts and medicine, every master upon his inception was required to swear to complete a period of 'necessary regency', i.e. to lecture for two years,[2] unless dispensed by the university. This system must be borne in mind in order to realize how large, youthful, and fluctuating a body the masters of arts really were, and in order to appreciate the resemblances in spite of diversity between the master-university of Paris and the student-universities of Bologna. At the end of his necessary regency, the master was at liberty to continue his lectures as long as he pleased; but only so long as he continued to give an 'ordinary' lecture every 'legible' day in one of the schools in or near the Rue du Fouarre throughout the 'grand ordinary' of each year (i.e. from 1 October, the Feast of S. Remigius, to Easter) or the greater part of it, did he retain his rights to take part in the deliberations of his nation or faculty or of the whole university.[3] His rights ceased on becoming a non-regent, but not so his obligations. The oath of obedience to the rector

[1] [*Auctarium*, i, p. xx; and cf. the account by Jean Petit of discussions during the Great Schism (1406). He emphasizes the value to the faculty of arts of the bachelors in higher faculties, i.e. who were masters of arts but were not yet masters or doctors in the higher faculty: 'un theologien est de la Faculté des ars jusques à ce qu'il ait le bonnet sur la teste'(A.Coville, *Jean Petit*, Paris, 1932, p. 80). The same was true of the nations. Ehrle thinks that membership of the nations lasted for life, even if a member had become a doctor in a higher faculty; cf. *op. cit.*, p. clxi. It is certainly the case that within the faculty of medicine the masters were still grouped according to their nations. For example, the dean of the faculty of medicine was chosen by electors delegated by the four nations, and the examiners in medicine were at one time chosen from different nations (Wickersheimer, *Commentaires*, pp. xx, li–liii). A non-regent master of arts of course remained a member (two years of non-regency counted for one of regency towards seniority in 1406, *Auct.* i. 933). But the right to vote in a nation depended upon the possession of the degree of master of arts, the regent masters in arts had most influence, and masters in higher faculties did not vote in the congregations of the nations.]

[2] *Chartul.* i, Nos. 501, 937. In practice the period appears to have been usually one year.

[3] Bulaeus, iv. 164 (*Chartul.* ii, No. 697), v. 71.

was of perpetual validity, and hence, when summoned by the rector, he was as much bound as the regent to attend a congregation and give his late colleagues the benefit of his advice and support. At first the summoning of the non-regents was a rare and extraordinary event. But, as the non-regents would always include a large number of persons highly placed in Church and State, their presence was naturally desired when anything like a demonstration was to be made. After the middle of the fourteenth century the attendance of non-regents seems to have become increasingly frequent, and eventually they were summoned on all occasions of importance except elections.[1] But they voted as members of their respective nations or faculties; and it is not clear whether their presence ever became legally necessary to the acts of the university, as at Oxford or Cambridge.[2]

Procedure in general congrega-tions. At these congregations the mode of proceeding was as follows. The rector notified the time and place of the meeting and the matters to be discussed at it, to the dean of theology by calling at his house in person or through a master of arts, and to the other deans and the proctors by sending them a *schedula* containing these particulars.[3] These officers in turn

---

[1] [On 28 August and 25 September 1349 we find non-regents joining in the election of the proctor, of the English nation, but this seems to have been exceptional: Bulaeus, iv. 314; *Auctarium*, i, col. 139. At any rate the reference to them is exceptional.] In the superior faculties non-regents had the right of voting in examinations. *Chartul.* i, No. 465.

[2] A Statute of 1312 directs the bedels 'nullum intrare vel accedere permittent, nisi magistros actu Regentes vel illos qui per Rectorem fuerint evocati'. Bulaeus, iv. 164; *Chartul.* ii, No. 697. In 1456 the privileges of regency were extended to 'Magistri et Paedogogi qui per longa tempora rexerint in vico straminis', except participation in the 'distributiones pro Missis et Vesperis', i.e. payments from the

funds of the nation or university to all masters who had attended the weekly university Vespers and Mass, sums which were spent in potations at a tavern immediately after the service. Intruders on these occasions were to be expelled, or if they had eaten or drunk anything before detection to be compelled 'ad solvendam cotam suam de propriis pecuniis'. Bulaeus, v. 617.

[3] If due notice of the agenda were not given, the proceedings might be annulled (Bulaeus, v. 527). In the fifteenth century the senior or French proctor, with the concurrence of the other proctors, claimed the right of summoning a congregation of the faculty of arts if the rector refused to do so. Bulaeus, v. 718–20.

summoned the masters of their respective faculties or nations by sending a bedel round the schools during morning lecture. In most cases the business to be discussed would have originated with one of the component bodies, who would either have arrived at a resolution and ordered its head to demand the 'adjunction' of the other faculties and nations, or simply referred the matter for further deliberation to the whole university.[1] When the university was assembled, the rector laid the question before it. In every church or convent where the university was in the habit of meeting, each faculty and nation had its accustomed place for separate deliberation. In the Church of S. Julien, for instance, there were chairs for the four proctors in the four corners of the nave. To these four corners upon a division the nations retired and held their separate congregations. The three smaller bodies— the doctors of the three superior faculties—repaired to other parts of the church. Debate took place only in these separate assemblies. On the reassembling of the congregation the vote or opinion of each nation[2] was reported by its proctor, the vote of each faculty by its dean. The rector then summed up the collective sense of the house, and pronounced the 'conclusion' of the whole university.[3]

[1] At times the proceedings were spread over several congregations. Thus in 1340 'cum idem rector alias tradidisset, in quadam congregacione generali magistris trium facultatum, videlicet medicorum, decretorum et theologorum, tres cedulas papireas, in quibus cedulis continebantur articuli et modus per quem detrahentes, malefactores et detractores scolarium beiaunorum corrigerentur, ut dicti magistri predictarum facultatum dictas cedulas corrigerent', &c. Jourdain, No. 567; *Chartul*. ii, No. 1032. This document gives a very clear and detailed account of a general congregation.

[2] It was taken by show of hands and shouting combined, 'et cuicunque placeret illud, levaret manum et diceret: ita.' *Chartul*. ii, No. 1072; but elsewhere—presumably when a poll was demanded or perhaps on personal 'graces'—we find allusions to secret voting. *Chartul*. ii, App., p. 672.

[3] An attempt of the dean of theology to 'conclude' in default of the rector was violently resented by the artists. Bulaeus, v. 589. The act of 'Conclusion' was made the more indispensable and the more difficult since no actual 'motion' or 'question' was commonly put before the retirement of the nations and faculties. Hence the rector's function was not merely to count or declare votes, but to sum up the collective sense of resolutions which might be variously worded. Where no majority appeared for any one resolution, the rector 'nihil conclusit'. He had no casting vote.

At first, as we have seen, the principle was that a majority was required in each faculty. The earliest instance of decision by a majority of faculties which occurs is an exception exactly of the kind which is said to prove the rule. It occurs in 1303, when only a majority of the faculties could be induced to support the appeal of the prelates of France against Boniface VIII's excommunication of the adherents of Philip the Fair in his struggle against the papacy. The language used in the Act of Adherence implies that the step was exceptional: it was rather a declaration of opinion by the majority to which they were emboldened or compelled by royal pressure to give

the sanction of the university itself.[1] The document to which the seal was appended was a mere academic protest or manifesto, not a statute claiming the obedience of individual masters. The precedent was no doubt not without its influence in the development of the new constitutional theory: at all events it illustrates the way in which the majority may have introduced the theory of majority-voting by the forcible creation of successive precedents. But as late as 1313 the Dominicans of Oxford allege in their pleadings against that university that at Paris the consent of the whole four faculties was requisite to the making of a statute, though from the same document it appears that the practice of majority-voting existed *de facto* in the University of Oxford.[2] But it is not till the year 1340 that we get a decisive instance of an attempt to carry a statute by a majority of the faculties only.[3]

[1] 'Ad notitiam singulorum volumus pervenire quod nuper nonnullis ex nobis maiorem partem facultatum nostrarum [et] tocius Parisiensis studii facientibus pro certis causis et negociis accedentibus ad presentiam excellentissimi principis domini Philippi ... recitatum fuit,' &c. Bulaeus, iv. 47. The original text appears to have no *et* (*Chartul*. ii, No. 634), but the passage can hardly be construed without it. The precautions taken in 1312–13 against abuse of the university seal (Bulaeus, iv. 163; *Chartul*. ii, No. 698) suggest the kind of way in

which a majority might forcibly attempt to override the minority: it is provided 'cuiuslibet facultatis teneatur unus magister cum clavi in loco sigillationis personaliter interesse'. All previous writers (Denifle does not touch on the question) have assumed (1) that voting by a majority of bodies dates from the earliest days of the university; (2) that on a division, a nation was equal to a faculty.

[2] See above, p. 394, n. 2, and below, vol. iii, chap. xii, § 2.

[3] 'Quatuor Facultates seu magistri earumdem dixerunt, ac etiam

Even now, however, the principle is only struggling for recognition. A statute or decree against the bullying of freshmen
was carried in spite of the dissent of the faculty of law from
a particular clause of it. But since the dissent of the faculty
from this part is specified in the official record, it is not clear
how far it was intended that the lawyers should be bound by
those parts of the statute to which they had not consented.
In the very same year, however, the theologians refused their
consent to a contribution or levy voted by the other faculties
for the expenses of an embassy to the Holy See. Though the
majority were determined to override the opposition of the
theologians, it was considered necessary to obtain their formal consent, and they were accordingly forced to yield by
the threat of being suspended from six ordinary lectures in the
event of continued recusancy.[1] Long before the end of the
century, however, the right of the majority of faculties to
bind the minority had ceased to be disputed.[2] The historians

---

concorditer pronunciaverunt quod
volebant et concordabant, quod
omnia in predicta cedula contenta
per modum ordinacionis decetero
tenerentur, hoc tantum excepto,
quod vir venerabilis et discretus
magister Nicholaus de Hamello,
doctor in decretis, qui non fuerat in
correctione predicte cedule, ut dice-
bat, nomine sue facultatis decretorum, sic dixit, quod non erat
bonum, quod magistri regentes
tenerentur, iniurias, minas vel
violencias beiaunis illatas, prout in
cedula continebatur, alicui revelare, quia non videbatur facultati
sue decretorum iustum nec con-
sonum rationi.' Jourdain, No. 567;
Chartul. ii, No. 1032. There are
traces of the practice before this.
In 1318 a document was sealed,
though an amendment had been
suggested by the theologians, but
it does not appear whether the
amendment was accepted. Bulaeus,
iv. 181; *Chartul.* ii, No. 774. Cf.
also Bulaeus, iv. 208 *sq.*; *Chartul.*
ii, No. 845.

[1] Bulaeus, iv. 261; *Archiv*, v.
246.

[2] In 1347 the majority claims
that a resolution (not a statute) has
been passed 'per dictam Universitatem seu maiorem et saniorem
partem ipsius', though the faculty
of decrees and two nations protested against it. (*Chartul.* ii, No.
1129.) But its validity is apparently
undisputed. See a clearer case in
1348 (*ibid.*, No. 1152). The principle is fully established by the
year 1379, when the university
resolved that no judgement in respect of the Schism question
should be binding without the
unanimous consent of the faculties
(Bulaeus, iv. 565, 566; *Chartul.* iii,
No. 1616). It would even appear
that the principle had been sanctioned by some statute which is not
extant, since the university enacts
'quod dominus rector in colligendo
vota, quando determinandum erit,
et concludendo, non concludat pro
tribus (sicut facit aliquando secundum quod potest per statutum,

CHAP. V, of the university have indeed pretended that the vote of the
§ 3. university was determined by the majority of the seven
corporations, each nation being thus placed on an equality
with one of the superior faculties;[1] but such a contention is
contrary to the most explicit statements in the medieval
documents which have come down to us.[2] The faculty of
arts did sometimes attempt, not unsuccessfully, to overcome
the opposition of the superior faculties by virtue of the rector's
authority over its individual members; but the constitutional
principle was that the vote of the faculty of arts was determined by the majority of nations, the vote of the university
by the majority of faculties. The whole history of the voting
arrangement in the University of Paris supplies an interesting
illustration (to borrow Lord Bryce's happy expression) of
constitutional development by usage.

Voting by Long before the principle of majority-voting finally
nations. triumphed in the university itself, we find it well established
as between the nations in the faculty of arts; though here the
minority-nation had the remedy of an appeal to the whole
university. But even after the establishment of the principle,
it did not by any means follow that a dissentient faculty or
nation would submit unhesitatingly or unquestioningly to the

quando materia non est tam gravis
et ponderosa), sed ita quod omnes
sint contenti; in ista materia
maxime ardua faciat consentire
omnes Facultates et Nationes'.
The clearest possible evidence of
the continuance of the same practice is supplied among other places
by Bulaeus, v. 725, 807, 831-2. The
last reference brings us to the year
1499. In explanation of the Bulaean
misrepresentation, it must be remembered that the faculty of arts
voted by nations, so that three
nations could carry the day against
one nation with the aid of two other
faculties, or with one faculty could
prevent a conclusion. The only
exception to the above generalizations which I have come across is
an occasion on which, in a dis-

pute between the superior faculties
and the faculty of arts, the rector
'requisitus saepius ab illis tribus
[Facultatibus] ut concluderet pro
illis, conclusit ad conclusionem
Facultatis Artium' (Bulaeus, Remarques sur la dignité du R.,
p. 88), but this appears to have
been an arbitrary stretch of
authority, not based on any constitutional theory as to each nation
counting as a faculty.
[1] Crevier, iii. 29; Thurot, pp.
24, 25.
[2] The principle was usually observed in the appointment of delegates to award benefices or legati to
represent the university (Bulaeus,
v. 347, 348, 583; Jourdain, No.
1385), but not in voting on a
statute or decree.

decision of the majority. It is indeed extremely difficult to CHAP. V, give the modern reader any adequate idea of the turbulence, § 3. the boisterousness, the quarrelsomeness of these academic assemblies, or of the chaotic condition of the constitutional principles by which they were supposed to be regulated. Here as in other departments of medieval life we constantly see side by side the strongest passion for legal chicane or constitutional subtlety and the most reckless defiance of all rule. Hardly any principle is so well established that it cannot be disputed. Not only corporations but even individuals at times put forth a claim to veto or at least delay the decision of the majority.[1]

There was one quasi-legal means of obstruction by which Constitutional obstruction. a dissentient faculty or nation might prevent the acts of the majority taking effect. The university seal was kept in a chest to which each faculty and nation possessed a separate key. When party feeling ran high, a dissentient faculty or nation would direct its dean or proctor to attend the rector's summons without his key, and obstinately to refuse to produce it. Under such circumstances there was no remedy but to direct the chest to be broken open.[2] A still more constitutional

[1] Thus in the register of the large nation of France we read, 'et quia unus nostrum, ut dictum est, reclamaverat, dictum statutum non fuit sigillatum'. Bulaeus, iv. 224 (cf. v. 387, 423); *Chartul.* ii, No. 897. [Cf. Boyce, p. 38.] Yet it is abundantly clear that, under ordinary circumstances, a majority-vote was considered sufficient: 'Conclusi a pluritate vocum in vigore statuti antiqui.' Bulaeus, v. 532. [The method of electing officials which prevailed in the Norman nation illustrates both the intricacies of elections and the problems suggested by majority decisions. In an elaborate way, designed to maintain secrecy and avoid fraud, each master was given a single bean. One bean was black, the others white. The master who received the black bean nominated

five electors. If the electors were divided, the consent of the minority to the election of the person chosen by the majority had to be asked. See the lengthy statute (1336) purporting to define ancient custom, in *Chartul.* ii, No. 455. At Bologna, voting in the colleges of doctors or faculties was made according to a common Italian custom, by black and white beans; cf. *Chartul.* iv, *passim*, and the document printed by Ehrle, *op. cit.*, p. 90—a decision of the faculty of theology in 1482.]

[2] Bulaeus, iv. 163; v. 555, 776. In some cases this manœuvre seems adopted to compel an appeal 'ad Universitatem ipsam melius congregandam'. Cf. also Bulaeus, iv. 579, 580. Sometimes this kind of opposition compelled the majority to agree to a compromise. Bulaeus, v. 555–6.

CHAP. V, method of resisting the decision of the majority was by
§ 3. lodging an appeal to the Holy See, a threat which, even when
not seriously meant, created delay, and meanwhile relieved
the conscience and character of those who refused to obey
from the imputation of perjury.[1]

Drinking of surplus. The origin of the university in a voluntary society of
teachers bound together at first merely by a body of unwritten
customs or class-law is eminently illustrated by the sources
of its revenue and the way in which it was spent. The fees
and expenses on taking degrees were really nothing more than
the money exacted by the masters from a new-comer on plea
of making him pay his footing, precisely on the level with the
demand of 'bejaunia' by the students from freshmen so often
condemned by the masters themselves.[2] Every favour that the
masters conferred had likewise to be paid for. For example,
the first time a master was appointed proctor or receiver
of his nation, he was expected to pay down a sum of money
which that august body immediately proceeded to spend in
drink at a neighbouring tavern.[3] Surplus revenues seem to
have been habitually disposed of in the same jovial fashion.[4]

Academical courts. It has been already pointed out that neither the rector nor
the cathedral chancellor held the position at Paris which the
chancellors of Oxford and Cambridge occupied in those
universities. The jurisdiction in causes which concerned
scholars—at Oxford and Cambridge merged in the Chancellor's Court—was divided between three tribunals (the

[1] In some cases when this threat
of 'appeal' is made, it is not clear
to whom the appeal was made.
Bulaeus, v. 633, 664.

[2] See below, vol. ii, ch. xiv.

[3] The books of the nations contain such entries as the following:
'M. Nicolaus solvit Nationi unum
scutum pro Procuratoria et statim
perpotatum fuit illud scutum per
Magistros in taberna ad imaginem
nostre Domine in vico S. Jacobi.'

[4] These drinkings were abolished in the German or English
nation in 1391 except the accustomed celebration of the feast of

S. Edmund. The statute provides
'quod decetero nulle fient pota-
ciones, nec speciales, nec generales
... de pecuniis recipiendis a magistris pro prima procuratoria, et pro
iocundo introitu, pro mensibus dis-
tribuendis in examine Sancte Genovefe'. The money was henceforth
to be reserved 'pro usu nacionis'.
Bulaeus, iv. 674. [Chartul. iii,
No. 1592. The statute was issued
in a time of distress and has parallels,
e.g. in 1370 (Auctarium, i. 361).
On the whole subject see Boyce,
chapters v and vi.]

rector's court being put aside as wielding in the main a merely academical or disciplinary and consensual jurisdiction, extending only to cases where both parties were members or clients of the university or owners of university hostels): (1) The Bishop's Court, (2) The Châtelet, (3) The Court of the Conservator of the Apostolic Privileges of the University.

To understand the distinction between these different jurisdictions, it is necessary to bear in mind that prior to any privileges from king or pope, the masters and scholars of Paris were presumed to be clerks, and as such entitled to all the ordinary immunities of ecclesiastics. This was the foundation of their exemption from the ordinary tribunals, though they managed to retain many of their privileges after other ecclesiastics had partially lost them.

(1) The bishop's official heard all ordinary criminal or ecclesiastical prosecutions against a scholar, and might hear civil cases in which he was engaged either as plaintiff or defendant.[1] A scholar, if plaintiff, might also appeal to the Bishop's Court, but if the defendant was a layman, the court could in that case only impose spiritual penalties, i.e. excommunication and penance as the condition of absolution. *The Bishop's Court.*

(2) The Châtelet as the Court of the Provost of Paris, the 'Conservator of the Royal Privileges of the University', tried all civil actions in which a member of the university was engaged, wherever the cause of action arose, which lay out of the jurisdiction of the ecclesiastical courts (e.g. actions affecting real property), and which (but for the royal privilege) would be heard by some other secular court in or out of Paris. Criminal cases in which a scholar was prosecutor, and in which he did not elect to be satisfied with such penalties as the ecclesiastical court could inflict, would also be tried by the provost or his lieutenant. A general power to protect scholars was, as has been mentioned, entrusted to the provost *The Conservator of the Royal Privileges.*

[1] There were of course changes in the extent of these various jurisdictions. Without attempting to trace them in detail, we may say that by the close of our period, the trial of civil causes had probably passed from the bishop to the rector and the royal conservator.

CHAP. v, of Paris by the charter of Philip Augustus in 1200;[1] but the
§ 3. right to bring up cases from secular courts in all parts of
France seems to have been first conferred by a royal charter
in 1341.[2] This jurisdiction was of course merely an extension
of the ordinary civil and criminal jurisdiction which the
Châtelet exercised over all inhabitants of Paris.

The Con- (3) Cases affecting a scholar in which the jurisdiction in
servator
Apostolic. the ordinary course belonged to the Holy See or to some
apostolic delegate out of Paris, were transferred to the Court
of the Conservator Apostolic in Paris[3]—subject to the reservation that a defendant might not be cited further than four
days' journey beyond his own diocese.[4] To this court belonged
also the right of interfering to protect either the university
itself, or any member of it, from the violation of any of its
papal privileges.[5]

To define the limits of these several jurisdictions with
greater precision would involve a treatise on a difficult and
complicated branch of medieval law. It is clear that in many
cases several ways of proceeding were open to a scholar or
a layman involved in a dispute with a scholar. But, whatever
difficulty there may be in distinguishing the cases which fell
to these different courts, the difference in the penalties
imposed by them is quite clear. The distinction between
academical, ecclesiastical, and secular jurisdiction was always

[1] See above, p. 295.

[2] Bulaeus, iv. 264; *Chartul.* ii,
No. 1044. As an example, we may
take a tithe-case affecting a curé
in the duchy of Normandy transferred from one of the civil courts
of the duchy. Bulaeus, iv. 682.
Power to protect scholars against
violence in all parts of the kingdom
was given in 1306. *Chartul.* ii, No.
657.

[3] The right of citing a defendant
before the conservator is often
called the 'droit de *Committimus*'.

[4] From 1317 the previous permission of the rector and university
or its deputies was necessary before application could be made by
an individual student to the Court

of Conservation. Bulaeus, iv. 178;
Chartul. ii, No. 736.

[5] A specimen of the kind of monition or prohibition which the
conservator addressed to persons
attempting to cite a scholar out of
the city is given in *Chartul.* i, No.
529. In explanation of the fact that
the privilege is limited to citation
before papal delegates out of Paris,
it must be remembered that by
ordinary canon law a person must
be cited in the diocese where he
resides, so that the scholars were
already protected from being cited
before all other ecclesiastical tribunals out of Paris—even in respect
of an offence committed in some
other diocese.

maintained, and never merged as it was at Oxford and Cam- bridge in the Chancellor's Court. The *ultimum supplicium* of the rector or the university was expulsion; that of the conservator apostolic and the bishop, in the case of laymen, excommunication followed by penance. The bishop's official could only imprison his own subjects, i.e. clerks, whether scholars or otherwise: he could only touch the goods or person of a layman by invoking the aid of the secular arm.[1] One class of cases of course formed an exception to the general exemption of scholars as of other ecclesiastics from lay tribunals. In the height of their power, the ecclesiastical courts were never allowed to take cognizance of a cause involving the right to a lay fee.[2]

We have already noticed some of the privileges which *Further* scholars enjoyed over and above the ordinary privileges of *privileges.* the ecclesiastical order in the ecclesiastical courts themselves, such as the requirement of two warnings before they could be excommunicated, and the prohibition of pecuniary penances for moral delinquencies. In addition to these privileges, for which the university could undoubtedly produce papal Bulls, it seems eventually to have claimed a right to demand that the bishop's official should in all cases liberate a scholar

---

[1] In 1347 a difficulty arose as to the powers of the conservator apostolic to imprison for contempt. It was decided that he was to imprison only in the bishop's prison, but without prejudice to his right 'eos questionibus subicere et torquere' (*Chartul.* ii, No. 1137). The case in which the difficulty arose was in connexion with a scholar who had counterfeited the conservator's seal (*ibid.*, No. 1129). I presume that the court could not have proceeded in this way against a layman. As to the attempts of the ecclesiastical courts to directly touch property, see Paul Fournier, *Officialités du moyen âge*, pp. 228, 229, and as to the whole question of the competence of these courts in France, *loc. cit.*, p. 64 *sq.*

[2] Other exceptions might no doubt be adduced, especially in the later Middle Ages, when the benefit of clergy was everywhere greatly curtailed. Thus in 1427 (Bulaeus, v. 381) a M.D. 'clerc non marié' was imprisoned by the Châtelet for contempt in falsifying a document under the seal of the court. The bishop claimed his surrender, which was decreed by the parlement, subject to the condition that he should not be discharged from custody and that 'seront deux des dits Conseillers de la Cour presens, avec l'Evesque ou son Official à faire le procez du dit M. Bernard'. [The case was a protracted one and the university had recourse to its weapon of *cessationes*; cf. *Chartul.* iv, No. 2298, note.]

CHAP. V, committed to his custody by the secular courts until trial
§ 3. upon his mere oath to appear.[1]

Officials   The officials of the university (even when not masters or
of the   scholars) enjoyed the full privileges of scholars. Of these the
uni-   most important were (1) the bedels whose duties were much
versity.   the same as those of the bedels at Bologna;[2] (2) the common *procurator ad litem* or *syndicus*, afterwards styled the
promotor universitatis, who was the chief permanent official
of the university, combining the functions of a university
counsel or solicitor with some of those which would now be
discharged by a registrar. (3) At a later date a *scribe* or secretary was appointed distinct from the syndic.[3] The duties of
registrar had in early days of the university been discharged
by the rector, who was also the collector and treasurer of the
common funds. (4) These last duties were afterwards delegated to a receiver (*receptor* or *quaestor aerarii*). The last
two offices are not mentioned till the beginning of the fifteenth
century. The nations and faculties had for a long time had
receivers of their own.[4]

The   Another office which calls for a passing mention is that of
Nuntii. university messenger (*nuntius*). The transmission of money
and goods to scholars must have been a business of considerable importance from an early period. Eventually it became
a regular university office, the scholars of each diocese electing
their own *nuntii*. Of these there were two classes. The *nuntii
maiores* would seem to have been merchants or bankers who
undertook to pay to scholars money advanced by their parents
in distant regions, and lent money to scholars on their own

[1] 'Ad cautionem iuratoriam, secundum formam Privilegii Universitatis' (Bulaeus, v. 533). The
university or rather the nation of
France declares, 'quod de eius-
modi re habebat declarationem a
summo Pontifice'.

[2] [The individual doctors of the
superior faculties had bedels of
their own, as at Bologna. (*Chartul.*
iii, No. 1702.)]

[3] Bulaeus, iii. 583, 585; *Remarques sur l'élection des officiers*, p. 9 *sq.*

[4] *Remarques*, p. 92 n. The receiver of the faculty of arts was also
receiver of the university. *Ibid.*,
p. 93. [The *receptor* of the English
nation is found from 1333, when
the Proctors' Book begins. He was
generally a senior non-regent
master and served for a year. He
rendered accounts to the masters of
the nation once a month. Boyce,
pp. 53–60, summarizes the extensive information printed in the
Auctarium.]

account;[1] while the 'petty', 'flying', or 'ordinary' messengers[2] actually travelled backwards and forwards with consignments of goods or money to scholars, and even took charge of the scholars themselves.[3]

Besides the actual members or scholars[4] (*suppositi*) of the university, and the officers, there was a numerous body of 'clients' who enjoyed the full privileges of membership, or at least a considerable portion of them.

The most important classes of clients were the *stationarii* and *librarii*, or booksellers, over whom the university established the same kind of control that existed at Bologna. The trade of the *librarius* consisted largely, if not entirely, in the sale of books for private individuals, the tradesman being remunerated by a percentage on the price obtained, while the *stationarius* employed the writers who actually produced new books which were either sold or much more often lent for a fixed sum on security for their value being deposited by the borrower.[5] The *stationarius* in fact combined the functions

---

[1] Crevier, vii, 158. Cf. de Lens, *Univ. d'Angers*, i. 108. [Boyce, pp. 70–2, protests against Rashdall's translation of *nuntius* as messenger, but the *nuntii* of whom he speaks are masters elected from time to time and placed under oath to transact the business of the university at the papal court and elsewhere. These are rather *nuncios* than the kind of official described above.]

[2] 'Parvi, volantes, ordinarii.' Bulaeus, v. 787–91 *sq.*

[3] Bulaeus, v. 807. So at Oxford, where the common carriers continued to be licensed by the University down to quite recent times.

[4] Strictly speaking, non-graduate scholars were not members of the university (*iurati Universitatis*) but only *suppositi* or subjects. The last term is often extended to the clients.

[5] The system is in the main established by 1275 (Bulaeus, iii. 419; *Chartul.* i, No. 462). This document shows that the power

claimed by the university rested solely on its right to forbid its own members from dealing with a recalcitrant trader. Other particulars are gathered from the more elaborate statutes of 1323 and 1342 (Bulaeus, iv. 202, 278; *Chartul.* ii, Nos. 733, 1064; cf. also Nos. 628, 642, 724, 825, 1064). In 1275 we hear of 'stationarii qui vulgo librarii appellantur'; in 1323 we have the names of twenty-eight 'stationarii et librarii', but the context seems to establish the distinction given in the text between the two terms, though both branches of the trade were no doubt followed by the same persons. M. Delalain, however, in his interesting monograph (*Étude sur le Libraire Parisien du xiiiᵉ au xvᵉ siècle*, p. xviii *sq.*) makes the *librarius* as well as the *stationarius* let books out on hire, while the characteristic of the *stationarius* is that he produces new books. The allusions to the 'correction' of books by the university

of publisher, bookseller, and circulating-library-keeper. No book might be let out on hire (whether for reading or for copying) till the correctness of the copy had been examined and the price or rate of hire fixed by a joint board, composed of four masters and four principal booksellers annually nominated by the university.[1] The stationer was forbidden to dispose of an authorized copy till he had informed the university assembled in general congregation of the intended bargain, in order that they might take measures to prevent it going out of their reach.[2] In order to check collusion between the *librarii* to the injury of those who had entrusted them with books, they were forbidden to sell a book (without the owner's express consent) to another person in the trade till it had been exposed for sale on four days at the Blackfriars' Convent during sermon-time.[3]

would seem to imply the existence of officials resembling the 'correctores peciarum' at Bologna. All stationers and booksellers were sworn to obey the university and were required to give security. The control of the university passed into a legal monopoly. Delalain, pp. 48 *sq.*, 55 *sq.* For the very similar Oxford regulations see Gibson, *Statuta Antiqua*, pp. 183–7. [See also T. G. Law, *Collected Essays and Reviews*, ed. P. Hume Brown, Edinburgh, 1904.]

[1] [*Chartul.* ii, No. 733. The university was especially concerned to safeguard the authorized copies or *exemplaria*, made from the author's manuscript or by the collation of existing copies. The so-called Paris text of the Vulgate is usually regarded as an early instance (cf. S. Berger, *Histoire de la Vulgate*, Paris, 1893; Denifle in *Archiv*, iv), but H. H. Glunz has given reasons to think that the Paris text was the text used by Peter the Lombard and the masters who carried on the tradition established by his teaching (*History of the Vulgate in England from Alcuin to Roger*

Bacon, Cambridge, 1933, pp. 259 *sqq.*). The *exemplar*, composed in Paris of unbound *peciae*, each of four folios or eight pages, was lent at a fixed sum (*taxatio*) for the purpose of copying. The idea was to establish the circulation of an authoritative text. Taxation-lists survive from *c.* 1275 and 1304 at Paris, Rome, Bologna, Padua, and Florence. On the significance of the system see J.-A. Destrez, 'La pecia dans les manuscrits du moyen âge', in *Revue des sciences philosophiques et théologiques*, xiii (1924), 182–97.]

[2] 'Item nullus stationarius exemplar aliquod alienabit, sine eo quod prius notificet Universitati in congregatione generali ut Universitas ordinet viam per quam ipse stationarius a profectu suo non impediatur et Universitas exemplaris usu non defraudetur' (*Chartul.* ii, No. 733). [For the four *librarii iurati* or *principales* cf. *Chartul.* iii, No. 1407 with note.]

[3] So, at Cologne, there were bookstalls on Festivals 'in ambitu Ecclesiae maioris'. Bianco, i, *Anl.*, p. 22.

As an illustration of the extent of the book-trade in medieval Paris, it may be mentioned that in 1323 there were twenty-eight sworn booksellers besides keepers of book-stalls in the open air, who were restricted to the sale and loan of books of small value. Books were no doubt bought and borrowed more extensively by masters than by scholars; but the statutes required every theologian to bring a copy of the Bible or Sentences, as the case might be, to lecture with him, at least during the first four years of his attendance. Many college statutes required the student attending logic or philosophy lectures to have a copy of the text.[1] So, at Vienna, a scholar attending lecture without his book lost his term.[2] The importance of oral teaching was no doubt greatly increased by the scarcity of books; but facts such as these warn us against the exaggerated and indeed absurd statements often made as to the booklessness of the medieval student. The difficulty arising from the expense of books was met by the system of lending libraries; and the expense even of purchase has been greatly exaggerated. The enormous prices often quoted in illustration of the dearness of books relate (so far as the university period is concerned) to the gorgeous illuminated works of art prepared for great personages or rich monasteries.[3]

[1] At Harcourt College, for instance, we find: 'Caeterum pro Artistis statuimus quod quilibet librum de quo audierit, sibi a principio ordinarii procuret et illum principali domus ostendat.' Bulaeus, iv. 159.

[2] 'Statuimus quod Scolaris non habens librum in Scolis ... non recipiat tempus suum.' Kink, *Wien*, ii. 132. So in most German statutes; but at Ingolstadt 'looking over' is recognized, it being permissible 'tres habere unum textum in qualibet eorum lectione, quod ita se complevisse iurabit quisque in congregatione facultatis ante admissionem ad examen', Prantl, *Gesch. d. Ludwig-Maximilians Univ.* ii. 74; [also at Tübingen and Freiburg (Kaufmann, ii. 412)]. The

first business of a student, in coming up, was to provide himself with books. Odofredus mentions the extravagance of a man who, on coming up with an allowance of 100 *librae* from his father, 'fecit libros suos babuinare (*sic*) de literis aureis' (ap. Sarti, 1888, 1. i. 167). [*Babuinare* means to adorn with grotesques or baboonery.]

[3] [It should be noticed that these are late instances. Except the wealthier students, only masters are likely to have had many books in earlier times: cf. Powicke, *Medieval Books of Merton College*, Oxford, 1931; and for the price of books, *ibid.*, pp. 38, 39, and especially J. de Ghellinck in *Revue d'histoire ecclésiastique*, xix (1923), 160–8, and the bibliography there given.]

CHAP. V,   The parchment-makers, illuminators, binders, and (later)
§ 3.   the paper-merchants and paper-makers of Corbeil and
Parch-
ment- Essones[1] were also under academical superintendence as
makers,
&c.   clients of the university. The parchment-makers were obliged
to bring the bales of parchment on their arrival in Paris to
the Hall of the Mathurines to be 'taxed' or valued by the
'four sworn parchmenters' of the university under the supervision of the rector, who also visited the great Fair of S.
Denis for the like purpose. The parchment had to remain
at the Mathurines for twenty-four hours, during which it
might only be sold at the appointed rate to members of the
university. By some means or other—probably by sheer
imposition afterwards sanctioned by law—the rector succeeded in levying a tax upon all parchment sold in Paris, which
formed the most important perquisite of the rectorial office.[2]

The chi-   Another body of clients were the surgeons. In northern
rurgeons. Europe the learned physicians[3] looked down upon the

---

[1] A document of 1415 (Bulaeus,
v. 279) shows that these mills were
set up about sixty years before that
date. Before that time, what paper
was used at Paris is said to have
been imported from Lombardy.

[2] Bulaeus, iii. 499 *sq.*; vi. 478;
Chartul. ii, No. 574, 575; Crevier,
ii. 130–2; v. 419. This duty consisted of 16 *denarii Parisienses* on
each *botte* of parchment. The
rector also received a 'cappa' from
each nation and a 'bursa' from each
'licentiandus' or 'magistrandus'
(Bulaeus, v. 304). He also received
an allowance of 40 *solidi Parisienses*
'pro stipendiis suae receptae' (iii.
589). This entertainment consisted
it appears, in *vinum et species* provided at his house for the masters
who accompanied him home after
his election. Du Boulay tells us
that in his day the feast had fallen
into desuetude, though the 'deductio' of the new rector was kept
up (iii. 573). (A similar ceremonial
is still observed after the admission
of the vice-chancellor and of the

proctors at Oxford. The masters
have, however, lost their 'wine and
spices', which at the vice-chancellor's admission have been superseded by a lunch for the 'heads' and
other magnates.) Further provision
might be made by the nation for
a rector chosen from the number
of its own masters. Cf. Bulaeus,
iv. 377.

[3] Besides the doctors, other physicians might be licensed to practise
by the bishop upon the recom-
mendation of the faculty; all other
practitioners were suppressed by
the Ecclesiastical Courts. *Chartul.*
ii, Nos. 900, 933. It is curious to
see the 'medical woman' question
fought out in a prosecution directed
by the medical faculty at Paris
against a woman who had cured
the royal chancellor and many
others for whom the physicians
could do nothing. She alleges *inter
alia* that 'mulier antea permitteret
se mori quam secreta infirmitatis
sue homini revelare', &c. *Chartul.*
ii, No. 814.

chirurgeons as mere manual operators, who were, according CHAP. V, to strict professional theory, only allowed to practise under § 3. the supervision of a doctor.[1] From the year 1436 the chirurgeons, hitherto merely clients, were admitted as actual 'scholars' of the university, provided that they attended (*ut moris est*) the lectures of the regent masters in medicine.[2] In 1491, however, elated by their newly acquired academical learning, the chirurgeons rebelled against the subordinate position to which the pride of the full-blown 'doctors' condemned them. The faculty retaliated by throwing open its lectures to the inferior class of barber-surgeons. To this the chirurgeons objected as an infringement of the statutes, since to be intelligible to these unlearned practitioners the lectures had to be given in the vernacular. The difficulty was got over by delivering the lectures first in Latin for the avoidance of perjury, and then in French for the edification of the audience. This expedient brought the chirurgeons to their knees, and in 1506 they again acknowledged themselves the humble 'disciples' of the doctors and were readmitted to the favour of the faculty.[3] The apothecaries were also under the supervision of the medical faculty, which was carried to the point of forbidding the sale of a 'laxative medicine' without a physician's order.[4]

During the earlier part of its history the university had Interference of papal legates. been subject to constant interference on the part of the Holy

---

[1] Bulaeus, iii. 400, 401; *Chartul.* i, No. 434. By an edict of Philippe le Bel in the year 1311 'nullus chirurgicus, nulla chirurgica' was allowed to practise without being examined by the 'magistri chirurgici iurati', under the presidency of the King's chirurgeon, and licensed in the Châtelet. *Ordonnances des roys de France*, i. 491. [See *Chartul.* ii, No. 692, with notes and references; cf. S. d'Irsay, *Hist. des Universités*, i. 163-5. On the whole question see especially Wickersheimer, *Commentaires de la Faculté de Médecine*, pp. lxxvi-lxxxiv. The first anatomical dissection known to have been made in the faculty

was in 1407; *ibid.* in *Bulletin de la Soc. de l'hist. de Paris*, xxxvii (1910), 159-69.]

[2] *Chartul.* iv, No. 2496; Pasquier, *Recherches de la France*, Bk. ix, ch. 30 (Paris, 1621, p. 865). The surgeons had a guild of their own and were admitted to the mastership by *birettatio* in much the same way as university graduates. [For the *prepositus* of the surgeons and their 'confraternitas Sanctorum Cosmae et Damiani' see *Chartul.* iii, Nos. 1231, 1250, 1296, royal charters of the years 1356-64.]

[3] Pasquier, pp. 868, 869.

[4] See the apothecary's oath, *Chartul.* ii, No. 817.

See. In the event of a dispute between different nations or faculties, the aggrieved party could always have recourse to the Pope or his legate, who would dispose of the matter almost independently of the King's consent. In the fourteenth century the royal prerogative began to assert itself in academical as in other matters. Papal injunctions were not invariably obeyed, and never without the royal concurrence. Hence, occasionally in the fourteenth century, and frequently in the fifteenth, we find the Parlement interfering in the affairs of the university. The university, however, claimed, as the *The university and the Parlement.* 'eldest daughter' (a very spoiled child) of the King of France, the right of pleading as a corporation before no secular judge but the King himself.[1] On more than one occasion it refused to obey a citation before the Parlement, or appeared only under protest. For a time the preposterous claim was, it would seem, admitted or rejected according to the humour of the court. But as taxation in France became heavier, and the wealth of the academic ecclesiastics attracted the attention of the fiscal officials, the court began to look unfavourably upon the exemptions enjoyed by regents and scholars. Whenever an attempt was made to tax a member or sworn client of the university, the matter was declared to be one of 'privilege'; the university appeared as an 'intervening party' and demanded audience of the King. These occasions at length became so frequent that in 1446 a royal edict put a stop to the nuisance, and definitively proclaimed the jurisdiction of the Parlement in the suits of the university.[2]

Arrogant abuse and consequent loss of privileges. This was only the beginning of its downfall from the proud

[1] 'Cum sola Regia Maiestas praesentialiter sui corporis causas solita sit tractare tanquam filiae primogenitae et perpetuae.' Bulaeus, v. 537–8.

[2] [The circumstances which led to the important Ordonnance of 26 March 1446 (last edited in *Chartul.* iv, No. 2608) are described in the proctor's book of the German nation (*Auctarium*, ii, cc. 641 *sq.*) and in a record of the proceedings in Parlement, 22–3 Feb. (*Chartul.* iv,

No. 2606). The university asserted that two doctors, on a frivolous complaint (*pro casu levi*) made by a former housemate of one of them, had been imprisoned by the Provost of Paris. They were claimed both by the university and by the bishop, and the Parlement intervened as between the two claimants. This action raised the whole question of privilege; and in the eyes of the university the royal ordonnance *visceraliter tangit nostra privilegia*

position once held by the university in the days when it CHAP. V,
§ 3.
could use the language of menace to kings and parlements,
and when rival princes or statesmen had thought it worth
while to court its favour. Under Charles VII, indeed, the
university still continued to be treated with great indulgence.
Though it had to admit the jurisdiction of the Parlement
when a matter was once brought before it, it still ventured
to exercise the terrible penalty of *privatio* against individual
members of its own body who carried their complaints from
the university tribunals to the supreme court of the realm.[1]
Never were its privileges more jealously, more factiously
asserted. Not content with the 'privation' or expulsion of
members who had violated its privileges, the children of the
offenders to the fourth generation were made incapable of
taking a degree, and the university sometimes persisted in
executing such a decree in spite of an order of Parlement.[2]
The spiritual thunders of the conservator apostolic were in
constant requisition against violators of privileges, and appear
at this time to have been launched as a matter of course,
without the exercise of any judicial discretion, against any
offender whom congregation had ordered to be delated.[3] On
one occasion the university even directed the conservator to
disregard the interim injunction of Parlement to raise an
excommunication pending an appeal to that court.[4] The old
remedy of a 'Cessation from Sermons and Lectures' was
exercised upon the slightest provocation with an alacrity
which does little credit to the zeal of the masters either for
the instruction of their pupils or for the edification of the
public. Since there could have been few preachers in Paris
who were not connected with the university, a cessation[5] of

---

(*Auctarium*, ii, c. 655). At one
point congregation considered the
suggestion that both the provost as
conservator of the privileges of the
university and the bishop should be
summoned to explain their conduct
in plena congregatione (*ibid.*, c. 643).
The records of the proceedings in
congregation give an excellent impression of the outraged dignity of

the university, *alma mater Parisiensis*.]
[1] Bulaeus, v. 588, 595.
[2] *Ibid.* v. 596–7; cf. 641.
[3] *Ibid.* v. 600, 635.
[4] *Ibid.* v. 597.
[5] It probably had to be obeyed
by all the regular orders who were
connected with the university
through any of their members.

CHAP. V, sermons must have meant the almost complete silencing of
§ 3. the pulpits throughout the capital. And since a large proportion of the judges and other government officials were also
graduates of Paris, the power of *privatio*—which involved the
publication of notices in all public places denouncing the
offender as perjured and excommunicated, or as 'an arid,
rotten, and infamous member'[1]—gave the university an
amount of power which it is surprising to find tolerated so
long in the capital of the most despotic sovereign in Europe.
One of the most serious of the disputes in which the university
was engaged at this period was its collision with the *Généraux
des finances*, charged with the administration of finance and
the collection of the *aide*. There appears to have been no
avowed attempt to interfere with the exemption of the university from this imposition; but it is obvious that there would
often be a difficulty in ascertaining the bona-fide character of
a claim to exemption; and the *Généraux* claimed to take cognizance of such disputed claims. The university contended
that they ought to go before the royal conservator. Those of
the *Généraux* who were university men—including a bishop—
were deprived, and all were excommunicated and compelled
to leave their parish churches on Easter Day before the
priests would begin Mass.[2] Even a royal ordinance does not
appear to have immediately put a stop to these proceedings;
and, though in the result the jurisdiction of the court was
upheld, so much consideration was shown to the wounded
amour propre of the sensitive corporation that the president
was appointed 'conservator of the exemption of the University
from the *Aides*', and ordered to take oath, like the provost of
Paris, to respect and enforce the privileges of which he was
constituted the guardian.[3]

Taste for   In the latter part of the fifteenth century the whole energy
university of the university was absorbed in constant conflicts with all
business.
manner of civil and ecclesiastical authorities on questions
of privilege. Many of these privileges were getting out of

---

[1] 'Quod affigeretur privatus per
Quadrivia et valvas tanquam mem-
brum Universitatis aridum, putridum, et infame.' Bulaeus, v. 713.
[2] Bulaeus, v. 634–8.
[3] *Ibid.* v. 644.

harmony with the temper of the age. But the university might chap. v,
probably have retained more of them than it did, had it been   § 3.
a little less outrageous and precipitate in the use of its formidable but antiquated weapons of self-defence. The 'idle and
thankless pursuit which they call doing university business'
(to borrow the phrase of a great censor of our own university[1])
had become a mania with the masters of that day. During the
conciliar period the academical dignitaries had really become
politicians of importance: the decisions of the university
congregation had been a matter of European interest. Now
the age of academical politics was over; but the taste for
'university business' remained.[2] The consequence was that
matter for agitation had to be made out of every trumpery
collision with the police or the tax-gatherers, and every
election to a university office.

The reign of Louis XI saw the extinction of the last relics   Humilia-
of the old independence and influence of the university, as   tion of the
university
of so many other ancient liberties. For a moment, in the   under
Louis XI.
stress of the first outbreak of the War of the Public Weal,
the King had sought to conciliate the capital by adding six
burgesses, six councillors of Parlement, and six masters of
the university to his own Privy Council;[3] but two years later,
in 1467, the King, alleging that some members of the university were caballing with his enemies, forbade the university to
meddle with politics, 'even in letters to their relations', and
demanded the revival of an old statute requiring that a royal
officer should be present at the rectorial elections.[4] It was
with difficulty that the university succeeded in protecting
its students from compulsory military service upon the
walls of Paris.[5] By a succession of minute interferences with
its internal affairs the way was prepared for an absolutely

---

[1] Mark Pattison, *Memoirs*, 1885, p. 331.

[2] As early as 1346 a Pope had found it necessary to remonstrate with the university on account of the number of congregations, in consequence of which 'perduntur et impediuntur lectiones, disputationes et alii actus scolastici, ac illi, qui deberent proficere, infructuose ut plurimum transeunt tempus suum'. *Chartul.* ii, No. 1125.

[3] Gaguin, *Rer. Gall. Ann.* (Frankfurt, 1577), p. 248.

[4] Bulaeus, v. 681.

[5] *Ibid.* v. 682–4; Gaguin, p. 246.

CHAP. V, unparalleled exertion of prerogative. For some two centuries
§ 3.   the university had behaved as if it owed its rights and privileges
to some *ius divinum* underived from any earthly authority,
civil or ecclesiastical. It was now to be rudely reminded that
privileges which the King gave, the King could take away.
In 1474 the King ordered that the rector should always be
a subject of his own; the order being disobeyed, the alien
rector was compelled to resign his office, and all the privileges
of the university were summarily suspended. They were
restored as soon as a new election had been made.[1] But the
measure had the desired effect. The spirit of the once haughty
corporation was completely broken. It is most instructive to
compare the tone which the university adopts in its dealings
with King and Parlement at the beginning and at the end
of this single reign. Hardly a rectorial election now passed
without a dispute as to its validity, and a schism of more or
less duration. Appeals to Parlement in such cases became
more and more frequent. The interference which the university had once resisted with so much vehemence, she now
seems positively to court, and we find congregation passing
hearty votes of thanks to the judges for the trouble they had
taken in adjusting university squabbles.[2] The university now
tamely submits to the orders of a body which the 'eldest
daughter of the King' had once insisted on regarding as its
'younger sister', on such matters as the censorship of plays
acted in college and the repression of wandering and froward
(*discholi*) scholars.[3]

Loss of   The university enjoyed somewhat more favour under
the right   Charles VIII, and was gratified by the degradation and
of cessa-
tion, 1499. punishment of his predecessor's barber, who had instigated
most of the late outrages upon academic privilege.[4] But on
the accession of Louis XII a final blow was struck at its old
prerogatives. It lost the right of cessation[5]—the great instrument of academic aggression. This punishment was provoked
by the opposition which it offered to an edict limiting its

[1] Bulaeus, v. 716–17.   [4] *Ibid.* v. 762; Gaguin, p. 282.
[2] *Ibid.* v. 745 *sq*.   [5] Already limited by Pius II.
[3] *Ibid.* v. 761, 811–12.   Bulaeus, v. 832.

privileges and guarding against their abuse. These privileges CHAP. V,
§ 3.
—including extensive exemptions from taxation[1]—had hither-
to been claimed by all members of the university, even non-
regent graduates, that is, practically by the greater number
of the lawyers, doctors, higher clergy, and higher government
officials residing in the capital, to say nothing of the fraudulent
use of scholars' names by traders and other private individuals.[2] It was now very reasonably enacted that these privileges should extend only to bona-fide students and regent
masters. The university notwithstanding ordered a cessation.
The Parlement cited the rector, deans, and proctors to appear
before it. These officers refused to obey, and in their absence
the court proceeded to order the withdrawal of the cessation.
The order was not immediately complied with, and a deputation was sent to the King. They met him at Corbeil on his
way back to Paris, and found that he had been informed (with
whatever truth) that seditious placards had been stuck upon
the walls of the capital by the scholars, and that he had been
denounced from the pulpit by some of the indignant doctors.
The deputation consequently found the King in such a
humour that they at once returned to Paris, and advised their
colleagues to propitiate the angry monarch by a speedy and
unconditional surrender. The cessation was revoked;[3] and
from this time forth the university never again ventured to
have recourse to such a measure. Thus, just at the epoch
which has been adopted for the purposes of this work as the
limit of the Middle Age, the subjection of the university to the
Crown and the royal court was completed, and there passed
away for ever one of the last relics of those privileged licences

[1] It is difficult to define the exact extent of these exemptions, which were matters of incessant dispute. The members of the university and their servants seem as a rule to have been exempt from all ordinary secular taxation; while they often gained special exemption from contributing to aids voted by the clergy. See, e.g., Bulaeus, iv. 361.

[2] Real or nominal members of the University abused their exemp-tion from the tax on imported wine to carry on a trade in that commo-dity. Bulaeus, v. 656, 686. There are incessant allusions to similar abuses.

[3] Bulaeus, v. 830–2. According to Richer (i. f. 131), the university tried to extend this cessation or compulsory strike not only to teachers and preachers but to physicians who were members of the university.

and uncouth, lawless liberties which so strangely tempered the iron régime of medieval feudalism. In the sixteenth century, governments were everywhere setting themselves to abolish the local immunities and class-privileges of the medieval system.[1] However much we may regret the temporary extinction of the spirit of liberty, there can be no doubt that a vigorous assertion of the principle of order was called for, and nowhere more so than in the streets of university towns.

[1] Exactly the same tightening of discipline was going on all over Europe. Riccobonus (f. 132) dates the cessation of student-riots at Padua from the execution of a scholar for the murder of a police officer during an attempted secession to Ferrara in 1580.

§ 4. THE STUDIES OF PARIS

In the regulations prescribing the courses of lectures which must be heard by the student at different stages of his career, we shall constantly be met by a distinction between 'ordinary' and 'cursory' lectures. The discussions which have taken place as to the meaning of this distinction would have been much simplified had the comparative method been more frequently employed in the exploration of University antiquities.

The 'cursory' lectures of Paris are the 'extraordinary' lectures of Bologna. The Bologna distinction between 'ordinary' and 'extraordinary' *books* was, as we have seen, confined to the faculty of law. In the faculty of canon law this distinction lasted at Paris in its oldest form even after it had been modified at Bologna. Ordinary lectures were confined to the Decretum;[1] lectures on all the other books were extraordinary or cursory. In the other faculties the same books might be the subject of both ordinary and extraordinary lectures. The distinction between them was mainly one of *time*: the ordinary lectures were those delivered by masters during certain hours of the morning on 'legible' days. In the faculty of arts the earliest hour was reserved for the masters: the time for ordinary lectures ending in winter usually at tierce, in summer going on till dinner-time.[2] In the vacation (when ordinary lectures were suspended) cursory lectures might be given at any time of day. The lectures of the masters of theology and canon law were also in the morning, though (in the case of theology) after tierce—later

---

[1] See above, p. 207. At Paris [whose practice was copied at Heidelberg] the doctors lectured as a rule only on the Decretum. The refusal of Paris to put the Decretals on a level with the Decretum is not without significance in relation to the development of Gallicanism. Cf. Péries, pp. 39, 72; Thurot, p. 181. So at Oxford (*Statuta Antiqua*, ed. Gibson, p. 45) it is ordered that lectures on the Decretals shall henceforth be given in the morning *quasi ordinarie*.

[2] The regulations were exceedingly complicated, varying with the season and according as the day was 'legible' or 'non-legible'. *Chartul.* i, No. 137; Bulaeus, iii. 194.

than the ordinary hours of the faculty of arts, so as to enable
them to be attended by masters of arts after giving their own
lectures.[1] The distinction continued to be primarily one of
time: ordinary lectures were those delivered at the hours
reserved originally for masters and always for the authorized
teachers of the faculty; extraordinary or cursory lectures
might be delivered (except on certain holidays) at any time
at which no ordinary lectures were going on, by either master
or bachelor.[2] Moreover, cursory lectures might be delivered
anywhere, while ordinary lectures (at least in canon law and
arts) had to be delivered in the recognized schools of the
nation or faculty. But though an 'extraordinary' lecture
meant originally nothing more than a lecture delivered out
of the close time reserved for the more formal lectures
prescribed by the faculty, the term 'cursory' came in time
to suggest also the more rapid and less formal *manner* of
going over a book usually adopted at these times as opposed
to the more elaborate and exhaustive analysis and exposition,
characteristic of the ordinary lectures.[3]

[1] Bulaeus, iv. 412, 413; [*Chartul.*
iii, No. 1334; a. 1367.]

[2] Mullinger (*Cambridge*, i. 358
sq.) was mistaken in supposing
that cursory lectures were *only*
given by bachelors, and ignoring the
fundamental distinction of time.

[3] Bulaeus explains the term
cursor 'quia cursum peragebant ad
Licentiam'. So in a statute of
Perpignan we read, 'Nemo censeatur
dignus ad cursandum legendo Sententias pro gradu', &c. (*Chartul.*
ii, App., p. 704.) But that the
term also implied a difference of
manner appears from the following
indications: (1) Robert de Sorbon
(Bulaeus, iii. 231) says: 'Non re-
putabitur aliquis Scholaris propter
lectiones *transitorias*, nisi audiat
ordinarias.' (2) So at Oxford: 'In
disputatione solemni (i.e. ordinaria)
non cursorie, solemniter et non
furtive, respondeat.' *Mun. Acad.*,
p. 390. So at Oxford 'festine' is a

synonym for 'cursorie' or 'extraordinarie'. Mr. Anstey (*Mun.
Acad.*, pp. cxxxix, 371) mistakenly
explains the expression 'Le. fe.'
in the calendar as a 'day on which
lectures were shortened'. [Cf.
Statuta Antiqua, ed. Gibson, pp.
lxxxi, 56.] (3) The expression in
the Paris statute of 1215 that certain books are to be read 'ordinarie
et non ad cursum', can hardly refer
only to the time of the lectures.
Bulaeus, iii. 82; *Chartul.* i, No. 20.
(4) Again, in a Statute of 1460 we
read: 'desides, ignavi, *cursores* et
discholi omni penitus Scholastica
disciplina carentes' (Bulaeus, v.
646), which seems to indicate that
the word carried with it the idea
of rapid, superficial treatment; cf.
the familiar English 'coach'. (5)
So the 'cursor' at Heidelberg swore
'*non extense* sed *cursorie* legere lit-
teram dividendo et exponendo'.
Hautz, *Gesch. d. Un. Heid.* ii. 335.

A comparison of the 'reforms' from time to time imposed CHAP. v,
§ 4. upon the university by papal authority supplies us with tolerably full information as to the nature of the university and arts curriculum and the changes which it underwent in the course of our period. In summarizing the results obtained from such a comparison, we shall confine ourselves for the most part to the characteristic studies of Paris, theology and arts. But a few words must first be said as to medicine and canon law.

Theology and arts the most important studies.

Medicine

A school of medicine situated in a great capital could not *Medicine.* fail to acquire considerable importance; and the medical doctors of Paris were a wealthy and influential body of men. But as a school of medicine, Paris never attained anything like the European reputation of Montpellier and Salerno: it did not attract students from distant lands. The standard of its examinations for bachelors cannot have been high if M. Thurot is right in inferring from the silence of the registers that no candidate failed to satisfy the examiners during a period of more than a century.[1] The earliest statute of the *The* faculty (*circa* 1270–4) requires thirty-two months of study *medical* for the bachelorship, and five and a half years of study for *culum.* the licence in the case of one who has already been licensed in arts, otherwise six years.[2] The books prescribed are the

The medical curriculum.

---

[1] From 1395 to 1500. Thurot, p. 189. [Rashdall might have given a more adequate and less slighting description of the faculty of medicine and its studies if he had studied the translation of the lost collection of statutes (1350) published by J. B. L. Chomel in his *Essai historique sur la médecine en France* (Paris, 1762), pp. 142 *sqq.* The *commentarii* or records of meetings of the faculty survive from 1395 and have been edited for the period 1395 to 1516, with a valuable introduction, by E. Wickersheimer, *Commentaires de la Faculté de Médecine de l'Université de Paris,* in the 'Collection de documents inédits sur l'histoire de France' (Paris, 1915). We have referred to this work as occasion

arose in other places in this volume. Here it may be noted that the academic exercises, and examinations, whether serious in fact or not, corresponded to those in other higher faculties. Failure was certainly contemplated as a possibility, and Thurot's argument from silence is not quite convincing. The faculty elected its dean from at least 1330, and from 1350 by means of electors drawn from the members of different nations (cf. above, p. 326). The faculty had no fixed home until 1470, when it acquired a house in the Rue de la Bûcherie.]

[2] *Chartul.* i, Nos. 452, 453. Elsewhere fifty-six months for the M.A., otherwise sixty months. *Chartul.* ii, No. 921.

CHAP. V, [*Ars medicinae*, or *corpus* of texts collected by Constantinus
§ 4. Africanus, with the *Viaticum* and the works of Isaac usually
associated with this collection, and the famous pharmacopoeia
or *Antidotarium* of Nicholas of Salerno. To these are added
a book of *Theoretica* and another of *Practica*.[1] A century or
so later (1395) the 'neo-Arabian' medical learning is found
well established in Paris—the treatises of Averroës and
Avicenna and of their Italian and French followers. They
were the text-books of a more rationalistic period, when
medicine was studied with all the rigour and apparatus of
the dialectic of the schools.[2]]

Scholasti-   In the great centres of scholasticism medicine also became
cism in
medicine. scholastic. The importance attached to disputations in the
medical curriculum of Oxford and Paris is by itself sufficient
to show the spirit in which medicine was here studied; on the
other hand we hear nothing even of the very occasional dissec-

[1] 'Debet audivisse bis artem
medicine ordinarie et semel cursorie exceptis *urinis Theophili*, quas
sufficit semel audivisse ordinarie
vel cursorie: *Viaticum* bis ordinarie,
alios *libros Ysaac* semel ordinarie,
bis cursorie, exceptis *dietis particu-
laribus*, quas sufficit audivisse cursorie vel ordinarie; *Antidotarium
Nicholai* semel. *Versus Egidii* non
sunt de forma. Item debet unum
librum de *theorica* legisse, et alium
de *practica*.' [For the *Ars medicinae* and its meaning, and for the
influence of Giles of Corbeil,
whose verses *de urinis* are here
mentioned, see above, pp. 81, 86;
also S. d'Irsay, *Hist. des Universités*,
i. 103–7, 162–3, with the references
to essays by him and other scholars.
This body of texts represented the
whole Arabic tradition, and was
known at Paris by 1200: see the
list of text-books, with notes, in
Haskins, *Studies in the History of
Mediaeval Science*, pp. 374–5. The
ars medicina included works of
Hippocrates and Galen and the
Byzantine Theophilus.]

[2] [*Chartul*. iv, No. 1723; *Com-

mentaires, p. 2, and cf. Introduction, pp. xxxv–xl. The catalogue of
the faculty library at the same date
is in Corlieu, *L'Ancienne Faculté de
Médecine de Paris*, 1877, p. 148. For
a typical physician's library cf. the
will of Simon Bredon (1372) in
Powicke, *Medieval Books of Merton
College*, pp. 82–6, 138–41, with
notes. The statutes of Cologne
usefully supplement the evidence
from Paris. Rashdall, after giving
a list of the books on which a bachelor was required to have lectured,
adds:] Before licence the bachelor
was required to swear 'quod non
sit excommunicatus nec infamis
nec homicida, nec publicus cyrur-
gicus operans cum ferro et igne,
nec transgressor statutorum, nec
uxoratus'. These statutes contain
quite a code of medieval professional
etiquette, e.g. the M.D. may not
attend a patient who has not paid
his bill to another physician; nor
'conversetur in practica cum iudeis
practicantibus, aut cum illitteratis
viris, aut mulieribus practicantibus'.
Bianco, *Die alte Universität Köln*,
i, Anl. 29, 31.

tions which were usual in the southern schools of medicine.
To the Parisian physician theory was everything. Arnald of
Villanova complains that he knew of an excellent northern
professor of natural science and medical theory in general,
who could not apply a clyster or effect the cure of the most
ordinary disease in particular.[1]

Canon Law

Law at the University of Paris was never studied in Canon
the scientific spirit which characterized the early School of law.
Bologna, and in a lower degree the other universities of the
Bologna type.[2] As a school of law, Paris always stood below
Orleans, Angers, and Toulouse. The prohibition of Honorius
III confined its students to the canon law, and the scientific
study of the canon law was not likely to flourish where the
civil law was not taught. The course of study and method
of teaching were of course derived from Bologna; the formalities of graduation were the same as in the other faculties
of Paris. Hence it is unnecessary to dwell upon them in

[1] 'Et propter hoc Parisienses et
ultramontani medici plurimum student, ut habeant scientiam de
Universali, non curantes habere
particulares cognitiones et experi-
menta. Memini enim vidisse
quendam maximum in artibus,
naturalem, logicum, et theoricum
optimum. In medicina tamen unum
clysterem seu aliquam particularem
curationem non novit ordinare, et
vix ephemeram [i.e. a fever recur-
ring daily at a certain hour] sciebat
curare.' Breviar., iv. 10; quoted by
Haeser, Gesch. der Medicin, 1875,
p. 653. [For Arnald see the interesting chapter in L. Thorndike,
History of Magic, &c., ii. 841 sq.]

[2] [For the statutes see Chartul.
iii, Nos. 1587 (1390) and 1697–
1712 (pp. 641–57). The Memoralia
of the faculty survive for the years
1415 to 1448: see Chartul. iv, pp.
v, vi, and M. Fournier and L.
Dorez, La Faculté des Decrets de
l'Université de Paris au XV⁰ siècle

(Paris, 1895–1902). By relying
unduly on later evidence and by
stressing the 'aristocratic' element
in the faculty, Rashdall gives a
somewhat unjust impression of the
activity and prestige of the Parisian
doctors from Hostiensis to the
influential canonists of the Conciliar period (cf. F. von Schulte,
Die Geschichte der Quellen und
Literatur des canonischen Rechts, ii
(1875), 540, 541. It is true, on the
other hand, that many of the more
distinguished canonists in the
fourteenth and fifteenth centuries
won their fame in other fields. The
most glowing testimony to the
concentration of purpose and in-
dustry of the faculty comes from
itself, in the case against the chapter of Notre Dame in 1384 (Chartul.
iii, No. 1486), when the faculty
resisted the claim of canons to
lecture on the canon law outside
the Clos Brunel.]

CHAP. v, detail. As in the other faculties, the exact period of study
§ 4. required for degrees varied from time to time. At the middle
of the fourteenth century, forty-eight months, extending over
a period of six years, was required for the bachelorship and
another forty months for the licence.[1] For those who had
studied civil law the period was shorter.

Abuses
in this
faculty.
Too many students of canon law at Paris were, however,
men with whom the attractions of the capital and the ecclesiastical influence of its university were recommendations
which far outweighed the scientific superiority of the great
provincial schools. It was to the faculty of decrees that the
great mass of the well-born, well-beneficed, or wealthy idlers
of the university belonged, whether their object was to get
on in the world and attain high preferment in the Church
or merely to pass their time pleasantly in a university town.
The cadet of a noble house, the wealthy merchant's son, or
the capitular dignitary who had got leave of absence from
his benefice for five years on pretext of study, enrolled himself
as a matter of course in the faculty of decrees. Hence it is
especially with reference to this faculty that we meet with
constant legislation—sometimes initiated by the faculty·itself,
more often imposed upon it from without—against sham or
'froward' (*discholi*) students and against bribery and corruption in the purchase of degrees or dispensations from the
statutable conditions for obtaining them. Cardinal Estouteville, for instance, in 1452, renewing an old statute, enacted
that no one should be accounted a student of the faculty who
did not attend morning lecture three times or at least twice
a week, and fixed a limit to the sum which might be paid by

[1] Bulaeus, iv. 428, 429. In the
prominence of teaching by bachelors the faculty imitated the Paris
theologians rather than the jurists
of Bologna. [The bachelors *legentes
de mane*, who began to lecture
on the Decretals at 'matins', without a candle, took precedence over
other bachelors. The doctors read
the Decretum at prime. A case
brought in 1386 by Aimé Dubrueil,
a doctor of decrees who insisted on
lecturing both on the Decretals at
matins by candle-light and as a
doctor at prime, throws much light
on the working of the statutes.
Dubrueil, who had 200 or 300
pupils who brought him an income
of about as many francs, lost his
action (*Chartul*. iii, Nos. 1528–31,
1546). The object of forbidding
the candle was to secure that the
lectures were rapid, and extempore;
cf. *ibid*., pp. 642, 646.]

wealthy men as the amount of their 'bursa' or weekly expenses CHAP. V, by which the dues payable to the faculty were regulated. The § 4. intentional over-estimation of the 'bursa' supplied an easy and frequent means of corruption.[1] In short, it would seem that it was easy to buy a Paris degree in canon law, provided that the social and financial standing of the candidate was beyond question.[2] The presents and fees paid by candidates made the position of regent in this faculty a lucrative privilege, which its possessors naturally sought to convert into a monopoly. Hence admission to the doctorate ceased to confer the rights of regency, and the regents became a co-opting professoriate something after the manner of the Bologna 'College of Promotion'.[3]

Arts

[See also L. J. PAETOW, 'The Arts Course at Medieval Universities with special reference to Grammar and Rhetoric', in *University of Illinois Studies*, iii (1910), No. 7; G. C. BOYCE, *The English-German Nation*, ch. iii.]

The first complete account of the studies required for a Statutes of master's degree in arts is contained in the statutes drawn up 1215. by the papal legate, Robert Curzon or de Courçon, in 1215.[4]

[1] Bulaeus, v. 568. [*Chartul.* iv, pp. 718–22.] In the sixteenth century we hear that this faculty 'spe maioris utilitatis et corradendae atque emungendae undique pecuniae, infra privatos parietes, imo saepe inter pocula suos Baccalareos promoveret'. Bulaeus, *De la Prés. du R.*, p. 117.

[2] In 1466 a statute was made requiring licentiates to swear that they would not incept 'nisi habueritis in reditibus octuoginta (*sic*) libras parisienses in portatis, sive in patrimonio, sive in beneficiis'. Another statute of this aristocratic faculty required an oath 'quod non sit mercenarius seu capellanus alicuius collegii vel Domini, ut per hoc magis servetur honor Facultatis et gradus doctoralis'. Doc. ap. Péries, p. 36.

[3] Péries, pp. 39–41. It is evident,

from the complaints made in the sixteenth century, that there was a great deal of corruption in the bestowal of these chairs, though ostensibly they were awarded after the 'concours' or competitive trial lecture. The students, moreover, had frequently to bring actions against the professors to compel them to lecture. Péries, pp. 150 *sq.*, 185, 190 *sq.*

[4] Bulaeus, iii. 81; *Chartul.* i, No. 20; [cf. No. 201. Robert Curzon was a well-known theologian and preacher of Paris, a pupil of Peter the Chanter, and later a distinguished cardinal legate. A family or families of this name existed in England, holding land in various counties in the early thirteenth century. See, for his *summa*, Grabmann, ii. 493–7, and G. Lefèvre in *Travaux et mémoires de*

CHAP. v, If the conclusions at which we have already arrived as to the
§ 4.   unformed condition of the university at the beginning of
the century are well founded, nothing approaching what we
understand by a 'curriculum' can well have existed at any
much earlier period. It is not improbable that the Bolognese
examinations in law—a subject wherein any examination is
necessarily an examination in set books—may have helped to
suggest the idea of prescribing a fixed cycle of books as the
subjects of examination in arts; though the medieval reverence for the *littera scripta* makes such a hypothesis not
absolutely necessary.[1] The medieval idea of knowledge, or
rather of its ultimate foundations, rarely went beyond knowing what somebody had said about something. At all events
it is hardly possible to exaggerate the importance of this
innovation in the history of education: the very idea of a
'curriculum' in the sphere of liberal education (so far as our
evidence goes) originates with the university legislation of the
Englishman Robert Curzon.

The cur-   The entire omission of the poets, historians, and orators of
riculum of   ancient Rome from the course now prescribed has been
1215.   already noticed. Instruction in the Latin language is limited
to 'grammar', which is to be studied in the 'two Priscians'[2]
or at least one of them. Logic forms the main subject of
instruction. The old and new dialectic of Aristotle, i.e. the
whole Organon together with the *Isagoge* of Porphyry, are
to be read *ordinarie*; rhetoric and philosophy are reserved by
way of a treat for festivals.[3] In rhetoric the only books specified

l'Université de Lille, x (1902),
mémoire 30, where the section on
usury is printed. Cf. Ueberweg-
Geyer, pp. 281, 712; and Powicke,
Stephen Langton, passim.]
    [1] [The system grew out of the
concentration upon more precise
methods of instruction (see above,
p. 68) and the tendency to the
comparative study of texts which
crystallized in the work of Peter the
Lombard. This has been examined
by Ghellinck, Grabmann, Martin,
and other scholars. For early references to examinations at Salerno

and Bologna cf. above, pp. 86, 232.
The 'list of textbooks' edited by
Haskins, *Studies in Mediaeval
Science*, pp. 372–6, reveals the
idea of comprehensive yet definite
programmes of study before 1200.
Rashdall hardly does justice to the
nature of this development.]
    [2] The first sixteen books were
called *Priscianus magnus* or *maior*,
the last two *Priscianus minor*.
    [3] 'Non legant in festivis diebus
nisi philosophos et rhetoricas et
quadrivialia et *barbarismum* et
ethicam, si placet, et quartum topi-

are the *Barbarismus* (i.e. the third book of the *Ars maior*) of CHAP. V,
§ 4.
Donatus and the *Topics*; philosophy apparently includes the
Nicomachean Ethics of Aristotle [i.e. the first three books, in
the translations known as the *Ethica vetus* (Book I) and the
Ethica nova (Books II, III)][1] and the subjects embraced in
the *Quadrivium*, i.e. arithmetic, geometry, music, and astrology, for which no particular books are prescribed. The newly
recovered *Metaphysics* of Aristotle and his works on natural
philosophy are peremptorily forbidden, together with 'the
doctrine' of Master David of Dinant, Amauri the heretic, and
Maurice of Spain.[2]

We have already seen reason for believing that this pro- Course of
1252.
hibition of the new Aristotle was removed about the year
1235.[3] A statute of the English nation in 1252[4] shows some
signs of this revolution (it was no less) upon the university
course. Unfortunately the document does not give us a complete curriculum, as it only relates to the studies required before 'determination', i.e. the degree of B.A. The *de Anima* is
the only one of the prohibited books prescribed at this stage.
The other books are the same as those of 1215, except that
the *Sex principia* ascribed to Gilbert de la Porrée is now
included in the old logic,[5] and that the *Divisiones* of Boethius

chorum.' It is thus clear that at this time there were extraordinary books (as well as extraordinary times), which afterwards disappeared. (The expression *libri ordinarii* in Bulaeus, v. 617, apparently means all the regular books of the faculty except those on grammar.) In the fifteenth century the *Ethics* was still reserved for holidays, but was read *ordi-narie* (*ibid.* v. 726). Thurot is in error on this point (p. 78). At Oxford masters might read *festine* on feast-days 'de aliqua parte libri ad lecciones extraordinarias specialiter reseruata' (*Statuta antiqua*, p. 56). At Vienna, mathematics were thought specially suitable for holiday afternoons: there is a curious statute beginning 'Quamvis Divinum officium sicut non debemus,

ita nolumus perturbare, tamen sanius reputamus quod nostri scolares simul et Baccalarii eciam diebus festiuis visitent Scolas quam Tabernas, dimicent disputando lingua quam gladio, Ergo', &c. Kink, *Gesch. d. Univ. Wien*, ii. 196.

[1] [On these see Grabmann, *For-schungen*, pp. 205, 214–17.]

[2] See above, p. 355.

[3] See above, p. 357.

[4] This very important docu-ment (with others) exists only in a MS. of C.C.C., Oxford, and is printed for the first time in *Chartul.* i, No. 201.

[5] 'Insuper quod audiverit libros Aristotilis de *Veteri logica*, vide-licet librum *predicamentorum* et librum *periarmenias* bis ad minus

appears as well as the *Topics*. But the most remarkable feature of this course is the large number of times which the student was required to have 'heard' each of these books; in most cases they are required to have attended one or two courses of ordinary and one of cursory lectures on each book. Under the circumstances one is not surprised to find that there soon grew up a regular system of wholesale dispensations.[1]

Subjects of lectures in 1255. The next statute bearing on the subject belongs to the year 1255, and gives us the list of books, in order, upon which a master was required to lecture at that date. The Aristotelian treatises mentioned in this statute in addition to the 'old[2] and new logic' and the *Ethics* are the following: *Physica, Metaphysica, de Anima, de Animalibus, de Caelo et Mundo, Meteorica, de Generatione, de Sensu et Sensato, de Somno et Vigilia, de Memoria et Reminiscentia, de Morte et Vita*. To these are added the *de Plantis* still included in editions of Aristotle though believed to be spurious, and (it is surprising to find) the extremely sceptical *Liber de Causis*. This work at first passed under the name of Aristotle, though it never had a Greek original, and was recognized by Thomas Aquinas to be a translation from the Arabic. Another translation from

ordinarie, et semel cursorie; librum *sex principiorum* semel ordinarie ad minus et semel cursorie; libros videlicet tres primos *topicorum* et librum *divisionum* semel ordinarie vel ad minus cursorie; libros *topicorum* Aristotilis et *elencorum* bis ordinarie et semel ad minus cursorie, vel si non cursorie, ad minus ter ordinarie; librum *priorum* semel ordinarie et semel cursorie, vel sit in audiendo . . . librum *posteriorum* semel ordinarie complete. Item quod audiverit *Prissianum minorem* et *barbarismum* bis ordinarie, et ad minus cursorie; *Prissianum magnum* semel cursorie semel (*sic*). (One 'semel' should follow 'et', two lines above.) Item librum *de anima* semel audiverit vel sit in audiendo' (*loc. cit.*). Porphyry is not men-

tioned, but is probably not deliberately excluded.

[1] Cf. the oaths in *Chartul*. ii, App., pp. 678, 679. A number of rubrics indicate the portions of the old regulations 'dispensed' or 'interpreted' away by the faculty. The document is of date anterior to the Reform of 1366. Among these dispensations it is interesting to notice that the necessary portion of the *Ethics* was reduced to the first four books now [1895] taken up for 'Pass Greats' at Oxford.

[2] Which here includes the *Isagoge* of Porphyry, the *Praedicamenta* and *de Interpretatione* of Aristotle, and the *Divisions* and *Topics* of Boethius. Bulaeus, iii. 280; *Chartul*. i, No. 246. As to this distinction cf. above, pp. 37, 64.

the Arabic occurs under the title *de Differentia Spiritus et* CHAP. V,
Animae.[1] The Priscians are prescribed, and 'three little books', § 4.
the *Sex principia*, *Barbarismus*, and Priscian *de Accentu*, might
be read together. Such are the books which were sufficiently
in use at Paris to be included in a statute prescribing the
length of time which the lecturer was required to spend over
each book.[2]

In 1366 a body of statutes was imposed upon the university Legatine
by the papal legates Giles de Montaigu, Cardinal of S. reform of
Martin, and John de Blandy, Cardinal of S. Mark. The list 1366.
contained in this 'Reform' represents, not (like the last) the
whole range of the lectures, or, at all events, of the ordinary
lectures usually given at Paris, but the books actually 'taken
up' at each stage of the student's career. For the 'two
Priscians' were now substituted the *Grecismus* of Eberhard
of Béthune and the new grammar or 'Doctrinale' of Alexander
of Villedieu, written in verse or doggerel, which retained its
place as the universal school grammar till the sixteenth
century.[3] The whole of the old and new logic (including
the *Topics* of Boethius) was taken up as before, and part or
the whole of the *de Anima*. For the licence were further
required the following Aristotelian books: the *Physica*, the
de Generatione et Corruptione, the *de Caelo et Mundo*, the
group of minor treatises known as the *Parva Naturalia* (viz.
the books *de Sensu et Sensato*, *de Somno et Vigilia*, *de Memoria
et Reminiscentia*, *de Longitudine et Brevitate Vitae*), the *Metaphysics*, and certain mathematical books not further specified.[4]

---

[1] The work of Costa ben Luca
[of Baalbek, 864–923; translated by
John of Spain in the twelfth century; ed. by C. S. Barach (Innsbruck, 1878). See Ueberweg-
Geyer, pp. 295, 296, 716.]

[2] *Chartul*. i, No. 246.

[3] Over one hundred editions of
or comments upon the whole or
parts of this work are enumerated by
Hain (*Repertorium Bibliographicum*,
1826, *sub voce*) as printed before
1500. It continued to be reprinted
till much later. [For the *Doctrinale*

(1199), ed. Reichling (Berlin,
1893), and the *Grecismus* (c. 1210),
ed. Wrobel (Breslau, 1887), see
Paetow, *op. cit.*, pp. 36–40, and
especially Manitius, iii. 747–51,
756–61. The *Morale Scolarium* of
John Garland, c. 14 (ed. Paetow,
pp. 321–4), shows that these books
were generally studied at Paris as
early as 1241. Cf. above, p. 73, note.]

[4] 'Librum Metaphisice, vel quod
actu audiat eundem, et quod aliquos libros mathematicos audiverit.' Bulaeus, iv. 388 [who read

CHAP. V, Moreover, the candidate for the licence was required to have
§ 4.   attended disputations at least throughout one 'grand Ordinary',
i.e. from 1 October to the first Sunday in Lent, and to have
himself responded in at least two disputations. The *Ethics*
(the greater part of it) and at least three books of the *Meteorics*
were reserved for the period between the reception of the
licence and inception.[1] This distribution is somewhat more
systematic than in the earlier lists; the course of instruction
may now be said to have been divided into three stages, which
may be thus characterized:

For B.A.—Grammar, Logic, and Psychology.

For the Licence in Arts—Natural Philosophy and Metaphysics.

For M.A.—Moral Philosophy, and completion of the
course of Natural Philosophy.

Reform of   The reform of Cardinal Estouteville in 1452 makes no
Cardinal
Estoute- important change in the curriculum; his insistence on verse-
ville, 1452. making may perhaps be taken as a sign of the times, but it was
probably always supposed to be taught under the head of
grammar.[2] His statutes are chiefly interesting on account of
the light which they throw upon the discipline and mode
of teaching in vogue at the time. These regulations exhibit
a laudable disposition, sometimes wanting in university reformers, not to insist on the impracticable. He follows indeed
the reformers of 1366 in sternly repressing the laxity which

erroneously 'Liber Mechanicae',
Chartul. iii, No. 1319]. A notice
in the book of the Chancellor
of Ste Geneviève prescribes 'centum lectiones de mathematica',
which was interpreted by the
faculty to mean the hearing of
Johannes de Sacrobosco (i.e. Holywood, generally identified with
Halifax in Yorkshire, †1256), *de
Sphaera*, and one other book. This
must have been introduced at some
time before 1366. *Chartul.* ii,
App., p. 678. [For John of Holywood see *D.N.B.*, s.v. 'Holywood';
Duhem, *Le Système du monde*, iii.
238-40; M. Cantor, *Gesch. d.*

Mathematik, ii (ed. 1913), 87; cf.
Haskins, *Mediaeval Science*, pp.
277, 279, 282-3, for the commentary on the *de Sphaera* ascribed to
Michael Scot.]

[1] 'Libros morales, specialiter librum Ethicorum pro maiori parte,
et librum Metheororum.' This
arrangement probably did not
supersede the ethical lecture on
festivals for students before licence.

[2] 'In arte metrificandi fuerint
competenter edocti.' Bulaeus, v.
573; [*Chartul.* iv, No. 2690, pp.
724 *sq.*]. This stage was to be got
over before logic was begun.

allowed boys in the art schools to sit on benches, and requires CHAP. V,
the old custom of making them sit on the ground to be strictly § 4.
enforced, 'that all occasion of pride may be taken away from
the young'.[1] But the uselessness of attempting to forbid by
legislative enactment modes of lecturing which were equally
in favour with the regents and their auditors was at length
perceived. A succession of statutes had peremptorily required
the master to lecture *ex tempore* instead of reading or
'dictating' his lecture. They had even gone so far as to pre- Dictation.
scribe the exact pace or rapidity with which the words were
to flow from the teacher's lips: he was to lecture not 'drawl-
ingly' (*tractim*) but 'rapidly' (*raptim*), that is to say, 'bringing
out the words as rapidly as if nobody was writing before him'.[2]
And the eagerness of the medieval undergraduate to take
full notes was so intense that it was considered necessary to
accompany this anti-dictation statute with penalties against
persons resisting its execution by 'shouting, hissing, groaning,
or throwing stones by themselves or by their servants or
confederates'.[3] Estouteville dispensed the regent master from
the statute against dictation (*legendo ad pennam*) and added
the moderate requirement that the teacher should take the

[1] 'Ut occasio superbie a iuvenibus secludatur.' Bulaeus, v. 573.
In 1387 the university had petitioned the Pope for a relaxation
of Urban IV's statute requiring
artists to sit on the ground, alleging
that 'plures tam nobiles quam alii
magni religiosi et honesti viri ex
verecundia moti, quia sedere habent
ad terram, dimittunt audire propter
defectum scannorum et bancarum'
(*Chartul.* iii, No. 1537).

[2] 'Sic scilicet proferendo, ac si
nullus scriberet coram eis, secundum quem modum fiunt sermones
in Universitate et recommenda-
tiones, et quem lectores in ceteris
facultatibus insequuntur.' Bulaeus,
iv. 332; [*Chartul.* iii, No. 1229
(1355)].

[3] 'Auditores vero huius nostri
statuti executioni obviantes cla-
more, sibilo, strepitu, iactu lapidum

per se aut per suos famulos vel
complices, seu quovis alio modo,
privamus et resecamus a nostro
consortio usque ad unum annum,'
loc. cit. The statute, however,
permits the 'nominacionem ad pennam alicuius determinationis, notabilis tractatus, vel expositionis,
quam in vico Straminis scribunt
quandoque iuvenes in diebus fes-
tivis'. Ramus lays down the following rules on the subject:

Philosophiam continua voce et per-
petua ratione praelegito.

Ne tractim nominato et dictato.

Discipulus Magistri verba mente
capito.

Manu et penna ne exarato.

Notabilis tamen sententiae dictan-
dae et excipiendae facultas esto.

Scholae in Liberales Artes, Basel,
1578, c. 1063.

trouble to read the lecture himself instead of handing his manuscript to a scholar who dictated it to the rest.[1] In the same way he allowed the theological bachelors to read their lectures or exercises for degrees, requiring only that they should not read word for word the *questiones* of another.[2] It may be observed that the discussion of *questiones* had by this time largely replaced—at least in the higher faculties—the older method of exhaustive analysis and textual comment. In the same practical spirit, the regulations on the subject of academical dress were relaxed. The enforcement of the

Marriage of M.D.s allowed. 'cappa' was now limited to masters. Equal common sense is exhibited in the abolition of enforced celibacy for doctors of medicine, as a condition of continuing to enjoy the privileges of regency. Nobody seems to have thought of extending

Abolition of superfluous oaths. this relaxation to the other faculties. In several trifling points an effort was made to reduce the enormous amount of conventional perjury involved by that reckless multiplication of oaths which characterized all medieval university legislation. Of about forty oaths required from inceptors by the reformers of 1366, Estouteville abolished some half-dozen, probably those whose obligations were most systematically neglected—

[1] Bulaeus, v. 572, 573; [*Chartul.* iv, No. 2690, p. 727]. 'Specialiter autem et sub pena excommunicationis inhibemus, ne quasdam quaestiones, quamvis bene compilatae existant, tradant uni de scholaribus suis ad legendum et nominandum ceteris studentibus; quod, ut accepimus, quidam facere non erubescunt in dampnum scholarium, et grave scandalum facultatis artium.'

[2] In the same way candidates for theological degrees were allowed to read their 'Principium' or 'Sentences', but provided they were written by themselves, 'cum memoria hominum labilis maxime circa subtiles theologie materias plerumque deficiat'. *Ibid.*, p. 565; [*Chartul.* iv, p. 717]. On the other hand, in the faculty of decrees, *baccalariandi* were still required to perform

their exercises and deliver their lectures 'corde tenus' and 'absque aliquo quaterno, sive codicello legendo sive expediendo'. *Ibid.*, p. 567; [*Chartul.* iv, p. 720]. At Greifswald lecturing or disputing 'ad pennam' is still [1895] forbidden; note-taking is allowed 'dummodo fiat sine pronuntiatura' (Kosegarten, *Greifswald*, ii. 301). At Ingolstadt special lectures seem to have been established to enable poor scholars to provide themselves with books: 'Conclusum fuit . . . quod statuantur duo magistri lectores textuum ad beneficium calami.' Prantl, ii. 73. An edict against 'dictation', still popular with the students, was issued at Padua by the Doge and Senate of Venice in 1596. Riccobonus, *De Gymn. Patav.*, p. 100.

such as the duty of attending the funerals of scholars, of saying a 'whole Psalter' on the occasion of every death among the regents, of incepting in a 'new cope not borrowed or hired',[1] of lecturing for two years,[2] and the requirement that each master should have a black cope of his own.

This sketch of the principal reforms introduced from time to time by the cardinal legates, will give the reader a fair notion of the general character of Parisian teaching and of the more important modifications which took place in the university curriculum during our period. He must, however, be warned that the picture is by no means complete.[3] The statutes of the German universities, which we know to have been in the main based upon Parisian usage, mention a considerable number of minor books which do not appear in any of the above-cited lists. It follows that in the periods intermediate between these university commissions various changes took place of which no account has reached us, or more probably that lectures were given upon a certain number of books not actually 'taken up for the schools'.[4] The most important of the books excluded from the above lists which may thus be presumed to have been studied at Paris are the *Politics, Economics,* and *Rhetoric* of Aristotle:[5] as to the first two we have positive evidence that such was the case.

Other text-books in use at Paris.

---

[1] 'Item iuramentum de incipiendo in cappa nova non accommodata, non conducta.'

[2] Du Boulay prints 'sex', but from other evidence it appears that the true reading must be 'duos' (ii for vi). Cf. *Chartul.* ii, App., p. 680. [Rashdall acutely anticipated the right reading, now in the *Chartul.* iv, p. 733.]

[3] [For comment on what follows see Additional Note at the end of this section.]

[4] Thus at Heidelberg we find a 'Pastus (table of fees) librorum quos non oportet scolares formaliter in Scolis ratione alicuius gradus audivisse' (in 1443), including the 'Parva logicalia Marsilii', the *Politics,* Petrus Hispanus, the *Econo-*

mics, 'de perspectiva, de Algorisimo, de bona fortuna, de proportionibus'. Alexander (de Villedieu) parts i, and ii, Donatus, 'de Theorica planetarum'. Hautz, ii. 355.

[5] A statute of Caen prescribes the *Politics* and *Economics* 'prout est solitum fieri Parisius' (*Bull. de la Soc. de Normandie,* xii. 497). All three appear at Prague (*Mon. Univ. Prag.* I. i. 56, 76), where also the *de Vegetalibus* is mentioned; at Leipzig the *Politics* and *Economics,* and in 1499 the *Rhetoric* (Zarncke, *Statutenbücher d. Univ. Leipzig,* pp. 399, 465). The tradition which makes Dante attend Siger's lectures on the Politics while at Paris is now quite discredited [see Mandonnet, *Siger de Brabant,* i (ed. 1911), 293].

CHAP. V, The rest are smaller and slighter books. They include the
§ 4. more popular treatises of Boethius such as the *de Consolatione
Philosophiae*, and occasionally even the spurious *de Disciplina
Scholarium*.[1] Then there are the short logical treatises or
text-books composed by the leaders of the various medieval
schools of thought. At this period the logical studies of every
young student began probably with one of these school-books,
even where they are not specified in the official curriculum.
The most important were the *Summulae* of Petrus Hispanus
(Pope John XXI)[2] and the *Parva Logicalia* of Marsilius of
Inghen.[3] Other medieval treatises used as philosophical text-
books were the *Tractatus* of the realist Albert of Saxony[4]
and the *Questiones* of Buridan.[5] The *Grecismus* of Eberhard
and another poetical work, the *Labyrinthus*,[6] are frequently

[1] *Mon. Univ. Prag.* I. i. 76, 77.
[Printed in Migne, *Patrol. Lat.*
lxiv. 1223–38; see Paetow, *Morale
Scolarium of John of Garland*,
p. 105.]

[2] At Prague for M.A., *Mon.
Univ. Prag.* I. i. 48. The first and
fourth books of Petrus Hispanus
were also called 'Parva Logicalia'.
Prantl, *Ingolstadt*, ii. 89. Goulet
(f. xix *b*) observes that *Summulae*
were usually read at the smaller
universities by students who afterwards came to Paris. But we also
find a class of *Summulistae* in the
Paris colleges. See Launoi, *Navarrae Gymn. Hist.*, 1677, i. 174. So
in the Cistercian College (1493):
'Similiterque ad logicam nullus
accedat, nisi qui ordinarie sub
magistro summularum glosas audiverit, et textum ex corde reddiderit.'
Félibien, iii. 174. It is obvious to
any one acquainted with the contents of the Organon and the youth
of the medieval student that any
real knowledge of it must have been
acquired by the aid of abridgements of some kind.

[3] See above, p. 447. At Heidelberg we find, in addition to those
which usually appear, lectures 'de
textibus suppositionum, Ampli-

ficationum et Appellacionum, De
consequenciis, De obligatoriis,
De insolubilibus' (Hautz, ii. 353);
also on 'textum cum glosa Bnn.
(Bottonis s. Bernardi Parmensis)
cum suis additionibus' (*loc. cit.*,
p. 339). The 'Parva logicalia Marsilii obligatoria et insolubilia' were
lectured on at Freiburg in 1465 as
well as '*Controversae* Marsilii et
theoreticae' (Schreiber, *Gesch. d.
Stadt u. Univ. Freib.*, 1857, II. i. 51).
[Marsilius of Inghen (d. 1396)
was the first rector of the University of Heidelberg.]

[4] e.g. at Freiburg, *loc. cit.* II. i.
45.

[5] The *Questiones Buridani* were
read at Prague *circa* 1370 (*Mon.
Univ. Prag.* I. i. 82). So at Cologne
bachelors were admitted 'ad legendum Summulas Petri Hispani et
Byridani et parva logicalia (? Marsilii)' (Bianco, i, *Anl.*, pp. 66, 67).
Leipzig used the 'Parva Logicalia'
of Maulfelt or of Greffinstein or
of Marsilius. Zarncke, *Statutenbücher*, p. 311; where also appears
'Logica Hesbri' (i.e. Heytisbury.
See above, p. 247 n.).

[6] *Mon. Univ. Prag.* I. i. 77. The
Labyrinthus is an elegiac poem *de
Miseriis Rectorum Scholarum* (ed.

added to the more classical treatises on grammar or rhetoric.[1] CHAP. v,
Moreover, these German lists enable us to supply the names §4.
of the 'mathematical books' vaguely required by the legatine
statutes. Such books were Euclid (the first six books), the
Almagest of Ptolemy, the *de Sphaera* of the Englishman, John
of Holywood,[2] the *Perspectiva Communis* (i.e. *Optics*) of
another Englishman, John Pecham[3] (written in 1280).
Instruction in algebra and arithmetic is also mentioned
in general terms. At the same time the mere fact that the
mathematical books are passed over with such scant courtesy
by the reforming cardinals seems to show what there are
other grounds for supposing, namely that mathematics was
more seriously cultivated in Oxford and some of the German
universities than at Paris.[4] Oxford and the German universities seem to have agreed also in requiring Boethius *de re*

Leyser, *Hist. Poetarum Med. Aevi,*
Halle, p. 796 *sq.*), consisting partly
of advice to schoolmasters, partly
of rules relating to figures of speech
and versification.

[1] In *Mon. Univ. Prag.* i. i. 77
the *Poetria Nova* of Geoffrey de
Vinsauf (*Vino Salvo*), a Norman, fl.
A.D. 1198–1216, ed. Leyser, *op. cit.,*
p. 861–978 [and by E. Faral, *Les
Arts poétiques du XIIᵉ et XIIIᵉ siècle,*
pp. 197–262; cf. Manitius, iii.
751–6]. At Ingolstadt a *libellus de
arte epistolandi* is prescribed. Prantl,
Gesch. d. Un. Ingolst. ii. 76.

[2] In 1340 a Swede is specially
authorized to lecture on this book
at Paris. In 1427 a Finlander lectures on the *Theorica planetarum* of
Campanus de Novara; but even a
lecture on geometry seems to be an
extraordinary thing at Paris. About
1378 Charles V founded two bursarships in the College of Maître Ger-
vais as mathematical lectureships.
Thurot, pp. 81, 82.

[3] Prague in 1390 required for
M.A. 'sex libros Euclidis, sphae-
ram, theoricam, aliquid in musica
et arithmetica, perspectivam com-
munem' (*Mon. Univ. Prag.* i. i. 56).

The works referred to are the *de
Sphaera* of John of Holywood, the
Theoria Planetarum of Campanus
of Novara, [written for Pope Urban
IV (1261–5); see Duhem, *Le système du monde,* iii. 317 *sq.*, 322–6],
and the *Perspectiva Communis* of
John Pecham, Archbishop of Canterbury. See an interesting account
of the manuscripts of this work in
Reg. Epist. Jo. Peckham, ed. Martin,
vol. iii, p. lviii *sq.* At Freiburg the
mathematical subjects include 'Lati-
tudines' and 'Proportiones' (of the
English archbishop Bradwardine
or its abridgement by Albert of
Saxony). Schreiber, *Gesch. d. Stadt
u. Univ. Freiburg,* II. i. 51. We find
lectures on 'Algorismus' and 'Alma-
nachus' (presumably the method of
finding Easter) at Prague (*Mon.
Univ. Prag.* i. 77), and again on
'Arithmetica accurata' (*ibid.*, p. 83);
cf. *ibid.*, p. 91 'algorismus de
integris'.

[4] The astronomical tables of the
Prague master, Johann Schmidel,
were of use to Tycho Brahe.
Tomek, p. 132. [Vienna should
especially be mentioned as a centre
of mathematical study.]

CHAP. V, *musica*, or some other musical work,[1] so as to keep up the
§ 4. theory that the arts course consisted of the complete *Trivium*
and *Quadrivium*. At Paris we hear nothing of music, and less
importance seems to have attached to the theory of the
Trivium and *Quadrivium*.

The We have already seen that the student's course was divided
bacca-
laureate. into two clearly marked periods, during the first of which he
was a scholar pure and simple, while during the second he
was allowed or required to undertake a certain amount of
teaching himself, though still continuing his studies under a
master. The baccalaureate perhaps originated in the superior
faculties. We have seen that it existed from an early period
in the law-schools of Bologna, though there the teaching by
bachelors never became much more than an academical
exercise. By the statutes of Robert Curzon students of theology were allowed to deliver 'private lectures' after five years'
study, though the word bachelor does not occur. In the
faculty of arts the baccalaureate does not appear till rather
Deter- later; neither the name nor the thing occurs in Robert
mination. Curzon's statutes, though it is probable that the custom of
employing the assistance of pupil-teachers was of great antiquity in the medieval schools.[2] There is, however, a provision
that no banquets should be allowed at the 'responsions or
oppositions of boys or youths'. These disputations, a kind
of imitation of the inceptions and other disputations of the
masters, took place during carnival-tide and Lent every year.
The name of the concluding act, in which the president
summed up or 'determined', was applied to the exercises, so
that they came to be technically known as 'determinations'.[3]

[1] At Prague the '*Musica* Muri'
[i.e. of John of Meurs, a French
writer on music, mathematics and
astronomy, who fl. 1321–45; see
bibliography in Thorndike, ii.
96]; *Mon. Univ. Prag.* I. i. 82, 83.
So at Leipzig, Zarncke, *Statutenbücher*, p. 311. The book is printed
by Gerbert in *Scriptores Eccles. de
Musica*, iii. 189 *sq.*

[2] [The *prepositus* or *clericus* of the
master is found in the twelfth cen-

tury. He was perhaps responsible
for the authoritative *reportatio*. In
1241 John Garland refers to unreliable *seniores* who deceive *doctores iustos* (*Morale Scolarium*, ll.
647, 648; ed. Paetow, p. 255).
Paetow (p. 161 n.) would identify
these with 'bachelors who had
finished their determinations'.]

[3] In 1476 we hear of determinations taking place between Martin-
mas and Christmas (Bulaeus, v.

On these occasions the 'determiner' was a bachelor entering chap. v, upon the next stage of his career, and the opponent a student § 4. of somewhat lower standing.[1] The determinations seem at first to have been voluntary, and may have originated with the scholars rather than with the masters.[2] At about the middle of the thirteenth century, however, they became at first a customary and then a compulsory part of the training of every

722), but this is so contrary to the usual practice that it seems probable that the preliminary responsions must be meant or that the occurrence was exceptional. [Determinations in Advent were not uncommon in the theological faculty.]

[1] Mr. Boase's explanation (*Reg. of the Univ. of Oxford*, i, p. viii), 'instead of disputing himself, he presided over disputations, and gave out his determination or decision on the questions discussed', is incomplete. The determiner was the leading disputant, though after debating the question with an opponent, he would appear to have wound up with certain 'conclusions' (*Chartul.* ii, App., p. 673, note). Mr. Clark (*Reg. Univ. Oxf.* ii. i. 50 *sq.*) gives a detailed and interesting account of the determination and its attendant ceremonies in the sixteenth century at Oxford. The last relic of determination was abolished (alas!) in 1855. 'Up to that time on Ash-Wednesday the Deans of the several colleges attended at a special Congregation and . . . read over a supplicat for all those of their College who had been admitted to B.A. during the year. These were then held to have lawfully determined, though they were no longer present in person, and though no exercises were performed' (Clark, *loc. cit.*, p. 63). [The master probably presided, at any rate in the thirteenth century. The early history of determinations is very obscure. The statute of 1275 (*Chartul.* i, No. 461) makes

a clear distinction between bachelors and bachelors licensed to determine or determiners. The latter had to have responded as bachelors to a master in disputations *ante Natale* before they could be admitted to the 'examen determinantium', which led to the licence to determine. The statutes of the English nation of 1252 appear to refer to the books prescribed for this examination. But, if this be so, it is hard to see at what stage the 'bachellarius non licentiatus' received the title of bachelor. Rashdall had this difficulty in mind when he suggested that the term 'bachelor' was at first used vaguely, and after 1275 came to imply a definite status or degree; below, p. 454. But more evidence on earlier usage is required. The first reference to the bachelor in the *Chartularium* is in No. 79 (Bull of Gregory IX, 1231): constitutions are to be made 'de bachellariis, qui et qua hora et quid legere debeant', where we find them lecturing; cf. No. 137 (1245): 'A quadragesimo vero, postquam bachellarii determinare inceperint.' These passages suggest a well-established, if not a compulsory, system.]

[2] A curious relic of this state of things survived till recently [1895] at Oxford. The *Collectores Baccalaureorum* were B.A.s supposed to manage these disputations under the proctors. They wore the full proctorial robes, i.e. the M.A. full dress. Cox, *Recollections of Oxford*, London, 1870, p. 242.

student in arts who wanted to become a master. In 1275 the earlier rules for determination were revised, and, four years later, it was made obligatory for students in arts to 'determine' before presenting themselves as candidates for the chancellor's licence,[1] though it had already been enforced for some time by particular nations.[2]

In 1275, if not earlier,[3] a preliminary test or 'responsions' was instituted to ascertain the fitness of those who wanted Respon-sions. to take part in the public performance.[4] At these 'respon-

---

[1] [*Chartul.* ii, Nos. 461, 485. The latter statute] enacts that an oath to this effect should be taken before the candidate was admitted to the examination at Ste Gene-viève, and before inception in the case of a bachelor who elected to be licensed at Notre Dame. The faculty does not venture to impose its regulations on the cathedral chancellor; it can only refuse to admit to its membership a licen-tiate who had disobeyed them. (Bulaeus, iii. 447; *Chartul.* i, No. 485.)

[2] See the statute of the English nation in 1252. *Chartul.* i, Nos. 201, 202. It is of course quite pos-sible that it was already enforced by the whole faculty. [The *re-sponsiones* of the proctor of the faculty of arts at the papal court in 1283–4 suggest that the obligation was a recent one. The chancellor objected to the determinations (*Chartul.* i, No. 515, especially, p. 611.]

[3] The statute of the English nation in 1252 runs: 'Item det fidem (before determination) quod per duos annos diligenter disputa-ciones magistrorum . . frequenta-verit, et per idem tempus de sophismatibus in scolis requisitus responderit.' (*Chartul.* i, No. 201.) [The significance of this text in the history of the *sophismata* has been pointed out by Mandonnet, who, however, seems to be wrong in

saying that the obligation, here imposed, to take part in sophistical exercises refers to the bachelor. It was one of the qualifications re-quired of the future bachelor before determination (*Siger de Brabant*, i. 122–4; cf. below, p. 496).] The obligation of 'sitting in the schools' during the *viva voce* examination of other candidates, which lasted at Oxford till a generation ago, was the last relic of the obligation to attend disputations [1895].

[4] 'Statuimus ut nullus dece-tero nisi prius in scolis publice magistro regenti actu de questi-one responderit ante Natale, ad examen determinantium admitta-tur.' Bulaeus, iii. 420; *Chartul.* i, No. 461. In Oxford, in the six-teenth century, the examination seems to have assumed the form of a disputation between the examinee and a senior scholar, before the 'Magistri Scholarum'. The dis-putations were in grammar and logic, and took place in the ninth term. The retention of the name 'Magistri Scholarum' and the *Testamur*, which (till abolished in 1893) stated that the candidate 'quaestionibus Magistrorum Scho-larum in *parviso* pro forma re-spondit' (see below, chap. xii, § 5) testify to the identity of the modern examination known as responsions or 'smalls' with this ancient institu-tion. The *four* masters of the schools at Oxford were possibly an

sions', which took place in the December before the Lent in which the candidate was to determine, he had to dispute in grammar and logic with a master. If this test was passed in a satisfactory manner,[1] the candidate was admitted to the *Examen determinantium* or *Baccalariandorum* which was conducted by a board of examiners appointed by each nation for its own candidates. The duty of the examiners was twofold, firstly to ascertain by inspecting the *schedulae* given by his masters that the candidate had completed the necessary residence and attended lectures in the prescribed subjects, and secondly to examine him in the contents of his books.[2] If he passed this examination he was admitted to determine. It was perhaps at about the period when determination was made a necessary preliminary to the mastership that the word bachelor, borrowed from the terminology of the guilds and hitherto applied vaguely to any student allowed by his master to teach in his school or to a student who was a candidate for the mastership,[3] came to be technically restricted in

Examination for B.A.

inheritance from the four nations of Paris. At Oxford a hood of plain black stuff (*simplex caputium*) was conferred with some ceremony after the disputation, by which the student became '*sophista generalis*'. This hood was worn in the final schools till 1860–70. See Clark, *Reg. Univ. Oxf.* II. i. 21, 22.

[1] The same regulation was adopted at Oxford in 1268; *Statuta Antiqua*, pp. 25–7. The examination is described in Bulaeus, v. 647 (1460): 'Item circa bacalariandorum examen statuimus et ordinamus quod maturius graviusque de cetero ipsi bacalariandi examinentur, videlicet in grammaticalibus quilibet ab unoquoque examinatorum, similiter in parvis logicalibus ab unoquoque examinetur. In aliis vero libris Porphirii et Aristotelis examinentur per ordinem, ita tamen quod quilibet in unoquoque librorum unam ad minus habeat questionem.' The examiners are at the same time

required to draw up a list of those who have passed immediately after the examination, for fear of their being moved 'multorum precibus importunis'. [Text as in the *Auctarium*, ii. 935–9, and in Boyce, *op. cit.*, Appendix ix.]

[2] [For the changes in the methods of electing examiners between 1252 and 1460 see the documents cited by Boyce, pp. 81–4; the selection took place in January or February, and in order to determine in a given year a student had to receive the examiner's licence by the Sunday next before Lent. In 1252 a determiner had to be twenty years of age, but before 1350 the age limit, unless the text of the oath is incorrect, was reduced to fourteen years; *Chartul.* ii, p. 673.]

[3] 'Mesme en Massonerie et tout autre mestier de France ou il y a maistrise, l'on appelle Bacheliers ceux qui sont passez Maistres en l'Art, mais qui ne sont pas Iurez, et

the faculty of arts to candidates who had, after passing the prescribed examination, been duly admitted to determine and permitted to give 'cursory' lectures.[1] The baccalaureate became in fact an inferior 'degree' to which the candidate was regularly admitted by the proctor of his nation, after taking the oath of obedience to the rector and faculty, and to his proctor and nation. Determination thus played the same part in the admission to this new degree that inception played at the final stage of his career. Part of the ceremony consisted in the determiner's putting on his bachelor's *cappa* and taking his seat for the first time among the bachelors.[2] It is important to remember that at Paris and in most continental universities the chancellor had nothing to do with the conferring of the bachelor's degree.

Deter-
mination.

Determination was a great period in the student's university life. The disputations took place in one of the schools of

lesquels pour amander le rapport fait par les Docteurs Iurez doiuent estre deux fois autant.' Claudius Falcetus, *De Origine Equitum*, c. 1, ap. Bulaeum, ii. 680.

[1] [Commenting on this passage, Boyce points out that in the proctors' lists the more precise caption 'nomina determinancium' did not give way to the words 'nomina baccalariorum' until the middle of the fifteenth century. Strictly speaking, it would seem that in the fourteenth and early fifteenth centuries, a student 'duly admitted to determine' did not become a bachelor until he had completed the determination (*op. cit.*, p. 80 note). Instead of the form of admission at Oxford, given by Rashdall, we add the words of a Paris certificate recently discovered in the binding of a book in the Merton College library. The document is clipped and imperfect at the beginning, but the text can be reconstructed with the aid of another, still more imperfect certificate which accompanies it and is of the same date,

January 1508: '. . . receptor venerande nationis Francie necnon vos examinatores eiusdem nationis: nos Ludouicus Dalbiac, eiusdem nationis procurator, mittimus ad vos Petrum Hamelin, diocesis Turonensis, qui audiuit omnes libros ad gradum baccalauriatus requisitos, nec non determinauit de una questione morali in Vico Stramineo, ut moris est, ut a suis preceptoribus nobis extitit facta fides: cuius bursa valet sex solidos Parisienses. In cuius rei testimonium sigillum nostrum procuratorie anno domini millesimo quingentesimo septimo die vero xxij^mo mensis Ianuarii duximus apponendum.' This certificate or schedule illustrates exactly the regulations of the German nation made in 1466; see Boyce, p. 207. For the receptor and the *bursa* see above, pp. 420, n. 4, 439; cf. Boyce, pp. 90, 164, 183.]

[2] So at least at Prague in 1371 (*Mon. Univ. Prag.* i. i. 52), and elsewhere. At Oxford the disputation had to be performed twice by each bachelor in the course of Lent. Clark, *loc. cit.* ii. i. 58.

the Vicus Stramineus (*Rue du Fouarre*). [The determiner,
among many other conditions which he swore to fulfil, undertook to begin his determination before the Wednesday after
the first week of Lent (*brandones*) and to continue his disputations throughout Lent, unless he had a sub-determiner; in
this case the deputy carried on from the middle of Lent.[1]
Unless the nation had granted permission for some other
master to act, the proceedings had to take place under the
presidency of a regent master.[2]] The determiner had to pay
his master—the master under whom (as the phrase ran) he
was determining—for the use of his school; and the master
expected to get back the greater part of his year's rent by the
fees which he received from his determining bachelors.[3] Even
after an official character had been given to determination by
the recognition of the faculty, it retained much of its primitive
character of a students' festivity. Every effort was made to
attract to the schools as large an audience as possible not
merely of masters or fellow students but if possible of
ecclesiastical dignitaries and other distinguished persons. The
friends of a determiner who was not successful in drawing a
more distinguished audience would run out into the streets
and forcibly drag chance passers-by into the school. Sometimes the halls were invaded by eager partisans for the same
purpose.[4] Wine was provided at the determiner's expense
in the schools, and the period ended in a feast given in imitation of the master's inception-banquets, even if dancing

---

[1] [*Chartul.* ii, pp. 673, 674; cf.
i, p. 611 (1283–4). Rashdall
erroneously described determination as taking place on a single great
day. Cf. the practice at Oxford in
1409: 'per totam Quadragesimam'
(*Statuta Antiqua*, p. 262), and
Boyce, pp. 87–90. For a discussion
of sub-determination see *ibid.*, pp.
96–100, and Appendix II.]

[2] 'De qualibet domo seu de
quolibet pedagogio unus assistat
magister regens, qui non permittat
in dictis disputationibus, aut eundo
vel redeundo, aliquas insolentias

fieri.' Bulaeus, v. 574; *Chartul.*
iv, p. 729. Cardinal Estouteville
was professedly following old
statutes and usage.

[3] [A master could not take more
than two *bursae* (*Chartul.* i, No.
461 (1275). For the practice in the
French nation see *ibid.* ii, No.
655 (1306). At Oxford a master was
forbidden to receive anything from
a determiner 'pro pensione scolarum' (*Statuta Antiqua*, p. 28).]

[4] *Statuta Antiqua*, p. 203
(Oxford); Bulaeus, v. 574.

or torch-light processions were forborne in deference to authority.[1]

A road to prefer-ment. A very interesting document has fortunately been preserved which shows us that a bachelor who cut a good figure in these boyish word-tournaments might win something more than applause or complimentary speeches. The document contains the pleadings on the part of the university in the great suit of 1283 against the chancellor. That official had complained of the requirement of determination from intending masters as an infringement of his prerogatives: he was acute enough to discern in the innovation the establishment of a new degree over the conferring of which he had no control. The faculty replies that 'since great men of every faculty come to their determination, magnates, such as archdeacons, chanters, and provosts of cathedrals and many others, they acquire that boldness of speech which is necessary to an artist, as well as acquaintance with the magnates, by which they used to obtain promotion to ecclesiastical benefices'.[2]

The legatine reform of 1366 prescribed the books which the bachelor had to study between determination and the examination for the licence. When he had completed five or six years of study from his matriculation, had 'heard' all the books prescribed by the faculty, and had attained the age of twenty, the student was free to present himself for the chancellor's examination.[3]

---

[1] Bulaeus, iii. 420; v. 575. Among the exuberances of spirits condemned (iii. 420) is the election of a 'capitaneum quocumque nomine censeatur; sed regimine Rectoris et Procuratorum sint contenti'. It is interesting to observe the masters of Paris repressing movements among the students exactly similar to those which led to the formation of the student-universities at Bologna.

[2] Jourdain, No. 274; *Chartul.* i, No. 515.

[3] [Above, p. 443; cf. *Chartul.* iv, p. 729. In the first edition Rashdall somewhat misunderstood *Chartul.* i, No. 202 (1252), which defines the qualifications of the incepting bachelor, and his obligations, if he were a member of the English nation, to his nation. On inception the bachelor was to swear that he would attend, as a master, the lectures of bachelors, and that he would never present (for the licence) an unworthy bachelor. The document proceeds to define the marks of an unworthy bachelor; one of these is non-attendance at lectures, another is, 'si non constiterit, ipsum saltem per biennium ante presentacionem suam de questione publice respondisse'.]

Enough has been said as to the contests between the chan- cellor and the university with regard to the conduct of these examinations.[1] We have already traced the steps by which the chancellor lost all real control over the licence which he conferred. It appears, however, clear that in the case of the faculty of arts there always was an actual examination—at one time a serious examination—by the chancellor or his deputy (*subcancellarius*) and four examiners in the books taken up, before the actual ceremony of conferring the licence, while at the ceremony itself some at least of the candidates were required to give expositions or lectures (known as 'colla- tions') after the manner of masters lecturing in the schools upon various portions of the texts, after which the chancellor himself might, if he wished, take part in the discussion of 'questions' arising therefrom.[2]

[1] In the agreement of 1213 (Jour- dain, No. 15; *Chartul.* i, No. 18) the artists are required to give their testimony as to the qualifications of candidates upon oath, the physi- cians 'dare fidem', the theologians and canonists merely 'dicere in ver- bo veritatis'. So far there is nothing to show that an actual examination in the modern sense took place, but the board of six masters in arts [in- stituted by the papal commissioner in 1213 (*Chartul.* i, No. 16) cer- tainly implies a definite form of testing candidates.] The *de Con- scientia* of Robert de Sorbon (*d.* 1272), moreover, in which the famous preacher draws a parallel between the examination for the licence and the Last Judgement, makes it plain that this was the case. 'Item si Cancellarius Parisien- sis examinet aliquem clericum in aliquo libro, sufficit quod reddat ei septem vel octo lectiones ... Item si aliquis respondeat coram cancel- lario de quatuor questionibus, ad tres bene transit et licentiatur,' ed. F. Chambon, Paris, 1902, pp. 12, 17; [cf. Dorothy Mackay in *Mélanges ... offerts à M. Ferdinand Lot*, Paris, 1925, pp. 491–500;

Haskins, *Mediaeval Culture*, p. 42 and *passim*.] It appears, however, that 'Cancellarius non audit omnes qui licentiantur in propria persona, sed facit eos audiri ab aliquibus aliis magistris' (*loc. cit.*). In the great suit of 1283 (Jourdain, No. 274; *Chartul.* i, No. 515) the masters relied upon a passage in the Bull of 1231 which they cited as ordering that 'De fisicis autem et artistis cancellarius bona fide *per- mittat* examinare magistros'; but it appears that the true text is '*pro- mittat*' (Denifle, i. 89). Bulaeus (iv. 280) tells us that in his own day the chancellor no longer ex- amined the theologians, but that the formal examination of the bachelors of arts was still kept up. [Grabmann has edited, from a Ripoll MS. at Barcelona, a thir- teenth-century Parisian collection of questions, 'que maxime in exa- minationibus solent queri', with answers (*Revue néo-scolastique*, xxxvi (1934), 211–29; cf. *Sitz. d. Bayerischen Akad. der Wissen- schaften*, Phil.-hist. Abth., 1933, p. 20).]

[2] [*Chartul.* ii, p. 679.]

CHAP. V,
§ 4.
Previous
examina-
tion by the
faculties. In the superior faculties the examination before the chancellor seems to have first been reduced to the barest formality, and then to have disappeared altogether;[1] the fate of the candidate was really determined beforehand at a meeting of the faculty in the absence of the chancellor. Eventually the faculty of arts claimed the same right for itself, though only as regards the licences given at Ste Geneviève. Four *temptatores* were appointed by and from the candidate's own nation to conduct an independent examination (*temptatores in cameris* or *in propriis*) which took place between the examination before the chancellor[2] (*in communibus*) and the 'collations' at the actual bestowal of the licence.[3] The first examination, conducted by the chancellor and four *temptatores* named by him but accepted by the faculty,[4] included an inquiry into the

[1] This was certainly the case in the faculty of medicine, in which the chancellor would naturally have been an inefficient examiner. See the long series of published documents relating to a great litigation between the chancellor and the faculty in 1330–2. *Chartul.* ii, Nos. 918–43. The chancellor had licensed a bachelor not presented by the faculty, which claims that it is customary for the bachelor 'ire per singulos magistros regentes Parisius in facultate predicta, antequam presentetur cancellario Parisiensi, et petere ab eisdem quod ipsi audiant de una questione solempni' (No. 921). The custom received the royal confirmation in 1331 (*ibid.*, No. 943).

[2] Or his sub-chancellor. The chancellor of Ste Geneviève, if not an M.A., was obliged to appoint a D.D. as sub-chancellor. The chancellor of Notre Dame also had a sub-chancellor who was a B.D. *Chartul.* ii, App., p. 676, note. [The phrases *in communibus* and *in propriis* point to examinations conducted by masters drawn from all the nations, and those conducted by masters elected by and from the nations.]

[3] [See *Chartul.* iii, No. 1468; cf. *Auctarium*, i, p. xxxi. This description applies to the period before 1350. In the early thirteenth century (*Chartul.* i, No. 16, a. 1213) we find a board of six masters who served for six months. Three were appointed by the chancellor of Notre Dame, three by the masters of arts. In 1259, on the ground that the chancellor of Ste Geneviève was granting the licence to their prejudice, the masters decreed that he must act with examiners appointed by themselves (No. 333). This was confirmed by Alexander IV, who said that four examiners were to be appointed by the 'universitas magistrorum facultatis' (No. 346).]

[4] These are spoken of as nominated by the chancellor. (*Chartul.* ii, p. 676, notes.) In 1260 (*ibid.* i, No. 363) the faculty had claimed to elect both sets of examiners; the appointment of examiners *in communibus* was evidently matter of dispute between faculty and chancellor, though they certainly had to be formally admitted by the latter. The above account in the main follows Thurot's (p. 53 *sq.*), which is, however, criti-

candidate's residence, attendance at lectures, and perform- ance of exercises, as well as some examination in the pre- scribed books; at its conclusion, the chancellor, guided by the votes of the examiners, admitted those who were judged worthy to the examination before the faculty, which was per- haps the more important examination in the modern sense of the word. The faculty appears never to have ventured on imposing an additional examination on the candidates at the 'inferior' or cathedral examination. There the only *tempta- men* was conducted by the four examiners chosen from the faculty by the chancellor, together with the purely formal public examination or collations on the day of the licence- ceremonial.[1]

The candidates who had passed their examination or examinations were sent to the chancellor to be licensed in batches of eight or more at a time, the names being arranged in order of merit. This order, which the chancellor was expected to follow in actually conferring the licence, was the only approach to a competitive examination which the Pari- sian university system admitted. The only 'honour' which a student could win in taking his degree was a good place in his *camera* or *auditio*.[2] The 'honours' of the university were, however, no more above suspicion than the degree itself. In 1385 a chancellor of Paris, defending himself against a charge of exacting illegal fees for the licence, numbers the supplica- tions and entreaties which he received from great persons on behalf of their relatives for precedence in their *auditio* among the most serious and oppressive burdens of his ill-

---

cized by Feret (*L'Abbaye de Ste Geneviève*, i. 286), whose book is based upon the older work of Moli- net. See also *Chartul.* ii, App., p. 675 *sq.* (with Denifle's notes), and below, Appendix iv. I have made an independent study of the Registers.

[1] [Cf. *Chartul.* ii, p. 676 note. Al- though there appears to have been no definite rule requiring candi- dates to appear before the chan- cellor of Ste Geneviève rather than

the chancellor of Notre Dame, they generally went to the former. In 1448 the proctor of the English- German nation refers to the exami- nation at Ste Geneviève as 'examen facultatis artium' (*Auctarium*, ii. 728). See Boyce, p. 103 and notes.]

[2] Goulet, f. viii *b*. At Prague we find the candidates in the bachelor's examination arranged in order of merit, and after the sixteenth cen- tury in *three classes. Mon. Univ. Prag.* 1, pt. i. 43, 44; pt. ii. 341.

CHAP. V, remunerated office. The right of determining the order of
§ 4. precedence was, it may be observed, still claimed by the chancellor, though the masters treated this last relic of his ancient
independence as a usurpation.[1] Between the 'private examination' and the licence, the *licentiandi* were required to maintain
a thesis chosen by themselves in S. Julien's Church, the ceremony being known as the *quodlibetica*, i.e. disputation on a
subject chosen by the candidate himself.[2]

The On the day appointed for the conferment of the licence,
licence. the successful candidates,[3] in full academical dress (*cappati*),
proceeded in state from the Mathurine convent to the episcopal palace or the abbey of Ste Geneviève, as the case

[1] Bulaeus, iv. 606. [See the lengthy documents in *Chartul*. iii, Nos. 1504–22, especially pp. 341, 351, 403–4.] Gerson indulges in a similar vein of self-commiseration, *Opera* (Paris, 1606), ii, c. 825. [The generalizations in the text are based upon slight evidence. The serious-ness of the examinations and the value of the order in the *auditio* would vary in different periods; and the claim of the chancellor in 1385 is worthy of note: 'quod se possit informare spacio trium men-sium tam per omnes magistros illius facultatis Parisius presentes, in qua petunt [bacalarii] licenciari . . ., quam per alios viros honestos ac literatos, per quos veritas sciri potest de vita, sciencia et facundia necnon proposito et spe proficiendi et aliis, que sunt in talibus requi-sita et requirenda' (*Chartul*. iii. 403, 404).]

[2] [There seems to be some mis-understanding here. In 1445 the faculty of arts decided to resume the *actus solemnis* of the quodlibets and to appoint masters from each nation as *quodlibetarii*, presumably to preside (*Auctarium*, ii. 632, cf. 669). In 1452 the resumption of this disputation in the church of St. Julien was ordered by Estoute-ville (*Chartul*. iv, p. 726). Although

claimed as an ancient custom, there is no earlier record of it in the faculty of arts, nor is it said to have been conducted by bachelors, though this is probable, as a similar dispu-tation existed by 1350 in the faculty of medicine; *Commentaires*, p. xxv; cf. *Chartul*. ix, No. 2614 (1446). Grabmann has suggested that the sophistical disputations corre-sponded in the faculty of arts to the quodlibets in the theological faculty: see his article on Simon of Faversham in the *Sitz. der Bayerischen Akademie der Wissen-schaften*, Phil.-hist. Abth., 1933, pp. 11–13.]

[3] In some universities the result of the degree examination was an-nounced to the candidates by the examiners sending them a candle, either an allusion to the parable of the light not to be set under a bushel, or to be offered in a church. At Leipzig a curious mode of voting was in use. The caps of the candi-dates were spread out on the table; each examiner passed down the table and put a pea (*pisum*) in the cap of the candidate for whose pass-ing he voted, a pebble in the caps of those whom he rejected. The can-didate's fate was decided by the predominance of peas or pebbles. (Zarncke, *Statutenbücher*, p. 319.)

might be, accompanied by the rector and proctors, and preceded by the bedels of the faculty. They were then presented
to the chancellor, and, after the formal 'collations' already
mentioned, received kneeling before him the solemn licence
in the name of the Trinity, to incept or begin to teach in the
faculty of arts, together with the apostolical benediction.[1]
This ceremony was in fact the same as that which is now
inaccurately termed taking a master's degree at Oxford or
Cambridge. The licentiate, as has been fully explained
already, did not become a full master until he had actually
entered upon the duties of his office and been incorporated
into the society of his new colleagues. An interval of half
a year commonly elapsed between licence and inception.[2] Inception.
Before the actual ceremony of the *birettatio* the licentiate had
to appear before a congregation of his nation and obtain its
placet for his promotion. This being granted, he was immediately sworn to obey the rector and his faculty and nation,
and to do or abstain from doing some scores of things which
had, from time to time, been enjoined or forbidden by university, faculty, or nation.[3] The evening of the day before
the inception he took part in a peculiarly solemn disputation
known as his 'vespers'. He was then free to give his formal

[1] The formula in Bulaeus is as
follows: 'Ego N. auctoritate Apostolica qua fungor in hac parte do
tibi potestatem docendi, regendi,
interpretandi, omnesque actus
scholasticos exercendi hic et ubique
terrarum', concluding no doubt 'in
nomine Patris, Filii, et Spiritus
Sancti' (Bulaeus, i. 278). But in the
book of the Chancellor of Ste
Geneviève (*Chartul.* ii, App., p.
679) it runs: 'Et ego auctoritate
apostolorum Petri et Pauli in hac
parte mihi commissa do vobis
licentiam legendi, regendi, disputandi et determinandi ceterosque
actus scholasticos seu magistrales
exercendi in facultate artium Parisius et ubique terrarum, in nomine,
&c. Amen.'

[2] [The editors of the Proctors'
Book (*Auctarium*, I. xxxi) give two

or three years as the customary
period. Boyce (pp. 109, 110), com-
menting on this, shows that the
period might vary indefinitely; he
cites one case in which licence and
inception occurred on the same
day. This section in the text is an
attempt to describe the licence and
inception from later evidence and
must not be read back into the
thirteenth century without further
evidence. It is also perhaps coloured by the further information
available for Oxford. Indeed, as
previous notes have shown, it is
hard to reconstruct the details of
the arts course generally before
1366.]

[3] The oaths occupy two folio
pages in Bulaeus (iv. 273–5). [Cf.
Chartul. i, No. 501; ii, p. 680.]

CHAP. V, §4. inaugural lecture or rather disputation in the presence of the faculty, to receive the magisterial *biretta* and the book from the hands of the presiding regent, to receive the kiss of fellowship, and to take his seat upon the magisterial cathedra.[1]

The inception banquet. The evening concluded with a banquet given at the expense of the inceptor or a party of inceptors to the masters and others, at which it is probable that the prohibitions which we find in some universities against dancing or the introduction of actors and trumpeters were not always strictly complied with.[2] There were others in which the latter form of jubilation was recognized by statute.[3]

Length of the course. The time occupied by the course in arts varied considerably at different periods. Robert Curzon fixed it at six years, requiring twenty years of age for the licence.[4] The statutes of the English nation in 1252 require the determiner to have passed five or at least four years in the study of arts, and to be at least nineteen years of age.[5] It is, however, certain that at Paris the tendency was towards shortening the course in arts, and towards an early baccalaureate. In the course of the fourteenth century the minimum period for the M.A. degree was reduced to five years and (after 1366) to four years and a half; yet even before this date we find the book of the chancellor of Ste Geneviève requiring only three years' study at Paris, with the reservation that the faculty inter-

---

[1] Bulaeus, v. 858.

[2] 'Quod tripudiare vel choreare nullo modo audeant publice vel occulte.' (Devic et Vaissete, *Hist. Gén. de Languedoc*, vii, 1879, Docs. c. 536). So, at Caen, 'mimi seu bucinatores' are forbidden. Comte de Bourmont, *Bulletin de la Soc. des Antiq. de Normandie*, xii (1884), p. 405.

[3] e.g. Toulouse: Devic, *loc. cit.*, c. 537.

[4] *Chartul.* i, No. 20: 'Nullus legat Parisius de artibus citra vicesimum primum etatis sue annum'; i.e. 20, not 21 as commonly stated. The age 12 given in Du Boulay's transcript of the statute of 1215 (iii. 81), upon which Malden, Prof.

Laurie, and others have based grave reflections, is an obvious misprint for 21. [The terms of the oath of determiners in *Chartul.* ii, p. 673: 'vos iurabitis quod vos estis 14 annorum' is almost certainly due to a scribal error. The bachelor swore that he was in his twenty-first year before he took the examination for the licence (*ibid.*, p. 678). Cf. i, No. 501 (c. 1280).]

[5] *Chartul.* i, No. 201. It is observable that the residence must be kept 'continue'; the abuse of completing residence by scraps of a few weeks at a time, which has been permitted by some modern universities, is thus guarded against.

preted the three years as two complete years and part of a third.[1] There was probably at all times so much discrepancy between the letter of the statutes and the liberal interpretation put upon them by the faculty as to add considerably to the difficulties of the university historian. Two years' residence in another *studium generale* which had at least six regents was reckoned as equivalent to one year's study at Paris.[2] Many students passed the earlier half of their university course in some minor university nearer home, and then came to Paris after taking their bachelor's degree, and thus avoided the examination for that degree at Paris, an examination which, if not severe, was something more than a form of which the substance consisted in the payment of fees. The time of those who kept their full residence of four years and a half at Paris appears usually to have been divided thus—they went up in October, took their B.A. in the spring of their second year, the licence two years after that, and 'incepted' towards the end of the same year. It is, however, certain that in the fifteenth century a man frequently took his bachelor's degree a year within after his coming into residence.[3] The tendency to an earlier baccalaureate and a

[1] *Chartul.* ii, App., p. 678. It is probable that this applied only to those who had kept some residence at another university [for in another oath the bachelor swore that he had determined at Paris or 'in alio studio generali'].

[2] In the fifteenth century students from other universities were frequently allowed to pass the examinations for the baccalaureate, the licence, and the mastership in the same year, even though 'neque Parisius, neque in aliquo studio solemni seu generali, libros audiverant requisitos ad huiusmodi gradus, neque studuerant per tempus requisitum'. Moved by jealousy of the new University of Caen, the nation of France provided against this abuse in 1444. (Bulaeus, v. 529–30.) [Cf. *Chartul.* iv, No. 2588: 'de aliquibus qui legunt

textum tocius logice, phisice aut metaphisice infra triduum vel biduum'.] Examples of similar laxity as to all manner of university regulations might be multiplied indefinitely. The case of each student who supplicated for this or that step was more or less considered on its own merits, and neither statutes nor oaths could really prevent a great deal of 'dispensation'. It may, or may not, be more than a coincidence that the English universities continued to place the bachelor's degree later in the course than Paris, and (consequently, perhaps) to attach more importance to it.

[3] See the statue of the German nation in 1461, Bulaeus, v. 646; [*Auctarium*, ii. 935–9]. In the German universities the usual period before the bachelor's degree seems to have been a year and a half (so

CHAP. V, still further curtailment of the arts course is observable after
§ 4. the medieval period. By the sixteenth century it had been
reduced to three years and a half.[1] On the Continent the
baccalaureate has eventually disappeared altogether or become practically equivalent to matriculation. In the older
English universities curtailment of residence made inevitable
by the improvement of grammar schools and the later age
for commencing the university course has been effected by
dispensing with residence after admission to the bachelor's
degree and reducing the final degree to an expensive
formality.[2]

Necessary   The obligations of a scholar to his university did not end
regency. with taking his degree. In the first place he was (in the early
period) bound to dispute or 'determine questions' for forty
days continuously.[3] Then he was required, after taking his

at Leipzig, Zarncke, *Statutenbücher*, p. 374) and two years more for the mastership. The statutes of Cornouaille College at Paris allow five years for the licence (Félibien, iii. 497) probably as a maximum.

[1] Bulaeus, v. 858; Launoi, *Regii Navarrae Gym. Hist.*, Paris, 1677, i. 272. At this time scholars in colleges were usually divided into four classes, each of them taught by one regent (*Summulista, Logicus, Physicus, Intrans*) in the manner of a form at a public school. This arrangement is still preserved in Scotland, where the bachelor's degree has likewise disappeared, though one of the classes was long called the bachelor-class. The same regent took his pupils through the whole course, changing his class every year. Ramus, *Prooemium Reformandae Parisiensis Academiae* in *Scholae in Liberales Artes*, c. 1116. Cf. below, chap. xi. The arrangement is probably much older than the time of Ramus.

[2] M. Thurot's statement that 'le baccalauréat n'était pas un *grade*, mais un état' (p. 137) seems to imply a somewhat transcendental conception of the nature of a 'de-

gree'. The fact is the term *gradus* was originally used *only* of the baccalaureate and perhaps the licence; they were so many *steps* to the mastership. Thus *c.* 1284 the faculty of arts declares that 'determinatio est unus honorabilis gradus attingendi magisterium'. Jourdain, No. 274; *Chartul.* i, No. 515.

[3] So in the English nation in 1252: 'Disputabit hora determinata, et questiones suas determinabit per quadraginta dies continue post inceptionem.' (*Chartul.* i, No. 202.) [The oath prescribed *c.* 1280 for all inceptors in arts runs to the same effect and continues, 'procedetis per xv dies (*one MS. reads* "XL dies") habitu predicto', i.e. the *capa rotunda* (*ibid.*, No. 501).] This requirement, which seems to have early become obsolete at Paris, left a curious trace behind it at Oxford. Every inceptor was bound to wear his full academical dress for forty days, which included, in the case of theologians and canonists, boots ('*botys*'), while inceptors of other faculties were bound to go 'cum sotularibus quodammodo conatis vulgariter nuncupatis Pynsons'. [*Statuta Antiqua*, pp. 288–9.]

degree, to stay up and teach in Paris for a certain number of years. An oath to teach for two years, unless previously dispensed, continued to be enforced upon inceptors[1] till it was abolished by Estouteville in 1452, though it had probably long since ceased to be strictly enforced. So long as the schools were merely rooms hired in the houses of the Rue du Fouarre by individual masters, there was no necessary limitation to the number of regents. If schools could not be obtained in the street thus consecrated to scholastic uses, schools in the immediate neighbourhood were recognized by the faculty as entitling the masters who occupied them to the privileges of regency.[2] But when the nations came to possess or at least to rent schools of their own, the regent was required to teach in these schools. After 1452, it would seem, no obstacle was placed in the way of those who wanted to 'go down' immediately after taking their degree, while those who wished to teach had to supplicate *pro regentia et scholis*, and if the petition was granted, to wait for their turn to succeed to the use of a vacant school.[3]

At this point it seems desirable to discuss one of the most important and yet most difficult questions which is suggested by our review of these Parisian exercises and examinations— the question 'What was the real difficulty of a medieval examination? What was the real value of a medieval degree?' With regard to the earliest part of our period, we are left to mere inferences from isolated expressions of contemporary writers. In the third quarter of the thirteenth century it would seem that the examination before the chancellor must have been a bona fide though by no means a strict or

Value of a medieval degree in arts.

---

[1] [*Chartul.* ii, p. 680. The obligation was laid down by Curzon (i, No. 20) and appears in the oaths of *c.* 1280 (No. 501).]

[2] Bulaeus, iv. 212; *Chartul.* ii, No. 872. By this time (1327) it would seem that the determiners paid directly to the nation, who provided schools for the masters. [The nations, as pressure on the space available in the Rue du Fouarre increased, began to buy property, as well as to rent schools, in the fourteenth century. See the very interesting history of the acquisition by the English nation of the 'new schools' (1368–9) and the schools of the seven arts (*c.* 1378) in Boyce, chap. iv. The proctors' books are full of detail about equipment, allotment of rooms, problems of lighting and repairs, &c.]

[3] Bulaeus, v. 858–9.

CHAP. V, inexorable examination. A very amusing sermon or treatise,
§ 4. addressed by Robert de Sorbon possibly to the scholars of
the college which he had just founded at Paris, consists of an
elaborately drawn-out parallel between the examination before
the chancellor and the Last Judgement. Infinitely more
severe as the latter examination was represented to be, the
illustration could hardly have been used at all had the chancellor's examination been a mere farce. The writer distinctly
contemplates the possibility of a candidate's rejection, though
he points out that in the earthly examination, unlike its
celestial antitype, the chancellor or his assistants were amenable to personal or pecuniary influences: even if a candidate
were discomfited, he could still by tears and entreaties and
presents to the chancellor's assistants induce him to recon-
sider the matter.[1] Moreover, he tells us that many magnates
were licensed without any examination at all.[2] It is probable
that in this passage the writer had chiefly in view the faculty
of arts, in which his hearers had already graduated. For at
this time the number of theological chairs at Paris was usually
fixed by papal authority, so that admission to the theological
doctorate really amounted to selection for a professorship,
for which there must have been many applicants; when this
limitation was removed, we get complaints both of the admission of unworthy and of the rejection of worthy candidates.[3]

[1] 'Si refutetur aliquis Parisius a Cancellario, hoc non est nisi per annum: qui si post annum redeat, si bene respondet, licentiatur. Item data sententia per preces aliquorum vel per dona vel per servitia aliquando data vel facta collateralibus Cancellarii vel examinatoribus aliis,' &c. . . . 'Item, si quis habet confusionem animi quando refutatur a Cancellario, delebilis est et traditur oblivioni per processum temporis.' [*De Conscientia*, ed. Chambon, pp. 5, 6. See above, p. 457 n.]

[2] 'Multis enim magnatibus fit aliquando gratia et licentiantur sine examinatione,' *op. cit.*, p. 2.

[3] Innocent III in 1207 limited the theological chairs to eight (Bulaeus, iii. 36; *Chartul.* i, No. 5), but from a document of 1218 (*ibid.*, No. 27) it appears that this regulation was not strictly observed. In 1221 Honorius III enjoins Archbishop Langton and his brother commissary to reimpose some limitation, since 'ad docendum non solum in aliis facultatibus set etiam in theologia interdum repulsis dignis admittuntur indigni et adeo excrescit numerus magistrorum, ut tum pro numerositate tum pro insufficientia eorumdem vilescat auctoritas magistralis'. *Ibid.*, No. 41.

But still the whole tone of the allusions to the mastership in CHAP. V,
the faculty of theology at this time is such as to imply that it § 4.
was not every student, not even the average student, who
could look forward to obtaining it as a matter of right, at
least unless he were supported by exceptional favour or direct
bribery.[1] Incorruptibility in the examination-room is as much
a late product of modern civilization as incorruptibility upon
the judicial bench. How much the value of a theological
degree sank in the course of the next two centuries, we shall
see hereafter. With regard to the faculty of arts, the mere
number of masters is sufficient to show that the standard
of learning expected in the candidates—and perhaps of
impartiality in the examiners—was very much lower, though
taking a degree is spoken of as not quite a matter of course.[2]
In the litigation which took place between the chancellor and
the faculty of arts in the last quarter of the century, the
masters accuse the chancellor of appointing incompetent
examiners at Notre Dame, while the chancellor retorts with
an accusation of venality against the examiners at Ste Geneviève.[3] This document and many statutes directed against
venality and corruption tend to show that, however lax the
examination, and however dubious the means adopted for
passing it, there really was an examination to be passed.[4] The
examiner's fangs still retained sufficient keenness to make it

[1] See, for instance, the statute of
the college of Rouen (or de Saana)
in 1268, which provides that fellowships shall terminate after six years
'nisi aliquis illorum in tanta prero-
gativa scientie emineat, quod possit
in scolis alicuius magistri theologie
publicas legere lectiones; et tunc
dimittatur ibidem, si voluerit, donec
ad cathedram valeat ascendere
magistralem'. *Chartul.* i, No. 423.
Later college statutes simply provide that fellows shall take their
degree as a matter of course.

[2] In 1261-8 the Pope complains
that 'magistri (no particular faculty
is mentioned) creantur subito, non
quos juvant morum scientieque
suffragia, sed quibus favor et preces

ne pretium dixerimus suffragan-
tur'; as a consequence of which 'in-
geritur convocationum necessitas',
pointing to frequent dispensations.
Ibid., No. 425.

[3] See above, p. 398 *seq.*

[4] At Freiburg (in the sixteenth
century) 'ultra quinque tentamina
observari non debent, neque etiam
durabit aliquod ex his ultra duas
horas'. Schreiber, ii. 47. At Greifswald there were thirty 'sessiones
pro baccalariatus gradu' (presumably for all the candidates together
or at least an *auditio*) of two hours
each, 'quia nullius aut minimi
fructus est disputationem adire et
statim recedere ab eadem'. Kosegarten, ii. 307.

CHAP. v, worth while to draw them. When we turn to the latter half
§ 4. of our period, the case is by no means equally clear; but the
evidence obtainable both from the registers of Paris and
from the records of the German imitations of Paris make it
tolerably certain that the actual rejection of a rich candidate
must have been a matter of the rarest possible occurrence.
At Paris we do occasionally get allusions to the rejection of a
candidate, but the exceptions are of the kind which prove the
rule; since we hear of such rejections only in connexion with
appeals to the faculty against the decision of the examiners,[1]
and it was a frequent practice in such cases to give the rejected a fresh chance before a special board of examiners. In
one of the German universities we get actual records of the
number examined and the number passed, and the figures
are identical year after year for long periods.[2] It does not
follow that the degrees did not imply a certain irreducible
minimum of attainment. The candidate really had to go
through a certain number of disputations, to hear a certain
number of lectures, and to get a master to present him for his
degree. From the registers of such universities as present us
with detailed statistics on this head, it is evident that as a
matter of fact only a certain proportion—at the outside half—
of the students who matriculated in the faculty of arts proceeded even to the B.A. degree, and of these again much less

[1] 'Supplicaverunt aliqui magistri pro aliquibus scolaribus cifratis ut eis fieret gratiam et per facultatem admitterentur.' MS. *Reg. Nat. Angl.* (No. 8), f. 94 *a, et passim.* [This passage may now be found in the *Auctarium,* ii, col. 614.]

[2] At Greifswald, where it appears that from 1456 to 1478 no candidate failed to satisfy the examiners (Kosegarten, ii. 232 *sq.*). On the other hand such an occurrence must have been not unknown at Ingolstadt, where a new statute was passed enacting 'ut nullus ad gradum baccalariatus rite reiectus proxima suae reiectioni sequente angaria (Ember season) per facultatem rursus ad examen pro eodem gradu admittatur'. Prantl, ii. 51. A statute of Caen allows the examiners 'differre licentiam et imponere illis lecturam certorum librorum' (*Bull. de la Soc. des Ant. de Normandie,* xii. 496). Other statutes forbid such conditional passes (*approbatio cum cauda*). No refusal of a degree is recorded in the fragmentary fifteenth-century register which we possess at Oxford, except one in 1455 when 'frater Philippus Herford ordinis predicatorum repulsus fuit a susceptione gradus bachellariatus in sacra theologia'. (Archives Aa, f. 90 *a.*) Friars stood in an exceptional position. See below, vol. iii, ch. xii, § 2.

than half went on to the M.A.[1] It is probable that incompetent students were more often prevented from entering at all by laziness or conscious incapacity or a hint from their masters than actually rejected at the examination itself.[2] On the whole it may be inferred that a student who was notoriously ignorant of the merest elements of Latin or logic would scarcely have found a master to present him for a degree, and the examinations, as may be presumed from the length of time which they occupied, were considerably less of a farce than the Pass Examinations of Oxford and Cambridge have been almost within the memory of persons now living [1895].[3]

It is clear, however, that there were degrees of laxity in the different universities and at different times, though complaints of extreme laxity are universal, especially in the fifteenth century.[4] We frequently find the universities themselves taking measures to check the growing unconscientiousness of examiners; and in one instance—at Leipzig in 1444— we find the chancellor arbitrarily suspending the examinations in consequence of the scandalous extent to which abuses

---

[1] There are many allusions to a practice of passing a candidate conditionally on his subsequently hearing certain lectures. The practice is forbidden at Aix: 'Quod Baccalaureus non approbetur cum cauda' (Fournier, iii, No. 1582). Paulsen computes that at Leipzig only one-fourth to one-third of those who matriculated proceeded to B.A., one-twentieth to one-sixteenth to M.A. But see below, vol. ii, ch. xiii.

[2] Thus in the S. Andrew's Register (MS. *Acta Fac. Art.* f. 24), which contains no instance of actual rejection, we find under the year 1441 that 'decanus facultatis ut moris est secundum formam statutorum inquisivit a regentibus an nouerint aliquos bacalarios ydoneos ad examen anno presente, ad quod respondetur negative'. In the colleges students were not allowed to enter the examination without

leave of the college. So at Angers: 'Item, quod huiusmodi pedagogi non permittant aliquem scholarium suorum subire examen alicuius gradus, nisi ipsi crediderint esse sufficientem et idoneum, quoad gradum obtinendum, sed ipsum exhortentur et moneant, ut non se subiiciat huiusmodi examini, ne contingat ipsum reprobari et inde diffamari.' *Statuts des quatre Facs. de l'Un. d'Angers*, p. 70 (1494).

[3] For an amusing account of an examination at Oxford in 1781 see *Letters of Radcliffe and James*, ed. Evans (Ox. Hist. Soc., 1888), pp. 160–1.

[4] One of d'Ailly's demands in his treatise *De Reformatione Ecclesiae* is 'ut gradus distribuerentur dignis sine favore aut acceptione personarum, et cum rigore examinis in scientia et moribus'. *Fascic. Rer. Expetend.*, i. Cf. von der Hardt, *Concil. Constant.* i, pt. iv, c. 427.

CHAP. V,
§ 4.

had recently been carried. A little later in the same university it became necessary to pass a statute to forbid the dean and vice-chancellor giving the candidates private information as to the questions which would be asked.[1] All this goes to show that the 'art of pluck', though little practised, was not quite unknown in the medieval university. From the frequent insistence on secrecy of voting and the oaths against taking vengeance upon the examiners it is evident that its practice was not unattended by personal risk.[2]

Privileges
of no-
bility.

It may be laid down as a general principle in all spheres of medieval life that rich and noble persons enjoyed in practice exceptional privileges. But it is not certain whether Toulouse borrowed from Paris the unblushing provision by which the chancellor of Toulouse was allowed to dispense with the public examination in the case of nobles who support companions in livery.[3] The University of Cambridge was probably the last university in the world to abolish the privilege which excused an examination to sons of nobles.[4]

Moral and
other
qualifica-
tions.

It should be added that the examination included an inquiry into the legitimacy, conduct and character of the candidates, and 'ploughing' for moral or disciplinary reasons appears to have been less infrequent than for intellectual incompetence. It must be remembered that the degree was not a mere certificate of having passed an examination but the admission to an official position. Thus at Vienna we find that in 1449 of forty-three candidates for the licence seventeen were rejected, one for having spoken uncivilly to a master, another for irregularities in the matter of academical dress, another for going out to see an execution in the middle

---

[1] Zarncke, *Statutenbücher*, pp. 367, 446. The faculty had shortly before ordered that examiners should be chosen by lot. *Ibid.*, p. 363.

[2] e.g. at Caen candidates are to swear that 'si contingat ipsos refutari post examen, nullum malum vel dampnum occasione sue repulse cuicumque magistro examinatori vel alteri per se vel per alium fieri

procurabunt'. *Bull. de la Soc. des Ant. de Normandie*, xii. 498.

[3] 'Nobilibus tenentibus socios de raupis' (i.e. robis). Devic et Vaissette, *Hist. de Languedoc*, vii, Docs., c. 591.

[4] The *ius natalium* which excused the 'general' examination and a year's residence was abolished in 1884.

of the examination, another for going about disguised and for the heinous offence of 'wandering by the Danube',[1] another for gambling, another for taking part in a knife-fight with certain tailors—none, apparently, for failure in the literary part of the examination.

Theology

[See especially A. G. LITTLE and F. PELSTER, *Oxford Theology and Theologians, c. 1282–1302* (Oxford, 1934), pp. 25–56, where Oxford and Parisian customs are described and compared.]

We have seen that in the faculty of arts the course had by the close of the medieval period come to be very much shorter than that prescribed by Robert Curzon in 1215. In the faculty of theology an opposite tendency was at work. M. Thurot attributes this to the influence of the colleges, whose bursarships were held only till the attainment of the doctor's degree, while in some cases a longer period of study was allowed than the minimum prescribed by the faculty.[2] More weight ought perhaps to be ascribed to the desire to limit the number and keep up the prestige of the theological doctors and maintain the value of their lucrative perquisities, at a

Increasing length of the course.

---

[1] 'Quia infra examen exiverunt ad locum, in quo plures fuerunt puniti crucis supplicio . . . quia etiam notatus fuit de mutatione habitus et de spaciamento ad Danubium' (Kink, I. i. 35). Moral, political, and theological considerations were frequent grounds for refusing a degree at Oxford in the sixteenth century. Cf. Clark, *Reg. Univ. Oxf.* II. i. 37 *sq.* So at Padua a candidate was objected to because he had called one of the doctors 'unus ignorans et lavator scutelarum'; and told another who had threatened not to present him for his degree 'quod nesciebat unam literam'. Gloria, *Mon. di Padova* (1318–1405), i. 271.

[2] *De l'organisation de l'enseignement*, p. 133. Paulsen (*Hist. Zeitschr.* xlv. 393) suggests that it

was considered simoniacal to take fees for lectures on theology and canon law. If so, this would account for the desire to thrust the teaching on the bachelors, but I know of no evidence for this. [The subject was frequently discussed by the canonists; and Gaines Post has collected evidence which strongly suggests that the secular masters of theology at Paris were paid fees; *Speculum*, vii (1932), 197, 198. This is confirmed by Stephen Langton. Referring to the tradition that Abraham acquired his riches by teaching astronomy to Egyptians, he says, on Genesis xiii. 2, 'sic ergo patet quod licet magistro a discipulis accipere bona, *et eciam querere*' (Durham MS. A. i. 7, f. 16 c). We owe this reference to Dr. B. Smalley.]

PARIS

472

CHAP. V, time when other restrictions on their multiplication were
§ 4. removed. Robert Curzon required five years' study as the
qualification for 'publicly giving private lectures' after tierce
on days on which masters lectured. For the doctorate eight
years of theological study were prescribed, so that the student
who took his final degree in the minimum period would spend
three years as a 'bachelor'.[1] Moreover the doctor was required to have reached the thirty-fifth year of his age.

We have not materials for tracing the gradual extension
of the period of bachelorhood and the gradual increase in
the number and complication of the exercises required for the
attainment of the high dignity of the theological doctorate.
By the reform of 1366 the complete course is made to extend
over a period of sixteen years, and this was reduced by only
one year under the statutes of Estouteville in 1452. Though
the exact number and character of the disputations, sermons,
acts, and exercises of one kind or another demanded of the
candidate varied slightly from time to time, the following
account will be applicable to the greater part of the fifteenth

---

[1] Such appears to me to be the plain meaning of the clause, which runs as follows: 'Circa statum theologorum statuimus, quod nullus Parisius legat citra 35 etatis sue annum, et nisi studuerit per octo annos ad minus, et libros fideliter et in scolis audierit, et quinque annis audiat theologiam, antequam privatas lectiones legat publice, et illorum nullus legat ante tertiam in diebus quando magistri legunt.' (Bulaeus, iii. 82; *Chartul.* i, No. 20.) Denifle, however (i. 100, 101), strangely understands by these words that the candidate must have studied eight years in all before becoming a 'Lehrer' (i.e. presumably doctor), i.e. three in arts and five in theology. But then there will be no time allowed for the cursory lectures which it is clear were to be delivered by persons who were not masters in theology. It is evident that 'legat' in the first sentence means to lecture *as a master*, and the advanced age required for the mastership makes it improbable that the minimum course was so short as five years. [In his constitutions of 1335, for the Cistercian order, Benedict XII cites a statute of the university: 'illo presertim statuto, quo in eodem studio Parisiensi cavere dicitur, quod nullus possit legere cursum Biblie, nisi ibidem studuerit septem annis, quodque non permittatur Sententias legere, nisi etiam inibi studuerit decem annis' (*Chartul.* ii, No. 992). These years could be spent in theological study and show a lengthening of the period required for the bachelor; but the passage lends some weight to the view that Curzon's statute refers throughout to the bachelor, and that Denifle (who probably meant by 'Lehrer' a bachelor) was right in his interpretation. The difficulty lies in the age prescribed.]

century.[1] It should be added, however, that this inordinately
protracted course of study was constantly curtailed by a
liberal employment of the faculty's powers of dispensation.[2]

As the time of study lengthened, the teaching more and
more devolved upon bachelors. The distinction between
'ordinary' and 'extraordinary' lectures became in the faculty
of theology purely one of time, even 'ordinary' lectures being
given by bachelors. By the sixteenth century it appears that
doctors of theology merely lectured once a year by way of
maintaining their regency.[3] The doctors had developed or
degenerated into mere dignitaries, who officiated at disputations, examinations, and other meetings of the faculty, while
the only real teachers were the bachelors. It may be observed
that abuses of this kind prevailed more or less in the higher
faculties of all universities in which the masters possessed
supreme and irresponsible authority. They were unknown
in the student-universities, in which there can be little doubt

---

[1] Two collections of statutes are
extant, the earlier one belonging to
the later fourteenth century in
D'Achéry, *Spicilegium* (1723), iii.
735 *sq.*, Bulaeus, iv. 425–8; a later
one in D'Argentré, *Collectio Judi-
ciorum*, ii. 462 *sq.*, both now more
accurately printed in *Chartul.* ii,
App., Nos. 1188, 1189, pp. 691–3,
697–703. [The brief statutes of
Urban V's commission of reform
in 1366 (*Chartul.* iii, No. 1319) and
the 'Statuta facultatis theologie
Paris. de admittendis ad lecturam
Sententiarum et de questionibus
faciendis', of 4 July 1387 (*ibid.*, No.
1534), are less comprehensive. The
whole body of material can now be
supplemented by the earlier statutes
of the theological faculty at Bologna
(1364) edited by Ehrle (*I più antichi statuti*, &c.) and frequently
referred to in previous pages. The
Bologna statutes were based on
those of Paris and were known to
the editor of the *Chartularium* (see
the valuable notes in ii, p. 693–5). As
Ehrle points out (pp. clxxvii–clxxx),

other theological statutes at Toulouse, Heidelberg, Cologne, Vienna,
and Perpignan were derived from
those of Paris and may also be compared with the strangely fragmentary Parisian records.]

[2] This may be inferred with certainty from the fact that later college statutes sometimes allow less
time for the licence or the doctorate
than the university statutes required, e.g. at Coll. le Moine, nine
years for the whole course (Félibien,
v. 610); at Narbonne, 'duodecim
annos ad licentiam obtinendam.'
(*Ibid.* p. 663.) At Plessis, however, ten years are allowed to
become *sententiarius.* (*Ibid.* iii.
376.) It should be added that some
religious orders had papal privileges curtailing the period of study
for their students (e.g. *Chartul.* ii,
Nos. 992, 1002), and still more extensive dispensations for their individual members were very common.

[3] Bulaeus, vi. 133. [On this see
further in Additional Note, below,
p. 495.]

that the most efficient teaching of the Middle Ages was to be found.

The theological student passed the first six years of his course as a simple *auditor*. For four years he attended lectures on the Bible, for two years on the Sentences of Peter the Lombard, these being the only text-books with which the theological doctor necessarily became acquainted during the whole of his fifteen or sixteen years of study.[1] How completely the Sentences were placed side by side with the Bible as the very source and fountain-head of all theology is illustrated by Albert the Great's disquisition on the knowledge possessed by the Mother of Christ. After demonstrating in detail that the Jewish peasant woman must have been acquainted with the *Trivium* and *Quadrivium*, the doctor proceeds to discuss the extent of her attainments in the faculties of medicine, civil and canon law, and theology; in the latter he holds that she must have had a 'summary' knowledge of the Bible and Sentences.[2] At the end of his first six years of study, provided he had attained the age of twenty-six or twenty-seven, the student might appear before the faculty with his certificates (*cedulae* or *schedulae*) of due attendance on the prescribed lectures and supplicate for his first course (*pro primo cursu*). He was then examined by four doctors, and, if passed, would be formally admitted by the dean to the reading of his 'first course', i.e. be made a bachelor. He entered upon his baccalaureate with a public exercise known as the *principium*,[3] and then began a course of lectures on a book of

[1] [Stress must be laid upon the words 'text-books' and 'necessarily', if this generalization is to be accepted as just. Collections of questions, postils, and commentaries were aids to study. See Additional Note, below, p. 490.]

[2] 'Beatissima Virgo Bibliam et sententias in summo habuit.' *Opera* (Lyons, 1651), xx. 80.

[3] [Before *c.* 1250, this exercise was called the *introitus*. For the *reportatio* of particular *principia* see M.-D. Chenu, 'Maîtres et bache-

liers de l'Université de Paris v. 1240', in *Études d'histoire littéraire et doctrinale du XIIIᵉ siècle*, i (Paris and Ottawa, 1932), 28–30. At Bologna the *cursor*'s *principium* consisted only of a 'commendatio scripture', while that of the bachelor proper comprised a 'collatio pro commendatione sacre doctrine vel librorum Sententiarum', followed by a 'protestatio fidei' and a *questio* which he 'proponit . . . et studiose pertractat' (Ehrle, p. 21). The masters and students were all

the Bible, which occupied a year, and in the following year CHAP. V,
a second course on another book. The bachelor was at this   § 4.
stage of his career described as a *cursor*. The secular theologian was in practice usually a master of arts,[1] who might be
thirsting for the time when he might once more bring his
logic and his philosophy into play upon the more congenial
questions suggested by the master of the Sentences. [At
Paris the seculars would seem as a rule to have confined themselves to the cursory lectures on the Bible, which were the
condition precedent to proceeding to the higher degrees; they
corresponded to the *cursores* of Bologna, whereas the 'ordinary'
lectures, given by the *biblici* at Bologna, were generally left to
regulars.][2] Each of the mendicant orders in Paris (as well as

present and no other scholastic act
was done on the days when *principia* were held. A *collatio* was in
its primary sense an informal and
short sermon; academically, it
came to mean an address or, more
usually, a disputation in which the
speaker discussed matters freely
without determining or coming to
a formal conclusion. One scholastic, cited by F. Pelster, uses the
phrase 'intendo solum dicere proba-
biliter et collative'. At Paris the *collatio* was also the informal discourse
on the theme of a sermon preached
earlier in the day on feast-days
when the theologians did not
lecture (*Chartul.* ii, p. 692); finally,
the *collationes* were private disputations where there was no *magister
determinans*, held by masters and
bachelors in the Sorbonne and conventual *studia*. See F. Pelster on
the *Collationes Parisienses* of Duns
Scotus in *Franziskanische Studien*,
x (1923), 21–7; and more fully in
Little and Pelster, pp. 54–6.]

[1] [At Bologna a secular admitted
to lecture on the Sentences had to
have the qualifications 'quod sit
magistratus in artibus vel examinatus et velut dignus magistrari
in artibus approbatus, et postea in
theologia audiverit studiosus ad

minus per quinquennium sub uno
vel diversis magistris in theologia:
—item quod ante Sententiarum
lecturam modo cursorio legat
Bononie duos libros biblie, per de-
canum magistrorum sibi assignan-
dos, faciendo publice solempne
principium' (Ehrle, p. 17).] The
statutes of Vienna, which are also
based on the customs of Paris,
require the B.D. to be M.A.,
'uel saltem quomodocumque ita
edoctus, quod sufficienter sciat in
Theologycis scolis et opponere et
respondere'. Kink, ii. 107.

[2] [This is the view of the editors
of *Chartul.* iv, p. x; but, as Ehrle
points out (p. clxxxv note), the evidence is not conclusive, and secular
biblici are found both at Toulouse
and Cologne. It is hard to see
exactly what the distinction between
the *cursores* and the *biblici* was in
terms of status. At Bologna the religious, who formed the great majority
of the students in the faculty, could
apparently proceed directly to lecture on the Sentences, if they had
studied for six years in a theological *studium* and three years in a
studium generale (of their order), and
then been appointed by their order
ad legendum Sententias (Ehrle, pp.
16, 17). Were the *biblici* selected

CHAP. V, the Cistercian College) was required to supply a fresh
§ 4. lecturer (*biblicus ordinarius*) every year.[1]

The In the course of his ninth year of study, the bachelor was
tentative. required to respond in a disputation known as the *tentative*,[2]
at which a master presided and assigned a question to be
disputed upon, while a number of bachelors awaiting their
licence (*baccalarii formati*) opposed the respondent's theses,
and afterwards conferred with the master as to whether the
exercise should be accepted by the faculty. Eventually this,
like all other academical disputations, reduced itself to a farce,
and consisted in a succession of complimentary speeches, after

from them to give ordinary lectures
on the Bible before they began on
the Sentences? The *biblici* at
Bologna certainly formed a group
between the *cursores* and the
bachelors, a name confined to those
admitted to read the Sentences; cf.
Ehrle, p. 21: 'Biblici autem inci-
piunt (at the *principia*) immediate
post omnes bachalarios', i.e. the
biblici were of lower standing than
the bachelors. Cf. Benedict XII in
1335: 'magistri, baccalarii et lectores
Biblie' of the Cistercians (*Chartul.*
ii, No. 992).]
   [1] Bulaeus, v. 564. Cf. *Chartul.*
ii, App., p. 692 *sq.*
   [2] [*Chartul.* ii, p. 669, n. 29. This
'tentative' corresponds to the requirement at Bologna of a 'tempus
preparationis', lasting for six
months before 1 October. But in
Bologna this period followed graduation. His own master had already
presented him to the chancellor and
testified on oath that he was worthy
and had taken the necessary oaths.
Then (*tunc statim*) the notary of the
theological *universitas* at the command of the chancellor entered his
name 'tanquam graduatum ad
lecturam' (Ehrle, pp. 17–19).] The
following statute of Valladolid
(*c.* 1350, confirmed by the Emperor
Charles V) may throw light on the
nature of the *tentative*, which is
first found in the fourteenth cen-

tury: 'Statuimus et ordinamus,
quod Licentiandus . . . faciat unam
publicam et solemnem disputationem quae tentativa dicitur, sub
Regentia Magistri in turno existen-
tis; hoc modo, Magister Regens . . .
Cathedram tenens, leget paululum
de aliquo textu sacrae Scripturae,
circa quem unus assistentium cui
fuerit commissum movebit quandam Theologalem questionem ad
utramque partem singulis mediis
ventilatis, quam remittet deter-
minandam tentativam facienti, quis
ad locum ante Cathedram deter-
minaturus veniens, ad determinationem dictae quaestionis aliqua
breviter notabit, ponetque pro eius
maiori decisione tres conclusiones,
singulis duo corollaria anectendo,
quorum ultimum sit responsivum,
probabit vero dictas conclusiones,
et corollaria ad nutum Regentis, et
his breviter peractis, arguat Regens
primo duobus vel tribus mediis,
manebitque verbum in ore eius, et
deinde arguant volentes, nec cessa-
bit actus ille, quousque nemo sit
qui arguat, si tamen copia sit oppo-
nentium, transactis horis tribus (si
Regenti visum fuerit) arguendi
finem imponet.' Here the act did
not count unless 'iudicio arguen-
tium sustentans per ipsum Regen-
tem fuerit approbatus'. *Estatutos
de la insig. Univ. Valladolid*, Valladolid, 1651, p. 43.

which the candidate was by acclamation pronounced *ingenio-*
sus et doctissimus.[1] The bachelor might now, after nine years'
study, be admitted to the ordinary reading of the Sentences,
entering upon each of the four books into which the Lombard's work was divided by a solemn *principium* or public
discourse upon some difficult theological problem,[2] to which
every doctor of the faculty was invited by the bedel while one
at least was obliged to be present. Sometimes these occasions
were further enlivened by an 'honest and moderate beer-
drinking' furnished by the lecturer.[3] The *sententiarii* of
the year followed one another in these *principia* in a regular
order, and, after each bachelor's own thesis had been laid
down in the first *principium*, the remaining three were largely
occupied with disputing against the positions maintained by
others or replying to attacks made upon himself.[4] [These
solemn exercises took place during the nine months devoted
by the bachelor to lecturing on the Sentences. In the words
of the statutes of Bologna (1364), 'Lectura vero Sententiarum
novem mensibus duret.']5

In the theological faculty there were practically three distinct degrees of bachelorship, to the first two of which there
was a regular admission quite as formal as the single admission to read cursory lectures in the other faculties—the
degrees of (i) *biblicus ordinarius* or *cursor* (according as he
was regular or secular), (ii) *sententiarius*, and (iii) *baccalarius*

---

[1] Bulaeus, vi. 19.

[2] At Vienna the *principians* 'col-
lacione brevi premissa subiungere
habet questionem, in qua conferre
. . . debet cum aliis sentencias
legentibus'. Kink, ii. 106. [For
Bologna see above, p. 475 n. For
the light thrown on *principia* by
extant commentaries on the Sentences see Ehrle, *op. cit.*, p. clxxxvii,
and especially the same scholar's
*Der Sentenzenskommentar Peters
von Candia* (1925).]

[3] 'Fiant cerivisia honesta et
moderata per incipientes primum
cursum Biblie et tertium sententiarum.' Stat. in Hemeraeus, MS.

Sorbonae Origines, f. 298.

[4] The *collationes* or constructive
part of these discourses appear to
have been privately circulated
among the bachelors of the year
before the public disputation. [The
statutes of Bologna prescribe that
the bachelors, 'gratia disputative
impugnationis non asserant aliquid
revocationi obnoxium, id est non
sane dictum seu etiam utcunque
suspectum' (Ehrle, p. 23). A
bachelor could impugn the dicta of
his colleagues, but not of a *magister
aulatus*.]

[5] [Ehrle, p. 19; cf. *Chartul.* ii, p.
692, n. 9.]

CHAP. V, *formatus*. This third term was applied to bachelors who had
§ 4. completed their course of nine months on the Sentences.
From this time to the licence the candidate was supposed to
remain in Paris, attending or taking part in disputations and
other 'public acts' of the faculty. [During this 'period of
preparation for the higher degree' the bachelor, according
to the statutes of Bologna, was expected to 'oppose' and
'reply' at disputations in each of the theological schools, to
'respond' publicly to each regent master at least once, and to
take part in the *aulatio* of at least one new master by replying
to the first question propounded in the course of the disputation.[1] The requirements at Paris seem to have been less continuous, if more precise, and] from the frequent renewal
of the statutes requiring these bachelors to reside continuously at Paris during the three or four years which elapsed
between the completion of the Sentences and the licence, it
may be inferred that the obligation of residence was at times
loosely observed. Some probably did little more than put in
an appearance now and then when it was their turn to take
part in one of the disputations in which each bachelor
was required to respond at this period of his career.[2] The

[1] [Ehrle, p. 19. For the period
see below, p. 479 n. One of the
questiones in the *Reportata Pari-
siensia* of Duns Scotus on the Sentences was originally a 'disputatio
in aula', in which Duns responded
as a bachelor; see Pelster, in *Fran-
ziskanischen Studien*, x (1923),
11 *sq.*]

[2] 'Responsiones de Quolibetis,
Sorbonica, ordinaria et aula.'
Chartul. ii, App., p. 701. At Caen
the 'ordinaria' took place 'sub
magistro incipiente de novo' (Stat.
of Caen, *Bull. de la Soc. des Ant. de
Normandie*, xii. 504), the 'aulica'
with an inceptor performing the
'aulica' for his own degree. [The
very detailed statutes edited in
the *Chartul*. (pp. 692, 700–2) imply
more activity on the part of the
bachalarius formatus than Rashdall
suggests. The statutes given on

p. 692 are certainly based on thirteenth-century practice: 'bachalarii
in theologia tenentur respondere de
questione in locis publicis aliis
bachalariis quinquies ad minus,
antequam licencientur', i.e. at an
aulatio, in a *vesperies*, at a formal
disputation at the Sorbonne during
vacation, at a *quodlibet* and once
in disputationibus generalibus. For
a more detailed analysis see Little
and Pelster, *op. cit.*, pp. 33, 34 and
note. Instead of the two years of
profectio or *perfectio* at Bologna
we find six, and later five years
at Paris (*Chartul*. ii, No. 822
(1323) and p. 700), but the latter
included the time spent in teaching on the Sentences and the
process of obtaining the licence.
See the editorial note, no. 38, on
p. 704.]

baccalareus formatus was also liable to be called upon to preach a university sermon, or to give what was called a conference (*collatio*) in the afternoon when a master had preached in the morning.[1] Medieval university sermons were not wont to err on the side of brevity. A statute of Ingolstadt, *de quantitate Sermonum*, provides that 'with a view to avoid prolixity' these discourses should be limited to an hour and a quarter;[2] at Vienna the preacher might go on for an hour and a half, or at most two hours.[3]

One of the disputations in which the bachelor was required, at any rate in the fifteenth century, to take part in this last stage of his career is too curious and characteristic an illustration of medieval ideas of scholastic prowess to be passed over. The favourite phrase *militare in scholis* was something more than a figure of speech in those days. A certain amount of animal combativeness and physical endurance was almost as necessary in the 'warfare of the schools' as in a tilt or a tournament. At this disputation, known as the *Sorbonic*, from its taking place in the hall of the Sorbonne, the respondent was required to reply standing, alone, and without the assistance of any moderator or judge except an audience which occasionally signified its approbation or disapprobation by stamping or clapping, to a succession of opponents who relieved each other at intervals from six in the morning till six in the

---

[1] [At Bologna the 'bachalarius formatus' was required 'unum pro forma sue perfectionis sermonem in universitate facere solempniter in ecclesia sancti Petri in primo anno duorum et unum in secundo' (Ehrle, p. 19).] In early times it would appear that no degree of orders was required even for D.D. (Bulaeus, iii. 601, 602). But when preaching became an essential exercise for the degree, the B.D. must have been at least in sub-deacon's orders. The German university statutes generally prescribe the order required at each stage in the theologian's career, but their exact provisions vary. At

Vienna (in 1389) the B.D.s must be 'acolyti et infra annum aut biennium subdiaconi' (Kink, ii, 104–5). The same statute informs us that graduates at Paris must be legitimate 'et non turpiter corpore viciati' (cf. *Chartul.* ii, App., p. 706). At Cologne the theologian must be an acolyte before B.D., and sub-deacon before licence (Bianco, i, *Anl.*, p. 37). Hemeraeus tells us that at Paris the dean was required to demand of candidates for the licence, 'si sint omnes in sacris ordinibus' (i.e. at least sub-deacons). MS. *Sorbonae Origines*, f. 298.

[2] Prantl, ii. 58.

[3] Kollar, i, c. 134.

CHAP. V, evening, an hour's relaxation only being allowed for refresh-
§ 4.   ment in the middle of the day.[1]

The   In the theological faculty licences were only conferred on
jubilee. or about All Saints' Day in every alternate year, which was
called the Jubilee. In the case of the superior faculties, all
the doctors had a right to be present and take part in the
examination, and, after the candidate had withdrawn, to
advise the chancellor as to granting or withholding the licence.
In the faculty of canon law, and still more in that of medicine,
the share of the chancellor in the examination must from the
first have been little more than formal and ceremonial; in
conferring the licence upon the lawyers and physicians, a
theologian would be obliged to accept the 'depositions' of the
doctors and confer or refuse the licence in accordance with
their advice. Under these circumstances it is probable enough
that the faculties from the first practically decided upon the
fate of the candidate in private, so that the examination in
the bishop's hall had become a mere formality by 1385; when,
roused by an attempt of the then chancellor to assert his independence of the doctors, all three superior faculties resolved
to hold previous meetings for the discussion of the merits of
candidates, and to present their recommendations in writing
to the chancellor.[2] In the faculty of theology we know that
these meetings included the non-regent members and that
a list of candidates was drawn up, about whom the chancellor
was to make private inquiries of the individual doctors.[3] But
neither before the chancellor nor before the faculty was there

---

[1] Ramus, *Scholae in Lib. Artes*, c. 1127; Crevier, ii. 242 *sq.*; Bulaeus, iv. 172. The institution in this form is probably much later than these writers represent [although solemn university disputations in the hall of the Sorbonne probably began in the early fourteenth century; see below, p. 510 n.]

[2] 'Magistri dictarum facultatum ante apercionem tentaminis et examinis domini cancellarii ecclesie Parysiens. seu vocacionem et de-posicionem magistrorum ad par-tem, deliberent inter se et ordinent de bachallariis et sufficiencia eorun-dem et de ordine licencie seu loco-rum.' Bulaeus, iv. 601. [*Chartul.* iii, No. 1504, Jan. 1385. For the accusations against the chancellor see above, pp. 400–1.]

[3] *Chartul.* ii, App., p. 683. Dur-ing this meeting the candidate stood at the door and bowed to the doctors as they entered. [The *de-positio* or testimony of the masters was prescribed by Gregory IX in 1231, and by Alexander IV in 1255; *Chartul.* i, Nos. 79, 247.]

any literary examination: the only questions were whether he had duly performed all the residence, exercises, and acts required by the statutes, and whether the reputation he had acquired during this university course for ability, character, and orthodoxy was such as to entitle him to the licence. In practice we may assume that at this stage the inquiry would as a rule limit itself to the question of residence and exercises. But it must be remembered that there was an examination for the first bachelor's degree (of *cursor* or *biblicus*),[1] and that the disputations or at least the more important of them, such as the *Tentative*, were in themselves examinations. The candidate who wished to proceed to lecture on the Sentences was not considered to have performed the *Tentative* unless he was pronounced by a majority of the *baccalarei formati* present to have acquitted himself satisfactorily.[2] However serious the consideration of candidates for the licence may have been earlier, by 1426 failure to 'satisfy the examiners' had become so unheard-of an event that a bachelor whom the doctors had refused to present for his licence petitioned the King in council, and boldly claimed the degree as the right of any candidate who had complied with the proper forms. In their answer the doctors maintain their right to exercise a discretion,[3] but it is not alleged that any one had actually within the memory of man been rejected for mere incapacity. In this exceptional case, the failure to 'satisfy

Action by a rejected candidate.

---

[1] 'Cum aliquis volens admitti ad legendum cursum suum primum, aut Bibliam, comparuerit in facultate, dabuntur quatuor magistri, a quibus examinabitur in generalibus theologie, et fiet per eos in facultate relatio.' *Chartul.* ii, App., p. 703. It seems probable that there was also an examination for *sententiarius*.

[2] *Chartul.* ii, App., p. 703; above, p. 476.

[3] Bulaeus, v. 377–81: 'Et ledit serment (i.e. of obedience to the faculty and its statutes) fait, ont ensemble deliberation et le examinent se bon leur semble'; after which

they allow or refuse to allow him to present himself before the chancellor. The plaintiff had alleged that when a candidate had kept his terms and performed the required sermons and exercises, 'On ne lui pouvoit ou devoit refuser ou denier ladite license et Maistrise, ainçois devoit estre presenté', &c. [These proceedings are reported as taking place at Paris before King Charles of France, but in 1426, as the editors of the *Chartularium* point out (iv, No. 2278 note), the council sat in the name of Henry VI of England.]

the examiners' was attributed by the candidate to *odium theologicum.*[1]

Value of theological degree. It is clear from the mere fact of such an action being brought—it is hardly necessary to add that it was unsuccessful—that an enormous decline had taken place in the standard of qualification necessary to the attainment of the theological doctorate. The only wonder is that the theological faculty of Paris should have retained the prestige which it actually enjoyed in the fifteenth century. We may suppose, perhaps, that though a candidate was never sent back when he was approaching the topmost rungs on the long ladder of promotion, though actual failure at an earlier stage may have been almost equally rare, a process of natural selection was neverthlesss brought into play. The examinations were really held, though no one was refused his *testamur*; the lectures had really to be attended or delivered; the disputations had really to be gone through, and that with great publicity, against opponents and in the presence of an audience who would be by no means delicate in their treatment of an embarrassed or hesitating disputant. This trial by ordeal may have been a rough and barbaric mode of testing intellectual capacity, but it was probably sufficient to shut the door of

[1] [At this point we come to a striking contrast between the surviving statutes of Paris and the Bologna statutes. The references to the *examen* for the licence at Paris are vague, and it is explicitly stated (*c.* 1343) that a bachelor who had performed all the statutory conditions of residence should only be rejected *propter mores* (*Chartul.* ii, p. 683). At Bologna, on the other hand, the statutes of 1364 laid stress on the rigour of the *examen* and describe it clearly. A master who felt doubtful about the merits of his bachelor was expected to delay his submission to the 'arduum examinis certamen'. The chancellor made searching and private inquiry regarding the career and conversation of the *bachalarii formati* before they sought the licence. Finally, before the masters gave their opinion on oath about the bachelor's sufficiency, he was subjected to examination before the chancellor and masters *in conclavi*. Three days before the dean of the faculty gave him two *distinctiones* or *puncta* from the Sentences with two highly debatable *questiones*. The day before the examination the bachelor circulated written conclusions to each master. On the day itself the dean and masters in turn argued 'contra positionem ad primam questionem per quattuor vel tres rationes, *ipsi examinando bachalario penitus inprecognitas*'; and impugned his replies in a formal manner; then they proceeded in a similar way to the second *questio* (Ehrle, pp. 31–2, 34–5).]

the faculty to hopeless incapacity or gross ignorance, except CHAP.V, in the case of very aristocratic or wealthy candidates. The §4. hired thesis which served till recently [1895] to make a D.D. in modern Oxford (though the institution was probably not altogether unknown at Paris) would hardly have been by itself sufficient to bring the highest degree which a university can bestow within the reach of the meanest capacity. Still, when all allowances have been made for the possibility of an indefensible system 'working well', the low standard of the degrees must be reckoned as one of the causes which contributed to the utter extinction of real intellectual life in the universities of the fifteenth century.[1] When a degree which was within the reach of every average man made its recipient a professor, the teaching of the university must have sunk to a lower depth of inefficiency than at Oxford in the days when every 'close' or 'founder's kin' fellow was qualified for a college tutorship. It is, however, worth noticing that even in the days of Louis XI the university had the spirit to refuse a D.D. which the King requested for a courtier of the King of Castile, nor did it ever carry the prostitution of academical grades so far as to confer a doctorate upon the sons of kings and princes for the mere accident of birth.

The ceremony of the licence itself has been sufficiently described in connexion with the faculty of arts, though graduation in the superior faculties was naturally attended with ampler pomp and circumstance.[2] On the day before this *The para-nymphus.*

---

[1] [In an additional note Rashdall (1st edition, i. 562) pointed out, with some exaggeration, that at Nantes, in 1461, 'the Vespers have become a comic entertainment': 'et teneat omnino ne aliquid turpe vel quod in infamiam possit vergere de ipso vesperisando dicat, sed pro risu modico et alleviatione audientium dicere possint aliqua de eo prosa levia et sine scandalo cuiuscumque risu digna' (Fournier, iii, No. 1595). This points to a dangerous tendency, but does not justify the conclusion that the disputation, for which see below, had become a farce.]

[2] The formula ran: 'Auctoritate Dei omnipotentis et apostolorum Petri et Pauli et sedis apostolice do vobis licenciam disputandi, legendi, et predicandi et omnes actus exercendi in theologica facultate qui ad magistrum pertinent. In nomine Patris et Filii et Spiritus Sancti.' After the ceremony, 'licentiati simul vadunt per domos omnium magistrorum ad regraciandum eis, et si aliquos non invenerint non est cura'. *Chartul.* ii, App., p. 683.

CHAP. V, function, a solemn assembly of the university was held, at
§ 4.   which the rector received the *paranymphus*,[1] a messenger of
the chancellor, who appeared in a gorgeous scarlet robe and
velvet cap, to invite the attendance of the *licentiandi* who had
passed the examination. The title recalls the idea that by
graduation a student was wedded to science. The *paranymphus* made an oration in praise of science, and then presented
the 'signeta' containing the names of the candidates whom
the chancellor was to license. The occasion, *more medii aevi*,
was further improved by a reception at the candidate's house,
at which cake and wine were kept going all day for the friends
who called to offer their congratulations, and the messenger
of the chancellor returned with divers 'spontaneous' fees for
his master, himself, and the rest of the chancellor's 'familia'.
Later on the candidates went round in person to invite the
attendance of the lords of Parlement and the canons of Paris
at the graduation ceremonial.[2]

The   The final stage of the theologian's career—his admission
aulatio. to the mastership—differed (as we have before noticed) in an
important particular from that of the masters of the other
faculties.[3] The ceremony of *birettatio*, in the case of the

[1] The bridegroom's messenger
or attendant at a wedding.

[2] The details are from Goulet,
f. xv *b* [E.T. pp. 86–91]; *Chartul.*
ii. App., p. 683. This elaborate
ceremonial only applied to the
superior faculties; [although the
artists also gave presents *pro audicione camere*. The procedure in its
earlier and simpler form, where
the chancellor's *nuntii* anticipate
the *paranymphus*, is described by
John Blanchart, the chancellor, in
his defence against the university
(1385). *Chartul.* iii, No. 1520, pp.
404, 405.]

[3] [The clearest account of the
exercises and ceremonies, *vesperiae*
and *aulatio*, in which the licentiate
in theology incepted as master, also
of the *resumptio*, or first exercise as
aulatus magister, is given in the
statutes of Bologna, pp. 40–6; cf.

Ehrle's introduction and notes, pp.
cxciv–cxcvii. Pelster has shown that
the description of the *aulatio* there
given corresponds in detail with the
reportatio of an actual *disputatio in
aula* at Paris in 1304–5 (see the
article, already cited, in the *Franziskanische Studien*, x (1923), 11–15).
The connexion between Paris and
Bologna is emphasized by the
definition, 'Aula sic vocatur quia
actus eius fiunt Parisius in aula
domini episcopi, Bononie vero in
ecclesia sancti Petri et utrobique in
mediis terciis' (p. 42). The *aula* or
aulatio was a continuation of the
vesperiae, for of four *questiones*
selected by the new master, two
were debated in the *vesperiae*, the
other two in the *aula*; in the first
academic acts of the master, the
second question was resumed, and
the third question (i.e. the first dis-

other faculties, took place in one of the schools and was performed by one of the regents; the chancellor took no part in the ceremony of incorporating the duly licensed master into the society of his fellow masters. In the faculty of theology the ceremony took place, like the licence, in the bishop's hall, and the chancellor himself, with the words *Incipiatis in nomine Patris, Filii et Spiritus Sancti, Amen*, placed the *birettum doctorale* on the head of the licentiate, who thereupon mounted his *cathedra* and, after an introductory 'harangue' in praise of Holy Scripture in general, maintained two theses of which due notice had previously been given to the members of the faculty.[1] A disputation or discussion followed, in which different parts were assigned, in accordance with a rather elaborate ritual, to the chancellor, the presiding master,

puted at the *aula*) was resumed and determined. Pelster has carefully analysed the elaborate procedure of the *vesperies* and the *aulatio* in Little and Pelster, *op. cit.*, pp. 45–7. The *resumptio*, in which the new master finished the *principium* or commendation of scripture begun at the *aula*, and returned to the questions, must be distinguished from the *resumptio* by a master who had given up his functions and wished to resume them where he had been regent or elsewhere. This also was a solemn affair, and, as between Paris and Oxford or Oxford and Cambridge, raises the thorny issue of the right to teach *ubique* without a new examination; *op. cit.*, pp. 52, 53.

At Bologna the *birettum* was imposed at the *aula* by the 'magister aulator, sub quo vesperiatus est'. He sat on the left of the new master, while the chancellor sat on his right. At this period, in Paris, Oxford, and Bologna, all the ceremonies were minutely ordered and solemn. At Oxford the *vesperiae* seem to have been regarded as *solempniores*. See Pelster on the Dominican Richard Knapwell or Clapwell, in *Zeitschrift für kath.*

Theologie, lii (1928), 480; and for both *vesperiae* and inception in theology at Oxford, A. G. Little, in *Archivum Franciscanum Historicum*, xix (1926), 27–30.]

[1] Kollar, i, c. 158. The following account of the *aulatio* is given in the statutes of Heidelberg, which may be taken as a faithful reflection of the Parisian custom: after the oaths and *birettatio*, 'novus magister faciat recommendacionem sacre scripture, qua finita aliquis magister in artibus (i.e. a student of theology) vel alius ad hoc idoneus surgens proponat questionem cum argumentis disputandam per novum magistrum ad quam unus de senioribus baccalariis respondeat cui et magister novus arguat et post eum magister qui biretum imposuit'. Afterwards other *questiones* were propounded by other masters. Hautz, *Gesch. d. Univ. Heid.* ii. 338. The *birettatio* does not seem to have been performed by the chancellor as at Paris. At Cologne it is performed by 'Cancellarius, vel ex commissione Cancellarii magister sub quo vesperiatus incipit'. Bianco, *Die alte Univ. Köln*, ii, Anl. p. 47.

the other masters present, and a bachelor whose performance on this occasion was one of the exercises for his own degree. The chancellor's interference in the *birettatio* of the new theological master is a curious relic of his ancient position as himself the principal, originally no doubt the only, authorized master of theology in the cathedral school.

Vesperiae and resumptio. The ceremony which has just been described was known as the *aulatio* of the new master, the actual disputation being known as the *aulica*. It was preceded, on the eve of the inception, by an equally elaborate and ceremonious disputation known as his *vesperiae*,[1] and followed at the beginning of the ensuing academical year, when he took possession of his regency, by a disputation called the *resumptio*. These public discourses before the assembled faculty naturally presented great opportunities for the display of ingenuity and subtlety. Nothing is more difficult than to combine originality with unimpeachable orthodoxy, and it is not surprising that the young theologian, ambitious of distinguishing himself at these imposing functions (especially the member of a mendicant order with its pet doctrines or cherished innovations), not unfrequently overshot the mark, and had humbly to recant his daring 'positions' before the faculty would allow him to proceed to any further step in his career.[2]

[1] The following description of vespers is found in the theological statutes of Heidelberg: 'Vesperie fiant post prandium hoc modo: Magister tenens vesperias disputet unam questionem ad quam respondebit unus de Baccalariis cui presidens arguat et breviter post hoc arguant omnes Baccalarii per ordinem et post argumenta Baccalariorum proposita soli seniori respondeatur. Item post hoc unus de magistris senioribus proponat questionem cum expositione terminorum et argumentis pro utraque parte, qua per vesperiandum determinata Magister proponens questionem arguat contra dicta aliqua et postea sequens magister contra alia, contra que per precedentem non est argutum: hoc facto fiat recommendacio vesperiandi per magistrum vesperias tenentem.' Hautz, *Gesch. d. Univ. Heid.* ii. 338. At Ingolstadt in 1475 (Prantl, ii. 70) the earlier part of the ritual is much the same, but the latter part is more elaborate. From the MS. Matrilogium at Caen, written in 1515 (f. 24 *a*), it appears that this disputation had already become an elaborate burlesque: 'Presidens tentando patientiam doctorizandi sibi multa vel puerilia facta dicta gesta ridiculosa dicit et in medium propalat quibus assistentes in risum prouocat.'

[2] [See the forms and rules of the *protestatio publica* and the *revocatio* at Bologna, Ehrle, pp. 46–52.]

We have already alluded to the method of taxation adopted by the university—the demand (when occasion required) of so many *bursae* from each master, bachelor, or student. The same method was adopted in fixing the fees payable to the respective faculties, on taking the bachelor's degree, on ad- mission to the licence, and at inception. These fees consti- tuted the most important part of the ordinary revenue of the university or its constituent bodies. A large part of them was, however, especially in the case of the superior faculties paid to the individual doctors who took part in the graduation- ceremonies. In the colleges it is clear that there could not be an indefinite variety in the scales of living which were open to the paying boarders who lived with the foundationers. These 'pensioners' or 'commoners' were eventually divided into two classes—'commensales magnae portionis' and 'commensales parvae portionis', corresponding roughly to the fellow commoners and pensioners of Cambridge and the gentlemen commoners and 'commoners' of most Oxford colleges.[1] In the fifteenth century this classification was adopted by the university: the 'bursa' of the former was esti- mated at eight *solidi Parisienses*, that of the latter at six. Besides these were three classes of very poor scholars, the martinets, the camerists, and the servitors, who paid only four. Noblemen and ecclesiastical dignitaries remained out- side this classification and were specially taxed according to their means.[2] No complete table of fees and other expenses of a degree at Paris is before us; it is obvious that a consider- able part of the expense, which consisted in the inception banquet, could not be precisely regulated. In the superior faculties there were also presents of robes to all the doctors and of caps to other dignitaries present. Ramus estimates the

[1] Bulaeus, v. 748, 825. Nothing is said here of the servitors (no doubt including college *beneficiarii*), who are, however, usually associ- ated with the *martinetae, came- ristae,* or *cameristae pauperes*. The *cameristae* exactly answer to the Oxford batteler (see below, chap. xiv). [For the *bursa*, and the formal oath of poverty required before dispensation by the English nation (1369), see Boyce, pp. 90–4, 164–7 (based on the Proctors' Book pub- lished in the *Auctarium*). The statutes of the theological faculty at Bologna contain lists of fees (Ehrle, pp. 52–62).]

[2] Péries, p. 34.

CHAP. V, expense of a master's degree at Paris in 1562 as 56 *livres* 13 *sols*
§ 4.   in arts (together with a mysterious 60 *livres* for 'locus nomina-
tionis in licentiatu'), 881 *livres* 5 *sols* in medicine, 1,002 *livres*
in theology. It must be remembered that this estimate includes only the cost of the licence and inception, and not
the smaller fees paid at earlier stages; but it is not clear for
what class of students the expenses are thus calculated.[1] At
Oxford we find the prior of a religious college paying £10 as
a commutation for the inception banquet.[2] The prior's position and the honour of his house must have demanded more
than a minimum scale of expenditure; but still the amount
can hardly have exceeded what would have been expected in
an ecclesiastic of good position. The entertainments given
by great noblemen on such occasions were on the scale of the
festivities which would take place on the coming of age of the
heir to a great title. George Neville, of Balliol, brother of
the Earl of Warwick, took his M.A. in 1452, when 'on the first
day there were 600 messes of meat, and on the second 300
for the entertainment only of scholars and certain of the pro-
ceeder's relations and acquaintances', in addition to 'provisions for the poor and other ordinary sort of people of the
University'. Any one who reads the varied menu given in full
by Savage and Wood will not be surprised to read that the
popularity of the young nobleman was such that he was 'the
next year Chancellor of the University, and three years after
that, though still only twenty-three years of age, Bishop of
Exeter'.[3] The Council of Vienne in 1311 had limited the
expenses of inceptors to 3,000 *livres tournoises* and required
every licentiate to take an oath that he would not exceed that
limit; but on such occasions as the above the University of
Oxford was gracious enough to dispense with the provisions
of the Pope and general council in a way which says much

---

[1] *Proaem. reform. Par. Acad.*
(*Scholae in lib. Artes*, c. 1110 *sq.*).
[2] H. E. Salter, *Registrum Cancellarii* (O.H.S. 1932), i. 146. Cf.
Bulaeus, v. 864.
[3] Savage, *Balliofergus*, p. 105;
Wood, *Hist. and Antiquities of the*

Univ. of Oxford, ed. Gutch, i.
598–9. Cf. Hearne's note in *Wal-
teri Hemingford* (i.e. Hemingburgh)
Hist., Oxford, 1731, ii. 515. He
was not consecrated till the age
of 27.

for the spiritual independence of the Anglican Church in the CHAP. V,
fifteenth century.[1]   § 4.

Vacations.
The length of the vacations gradually increased during the medieval period. In 1231 Gregory IX ordained that the summer vacation should not exceed one month,[2] but papal thunders failed to check the rapid elongation of the 'great vacation'. We find from a calendar belonging to the end of the fourteenth century that the long vacation then began at tierce on the vigil of S. Peter and S. Paul (28 June) and lasted in the faculty of arts to the morrow of S. Louis (25 Aug.) or to the morrow of the Exaltation of the Holy Cross (15 Sept.) in the case of theology and canon law. But it appears that this beginning of term was of a more or less formal character: it was at this time that ordinary lectures *might* be recommenced. We always find the feast of S. Remigius (1 Oct.) treated as the real inauguration of the winter term,[3] when the courses of the year were usually begun. The period from 1 October till Easter was styled the 'grand ordinary', the period from Easter till the end of June constituting the 'little ordinary'. Only a few days' holiday is officially recognized at Christmas and Easter, and even in the long vacation cursory lectures might be delivered except upon certain festivals. Numerous festivals in term-time were observed by a total suspension of lectures, or by a suspension of ordinary lectures only.[4]

[1] 'Non teneatur . . . ad stratitudinem statuti de tribus millibus turonensium grossorum.' Oxford Archives, Aa. f. 66 *a*.

[2] Bulaeus, iii. 141; *Chartul.* i, No. 79, and the Calendar, *ibid.* ii, App., p. 709.

[3] Crevier, ii. 141. At Heidelberg the period from 25 Aug. to 9 Oct. is styled a 'Parvus Ordinarius in Cappis Nigris'. Toepke, *Matrikel d. Un. Heid.* i. 629 *sq.*; and by the statute of 1245 at Paris, 'a festo . . . B. Johannis Baptiste usque ad festum B. Remigii quilibet suas lectiones ordinet, prout melius sibi et auditoribus suis viderit expedire'. Bulaeus, iii. 280; *Chartul.* i, No. 246. M. Thurot

(p. 66) is thus wrong in confining ordinary lectures to the 'grand ordinary'. At Oxford the terms corresponded roughly with the existing statute terms, except that there was a vacation of eleven days at Whitsuntide. See Calendar in *Statuta Antiqua*, pp. 1–14, and the editor's introduction, pp. lxxx–lxxxii. A student of Nantes gives us the *rationale* of the long vacation: 'cum opportunitas temporis in omnibus sit querenda, et post collationem messium ceterorumque victualium sit ad studium exercendum tempus congruum' (Fournier, iii. 1595).

[4] [The statutes of the faculty of theology at Bologna (pp. 23–30)

Additional Note

[Since the first edition of this book was published much has been written bearing upon the studies of Paris. We have done our best to incorporate in the text and notes the more important evidence which can be gathered from the last two volumes of the *Chartularium*, from the *Auctarium*, and from the statutes of the theological faculty at Bologna. This does not materially modify Rashdall's narrative. More should be said, however, about the bearing of the extensive literature which is now available upon such matters as the disputations, the activity of the masters in arts and theology, the texts which bachelors and masters had at their disposal, and the significance of the incessant debate which went on in medieval universities, and especially at Paris. Rashdall, partly because he was obliged to depend largely on late evidence, took an unduly sceptical view of the value of a university education and of the influence of the masters during the thirteenth and fourteenth centuries.

As the almost innumerable manuscripts of the early scholastics, from the second half of the twelfth century onwards, are examined, and the more famous thinkers—Albert the Great, S. Thomas, Duns Scotus, William of Ockham—are fitted into their academic environment, the vivacious energy of life in the University of Paris is gradually revealed. Medieval thought was directed by conditions in the schools and in the *studia* of the mendicants. The formal *lectio* tended to become a series of *questiones* raised by the master or his hearers, and solved as he proceeded. The *questiones* of Stephen Langton (before 1206) were lectures of this kind. As studies came to comprise the writings of Aristotle and other text-books, the range and complexity of these *questiones* increased. The lectures or their *reportationes*, for which the *clericus* or, later, the bachelor of the master may have been especially responsible, were copied and distributed. In due course official *exemplaria* were prepared for the use of the stationers and those to whom they lent them (above, p. 422). The surviving texts of the numerous *questiones* on the books of Aristotle originated in this way. The variety of other texts used by the masters for purposes of comment and comparison was considerable. The list of text-books compiled about 1200 (Haskins, *Mediaeval Science*, pp. 372–6), ascribed to Alexander Neckam, becomes insignificant if it is set beside the ideal library or *Biblionomia* of Richard of Fournival (Delisle, *Cabinet des manuscrits*, ii. 148 *sqq.*) —which Birkenmayer, *Bibljoteka Ryzarda de Fournival* (Cracow, 1922), considers to be in fact a description of the library of the well-known secular theologian, Gerard of Abbeville, who died in 1271— and the great catalogue of the Sorbonne Library (*ibid*. iii. 9–114,

give a very clear idea of the 'legible' and 'disputable' days, the days on which the *bachalarius formatus* might give his statutory sermon, and the like; also of the exercises permissible in vacation and on non-legible days.]

begun in 1321). The college libraries of Paris, Oxford, and Cambridge were lending libraries. Out of 1,722 books, ranging over the subjects of the faculties, in the Sorbonne Library, only 330 were kept apart in the library proper; the others were distributed in accordance with a system of *electiones* afterwards adopted by the colleges in the English universities (Delisle, ii. 178 *sq.*; Powicke, *The Medieval Books of Merton College*, pp. 9–18, 60–82). Although private libraries were not common, and were usually small, is it clear that many students owned books, both the prescribed texts and others. For example, the manuscript which contains the only known copy of the statutes made by the English nation at Paris in 1252 was owned by a student belonging to the nation, and comprises, in addition to earlier texts of Cicero and Gregory the Great, Euclid with a commentary, astronomical tables and other scientific matter (C.C.C. Oxford, MS. 283). Again, the Amplonian library at Erfurt contains many books originally possessed by scholars at Paris. The students, before they could determine in arts or qualify as *cursores* in theology, had to frequent the lecture-rooms (*scholae*) and to listen to the disputations of bachelors and masters; the latter, whatever value may attach to their discussions, had to hold their own among keen-witted colleagues to whom, during a long period of study and debate, the learning of the age was familiar. The bachelor's arduous determination in arts was a long process; the *sententiarius*, in his nine-months' course of lectures on the Sentences, was expected to cope with problems which he had heard discussed by men whose treatises still hold a place in the history of thought; and the 'formed' bachelor of theology displayed his powers in the schools of the masters, and doubtless continued his studies, during a period of three or four years. In both arts and theology the masters were the leaders. Rashdall's acceptance of the view that the masters in theology left the theological teaching to bachelors is due partly to his generalization from later evidence, partly to over-emphasis on the duties of the *sententiarius* or bachelor. There is no certain evidence that the masters ceased to concern themselves with the Sentences, although, as Rashdall observed (1st edition, i. 562), it would appear from a document of 1386 (*Chartul.* iii, No. 1528) that the lectures of the doctors in theology were always on the Bible. Some issued their lectures as bachelors in a revised and mature form. In any case even the senior masters took their part in the theological training of students. Before the secular could be admitted to lecture as a bachelor, according to the statutes of Bologna, 'in theologia audiverit studiose ad minus per quinquennium sub uno vel diversis magistris in theologia' (p. 17; cf. Ehrle, pp. clxxxviii–cxc). Only a master could 'determine', that is, give a formal conclusion in a disputation. The 'determination' of a bachelor in arts was a discipline guided by rules of its own (above, p. 451, note).

The text-books, e.g. the *Summulae Logicae* of Petrus Hispanus (Pope John XXI), on which the Englishmen Robert Kilwardby and Simon of Faversham wrote commentaries, reflected and extended contemporary movements of thought. They helped to define tendencies in scholastic method, just as, in a more important way, Abelard and Petrus Lombardus had given a direction to earlier method. Dialectic according to rules might spend itself in sophistical or unprofitable forms of logic, like the Oxford dialectic of the fourteenth century, which was to influence Italian thought until the seventeenth century, or it might lead to scientific speculation of the greatest importance. John Buridan of Béthune, the chief influence at Paris in the fourteenth century, based his *compendium* of logic upon the work of Petrus Hispanus, and in his commentaries upon Aristotle developed a theory of 'impetus' which, according to Duhem and other modern scholars, makes him and his school the real founders of modern physics and astronomy (P. Duhem, *Études sur Léonard de Vinci*, vol. iii; the same, *Le Système du monde*, iv. 124 *sq.*; Ueberweg-Geyer, pp. 596 *sq.*, 783 *sq.*; cf. Michalski's papers in the *Bulletin international de l'académie polonaise des sciences et des lettres: classe de philologie*, &c., 1919-20, pt. i (Cracow, 1922) 59-88, and 1926: 'Le criticisme et le scepticisme dans la philosophie du xive siècle', offprint; also Powicke, *op. cit.*, p. 27 note. For the development of disputation in the thirteenth century see especially Mandonnet, *Siger de Brabant*, and the later work on Siger by Grabmann and others, noted in Ueberweg-Geyer, pp. 757-8.) The ruling principle in the study of science was laid down by S. Thomas in his commentary on the *De caelo* (book i, lect. 22): 'The end of philosophy is not to know what men have thought, but what is the truth of things.' This principle, involving personal observation and experience, had fruitful results in the minds of the wiser men. The scepticism to which it gave rise often ran wildly into aridity or perversity in the minds of lesser men. But in either case it set free vigour and energy in the lectures and disputations in the schools of Paris. Similarly, even in the study of grammar, some text-book writers were more enlightened and humane than others. Paetow has entered a protest against the confusion in a common condemnation of the *Doctrinale* and *Grecismus* with the work of the famous grammarian and classicist, John Garland, who died in Paris *c.* 1272 (*Morale Scolarium of John of Garland*, Berkeley, California, 1927, especially pp. 98-106). But John Garland was involved in the fight for the classics against prevalent Parisian studies, a matter with which we are not here concerned.

Rashdall made no detailed study of the disputations, which had more influence even than the lectures in 'forming' the bachelors and giving influence to the masters. The nature and rules of these exercises, and their place in the academic work of Paris, had been defined by the end of the thirteenth century. Modern scholars have paid more attention to the disputations in the faculty of theology, in which the developments from the lectures on the Bible in the twelfth century can be traced, but the tendency can also be seen in philosophical teaching from the middle of the twelfth century. The dialogue form, perceptible in some of the works of the early masters, gave way on the one hand to a lecture which, though still studded with questions, was primarily an exposition, and on the other hand to the formal *questiones disputatae* and *quodlibetae*. The lectures gave rise to the commentaries, short tracts, and elaborate treatises or *summae*, the disputations to collections of *questiones* (cf. Ueberweg-Geyer, pp. 354–6). A well-known passage in John of Salisbury's *Metalogicon*, referring to the teaching of Alberic (of Reims?) and Robert of Melun on the Mont Ste Geneviève (1137–9) is a good starting-point:

> Sic ferme toto biennio conuersatus in monte, artis huius preceptoribus usus sum Alberico et magistro Rodberto Meludensi (ut cognomine designetur quod meruit in scolarum regimine, natione siquidem Angligena est); quorum alter, ad omnia scrupulosus, locum questionis inueniebat ubique . . . alter, autem, in responsione promptissimus, subterfugii causa propositum numquam declinauit articulum, quin alteram contradictionis partem eligeret aut determinata multiplicitate sermonis doceret unam non esse responsionem. Ille ergo in questionibus subtilis et multus; iste in responsis perspicax, breuis et commodus. Que duo si pariter eis alicui omnium contigissent, parem utique disputatorem nostra etate non esset inuenire. (*Metalogicon*, ii. 10, edit. C. C. J. Webb, pp. 78, 79.)

Beside this may be set a passage from a sermon found by Landgraf in an early fourteenth-century collection (Bruges MS. 129):

> [Christus] tenuit disputationem suam, quemadmodum faciunt magistri in theologia Parisius in tempore Quadragesime. Circa tertiam vel sextam ascendunt magistri cathedram suam ad disputandum et querunt unam questionem. Cui questioni respondet unus assistentium. Post cuius responsionem magister determinat questionem et quando vult ei deferre et honorem facere, nichil aliud determinat quam quod dixerat respondens. (Landgraf, in *Zeitschrift für kath. Theologie*, liii (1929), quoted by Pelster in *Scholastik*, v (1930), 61.)

Here we have the *questio* in its simplest form, after the appearance of the *respondens*, who in the early thirteenth century cannot be distinguished from the master himself. Originally the master raised or invited questions; later his *determinatio* followed a formal *responsio* by a student or bachelor, and the *questio disputata* took place on definite occasions in the academic year or on disputable days, on feast days and in vacation. As Pelster has shown (*op. cit.*, pp. (59–67), more than one question might be propounded during

CHAP. V, one session, provided that it related to the same matter, and, except
§ 4.   on very solemn and formal occasions, such as the *aulatio*, the determination generally followed on the same day in the same session.
On these more solemn occasions more disputants took part, according to rules. (Cf. the same writer in *Zeitschrift für kath. Theologie*,
xlvi (1922), 361 *sq.*) During their course students attended the
ordinary *questiones disputatae* as well as the more solemn and
formal exercises. The records survive in very numerous manuscripts of the *questiones disputatae* of the masters whose work is
gradually being brought to light.

As has been seen, questions might be asked by the taught as well
as by the teacher, although in the ordinary disputation this appears
to have become unusual or to have ceased. Hence some writers,
reverting to Grabmann (*Geschichte der scholastischen Methode*, ii.
328), have refused to follow Mandonnet in his effort to show that
the *quodlibet*, the other chief form of disputation, owes its origin to
S. Thomas Aquinas (*Revue des sciences philosophiques et théologiques*, xv (1926), 477–506; xvi (1927), 5–38). Pelster (*Scholastik*,
v. 63–7) has found early allusions to *questiones* 'de quolibet', or
whatever-you-please, which in his opinion strengthen the case
for a gradual development of the *quodlibet*, alongside the *questio
disputata*, from the twelfth-century lecture-room. However this
may be, the *quodlibet* in S. Thomas's time at Paris was a recognized
form of disputation, held in the second week of Advent and from
the fourth week in Lent to Palm Sunday (see the important work of
P. Glorieux, *La Littérature quodlibétique de 1260 à 1320*, Kain,
1925; and the criticisms noted in Ueberweg-Geyer, p. 690). It
differed from the *questio disputata* in its freedom and in the variety
of the *socii* or disputants, who comprised masters, bachelors, and
distinguished visitors. It was a *disputatio generalis* or *communis* at
which any question might be propounded. The presiding master
determined at another session. Naturally enough, the reports of the
quodlibets are especially valuable as evidence of the matters, including social and ecclesiastical problems, which were 'in the air',
and of the various views taken about them.

Lastly, something should be said about the relation between the
questio, and especially the theological *questio*, and the study of the
Bible in the schools. In spite of the strictures of Roger Bacon, who
rightly attacked the neglect of textual criticism in the best sense of
the term, and deplored the preference of teachers in the schools for
theological subtleties which had no solid basis in scriptural knowledge (*Fr. Rogeri Baconis Opera quaedam hactenus inedita*, edit. J. S.
Brewer, 1859 (Rolls Series), pp. 329, 330), modern scholarship
does not justify the view that the Bible was not 'the basis of the
teaching of the masters of theology' (Denifle, in *Revue Thomiste*, ii
(1894), 149–61). The amount of time which the students were
expected to give to attendance on Biblical lectures, the period of

lectures demanded from the *cursor* and *biblicus*, and the vast
commentaries of the theological masters go to show the contrary.
Although the greatest commentators were Dominicans and Franciscans, the academic tradition had been established by the great
seculars, Peter the Lombard and Stephen Langton, and Rashdall
went too far in asserting, in the first edition of his book, that the later
seculars made no contribution to Biblical study. Mandonnet raised
another problem in his contention, which is now finding much
confirmation, that the theological *questio* as such developed from the
twelfth-century lectures on the Scriptures (Introduction to edition
of the *Questiones disputatae* of S. Thomas, Paris, 1926, especially
pp. 1–8). The Lombard's *magna glossatura* on the Epistles of S.
Paul were very important in the history of this development, for
commentaries on this gloss raised theological questions whose
discussion helped to give form to the *questiones disputatae* (cf. G.
Lacombe on Langton's *questiones* in *The New Scholasticism*, iv (1930),
129 *sq.*). Later collections of *questiones* show that the close connexion
between Biblical exegesis and the theological disputation was well
maintained in the thirteenth century (cf. Pelster, in *Scholastik*, v.
62, 63; and H. H. Glunz, *History of the Vulgate in England from
Alcuin to Roger Bacon*, Cambridge, 1933, *passim*).

A few recent studies may be mentioned by way of illustration of
the general statements made in this note. The nature of the 'questio
disputata' is shown abundantly in Assisi MS. 158, containing more
than 200 *questiones* disputed at Oxford, 1280–90, by sixty-five
scholars, first described by F. M. Henquinet in *Archivum Franciscanum Historicum*, xxiv (1931), 91–108, 215–54, and, more elaborately,
together with a description of the similar manuscript in Worcester
Cathedral Library Q. 99 (*c.* 1300–2), by A. G. Little and F. Pelster,
Oxford Theology and Theologians (Oxford Historical Society, vol.
xcvi, 1934). P. Glorieux has done similar work for Paris in his
paper, 'À propos du vatic. lat. 1086 : le personnel enseignant en Paris
vers 1311–4', in *Recherches de théologie ancienne et mediévale*, v
(1933), 23–39. Father M.-D. Chenu has analysed a series of lectures
on the Sentences and the Bible given by a dozen bachelors and
masters at Paris, *c.* 1240, and preserved in Paris, B.N., MS. lat.
15652, in *Études d'histoire littéraire et doctrinale du XIIIᵉ siècle*, i.
11–39 (Paris and Ottawa, 1932). A paper by Dr. Martin Grabmann,
'Die Aristoteleskommentare des Simon von Faversham (†1306)'
(*Sitz. d. Bayerischen Akad. der Wissenschaften*, phil.-hist. Abth.
1933, pp. 1–40), is of especial value in illustrating the great extent
of unpublished lectures and *questiones* on Aristotle, and in showing
the different kinds of commentary made by a single scholar. Simon,
who lectured at Paris and Oxford, and died as chancellor of the
University of Oxford, was very active as a teacher. Some manuscripts contain *lecturae*, in which the *questio* only appears in the
form of a doubt (*dubia*) : these are exegetical commentaries (cf. the

terminations 'terminatur sententia lectionis' and 'hec est sententia
lectionis'); some contain 'questiones disputatae'. Some give lectures
as written (*scripta*) by the author, others give them as taken down
by the hearer (*reportata*). A Munich MS. (Clm. 5852) contains a
series of *sophismata* by Simon, Siger of Cambrai, and others. Grabmann aptly describes the *sophisma* as a form of exercise in the
faculty of arts which in its character as a disputation corresponded
in that faculty to the *quodlibet* in the theological faculty (p. 11).
Simon of Faversham was only one of many whose lectures and
questiones survive, and who took part in sophistical disputations or
tournaments. This mass of literature is a convincing testimony to
the activity of the artists in the schools of Paris and Oxford. On
the developments generally see also Grabmann's *Mittelalterliches
Geistesleben* (1926).

§ 5. THE COLLEGES OF PARIS

A large quantity of documentary material for the colleges, not contained in Bulaeus, is to be found in FÉLIBIEN, *Histoire de la ville de Paris*, Paris, 1725, to which Jourdain (*Index Chartarum*, &c.) makes large additions. For the Sorbonne I have consulted the MS. *Sorbonae Origines*, by HEMERAEUS, in the Bibliothèque Nationale at Paris, Cod. Lat. 5493; and the MS. Register (*ibid.* 5494 A). Many of the documents contained in it (including the statutes of 1274) are now printed in the *Chartul. Univ. Paris.* FRANKLIN, *La Sorbonne*, Paris, 1875, contains a short account of the foundation, but is chiefly a history of the Library. GRÉARD, *Nos adieux à la vieille Sorbonne* (Paris, 1893), is a more elaborate, and an eloquently written, work, but more valuable for later periods than for ours. The *Histoire de la Sorbonne* by Duvernet (Paris, 1790) is a tendentious account of the theological faculty of Paris. A somewhat detailed account of the college and its founder is given in *Hist. Litt.* xix. 291 *sq.*

For the College of Navarre there is a very full history by LAUNOI, *Reg. Navarrae Gymnasii Historia*, Paris, 1677. SAUVAL, *Hist. et Recherches des Antiquités de la ville de Paris* (Paris, 1724), gives a list of colleges (ii. 372) and some documents in vol. iii. Cf. LEBEUF, *Hist. de la ville de Paris*, ed. Cocheris, Paris, 1890; BERTY, *Topographie du vieux Paris*, Paris, 1866–97.

There are also the following monographs: Marquis de BELBEUF, *Notice sur le C. du Trésorier*; GEFFROY, 'Les Étudiants suédois à Paris' (*Rev. des Soc. Savantes*, iv (1858), 659); QUICHERAT, *Hist. de Sainte-Barbe*, Paris, 1860; ROLLAND, *Recueil des délibérations du C. Louis-le-Grand, Mémoire donné par le bureau d'administration du C. Louis-le-grand*; CHAPOTIN, *Le Coll. de Dormans-Beauvais*, Paris, 1870; JOURDAIN, 'Le Coll. du Cardinal Lemoine' (*Mèm. de la Soc. de l'hist. de Paris*, iii (1877)); BOUQUET, *L'ancien Collège d'Harcourt*, Paris, 1891. Cf. also *Mém. de la Soc. de l'hist. de Paris*, i (1875), 93 *sq.* In compiling the list at the end of the section I am specially indebted to Jourdain's Catalogue, with its indications of other authorities. I have been obliged to insert several colleges on the authority of Félibien or others, without having seen the original authority for their existence or date. Two or three are due to the *Histoire littéraire de la France*.

[The unprinted work by Jerome BESOIGNE († 1763), *Les Recherches sur l'Université de Paris*, i. *Collèges*, in Bibl. Nat. MS. fr. 14491, is excellent and especially valuable because the author made use of materials which have since disappeared.

For Robert de Sorbon see F. Chambon's edition of the *De conscientia*, Paris, 1903; cf. Hauréau in the *Mémoires de l'Académie des Inscriptions*, xxxi, pt. ii, 133–49. For the Sorbonne P. FERRET, in *Bulletin du comité d'histoire du diocèse de Paris*, 1884, pp. 98–118; J. BONNEROT, *La Sorbonne: sa vie, son rôle, son œuvre à travers les siècles*, Paris, 1928; R. THAMIN in *Revue des Deux Mondes*, xxxix, 1927, pp. 591–511, 855–75. See also P. DE LONGUEMARE, *Notes sur quelques collèges parisiens de fondation normande au XIIIᵉ, XIVᵉ et XVᵉ siècles*, Rouen, 1911; P. ANGER, *Le Collège de Cluny*, Paris, 1916; M. GODET, *La congrégation de Montaigu* (1490–1580), Paris, 1912; Raoul BUSQUET, 'Étude historique sur le collège de Fortet', in *Mémoires de la Soc. de l'hist. de Paris*, xxxiii (1906), 187–290, xxxiv (1907), 1–151: an excellent account of the foundation, constitution, and life of a medieval college; Ch. JOURDAIN, 'Le collège du cardinal

CHAP. V, Lemoine', *ibid*. iii (1876), 42–81; Marcel POÈTE, *Une vie de cité: Paris de*
§ 5. *sa naissance à nos jours*, Paris, 1924–31, i. 169–71; iii. 40–59.

Several of the colleges have been the subject of theses in the École des
Chartes. Summaries are given in the printed *Positions de thèses*: A.
HUGUES, *Le Collège d'Autun* (1885, 1886); A. RASTOREL, *Le Collège des
Cholets* (1899); G. CRÈPY, *Le Collège de Boissy* (1904); H. CAHEN, *Le
Collège de Laon* (1906); P. LÈVY, *Le Collège de la Marche et de Winiville*
(1921).

For the Swedish colleges, Henrik SCHÜCK, *Svenska pariserstudier under
medeltiden* (Kyrkohistorisk Areskrift, i, 1900). Cf. L. MAURY, 'Les
étudiants scandinaves à Paris (xie–xve siècles)' in the *Annales de l'Université*, no. 3 (May–June, 1934).]

Paris the home of the collegiate system.

EVEN learned historians have sometimes allowed themselves
to speak of colleges as institutions peculiar to the English
universities.[1] The reader of the present work will by this
time be aware that colleges are not even peculiar to the class
or family of universities to which Oxford and Cambridge
belong. Few of the Italian and other student-universities
continued long without colleges or endowed residences for
poor students being provided by pious founders. The earliest
of them, however, arose somewhat later than was the case at
Paris. They were, with a few exceptions, small foundations,
and exercised comparatively little influence over the educational system and constitutional development of the universities in connexion with which they were established. The
true home of the collegiate system is Paris; from Paris it
passed to those universities upon which it has obtained its
longest and firmest hold.

The hospicia. To understand what the colleges were, it is necessary in
the first place to appreciate the social conditions of the universities wherein they arose. It has been usual to trace back
the system of boarding in masters' houses, which was nearly
universal at Paris before the close of the medieval period, to
the earliest days of the university; and when the extreme
youth of the Parisian arts-student is considered it is no
doubt difficult for persons familiar with modern ideas of
education to believe that he was allowed to live in a great city
without some kind of domestic supervision. It is, however,
quite certain that in the thirteenth century the Parisian
arts-student of fourteen was, so far as the university was con-

[1] e.g. Malden, p. 109.

cerned, as free to live where and how he pleased as the canon or rector of twenty-five or thirty who had left his benefice in the country to read canon law at Paris or Bologna. Nor is it clear that the earliest *hospicia* or houses or residence hired by parties of students at a rent fixed by a joint university and city board[1] differed fundamentally, even when occupied by arts-students, from the *hospicia* of the Bologna law-students. Where, however, a large number of boys and young men were packed together into a very narrow space, the necessities of the case must inevitably have evolved some kind of government, whether democratic or aristocratic.[2] The usual practice from the first was no doubt to live with a party of other students in a *hospicium*; and gradually residence in a house presided over by a master became universal except for two classes of students—the richest, who lived in their own houses with a private tutor, and the poorest, who could not afford the expense of the *hospicium*, and lodged or boarded in some miserable garret of a townsman's house. Eventually the university attempted to suppress this last class altogether.[3]

[1] By Curzon's statute of 1215 (Bulaeus, iii. 82; *Chartul.* i, No. 20) the scholars are authorized to make statutes 'pro taxandis pretiis hospitiorum'. By the Bull of Gregory IX in 1231, the taxation is to be by two masters and two burghers, 'sive, si burgenses non curaverint interesse, per duos magistros, *sicut fieri consuevit*'. (Bulaeus, iii. 143; *Chartul.* i, No. 82. Cf. Nos. 429, 511; [and ii, No. 556.) See also C. Jourdain, 'La taxe des logements dans l'université de Paris', in his *Excursions historiques et philosophiques à travers le moyen âge* (Paris, 1888), pp. 247–63.]

[2] [A list of *bursae*, dating 1329–36, gives a very good idea of the extent to which scholars lived together (*socii*); and it is noteworthy that some of the recently founded colleges come in this list, e.g. the Collège de Bayeux (1309) appears as 'domus Guillelmi Boneti' (*Chartul.* ii, No. 1184, pp. 662 *b* and 671,

note 15). In 1391 a *paedagogus*, Master William Veulet, had a house in which 'parvi scholares circa 50 tanquam in collegio aluntur' (*Chartul.* iii, No. 1599). On the other hand we find highly-organized *collegia* of a few scholars, such as the eight of Collège de Fortet; cf. also *Chartul.* iii, No. 1327, for a proposed foundation of this kind in 1366.]

[3] At Paris no legislation about the authority of principals or the internal management of halls occurs till the fifteenth century. [In a lawsuit of 1336 a master had hired a house 'tanquam principalis dicte domus' (*Chartul.* ii, No. 1007). For a criticism of Rashdall's argument in the first edition that students. could be principals of a hall see Emden, *An Oxford Hall in Medieval Times*, pp. 19–21. Medieval letters throw some light on the private lodgings in which students lived in early times; cf. Haskins, *Mediaeval Culture*, pp. 21, 22.]

CHAP. V,   As to the internal government of these communities, we
§ 5.   have in regard to Paris hardly any direct evidence before
Origin of
colleges. the period when the head was usually a master and when
his authority over his fellows (*socii*) was more or less
backed up by the university as a whole. Even for that
period the evidence is very scanty.

The college was, in its origin, nothing but an endowed
hospicium or hall. That students at the universities should
live together in societies was established by custom before
the first college arose. But for this circumstance there was no
reason why endowments for the benefit of poor students
should have assumed the form of colleges.[1] The object of
the earliest college-founders was simply to secure board and
lodging for poor scholars who could not pay for it themselves.
At Paris the endowed scholars' home always had a master at

[1] [This is doubtful if it implies
anything more than a few students
living together for convenience.
The late Professor L. J. Paetow
believed that the formative influence in the beginning of 'endowments for the benefit of poor
students' was the hospitals, which
furnished the material bases for the
college: the method of endowment,
the habit of giving alms at stated
intervals, the living from a common
chest. It was not until the foundation of the Sorbonne in 1257 that
the college became an organization
independent of an ecclesiastical
corporation other than the university. Hospitals were not merely
places for the sick. Boys far from
home, in a city where the growing
population outran the means of
housing it, and where rents were
high, were inevitably thrown upon
the hospital for support.

The possession of house property
by the nations was important in
later developments at Paris. A 'college' of foreign students, e.g. the
Swedish College, might be housed
in property owned by the nation.
In 1392 a committee was appointed

to look after the houses belonging
to the nation, 'that had been forsaken by the customary student
inhabitants': Boyce, p. 140, referring to *Auctarium*, i. 661. The
share of the nation in providing
opportunities for corporate life
should not be overlooked in any
comparison between the colleges
of Oxford and Paris. For similar
arrangements in German and Polish
universities see the passages quoted
in the first edition of this work: a
statute of Rostock (E. J. de West-
phalen, *Monumenta inedita rerum
Germanicarum*, iv, c. 1027: 'omnia
clenodia et utensilia regentiae com-
parata per rectorem domus de communi collecta scholarium debent
manere in dicta regentia mutato
rectore et alio succedente'), and the
purchase of furniture with the consent of the community of a Hall or
Bursa governed by an elected *Senior*
and four *Conciliarii* (*Registrum
Bursae Cracoviensis Hungariorum*,
Buda, 1821, pp. 1-5, 51, 61, 68, &c.).
Here we approximate more closely
to the democratic system which
Rashdall supposed to have existed
in Paris.]

its head; but the instruction which he was supposed to give
was entirely subordinate to that of the public schools. The
colleges introduced no innovation into the educational system
of the universities; nor were their founders primarily influenced by the enlightened and far-reaching design which
has sometimes been attributed to them, of correcting by a
system of domestic instruction and supervision the dangerous
licence allowed by the earlier form of the university life,
though of course they took precautions to secure that their
bounty was not thrown away upon idle or ill-conducted
students. Eventually the college system did, as we shall see,
exercise a most important and on the whole salutary influence
both upon the education and upon the morals of the universities in which it took root. But originally the college was
nothing more than an endowed *hospicium*.

The earliest Parisian college-foundation was one of the
very humblest description. At right angles to the west front
of the Cathedral of Notre Dame there stood already in the
twelfth century (and still stands under a strangely altered
régime) the 'Hospital of the Blessed Mary of Paris', commonly known as the Hôtel-Dieu. In this hospital a single
room was customarily set apart for 'poor clerks'. Many, perhaps most, of these must have been scholars, but there was
no express limitation to this particular class of clerks. In the
year 1180, however, a visit was paid to the hospital by
'dominus Jocius de Londoniis', just returned from a pilgrimage to Jerusalem. As the result of this visit, the pious
Londoner, after taking counsel with the dean and the chancellor, determined to buy the room from the hospital and
appropriate it for ever to the support of 'eighteen scholar-
clerks', the proctors of the house agreeing with the benefactor
to supply the eighteen with 'sufficient beds' (how many beds
is left doubtful), and to pay them twelve *nummi* a month out
of the alms collected in the hospital chest.[1] The college (if

Collège
des Dix-
huit, 1180.

---

[1] 'Tali facta conditione, quod eiusdem domus procuratores decem et octo scolaribus clericis lectos sufficientes et singulis mensibus duodecim nummos de confraria que colligitur in archa, perpetuo administrabunt.' (From the deed of the dean and chapter accepting

CHAP. v, such it can be called) was obviously a very simple affair—
§ 5. intended for the very poorest class of clerks. At first the
scholars were under no special rule or government except that
under which other inmates of the hospital were placed: their
sole statutable obligation was to take turns in bearing the cross
and holy water at the funerals of those who died in the house,
and nightly to say the seven penitential psalms and other
customary prayers. By the year 1231, however, we find the
community established in a house of its own near the church
of S. Christopher.[1] It was henceforth known as the 'Collège
des Dix-huit'.

S. Thomas   The next college-foundation or attempt at a college-founda-
de Lupara,
c. 1186. tion is perhaps the College of S. Thomas of the Louvre.
About the year 1186, Count Robert of Dreux, with the
approval of King Philip Augustus and of Urban III,[2] established a hospital in some houses of his own near the Palace of
the Louvre. The house was designed for the benefit of 'poor
clerks'. It does not, however, appear distinctly whether these
clerks were scholars, and the foundation was originally of the
nature of a hospital, apparently for clerks, under a Com-

the endowment, first printed from
a manuscript copy in the National
Archives by Denifle. *Chartul.* i,
Introd., No. 50. [A London citizen,
Josce the vintner, who had appar-
ently lately died, is mentioned in
Pipe Roll 2 Ric. I, p. 158.]

[1] Doc. in Brièle, *Cartulaire de
l'Hôtel-Dieu*, No. 260. [The college had a continuous history from
1180 until 1789, when it was absorbed with other small colleges
into the College of Louis-le-Grand.
The statutes of 1330 require a
mass and vigils 'pro Joncio de
Londonis, qui fundavit domum
istam' (E. Coyecque, 'Notice sur
l'ancien collège des Dix-huit', in
*Bulletin de la société de l'histoire de
Paris*, 1887, p. 182). The removal
of the poor scholars to a house of
their own was probably made when
the old Hôtel-Dieu was pulled
down to make way for the new

cathedral and the Rue Neuve
Notre Dame was cut (M. F. Hoff-
bauer, *Paris à travers les âges*, i. 50).
The house stood in this street.
Throughout its history the college
remained under the tutelage of the
hospital (Coyecque, *L'Hôtel-Dieu
de Paris au moyen âge*, 1889, ii.
374). According to J. du Breul (*Le
théâtre des antiquitez de Paris* (1612),
p. 634) later students were wont to
pause as they were leaving their
house to sprinkle holy water on the
corpses which were exposed at the
gates of the hospital and to say
brief prayers over them. This was
a link with the earlier obligations
mentioned in the text.]

[2] The Bull of Urban III alone
survives (without date). Bulaeus,
ii. 463–4; *Chartul.* i, Introd., No.
14: cf. No. 18. [See especially the
note on p. 11.]

munity of Brethren, who are described as 'religious persons',
i.e. (as was usual in hospitals) canons regular.[1] At what date
(if not from the first) scholars were admitted to the foundation
cannot be precisely determined; but in 1210 the community
is described in a Bull as the 'Provisor and Brethren of the
Religious House of the poor scholars of S. Thomas the
Martyr at Paris';[2] and in 1228 abuses had sprung up in this
scholastic community which called for the peremptory interference of the bishop of the diocese. 'We have found', says
that prelate, 'that certain scholars who had long since lived
of the goods of the same House, have been carried to such
a pitch of insolence that they have attempted to break the
doors of the House of the Brethren by night and violently
to effect an entrance; others, as though secure of their
victuals through having unduly long eaten the bread provided for students, making little progress and unwilling to
study, burdensome to the real students, were molesting in
various ways the quiet and studies of others.'[3] Evidently
the college is by this time an established institution: already
its 'burses' have degenerated into 'idle fellowships', and the
bishop is obliged to make them terminable at the end of the
year, unless specially prolonged by delegates appointed by
himself.

According to Félibien, the historian of the City of Paris, S. Nicho-
the scholars of S. Thomas of the Louvre were in 1217 re- las de
moved from the hospital and established as a separate com- Lupara.
munity under the title of 'The Scholars of S. Nicholas in
the Louvre',[4] although until 1284 the scholars were still

---

[1] The object of the Bull is to
authorize the benediction of a ceme-
tery 'ad opus fratrum et familie
ipsius atque infirmorum decumben-
tium'. *Ibid.*, No. 14.
[2] Bulaeus, ii. 465; *Chartul.* i,
No. 10.
[3] Guérard, *Cart. de Notre Dame
de Paris*, i. 350; *Chartul.* i, No. 60.
Colleges were not peculiar to universities. A 'Collegium Bonorum
Puerorum' was founded in connexion with the Cathedral Schools

of Reims before 1245. Varin,
*Archives administratives de la ville
de Reims*, i. 663 *sq.* If we may trust
Hemeraeus, a college with a similar
title, in connexion with the Church
of S. Quentin, dates from 843. See
his *De Scholis publicis pro regali
ecclesia S. Quintini*, Paris, 1633,
p. 161.
[4] Félibien, i. 211. [In the first
edition Rashdall accepted, with some
hesitation, the view of Bournon,
Rectifications et additions à Lebeuf

CHAP. V, occasionally described as the Scholars of S. Thomas in the
§ 5. Louvre.[1] Then the old name disappears. If we may assume
that the statutes of 1316 are a safe guide to its earliest condition, it is clear that here at least we have a college for artists
attending the schools of the university.[2]

'The Good   Of much the same type is the College of the 'Good Children
Children
of S.   (Paris, 1890), i. 27, that the colleges   of S. Thomas obviously was in
Honoré',   of S. Thomas and S. Nicholas were   1284 should have suddenly dis-
1208–9.   separate foundations. There seems,   appeared without leaving a trace.]
           however, to be good reason to fol-   [1] In the episcopal ordinance of
           low Félibien, as Denifle does   1228 (above, p. 503), in the will of
           (Chartul. i, Introd., pp. 11, 70,   S. Louis (1270), by which they
           notes). In 1210 Innocent III gave   were left 15 librae (Bulaeus, iii.
           the poor students of S. Thomas the   393; Chartul. i, No. 430 a. Cf. also
           right to construct a chapel (ibid. i,   No. 83) [and in a confirmation by
           No. 10). In 1212 a separation was   the 'officiales curiarum' of Paris,
           effected between certain property   1284 (ibid., No. 514)]. An identity
           which the Brethren and the Canons   is, however, supported by a docu-
           of S. Thomas had hitherto held in   ment of 1419 (Bulaeus, v. 345), in
           common (Dubois, ii. 184). In 1217   which the College of S. Nicholas de
           an episcopal brief, beginning 'no-   Lupara is spoken of as the oldest in
           tum facimus quod, cum rector et   Paris. [This is correct, for the poor
           fratres hospitalis sancti Thome   clerks of the Hôtel-Dieu did not
           Martyris de Lupara', authorized   obtain a home of their own until
           the construction of the chapel (ibid.).   after 1186, when the hospital of
           This was built on a site which, as   S. Thomas, afterwards the College
           it was liable to be flooded, was   of S. Nicholas, was founded.]
           dedicated to S. Nicholas, the patron   [2] Bulaeus, iv. 139. It is governed
           saint of inundated places. The site   by a master and procurator, after
           was probably the 'Verger . . . ante   the manner of later Colleges of
           ianuam ecclesiae' mentioned in a   Artists. [In the document of 1284,
           papal confirmation of 1192 (Dubois,   mentioned in the last note, the
           i. 183). In order to avoid the con-   'domus pauperum scholarium
           fusion between a collegiate church   Sancti Thome' (the last appearance
           of S. Thomas on one side of the   of this name) consisted of a pro-
           street and a college of S. Thomas   visor, six magistri, who are named,
           on the other, the latter gradually   and a group of scholars, twelve of
           took the name of the patron saint   whom are named and described
           of its chapel. The 'hospitale pau-   as clerici. In 1350 Barthélemy of
           perum scolarium Sancti Nicolai   Bruges founded three new bursar-
           de Lupara' of 1247 (Chartul. i, No.   ships in the College of S. Nicholas.
           168) and of a papal Bull of 1263   In 1541 the Cardinal du Bellay
           (Bulaeus, iii. 370) illustrates the   transformed the college into a
           transition. This is the explanation   chapter with a provost and nine
           given by Adolphe Berty (Louvre,   prebends. Finally, in 1740, this
           i (1866), 109–12). If there were two   chapter was reunited with that of
           colleges, it would be very hard to   S. Thomas, with which it had
           explain why S. Louis mentioned   been originally associated as a hos-
           only one in his will, and why such   pital of clerks in 1186 (Berty,
           a flourishing society as the College   Louvre, i. 110, 111).]

of S. Honoré', founded in 1208–9 by a citizen of Paris, Étienne Belot or Berot and his wife,[1] to contain thirteen beds, whether to be used singly or otherwise does not appear. The only difference is that, instead of being attached to a religious hospital, the boys were placed under the government of the secular chapter of the Church of S. Honoré; the 'Provisor' was to be one of the canons, appointed, after the death of the founders, by the Bishop of Paris. As to the educational character of the House of S. Honoré we are completely in the dark. We do not know whether its scholars studied grammar or arts, or whether they were taught in the house or out of it. But in all probability they were merely grammar boys. It is not clear whether they originally lived under the supervision of a master, though they certainly did so at a later date.[2]

One of the earliest independent foundations at Paris was S. Victor. the 'College of the Good Children of S. Victor', about the origin of which we know nothing except that it existed in 1248, when Innocent IV allowed them a chapel of their own,[3] and that it was placed under the supervision of the Chancellor of Paris.[4] From its designation we may assume that this, too, was a college for grammarians. Another independent society, if it actually existed, was the College of Constantinople. It College of is supposed that the foundation of this college was connected Constanti- with the Latin conquest of Constantinople in 1204, and the nople. consequent projects of Innocent III for the reunion of Christendom. A host of Parisian ecclesiastics, armed with missal and breviary, was to be dispatched into the East;[5] while Greek youths were to be sent to Paris to be indoctrinated with the theology of the West. That such a project was formed is an historical fact: its connexion with the foundation of the College of Constantinople appears to be no more than a conjecture, though a very probable one. Of the

[1] Bulaeus, iii. 45; *Chartul.* i, No. 9 (where the text is corrected).

[2] Sauval, iii. 119; Jourdain, No. 711; Félibien, i. 246 *sq.*

[3] Dubois, *Hist. eccl. Paris*, ii. 511.

[4] Bulaeus, iii. 217; *Chartul.* i, Nos. 184, 323.

[5] In 1205 Innocent III issued a Bull to invite Parisian ecclesiastics to go on this mission. *Chartul.* i, No. 3.

CHAP. V, subsequent history of the college little is known till the year
§ 5. 1363, when the single 'bursar' or foundationer who was found quartered in its ruined and dilapidated buildings was persuaded to make over its property to the founders of the Collège de la Marche.[1]

Influence of the regular colleges. The secular college would never perhaps have developed into the important institution which it actually became but for the example set by the colleges of the Mendicants. We have already noticed the formation of the mendicant convents in Paris, beginning with the establishment of the Dominicans in 1217.[2] A little later some at least among the older monastic orders, which had hitherto stood aloof from the new academical learning, became anxious to remove the reproach of ignorance freely hurled against them by the more ambitious and progressive friars. In 1246 a Cistercian college, known as the Collège du Chardonnet, was founded by the Englishman Stephen of Lexington, Abbot of Clairvaux, for students of his house.[3] Subsequently, however, he was deprived of its management by the chapter general of the Cistercians, and the college thrown open to the whole order. The students in this and other monastic colleges were supported by pensions derived from their respective monasteries. In these Parisian houses of the monks and friars the monastic life was adapted to academical needs. A convent inhabited by students necessarily assumed the form of a college;[4] and the 'regular' college may have done much to suggest the idea of the more elaborate secular foundations which began to

[1] Bulaeus, iv. 366–7. [Cf. C. Jourdain, in *Revue des sociétés savantes*, 1863, pp. 350–8. The editors of the Chartularium identify the college with the endowment for ten *pueri orientales* (1248) or ten clerks versed in Arabic and other Oriental tongues (1286), mentioned in Bulls of Popes Innocent IV and Honorius IV: *Chartul.* i, Nos. 181, 182, 527.]

[2] Above, p. 347.

[3] Brother of Robert and John of Lexington, judges in England, and Henry, Bishop of Lincoln. Bulaeus,

iii. 184. The Pope's approval was given in 1244. *Chartul.* i, No. 133. Cf. Nos. 146, 148, 157, 166, &c. See also Félibien, i. 309 *sq.*; iii. 160 *sq.* The Cistercians petitioned for a Dominican Doctor of Theology; a significant indication of the standard of learning in the old orders and the new. *Chartul.* i, No. 151.

[4] The ordinary monasteries also received students of their order. According to Péries (p. 18), students from all parts were received at S. Germain-des-Prés.

come into existence about the middle of the thirteenth century. In particular it is to these regular colleges that we must
look for the origination of the idea of a college of theologians.
The earlier foundations were, as we have seen, mere eleemosynary institutions for poor boys. The college founded about
the year 1257[1] by S. Louis's chaplain, Robert de Sorbon (canon
of Cambrai and afterwards of Paris), was a college for men
who had already taken the degree of master of arts and were
desirous of entering upon the long and laborious career which
led to the theological doctorate. In face of the attractions The
offered to the pious by the Mendicant orders and to the Sorbonne,
worldly by the lucrative profession of a canonist, some such *c.* 1257.
institution was absolutely needed if the class of secular theologians was to be kept from entire extinction. From this
point of view the establishment of the 'Sorbonne' was an
event of European importance.

'The House of Sorbonne' was originally designed for six- The
teen students of theology, four from each nation. This ab- Sorbonne,
sence of narrow local restrictions is an unusual feature in 1257-70.
Parisian college constitutions, and perhaps laid the foundations of the future greatness of the college. Its numbers were
soon increased by supplementary benefactions to thirty-six.[2]
Indeed, a large number of purses contributed to the erection of this illustrious house. S. Louis gave part of the site,
close to the ancient Palace of Julian (the *Palatium Therma-
rum*), south of the Seine, and otherwise contributed to its

[1] S. Louis's gift of adjoining houses and stables 'ad opus scholarium qui inibi moraturi sunt', is dated 1250 by Hemeraeus (MS. Hist., f. 9) and Bulaeus (iii. 224). But its true date seems to be Feb. 1257 (see Jourdain, No. 150, and *Chartul.* i, No. 302). According to Richer (i, f. 411 *b*) the traditional date of foundation, preserved in an inscription in the library, was 1252. But it is evident that the arrangements for the purchase were spread over a considerable period. The house is still spoken of as future in 1258 (*Chartul.* i, No. 325), and the formal donation of the property did not take place till 1270 (Jourdain, No. 222; *Chartul.* i, No. 431); but the college no doubt existed, its founder being the first provisor—a fact which goes a long way to explain the position of that official.

[2] Franklin, p. 19. [Robert appears to have begun his work about 1245. The date of the royal charter is February 1267 (n.s.). For the growth of the buildings see Bonnerot, pp. 4–7. The 'little Sorbonne' or College de Calvi was founded by Robert in 1271 for young scholars.]

CHAP. V, endowment.[1] One of many early benefactors was Robert
§ 5. Geoffrey of Bar, one of the four champions of the secular clerks
in their battles with the Mendicants,[2] all remembrance of
whose former heresies was now extinguished beneath a
cardinal's hat. He was also the founder's executor for the
completion of the undertaking.[3] Collections on behalf of the
pious object were even made in the churches by the aid of
papal and episcopal indulgences.[4] Besides the full bursars, a
certain number of *Beneficiarii* were supported by the broken
meats of the hall dinner and supper, in return for which they
performed some menial services to the fellows. At a later date
each fellow had a 'poor clerk' as his personal attendant, sharing
the chamber in which he lived and slept.[5] Though the 'Bursars'
were associated in the government of the house, they hardly
possessed the independence of an Oxford or Cambridge college.
The supreme government of the foundation and the filling up
of its 'burses' was entrusted to a body of external governors—the Archdeacon and Chancellor of Paris, the doctors
of theology, the deans of the other two superior faculties, and
the rector and proctors of the university.[6] The ordinary
administration of the house and the management of its
property was vested in a provisor, appointed by the governors, in conjunction with the Sorbonnists themselves. The
position of the provisor was apparently something between
that of an Oxford visitor and that of an Oxford head. He was
not a member of the community, but some important ecclesiastic who governed it from the outside; on the other hand he
possessed, though he rarely exercised, disciplinary powers
more like those of the medieval master or warden at Oxford.
The internal presiding officer of the society was an annually

[1] *Chartul.* i, Nos. 302, 329, 347.
[2] Franklin, p. 17.
[3] Franklin, p. 19; *Chartul.* i, Nos. 515, 519.
[4] Jourdain, Nos. 180, 189; *Chartul.* i, Nos. 348, 378.
[5] Hemeraeus, MS. Hist., f. 31; Richer, MS. i, f. 448. It would seem that the *beneficiarii*, who originally lived in a separate but ad-joining house (Hemeraeus, f. 37), passed into the *clerici convictores* of a later date.
[6] In practice it would appear that the provisor was usually left to act by himself, and the governing body rarely interfered with the college, unless appealed to. MS. Reg. *passim.*

elected prior or *lator rotuli*,[1] the financial administration being entrusted to two greater and two lesser proctors.[2]

A word must be said as to the later history of this illustrious society, though it hardly falls within our period. Originally, as we have seen, the 'Sorbonne' was nothing more than a college of theologians like University or Oriel College in Oxford. In the sixteenth and seventeenth centuries, however, the title came to be popularly applied to the whole theological faculty of Paris. This usage was, it would appear, due to two causes. In the first place, the college early took to receiving as *Hospites* students or rather bachelors of theology who had passed their 'Tentative' to live with the foundation-members. Others became full members without endowment (*socii sine bursa*); and in time the value of the burses fell off to such an extent that their possession ceased to carry with it any considerable pecuniary advantage. Membership of the Sorbonne thus became an honorary distinction which was usually sought by most of the theological doctors of the university.[3] And, secondly, the hall or schools of the Sorbonne became the scene of disputations and other public acts of the theological faculty, especially of its meetings to discuss and pronounce judgement upon heresies or theological novelties. This circumstance especially led to the habit of speaking of the judgements of the theological faculty upon matters of faith as judgements of the Sorbonne.[4]

[1] Franklin, p. 19; *Chartul.* i, No. 421. For the identification see Hemeraeus, MS., f. 241 *b*; Richer, MS. i, f. 432 *a*.

[2] Hemeraeus, f. 239. The statutes of the Sorbonne (1274) are now printed in *Chartul.* i, No. 448.

[3] Hemeraeus, ff. 40–8 *b*. The election was by ballot among the members, after a 'probatio morum et doctrinae' (Hemeraeus, f. 52 *b*). It should be observed that whereas the 'bursarii' were compelled to retire from the college after graduation, the honorary membership of the Sorbonne could be granted for life (*ibid.*, f. 54). A peculiarity of the domestic economy of the Sorbonne, likewise due to the insufficiency of the original bursa of 5 *solidi*, 6 *den.*, was that the common life had eventually to be abandoned in favour of a system of dining (as we should say) by 'commonses' (i.e. *à la carte*), which continued down to Hemeraeus' time (*ibid.*, ff. 39, 44 *b*). But this usage is post-medieval.

[4] Launoi (i. 452) dates this usage from the time of Francis I. According to Richer (f. 423), all doctors of theology in his time styled themselves doctors of the Sorbonne, 'propter illum actum Sorbonnicum

CHAP. V,   A far more extensive and splendid foundation than the
§ 5.   subsequently more famous Sorbonne was the College of
College of
Navarre, Navarre, founded in 1304 by Joanna, Queen of Navarre, the
1304.   consort of Philip the Fair. The foundation of this college
forms the same kind of epoch in the history of Paris college-
building that the foundation of New College (suggested perhaps by its Parisian prototype) constitutes in our Oxford
history. Its organization illustrates more markedly than the
Sorbonne the points of resemblance and of contrast between
the Parisian and the English college. The object of college-
founders in both countries was to help poor students, and to
ensure a supply of educated secular clergy to the Church.
The lucrative professions of medicine and law needed no
artificial encouragement. Comparatively few fellowships or
bursarships either in England or at Paris were founded for
canonists, fewer still for students of medicine. The grammarians at Paris, however, formed a more important element
in the Parisian colleges than was the case at Oxford. The
only representative of this youngest class of students in the
Oxford and Cambridge colleges are the choristers of New and
other colleges; since the full foundationers were generally
admitted only after entrance upon the arts course, and usually
when already bachelors. At Paris some of the colleges were
(as we have seen) founded entirely for grammar boys. Thus
the founder of the little College of Ave Maria (A.D. 1339) for

qui die Veneris a sexta matutina ad
sextam serotinam aestivo tempore
absque ulla intermissione con-
tinuat'. [The localization of the
faculty of arts in the Rue du
Fouarre, and of decrees in the
Clos Brunel, doubtless assisted the
tendency to identify the faculty of
theology with the Sorbonne in the
fourteenth and fifteenth centuries.
A similar differentiation took place
in Bologna. The Sorbonne (*aula
Cerbonitarum*) was used for university disputations from at least
the early years of the fourteenth
century (*Chartul.* ii. 693 and
Denifle's note, p. 695. Cf. also a

statute of 1387, *ibid.* iii, No. 1534).
These disputations, which were
also styled *Sorbonicae* (*ibid.* ii, p.
701), must be distinguished from
the better-known *Sorbonica*, first
regulated in 1344 (*ibid.* ii, No.
1096), which has a more informal
disputation or *collatio* held on
Saturdays among members of the
college and visitors. See Little
and Pelster, *op. cit.*, p. 56 (cf. above,
p. 179 and note). It should be
observed that, though distinguished
in the text, the index of this work
treats the university and college
exercises as identical.]

a master, chaplain, and six 'young and poor boys', provided that they should be admitted at the age of eight or nine and superannuated on the completion of their sixteenth year, the age at which, according to the founder's melancholy experience, boys 'commonly begin to incline to evil'.[1] Most colleges, however, had burses for artists as well as grammarians, or for artists and theologians, and the larger ones for all three classes of students. At Navarre there were to be twenty students in grammar with a weekly allowance of four *solidi*, thirty in arts with six *solidi* a week, twenty in theology with eight *solidi*. Each class of students was presided over by a master, whose salary was fixed at double the allowance of a scholar of his faculty.[2] The master of the theologians was rector or 'grand master' of the whole college. Each class of students had its separate hall, kitchen, and dormitory:[3] they met only in the chapel, for the services of which four chaplains and four clerks were appointed.[4]

The most characteristic differences between the colleges of Paris and those of Oxford were constituted by (1) the entire separation between the faculties prevalent at Paris, (2) the totally different position of the head, (3) a difference in the mode of filling up vacancies. At Paris the colleges were essentially colleges for students: the burse usually expired as soon as the candidate had finished his course of study and (in the case of the two higher classes of students) taken his degree. If he wanted to proceed to a higher faculty, a fresh election was necessary, though the existing members of the college had a preferential claim to succeed to vacancies in the higher divisions.[5] Where students from more than one faculty were embraced in the same college, each division had a master of its own, though the master of the highest faculty governed the whole college; and these masters were actual teachers who presided over the studies and disputations, and supplemented by their private instruction the public lectures of the schools. At Oxford the head was primarily a

Difference between a Parisian and an Oxford college.

---

[1] Bulaeus, iv. 261.
[2] Launoi, i. 8.
[3] *Ibid.* i. 11.
[4] Originally two of each. *Ibid.* i. 9, 11, 17, 25.
[5] *Ibid.* i. 28.

CHAP. V, governor and administrator of the property of the house; at
§ 5. no period had he any direct concern with the studies of the
scholars.[1] The different position of the Paris head was connected with the rather inferior degree of autonomy enjoyed
by the colleges of that university. The details varied at different colleges; but it would appear that, at least in many cases,
the property of the Paris college was far less the common
property of the head and fellows than was the case at Oxford
and Cambridge: the powers of the external visitors or governors were usually much greater than those of the Oxford
'visitor'. Nearly always the patronage of the college—the
appointment to the mastership and the bursarships or scholarships—rested either with the bishop or other ecclesiastical
dignitaries in the province or diocese to which the burses
were reserved, or with some dignitary in the immediate
vicinity of Paris.[2] These patrons might or might not be
identical with the external governing or visiting body. At
Navarre the body entrusted by the founder both with the
government and the patronage of the college was the theo-

[1] [The preceding generalizations should be modified by considera-tion of the difference between the conditions of life in the large and the conditions in the much more numerous small colleges. Thus there was no separation of the students of various faculties, nor was teaching always provided in such small societies as the Collège de Dix-huit and, so far as the records go, in the Danish and Swedish col-leges (Coyecque in *Bulletin de la Soc. de l'hist. de Paris*, 1887, pp. 180, 181; *Auctarium, passim*). Even in the larger College of Narbonne, there was no separation of students, the earliest statutes forbid it, and as late as 1379 it is forbidden to have separate *bursae* or expenses, 'nisi separatio scientiarum vel faculta-tum ... aliud requireret in futurum' (Félibien, v. 669, 674). Secondly, the position of the head differed in various colleges; naturally he had more duties in the smaller societies.

At the College of Harcourt, on the other hand, it was not the head or provisor but the prior who had charge of the arrangements for masses, sermons, fast days, dispu-tations, *collationes* among artists and theologians (Bouquet, *L'ancien col-lège d'Harcourt*, p. 588; cf. the statutes of the College of Narbonne, when it is his duty generally 'rem publicam gubernare': Félibien, v. 672). Rashdall's observations are generally true, not of the small colleges, but of the larger, more organized societies, and not always of these.]

[2] Or in some cases to the founders' heirs, e.g. at Tréguier. Félibien, i. 540. [The bursars of the Norman College of the Trea-surer were chosen by the two arch-deacons (the greater and the lesser) of the 'pays de Caux': D. Pom-meraye, *Histoire de la cathédrale de Rouen*, p. 266, cited by Coville, *Jean Petit*, p. 6, note.]

logical faculty of Paris.[1] Afterwards their powers were trans- ferred to the Bishop of Meaux together with the Chancellor of Paris, the Dean of the Theological Faculty, and the Grand Master.[2] But after numerous changes the government and patronage were arbitrarily assigned by the King to his Confessor.[3] The management of the property would seem to have remained with the royal *Gentes Computorum* or masters of the Exchequer, who paid over the annual revenues to a provisor[4] appointed by the external governors. Even where a college had the management of its own property, it usually had to account for its administration of the revenues at the end of the year. At Navarre and elsewhere the theologians were to a certain extent associated with the master in the government of the house;[5] but the artists usually seem to

[1] Launoi, i. 8, 9.

[2] *Ibid.* i. 28, 29, 54, 152, 183. At Narbonne, the 'Procurator domus' merely received his weekly supply of funds 'a mercatore qui tenebit pecunias domus'. Félibien, v. 674. At the College of Plessis the consent of the Abbot of Marmoutier at Tours is required for all important transactions relating to property (*ibid.* iii. 386). At the College of Boncour it seems contemplated that the external 'Provisores' may interfere with the details of internal discipline (*ibid.*, p. 442). Occasionally we find the master elected by the college, e.g. at Laon (Jourdain, No. 500). [The 'provisores', appointed by the Chapter of Notre Dame, exercised a close supervision over the Collège de Fortet, although the right *bursarii* or scholars of the college enjoyed a good deal of self-government: see R. Busquet in *Mém. de la Soc. de l'hist. de Paris*, xxxiii. 232–3, where the difference between this college and that of Saint-Barbe is pointed out; also the statutes of 1396, *ibid.* xxxiv. 142–9.]

[3] Launoi, i. 56, 112 *sq.*

[4] In Launoi, i. 22, we read 'Pro-

visor seu Magister', but from later documents it would appear that the master was the head, and that the provisor occupied the position of an Oxford 'bursar', ranking second in the college. In the eighteenth century the ordinary administration was in the hands of the officers (i.e. grand master, provisor, and the two principals) and a body of elected deputies. But the whole college was summoned on rare occasions. Register in Archives Nationales (MM. 469).

[5] From Launoi, i. 159, it appears that the consent of the theologians was usually asked to the admission of non-foundation theologians, and so with the artists; but in general the artists were admitted to less active participation in the college affairs than at Oxford, where the artists who were full *socii* were usually B.A. before admission. The absence of all allusion to a college seal in the Navarre Statutes is significant. [This distinction between the colleges of Paris and Oxford represents a general tendency rather than the facts of medieval college organization. The absence of allusion to seals does not prove that even the smaller colleges had no

occupy a position more like that of the later 'scholars' of Oxford colleges, when there came to be a body of scholars distinct from the fellows. The ideal of the Parisian founder was a body of students governed by a master,[1] though the character of this rule naturally varied with the age and status of those students. The idea of an Oxford college was rather a self-governing corporation whose ordinary administration, like that of a monastery, was in the hands of its elected head with the assistance of a certain number of the seniors, while the consent of all was required for the more important legal acts. Even the youngest full member of the foundation took part in the election of the master or warden.

Internal arrangements. The internal arrangements of the colleges at Paris were, however, as might be expected, very similar to those of Oxford and Cambridge colleges, of which we shall have more to say hereafter. The most notable differences arose from that sharp separation between the faculties which has been already noticed. In our own colleges the younger members of the society—whether full 'fellows' or inferior members of the foundation like the demies of Magdalen—instead of being placed under the government of a master of the artists, lived under the general supervision and, at a later date, instruction of the older students of theology. The usual arrangement at Oxford was to put three, four, or more students in a room with one senior in each. At the College of Navarre, however, and some other Parisian colleges, the students slept in large dormitories, one for each faculty, though elsewhere we hear of students living two in a room or even enjoying the luxury of single apartments.[2] The

seals; e.g. the seal of the College of S. Nicholas in the Louvre survives (Berty, *Louvre*, i. 110, 111, c. 1350). There were varieties of self-government, but regular meetings of the house seem to have been held in all colleges. The College of Dix-huit was self-governing, and until 1430 its only official was a *procurator* elected by the students. The statutes of the College of Bayeux (Félibien, v. 626–8) reveal a large measure of self-government.]

[1] This was not the case with the Sorbonne. See above, p. 508.

[2] 'Bini et bini habeant suas cameras in quibus studeant et jaceant' (Félibien, iii. 442). At Narbonne College, only 'in casu necessitatis . . . poterit una camera duobus juvenibus bursariis assignari ad tempus' (*ibid.* v. 671).

'Beneficiarii' of the Parisian college always remained mere CHAP. V, servitors like the medieval 'choristers' of New and other § 5. colleges,[1] and never developed into an important class of inferior foundationers like the 'scholars' of our present system. How important an influence these two distinctions exercised over the subsequent development of the two university systems the sequel will show.

The statutes of the College of Harcourt (1311) are dated Common-a few years later than those of Navarre, though the founda-ers or pen-tion itself belongs to the year 1280. Here we find a provision sioners. which became of great importance at a later date.[2] The master is allowed to receive into the house 'any suitable scholar of whatever country who may wish to dwell with the said scholars' of the foundation, upon his paying the amount of his keep (*bursa*), the rent of his rooms, and such a contribution towards the expenses of the establishment as shall be determined on by the master and fellows. At first the

---

[1] The duty of waiting on the fellows was usually combined with that of singing in chapel. See the Statutes of New College, p. 78. At Winchester the 'choristers' still wait at table.

[2] 'Item statuimus quod si aliquis scholaris idoneus undecumque fuerit oriundus, desideret cum dictis scholaribus habitare, recipiatur a nobis, vel a deputato a nobis quamdiu vixerimus, et post decessum nostrum a magistro dictae domus secundum quod loca domus ad hoc se potuerint extendere, ponendo bursam suam, ac conducendo cameram suam, ac emendo tantum de munitionibus, quantum reperietur tempore receptionis suae proportione cuiuslibet scholaris iuxta aestimationem magistri et sociorum' (Bulaeus, iv. 154). In the statutes of 1317 for the College of Narbonne a similar provision is made (Félibien, v. 674), while in 1379 we find a statute against keeping horses by any student 'nisi socius commensalis', as if the institution

was quite established (*ibid.* v. 670). So in 1380 the statutes of the College of Cornouaille forbid injuries 'alteri conscholari suo, nec etiam hospiti suo intraneo qui debito modo fuit ad manendum et convivendum inter ipsos receptus' (*ibid.* iii. 500). So the statutes of Dainville College in the same year provide for the lodging of 'foranei scholares . . . sicut in aliis collegiis Parisiensibus est aliquando fieri consuetum', but here only decretists in priest's orders are to be received, though the college includes artists and grammarians (*ibid.* iii. 511). [Earlier than any of these statutes, those for the College of the Treasurer (1280) contemplate the admission of *hospites*, provided that they are peaceable persons: 'si autem predicti scolares nostri aliquem divitem pacificum secum receperint, volumus quod pro camera sua viginti solidos parisiens. solvere teneantur' (*Chartul.* i, No. 499).]

reception of such 'commoners' or 'pensioners', or as they were usually called at Paris 'guests', was no doubt an exceptional thing—confined for the most part either to students in the superior faculties as at the Sorbonne, or, among the students of arts, to the richer class. The collegian, however, evidently possessed many advantages over the pupil of a private hall and still more over the 'martinet', as the student was called who lodged with townsmen instead of in a regular *hospicium*. He was under stricter discipline than the young master anxious above all things to fill his hall would have the inclination or the power to enforce. He enjoyed the advantage of a private tutor besides the public regent selected for him by the head of his college.[1] At Navarre, the master, or, as he was usually called, principal of the artists, was required 'diligently to hear the lessons of the Scholars studying in the Faculty of Arts and faithfully to instruct them alike in life and in doctrine'.[2] He was also to answer their questions and to read with them some 'Logical, Mathematical or Grammatical book' agreed upon by the majority of the scholars in addition to the lectures of the public schools. Then there were advantages in the greater numbers of the larger colleges. Thus at Navarre those who attended the same lecture were upon their return to college 'to meet together and peaceably go over it', and he who could best repeat it was to be listened to by the rest.[3] There was more chance of the rule requiring scholars 'commonly to speak Latin' being enforced than in the private hospice. The colleges, too, had libraries, the want

---

[1] By the 'Reformatio' of S. Nicholas de Lupara in 1310, the master is 'assignare libros quos audiant' (Bulaeus, iv. 139).

[2] Bulaeus, iv. 93.

[3] Launoi, i. 33, 34. So in the College of Dainville (1380): 'Quod statim finita lectione ad domum redeant, et in uno loco pariter conveniant ad suam lectionem repetendam; ita quod unus post alium totiens lectionem repetat, quod ipsam eorum quilibet bene sciat, et quod minus provecti magis provec-

tis lectiones quotidie reddere teneantur' (Félibien, iii. 512). We hear of the custom of *repetitio* as early as c. 1284, when the masters, in their suit against the chancellor, say that if two lectures are given one after another 'pueri doctrinam recipientes in una materia, antequam habituati sint in eadem ex repetitione sequente, suam doctrinam amittunt' (Jourdain, No. 274; *Chartul.* i, No. 515, p. 607). [Cf. above, p. 68, for the method of Bernard of Chartres.]

of which had long been felt as putting the secular masters at CHAP. V,
a disadvantage compared with their rivals, the regulars.[1] § 5.
Then there were disputations on winter evenings or (in some
cases) during dinner or supper. These advantages might
naturally induce parents who wanted their sons to be kept
out of mischief and to make the most of their time in the
university to send them into the colleges as 'pensioners' or
'commoners'.[2]

[1] The advantage which the regulars enjoyed in this respect was a sore point with their secular critics. Bonaventura in his reply to their advocate (*Opera*, vii. 384) says: 'Videntur tibi fratres in hoc Regulae contraire, cum tibi videantur pecuniam per interpositam personam recipere, libros habere et domos, cum non possint harum rerum quas habent Dominos assignare. In labore etiam manuum sibi iniuncto, ut videtur, sub praecepto culpabiles tibi videntur, cum nec laici laborent in operibus mechanicis, nec clerici manu propria in libris scribendis, quin potius cum magnis sumptibus faciunt eos scribi, ac si per se haberent numismatum percussores.'

S. Louis divided the large library (consisting of about 1,200 volumes, Hauréau, P. II, t. i, p. 186), which he had been incited by the example of the Saracen Sultan to form in the library of the Royal Chapel, between the Dominicans, the Minorites, and the Cistercian House (of Royaumont) of his own foundation (Bulaeus, iii. 658).

Similar complaints were made at Oxford. Richard of Armagh tells us (1357) 'quod non reperitur in Studiis communibus de Facultate Arcium, sacre Theologie et Juris Canonici aut etiam, ut fertur a pluribus, de Facultate Medicine atque Iuris Civilis, nisi raro, aliquis utilis multum liber venalis, set omnes emuntur a Fratribus, ita ut in singulis Conventibus sit una

grandis ac nobilis Libraria et ut singuli fratres habentes statum in studiis . . . nobilem etiam habeant Librariam'. Two or three rectors of his diocese whom he sent to Oxford returned because they could not find a decent copy of the Bible or other theological books for sale. *Defensorium Curatorum* in Brown's *Appendix ad Fasciculum Rerum Expetendarum*, London, 1690, p. 474. (The text is corrected from MS. Bodley 144, f. 261; but 'nobilem' ought no doubt to be 'notabilem' as in Bulaeus, iv. 339.)

At Paris the difficulty was largely met by the college libraries. The library of the Sorbonne was partly formed by its original benefactors, and by 1338 amounted to 1,700 volumes (Franklin, p. 56). At Navarre the surplus revenue was to be spent in books (Launoi, i. 37). The library is mentioned in many other college statutes. While some of the books were chained in the library, others could be taken out by the fellows and retained for long periods, so that they were dispensed from the necessity of buying even text-books for lectures. [Cf. above, p. 491.]

[2] [Rashdall considers only the point of view of the pensioner or *hospes*. In fact the colleges, in order to add to their prestige and income, as often as not invited *hospites* and efforts were made to keep them contented with their accommodation; cf. the statutes of the College of Narbonne, 1379: 'nec aliquis per

The tendency was connected, partly perhaps as cause and partly as effect, with a change which came over the educational system of the university in the course of the fifteenth century. The theological masters at the Sorbonne and at Navarre[1] appear to have lectured in the college, and it is possible that these lectures were open to outsiders. At all events they counted as regular lectures of the faculty. The grammarians, not having begun to keep terms in the arts schools, were, it would appear, taught exclusively by their own master in the college. The students of arts were, however, bound to complete the courses of 'ordinary' lectures required by the faculty in the public schools in or near the Rue du Fouarre;[2] and it is quite clear from the statutes of the earlier colleges that it was contemplated that they would have to go outside the house for lectures like the members of halls or paedagogies.[3] The college instruction was merely supplementary to that of the public schools. Gradually, however, the lectures and still more the catechetical lessons or 'repetitions' given in the college or hall became more and more

suum juramentum audeat tales bonos et alios honestos hospites scholares aliquo modo impedire, cum domus lucretur et honoretur per tales' (Félibien, v. 663). Another type of *hospes* was the student who had graduated and wished to remain in residence 'de proprio suo'; cf. the statutes of the Collège des Cholets, 1296 (*ibid.* iii. 301). Jean Petit, for example, lived, as doctor of theology, in the College of the Treasurer (Coville, *Jean Petit*, p. 6).]

[1] 'Qui in domo praedicta legere teneatur' (Launoi, i. 44). [The first statutes of the Sorbonne (1274) suggest that the scholars went only to the schools and that there were no lectures in the college (*Chartul.* i, No. 488). The statutes of 1321 show that there was public teaching in the 'schools of the Sorbonne' (Feret, *La faculté de théologie*, iii. 599).]

[2] Thus a statute of 1276 forbids lectures 'in locis privatis' except 'in gramaticalibus et logicalibus'. Bulaeus, iii. 430; *Chartul.* i, No. 468.

[3] It is impossible to say how often the *paedagogus*, or master of the college, himself acted as *proprius magister* to the boys in his own house, though obliged to go to the Rue du Fouarre to give them their lectures. A statute of 1456 forbids a master to participate in the banquets of the nation: 'nisi fuerit verus actualis et continuus Regens habens proprios Scholares *quos continue ducat ad vicum Stramsnis* et quibus legat libros Logicales', &c. Bulaeus, v. 616–17. On the other hand, at the College of Dainville (in 1380) the master is to choose the regents whom his scholars are to hear. Félibien, v. 512.

important, and the lectures out of it more and more formal CHAP. V,
and perfunctory. To assist the master of the college or the §5.
master of the artists other 'regents' were taken into the college,
and the masters of the paedagogies also employed assistant
regents to teach their students. It is difficult to give exact
dates for the beginning or the completion of this educational
revolution. It is certain that many boarders were received
by the colleges in the fourteenth century. But it was in
the course of the fifteenth century,[1] and especially towards
the middle of that century, that the pensioner-system and the
new educational methods which accompanied it, attained
their fullest development. In 1445 we find[2] the university
declaring in a petition to the King that 'almost the whole
University resides in the Colleges'. In 1459 the excessive
multiplication of non-bursarial students in the College of
Navarre led to disorders which called for the appointment
of a Royal Commission.[3] The growth of the system is the

[1] The reception of pensioners
(and also of non-boarders for instruction) is mentioned as common
in other colleges by the statutes of
the College of Beauvais, c. 1370
(Chapotin, p. 77). The appointment of a sub-magister in arts at
Navarre in 1404 suggests that
college teaching was increasing in
quantity and importance (Launoi,
i. 103). In 1428, however, it is still
contemplated that scholars in the
Collège de Séez will have to go to
the Rue du Fouarre. Félibien, v.
691.

[2] 'Item precipue apperiatur quo-
modo ipsa Universitas Parisiensis
in suis Collegiis maxime fundata
est, in quibus quasi tota residet,
ymo et durantibus guerrarum dis-
cidiis iam ipsa periisset, si in ipsis
Collegiis non esset conservata'
(Bulaeus, v. 536). [*Chartul.* iv, No.
2592, p. 648: instructions of Dec.
1444 to ambassadors.] The war
with England leading to the de-
sertion of the halls, which must
then have passed to other hands,

may have contributed to the growth
of the pensioner system when the
university began to fill again. So
in England the depopulation of the
universities, consequent upon the
Reformation, led to the extinction
of all the Cambridge, and most of
the Oxford, halls.

[3] The Commission issued in
1459 (*ap.* Launoi, ii. 165); the
edict of Louis XI enforcing its
recommendations appeared in 1464
(*ibid.* ii. 170 *sq.*). The following
extract illustrates the spontaneous
way in which the system had grown
up: 'Item, ad tollendam excessivam
Scholarium non Bursariorum mul-
titudinem quae confusionem parit
et magna affert incommoda, usque
etiam ad destructionem morum,
scientiae et aedificiorum dicti Collegii, obstruetur infra festum beati
Remigii proxime venturum ille
ingressus seu illa muri apertio,
quam Magister Grammaticorum
fieri fecit citra viginti aut sexde-
cim annos, ut de suis privatis et
acquisitis domibus ad Domum

more remarkable if (as du Boulay states) it had only been introduced into that college some ten years before.[1] From the report of the commission it appears that many dined and attended lectures in the college without sleeping in it; and it was now ordered that none should dine in college except those who lodged in it or in an adjoining house. By the beginning of the sixteenth century it seems to have been possible to obtain a degree without attending any but college lectures.[2] Eventually the schools of the Rue du Fouarre were deserted except for formal acts such as determinations and inceptions. Ramus, the great assailant of the Aristotelian traditions of medieval Paris, lived to see the death of the last regent who had taught in the schools of the Vicus Stramineus.[3] The assault on the old scholastic ideas and the metamorphosis of the educational system by which they had been kept alive, were connected by something more than an accidental synchronism. It was, in part at least, the revival of classical studies, and the new and more individual method of instruction which that revival brought with it, that led to the substitution of college teaching for the old university lectures. Perhaps, indeed, the earliest phase of their revival was not itself due to the better discipline and elementary instruction of the colleges.[4]

collegialem Scholares non Bursarii transire possent, quatenus Collegium predictum ad modum et statum quos, dum maxime floreret, habuit, ponatur et reducatur' (ibid., p. 171). It will be observed that here the pensioners are the private boarders of the master, rather than of the college, like the non-foundation boarders received by the head master of a foundation-school.

[1] 'Convictores nobiles tum primum accepit, Scholares extraneos et professores.' Bulaeus, iv. 97.

[2] None but college lectures seem contemplated by the statutes drawn up for the College of Montaigu in 1501. Félibien, v. 727 sq.

[3] Ramus, Prooem. reform. Par. Acad. (Scholae in lib. Artes, c. 1116).

The only survival of the university lectures in the faculty of arts was the ethics lecture which passed into a sort of professorship filled by annual election of the nations in turn. We hear that a new rector in 1458 'supplicavit Nationi cuius vices erant pro lectura Ethicae' (Bulaeus, v. 630. Cf. p. 726). An Oxford parallel might be found in the moral philosophy professorship, long held at Oxford (from 1673) by the senior proctor for the time being.

[4] [A very interesting description of university life at Paris under the college system of the sixteenth century may be read in M. Poëte, Une Vie de Cité, iii. 40 sq. The career of John Standonck of Malines

The stricter discipline of the colleges gradually reacted CHAP. V, upon the discipline of the university generally. The univer- § 5. sity was in its origin a voluntary association of individual Influence masters rather than a single educational institution conducted colleges by an organized staff. The university prescribed the studies university. which were to lead to the master's chair; but it did not attempt to interfere with the discipline of the scholars. In a sense all scholars were regarded as members, though not as governing members, of the 'University of Masters and Scholars'; but as primitive society recognized only heads of families, so the primitive university recognized only masters. The discipline of the streets was left to the ordinary police and the ecclesiastical tribunals. The discipline of the schools and the hospices (in so far as such a thing existed) was left to their respective masters or principals and the autonomous societies over which the latter presided. When a dispute arose as to whether a captured clerk was entitled to the university privileges, the sole question was whether any of the masters would claim him as a pupil. It was not till 1289 that the university required the names of all students together with an inventory of their property to be inscribed on the list or *Matricula* of some master as a condition of enjoying those privileges.[1] There

illustrates the possibilities of the new régime. Standonck was educated by the Brethren of the Common Life at Gouda. He studied at Paris and in 1483 was made head of the ruined College of Montaigu, which was rebuilt and revived under his care. A hospice for poor boys which he had formed at his own house grew into a large establishment attached to the college. When he drew up the statutes of 1503, the college contained more than 200 students, and was the centre of a reformed congregation which sent out reformers to the Dominican, Franciscan, and other orders and was inspired by the traditions of the Brethren of the Common Life. Calvin (1522–8) and Ignatius Loyola (1528) were both members of the

College of Montaigu. See A. Renaudet on Standonck in the *Bulletin de la société de l'histoire du Protestantisme français* (1908), pp. 5–81; M. Godet, *La Congregation de Montaigu* (Paris, 1912); A. Hyma, *The Christian Renaissance* (New York, 1925), ch. vii. Mention may here be made, for the later Jesuit system of teaching, to G. Dupont-Ferrier, *La Vie quotidienne d'un collège parisien pendant plus de trois cent cinquante ans: Du collège de Clermont au Lycée Louis-le-Grand*, i (1921), *Le Collège sous les Jésuites* (1563– 1762).]

[1] Bulaeus, iii. 449; *Chartul.* ii, No. 561. (Date wrong in Bulaeus.) In 1341 the inceptor is further to swear, 'Non dabitis testimonium de aliquo scolari, nisi vobis iuraverit, quod intendit esse vester scolaris

CHAP. V, was no university *Matricula* as in the Italian or German uni-
§ 5. versities. As late as 1461 we find the English-German nation providing, apparently for the first time, that students wishing to begin the course in arts shall appear before the congregation of the nation on the first day of the grand ordinary—or, as we should say, of the October term—and have their names inscribed in the register of the nation by the proctor.[1]

Improved discipline. In the fifteenth century, however, the university, or rather the faculty of arts, began, as it had never done before, to make in its corporate capacity a serious effort to put down the violent encounters between armed student-mobs or between students and townsmen which had hitherto been affairs of almost everyday occurrence in the streets of Paris. On these occasions neither college nor paedagogy afforded that sanctuary against the pursuit of proctorial justice which is supplied by the walls of an Oxford or Cambridge college.[2] The rector and proctors were empowered by the university to enter the college or hospice and there superintend the enforced chastisement of the offenders;[3] while masters who had participated in these exuberances of youthful spirits were deprived of their regency.

Authority of the university over the colleges. One of the most remarkable features of the Parisian as compared with the English college system is the extent to which at Paris the university or its constituent faculties and nations managed to acquire complete control over the colleges, to enforce regulations for their internal government,[4] and to

vester.' *Chartul.* ii, p. 680. [The responsibility of the master was fundamental. (Cf. above, pp. 283–6.) It had the authority of the Authenticum *Habita* of the Emperor Frederick I and was emphasized at Paris in the statutes of 1215: 'forum sui scolaris habeat'. It is a frequent subject of comment or illustration in sermons and academic writings in the thirteenth century. Paul Viollet assimilates it to 'family' law: *Hist. litt. de la France*, xxiii. 140.]
    [1] Bulaeus, v. 646–7; [*Auctarium*, ii. 935–9. The registration by the proctor of the nation of bachelors

on inception was, of course, much older; cf. the statute of the French nation in 1341. *Chartul.* ii, No. 1054; and Boyce, p. 105 and note.]
    [2] By custom, perhaps not by law.
    [3] Bulaeus, v. 704, 713, 726.
    [4] The faculty of arts for instance forbids the celebration of 'festa . . . cum minis [? mimis] seu instrumentis altis [? aliis] cum tapetis et brevibus seu quibusvis dissolutis habitibus animum scholarium distrahentibus a profectu et inducentibus ad lasciviam'. Bulaeus, v. 560. The bedels are directed to read the

remove their officers or foundationers, sometimes even with- out consulting the visitors named by the founder.[1] On one occasion the university actually sold the property of a college which had fallen into decay.[2] The right of visiting the colleges thus acquired by the university rested upon sheer usurpation—a usurpation which was made possible by its undoubted authority over the individual officers and members of the college.[3] It is obvious that such claims had only to be asserted to be irresistible, since expulsion from the university

statute in the presence of the principal and the assembled scholars. [On the relations between the University of Paris and the colleges, and Rashdall's view of the former's usurpation, see the Additional Note at the end of this section.]

[1] e.g. in 1466, when the French nation appointed a master of the Collège de la Marche. Bulaeus, v. 679–80. In one case, indeed, the nation in asserting its right to fill a vacant headship inserts the qualification 'maxime in absentia Collatorum seu Provisorum'. Bulaeus, v. 385. Cf. Jourdain, No. 1202.

[2] The College of Constantinople, in which in 1363 a single bursar survived, who assents to the transaction as 'Scholaris unicus Constantinopolitanus ac gubernator solus'. Bulaeus, iv. 366.

[3] Thus the nation of France in 1419 resolved that 'Collegium illud [de Lupara] erat Nationis, quia maior pars Scholarium debent esse de Nàtione', and further, 'quod Universitas et Nationes habent reformare sua Collegia' (Bulaeus, v. 345). The confusion into which the colleges had fallen during the wars, and the consequent ruin of their estates, probably contributed to enable the university to strengthen its hold upon them. Thus in 1421 the nation of France decreed a 'Reformatio' of a number of colleges which had fallen into ruin. This 'reform' was inaugurated by an

inquiry, carried out with all the thoroughness of a modern University Commission, into the state of the college revenues. It required a return ('codicillos') as to the statutes and property of the colleges, respecting, however, the 'secreta ipsorum Collegiorum, sicut vasa argentea, Iocalia Capellarum, thesaurus sive pecuniae eorum'. In some cases deeds of foundation and title-deeds had been lost and were recovered by the inquiries of the commission. The nation also ordered 'quod omnes viri Practici tam Magistri quam Scholares similiter et Officiarii Regii qui non studii gratia loca occupant Collegiorum, a dictis Collegiis expellantur' (Bulaeus, v. 350–2). How different might not the history of Oxford have been had there been medieval precedents for a similar interference by the university with college abuses. For other instances of such university visitation see Bulaeus, v. 384–6. Even where the visitor or 'collator' had appointed, his nominee came to the nation to obtain its authorization for his installation as master. *Ibid.* v. 385–6. [The English nation owned the short-lived College of Upsala, the more important College of Skara, also for Swedish students, and the *domus Dacie*; the Emperor Charles IV tried to get the nation to found a college for Germans. See Boyce, pp. 140–5.]

CHAP. V, would have prevented the accomplishment of the purpose
§ 5. for which students entered the college.

Legislation of 1452. In the Reform of 1452 the internal discipline of the colleges is thoroughly dealt with; and the duty of 'paedagogues' with reference to the moral well-being of their boarders is enforced in a manner which is in marked contrast with the absolute silence of the legates who had legislated for the university at previous visitations. The reformers descended to such details as the price, quality, and equal distribution of provisions.[1] At the same time the Commission ordered [the rector to summon every October a special congregation of the faculty of arts for the election of four visitors of colleges and paedagogies in which artists resided. The visitors were to be experienced masters of arts who were also graduates in one of the superior faculties, and were to be chosen one from each nation.][2]

Disorders in the Collège de Boissi. If the visitatorial claims of the university constituted a violation of the older college autonomy, the state of matters revealed by one of the first of its visitations shows that some such usurpation was not uncalled for. A student in the College of Boissi had been in the habit of leaving the college by day and by night without permission of the master; at times he had come accompanied by a party of boon companions armed with great swords and had assailed the college gates, which he found closed against him, with heavy stones.[3] Excommunicated for an assault upon one of his fellow scholars, he had refused to seek absolution and had tried to enter the chapel. Upon being forcibly ejected, he retired to his chamber while the others were engaged at mass, and set fire to his bed, so that the college narrowly escaped being burnt to the ground. On another occasion he had thrown big stones on to the roof of the hall during supper with so

[1] 'Quodque iustum et moderatum pretium pro victu secundum rerum et temporum qualitatem a scolaribus exigant; victualia munda, sana atque salubria scolaribus subministrent, et ex illis, honesta frugalitate servata, prestent cuique congruam portionem.' Bulaeus, v. 572; [Chartul. iv, No. 2690, p. 726. For a criticism of the word 'usurpation' in the text see below, Additional Note.]

[2] Bulaeus, v. 571; [Chartul. iv. 725].

[3] Bulaeus, v. 93.

much force that the food was covered with dust.[1] Similar annoyances had compelled the students to give up attending their lecture-rooms. Finally, being summoned before the rector to answer for these enormities, he had stationed his brother and a party of eight or ten armed men[2] between the Bernardine convent, where the university court assembled, and the rector's house—a measure which had the desired effect of preventing that official from attending the court. Even this catalogue of offences was not visited with deprivation till it was ascertained by examination that he was of 'rude intellect, not fitted or apt for acquiring proficiency';[3] and even then the sentence was merely deprivation of his bursar's place in the college, not expulsion from the university—a further punishment which was held over his head *in terrorem* in case he should refuse to quit the college within four days.

There was one great difficulty in the way of the university reformers who were trying to bring up the general discipline of the university to the stricter standard aimed at in the best colleges: this was the absolute liberty of migration enjoyed by the students in the hospices or paedagogies. The imagination declines to picture to itself the state of a public school in which a boy who found his housemaster's régime too exacting and restrictive should be perfectly free to transfer himself to the boarding-house of a more easy-going pedagogue. Yet such was the state of things which prevailed in the University of Paris with students of the same age as the modern fourth-form boy up to the year 1452. In that year Cardinal Estouteville, whose regulations for the internal conduct of *hospicia* have already been referred to, enacted that no paedagogue should receive into his house a student who had left his former master 'to avoid correction'.[4] One more

Prohibition of migration, 1452.

---

[1] 'Et dictis Scholaribus in prandio existentibus plancherium (ceiling) desuper cum grossis lapidibus percutiebat, pulveres super eorum cibaria cadere faciebat.' *Ibid.*, p. 94.

[2] 'Magnis ensibus et aliis armis invasivis munitos.'

[3] 'Rudis intellectus, non idoneus,

nec habilis ad proficiendum.' *Ibid.*, p. 93.

[4] 'Quatenus correctiones et disciplinas scholasticas faciant erga suos scolares secundum exigentiam culparum . . . Sed non liceat scolari juste ob culpam negligentiamve correcto, ad evitandam disciplinam ac correctionem, nisi

CHAP. V,
§ 5.
Suppres-
sion of
'mar-
tinets',
1457. step was wanted to complete the triumph within the university of order over anarchy, and that was the enforcement of
residence either in a college or a paedagogy. This step was
taken in 1457.[1] It seems probable that by this time the paedagogies had already become so far an essential part of the
university system that even the martinets went to some
college or paedagogy for lectures and other exercises, though
their own masters out of school.[2] It was now ordered that
the martinets 'should be bound to live in the Paedagogy or
adjoining places'.[3] At the same time the migration from one
master's house to another was forbidden in all cases except
with the leave of the scholar's nation or faculty. Moreover,
the mastership of a paedagogy was for the first time recognized as a university office by the provision that no one should
open a new paedagogy without the permission of the faculty.
In 1463 actual residence within the paedagogy or college was
explicitly required, except in the cases of those who lived in
the house of relatives or of some 'notable person' himself a
regent or student of the university.[4]

It is instructive to notice that Oxford purged itself or
attempted to purge itself of its 'Chamberdekyns' twenty
years before the suppression of the corresponding class of
martinets at Paris; while the history of every German university of which we possess any detailed record exhibits, through

alia causa sufficiens et honesta
suppetat, ad alium transire peda-
gogum; inhibentes ne talis ab alio
pedagogo recipiatur in domo sua,
qui propter correctionem debitam
prioris magistri domum exierit.'
Bulaeus, v. 572. A principal thus
bereft of his pupil was to reclaim
him, 'coram cancellario vel eius
officiali' [*Chartul.* iv. 726, 727].

[1] Bulaeus, v. 622. The resolution is one of the nation of France,
but was intended for adoption by
the faculty of arts.

[2] As much seems to be implied
in the name, which is derived from
their habit of roosting under the
eaves of the paedagogy instead of
inside, or (according to others)

from their flitting from one house
to another.

[3] 'Voluit insuper Martinetos ad-
stringi Paedagogia aut loca vicina
inhabitare.' *Ibid.* v. 622.

[4] 'Quod nulli de caetero in ipsa
Artium Facultate tempus acquirent,
neque eisdem sigillum Rectoris, aut
Procuratoris, aut signeta Paedago-
gorum et Regentium pro examinan-
dis ad gradum Baccalaureatus aut
licentiae expedientur, nisi per tempus sufficiens ad gradum obtinendum moram traxerint in Collegio,
Paedagogio aut domo suorum
parentum, aut alicuius notabilis
viri in aliqua 4 Facultatum Regentis
aut studentis, gratis serviendo.'
Ibid. v. 658.

the whole of the fifteenth century, a similar course of in- CHAP. V,
creasingly severe legislation for the enforcement of college § 5.
discipline or its equivalent upon all students of the faculty
of arts.[1] It should be observed that at Paris, as at Oxford and
elsewhere, these statutes had constantly to be renewed; so
that it was only by slow degrees that this lowest, idlest, and
most lawless class of students was improved away.[2]

There was, however, one most important feature in which Colleges of full exercise and 'combined lectures'.
the Parisian system of college education differed from the
system which was growing up at the same time in the English
universities. That difference was a necessary outcome of the
difference in the original constitution of the two kinds of
college. At Paris, as has been said, the original constitution
provided the arts students of a college with one master and

[1] As to Oxford, see [*Statuta Antiqua*, p. 208; and the introduction, p. lxxxii]. At Vienna, in 1410 (Kink, ii. 236), scholars not residing in a master's house are deprived of the privileges of the university in the event of arrest or imprisonment, except 'honestae personae notae tamen in suis Statibus, quibus in priuatis domibus stare solitarie sua cum familia aut cum aliis habitare placuerit', who are required to obtain the licence of the rector. The rector is given the power of deposing or depriving 'negligentes hospites', whether masters or not. A scholar expelled from one 'Bursa aut habitatio Studentium' is not to be received into another without leave of rector and dean. An elaborate statute of 1413 regulates the discipline of these 'Bursae'. The punishments are fines, and, in the last resort, expulsion from the house. The mildness of the discipline now imposed is a sufficient illustration of its previous absence, e.g. for laying violent hands upon the 'Conventor Bursae' (i.e. the master) 'absque tamen sanguinis effusione aut alias notabili corporis laesione', the penalty is expulsion and a fine of 24 grossi (p. 249): 'si

quis Bursalium cum muliere suspecta in Bursa occulte deprehensus fuerit', 3 grossi (p. 253), &c. It is satisfactory to find, however, that a student who 'invasit suum conventorem cum cultello et fugavit eum ad tertiam domum' was actually imprisoned (*ibid*. i, pt. i, p. 38). The statute of 1413 further orders 'quod non stent plures simulquam quatuor sine Magistro, Baccalaureo aut alio, cui tanquam Rectori obediant' (iii. 255). Provisions were made for enforcing some decency of behaviour on those who lived 'cum hospite' or 'in domibus pauperum'; in these cases alone is corporal punishment contemplated (they were probably the poorest scholars). They may be punished 'vel in pecunia, vel in corpore, vel in carceratione, seu in promotionibus, prout Rectori', &c. The visitors of the university appointed by the Council of Basel in 1436 made further provisions for domestic discipline, e.g. bachelors of arts were not allowed to preside over a hall (p. 281); and in 1509 (p. 316) every student was placed under the supervision of a tutor (*praeceptor*).

[2] See Bulaeus, v. 810, 812.

CHAP. V, only one. Even if the college had other masters of arts on its
§ 5. foundation as students of theology, these had nothing to do
with the discipline or instruction of the artists; and many
Paris colleges were colleges of artists only, some of them very
small ones. It is obvious that the single master could not
supply the whole of the instruction needed by all his pupils
through the whole of their course. At Oxford the instruction
of the junior members of the foundation and of non-founda-
tioners (in so far as it was conducted within college walls)
was entrusted to the numerous M.A. fellows, who had always
been closely associated with the students in arts. The system
of university teaching was gradually supplanted by the
tutorial system which has lasted down to our own day.[1] At
Paris the bigger colleges—especially no doubt those who had
succeeded in attracting a large number of paying students—
hired additional regents to lecture to their men in college, and
these regents gradually took the place of the regents in the
Rue du Fouarre with less change of educational method than
was ultimately necessitated at Oxford by the responsibility
of the single tutor for almost the whole work of his pupils.
Meanwhile, the smaller colleges and the paedagogies were
glad to send their members for lectures to the larger and
better-equipped establishments. And the number of colleges
which supplied a full course of instruction to their members
continually diminished till, before the end of the fifteenth
century, the 'Collèges de plein exercice' (as those which provided a full educational course were called) had reduced
themselves to eighteen, though the whole number of colleges
were considerably over fifty. In the faculty of theology lecturing had likewise become confined within the walls of two
secular colleges—the Sorbonne and the College of Navarre—
together with the houses of the regulars.[2] Thus, in place of
the system of college isolation which prevailed until recently
in Oxford, the system of education in the University of Paris
resolved itself (so far as the faculty of arts was concerned)

[1] It was, however, only gradually
that instruction passed into the
hands of the pupil's single tutor.
In the sixteenth and seventeenth
centuries there was often a well-
organized system of *Praelectors*.
[2] Goulet, f. xiiii; Bulaeus, v. 827,
857; Launoi, i. 263, 265.

into a system of inter-collegiate lectures—a system which the CHAP. V,
University Commission of 1882 reproduced in Oxford as the § 5.
best practicable means of combining the advantages of college teaching with that of a purely professorial or university
system. Of course, no comparison is intended between the
details of the two systems. At Paris the larger colleges came
in the sixteenth century to be organized very much after the
manner of large schools divided into classes, each of them
comprising the students of one year and taught by a separate
regent, while the smaller colleges and paedagogies reduced
themselves to boarding-houses dependent on the 'Collèges de
plein exercice'.

While the system of college-teaching had many advantages Advan-
from the point of view of the student or at least from that of the system
his parents or guardians, it was no less attractive from the to masters.
point of view of the master; and these advantages no doubt
contributed largely to its growth and also to the eventual
concentration of teaching in the larger colleges. Originally,
the schools or lecture-rooms of the university were merely
rooms hired from private individuals. The master depended
for his support (if not beneficed) upon the fees of his students,
while for the payment of the rent he depended mainly upon
the fees of his bachelors at determination.[1] When the nations
acquired schools of their own near the Church of S. Julien,[2]
the situation was not materially altered, except that the master
was responsible for the rent to the nation instead of to the
landlord. The colleges at least freed the regent from anxiety
as to his rent; while, as the practice of boarding in colleges
began with the richer scholars, it is probable that they were
able to offer larger as well as less precarious incomes to competent teachers. The superior ability and experience of the
more permanent college regents no doubt enabled them to

[1] In 1306 the French nation provided that if a master's determining
bachelors were insufficient to pay
the rent, the deficiency should be
supplied 'de bursis determinantium vel de aliis obventionibus'.
Bulaeus, iv. 100; *Chartul.* ii, No.
655. [Cf. above, p. 455.]

[2] Towards the end of the fourteenth century we find the various
nations beginning to buy or build
schools of their own. The movement in favour of university buildings appears to have begun at about
this time, or a little later, all through
Europe. [Cf. above, p. 406.]

compete at an advantage with the young master who was teaching for a year in the Rue du Fouarre to satisfy the statutes of the university, and even with the keeper of the private-adventure paedagogy.

Position of the college regent in the university.
By accepting a college appointment of this kind and giving up his school in the Rue du Fouarre, the regent lost the rights of regency. It appears, however, that considerable laxity prevailed in the enforcement of this regulation. For, though every duly incepted master had a right to the position of regent, he had to supplicate for 'Regency and Schools', and, since the number of schools at the disposal of the faculty was limited, the *supplicat* could not invariably be granted, and masters who were thus kept waiting for schools were provisionally admitted to all the rights of regency.[1] There were thus a considerable number of regent masters not actually teaching in the Rue du Fouarre: hence it is easy to understand that, under cover of this exception, many college regents may have continued to enjoy their university privileges, though they had no intention of ever teaching in the schools of their faculty. This state of things no doubt contributed to the growth of the college system. In 1456, however, an attempt was made to check these growing irregularities by enacting that no regent who did not 'continuously conduct pupils to the Rue du Fouarre' and lecture to them there, should enjoy the privileges of regency.[2] An exception is, however, made in respect of the 'Masters and Paedagogues' who had long lectured in the Rue du Fouarre. These were to enjoy all the privileges of regency except a share in the weekly distributions at the national vespers and mass, and were henceforth called honorary regents. The resolution is interesting as an

[1] Bulaeus, v. 858, 859.

[2] *Ibid*. v. 617. (See above, p. 410, n. 2.) The regulation was renewed in 1474, *ibid*., pp. 711, 712. The resolutions are silent as to the power of voting in congregation, but it would seem that college regents must be excluded since their position must have been different from that of the honorary regents who were likewise excluded from distributions, and complaints were made that collegians suffered through being examined by 'Paedagogi suos baccalarios habentes domesticos et commensales'. *Ibid*., p. 575. It is implied that college regents could not be examiners, presumably because not full regents in the university sense.

indication of the growth of college teaching. The college regents are now a numerous body, but presumably not in a large majority, though it is of course conceivable that they may have taken a less active part in the affairs of the university than the more constitutional, but less employed and more needy, regents of the Rue du Fouarre. Nothing, however, is said as to the exclusion of the pupils of the college regents from the university degree: hence we may conclude that by this time college lectures have acquired a tacit recognition as 'ordinary lectures' of the university.

In 1486 the constitutional position of the regents again attracted the attention of the university. *De facto* the status of the regents was simply that of the assistant-master in a modern English public school. Under these circumstances it is not surprising that the principal of the College of Lisieux should have thought he had a right to dismiss his regent. The deprived regent, however, appealed to the faculty of arts, which, conformably with its general claim to supervise the colleges, determined that in future regents in colleges, though nominated by the principal, should receive their appointment from the faculty and be removable only by that body. It was further enacted that none should be allowed to teach arts in the colleges who were not actual members of the faculty.[1] Hence the system of college teaching at Paris was further differentiated from the college system of Oxford by being subject to university supervision,[2] which extended at times even to the actual inspection of college lectures.[3]

A more detailed account of these extinct Parisian colleges would not be interesting to the English reader. A list of

[1] *Ibid.* v. 771–4. The superior faculties, however, asserted the right of their graduates to preside over colleges or paedagogies of artists. Crevier, iv. 424.

[2] It is true that by the Oxford statutes a college tutor (not lecturer) could not be dismissed without the consent of the Vice-Chancellor, but since it rested with the head to assign pupils to different tutors, and as each tutor was paid solely by the fees of his pupils, the statute was inoperative. The Provost of Oriel was thus able virtually to deprive Newman of his tutorship.

[3] In 1498 a statute of the French nation reciting that 'multi (Regentes) sunt qui dicunt se habere materias qui forte non habent', appoints delegates 'visitare Lectiones singulorum Collegiorum'. Bulaeus, v. 827.

CHAP. V, the colleges with their founders and dates of foundation is
§ 5. appended to this section. It will at all events serve to impress
upon the reader's mind their very large number, and to warn
him against exaggerating the peculiarities of the English
college system. It must, however, be added that the list is
very probably incomplete. More than one college mentioned
in it is revealed to us only by a single accidental allusion.
There can be no more interesting illustration of the contrast
between English and French history than the fate of the
Oxford and of the Paris colleges respectively. Some of the
Parisian colleges may be said to have enjoyed only an intermittent existence. From time to time war emptied the college rooms, or prevented the collection of the revenues from
the country estates.[1] We constantly hear of colleges falling
into total decay.[2] Sometimes the scanty remains of their
property (occasionally nothing was left but a dilapidated
building) were merged in some wealthier foundation. And

[1] How war affected the universities is indicated by a Paris college
statute of 1397, which provides that
there shall be 'unus parvus cofrus
catenatus pro pecuniis servandis,
qui ponatur in aliquo loco tuto,
quando propter generales guerras,
vel alias, essent pauci scolares
ydonei in domo'. Félibien, v. 667.

[2] So in 1430 the College of Hubant was so much overwhelmed by
debt and dilapidation that all payments to bursars had to be suspended (Jourdain, p. 253). The
College of Montaigu was in ruins
and without revenues in 1483, when
Jean Standonck became master,
took rich boarders, and made them
support the 'Pauperes' (ibid., p. 301,
note; above, p. 521 n.). In 1463
the Collège de Coquerel was found
to have no bursar and to be full
of workmen and their families who
had occupied the empty rooms
(ibid., p. 290, note). In 1445 the
English had applied the revenues of
college estates in Normandy to the
support of the rival University of

Caen, to which all Norman students
were now compelled to go. Bulaeus,
v. 536, 537.
The following resolutions of the
university may be left to speak for
themselves:
'Tertium Caput rerum ab Universitate hoc anno gestarum fuit
lustratio et reformatio Collegiorum,
quorum pleraque calamitate temporum aut funditus ruebant, aut
Praefectos non habebant, aut re-
ditus non percipiebant, aut prave
administrabantur.' Bulaeus, v. 350,
an. 1421.
'Item placuit Nationi quod omnes viri Practici, tam Magistri quam
Scholares, similiter et Officiarii
Regii qui non studii gratia loca
occupant Collegiorum, a dictis Collegiis expellantur.' loc. cit.
'Item placuit Nationi quod Collegiis in quibus nulli vel pauci
et antiqui habitant, praeficiantur et
ordinentur ad eorum regimen et
salvationem utensilium, librorum,
redituum et litterarum duo vel 3
notabiles Magistri.' loc. cit.

at the Revolution the collegiate system as a whole fell with
the other institutions of medieval France—never (like so
much of the *ancien régime*) to reproduce itself under altered
forms in modern times. In England—thanks to our insular
position and the comparative mildness of our civil wars—no
college ever disappeared through a failure of revenue:[1] in
most of them the increasing value of their estates has (till
recently) more than kept pace with the rise of prices: a few
of them have at times been scandals of corporate opulence.
Of all the secular foundations which medieval piety bequeathed to Oxford[2] she has lost not one. During the last
hundred years the college buildings and the college system
alike have silently adapted themselves to the altered needs of
the present with that power of spontaneous self-development
which is the happy peculiarity of English institutions. It is
with a melancholy feeling that the dweller in Oxford quad-
rangles wanders through the old Quartier Latin of the Mother
University and finds scarcely anything left to remind him of
the historic colleges and schools and convents which once
occupied the sites now covered by dirty slums or trim boule-
vards, save the street-names—always the most durable
landmarks of urban history. Those silent witnesses of the
past will remain there to remind modern students of the rock
whence they were hewn and the hole of the pit whence they
were digged, until the fertile brain of some municipal coun-
cillor is fired with the ambition of replacing them by names
less contaminated by clerical associations.

Additional Note

[The following note on the relations between the university and
colleges of Paris was written by the late Professor Paetow, with
special reference to Rashdall's observation that 'the right of visiting
the colleges thus acquired by the University rested upon sheer

[1] Except the very modern Hertford College (founded 1740) and
that only for a time. It is said that
during the decay of this college,
when there was only one (insane)
fellow left, all sorts of unauthorized persons took up their abode in
the ruinous buildings (Cox, *Recol-*

lections of Oxford, 1870, p. 190).
See below, vol. iii, App. on 'Lost
Colleges at Oxford'.

[2] The same might be said of
Cambridge but for the merging of
older colleges in Trinity and the
merging of Godshouse in Christ's
College.

usurpation—a usurpation which was made possible by its undoubted authority over the individual affairs and members of the College' (above, p. 523).

'Although Rashdall modifies this statement somewhat by giving other reasons also, I think that this theory does an injustice to the university and neglects a great mass of evidence of statutory rights given freely to the university by founders of the colleges and their representatives.

'The university had very definite statutory rights in the Sorbonne from the earliest years:

' "Nichilominus quoque statuimus et etiam ordinamus ut te, fili, provisore obeunte nullus in locum tuum per fraudis astutiam apponatur, nisi quem . . . loci archidiaconus . . . cancellarius Parisiensis ac magistri Parisius actu regentes in theologica facultate, necnon decretistarum et medicorum decani . . . rector Universitatis Parisiensis, et procuratores quatuor nationum communiter vel major pars eorum duxerint apponendum . . . qui etiam de dictorum magistrorum receptis et expensis annis singulis archidiacono, cancellario et aliis supradictis vel aliquibus ab ipsis vel a maiori parte ipsorum qui ad hoc extiterint deputati teneatur reddere rationem. Archidiaconus insuper, cancellarius et alii memorati seu maior pars eorum provisorem quem duxerint statuendum amovere valeant prout viderint faciendum" (*Chartul*. i, No. 421).

'Each of the four nations had the right of presenting students to the Sorbonne by statute (*Auctarium*, i. 162, 163).

'In the case of the College of Harcourt "approbatores" were named by the founder, the chancellor, the rector, and the senior master of the faculty of theology belonging to the Norman nation (Bouquet, p. 587). The faculty of theology and the chancellor had wide powers in the College of Navarre also. Hence the three largest and most influential colleges at Paris were definitely linked with the university.

'The aid of the university in maintaining discipline was frequently sought by the founders. Thus at the College of Narbonne in 1379: "Quod si quis in profundo malorum lapsus, ad vindictam vel ad aliam violentiam propter premissa contra aliquem haspiraret, minas inferret; confestim ad auxilium provisoris vel universitatis recurratur . . ." (Félibien, v. 669).

'The final submission of the colleges to the control of the university was the result of a series of developments in which the university and the nations, to be sure, played their part; but in which the college founders and college members shared also—and not against their will; and to which the accidents of war and other times of stress gave a strong impetus.

'In his account of the University of Oxford Rashdall attributes the difference in the position of the chancellor at Oxford and the chancellor at Paris to the existence of a cathedral church at Paris administered by a bishop and a body of canons. It seems to me that in this different position of the chancellor at Paris lies the key to the difference between the independent Oxford college and the Parisian college subject to the university. The chapter of Paris and particularly the chancellor stood as intermediaries between the college and the university. It was the rule—there are few exceptions—to appoint the chancellor or some other member of the chapter to visit the college. It should be said that these powers were given the chancellor rather as a representative of the Church of Paris than as chancellor of the university; but in the actual exercise of the powers there would be no such distinction. In any case it was probably not the constitutional consideration that was uppermost in the minds of the founders. If they were indeed in Paris at the time the statutes were made they were presently going on to other parts of France, to Scotland, to Upsala, or to Italy to be occupied with other business. Here was an important ecclesiastic of the Church of Paris on the ground upon whom, by virtue of his connexion with the university also, they could depend upon to have a perpetual interest in the welfare of the students who were, perhaps, to be pupils in his classes. When he was associated with other dignitaries living at a distance from Paris he soon acquired complete control. Since he was always at Paris and continually dealing with student affairs, it was natural that he should take the responsibility. In 1380 the Archbishop of Reims, who had rights in the College of Cambrai, resigned all power into the hands of the venerable man and master, John de Calore, Chancellor of the Church of Paris (Jourdain, *Index Chronologicus*, p. 178).

'Furthermore, there is no evidence that it was the chancellor who took the initiative in securing these rights. In the early years of the university, when the good behaviour of students outside the classroom was no concern of the university, he probably regarded his duties in this direction as unpleasant and unnecessary and either neglected them a great deal or assigned them to some one else. The statutes of the College of Cambrai suggest as much:

'"Ut autem praedicta et infra scripta omnia et singula futuris temporibus securius et fructuosius observentur, cancellarium dictae ecclesiae Parisiensis nunc vel pro tempore existentem, facimus, constituimus ac deputamus perpetuo specialem et immediatum protectorem, defensorem et visitatorem, correctorem, reformatorem et superiorem dictae domus et collegii supradictorum; et nihilominus statuimus et ordinamus, quod magister dictae domus, et capellanus, et scholares omnes dictae domus, omnes et singuli, praesentes et futuri, teneantur et debeant anno quolibet requirere et rogare ipsum cancellarium qui erit pro tempore, et erga eum semel et pluries insistere cum effectu, ut accedat ad domum eamdem personaliter, et in ea officium visitatoris, correctoris, et reformatoris impendat. Cui cancellario, cum ad ipsam domum causa exercendae visitationis accesserit, ostendi et legi· debeat de verbo ad verbum praesens capitulum super hoc in fundatione dictae domus per nos specialiter ordinatum. Item, cancellarius, vocatis secum aliquibus honestis

536 PARIS [514]

personis, super statu domus, ac vita et moribus magistri et scholarium
et sacerdotis dictae domus, et observatione statutorum et ordina-
tionum factarum vel faciendarum et scholasticae disciplinae et
super aliis quae sibi videbuntur, inquirat simpliciter et de plano
sine strepitu iudicii et figura; et quae corrigenda viderit, corrigat et
emendet; ipsique cancellario visitanti magister, scholares, et sacerdos
et caeteri domus eiusdem familiares obedire et parere in praedictis
totaliter teneantur" (Félibien, iii. 434, 435).'

Professor Paetow concluded that there 'would be no act of aggression or "usurpation" if the authorities of the University visited the
College of Cambrai'. Rashdall, who minimized unduly the influence
of the chancellor in the university, would doubtless have pointed
out that the conclusion does not follow, and from a strictly constitutional standpoint, he would (so far as this particular case goes) have
been right. Yet Professor Paetow's main contention, that the intervention of the university in college affairs cannot appropriately be
described as usurpation, seems to us to be sound.]

LIST OF THE COLLEGES FOUNDED
BEFORE A.D. 1500

[* denotes a college for Monks. The Mendicant Colleges are not included
in this list.]

Colleges.	*Date.*	*Founders.*
Collège des Dix-huit	1180	Jocius de Londoniis.
S. Thomas du Louvre, later		Robert, Count of Dreux.
S. Nicholas du Louvre	c. 1186	
C. de Constantinople	c. 1204 (?)	
C. des Bons Enfans de S.		
Honoré	120⅔	Étienne Belot and wife.
*Maison de l'Ordre du Val		
des Escoliers (Austin		
canons)	c. 1228	
*C. du Chardonnet	1246	Stephen Lexington, Abbot of Clair-vaux.
[C. des Bons Enfants de S.		
Victor.	*ante* 1248]	
*C. des Prémontrés	c. 1252	John, Abbot of Prémontré.
C. de la Sorbonne	1257	Robert de Sorbon, Canon of Paris, Royal Chaplain, &c.
*C. de Cluny	1260–2[1]	Yves de Vergi, Abbot of Cluny.
*C. de S. Denis	c. 1263	
C. du Trésorier (*or* de Saône,		
or de Rouen)	*ante* 1266	Guill. de Saône, Treasurer of Rouen.
C. d'Abbeville	1271	Gerard d'Abbeville, Archdeacon of Ponthieu.

[1] [For the dates see *Chartul.* i, Nos. 361, 370. In 1286 the college contained 40 students of theology: *ibid.*, No. 486, note.]

Colleges.	Date.	Founders.	
C. de Calvi (*or* La Petite Sorbonne) . . .	1271 (?)	Robert de Sorbon, Canon of Paris, Royal Chaplain, &c.	
C. des Daces (*domus Dacorum*)	1275[1]		
[C. of Upsala[2]. . *ante*	1280]		
C. d'Harcourt . . .	1280	Raoul d'Harcourt, Doctor of Decrees, Canon of Paris, Archdeacon of Coutances, Chancellor of Bayeux, Chanter of Evreux, Grand Archdeacon of Rouen.	
[C. des Bons Enfants d'Arras[3] . . . *ante*	1282]		
C. des Cholets (*or* de Beauvais)	1295	Jean Cholet, D.U.J., Cardinal and Papal Legate in France.	
C. du Cardinal Lemoine .	1301	Cardinal Jean Lemoine.	
C. de Navarre . . .	1304	Joanna, Queen of Navarre and Consort of Philip IV.	
C. de Bayeux . . .	1309	Guill. Bonet, Bishop of Bayeux.	
C. de Laon ⎫ ⎬ . . 1314 ⎨ C. de Prêles ⎭		Gui de Laon, Canon of Paris, Laon, and the Sainte Chapelle. Raoul de Presles, King's clerk. (Originally these two foundations were a single college; separated in 1323.)	
C. des Aicelins, *afterwards* de Montaigu . .	1314	Giles Aicelin, Archbishop of Rouen; restored in 1388 by Pierre Aicelin de Montaigu, Bishop of Nevers and Laon and Cardinal.	
C. de Narbonne . .	1317	Bernard de Farges, Archbishop of Narbonne.	
C. de Linköping . .	1317		
C. de Skara, early fourteenth cent.			
C. de Cornouaille (*or* Quimper)	1321	Nicolaus Galeranus, clerk.	
C. du Plessis . . .	1322	Geoffroi du Plessis, Notary Apostolic and Secretary of Philip the Long.	

[1] [*Chartul.* i, No. 464 and note.]
[2] [*Ibid.*, No. 496 and note. According to Schück, this college, known also as the Collège de Suesse was definitely founded in 1291, and this date appears on the plaque recently placed on its site in the Rue Serpente.]
[3] [The hostel at Paris of the Bons Enfants of Arras, founded at Arras in the middle of the century and controlled by the chapter. (The college came to an end before 1441.) See A. Guesnon, 'Un Collège inconnu des Bons Enfants d'Arras à Paris du XIIIe au XIVe siècle', in *Mém. de la Soc. de l'histoire de Paris*, xlii (1915), 1–37.]

CHAP. V,	*Colleges.*	*Date.*

Founders.

C. de Maclou . . *c.* 1323 — Jacques Rousselet, Archdeacon of Reims, executor of Raoul Rousselet, Bishop of Laon.

C. de Tréguier . . 1325 — Guill. de Coetmohair, Chanter of Tréguier.

C. des Écossais . . 1326 — David, Bishop of Moray.

*C. de Marmoutier (*or* de S. Martin) . . *c.* 1329 — Geoffroi du Plessis (for the monks of the Abbey of Marmoutier at Tours).

C. d'Arras . . . 1332 — Nicholas le Caudrelier, Abbot of S. Vast.

C. de Bourgogne . . 1332 — Joanna of Burgundy, Dowager of Philip the Long.

C. de Tours . . . 1334 — Étienne de Bourgueil, Archbishop of Tours.

C. des Lombards . . 1334 — Andrew Ghini (of Florence), clerk of Charles le Bel, Bishop of Arras and Tournay, and Cardinal; François de l'Hôpital (of Modena), clerk of the Royal Cross-bowmen (*Albalêtriers*); Renier Jean (of Pistoia), Apothecary; Manuel de Rolland (of Piacenza), Canon of S. Marcel in Paris.

[Hostel for the canons of Saint-Jean des Vignes, Soissons[1] . . . 1335 — Jeanne de Chastel.]

C. de Lisieux (*or* de Torchi) 1336 — Gui d'Harcourt, Bishop of Lisieux; absorbed in the college founded (1414) by Guill. d'Estouteville, Bishop of Lisieux, Estond d'Estouteville, Abbot of Fécamp and their brother, the Seigneur de Torchi.

C. d'Hubant (*or* de l'Ave Maria) . . 1336 *or* 1339 — Maître Jean de Hubant, President of the *Chambre d'Enquêtes.*

C. de Bertrand (*or* d'Autun) 1341 — Pierre Bertrand, Bishop of Nevers and Autun and Cardinal.

C. de S. Michel (*or* de Chanac) . . . 1343 (?) — Guill. de Chanac, Bishop of Paris and Patriarch of Alexandria.

C. des Allemands . *ante* 1348 — (A *Domus Pauperum.*)

C. des trois Évêques (*or* de Cambrai) . . . 1348 — Hugues de Pomare, Bishop of Langres. Hugues d'Arci, Bishop of Laon and Archbishop of

---

[1] [Jeanne de Chastel was the widow of Raoul de Presles. See H. Omont, *Bibliothèque de l'École des Chartes,* lxxxvii (1926), 367–71.]

Colleges.	Date.	Founders.	CHAP. V,

Reims, Guill. d'Auxonne, Bishop of Cambrai and Autun.

Colleges.	Date.	Founders.
C. de Maître Clément	1349	Maître Robert Clément.
C. de Tournai.	c. 1350	
C. de Mignon .	ante 1353	Maître Jean Mignon.
C. de Boncour (or Bécond)	1353	Pierre Bécond, Chevalier.
C. de Justice .	1358	Jean de Justice, Chanter of Bayeux and Canon of Paris.
C. de Boissi	1359	Étienne Vidé de Boissi-le-sec, Canon of Laon.[1]
C. de la Marche	1363	Maître Jean de la Marche (an Ex-Rector). (Absorbing the ruined College of Constantinople.)
C. de Vendôme	ante 1367	
C. de Dormans (or de Beau-vais) .	1370	Jean de Dormans, Bishop of Beau-vais and Cardinal.
C. de Maître Gervais	1370	Gervais Chrestien, First Physician of Charles V.
C. de Dainville	1380	Gerard de Dainville, Bishop of Cambrai, and Jean de Dainville, Knight.
C. de Fortet .	1391[2]	Pierre Fortet, M.A., Lic. U.J.
C. de Tou (de Tulleio)	ante 1393	
C. de Tonnerre	ante 1406	The Abbot (Richard de Tonnerre) and Convent of S. Jean en Vallée.
C. de Reims .	1409	Gui de Roye, Archbishop of Reims.
C. de Donjon .	1412	Olivier de Donjon. (Afterwards united with Tréguier.)
C. de Thori .	ante 1421	
C. de Kerambert (or de Léon) .	ante 1421	(United to C. de Tréguier.)
C. de Séez	1428	Grégoire l'Anglais, Bishop of Séez.
C. de Rethel .	ante 1443	(In that year united to College of Reims.)
C. de Lorris .	ante 1444	
C. d'Aubusson	?	
C. de Saint-Barbe	1460	Geoffroy Lenormant, Master of Grammarians at Coll. of Navarre.
C. de Coquerel	1463	Nicolas de Coquerel, B.D., Canon of Amiens.
C. de Boucard.	1484	Jean Boucard, Bishop of Avranches.

[1] [The *rotulus* of the French nation, 1379, states that the college was founded by 'dominum Gode-fridum et eius nepotem magistrum Stephanum de Boissyaco': *Chartul.* ii. 252.]

[2] [This is the date of the foun-der's will. The college dates from 1394. See Raoul Busquet, in *Mém. de la Soc. de l'hist. de Paris*, xxxiii (1906), 187 *sq.*]

§ 6. THE PLACE OF THE UNIVERSITY IN EUROPEAN HISTORY

[The fifth volume of the *Chartularium Universitatis Parisiensis*, now in course of preparation, will comprise documents from 1396 to *c.* 1450, and will be the main textual authority on the university during the period of the Schism and Councils, to which Rashdall gives much attention in this chapter.]

CHAP. V, ALONE among the earliest university towns, Paris was a great
§ 6. capital. It occupied indeed more completely the position of
Political
influence a modern capital than any other city of continental Europe.
of the uni-
versity: It is hardly too much to say that the descendants of Hugh
due to its
situation Capet eventually succeeded in making themselves the real
in a great masters of France, just because, when their power was at its
capital.
lowest, they were still masters of Paris. The political position
of Paris gave its university a place in the political and ecclesiastical world which no other university has ever occupied.
Its masters played as important a part in medieval politics as
men of the pen or of the tongue could well play in an age
Period of which was governed by the sword. The influence of the
this in-
fluence. university in this direction was most strongly felt after the
period of her greatest intellectual brilliancy. In the thirteenth
century the university was too cosmopolitan a body to concern itself much with French politics. The French king protected foreign clerks, even when he was at war with their
country.[1] In the twelfth and thirteenth centuries scholars
were, indeed, to a degree which is hardly intelligible in
modern times, citizens of the world. Though almost all the
greatest schoolmen from the time of Abélard onwards taught
in Paris at one period or other of their lives, hardly one
Parisian scholastic of the very first rank was a Frenchman by
birth.[2] Moreover, just at the period at which the university
was growing into a great corporation, the influence of the
Friars—at the Court of Rome, at the Louvre, and everywhere
else—was at its zenith. During the first century of its corporate life the university had enough to do to make good its

[1] See, e.g., *Chartul.* ii, Nos. 718–
20. [In 1315, with special reference
to Flanders, No. 719.]

[2] Bretons of course being excluded. But cf. below, p. 562, n. 3.

right to an independent existence.[1] An age of friars succeeded CHAP. V, an age of monks; and the age of doctors was not yet come. §6. But just as the Papacy exercised a really more commanding and certainly a more elevating influence over European affairs in the days of Hildebrand than in the days of the bolder and more arrogant usurpations of Innocent III, and a more powerful influence under Innocent III than in the days of Boniface VIII or of the Avignon Schism, so the intellectual ferment of the schools of Paris was most vigorous, the genius which inspired its teaching most brilliant, its monopoly of the highest education most complete, almost before a university existed at all. The political influence of the university did not begin till the greatest Parisian schoolmen were in their graves; while just as its influence, its privileges, and its pretensions rose to their highest point, the period of intellectual decadence set in.

This organized scholastic democracy became politically The university an organ of public opinion. important in much the same way that the Corporation of London acquired so much political importance under the Stuart kings of England. Here under the very palace of a despotic king, in the midst of subjects almost without municipal privileges, and placed under the arbitrary authority of the royal provost,[2] was a body of educated men protected by the sanctity of their order against the hand of secular justice, possessing the right of public meeting, of free debate, and of access to the throne. And the tendency of a body so situated to become a great organ of public opinion, a channel through which the Court might address itself to the nation and the voice of the nation might reach the Court, was strengthened by the deliberate policy of the House of Valois—with whose accession this tendency became for the first time distinctly visible—the policy of depressing the nobility and conciliating the support of the clerical and lawyer classes.

[1] [See, however, S. d'Irsay, 'L'Opinion publique dans les universités médiévales: étude sur l'activité politique de l'université de Paris à ses débuts', in the Revue des études historiques, xcix (1932), 237-56.]

[2] [The words 'arbitrary author-ity' are misleading in so far as they suggest that the jurisdiction of the royal officials in Paris was not influenced by local custom: see Olivier Martin, Histoire de la coutume de la prevôté et vicomté de Paris, i (1922), 42-74.]

CHAP. V,
§ 6.
'The eldest
daughter
of the
King.'
At all public ceremonials, in those great assemblies of notables which the French kings from time to time gathered around them, in the councils of the National Church, and even in the States General, the universities were fully represented. We find a symbol of this new position of the university in the title 'eldest daughter of the King', which was first assumed under Charles V. But it was especially in the paralysis of the royal authority which ensued upon the death of that monarch in 1380 that the university, emboldened by the royal favour and widely diffused prestige to which it had become accustomed, most conspicuously asserted itself as a factor in the political forces of the age. To enumerate all the instances between 1380 and the reign of Louis XI in which the university played, or attempted to play—for it is needless to say that it met with some rude rebuffs when its presumption was unwelcome to the ruling powers—a political role, would involve a review of the whole course of French history. An illustration or two must suffice.

More than once during the Burgher rising under Étienne Marcel, in 1357-8, the good offices of the university were sought as mediators between the Court with which its real sympathies lay and the rebellious provost of the merchants in whose power it for the moment found itself.[1] In 1382, after the suppression of the Maillotin rising against the tyranny of Anjou, the intercession of the university was implored, together with that of the clergy, on behalf of the convicted rebels. The rector and the bishop appeared as the representatives of the two bodies, and pre-audience was given to the 'Orator' of the university. An amnesty was granted to all but the ringleaders.[2] In 1418, when Rouen was besieged by the English and on the point of surrender, the hard-pressed citizens implored the assistance of the university as

[1] Bulaeus, iv. 344; [*Chartul.* iii, No. 1239; *Auctarium*, i. 236]. Jourdain in his article 'L'Univ. de P. à l'époque de la domination anglaise' (*Excursions Historiques*, pp. 339–61) collects other evidence as to the part played by the university at this crisis, and shows that historians are mistaken in attributing to the university an active sympathy with Étienne Marcel.

[2] Bulaeus, iv. 585, 586; *Chartul.* iii, No. 1465 and note.

the one body in all France whose intercession might move their sovereign to come to their relief.[1] As a rule, of course, the sympathies of the university were with the powers that be, with the nobles and the prelates rather than with the burghers or the peasants, but it must not be supposed that the attitude of the university towards the throne was one of unvarying sycophancy. Medieval Paris was not Royalist after the fashion of seventeenth-century Oxford. There were many occasions when the university united with the citizens of the capital in deputations to the sovereign, and on such occasions its views on the conduct of affairs were expressed with a freedom which frequently excites the unfeigned amazement of Crevier, the courtly academic historian of the age of Louis XV.[2]

During the dismal period of conflict between the Armagnac and Burgundian factions, it is commonly alleged that the sympathies of the university were on the Burgundian side. This, to say the very least, has been much too absolutely stated.[3] In the first place, when the sympathies of 'the clergy' are set down as Burgundian, too little account is taken of the never-dying antagonism between the secular clergy and the regulars. The strength of the Burgundian party lay in the support of the populace of Paris and of the Mendicant Orders:[4] the university would therefore be inclined to the

[1] Bulaeus, v, 334; [Chartul. iv, Nos. 2111, 2120; cf. J. H. Wylie and W. T. Waugh, The Reign of Henry V, iii (1929), 130, 135, 140].

[2] See the oration of Jean Courtecuisse, in Bulaeus, v. 83–93, wrongly referred by Bulaeus to 1403. It was really delivered on the occasion mentioned below in 1413. See Coville, L'Ordonnance Cabochienne, Paris, 1891, pp. iv, 211 sq. For other instances cf. Lea, Hist. of the Inquisition in the Middle Ages, ii. 135 sq. Mr. Lea is, however, mistaken in supposing that the university ever possessed or claimed for itself the power of excommunication.

[3] [See especially Auctarium, ii.

162–7, with notes: deliberations of January and February 1414.] An exception must be made as to the nation of Picardy, which was largely composed of the Duke of Burgundy's subjects. [Chartul. iv, No. 2005; cf. Auctarium, ii. 169, 170.]

[4] Censures et conclusions de la faculté de théologie touchant la souveraineté des rois, Paris, 1720, p. 247 sq.; Gerson, Opera (Paris, 1606), i, cc. 396 sq., 409 sq.; Bulaeus, v. 257 sq. Bishop Creighton, if I may venture to criticize the admirable account of this period in his History of the Papacy during the period of the Reformation, London, 1882, i. 372 sq., seems to me not to have quite appreciated this

CHAP. V, Orleanist party by the tie of common enmities. The great
§ 6. democratic rising of the Cabochiens in 1413 is known to have
been largely inspired or at least aided by the Carmelites,
whose convent lay in the butchers' quarter—the headquarters
of the Burgundians. In the Carmelite Doctor Jean de Pavilly
the rioters found their mouthpiece. Then it is forgotten
that in the university as outside it public opinion was liable
to fluctuations. Private individuals were not committed irre-
vocably to one or the other side, nor were they in all cases
prepared to follow the party which they favoured to all
lengths. The great crises at which we find the university as
a body unmistakably identifying itself with the Burgundian
cause occur at moments when the outrageous misgovernment
of the Orleanist Princes had driven even the most conservative classes of Paris and of France generally into the arms of
the Burgundian faction. This was eminently the case on the
occasion of the Cabochien rising. It is true that the university
as a corporation backed up the Cabochien demands, and that
prominent seculars had a share in the compilation of the
famous 'Ordonnances': it does not follow that the university
must be looked upon as an assembly of Burgundian partisans.
In the very year in which the 'Ordonnance Cabochienne' was
published, the theological faculty, by a large majority, condemned the work of Jean Petit, the apologist of the murder
of the Duke of Orleans, and their judgement was embodied
in a formal sentence against the book (its author was now

element in the party divisions of
the time. The advocate of Petit's
propositions at Constance defended
them 'authoritate Menticantium
qui subscripserant illarum veritati'
(Bulaeus, v. 284); while Gerson
declared 'non esse cum eis duos
Magistros in Theologia seculares;
vel si veniant ad ternarium, totum
est' (*ibid.*, p. 289); [cf. *Chartul.* iv,
No. 2072]. Cf. Launoi, *Reg. Navar.
Gymn. Hist.* i. 126; Dubarle (1829),
i. 238 *sq.* Ample materials for the
study of the subject are now provided by the very careful study
of M. Coville, *Les Cabochiens et*

l'Ordonnance de 1413, Paris, 1888,
to whom the reader may refer for
references to the original authorities. M. Coville has also edited the
Ordonnance itself (*L'Ordonnance
Cabochienne*, Paris, 1891). Bulaeus
systematically represents the university as throughout Orleanist and
anti-English. (Cf. also *Hist. Litt.*
xxiv. 60.) This may be an exaggeration on the other side, but it is evident to me that the Burgundian
sympathies of the University, even
in the earlier part of the conflict,
have been greatly overstated.

dead) by the bishop and inquisitor.[1] At Constance the uni- versity exerted itself to procure the condemnation of Petit; but not all the influence of Gerson or of the University of Paris in the height of its power could extract from the Council, which exhibited in so practical a manner its zeal against heresy any proof of its sincerity in condemnation of political assassination. The influence of the Duke of Burgundy and his partisans was strong enough to prevent the Council coming to a definite decision on the matter. It even imposed silence on both parties to the controversy for a period of forty years, and reversed the decision of the Bishop of Paris in so far as the personal honour of the duke was concerned. The strength of the feeling against Petit at Paris may be measured by the unusual form of manifesto adopted on the occasion; the condemnation was subscribed not only by doctors, but by the bachelors of the theological faculty to the number (in all) of 140.[2] Nor is there any evidence that, even on occasions when the university sided with the Burgundians, there was anything like unanimity in its ranks. Every party had its representatives among the masters of Paris; every faction-leader among the princes and the nobles naturally sought for his tools among the educated clergy. Moreover, it must be

---

[1] Petit's *Justificatio Ducis Burgundiae super Caede Ducis Aurelianensis* is printed in Gerson, *Opera*, Antwerp, 1706, v, col. 15 *sq.*, where it is followed by the proceedings against Petit in the University and Council of Constance *in extenso*. [The full story has now been told by Coville, *Jean Petit* (Paris, 1932), pp. 431–561, in the light of all the available evidence, especially of the documents in the *Chartularium*, iv, Nos. 1928, 1988–90, and onwards. In 1411 the Duke of Orleans appealed to the university, but the faculty of theology was divided, and it was not till 1413 that the energy of the chancellor, Gerson, brought the matter to a head. The 'Council of Faith' which condemned Petit's book was presided over by the bishop and inquisitor, and consisted mainly of doctors; it was not, of course, a university assembly. The university as a whole did not deliberate (Coville, p. 443). Preliminary discussions took place in the superior faculties and the nations. The chief obstacle to Gerson's campaign was the faculty of decrees or canon law, the Picard nation, and some of the leading Mendicants. The opposition was mainly political and did not necessarily imply approval of political assassination.]

[2] [*Chartul.* iv, No. 2072. The roll was signed on dates between 19 Aug. and 22 Oct. 1416. See Coville, *op. cit.*, p. 552. The 140 comprised 40 doctors, 4 licentiates in theology, 27 bachelors *formati*, and 69 bachelors.]

remembered that not every formal decision of the university congregation represents the real opinion of its members. By the fifteenth century the approbation of the university had come to be considered essential to the party in power at any important political crisis; and consequently had to be forcibly extorted when it was not freely forthcoming. Thus in 1418 the Burgundian triumph was followed by the arrest or proscription of many leading masters, while the College of Navarre was pillaged by the Burgundian mob.[1] What was left of the university revoked the edicts against the Duke of Burgundy and Petit, in a document which alleges that they had only been obtained by force and by the wholesale imprisonment of opponents. There may of course be truth in the allegations of violence on both sides: at all events the facts are quite inconsistent with the idea that the university was unanimous in the matter.[2] So again in 1430, during the English occupation, while the majority of the masters fled (many of them to Poitiers, where a new university was called into existence to receive them), those who continued teaching in Paris were compelled to assent to the infamous proceedings against the Maid of Orleans.[3] On the whole it must be

[1] *Chronique du religieux de Saint-Denys*, ed. Bellaguet (1852), vi. 234. [On the Burgundian control of Paris and the reversal of the attitude of the university, see Coville, *op. cit.*, pp. 558–61; Lavisse, *Hist. de France*, IV. i. 374–8.]

[2] Bulaeus, v. 331, 332, 334; [*Chartul.* iv, No. 2107, 9 Aug. 1418]. It is alleged that when the Norman nation attempted to mediate between the parties its proctor was imprisoned and many principals of halls 'proscribed'. But it was, it would seem, only the Picard nation who actually voted against the condemnation, which seems to imply that in the other nations and faculties the majority was in favour of it.

[3] Documents in Quicherat, *Procès de Jeanne d'Arc*, Paris, 1841, i. 8 *sq.*, 17, 407 *sq.*; ii. 498–9; Bulaeus, v.

395 *sq.*; [*Chartul.* iv, Nos. 2369–90]. Considerable fees were paid by the English king to the Parisian doctors who assisted at the trial (*ibid.* v. 197 *sq.*). [Coville, *op. cit.*, p. 452, points out that several of the university doctors among the Maid's judges had taken part in the process against Jean Petit twenty years earlier. On the action of the university cf. Denifle and Chatelain in *Mém. de la Soc. de l'hist. de Paris et de l'Île de France*, xxiv (1897), 1–32; and *Chartul.* iv. 510–14.] Neither Mr. Lea (*Hist. of Inquisition*, iii. 357 *sq.*) nor Ch. Jourdain (*Excursions Historiques*, p. 311) seems to recognize that 'the University of Paris' was composed of different persons at different times. Not only were the opponents of the dominant portion liable to be silenced, but in 1436, after the

pronounced exceedingly doubtful whether—putting aside the CHAP. V, Mendicants and the Picard nation, which was largely com- § 6. posed of the Duke of Burgundy's subjects—there is sufficient evidence for attributing to any large majority of the university a strong and definite Burgundian partisanship.

It is its political and ecclesiastical importance as a great Unique corporation that places Paris in a unique position among the position of universities of the Middle Ages. Many of the early jurists of Paris. Bologna were individually prominent politicians; and at a later time great weight was often attached to the opinion of the college of doctors on points of canon or public law. But the doctors were not a numerous body, and the universities proper were universities of students. The exclusion of citizens of the towns in which the Italian universities were situated prevented the exertion of political influence by the universities as corporations. The strength of Paris lay first in its situation within the walls of the French capital, and secondly in an organization by which the weight attaching to the judgement of the greatest school of theology in Europe was backed by the weight of numbers. The importance of the first of these causes is well illustrated by the contrast which the influence of Paris presents to the political insignificance of the English universities;[1] that of the second by the contrast in this respect with Bologna.

The influence of Paris, considerable in secular and domestic Ecclesias- affairs, was naturally greatest in the sphere of ecclesiastical tical influ- politics. General councils were extraordinary remedies for ence. extraordinary evils. Even national councils met but rarely, and then not without the 'commandment and will of princes'. When no council was sitting, the University of Paris was able to act as a sort of standing committee of the French, or even of the Universal, Church.

That it was able so to act, and to act with effect, is a proof 'The first of the revolution which had taken place since the thirteenth School of the Church.'

---

expulsion of the English, we read that 'Natio Gall. decrevit ut e libris seu Actis suis eraderentur eorum nomina qui regnante Anglo per vim inscripti fuerant'. Bulaeus, v. 439.

[1] It is true that at such a crisis as the Barons' War the students of Oxford might take a side. What I have said applies to corporate and official influence.

century in the relations between the Church and the schools. We have seen with what suspicion the disputations of the Parisian schools were watched by the ecclesiastical authorities after the first great outburst of Averroistic speculation. For a moment it looked almost as if the revolt of the human mind against the intellectual despotism of the Church had come already. Ere long, however, persecution, bribery (in the shape of patronage), the natural tendency of any unusual stimulation of intellectual activity to wear itself out, and above all the genius of the great orthodox schoolmen prevailed over a purely speculative movement rarely backed by much moral or religious earnestness, and almost entirely unconnected with the main currents of intellectual and religious life in the nation at large. The new scholastic theology triumphed alike over the sceptics and over the mystical reactionaries; and Paris became 'the first School of the Church'—the theological arbiter of Europe. However much the theological dictatorship assumed by the university may have blasted the fair prospects of the twelfth-century 'illumination', it is by means of this theological dictatorship that Paris conferred on France —and indeed on all northern Europe—one of the most memorable services which she rendered to the cause of enlightenment, of civilization, and of humanity. It was largely to the influence of the university that northern France owed her comparative immunity from the ravages of the Holy Inquisition.[1] The inquisition was, indeed, in existence at Paris, but it was never very powerful: its work was largely done for it in far milder fashion by the university. In that age a theological dictatorship of some kind was inevitable. It was something that such a dictatorship should be vested in

[1] This is well pointed out by Mr. Lea, *History of the Inquisition in the Middle Ages* (1888). I must take the opportunity of expressing my profound admiration (in spite of occasional lapses in matters of ecclesiastical technicality) for this truly learned and valuable work. [See, for the attitude of the university, the documents relating to certain heretical sorcerers at Paris in 1425–6: *Chartul.* iv, Nos. 2262, 2265, 2272, 2273. The university, as in the case of Jeanne d'Arc, was accustomed to be asked for its opinion in the matters of heresy, and to be associated with the local inquisitor. It resented intervention from outside; cf. *ibid.*, No. 1993.]

a large and popularly constituted body of secular theologians, CHAP. V, eminently amenable to the influences of public opinion and § 6. always favourable within certain limits to free discussion and theological ingenuity, and without motive for unnecessary or malignant persecution. Paris—and in a measure that northern world of which Paris was the centre—suffered little from the most cunning instrument that has ever been devised for the suppression of religious and intellectual life and for the gratification not merely of theological passion but of personal malice, of unhallowed greed, and of that terrible blood-lust which sometimes gets possession of the human soul under the guise of religious zeal.

In matters of ecclesiastical polity and discipline, indeed, Its theo- the Mendicants were often too strong for the university: she logical dictator- could only keep alive a kind of constitutional opposition ship. against the dominant impulse towards autocracy and centralization. But in matters of pure theology the conflicting tendencies of the great Mendicant orders neutralized the influence which they might have had if united. There it was left to the theological faculty of Paris to hold the balance between them, and on such questions her will was almost supreme. Again and again Paris led the way and Rome followed.[1] In the main it was no doubt the theology of the great Dominican Doctor S. Thomas which became the accredited theology of the Church. In one matter, however, Franciscan teaching was too completely in harmony with the tendencies of popular religionism to be extinguished beneath

---

[1] Thus a controversialist of the conciliar epoch says 'dum inde trahitur causa fidei per appellationem ad Curiam Romanam, solet remitti ad Universitatem Parisiensem, sicut visum est pluries temporibus nostris' (Launoi, *De Scholis celebrioribus*, p. 231). And Gerson goes further, 'Nec Papa nec Doctores Iuris Canonici, si non sint Theologi, circa ea quae sunt fidei, aliquid canonice discutiunt, vel authentice determinant sine Theologorum doctrinali determinatione praevia, cum Papa in haeresum condemnatione consueverit reddere Theologicam rationem' (Bulaeus, iv. 900). Cf. also a passage in the Edict of Charles VI against the doctrines of Jean Petit: 'Cognovit etiam ipsa quandoque Romana sedes, dum olim et nuper, si quid apud eos ambiguum in doctrina Christianae Religionis obtigerat, certitudinem ab ipso consilio fidei Parisiis causa existente postulare, nec puduit, nec piguit' (*ibid.* v. 259).

CHAP. V,
§ 6.
The Im-
maculate
Concep-
tion.
the inquisitorial frown of the Dominican. In the great controversy on the doctrine of the Immaculate Conception which
began to rage during the latter part of the fourteenth century,
Paris declared herself against that absolute negation of the
popular opinion on which the conservative Dominicans insisted (1387).[1] In this as in similar cases we find the faculty
of theology taking upon itself the theological police of the
Church.[2] For once, the inquisitor as a Dominican sympathized
with the accused, but the faculty proceeded against John de
Monson (de Montesono), the friar who had taken the lead in
the recent preachings against the rising Mariolatry,[3] before
the bishop and procured his condemnation. An appeal to
Avignon, where the university was represented by Peter
d'Ailly, went against the Dominican doctor;[4] he was excommunicated, fled to his native Aragon, and afterwards found
protection with the rival Pontiff. His brethren refused to
subscribe the judgement of the faculty and were expelled the
university. For sixteen years the Black Friars as a body clung
to their unpopular orthodoxy, and during that time something
like a persecution raged against them throughout the length
and breadth of France. But at last, in 1403, as was the wont
sooner or later of beaten theological parties in the Middle
Ages, they surrendered, and their doctors were readmitted
by the university. Their recantation was conducted with

[1] Bulaeus, iv. 618 sq.; d'Argentré,
Coll. Judic. i. ii. 61 sq.

[2] On this same occasion the following position, which had been
maintained by John de Monson,
was condemned: 'Asserere aliquod
fore verum quod est contra sacram
scripturam est expressissime contra
fidem.' It was condemned 'tanquam falsa et iniuriosa sanctis et
doctoribus si eam intelligat univer-
saliter' (Bulaeus, iv. 620; [Chartul.
iii, No. 1559, p. 494]). This is a
good illustration of the conservative character of Dominican orthodoxy.

[3] [In 1362 the Dominican Jean
l'Eschacier had asserted that those
who accepted the Immaculate Conception were heretics (Chartul. iii,
No. 1272). The very interesting
revocations of 1389 are in ibid.,
Nos. 1571–9. One Dominican,
John Ade, revoked his exclamation:
'en volés-vous faire une deesse?'
(ibid., No. 1577).]

[4] [John de Monson had maintained his views at his Vesperiae
and in the later resumption. Peter
d'Ailly's lively account of the
affair is in Chartul. iii, No. 1557;
see also for the whole story, Nos.
1559, 1560, 1562–4, 1566 sq. A
good history of the medieval controversies is in Father X. le
Bachelet's article on the Immaculate Conception in the Dict. de
Théologie Catholique, vii.]

every circumstance of ignominious publicity; the order was degraded to the lowest place in university processions, and the triumph of the university was enhanced by the fact that the King's Confessor and a Dominican bishop was among the penitents.[1] Opinion at Paris soon abandoned the merely negative attitude which it hitherto professed to take, and insisted upon positive adhesion to the doctrine of the Immaculate Conception. Less than a century afterwards, three centuries and a half before the Immaculate Conception became a dogma of the Roman Catholic Church, an oath to defend it was exacted from all candidates for theological degrees at Paris.[2]

More often it was against extreme developments of Franciscan tendencies that the university was called upon to defend the dominant creed of the Church. We have seen how the theologians of Paris compelled Alexander IV to condemn the Franciscan 'Everlasting Gospel'.[3] But the leaven of Joachimism went on working in the Franciscan body; and it was necessary for the university to procure from John XXII the condemnation as a heresy of the doctrine of the absolute poverty of our Lord and his Apostles—a measure which drove the extreme party among the Franciscans into open schism, into the avowed advocacy of the most violently anti-papal and anti-hierarchical, though not anti-sacerdotal, theology— a theology (if the chaotic body of ideas which emanated from the Franciscan interpretation of the dreams of Joachim deserve that name) which, in spite of all suppressions, went on working like a mighty undercurrent beneath the smooth surface of medieval orthodoxy, occasionally coming to the surface in the teaching of the Fraticelli, the Beguines, and the like.[4]

Franciscan heresies.

---

[1] [*Chartul.* iv, No. 1781; cf. Benedict XIII's Bull, No. 1842 (1407). The relegation of the Dominicans to the last place had been decreed early in 1389 (*ibid.* iii, No. 1568, but did not take effect until 1403. Some individual submissions were made in 1389 (Nos. 1571–8), but the Dominican order remained in exile from Paris, and

university sermons were preached in the church of the Franciscans during the interval.]

[2] In 1497. Bulaeus, v. 815. Again the controversy was aroused by the preaching of a Dominican.

[3] See above, p. 386.

[4] As to the relations between the earlier Spiritual Franciscans and the Fraticelli—i.e. the rebels against

CHAP. V,   It required but little pressure to procure the condemnation
§ 6.   of the ultra-Franciscan dreams of universal brotherhood and
John
XXII   a pauper clergy from the monarch of that Babylon against
and the
heavenly   which much of the prophetic wrath of the visionaries had
vision.   been launched. A more striking instance of the power of the
university to force the hand of the supreme pontiff is afforded
by the fate of the curious Franciscan doctrine[1] of the 'retardation of the heavenly vision'. The popular view was that the
Saints and all who had no need of purgatorial purification,
passed at once—without waiting (like ordinary souls) for the
day of judgement—into the full enjoyment of the beatific
vision of the Blessed Trinity, a doctrine which was supposed
to have incurred the peculiar . displeasure of the reigning
Pontiff, John XXII. The Pope himself originated the controversy by attacking the received opinion in a sermon at
Avignon. From Avignon the controversy passed to Paris.
The Franciscan General, Gerald Otho, excited the popular
indignation by preaching a doctrine which appeared deroga-
tory to the honour due to the saints; while he moved the

John XXII's condemnation of the doctrine of the absolute poverty of Christ—the reader may be referred to the important researches of Ehrle in the *Archiv für Litt.- u. Kirchengesch. des Mittelalters*. Cf. Lea, *Hist. of Inquis.* iii. 1–180. [The opinion of certain masters of theology in 1318, printed in the *Chartul.* ii, No. 760, did not emanate from the university, but is the judgement of a commission appointed by Pope John XXII. The share of the university in the controversy about the poverty of Christ was most emphatic during the conflict between John XXII and Michael of Cesena. The Pope sent his constitutions to be read in the schools by the masters of decrees and theology (*ibid.*, Nos. 833, 836, Nov. 1324, Jan. 1325). A document which Gerard Rostagni, a disciple of Michael, had affixed to the door of Notre Dame, was publicly burnt in the presence of the bishop and chancellor (*ibid.*, No.

895; Douie, *The nature and the effect of the heresy of the Fraticelli*, Manchester, 1932, p. 174). Among the numerous tracts of this time, a treatise by the Parisian doctor of theology, Jean d'Anneux (*Hist. litt. de la France*, xxxv. 455), may be mentioned as an example of academic controversy. Miss Douie's book, with its full bibliography, shows the development in the study of this intricate subject since Ehrle's important articles appeared.]

[1] It is interesting to find the usual state of things reversed by the imprisonment of a Dominican, Thomas Walleis or 'Anglicus', by Franciscan Inquisitors at Avignon. The Pope alleges that he was imprisoned for other heresies, but it was generally believed that his denial of the papal tenet was his real offence. *Chartul.* ii, No. 973 *sq.* [For Thomas Walleys see the *Dict. Nat. Biog.,s.v.* Wallensis, Thomas.]

wrath of the theologians of Paris by calling in question the
view for which their faculty had (by implication) pronounced as long ago as 1241.[1] The General was believed to have been sent to Paris for the express purpose of inculcating the theological crotchet of this cruel and avaricious pontiff. The question was debated with so much fury as to call for the interference of the civil government. In December 1333 Philip of Valois summoned a number of prelates and doctors of theology to Vincennes, and called upon them to settle the matter among themselves once for all, one way or the other.[2] The faculty reaffirmed the judgement of their predecessors, and thirty doctors signed the condemnation of the retardation theory, which the King dispatched to Avignon with the peremptory request that the Pope would endorse their decision, and punish those who dared to maintain the contrary.[3] The doctors of Paris, he told his Holiness, knew what ought to be believed in matters of faith much better than the lawyers and other clerks about the Pope, who knew little or no theology. The reply of John XXII is as humble and apologetic as if he were a young student at Paris in danger of losing his bachelor's degree for heresy. He apologizes for venturing to express an opinion upon a theological question when he was not a doctor of divinity,[4] denies that the Franciscan General's utterances were inspired by him, and declares that he had in his sermon only explained the two views taken on the subject by different fathers without positively committing himself to either side of the question. He

---

[1] It had condemned the proposition 'Quod anime glorificate non sunt in celo empireo cum angelis, nec corpora glorificata erunt ibi, sed in celo aqueo vel crystallino, quod supra firmamentum est, quod et de beata Virgine presumitur'. *Chartul.* i, No. 128.

[2] Peter d'Ailly boasted at Constance that the King had caused an intimation to be made to the Pope 'qu'il se revoquast, ou qu'il le feroit ardre' (Bulaeus, v. 238).

[3] *Ibid.* iv. 235–8. A number of

additional documents relating to the affair are published in *Chartularium*, ii, Nos. 970–87. [See N. Valois on Pope John XXII in *Hist. litt. de la France*, xxxiv. 609–12, 617–18; and, for a good short account, G. Mollat, *Les papes d'Avignon*, Paris, 1912, pp. 57–60.]

[4] 'Et quia, fili dilectissime, forsan tibi dicitur, quod nos non sumus in theologia magister, audi quid unus sapiens dicat: "Non quis, inquit, sed quid dicat intendite."' *Chartul.* ii, No. 978.

refused, however, to condemn the opinion to which he personally leaned. But in the following year it is said that, being
on his death-bed, he published an express recantation of all
that he might have said in favour of the Retardation hypothesis.[1] This document, however, was not published till the
accession of his successor, who pronounced decidedly against
his predecessor's view, and is of somewhat doubtful authenticity. The combination of King and university against
John XXII already seems like a shadow of the coming events
which culminated in the deposition of John XXIII at Constance. It is a significant indication of the change which had
taken place in the mutual relations of the university and the
Holy See that John's successor, Benedict XII, a D.D. of the
Cistercian college at Paris, began the custom of officially
notifying his election to the university, which was thus recognized as one of the great powers of Europe.[2]

The uni-
versity a
champion
of the
secular
clergy.
Divided in matters of speculative theology, the Mendicant
Orders were (as has been said) equally obnoxious to the
secular clergy by reason of those exemptions and privileges
which carried confusion into the discipline of every diocese
and parish in the kingdom. In the long struggle of the prelates and parochial clergy against the Papal Bulls enabling
the Mendicants to hear confessions, to preach, and to give
burial without the consent of diocesan or curate, the university formed the rallying point for the opposition of the
seculars. The bishops and curates of the future naturally
sympathized with the bishops and curates of the present.[3] It

---

[1] The retreat is a little masked by
the position that the 'anime purgate
separate a corporibus sunt in celo . . .
et vident Deum . . . ac divinam es-
sentiam facie ad faciem clare in
quantum status et conditio compati-
tur anime separate'; but the document proceeds, 'si qua alia sermo-
cinando, conferendo, *dogmatizando*,
docendo seu alio quovis modo dixi-
mus . . . in quantum essent a pre-
missis fide catholica, determinatione
ecclesie, sacra Scriptura vel bonis
moribus aut aliquo ipsorum dis-
sonantia, reprobamus' (*Chartul.* ii,

No. 987). The genuineness of the
document has been denied, and
the older printed copies represent
the interpolated edition in Benedict
XII's Register. The existence of
such copies is an argument for the
genuineness (which is defended by
Denifle) of the original in John
XXII's Register, though it is admitted not to have been sealed till
after his death.

[2] Bulaeus, iv. 242.

[3] [See above, p. 396, for John of
Pouilli and the history of John
XXII's Bull *Vas electionis*.]

was, as has been suggested elsewhere, the support given to CHAP. V, the Mendicants by the Papacy in their quarrel with the § 6. university which for the first time brought the masters of Paris into antagonism with the authority to which they owed a large part of their own privileges—nay, their legal existence —as much as the religious orders themselves. It was, indeed, the continual growth of Mendicant pretensions, together with the steadily increasing drain upon the revenues of French benefices involved in the papal system of annates, provisions, expectatives, tenths, and the like, which produced between the age of S. Louis and the close of the fifteenth century a complete revolution in the attitude of the Gallican Church towards the see of S. Peter.

The opposition of the university to those ecclesiastical The usurpations of the papacy which went on increasing in exact *rotulus benefici-* proportion to the decline in its political power was long *andorum.* bought off by an ingenious system of patronage. When·the seat of the Papacy was transferred to Avignon the French universities were allowed to profit by its abuses. The papal power of 'provision' was largely exercised in favour of Parisian graduates by John XXII, and on the accession of Clement VI (if not before) the custom began of sending to the papal court a *rotulus nominandorum* or roll containing the names of graduates to whom the Pope was invited to give provisions or expectative graces to benefices in ecclesiastical collation. The roll eventually became an annual affair.[1] The names of the applicants were placed on the roll in order of seniority, but with a preference for regents over non-regents and for

[1] It is disputed whether the custom began under John XXII or under Clement VI. See the dissertation in Bulaeus, iv. 901. About 1322 we find Oxford petitioning John XXII that he would bestow on Oxford graduates the same favours which had been conferred upon 'doctores tam philosophos quam theologos' at Paris (*Chartul.* ii, No. 818), and there is a general injunction to prelates to promote graduates (*ibid.*, No. 729); but the first actual benefice-roll sent by the university belongs to the Pontificate of Clement VI (*Chartul.* ii, No. 1062 and note). Several Oxford rolls sent to Clement VI are among the Roman transcripts sent to the Public Record Office by Mr. Bliss. [Something of the kind seems to be implied in the numerous provisions for fellows of Merton College, Oxford, in 1317. See *Cal. of Papal Letters*, ii, index, *s.v.* Oxford, Merton College.]

residents over non-residents.[1] A special petition was presented on behalf of the rector for the time being.[2] A deputation of masters was appointed to carry the roll to the papal court, and to occupy themselves for two months amidst the swarm of greedy and simoniacal benefice-hunters in pressing the claims of the absent masters on the Pope and cardinals. That these claims should really have been attended to is no

[1] Of the petitions prefixed to the roll specimens are given in Bulaeus (iv. 901–11 and v. 366–73). [In 1359 the faculty of theology describe the roll as follows: 'quando pro parte Universitatis super promotione magistrorum eiusdem, domino pape per rotulos, ut consuevit, supplicatur, in (dictis) rotulis est ordo prioritatis et posterioritatis.' The rolls of the faculties had an order of precedence, beginning with theology, and the *supplicatio* of the rector appeared among those of the faculty of arts (*Chartul.* iii, No. 1246, p. 63). For the nature and order of the rolls see *ibid.*, Nos. 1427–38 (1379) with notes; iv, Nos. 1783–99 (1403). On 14 Nov. 1378 Clement VII ordered that the roll of the University of Paris should precede the rolls of other universities by one day (Ottenthal, *Regulae Cancellariae Apostolicae*, p. 90). In order to prevent private or irregular solicitation the university decided in February 1396 that no faculty, nation, college, or congregation should send rolls to the Pope without the consent of the university (*Auctarium*, i. 715 note).] A usual request in these rolls (e.g. 1424) is the petition that every master whose name is inscribed therein may have the power of choosing a confessor 'qui possit eos et eorum singulos absolvere ab omnibus peccatis suis et etiam plenam indulgentiam saltem semel in mortis articulo eisdem concedere' (Bulaeus, v. 370). Another clause of the earlier roll of 1414 is interesting as an indication of the number of grammar schools throughout the country (*ibid.* iv. 909):

'Item cum in nonnullis partibus iam inoleuerit consuetudo, imo potius abusus intolerabilis, quod scholae magis danti licet tamen ignoranti distribuantur, vel potius vendantur in graue Doctorum, Doctrinae, Iuuenum et Reipub. et totius Ecclesiasticae politicae [*sic*] detrimentum, dignetur S.V. tale remedium apponere quod amplius non ita distribuantur, sed pauperibus Magistris scientificis mere gratis conferantur.' It is clear that this cannot refer to the schools of the university, which were entirely under the authority of the masters themselves.

[2] At first the exact amount and nature of the papal benevolence was left to the donor; but later rolls often specify the patron to whose benefices they aspired or the Church in which they wanted a prebend. Sometimes even at Paris the roll includes non-graduate students (*Chartul.* iii, No. 1378), and this was habitually the case in Germany and in the student universities. Thus in a roll from Florence in 1404 we find the scholars asking for 'one, two, three, or more benefices', in one or more specified dioceses up to a certain value, which varies in different cases. Thus the rector specified 300 florins as the goal of his ambition, though he already enjoyed a prebend and parochial cure which brought in between them some 120 florins. The most modest limit their expectations to 150 florins (*Stat. Fiorent.*, p. 383).

small evidence of the extraordinary influence which the university had acquired. From the complaints which began to be made immediately after the withdrawal of obedience,[1] it is evident that the most corrupt Popes were much better patrons of learning than the Gallican bishops. The bishops had between them more nephews and dependants than the Pope, and fewer personal or political ends to serve by the promotion of able men and the propitiation of the most powerful corporation in the Gallican Church. That the *carrière ouverte aux talents* should have been secured by the system of provisions[2] is a striking illustration of the indirect

[1] Among other indications of this feeling we find the university in 1399 decreeing a cessation of lectures, which lasted till Lent, because a royal edict had restored the collation of benefices to the Ordinaries (Bulaeus, iv. 884; *Grands Chroniques de S. Denis*, ii. 746). So in 1411, when a discussion arose as to whether a roll should be sent to John XXIII, the majority determined in favour of the proposal 'aientes Pontificum Gratias et favores certiores esse quam Praelatorum: quippe Universitatem experientia propria didicisse, spretis suis suppositis, Episcopos aliosque Beneficiorum Collatores et Patronos conferre solitos famulis suis et illiteratis hominibus' (Bulaeus, v. 221. Cf. also *ibid.*, pp. 186–8). [That this attitude was not inconsistent with the display of Gallican feeling in the university is clear from the proceedings in a congregation of Nov. 1410: *Auctarium*, ii. 93, 94 and notes.] After the deposition of John XXIII, in 1417, a Royal Ordinance again restored the collation to the Ordinaries, when the university appealed to the Pope. The rector and deputies of the university were summoned before the Parlement to answer for their conduct, and were, by the orders of the Dauphin, who was present, arrested for high treason; they were only

released on abandoning the appeal (Bulaeus, v. 307 *sq.*; [*Chartul.* iv, Nos. 2096–2102]).

[2] [The procedure by which graduates obtained benefices, dealt with in the next note, led Rashdall here to a generalization which is not in accordance with the results of detailed local studies. Provision to canonries and prebends, which one would especially expect to be the means of securing a *carrière ouverte aux talents*, and which in the twelfth and early thirteenth centuries was frequently urged upon the bishops as a suitable aid to scholars, was not in fact a common reward of unrecognized merit when the system of papal provisions was in full force, in the fourteenth century. The Curia paid much attention to the wishes of the local chapter and tended to provide men from important local families, e.g. persons of noble birth who were otherwise debarred on grounds of youth or illegitimacy. When graduates were provided, they were generally men who had already won distinction. Moreover, the proportion of provided canons was not so high as is usually supposed; it has been calculated that at Constance during the period 1316 to 1378 the ratio of provided to non-provided was 37 to 20. See Karl Rieder, *Römische Quellen zur*

CHAP. V, utilities which were often bound up with the most indefen-
§ 6. sible and most corruptly intended of papal usurpations.[1]

The The Schism made the Avignon Popes more than ever
Schism dependent upon the support of the King and Church of
(Sept.
1378). France. On the arrival of the news of Clement VII's election,
much difference of opinion was expressed among the doctors
of Paris. A paper warfare immediately broke out between
the partisans of the rival pontiffs. Sufficient indications of the
existence of an Urbanist party were given to elicit from the

Konstanzer Bistumsgeschichte zur Zeit der Päpste in Avignon (Innsbruck, 1908), pp. lxxxii, lxxxviii; similar conclusions are drawn by W. Kothe, Kirchliche Zustände Strassburgs im vierzehnten Jahrhundert (Freiburg i. B., 1903), pp. 12, 31, and by W. Kisky, Die Domkapitel der geistlichen Kurfürsten (Weimar, 1906), p. 16. More local studies are needed.]

[1] [From the twelfth century onwards the popes, in suggesting and, later, in granting provisions, paid special attention to the claims of scholars (cf. Powicke, Stephen Langton, pp. 31–4; and for the views of canonists on the relation between benefices or salaries and fees, Gaines Post in Speculum, vii (1932), 189–92). There was nothing scandalous or 'political' in this. Clerks at the schools required encouragement and were often out of touch with their diocesans. The administrative system regarding provisions paid methodical heed to the needs of graduates. It comprised fixed rules for the classification of academic qualification and graduates were excused the examination which the ordinary pauper clericus had to undergo (Tihon, 'Les Expectatives in forma pauperum', in Bulletin de l'institut historique belge de Rome, fasc. 5 (1925), 51–118; cf. for the examination H. von Grauert 'Magister Heinrich der Poet in Würzburg

und die römische Kurie' in Abhandl. d. Königlichen Bayerischen Akad. der Wissenschaften, Philos.-philol. und hist. Klasse, xxvii. 1, 2 (1912), pp. 296–9; E. von Ottenthal, Regulae Cancellariae Apostolicae (1888), passim. The policy of the bishops was quite different and complaints of their disregard of learning were frequent. The fixed rules of the papal chancery recommended the papal system of provisions to the graduates, and it is improbable that 'Gallican' tendencies at Paris affected their preference for it. The university rotuli, which became general in Paris, the German universities, and elsewhere in the fourteenth century, were, therefore, a natural development. Cf. L. Thomassin, Vetus et nova Ecclesiae disciplina, II. i, cap. 53 (de graduatis). Rolls of a similar kind, classifying petitions from particular quarters, had been used originally in order to simplify chancery routine, in the thirteenth century (cf. H. Bresslau, Urkundenlehre, 2nd ed. ii. 8), although academic rolls begin only under the Avignon Popes. The rotulus beneficiandorum became, indeed, in practice a class-list of graduates beginning their regency. (Cf. Boyce, The English-German Nation, p. 139.) We owe part of this and the preceding note to Mr. G. Barraclough.]

Roman Pope a letter of warm thanks to the university for not CHAP. V, § 6. having joined the schismatics.[1] The academic body seems at once to have appreciated the importance of the position in which it was placed by the Schism. It resolved to petition the court, which had very decidedly taken the side of the Avignon claimant, not to insist upon a hasty conclusion. It determined, moreover, as if with the express view of lengthening the period of its neutrality and adding to the weight of its eventual judgement, that the rector should not 'conclude' for either side without the unanimous vote of all the Faculties and Nations.[2] The proposal to adhere to Clement VII encountered strenuous opposition from the two nations, Picardy and England, which were chiefly composed of the subjects of Urbanist sovereigns. In spite of the eagerness of the court, whose policy required a close alliance between France and Avignon, more than six months elapsed before a very peremptory letter from the King compelled the university to declare by a majority consisting of the three superior faculties with the nations of France and Normandy, in favour of Clement VII.[3] And it was not till September or October 1379 that the university, as a whole, committed itself to the Clementine faction so far as to send a roll of petitioners for benefices to Avignon.[4]

[1] Bulaeus (iv. 565) says, 'Universitas quandiu non est de Urbani electione dubitatum, *ei quoque adhaesit*; deinde ut dubitari coepit, nec statim ei adhaerere destitit.' But this was before the election of Clement. Cf. *Chartul*. iii, Nos. 1605–16.

[2] Bulaeus, iv. 565. *Chartul*. iii, No. 1616.

[3] *Chartul*. iii, Nos. 1616–27. In accordance with the previous resolution, or because the rector was a German, there was no technical 'conclusion', but the King was informed that what was done by the three faculties and two nations was considered the act of the university.

[4] The King declared his adherence to Clement VII on 16 Nov.

1378. The declaration of temporary neutrality by the university was voted 8 Jan. 1379 (*Chartul*. iii, No. 1616): the adhesion to Clement VII was handed in to the King at Vincennes on 30 May 1379 (Nos. 1427, 1627). The nation of France and some members of the faculty of medicine had already sent a roll to Clement VII (*ibid*., No. 1622). Denifle points out that the revulsion of feeling in the university against Clement was due to his consent to the King's imposition of a tax upon the clergy, including the university (*ibid*., No. 1636). [Rashdall pointed out in the first edition that he might have dealt with the attitude of the university in more detail if the third volume of the

But, in spite of this forced adhesion, there can be no doubt that there was a strong feeling in the university against the Avignon cardinals and their nominees, and that this feeling deepened enormously the growing indignation against the now doubly onerous exactions of the papal court. As the Schism went on, this indignation found ever louder expression in the discussions of the Parisian schools and the writings of Parisian doctors. In accordance with the traditional policy of the French kings towards the foreign students in their capital, the scruples of the foreign students were respected. The English nation eventually consented to send a roll to Clement, but till the year 1382 it continued in its corporate capacity neutral, while its members were allowed as individuals to acknowledge and send rolls to Urban VI.[1] After that date it adopted a wavering and uncertain attitude. The existence of this Urbanist minority within the university itself must have had an important influence in keeping the existence of the Schism and its attendant evils constantly before the minds of the Parisian theologians, and in stimulating discussion as to the best means of terminating it.

Chartularium and the first volume of the *Auctarium* had appeared earlier. Since he wrote, the whole matter has been discussed by N. Valois, *La France et le Grand Schisme d'Occident*, 4 vols. (Paris, 1896 to 1902). Cf. L. Salembier, *Le Grand Schisme d'Occident* (4th ed., Paris, 1921), for a good short account and bibliography.]

[1] Bulaeus, iv. 591, 592; v. 65. [A mission to Urban VI before the declaration of the university for Clement VII comprised the three Germans, Marsiglio of Inghen, Conrad of Gelnhausen, and Gerard of Calcar (Valois, i. 121 *sq*.). Between 1379 and 1381 Conrad of Gelnhausen wrote his *Epistola Concordiae*, and Henry of Langenstein, another doctor of Paris, his *Epistola pacis* and *Epistola Concilii pacis* (*ibid*. i. 324, 325, 326). All of them declared for a council. The hosti-lity of the English-German nation to Clement VII made them refuse to recognize the Chancellor of Notre Dame. A scholar who had sought his licence at Notre Dame was not allowed to incept under the masters of the nation and the proctor was ordered to refuse his burse: *Auctarium*, i. 619, 651; cf. pp. 631–8 for a discussion on the admission of students licensed at Notre Dame in 1378. See Boyce, p. 104. As Rashdall pointed out (1st ed. i. 557 note), 'the difficult position in which the Schism placed the Germans in Paris contributed to the growth of universities in Germany'. In 1444 Albert of Does-borch, the rector, complained of scandalmongers who said 'quod ipse vellet transferre istam Univer-sitatem ad partes Almanie' (*Auc-tarium*, ii. 597).]

The Schism, indeed, by the reaction which it induced against the intolerable scandals and abuses of the ecclesiastical system in which men had hitherto tacitly acquiesced, exercised a stimulating effect upon the intellectual, if not upon the educational, life of the university. We have seen how, with the complete enslavement of the academic mind to the dogmatic system, the freshness and vigour of its intellectual life began to decline; and in the first half of the fourteenth century, though the privileges and apparent splendour of the university never stood higher, this decline appears to have been very rapid indeed. Throughout the fourteenth century, Oxford, not Paris, was the headquarters of scholastic activity. Richard of Bury,[1] for instance, an Oxford man, it is true, but one who speaks with the utmost enthusiasm of his earlier visits to Paris, describes in the most forcible language the utter extinction of intellectual life and original thought which had taken place there within his own memory. Its lectures and disputations, he tells us, had degenerated into sterile logomachies or else into a dull and unacknowledged reproduction of contemporary English speculation. Minerva had forsaken Paris as completely as she had forsaken Egypt and Athens.[2] Towards the end of the century, however, a marked improvement is noticeable. Several distinct influences combined to produce a certain revival of intellectual life. The first of these was the growth of nominalism. Nominalism was, no doubt, one of the Oxford importations which Richard of Bury recognized on his later visits to Paris;

---

[1] Or Robert Holcot, if he was the real author of the *Philobiblon*. [Holcot's authorship is not now accepted, although some scholars are inclined to allow a measure of co-operation with Bury. See the edition by Axel Nelson (Stockholm, 1922) and J. de Ghellinck in *Revue d'histoire ecclésiastique*, xviii (1922), 34; xix (1923), 239–41.]

[2] 'Isto, pro dolor! paroxysmo, quem plangimus, Parisiense palladium nostris maestis temporibus cernimus iam sublatum: ubi tepuit, immo fere friguit zelus scholae tam nobilis, cuius olim radii lucem dabant universis angulis orbis terrae. Quiescit ibidem iam calamus omnis scribae, nec librorum generatio propagatur ulterius, nec est qui incipiat novus auctor haberi. Involvunt sententias sermonibus imperitis et omnis logicae proprietate privantur, nisi quod Anglicanas subtilitates, quibus palam detrahunt, vigiliis furtivis addiscunt' (*Philobiblon*, ed. Thomas, p. 89).

CHAP. V, and it is always in the English, or, as it was afterwards called,
§ 6. the German, nation, that we find nominalism most prevalent.[1]

Growth of In the rest of the university the realists were at present in a
nominal-
ism. majority. In 1339 the exposition either in public lectures or
'private conventicles' of the writings of William of Ockham
was forbidden;[2] and in 1346 Nicholas of Autrecourt (*Ultri-curia*), who, with a much more brilliant metaphysical genius
than Ockham, anticipated the system of Berkeley, was com-
pelled to retract his extremely enlightened errors.[3] But, in

[1] It is significant that the oath 'contra scientiam Okamicam' which appears in the British Museum *Liber Rectoris* is omitted in the English Masters' book. *Chartul.* ii. 680. [This argument is not convincing, for, in the first place, the oath against the teaching of Ockham is embedded in a long series of omissions from the book of the proctors of the English-German nation; and, secondly, one of the leaders against this teaching was John Lutterell, Chancellor of the University of Oxford (1317–22). Lutterell in 1323 went to Avignon to protest against 'quandam doc-trinam pestiferam' (letter of John XXII, 26 Aug. 1325), and was one of a commission of masters in theology who reported in 1326 at Avignon upon 51 articles selected from Ockham's writings and pre-sented to the Pope by Jacques de Concoz, Archbishop of Aix. See A. Pelzer, in *Revue d'histoire ecclésiastique*, xviii (1922), 240 *sq.* Finally, the condemnations of the faculty of arts at Paris in 1339 and 1340 (*Chartul.* ii, Nos. 1023, 1042) were sealed with the seals of all the four nations.]

[2] Bulaeus, iv. 257; *Chartul.* ii, No. 1023. Cf. No. 1042.

[3] Bulaeus, iv. 308. *Chartul.* ii, No. 1124 (only a fragment appears in Bulaeus). Autrecourt is in the diocese of Verdun. Among the re-tracted positions are the following: 'quod de rebus per apparentia naturalia quasi nulla certitudo po-test hab(eri; illa tamen) modica potest in brevi haberi, tempore si homines convertant in(tellectum suu)m ad res, et non ad intellectum Aristotilis et Commentato(ris). . . .' 'Quod de substantia materiali alia ab anima nostra non habemus certi-tudinem evidentie. . . .' 'Quod nescimus evidenter quod aliqua causa causet efficienter que non sit Deus', and a number of other propositions tending to the denial of the 'necessary connexion' be-tween phenomenal cause and effect. At times his scepticism seems to have been carried further, e.g. in the proposition 'Deus est, Deus non est, penitus idem significant, licet (alio modo)'. He also divined that light has velocity, in which he was anticipated by Roger Bacon (*Op. Maj.*, ed. Jebb, pp. 248, 300), to whom he is not likely to have been indebted. Some of his views are ascribed by Denifle to the in-fluence of Bradwardine. Nicholas was deprived of his mastership in arts by papal authority, his books burned in the Pré-aux-clercs, and a solemn recantation took place thereon before the assembled university. [For Nicholas see Ueberweg-Geyer, pp. 591–4, and the bibliographical note on p. 783. In 1907 Rashdall contributed a paper, 'Nicholas de Ultricuria, a medieval Hume', to the *Proceedings of the Aristotelean Society*, new series, viii. 1–27.]

spite of all repression, Ockhamism seems to have made way; CHAP. V, §6.
and, at the beginning of the fifteenth century, many of the
leading spirits in the university, notably d'Ailly and Gerson,
were avowed nominalists. Possibly the growing anti-papal
feeling may have helped to procure toleration for the anti-
papal and imperialist friar. Thus, for the second time in her
history, nominalism infused new light and new life into the
torpid traditionalism of the Parisian schools.[1]

[1] [Just as Rashdall distinguished too sharply between the English and the French attitude to Ockham, so he laid too much stress upon the effects of the papal Schism in explaining the growth of nominalism at Paris. Richard of Bury's sympathy with the *via moderna*, as the teaching of the nominalists came to be called, no doubt contributed to his pessimistic feeling about the state of the Parisian schools, yet, when he wrote, the nominalists were already very active, and Paris was anything but a home of 'torpid traditionalism'. Indeed the definitions of philosophical and theological orthodoxy in the thirteenth century were followed at once by a period of intense activity, in which the Thomists (and Scotists) and the followers of Ockham gradually became the chief protagonists. Of the latter Buridan (see above, p. 492) was rector in 1327, 1348, and 1358, Gregory of Rimini was master of theology in 1345, John of Mirecourt lectured on the Sentences in 1345, and his theses were condemned in 1347 (*Chartul.* ii, No. 1147; also Ueberweg-Gèyer, pp. 590-1, 783, and the text of his two *apologiae*, edited by F. Stegmuller in *Recherches de théologie ancienne et médiévale*, v (1933), 40-78, 192-204), Nicholas of Autrecourt was his contemporary, Albert of Saxony was rector in 1353, and Nicholas of Oresme was a master of theology by 1362. Albert of Saxony carried the new teaching to Vienna, of which he was the first rector in 1365, and before 1386 Marsiglio of Inghen (rector at Paris in 1367 and 1371) was the first rector of the new University of Heidelberg. The struggle between the *via antiqua* and the *via moderna*, with its far-reaching consequences in Italy and Germany during the developments of modern science and Protestantism, was an intellectual movement of great importance, rooted in the study of first principles and independent of, though not uninfluenced by, political and ecclesiastical events. It is unfortunate that Rashdall was unable to study the history of the German universities in the light of recent investigation. Here we can merely refer to the very full account and the extensive bibliographies in Ueberweg-Geyer, pp. 583-612, 782-6. The most illuminating works are F. Ehrle, *Der Sentenzenkommentar Peters von Candia, des Pisaners Papstes Alexander V* (Franzisk. Studien, ix. 1925); G. Ritter, 'Studien zur Spätscholastik', in the *Sitzungsberichte d. Heidelberger Akad. d. Wissenschaften*, Phil.-hist. Klasse, 1921, 1922; and the writings of Michalski and Duhem, previously noted. Cf. also Denifle,. *Luther et le Luthéranisme*, French trans., iii (1912), 191-232; Rudolf Stadelmann, *Vom Geist des ausgehenden Mittelalters* (Halle, 1929), especially pp. 30-9; E. F. Jacob in *History*, xvi (1931), 219-21. But the literature is very extensive.]

CHAP. V,
§ 6.
Nominal-
ism and
enlighten-
ment. It is interesting to notice that as soon as the impetus imparted to the intellectual activity of Paris by the discussion
of the really important questions of ecclesiastical polity and
discipline raised by the Schism and the Councils died away,
we find Ockhamism again proscribed as a heresy, now not
merely by the university, but by the King, who was under
the influence of a realist confessor, and the Parlement. This
association of the rise and fall of nominalism with the rise
and fall of intellectual activity may be supposed to lend
some colour to the theory put forward by the late Mr. Pattison
as to the intrinsic connexion between nominalism and intellectual progress on the one hand and between realism and
religious or political reaction on the other.[1] But if in the
annals of medieval Paris the prevalence of nominalism may
to some extent be taken as an index of intellectual vitality,
that is simply because opposition to an established philo-

---

[1] Bulaeus, v. 678, 679, 706–10;
Dubarle, i. 310. By the edict of
Louis XI, published on 1 March
1474, masters are enjoined to teach
the doctrine of Aristotle 'and his
Commentator Averroes, Albertus
Magnus, Thomas Aquinas, Aegi-
dius Romanus, Alexander of Hales,
Scotus, and Bonaventura, and other
Realist Doctors', instead of that of
William of Ockham, 'Monachus
Cisterciensis', [John of Mirecourt],
Gregory of Rimini, Buridan, Peter
d'Ailly, Marsilius, Adam Wodeham,
John Dorp, Albert of Saxony, and
other 'Nominalists or Terminists'.
The teaching of the latter is strictly
forbidden under pain of perpetual
banishment and other 'arbitrary
penalties'; and all nominalistic
books are to be surrendered to the
officers of Parliament and chained
up so that they cannot be used
(Bulaeus, v. 708, 709). All regents
were required to swear obedience
to the statute, which they did
'exceptis paucis (Theologis) qui
sustinet Nominales qui nihilominus
conditionaliter iuraverunt'. The
faculty of arts, however, protested

against the 'Excatenatio' of the
books; and ordered that only one
volume should be surrendered
from each library, and at last the
king was persuaded to be satisfied
with this merely symbolical muzz-
ling of the offensive writers (ibid.
v. 711, 712). The decree was procured by the influence of the King's
confessor, the Bishop of Avranches.
It was, however, revoked in 1481,
and the imprisoned books restored
(ibid., 739, 740, 747). The German
proctor goes into raptures in re-
cording the joy of his nation 'doctrinam illam salubrem, Christianam,
Universitatis fulgorem, totiusque
machinae mundi lucernam super
candelabrum poni', &c. (ibid., p.
740). We find measures spontaneously taken against nominalism by
the university before the edict of
1473 (ibid., pp. 678, 679), which
shows that the majority, then as
always, except in the German
nation, were realists, though no
doubt some of the ablest men were
on the other side. [See on all this
Ehrle, Peter von Candia, pp. 305–
26.]

sophy, whatever be its character, is a sign of intellectual vigour; but the heresy tends to lose its vitality as soon as it becomes an orthodoxy. At Prague we shall find an established nominalism associated with the narrowest and most intolerant ecclesiasticism, while realism (though its religious earnestness might have destroyed for some minds its claim to any association with progress) was certainly the creed of some of the ablest men and the most fearless reformers that ever made their appearance in a medieval university. Ockham no doubt possesses an importance in the history of philosophy which cannot be accorded to John Hus or even to his master Wyclif, but this importance does not extend to the nominalist opponents of Wyclif at Oxford or the nominalist burners of Hus at Constance.

Moreover, at this time a first faint breath of that Renaissance which was already an accomplished fact in Italy reached the schools of Paris. We have already noticed the decline of Latin style and the extinction of classical education under the influence of the wider scholasticism which followed the introduction of the new Aristotle into the schools of Paris. Now—perhaps through the mere rumour of the new enthusiasm for Cicero and Virgil which was springing up beyond the Alps, but more probably through an independent operation of the same Renaissance spirit[1]—Paris could once again boast, in Nicholas of Clémenges, of a scholar whose style, though of course not critically faultless, bore the classical ring more decidedly than the style of Abélard's Letters or even John of Salisbury's 'Metalogicon'.[2] Though Clémenges' *The new classicism.*

---

[1] [There is sufficient evidence to establish some direct influence from Italy. See especially A. Coville, *Gontier et Pierre Col et l'humanisme en France au temps de Charles V* (Paris, 1934), ch. viii, pp. 140–86.]

[2] [It is very difficult to analyse with justice the reaction of the university to the gradual development of humanism in France, especially in court circles, from the time of King Charles V. The invitation given to Petrarch in 1340 by his friend Roberto dei Bardi, the chancellor (1336–49), to come to Paris to be crowned poet (*ad percipiendam lauream poeticam*) gives no indication, of course, of the general feeling in the university (*Chartul.* ii, No. 1038; cf. for the Florentine Roberto dei Bardi, No. 998 and note; also E. H. R. Tatham, *Francesco Petrarca*, ii. 113 *sq.*). On the whole it is doubtless true that a man like Jean Petit was, as his biographer says, more typical of

CHAP. V, scholarship exerted, so far as appears, very little influence on
§ 6. the ordinary education of the schools,[1] it contributed towards
a great improvement in the theological writing of the period.
The Wycliffite heresy had aroused in all reflecting men some
consciousness of the scandal arising from the prevalence of
simony, from the avarice and extortion of the papal collectors, and from the flagrant immorality of the clergy; and in
men like Clémenges and Gerson this consciousness inspired
a real desire for reunion and reform. In the presence of such

the university than were the enlightened spirits, Gerson, d'Ailly,
and Clémenges (Coville, *Jean Petit*,
p. 276, and his *Gontier et Pierre
Col*, pp. 103, 140). During the fifteenth century, however, particularly in the colleges, interest in the
'humanities' grew. Nicholas of
Clémenges taught in the College of
Navarre after his return to Paris in
1426 till his death in 1437. Gregorio
Tifernas lectured on Greek from
1458, and was followed by his pupil,
George Hermonymus of Sparta,
not a great teacher, but the master
of Reuchlin, Budaeus, and Erasmus. The movement culminated
in the establishment by King
Francis I in 1530 of Chairs in the
university, the beginning of the
Collège de France. See S. d'Irsay
op. cit. i. 261–74, with bibliography
of Tifernas and Hermonymus; L.
Thuasne, *Roberti Gaguini epistolae
et orationes* (Paris, 1904); A. Le-
franc, *Histoire de Collège de France*
(Paris, 1893), and his paper in the
Mélanges Pirenne (Brussels, 1926), i.
291 *sq.*; P. S. Allen, *The Age of Erasmus* (Oxford 1914), who is somewhat sceptical about the value of
these early developments. We have
already referred to the importance
of the mysticism of the Low Countries in the life of Paris and to the
College of Montaigu (above, p.
521 n.).
Something should also be said
about the establishment of chairs
in languages in order to promote

biblical exegesis. Pope Innocent
IV and the Dominicans prepared
the way by encouraging the study
of Oriental languages (*Chartul.* i,
Nos. 180, 279; Reichart, *Monumenta*, iii. 98, 290; iv. 50). Clement
V ordered teachers of Hebrew,
Greek, Arabic, and Chaldaean to
be appointed in the Universities of
Rome, Paris, Oxford, Bologna, and
Salamanca (*Corpus Juris Canonici*,
ed. Friedberg, ii, col. 1179; a canon
of the Council of Vienne (1311)
included in the Clementines, lib. v,
tit. i, c. 1). See also S. d'Irsay,
op. cit. i. 161, 261; B. Altaner in
Zeitschrift für Kirchengeschichte, lii
(1933), 226–36; and, with reference
to the suggestions of Pierre Dubois,
some interesting pages in R. Scholz,
*Die Publizistik zur Zeit Philipps des
Schönen und Bonifaz' VIII* (Stuttgart, 1906), pp. 427–36. The movement became really important
when the 'trilingual colleges' were
founded by Ximenes (Alcalá)
Fox (Corpus Christi College, Oxford), Busleiden (Louvain), Faber
(Vienna), and others. See P. S.
Allen, 'The Trilingual Colleges of
the Early Sixteenth Century', in
*Erasmus: Lectures and Wayfaring
Sketches*, Oxford, 1934, pp. 138–
63.]
[1] D'Ailly at the Council of Constance urged the appointment of
'institutores Rhetoricae et lingua-
rum Graecae et Latinae' (Von der
Hardt, vol. i, pt. iv, c. 427).

problems, the more earnest minds began to turn away in contempt or disgust from aimless and incessant disputations over
the serious questions of a bygone age, and from the increasingly subtle and increasingly frivolous discussions which
amused the schoolmen of the present. Gerson deplores
the 'useless speculation without fruit or solidity', and the
increasing subtlety and technicality of the theologians
of the day, whom he goes so far as to call 'verbose and
fantastic sophists'.[1] In his own treatises he inaugurated a
new school of theological writing which occupied itself not
with debating in dry logical and syllogistic form the speculative questions of the schools, but with the discussion in a
more popular style and a more practical spirit of the ecclesiastical questions of the day and the principles of Church
government upon which their solution was to be based. By
the time of Gerson the knell of scholasticism was already
sounded; an age of controversial but literary theology was
setting in.

A favourable political situation was, of course, necessary Growth of
to enable the views of the little group of reforming Gallican Gallican-
ism since
theologians to pass out of the region of speculation into that the reign
of Philip
of action. But a comparison between the part which the IV.
university played at this time with its attitude in an earlier
quarrel between France and the Papacy will show the enormous change which a century had effected in the position of
the great corporation and in the theological temper of its
masters. During Philip IV's quarrel with Boniface VIII
the university had merely joined, by a majority[2] and with

[1] Gerson asks: 'Cur ob aliud
appellantur Theologi nostri temporis sophistae et verbosi, immo et
Phantastici, nisi quia relictis utili-
bus et intelligibilibus pro auditorum
qualitate transferunt se ad nudam
Logicam vel Metaphysicam, aut
etiam Mathematicam, ubi et quando non oportet, nunc de intentione
formarum, nunc de divisione con-
tinui, nunc detegentes sophismata
theologicis terminis obumbrata'
(*Opera*, Paris, 1606, i, c. 502).

He speaks of this evil as specially
rife in England. For similar complaints of Clémenges see Bulaeus,
iv. 889.

[2] 'Nonnullis ex nobis maiorem
partem facultatum nostrarum tocius Parisiensis studii facientibus
pro certis causis et negociis accedentibus ad presentiam excellentissimi principis domini Philippi', &c.
(Bulaeus, iv. 147; *Chartul.* ii, No.
634, 21 June 1303). We are not
told which faculties dissented: the

CHAP. V, considerable reluctance, in the King's 'subtraction of obedi-
§ 6.   ence' and appeal to a General Council, 'and to a future true
and legitimate Supreme Pontiff'. The step was forced on the
university as upon the clergy at large by the policy of the
King and his lawyer advisers. The university took no part
whatever in leading opinion on the subject. But at the end
of the fourteenth century the views of the university were far

The uni- in advance of those of the court. The idea of forcing a
versity's
efforts to termination of the Schism on the reluctant Pope of Avignon
terminate
the Schism. may be said to have originated in the university, or at all
events to have been kept alive only in the university after
the death of Charles V. The Duke of Anjou, the first of the
regents by whom the government was carried on during the
unhappy reign of Charles VI, was a Clementine who was
anxious to perpetuate the alliance between Avignon and the
French crown for the plunder of the French Church. The
first 'Orator' who ventured to appear before the regent with

words might mean a majority in
each faculty. [Boniface VIII retaliated on 15 Aug. 1303 by suspending the right of the university
to grant the degree of master in
theology and canon and civil law.
His successor, Benedict XI, withdrew the ban on 18 April 1304
(*Chartul.* ii, Nos. 636, 645). See
generally Scholz, *Die Publizistik*,
&c.; J. Rivière, *Le Problème de
l'église et de l'état au temps de
Philippe le Bel* (Louvain, 1926),
pp. 110–14; H.-X. Arquillière,
'L'Appel au concile', in *Rev. des
questions historiques*, 1911, pp. 28–
37; and for the division of opinion
among the Dominicans and Franciscans in Paris, Picot, *Documents
relatifs aux États Généraux* (Paris,
1901); E. Longpré, 'Le b. Jean
Duns Scot. O.F.M. pour le Saint
Siège contre le Gallicanisme', in
La France franciscaine, xi (1928),
137–62; A. G. Little, 'Chronological Notes on the Life of Duns
Scotus', in *Eng. Hist. Rev.* xlvii
(1932), 575–7. The chief academic

supporter of Philip IV was John
Quidort of Paris, a Dominican,
formerly a well-known secular
master in the faculty of arts, whose
tract *De potestate regia et papali*
was written in 1302–3 (Scholz,
pp. 275–84, 298; Rivière, p. 148).]
    Bulaeus, as usual, asserts that the
university took a more prominent
part in these proceedings than is
warranted by the documents which
he produces. The tractate *De
potestate Papae* or 'Rex pacificus',
printed in Bulaeus, iv. 935 *sq.*,
[though it may have been written
by a doctor of canon law in the
university (Scholz, p. 256)], cannot
be assumed to represent the opinion
of the university as a whole. A few
doctors in 1297 had 'determined'
that Boniface's election was invalid,
as his predecessor could not canoni-
cally resign; see Denifle's note in
Chartul. ii, No. 604. [They were
answered by Giles of Rome in his
De renunciatione Papae (Roccaberti,
Bibliotheca pontificia maxima, ii.
1–64).]

a resolution of the university in favour of a General Council— one John Rousse or Ruysche—was the next night dragged from his bed in the Collège Lemoine, and lodged in prison by order of the regent. He was only released on promising to recognize the claims of Clement; and the rector was threatened with the same penalty for having received a letter from Urban and read it before the assembled university.[1] Both the rector and Rousse eventually took refuge in the court of Urban VI. The Schism, however, and the method to be adopted in healing it continued to be the one absorbing subject of thought and discussion in academic circles, and gradually the chaotic body of opinion shaped itself into certain definite schemes for its immediate termination; so that, when early in 1394 the university was at length allowed openly to discuss the subject, the question was ripe for settlement.[2] In order to allow of greater freedom in the expression of individual judgement, a novel expedient was adopted. In January a chest was placed in the Mathurine convent, into which members of the university—even, it would appear, mere students —were invited to place their written opinions.[3] The deputies appointed to examine these papers reported that the expedients recommended fell for the most part under three

[1] Bulaeus, iv. 583; *Chronique du Religieux de S. Denis*, i. 86; *Chartul.* iii, Nos. 1637, 1640. [See above, p. 560, note, for the works of Henry of Langenstein and Conrad of Gelnhausen advocating a council. Similarly Pierre d'Ailly claimed many years later (1412) that he had been the first to urge 'materiam concilii generalis in concilio Franciae . . . ex parte Universitatis' (P. Tschackert, *Peter von Ailli*, Gotha, 1879, App. xii, p. 37).]

[2] The university had met with another rebuff in 1391. *Chronique du Religieux de S. Denis*, i. 692, 694. [For Jean Gerson's sermon before Charles VI on 6 Jan. 1391, when he implored the court to give heed to the university and to seek means to end the Schism, see Valois, ii. 395, 396. Early in 1393

Gilles des Champs, speaking in the name of the university, went farther and pressed for action as the duty of all who would not be considered heretics. A Pope who insisted on his claim should be deposed: *Chartul.* iii, No. 1666; Valois, iii. 404.]

[3] 'Cedulas repertas, que decem mille numerum excedebant.' Such is the printed text of the *Chronique du Religieux de S. Denis*, ii. 100; [*Chartul.* iii, No. 1678. Gerson tells of a scrutiny of this kind, in which the same person put in a hundred schedules 'tamquam diversi posuerint, ut secundum pluralitatem schedarum iudicetur'; quoted *ibid.*, p. 504, note. Contemporaries estimated the masters in arts at 1,000, doubtless with much exaggeration.]

CHAP. V,
§ 6.

heads: (1) The way of 'Cession', or concerted abdication by both pontiffs; (2) The way of Arbitration; (3) The way of a General Council. A letter, setting forth these three methods, and adding that if the Pope refused to adopt one of them he ought to be held a schismatic, was immediately drawn up in the name of the university by Clémenges, and presented to the King.[1] The presentation of a similar letter to Clement himself, coupled with the news that the College of Cardinals had all but unanimously assented to the action of the university, produced an explosion of wrath which contributed to hasten the end of the unfortunate pontiff (16 September), and so, as it seemed for the moment, to give practical effect to the views of the remonstrants.[2] But the hurried election of Benedict XIII by the Avignon cardinals speedily dashed to the ground the hopes which began to be entertained of a peaceful solution of the difficulty, and compelled the university to renew its efforts for the extinction of the Schism.

Declares for the *via cessionis*, 1395.

In 1395 the *via cessionis* was definitely adopted as the best of the three methods already laid before the Pope, first by a council of the national Church, and then by the university.[3] At present the project of a General Council did not find much favour with the academical divines; for, if precedent was to be followed, such a council would be composed exclusively of bishops, or at most of bishops and abbots, and no theory of conciliar infallibility seems to have blinded French churchmen to the probability that, if it came to a counting of heads, the Italian 'Bishoplings' would inevitably outnumber the rulers of the larger dioceses of northern Europe. Moreover,

[1] Bulaeus, iv. 683, 687; *Chartul.* iii, Nos. 1678-86. The order of the method above given expresses the order of preference.

[2] Bulaeus, iv. 699, 703; *Chartul.* iii, No. 1690; *Chron. du Rel. de S. Denys*, ii. 184; [Salembier, pp. 135-41.]

[3] Bulaeus, iv. 729, 732, 747, 773; *Chron. du Rel. de S. Denis*, ii. 218 sq. [For the assembly of the clergy (Feb. 1395) and the embassy to Benedict XIII of May and June see

Valois, iii. 44 sq., and Coville, *Jean Petit*, pp. 36-43. Ten delegates of the university were included in the embassy, which was headed by the Dukes of Berri, Burgundy, and Orleans. Jean Petit gave an account of it in discourses delivered in 1406 (cf. Coville, p. 67). Ehrle printed the *Informatio seriosa*, composed by a partisan of Benedict in 1396, in *Archiv für Litt.- und Kirchengeschichte*, v. 400.]

it never seems to have occurred to the strongest churchmen of that day that episcopal consecration could prove a substitute for theological or legal training; and the masters of Paris did not relish the prospect of handing over the decision of the momentous question to an assembly which would have been largely composed of uneducated or half-educated men.[1] As soon as this decision taken at Paris became known, Benedict began to initiate proceedings against the members of the university, with a view to deprivation of their benefices; whereupon the university in 1396 appealed to the 'next sole, true, orthodox, and universal Pope'. The university thus openly declared war against the Avignon claimant of the Papacy.[2]

Appeal against Benedict XIII, 1396.

To record the successive efforts of the university, first to force a simultaneous resignation upon the rival pontiffs, and then, as experience proved the hopelessness of bringing about any scheme which required the co-operation of the two—or, after Pisa, three—claimants, to bring about the convocation of a General Council, would lead us farther than our limits would allow into the general history of the period.[3] During

The university a European power.

---

[1] Thus, the writer of the first appeal of the university from Benedict XIII dwells upon the difficulties involved in the summons of a General Council. There would be no agreement as to where it was to meet, who was to summon it, or who were to sit. A council composed of bishops must include 'Episcopellos Italicos Iuris ignaros quorum infinitus est numerus, Bellacores [sic], Alemannos caeterosque de Maevii promotione puerulos Gallicanos' (Bulaeus, iv. 817, 818). We should read perhaps 'Bellatores Alemannos'.

[2] Another of the letters of the university had, however, already suggested that an equal number of doctors of theology and law should sit with the prelates, 'quia plures eorum, proh pudor! hodie satis illiterati sunt'. *Ibid.* iv. 690; *Chartul.* iii, No. 1680.

[3] [The study of the Schism and of the conciliar movement, with the publication of new texts, has been greatly advanced since Rashdall's book first appeared. Perhaps the most convenient introductions to the new literature are the notes in Hefele-Leclercq, VI. ii and VII. i, and the bibliographies in Salembier, *Le Grand Schisme* (new edition, Paris, 1921), and in Gustav Schnürer, *Kirche und Kultur im Mittelalter*, iii (Paderborn, 1929), 436, 445. In addition to the various works of Valois and Coville, J. Haller's *Papstthum und Kirchenreform* (1903) should especially be consulted. The great work of E. H. von der Hardt, *Magnum Constantiense Concilium*, in six volumes (Frankfurt, 1700), has now been supplemented by the *Acta Concilii Constantiensis* of H. Finke, 4 vols. (Münster, 1896–1928), with

the twenty years which preceded the meeting of the Council of Constance, the history of Europe centres round the debates of the Parisian Congregations. In the work of preparing for the reformation of the Church 'in its head and members', the university played the part of a European potentate. Her ambassadors travelled to all parts of Europe—at one time they are found as far north as Scotland—with dispatches or missions to emperor, pope, or king, to princes, prelates, and universities, in the hope of establishing a European concert. And that such a concert was ultimately established is due in very large measure to the peculiar and unique prestige of the university, and the excellent use which for once was made of that prestige under the guidance of men like Clémenges and d'Ailly, and later of Gerson and Jean Courtecuisse. In the main, the subtraction of obedience by the Gallican Church from Benedict XIII in 1398[1] was directly the work of the university, while the assembling of the Council of Pisa and more decidedly of the Councils of Constance and Basel were results partly of the actual diplomacy of the university, and still more largely of the ideas which had gradually shaped themselves into something like a new theory of ecclesiastical polity in the minds and the writings of the Parisian theologians. Of course, there were more powerful political forces working in the same direction, and, above all, due credit must be given to the determination of the Emperor Sigismund.[2] But the Council of Pisa did not spring out of the discontent of a few cardinals; nor was the Council of Constance the result of the mere *fiat* of sovereign princes. The councils were emphatically the work of public opinion. But a mere

The great councils the work of the university.

his studies, *Forschungen und Quellen zur Geschichte des Konstanzer Konzil* (Paderborn, 1889) and *Bilder vom Konstanzer Konzils* (Heidelberg, 1903). Of the numerous detailed studies on the share of particular universities in the conciliar movement, the more general essay of L. Dax, *Die Universitäten und die Konzilien von Pisa und Konstanz* (Freiburg i. B., 1910), should be noted.]

[1] [27 May 1398, at a synod which had met in Paris on 23 May. For the problems which this act created, including that of provision for university graduates, see G. Barraclough, 'Un Document inédit sur la soustraction d'obédience de 1398', in *Rev. d'hist. ecclésiastique*, xxx (1934), 101–15, especially pp. 110, 111.]

[2] Strictly King of the Romans.

floating mass of unarmed opinion can never become operative CHAP. V,
§ 6. unless it finds definite and concentrated expression through recognized organs. At this crisis in the history of Europe the universities performed the function which is discharged at the present day by the press, by the platform, and even by the polling-booths. Two conditions had to be fulfilled by any body or institution which aspired to constitute itself the mouthpiece which the growing discontent against the protracted Schism demanded. It must be more than a merely national institution, and it must be to some extent an ecclesiastical body. The University of Paris with its four nations, the common mother of all northern universities, the recognized fountain-head (as it was constantly styled in official rhetoric) of 'the streams of knowledge' which watered the whole Christian world, could claim something of that international character which medieval theory accorded to the Papacy and the Empire. Never, indeed, did the university more completely justify the position so often assigned to her by medieval panegyrists as the third of the great powers or organs of the European system—France's equivalent for the Italian Papacy and the German Empire.[1] Now, in the paralysis of one member of the mysterious triad, it seemed the natural office of the other two to unite in restoring health to the disordered European system. And the second condition of success was no less happily satisfied by the peculiar relations of the university to the ecclesiastical system. Its theological faculty of scarlet-robed priests, the clerical status of all, and the high ecclesiastical rank of many of its members sufficiently guarded against the danger of wounding clerical susceptibilities or rousing genuine scruples in devout minds as to the lawfulness of disregarding papal censure and setting up the authority of a General Council—long considered a mere adviser of the Papacy—against the Vicar of Christ. In the Middle Ages intellect, learning, common sense, were not

An international institution.

Advantages of its ecclesiastical character.

---

[1] Cf. Budinszky (p. 25), 'Darf es uns nach dem Gesagten Wunder nehmen, wenn der Nimbus, der unsere Universität umgab, sie geradezu als genügende Entschädigung für Papstthum und Kaiserkrone auffassen liess, welche den beiden andern Nationen des Reiches Karls des Grossen als Erbtheil zugefallen waren.'

CHAP. V, forces strong enough to demand a hearing in their own right.
§ 6. They had to clothe themselves with some semblance of sacerdotal sanctity, and to speak with some tone of spiritual authority before they could command the reverence of the world. It is curious to observe the extent to which this mere semblance of traditional and ecclesiastical authority, which had gathered about an institution not three centuries old, succeeded in blinding the clerical mind to the partly secular, partly papal origin of the universities whose voice was now raised against the system of ecclesiastical government which had been dominant in Europe at least since the time of Hildebrand. The hand of secular power which first attempted to force the rival pontiffs into abdicating, and which then compelled John XXIII to convoke a General Council of Constance, wore a glove of quasi-spiritual authority. Probably no theory of ecclesiastical polity that ever was expressly formulated found a place for universities in its system of divinely authorized councils and synods, or elevated doctors as an order of its divinely commissioned ministry to the side of bishops and presbyters. Yet when the scheme of 'Cession' broke down and all thoughts were turned to the plan of a General Council, so subtly had the universities insinuated themselves into the ecclesiastical system of western Europe that no serious opposition seems to have been offered to the Parisian suggestion that their representatives must take their seats on the supreme tribunal of the Church beside the older hierarchy of bishops and abbots.[1]

The university at Constance, 1415.
The most important part which was played by the great university and the other universities associated in the movement lay in preparing the public mind for the ecclesiastical revolution implied in the convocation of a council by the College of Cardinals and in the deposition of a Pope on other grounds than heresy.[2] When the councils were once assembled, the universities had no doubt called into existence

[1] See the letters to and from the university in the *Chartularium* (esp. iii, No. 1680, pp. 614, 615, where an equal number of prelates and academic members is suggested), and

Correspondence of Thomas Bekynton, ed. Williams, London, 1872.
[2] It was thought advisable, however, to invent the doctrine that obstinate Schism amounts to heresy.

forces which they could not completely control; and it would be too much to say that the leading part in the deliberations of the councils was always taken by the actual delegates of the existing body of masters. Still, even at Pisa, the Council which was less directly the work of the university than Constance, we are told that out of 123 theologians present, eighty had graduated at Paris.[1] At Pisa and in the earlier sessions of Constance the moving spirit was Cardinal d'Ailly. This ambitious politician had been to some extent estranged from the Parisian Reformers by the offer of a cardinal's hat. Their left wing had, indeed, advanced beyond the theological position, not only of d'Ailly, but of Clémenges and Gerson.[2]

[1] So Bulaeus, v. 193. [For the evidence see Hefele-Leclercq, VII. i. 3–6, notes. Valois doubts if at any time the French contingent was ever more than one-third or, at the most, two-thirds of the whole assembly. At the beginning of June 1409, of the 500 or less assembled, not more than 150 were French or Provençals: Finke, *Acta Concilii Constantiensis*, i. 283. The effective element from Paris was probably small. John of Segovia suggests that thirty-one theologians from Paris took part in the Council.] The idea that the cardinals of both obediences might without the consent of the Pope summon a General Council is said to have been first suggested by the Parisian theologian, Henry of Hesse or Langenstein (Crévier, iii. 76), though this has been disputed. [Priority probably belongs to Conrad of Gelnhausen, whose *Epistola Concordiae* was composed in May 1380 (Valois, i. 324). By 1409 Cardinal d'Ailly, who had been attacked as a friend of Benedict XIII, Gerson, and others had rallied to this scheme, which was supported with vigour by Dietrich of Niem. See A. Kneer, *Die Entstehung der konziliaren Theorie zur Geschichte des Schismas und der Kirchenpolitiken* (Rome,

1893) and *Kardinal Zabarella* (Münster, 1891). Dietrich of Niem gave priority to the Emperor, next to the Pope, among those who had the right to summon a council: see H. Heimpel's edition of his tract (1413–14) on the calling of a council in his 'Studien zur Kirchen- und Reichsreform des 15. Jahrhunderts', i (*Sitzungsberichte der Heidelberger Akademie*, 1929). But, alongside his patriotic suspicion of the claims to authority of the University of Paris, Dietrich was much influenced by Cardinal d'Ailly: Heimpel, *Dietrich von Niem*, Münster, 1932, pp. 155, 169, 177.]

[2] Pierre Plaoul, for instance, in 1406 contended 'Dioecesim Romanam non aliter esse Dioecesim quam Parisiensem et eum qui Episcopatum obtinet Romanum, toti ecclesiae presidere', and that the King could summon councils 'in negotiis etiam fidei': Bulaeus, v. 132. [Good accounts of the important assembly at the end of 1406 and of the share of the university will be found in Valois, iii. 449 *sq.*, and Coville, *Jean Petit*, pp. 65–81. The discourse of Petit, cited by Coville (especially pp. 79, 80) throws much light on university procedure and the position of the nations.]

Still d'Ailly could never have played his part as an inter-
mediary between the Curialist cardinals and the conciliar
party but for his Gallican education and his early relations
with the Gallican leaders. And in the later sessions it was the
actual delegates of the university who took the lead. In particular, there was one critical moment when the university
was able to interpose with decisive effect. The right of presiding in a General Council was conceded by moderate
Gallicans, as it is still theoretically conceded by some Angli-
cans, to the occupant of St. Peter's Chair; and it was only
the firm attitude of the academical delegates, together with
the strenuous efforts of Sigismund, which prevented the dissolution of the Council after the flight of John XXIII.[1]

'Voting by nations' suggested by the university organization. But there was one matter in which the university was able
by the mere accidents of its constitution to exercise at Con-
stance a more powerful effect on the moulding of the destinies
of Europe than it exercised by any express utterance of its
delegates. We have already seen how long the convocation
of the Council was prevented by the fear that the enormous
number of petty Italian sees would give to the Curialist party
a representation out of all proportion to its real strength. It
is difficult to divine by what means this catastrophe could
have been evaded, had not the expedient of imitating the
system of voting by nations, which had been copied from
Paris in almost all her daughter-universities, suggested itself
to that assembly of graduates. The division into four nations,
likened by the medieval imagination to the four streams
which watered the Garden of Eden, seemed by this time so
completely a part of the eternal constitution of things, that
it was without difficulty assumed that the voice of the Universal Church—nay, the voice of the Holy Spirit Himself—
would be heard unerringly through an organ of similar constitution. The anomalies of the Parisian system of voting were
faithfully reproduced at Constance. In 1439, for instance,

[1] Von der Hardt, ii, c. 265 *sq.*
(erroneously numbered 165); iv, p.
75 *sq.* [See Hefele-Leclercq, VII. i.
197 *sq.*, and the authorities there
cited. The special claims of the
doctors in theology and law to a
vote was voiced emphatically by
Cardinal d'Ailly; see Von der
Hardt, ii, c. 224; iv, p. 15.]

the English, or, as it was then called, the German, nation at
Paris happened for the time to have dwindled to a single
master; yet he was allowed to elect himself proctor and to
vote on behalf of his nation on a level with the representative
of a hundred or more French masters in a rectorial election.[1]
At Constance the seven representatives of the English nation
enjoyed a voting power scarcely less out of proportion to its
numerical strength. The adhesion of England to the Council
was secured, as it could hardly have been secured otherwise
in the hey-day of English ascendancy on the Continent, by
an arrangement which thus neutralized the disadvantage it
would otherwise have been under owing to its distance from
the place of meeting.[2]

To sketch even in briefest outline the position of the Revolu-
Council of Constance (including its continuation at Basel) as tionary
a turning-point in the history of the Western Church would of the
lead us far beyond the limits of the present work. It will be conciliar
enough to indicate how these Councils form the turning- movement.
point in the history of the university to whose activity they
in so large a measure owed their existence. The Council of

[1] See the very amusing account
of the incident in the German Proctor's Book for 1439 (Jourdain, No.
772). A German master coming
into residence found that the only
master of his nation who had lately
been resident had gone out of town
for some time. He had left the
book, key, &c., of the nation with
the *bedellus*, with instructions that
they were not to be surrendered to
any one master but himself. The
new-comer's claim was, however,
recognized by the faculty of arts.
[The exodus was due to scarcity
and plague, which the depredations
of the *Écorcheurs* had intensified
(*Auctarium*, ii. 506–17 and notes).
Although it is impossible to estimate the fluctuations in numbers
exactly, it appears that 'during the
centuries for which the proctors'
accounts remain, the total membership varied at various times from
one to over twenty' (Boyce, pp. 36,

37). The congregation of the nation
was a small gathering which had no
fixed meeting-place and might vary
indefinitely in numbers for various
reasons, just as a college debating
or literary society does to-day. Each
resident master was summoned by
the beadle, but attendance at the
weekly meetings does not seem to
have been regarded with the sense
of obligation which pervades the
members of a college meeting at
Oxford or Cambridge.]

[2] [See especially Finke, *Forschungen*, chs. iii and iv, for the part
played by the first English delegates
in bringing about this method of
voting. In April 1416, after a
complaint from Constance that the
English delegation was too small,
the Bishop of London and others,
including twelve *doctores*, were
sent: Reg. Chichele, ii, f. 4. We
owe this reference to Dr. E. F.
Jacob.]

Constance represents the fleeting triumph of Gallicanism. By the time that Council met, the theology of Paris and the Parisian universities, the theology which had grown up in the secular faculties of theology, had become the theology of the clergy—at least of the secular clergy—everywhere beyond the immediate entourage of the papal court. At Constance the German ecclesiastics were louder even than the French in their opposition to papal abuses and their demands for reform. That the effort would fail, that the clergy would never reform themselves, might have been predicted by any one acquainted with the state of morals and religion among the clergy of that age. Had there been any doubt about the matter before, the hopelessness of expecting serious results from such assemblies became apparent enough when it was discovered that the mere presence of so many reforming ecclesiastics had bred a moral pestilence in the place of their assembly.[1] The conciliar movement was at bottom a merely clerical movement, the outcome of no deep convictions, supported by no widely spread religious fervour, entirely without root in popular sympathy. Nor were even its leaders (with the exception of Gerson and a very few others) actuated by any passionate zeal for those objects for which churches are supposed to exist. They were for the most part at best respectable ecclesiastical politicians and pamphleteers, who had little or no regard for the spiritual destitution of the people. D'Ailly, for instance, held more than fourteen benefices, and Pierre Plaoul was accused of scandalous corruption in university examinations.[2] The real reformers of the age

---

[1] The 'meretrices' attracted by the Council were variously estimated at from 450 to 1,500. See authorities in Robertson, *Hist. of of the Christ. Ch.* (1875), vii. 345. [Rashdall, in his epigram about the 'reforming ecclesiastics', overlooked the fact that at this time Constance was crowded by princes and their suites and by laymen of all kinds, who far outnumbered the clerical element. The total number of clerics who were members of the Council was about equal to the number of prostitutes, seven hundred, mentioned by Ulrich of Reichenthal. It has been calculated that the ecclesiastics and their suites alone were 18,000 in number, i.e. their followers were more than 17,000. In addition there were the lay princes and their followers. See Hefele-Leclercq, VII. i. 195 and notes.]

[2] *Chartul.* iii, No. 1511. Cf. note, *ibid.*, p. 340.

were more harshly treated at Constance in all probability than CHAP. V, they would have been treated at Rome or Avignon. The § 6. most conspicuous achievement of this vast assemblage of clergymen, beyond the termination of the Schism, was the burning of two heretics, one of whom had come to the place with the Emperor's safe-conduct, which the Council had taught him to violate.[1] The refusal of the Council to condemn Petit shows how little the divines so eager for orthodoxy cared for morality in comparison with the political interests of their order. With too many of its members all this talk about reform meant little more than a desire to protect the pockets of the clergy against papal extortion. The most respectable feeling by which the mass of the Fathers were actuated was a professional dislike of irregularities which (as they phrased it) generated scandal against the clergy.

Nor were the Councils much more successful in their merely political action against papal usurpation. The Council of Constance found itself powerless as soon as it had elected Martin V. The Council of Basel was defeated by the policy of Eugenius IV. The fact is that a Council could not diplomatize. Already at Constance Martin V succeeded in breaking the opposition against him by creating division in its ranks and entering into a separate Concordat with the German nation. And the Council of Basel ceased to be a serious business from the moment (1440) when Charles VII of France adopted the policy of semi-neutrality, recognizing the already-made decrees of the Council, but adhering to Eugenius IV against the conciliar anti-Pope Felix V.[2] The

Failure of the Councils.

---

[1] Mansi, *Concilia* (1784), xxvii, col. 799. The much more explicit sanction to perjury in the interests of dogma given by L'Enfant (*E.T.* i. 514) does not appear in the printed Acts, and there seems to be no evidence that it was actually passed. But even the first-mentioned decree assumes that the secular arm is to carry out a temporal sentence in spite of having given a safe-conduct. [See the full discussion in Hefele-Leclercq, VII. i.

340–51. The point of the decree was that, although a prince who gave a safe-conduct was bound to see that it was observed so far as possible, the safe-conduct could not ensure the safe return of a man who, after trial, was found guilty.]

[2] *Ordonnances des roys de France*, xiii. 321, 324; Bulaeus, v. 449. [Cf. G. Pérouse, *Le Cardinal Louis de Aleman*, Lyons, 1904, pp. 357, 358. For the importance of the provision of benefices in university policy cf.

CHAP. V,
§ 6.

University of Paris was compelled to acquiesce in his decision, and withdraw its envoys from the Council. From this time forth it became apparent that no great measure of Church reform was to be looked for from the united action of the clergy of Christendom. The real religious reform of the Roman Church had to wait till a schismatical Reformation movement had awakened a religious reaction. For the mere protection of the national Churches against pillage by the Pope and cardinals, the clergy had to look henceforward to their respective sovereigns. The Popes more and more degenerated into Italian princes. With the secular sovereigns of Europe the awe of their spiritual thunders was a thing of the past; but as an Italian prince and as the head of the ecclesiastical order throughout Europe, the Pope could still do much to aid or thwart political designs of rival monarchs. At the same time, within their respective kingdoms, the control of the secular princes over their own clergy was becoming stricter. Hence diplomatic agreement between King and Pope for the settlement of the ecclesiastical relations of the national Churches with the Papacy took the place of independent movements on the part of the clergy. The age of councils was succeeded by an age of concordats.

Policy of
Louis XI.

This nationalization of the Catholic Church throughout Europe—this breaking down, so to speak, of the solidarity of the ecclesiastical order—almost involved the destruction of the ecumenical character of the University of Paris. And the nationalization of the university was completed by the deliberate policy of Louis XI. Previous sovereigns had used every endeavour to protect the foreign students in their capital even when at war with the countries from which they came. In 1470, Louis XI, with the morbid suspicion which was one of his strongest characteristics, compelled all the subjects of the Duke of Burgundy to take the oath of obedience to himself as the condition of remaining in Paris. Some four hundred Burgundian scholars who declined the oath were allowed to leave the country, but, with extraordinary mean-

Petit-Dutaillis, in Lavisse, *Hist. de France*, IV. ii. 270, and G. Barra-   clough, *Papal Provisions*, Oxford, 1935.]

ness, their modest goods were confiscated.[1] Not long afterwards the edict which has been referred to in another chapter
required that no alien should be elected to the rectorship or
any other university office.[2] The multiplication of universities throughout Europe in the course of the fifteenth century
tended in the same direction—towards the nationalization of
Paris as of all other universities.[3]

The effect of this nationalization, combined with the
growth of centralization and absolutism, was completely to
destroy the influence of the university beyond the borders of
the French Church. Within those limits, the theological
faculty—though, like every other part of the ecclesiastical
system, henceforth completely subservient to the Crown—
retained at least as much importance as formerly. The university itself, indeed, the great scholastic democracy of the
Middle Ages, could not live in the France of Henry IV or
Louis XIV. The functions of its Congregations were more
and more transferred to what was called the tribunal of the
university—a court composed of the rector, the four proctors,
and the three deans. Its constitution thus became practically
almost as oligarchic as that of Oxford under the Laudian
Hebdomadal Board. More completely even than at Oxford
the university passed into an aggregate of colleges; and the
colleges of artists sank, as the colleges of Oxford with their
perpetual fellowships never could sink, into mere boarding-
schools for boys. Even as schools they were eclipsed in
scholastic fame and in social estimation by the schools of the
Jesuits. But the theological faculty—now centred in the
restored College of the Sorbonne—continued for the French
Church to give oracles which often emboldened king and
people to defy the thunders of the Vatican. 'The Sorbonne'
was a less dangerous, more manageable, and even more venerable authority to pit against the autocracy of Rome than the
resolutions of prelates too feudal and of councils too popular
to find favour in the eyes of absolutist monarchs.

We have seen how after the break-up of the Council of

---

[1] Bulaeus, v. 692.   [2] *Ibid.*, p. 716.
[3] [For developments earlier in the century cf. S. d'Irsay, *op. cit.* i. 207.]

CHAP. V,
§ 6.
The uni-
versity be-
comes the
home of
Gallican-
ism.
Basel a European concert on the great Roman question became impossible. The attitude of the French kings for a time wavered, like that of other princes, with the political exigencies of the moment. The Pragmatic Sanction of 1438, with the maintenance of which the newly developed Gallicanism became practically identified, was alternately withdrawn and reinforced. But in the main the tendency of political requirements outside France was in the direction of alliance with the Vatican; and as a consequence the tendency of Catholicism outside France was to become more and more completely Roman or Ultramontane.[1] In France, equally from political considerations, the tendency was in favour of resistance to papal encroachments. It was in the main political causes that determined this bifurcation of the theological tendencies of Europe. At the end of the fifteenth century the theology of the secular clergy throughout northern Europe was almost everywhere as anti-Roman as that of France. But the prestige of the university and its theological faculty enormously facilitated the opposition of the French kings to Roman encroachments. The Sorbonne became the home of a distinctively national school of theology. The Gallicanism of earlier ages had, indeed, to undergo a change; the older ecclesiastical liberties—the free elections to bishoprics and abbacies, the frequent councils and synods, and the right of free debate in them—were as offensive to the kings of the sixteenth and seventeenth centuries as papal interference. The Gallicanism which the great name of Paris and the cherished traditions of the Gerson epoch still kept alive was an erastianized Gallicanism. But in the preservation of this Gallicanism the most potent spiritual force was 'the Sorbonne', as the most potent material instrument was its younger, but now more powerful sister, the Parlement of Paris.[2]

[1] Thus at Vienna graduates were required to swear: 'Item abnego et reuoco illas propositiones indistincte positas, videlicet quod concilium est supra papam; item quod papa non potest reuocare per concilium generale conclusum' (Kink, I. ii. 26).

[2] As an illustration of the growth of Gallicanism see Bulaeus, v. 807, where the university (in 1491) resolves, in accordance with the decision of the faculties of theology and canon law, that an excommunication threatened by the Pope should not be feared or obeyed. In 1502 the resolution was repeated, when Alex-

One of the last occasions on which we find the university
still standing forth, at least in the imagination of men, as the theological oracle of Europe, was in the course of Luther's controversy with the papal legate. Luther pitted the authority of Paris against Rome;[1] and at one time he seems to have entertained hopes of finding support for the Reformation movement in the old adversary of Benedict XIII and John XXIII. But of this there was never any real probability. The very virtues of the university, the very services which she had performed for the French Church, tended to check the progress of the Reformation in France. While throughout southern Europe theological education and theological study were practically abandoned to the Mendicant orders, the theological schools of Paris kept alive some knowledge of the theology and discipline of earlier ages, while her colleges secured theological training for large numbers of the higher clergy, a class which in Italy, for instance, was mainly given up to the demoralizing education of the canonist. The academic conflicts with the Mendicants and their incessant cabals against the right of the secular clergy filled the Parisian scholar with an instinctive dislike for a friar, and consequently with a traditional suspicion of the great source of Mendicant immunities.

Paris was proud of her university. We have seen with what effect upon occasion that curious device, the cessation of sermons, was employed as a lever to move public opinion. From the eagerness sometimes exhibited by a parish struck with this peculiar interdict to be readmitted to the favour of the university,[2] it would seem as if the greater frequency of sermons, their superior quality, and the fact that they were

ander VI had actually excommunicated the French clergy for refusing a tenth (D'Argentré, I. ii. 346).

[1] On account of its recent appeal in 1517 against the Pope's condemnation of the Pragmatic Sanction to a General Council (Bulaeus, vi. 88).

[2] *Ibid.* v. 598. The cessation usually extended to the whole city, but on this occasion it was limited to the parishes in which certain

outrages on scholars had been perpetrated. The representatives of these parishes were twice refused audience, but on the third application they were admitted and the cessation relaxed on condition that a tablet with a sculptured or pictorial representation of the penance ('unum epitaphium imaginibus et scriptura descriptum') should be set up in one of the parishes.

CHAP. V, not all delivered by Mendicants—all three advantages secured
§ 6. by the presence of the university—had done something to
diminish in Paris the popular hatred of the clergy at the time
so prevalent in the great towns, notably in London, and to
indoctrinate minds elsewhere deprived altogether of spiritual
nutriment with the theology of which the university was the
accredited guardian. It is sometimes said that the ineradi-
cable Catholicism of Paris was the decisive weight which
turned the scale against the Reformation in France. At all
events the national feeling, which was elsewhere such a
powerful ally of the Reformation movement, was in France
satisfied with resolutely maintaining the attitude which the
university had taken up at Constance and at Basel, and nowhere did the support of the university tend to identify itself
with patriotism so closely as in Paris itself. Of course, many
of the circumstances just enumerated might have told in the
opposite direction had there arisen in the university itself a
strong party in sympathy with the Reform movement outside.
For the absence of such a movement no reason perhaps can
be given but the non-appearance of the men to lead it. However the fact be accounted for, the University of Paris never
did see within its college walls the growth of a really religious
movement at all comparable to the Wycliffite movement at
Oxford, to the movement of which Hus was the product
rather than the author at Prague, or even to the quieter
religious revival inaugurated in the sixteenth century by men
like our Oxford Tyndale and the Cambridge Reformers. The
comparative isolation of the intellectual life of Paris from
contact with the stronger currents of popular religious feeling
outside is one of the strangest facts of her history.[1]

[1] [Until the expulsion of Calvin and Nicholas Cop, the rector of the university, after the address, written by the former and spoken by the latter, 1 Nov. 1533, it would hardly be correct to say that the university was isolated from the new movements. It was affected by the work of men like Lefèvre of Étaples and by the circle of Mar- garet of Navarre. See especially E. Doumergue, *Jean Calvin*, i (Lausanne, 1899)—for Cop's ad- dress, pp. 331–6; A. Renaudet, *Préréforme et humanisme à Paris pendant les premières guerres d'Italie, 1494–1517* (Paris, 1916); T. M. Lindsay, *History of the Reforma- tion*, ii (Edinburgh, 1908), 136–51, with bibliography.]

APPENDIXES

I

SOME BOLOGNA DOCUMENTS

(To illustrate pp. 155, 170–1, 221)

A. *Bull of Honorius III in 1217 to the Student-Guild of Rome,*
Campania, and Tuscany at Bologna. (Cf. above, p. 155.)

(Vatican Register, No. 9, f. 110 *b*, Ep. 453. Procured for Dr. Rashdall by Heinrich Denifle.)

HONORIUS III

Scholaribus universis de Urbe, de Campania, et de Tuscia
Bononie commorantibus.

Etsi multam honestatem, immo necessitatem, sicut asseritis, causa contineat, que vos ad contrahendam societatem induxit, quia tamen interdum ea que bono inchoantur principio in pravum deducuntur exitum per abusum, diligenti vos decet sollicitudine precavere ne occasione societatis ipsius a vobis aliqua presumantur que Scolasticam in aliquo dedeceant puritatem.

Quapropter Universitatem vestram monemus et exhortamur in Domino per Apostolica vobis scripta mandantes quatenus in actibus vestris eam de cetero modestiam observetis, ut et infamie notam et rerum dispendium omnino vitetis, de Civitate exire quam periurii reatum incurrere potius eligentes si ad alterum predictorum per Potestatem vos contigerit artari. Vos enim Societatem dissolvere aut Statutum illud contra libertatem Scolarium vestris Statutis inserere non potestis qui utrumque servare, et quam potestis diligentius procurare, fide interposita promisistis.

Datum Anagnie sexto Kal. Iunii Pontificatus nostri anno primo.

B. *Bull of Honorius III authorizing the Archdeacon of Bologna
to absolve for assaults on clerks, 1219.* (Cf. above, p. 221.)

(*Ibid.*, f. 107 *b*, Ep. 510.)

ARCHIDIACONO BONONIENSI

Consideratis circumstantiis temporum et locorum rigor iustitie debet aliquando mansuetudine temperari, ut vini compunctio lenitate olei mitigetur, et peccator in profundum non veniat et contempnat, presertim cum sine dispendio Ecclesiarum usquequaque servari non possit vigor Ecclesiastice discipline. Sane cum sepe contingat, quod in civitate Bononien. plures doctores et Scolares propter violentas iniectiones manuum in clericos excommunicati decedant, ac alii redeuntes ad propria promoveantur ad Ordines, absolutionis beneficio non obtento; unde preter irregularitatem quam incurrunt, improvide in huiusmodi multi nolentes suum confiteri delictum, paupertate vel infirmitate gravati vel alias imbecillitate animi dormientes ac confessi ad Sedem Apostolicam transmittantur in peccatis suis miserabiliter moriuntur. Nos igitur super huiusmodi periculis volentes eisdem Doctoribus et Scolaribus paterna sollicitudine providere, quorum nolumus, sicut nec expedit, studium per absentiam impediri, auctoritate tibi presentium indulgemus ut ipsis, qui ad invicem in se aut in alias personas Ecclesiasticas manus iniecerint violentas, nisi tam gravis fuerit aut enormis excessus ut merito sint ad Sedem Apostolicam destinandi, iuxta formam Ecclesie beneficium absolutionis impendas. Nulli ergo omnino hominum liceat hanc paginam nostre concessionis infringere vel ei ausu temerario contraire.

Si quis autem hoc attentare presumpserit, indignationem Omnipotentis Dei ac Beatorum Petri & Pauli Apostolorum eius se noverit incursurum.

Datum Reate v. Kal. Iulii Pontificatus nostri anno tertio.

C. *Bull of Honorius III giving right of promotion to the Archdeacon of Bologna, 1219.* (Cf. above, p. 221.)

(Ibid., Ep. 509.)

Cum sepe contingat ut in civitate Bononiensi minus docti ad docendi regimen assumantur, propter quod et Doctorum honor minuitur et profectus impeditur Scolarium volentium erudiri; Nos eorumdem utilitati et honori utiliter prospicere cupientes auctoritate presentium duximus statuendum, ut nullus ulterius in civitate predicta ad docendi regimen assumatur, nisi a te obtenta licentia, examinatione quoque prehabita diligenti, tu denique contradictores si qui fuerint vel rebelles, per censuram ecclesiasticam appellationis remedio compescas. Dat. Reate iiii. Kal. Iulii [Pontificatus nostr]i anno tertio. Nulli ergo, &c., nostre constitutioni infringere. Si quis autem, &c.

D. *Bull of Honorius III in favour of the University of Bologna, 1220.* (Cf. above, p. 170.)

(Ibid., f. 179, Ep. 728 bis.)

POPULO BONONIENSI

Ex relatione Ven. Fratris nostri . . . Ostiensis Episcopi, devotione quam ad Romanam Ecclesiam geritis intellecta, tanto ad ea

que vestram salutem respiciunt & honorem ferventius aspiramus,
quanto vos tanquam obedientie filios ad eiusdem obediendum
mandatis cognoscimus proniores vos ab hiis retrahere satagentes,
que & famam vestram obnubilant, et afferre vobis possent inco-
modum et iacturam. Sane cum ex studio literarum preter infinita
commoda, que sentitis, ex eo vestra civitas inter alias sit famosa, et
in universo mundo nomen annuncietur ipsius, factaque sit altera
Bethleem, domus videlicet panis qui parvulis frangitur in eadem,
ex qua exeunt duces qui regant populum Domini, quoniam in
studio eruditi assumuntur ad regimen animarum, non solum
debetis a scolarium gravaminibus conquiescere verum etiam illos
honoribus prevenire, attendentes, quod ipsi gratuito ad studendum
vestram preelegerint civitatem, que cum prius esset humilis per
eos ibidem congregatis divitiis fere supergressa est civitates provincie universas; verum vos ad hec, sicut ex parte Universitatis
ipsorum fuit propositum coram nobis, debitum non habentes
respectum, gratiam ipsorum in debitum et libertatem in servitutem molientes reducere, statuistis ut si quis inventus fuerit sectam
pactionem vel conspirationem pro studio a civitate Bononiensi ad
locum alium transferendo facere vel fecisse; et si Scolaris quispiam vel alius quemquam Scolarem adstrinxerit modo quolibet,
quo precipere possit ei ut causa Studii eamdem exeat Civitatem
perpetuo banniatur, et omnia bona eius que Bononie vel in eius
districtu habuerit publicentur, et eorum tribuatur medietas ac-
cusanti: preterea Societatem vel Rectores Scolares non permit-
tantur habere, nisi hoc capitulum in eorum iuramento ponatur;
videlicet quod non dabunt operam, ut Studium ad locum alium
transferatur, nec cuiquam Scolari precipiant, ut gratia studii
abscedat a Civitate predicta et numquam huiusmodi mutabunt
capitulum cum consilio vel sine consilio eorumdem; ac si aliquis
contrafecerit, modo simili banniatur, et bona publicentur ipsius:
Potestas quoque infra duos menses ab ingressu sui regiminis
teneatur predictum Capitulum iurari facere a Rectoribus Scolarium, si qui fuerint, vel infra quindecim dies, ex quo extiterint
Rectores electi et in Societatum Scolarium scriptis poni, nec
permittant Bononiensem aliquem vel extraneum, nisi primo iuraverit quod non leget alibi, extraordinariam aliquam legere lectionem. Unde ex hiis dilectus Filius nobilis vir W. de Pusterula
Potestas, vestra occasione assumpta in eos indebitam iurisdictionem usurpans, libertatem ipsorum infringere nititur, et contra
eamdem pretextu ipsorum pro quorum observatione asserit se
iurasse illos in pluribus aggravare. Verum quia Statuta huiusmodi
procul dubio sunt iniqua et manifeste obvient Scolastice libertati,

et iuramentum super observatione ipsorum prestitum non est, utpote illicitum observandum cùm nec iudicium habeat nec iustitiam; eundem W. monendum duximus et hortandum Apostolicis sibi dantes litteris in preceptis, ut Scolares predictos contra libertatem hactenus habitam occasione Statutorum ipsorum, que velut iniqua duximus reprobanda, de cetero non molestet, libertatem eandem modo quolibet infringendo, ut studium eorum impediri non possit sed potius floreat ad Dei honorem, ac profectum Studentium nec non ad ipsius gloriam civitatis, ne si secus attemptare presumpserit nos super hoc cogamur aliud cogitare. Quo circa Universitatem vestram monemus et exhortamur attente quatenus, consideratis utilitatibus et honore ex Scolaribus vobis et civitati vestre provenientibus, ipsos caritatis brachiis amplexemini, et pretextu Statutorum ipsorum, que dicenda sunt potius destituta, contra libertatem antiquam et habitam hactenus ipsos nullatenus molestetis, nec faciatis per Potestatem eamdem, remisso sibi iuramento predicto de cetero molestari, permittentes eosdem solita libertate gaudere ut quieto animo possint inherere Scolasticis disciplinis et nos devotionem vestram possimus in Domino commendare, ne si secus egeritis, quod non credimus, contra voluntatem nostram cogamur faciem nostram vobis ostendere duriorem.

Datum Viterbii viii. Id. April. Pontificatus nostri anno quarto.

II

FORM OF CONFERRING THE DOCTORATE *IN UTROQUE JURE* AT BOLOGNA

(From Gaggi, *Coll. Bon. Doctorum Origo et Dotes*, Bologna, 1710.)

Cum mihi fueris praesentatus in utroque iure examinandus, et legitime approbandus per Illustrissimos, et Excellentissimos D.D. (*nominando Promotores*) Equites auratos, Comites Palatinos, Doctores celeberrimos, et cum inde subieris arduum et rigorosum examen in quo tam docte quam egregie te gesisti, ut caetus iste Illustrissimorum et Excellentissimorum P.P. nemine penitus, dico penitus disentiente te dignum laurea iudicaverint, ideo auctoritate qua fungor Archidiaconi huiusque Studii maioris Cancellarii te N.N. in praedictis facultatibus Doctorem creo, publico, et nomino, dans tibi omnimodam facultatem legendi, Magistralem Cathedram ascendendi, glosandi, interpretandi, et avocandi, necnon omnes actus Doctoreos exercendi hic et ubique terrarum et locorum; insuper iis omnibus utendi privilegiis, quibus uti, et frui soleant illa felicia capita, quae in his almis Collegiis promerita fuerunt.

Quae omnia in tuae augmentum famae, Collegiorum nostrorum APPENDIX
decus, ad laudem et gloriam Omnipotentis Dei et Beatae semper II.
Virginis Mariae Collegiorum protectricis perpetuo eventura
desidero.

III

SECESSIONS FROM BOLOGNA

(Towns which became permanent *Studia Generalia* are printed in capitals.)

Ante 1182. Pillius retires to Modena from Bologna.

1188. Jacobus de Mandra contracts to come to REGGIO and
bring his scholars with him—probably from Bologna.

1204. Migration from Bologna to VICENZA.

1215. Roffredus of Benevento secedes from Bologna to
AREZZO, in consequence of severe punishment of Lombard *v.*
Tuscan Riots.

1222. Migration from Bologna to PADUA.

1228. Migration from Padua to VERCELLI.

1282. Scholars absolved from an oath which they had taken to
leave Bologna for five years (Sarti, 1. ii. 106).

1306. Total suspension of the *Studium* for three years (*Acta
Nat. Germ.* p. 59).

1312. Migration from Bologna 'timore novitatis' (*Acta Nat.
Germ.* p. 65).

1316. Migration from Bologna to Argenta.

1321. Migration of nearly the whole University of Bologna to
Imola and thence to SIENA, the existing University of Perugia,
which obtains *ius ubique docendi* in all Faculties, Padua, and other
places. F. Filippini in *Studi e memorie*, vi. 101 *sqq.*, and A. Favaro
in *Atti e memorie della Reale Deputazione di storia patria per le
provincie di Romagna*, x (1892).

1338. Interdict on Bologna and suspension of *Studium*—
Secession to Castello S. Pietro; and consequent foundation of PISA
and FLORENCE.

This list does not profess to be complete.

IV

THE EXAMINATIONS AT PARIS ILLUSTRATED
BY BOURGES

(Additional note, p. 458.)

The nature of the two examinations at Ste Geneviève comes out
much more plainly in the statutes of some of the minor French

universities, which were based on the customs of Paris, than in the registers of Paris itself. The clearest that I have found is the following statute of Bourges, probably *circa* 1468–80 (from Fournier, *Statuts et priv. des univ. franç.* iii, No. 1863). It will be observed how the list of books required has shrunk. Bourges may well have adopted a lower standard than Paris; but still it is probable that the requirements of the faculty even at Paris (especially at this late date) were *always* in practice less severe than on paper:

'Item, statuimus quod, antequam aliquis accedat ad gradum licentie, tenebitur audivisse alios quatuor libros *Phisicorum*, tres libros *De Celo*, duos *De Generatione*, tres primos *Meteororum*, tres *De Anima*, *De Memoria*, *De longitudine et brevitate vite*, cum sex primis libris *Metaphisicorum* et sex primis *Ethicorum*, cum parte *Euclidis* et cum libro *De Sphera*.'

(For B.A. the statutes require: '*Isagogen* Porphyrii, *Predicamenta* Aristotelis, duos libros *Periarmenias*, primos *Topicorum*, duos *Ethicos* . . . tres primos *Phisicorum* cum parte quarti *Periermenias*.')

'Item, statuimus quod tenebuntur licentiandi respondere bis palam et publice, et poterunt esse quinque ad maius in uno die et in eadem disputatione; tamen sufficient quatuor. Et tenebuntur respondentes solvere presidenti suo quilibet unum scutum auri.

'Item, statuimus quod, his peractis, Facultas deputabit quatuor magistros qui iam attigerint tertium annum a suo magisterio et qui non habeant scholares illo anno licentiandos ex sua regentia propria, qui deputati experimentum capient de sufficientia omnium licentiandorum. Et iurabunt dicti deputati quod recipient sufficientes et repellent insufficientes.

'Item, statuimus quod, his sic peractis, ad relatum dictorum deputatorum sub suis signis manualibus fideliter traditis, cancellarius ordinabit dictos licentiandos secundum ordinem sibi per dictos deputatos datum, preponendo semper meliores et sufficientiores aliis, ut detur studentibus occasio bene studendi, et nemini fiat iniuria pro loco.

'Item, statuimus quod, antequam procedatur ad licentiam ipsorum licentiandorum, artium Facultas congregata ordinabit quatuor alios magistros a primis, qui in cameris deputatis examinabunt dictos licentiandos in propriis personis; et si non repererint eos tales quales primi examinantes retulerint reperiisse, referent Facultati, insufficientiam allegantes, qua Facultas cognoscet de errore primorum; quos si invenerit errasse, eorum errores poterit corrigere, loca mutando aut totaliter repellendo, si videantur insufficientes.

'Item, statuimus quod, approbatione vel reprobatione facta per dictos secundos examinatores, in una sedula ponent suos licentiandos secundum ordinem debitum et signata suis propriis signis, et eam clausam tradent cancellario, cui licitum non erit divertere ordinem, sed secundum positum ordinem in sedula eos licentiabit.'

From this document, taken in connexion with others, it would thus appear that the process of taking the degree of Ste Geneviève involved the three following steps: (1) *examinatio in communibus* (so called because the candidates were not at present divided into *camerae* or batches); an examination into performance of statutable conditions as well as a literary examination, before the chancellor and examiners, in which the candidates were divided into *camerae* or classes, and arranged in order of merit within each *camera* or *auditio*. (2) Each *camera* or *auditio* was then subjected to a more detailed examination in the books by the examiners of the faculty (*temptatores in cameris* or *in propriis*). It would seem that these examiners might, if they pleased, change the order of the candidates in the same *auditio* (see Fournier, iii. 166). (3) The candidates were then sent to the chancellor, who, upon the report or *depositiones* of the examiners *in cameris*, and after hearing their formal *collationes*, admitted them to the licence in the order in which they were presented to him. Such at least was the view of his duty taken by the faculty, though it is not improbable that he sometimes rebelled against it, as was constantly done by the Chancellor of Notre Dame.

At Nantes (1461) there were two examinations, no doubt more or less corresponding to the two examinations at Paris. At the first of these the 'cedulae' of attendance at lectures, of determination, and of responsions were produced, and the candidate examined 'per singulos libros'. After this the candidate received his 'cappa'. At the second examination he was examined 'particulariter et de specialibus et finaliter de metrificatura' (*ibid.*, No. 1595).

V

DOCTORES BULLATI: PAPAL INTERVENTION IN THE PROMOTION TO DEGREES[1]

The regulation of the *licentia docendi* was the work of the Papacy. Alexander III's decretal *Quanto Gallicana*, the Third Lateran Council in 1179 (*Chartul. Univ. Paris.* i, Introd., Nos. 4, 12), the instructions of Honorius III to the archdeacon of Bologna, and the earliest statutes of the University of Paris show how local

---

[1] This appendix has been revised and slightly enlarged.

ecclesiastical authorities were enjoined not to refuse the licence to worthy candidates and how later the corporations of masters were empowered by papal authority to give their sanction to the grant of the licence. It is not surprising, therefore, to find the Pope intervening from an early period in the ordinary working of the academical system in order to promote the conferment of degrees upon favoured individuals. One of the earliest instances occurs in 1218, when Honorius III specially directed Peter of Capua, William of Pont de l'Arche, and Richard the Englishman, doctors of Paris, to examine Matthew *de Scotia*, and if he were found sufficient in learning, to admonish the Chancellor of Paris to license him in theology (*Chartul.* i, No. 27). In other cases, the Bull merely dispensed the candidate from some of the statutable conditions, e.g. directed that he should be admitted at once to the reading of the Sentences. It became a regular system to grant this privilege to friars who had received, or were supposed to have received, the earlier stages of their theological education in the *studia* of their order. At other times the Papal Bull authorized certain ecclesiastics not only to examine but actually to confer the mastership upon his candidate (Wadding, *Annales ordinis minorum*, viii. 585; x. 477).

By the fifteenth century such commissions to confer degrees, whether permanent and general or simply *ad hoc*, had been multiplied. Thus the *Statuta Artistarum* of Padua, Venice 1596 (f. xxviii *a*), recite that 'plerique uel paupertate coacti uel alia causa inducti quum non possint uel nolint ex aliqua causa se subiicere examini clarissimi collegii in artibus medicinae bacchalariatus uel doctoratus gradum sumunt ab aliquibus qui ex apostolica uel imperatoria auctoritate facultate[m] et priuilegium habent huiusmodi baccalarios uel doctores creandi'. The statute goes on to enact that nobody in the Paduan territory is to take such degrees without paying to the university the fees which he would have had to pay for graduating in the regular way. Again, in 1481, the faculty of theology at Bologna decreed 'quod quilibet magister incorporatus in collegio universitatis predicte [i.e. theologorum], qui decetero se aliqualiter verbo, facto uel opere immiscuerit in examine uel aula aut doctoratu alicuius magistrandi in theologia, vigore aliquarum litterarum apostolicarum, cuiuscunque tenoris existant, et non per collegium universitatis predicte, quod sit ipso iure et facto in perpetuum privatus honore et emolumento ac commodo dicti collegii', &c. (Ehrle, *I più antichi statuti*, p. 90). The Cologne statutes of 1398 had laid down 'quod bullandi et bullati post tempus ordinationis presentium statutorum . . . hic non habeantur pro regentibus nisi de speciali gratia facultatis'

(Bianco, I. ii. 41, quoted Kaufmann, *Geschichte der deutschen Universitäten*, ii. 316 note); the doctors of Bologna a century later went farther and ejected the examiners of such persons from their body.

In England (Rot. Claus. Ric. II. 14 m. 32) the King complains that certain Dominicans 'in lege diuina minime approbati seu instructi set apotastate (*sic*) et notorie viciosi et . . . per ordinem predictum carceribus condempnati mare transeuntes gradum sibi magisterii ac alias gracias exemptorias subdole ac fraudulenter impetrant et procurant'.

Complaints of the multiplication of these *Doctores bullati* might be produced to any extent.

It appears that the Emperor likewise (but more rarely) exercised the right of making *Doctores bullati*, and even delegated it to others, e.g. the Count Palatine (Itterus, *De honoribus sive gradibus academicis*, pp. 134 *sq.*, 347).[1]

---

[1] The appendixes in this volume correspond to Appendixes IV, V, VII, XIII, XVII in the first edition (vol. ii, pp. 731, 734, 736, 742, 750).